D0771194

GERMAN

A Structural Approach

SHORTER EDITION

WALTER F. W. LOHNES

AND F. W. STROTHMANN

Stanford University

GERMAN

A Structural Approach

SHORTER EDITION

 W · W · Norton & Company · Inc · New York

CONTENTS

The Present Tense—**sein** and **haben**—Gender—Verb-Second Position—Intonation Patterns—**auch** and **denn**   **UNIT 1**

PATTERNS 1

CONVERSATION 5

READING 5

ANALYSIS (Sections **1-15**) 6

The Infinitive   Personal Pronouns   Inflected Verb Forms   Absence of Progressive and Emphatic Forms in German   Future Meaning of Present-Tense Forms   Variations in Personal Endings   **sein** and **haben**   Gender of Nouns   Position of the Inflected Verb   Word Stress   Syntactical Stress and Intonation of Assertions   The Grammatical Structure of German Questions   The Intonation of German Questions   **auch**   **denn**

EXERCISES 18

VOCABULARY 21

Plural of Nouns—Nominative and Accusative of Personal Pronouns and of **ein**-Words and **der**-Words—Adverbs and Predicate Adjectives—Sentence Structure—**doch**   **UNIT 2**

PATTERNS 23

CONVERSATION 28

READING 28

Eine Frau lügt nicht 28

UNIT 7

Prepositions with Dative or Accusative—The Genitive Case—**ein**-Words without
Nouns—The Indirect-Discourse Subjunctive

UNIT 8

Relative Pronouns—**wann, ob, als, wenn**—**gar**—**da**-Compounds—**wo**-Compounds—
Prepositional Objects

The Passive—**es** in the Front Field—Pre-Noun Inserts

PREFACE

The extremely favorable response to *German, A Structural Approach* has prompted us to provide a shorter edition of the text for the convenience of those whose classes meet only three times a week or who want to place more emphasis on reading toward the end of the first year of instruction. The parent volume was used at Stanford University in several successive mimeographed versions from 1962 to 1967. Since its publication early in 1968, it has been widely adopted across the United States.

The main difference between this version and its parent volume is simply a matter of length. We have reduced the number but not the variety of patterns, omitted some of the reading selections, and cut back on the exercise material. Many of the conversations have been shortened so that they may be assigned for memorization as well as classroom drill. We have rewritten several of the analysis sections without eliminating any explanations that we feel properly belong in the first-year course. Words in the end-of-unit vocabularies have been divided into two categories: "basic vocabulary" and "additional vocabulary." The laboratory exercises for this version, including all the patterns from the text that have been tape recorded, appear in a separate student's Laboratory Manual, and a special tape program adapted to this version is available. We have also prepared a Teacher's Manual specifically for this shorter edition.

Our special thanks are due to Miss Linda Bartz of the University of Wisconsin, Professor Eugene Weber of Harvard, and Professor Ralph Reed III of the University of Texas, who critically read the parent volume and provided us with many helpful suggestions for this shorter edition. We also owe a debt of gratitude to many other users of the regular edition who have supplied us with valuable comments, and to Miss Ingrid Gustus and Miss Marilyn Rose of Stanford University, who assisted us in the tedious and time-consuming job of putting together the final copy for this shorter version.

The authors are indebted to the Embassy of Lebanon for permission to reproduce the photograph that appears on page 142 and to the German Information Center for use of the photographs on pages 37 and 43. The many photographs of German scenes that appear throughout this book were obtained and reproduced through the courtesy of the Deutsche Zentrale für Fremdenverkehr.

Stanford, California   W. F. W. L.
November 1969   F. W. S.

INTRODUCTION

This shorter edition of *German, A Structural Approach* has the same aims as its parent volume: developing the skills of listening, speaking, reading, and writing. We are convinced that the "structural approach" leads to a more rapid and thorough acquisition of these skills than any other method.

In the structural approach we do not abandon audio-lingual techniques; but we go beyond those techniques in order to help the student acquire a real command of German.

In learning our native language, we absorb its syntactical principles by osmosis. We have no conceptual knowledge of many of these principles, and we certainly do not think of them every time we utter a sentence. Nevertheless, we know when to say *He thinks not* and when to say *He doesn't think*. By a series of "pattern drills" which stretches from birth into adolescence we learn how to use a linguistic code without necessarily having a conceptual knowledge of that code.

A first-year student must certainly drill the structural patterns of German sentences intensively and over a long period of time before he can approach active control and native fluency. But since college students are linguistic adults who already speak one language, they cannot be exposed to the nonconceptual learning process a German infant is exposed to.

In the first place, our students do not have that much time. In one year of college German, an American student cannot afford to learn German by trial and error and from context only; he has to resort to grammar if he wants to master German quickly.

In the second place, the linguistic "code" of English which our students have absorbed acts as a perpetual source of interference; it prevents them both from understanding many German sentences they hear and from actively using German sentence patterns correctly. This is to be expected, for once we have absorbed one linguistic code by osmosis, we cannot learn a totally different code without a contrastive analytical knowledge of that new code.

In the third place, college students who want to learn German have reached an age at which they are both able and eager to grasp the systematic concept behind the individual phenomenon. When they play around with the simple sentence **Ich bleibe heute natürlich zu Hause,** they want to know why it is perfectly acceptable to say **Zu Hause bleibe ich heute natürlich nicht,** but impossible to say **Zu Hause bleibe ich heute natürlich.** A conceptual understanding of German sentence structure is a time-saving short cut, and we see no virtue in postponing the immediate comprehension of German syntax by refusing to tell the student, as he manipulates structural patterns, what the principles underlying these patterns are. We are very much in favor of "keeping grammar out of the classroom"; but since we are also against "teaching grammar behind closed doors," we suggest that structural analysis be handled in a new way.

PATTERN SENTENCES make up the first large part of each unit. Work with these patterns must occupy the greatest amount of classroom time, for it is here that the student will transform his concept of the language into an instrument of communication. Each pattern group contains a sufficient number of examples to illustrate a grammatical point, and there are cross references in the page margins to relevant discussions in the analysis.

From the very beginning, we aim at the student's ability to comprehend, speak, read, and write not only the German he will see in formal print, but also the German he will hear in informal speech, and we have not shied away from the colloquial German used by educated people in everyday speech. Colloquial as well as literary German is recognized as socially acceptable, and the students are taught that **Wo kommen Sie denn her?** and **Wo willst du denn hin?** are just as correct as **Woher kommen Sie?** and **Wohin willst du?**

We have attempted not to write typical classroom German, and we have never yielded to the temptation to produce unidiomatic expressions for the sake of making our patterns fit into a preconceived mold. For instance, the use of the attributive genitive must obviously be illustrated, but this is no excuse for introducing sentences like **Die Farbe meines Kugelschreibers ist blau** as starting points for pattern drills as long as there is available a wealth of idiomatic phrases such as **ein Freund meines Mannes, gegen Ende des Jahres,** and **der Erfolg der neuen Methode.** We have mitigated the rigidity—and perhaps also the boredom—of many pattern drills by insisting that the student create sentences that could occur in actual speech. It serves no purpose to have a substitution drill end with **Sie werden ihre Tränen getrocknet haben.** On the other hand, we do expect the student to be able to handle complex structures such as **Seine Frau soll sehr aufgeregt gewesen sein** or **Ich hätte natürlich auch zu Hause bleiben können,** for such structures do belong to the living language as it is actually spoken.

Some pattern sections either contain built-in variations or are followed by a separate set of variations. These are designed in such a way that they can be used in class immediately after a group of pattern sentences has been introduced.

ANALYSIS is the intellectual core of each unit. The analysis sections have intentionally been written as detailed and unhurried discussions of grammatical points. Pains have been taken to explain grammar in terms the student will understand. We have shied away from short, terse rules that would force the teacher to spend precious classroom time for elaboration of these rules. The analysis sections should be assigned as outside reading as the new patterns are introduced in class, so that the student, while he works on the patterns, will have the feeling that he knows what he is doing and why he is doing it.

In the analysis, our first and foremost concern is syntax; in addition, we present all the major features of German morphology. After an introductory section on the pronunciation of individual sounds, Unit 1 deals with sentence intonation; in the following units, the basic structure of German sentences is developed. A discussion of the two-part predicate, the most characteristic feature of German syntax, is followed by an analysis of word order in the inner field of a sentence. Negation and time phrases are dealt with at length. Modal auxiliaries and the subjunctive—indispensable in "real" German—are introduced very early. A number of sections deal with sentence adverbs like **doch, ja,** or **denn.** Other sections are devoted to principles of word formation.

In order to contrast German structures with corresponding English structures, we have occasionally spent much time analyzing English usage from a German point of view. We want to call attention to those features of English that differ from German, and are therefore the primary cause of error.

EXERCISES are provided in addition to the variations in order to reinforce the student's control of each structural element. Their sequence is the same as that of the patterns and the analysis sections. Unlike the variations, however, the exercises should not be done until the student has thoroughly drilled and studied the corresponding patterns. We have intentionally included more exercises than most teachers will want to use, in order to save the teacher the time-consuming effort of writing practice drills of his own. A separate set of exercises appears in the Student's Laboratory Manual. These exercises are keyed to each unit; the student is given full instructions for these exercises, but their texts appear only in the Teacher's Manual. Thus their use is not restricted to the language laboratory; they can also be used for further oral drill in the classroom. In addition to the laboratory exercises, the Laboratory Manual also contains those pattern sections, conversations, and reading selections that appear on the tape recordings for this shorter version.

CONVERSATIONS are included in all but the last few units; they are based upon the contents of the unit in which they appear, and demonstrate to the student how the material he has learned can produce lively, colloquial, and idiomatic talk. Most of the conversations are set up in such a way that they can be used for memorization if so desired.

READING, as the book progresses, becomes a major concern. We have used a wide variety of topics in our reading selections, some of which give brief glimpses of the contemporary German scene. The story by Matthias Koch may be used as a starting point for excursions into recent German history. Though it follows Unit 13, it may be used in conjunction with Units 10 through 13. Details are given in the Teacher's Manual.

WRITING should be practiced from the very beginning. At first the student should be encouraged simply to copy from the text. Later on, dictations should be given regularly. A number of the lab exercises are dictations as well. From Unit 7 on, we have provided a number of structured compositions, based on the material of the conversations and the reading.

VOCABULARY study is essential to the successful completion of a German course. In the pattern sentences the vocabulary has purposely been restricted so that the student can concentrate on learning the structures introduced; the conversations and reading selections provide most of the new words and phrases. All vocabulary is introduced in the context of whole sentences, and vocabulary should be *practiced* in context only. We do, however, recommend very strongly that the student memorize the "basic vocabulary" at the end of each unit. Less frequently used words and phrases appear under the heading "Additional Vocabulary."

ILLUSTRATIONS for the book have been selected either to demonstrate linguistic points or to show the student some of the places where the reading selections take place. We have deliberately not chosen typical "tourist" pictures, devoid of any linguistic message.

THE STUDENT'S LABORATORY MANUAL contains all those patterns, conversations, and reading selections that appear on the tapes for this shorter version. It also contains the laboratory exercises described above.

A TEACHER'S MANUAL is available which contains a number of detailed suggestions on how to teach individual parts of this book, outlines for typical lesson plans, and the scripts for all those lab exercises that do not appear in the printed text.

SUGGESTIONS FOR USING THIS BOOK

Each of the 13 Units of this book can be taught in an average of two weeks, thus leaving about two to three weeks of the academic year for review and testing. In colleges on the quarter system, Units 1–5 should be taught during the first quarter, 6–9 during the second quarter, and 10–13 during the third quarter. For the semester system, we recommend working with Units 1–7 during the first semester, and Units 8–13 during the second semester. This edition can be used in courses ranging from three to five class periods per week. Detailed lesson plans are provided in the Teacher's Manual. The Laboratory Exercises should be sufficient to meet any needs. The tape program runs approximately ten hours.

We have provided enough text, both in the Patterns and in the Exercises, to eliminate the need of preparing additional practice material. If a teacher wants to cut down, we strongly suggest that, rather than leaving out entire sections, he eliminate only parts of sections; for example, in a Pattern section containing 15 sentences, 7 or 8 may suffice to drill the grammatical point in question. The student can then work with the remaining sentences outside the classroom or in the language lab.

Not too much time should be spent at the beginning on the section "The Sounds of German"; one should not expect perfect pronunciation before starting Unit 1. It will be more fruitful to review this section periodically throughout the year. The students should be encouraged to listen to the pronunciation tapes as often as possible.

The grammatical material of Unit 1 has to be dealt with as one block: the entire analysis of this Unit is illustrated in each section of the Patterns. From Unit 2 on, however, each group of Patterns should be introduced with the corresponding Analysis section. At the beginning of each Unit, the students should be advised to read, at home, the entire Analysis section to get an idea of the linguistic principles introduced in the Unit. In the classroom, the Patterns should be introduced and drilled with their variations; and while this work is going on, the students should be asked to keep their books closed as much as possible. Homework should always consist of further practice with the Patterns as well as a thorough rereading of the applicable parts of the Analysis. We have found that it is rarely necessary to discuss any of the Analysis sections in class. Class time should definitely be used for active work with the language.

The Conversations and the Reading selections are best taught at the end of each Unit. They always serve as a review of the grammatical material presented in the Unit, and they introduce new vocabulary which will re-appear in the Pattern sections of the following Units.

The Exercises at the end of each Unit are extensive enough to be dis-tributed over the two-week period devoted to each Unit. They should not be done, however, until after the students have thoroughly mastered the corresponding Analysis sections. The English-German translations found at the end of each Unit serve as a review of the material covered. We have found that if the students have mastered the material of a Unit, these English sentences will enable them to generate German equivalents spontaneously. We believe that this kind of exercise serves a very useful purpose: as long as translation is not transliteration, the student is forced to express entire ideas in the target language.

Although all new vocabulary is, of course, introduced and presented in context, we consider it necessary to hold the students responsible for all but the "Additional Vocabulary" of each Unit. Native Germans acquire their basic vocabulary by "osmosis" rather than by memorizing word lists, but this painless process takes years and cannot be imitated in a few hours a week in an American classroom.

Further suggestions for using this shorter edition are provided in the Teacher's Manual.

Throughout this book, major emphasis is placed on the intonation of entire utterances, on the characteristic sound of whole German sentences. The pronunciation of the individual sounds that make up those complete sentences is dealt with only in this section. It is imperative that you practice these sounds, with the help of your teacher, and that you listen to the accompanying tapes until you have mastered the sounds. You should review this section frequently as you work your way through the book. After four weeks or four months you will find that this section on pronunciation may be even more useful to you than at the outset.

We have avoided all technical discussion of the German sounds; instead, we have provided a large number of contrastive drills to show the distinction between two or more different German sounds which, to the ear of an American student, very often sound alike when he first hears them. Many German sounds are sufficiently similar to English sounds so as not to cause the beginner great trouble. Our main concern will be those German sounds which either have no equivalent at all in English or tend to cause an American accent if pronounced like their English spelling equivalents. In many cases, an American accent will not make the German sound unintelligible (though you shouldn't take this as an excuse to retain an American accent); in some cases, however, the wrong pronunciation of certain sounds will produce unintended results. If you mispronounce the **ch**-sound in **Nacht**, as many Americans tend to do, you will not produce the German word for *night,* but the word **nackt,** which means *naked.*

Good pronunciation is essential if you want to speak German correctly and naturally. With patience and lots of practice, you should easily be able to overcome your initial difficulties. Don't worry about making mistakes at the beginning; you'll learn more from them than from not speaking at all.

German Vowels

German has long and short vowels, and diphthongs. The distinction between long and short vowels is very important, but unfortunately it is not always indicated by spelling. As a rule of thumb, however, you can assume that a vowel is short if it is followed by a double consonant (for example, **bitte**) or by two or more consonants (**binde**). German vowels are either quite long or very short.

In the following table, all German vowel sounds appear in words. On the tape, this is Pronunciation Drill 1. All the pronunciation drills in this section appear on tape. You should listen to them repeatedly and review them periodically. It is just as important, however, that you listen carefully to your instructor as he drills these exercises with you in class.

		LONG	SHORT	UNSTRESSED ONLY
PRONUNCI-ATION DRILL 1	a	Saat	satt	
	e	Beet	Bett	
	/ə/*			-be (gebe)
	/ʌ/*			-ber (Geber)
	i	ihn	in	
	o	Ofen	offen	
	u	Buhle	Bulle	
	ä	bäte		
	ö	Höhle	Hölle	
	ü	fühle	fülle	DIPHTHONGS
	au			Baum
	ei (ai)			kein (Kain)
	eu (äu)			Heu (Häuser)

NOTE: The two dots over **ä**, **ö**, and **ü** are called Umlaut. Occasionally, especially in names, these sounds are spelled **ae**, **oe**, **ue**.

As the table shows, there are twenty different vowel sounds, of which two occur only in unstressed positions. These two are here represented by the symbols /ə/ and /ʌ/, which are not letters in the German alphabet, but are written as **-e** and **-er**.

All German vowels are "pure"; that is, they are monophthongs and do not have any diphthongal glide at the end as do the English letters *a* and *o*. As you hear the following examples, the difference will become clear.

	ENGLISH *a*	GERMAN LONG **e**
PRONUNCI-ATION DRILL 2	gay	geh
	ray	Reh
	stay	steh
	baited	betet

* We are using phonemic symbols here; in the alphabet /ə/ is **-e** and /ʌ/ is **-er**.

ENGLISH *o*	GERMAN LONG **o**
moan	**Mohn**
tone	**Ton**
tote	**tot**
boat	**Boot**

Long **a** vs. short **a**

Many American students have real difficulty in hearing the difference between these two sounds and consequently have trouble pronouncing them. Yet very often the difference between long **a** and short **a** is the difference between two totally unrelated words, as the following examples show.

PRONUNCI-
ATION
DRILL 3

LONG **a**	VS.	SHORT **a**
Saat (planting)		**satt** (satisfied)
rate (guess)		**Ratte** (rat)
Rabe (raven)		**Rappe** (black horse)
Wahn (insanity)		**wann** (when)
fahl (pale)		**Fall** (fall)
kam (came)		**Kamm** (comb)
Maße (measures)		**Masse** (mass)
Bahn (track)		**Bann** (ban)

Now say these words again, but stretch the long **a** sound. Instead of **Saat**, say **Saaaat**, etc. You cannot do this with the short **a**: if you stretch the words in the second column, you have to stretch the consonant; for example, **Kamm** will become **Kammmm**.

Long **e**, long **ä**, short **e** and **ä**, unstressed **e** /ə/ and **er** /ʌ/

This group of vowel sounds will need your special attention.

Remember that the long **e**, like all other vowels, does not end in a glide: **geh,** not *gay.*

Some Germans do not really distinguish long **ä** from long **e**, except where there is a difference in meaning, for example, in **Gräte** (fishbone) vs. **Grete** (the girl's name Greta).

Short **e** and short **ä** represent the same sound: the **e** in **Kette** is indistinguishable from the **ä** in **hätte**.

The unstressed /ə/ occurs most frequently in endings and in prefixes; it is quite similar to the unstressed English *a* in *the sofa*. If /ə/ appears in front of final **-n**, it often all but disappears; thus **nennen** sounds like **nenn'n** and **kommen** like **komm'n**. These forms are hard to hear and hard to distinguish from forms without the **-en** ending. Yet very often it is essential to realize the distinction, as in **ihn** vs. **ihn(e)n**, **den** vs. **den(e)n**.

The unstressed /ʌ/, which is written as **er**, is one of the most difficult sounds for most Americans to produce. At first, you will have difficulty hearing the difference between /ə/ and /ʌ/, but the distinction is there and may be crucial, as in **bitte** (*please*) vs. **bitter** (*bitter*).

The following drills are designed to show you the differences between the various sounds of this group.

PRONUNCI-ATION DRILL 4

LONG e vs.	SHORT e
Beet	Bett
Wesen	wessen
reden	retten
wen	wenn
den	denn
stehen	stellen

Note again that short **e** and **ä** represent the same sound:

PRONUNCI-ATION DRILL 5

SHORT e vs.	SHORT ä
Wetter	Blätter
kenne	sänne
hemme	Kämme
Schwemme	Schwämme

no difference (handwritten annotation)

PRONUNCI-ATION DRILL 6

LONG ä vs.	LONG e vs.	SHORT e OR ä
Gräte	Grete	rette
Ähren	ehren	Herren
bäte	bete	bette
wähne	Vene	Wände

PRONUNCI-ATION DRILL 7

/ə/ vs.	/ʌ/
bete	Beter
Rede	Reeder
nehme	Nehmer

don't really pronounce r (handwritten annotation)

THE SOUNDS OF GERMAN

/ə/	vs.	/ʌ/ (cont.)
gebe		Geber
Esse		Esser
Messe		Messer
Summe		Summer
Hüte		Hüter
führe		Führer
Kutte		Kutter
gute		guter
Güte		Güter
Liebe		Lieber
Spitze		Spitzer
Pfarre		Pfarrer
gehören		(erhören)
gearbeitet		(erarbeitet)
gegessen		vergessen
gestört		zerstört

Long i and ü, short i and ü, long and short u

The two i-sounds are not very difficult to produce. They resemble the English vowel sounds in *bean* and *bin*.

The ü-sound, on the other hand, does not exist in English. To produce it, say i (as in English *key*); then freeze your tongue in that position and round your lips; or, to put it another way, say English *ee* with your lips in the English *oo* position. If you are musical and can get B above C above middle C on a piano, whistle it, and your tongue and lips will be in perfect ü-position. The letter y, which occurs mostly in foreign words, is usually pronounced like ü.

The long u-sound is similar to English *oo* in *noon;* the short u-sound is— to oversimplify matters a bit—just a very short version of the same English *oo*-sound, but again both sounds are much more clearly articulated in German.

LONG i	vs.	SHORT i
Miete		Mitte
biete		Bitte
riete		ritte
ihnen		innen

**PRONUNCI-
ATION
DRILL 8**

PRONUNCI-ATION DRILL 9

LONG i	vs.	LONG ü (y)
Miete		mühte
Miete		Mythe
Kiel		kühl
schiebe		Schübe
Stiele		Stühle

PRONUNCI-ATION DRILL 10

SHORT i	vs.	SHORT ü		SHORT i	vs.	SHORT ü
Kissen		küssen		Liste		Lüste
missen		müssen		Gericht		Gerücht
sticken		Stücken		springe		Sprünge
Bitte		Bütte		Kiste		Küste

PRONUNCI-ATION DRILL 11

LONG ü	vs.	SHORT ü		LONG ü	vs.	SHORT ü
Hüte		Hütte		Wüste		wüßte
rügen		rücken		Düne		dünne
pflügen		pflücken		Füßen		Füssen
kühnste		Künste		fühle		Fülle

PRONUNCI-ATION DRILL 12

LONG u	vs.	SHORT u		LONG u	vs.	SHORT u
Mus		muß		schuf		Schuft
Ruhm		Rum		spuken		spucken
sucht		Sucht		Buhle		Bulle
Fuder		Futter		Buße		Busse

PRONUNCI-ATION DRILL 13

LONG u	vs.	LONG ü		LONG u	vs.	LONG ü
Mut		Mythe		Schub		Schübe
Hut		Hüte		tuten		Tüten
gut		Güte		Huhn		Hühner
Schwur		Schwüre		Kuhle		Kühle

PRONUNCI-ATION DRILL 14

SHORT u	vs.	SHORT ü		SHORT u	vs.	SHORT ü
Mutter		Mütter		mußte		müßte
Kunst		Künste		wußte		wüßte
durfte		dürfte		Bund		Bünde
kurze		Kürze		Luft		Lüfte

Long and short **o**, long and short **ö**

Remember that the German **o**-sound does not end in a glide toward **u:**
Mohn, not *moan.* To produce an **ö,** say a long German **e,** then freeze your
tongue and round your lips. Note also the clear distinction between German **a** and German **o.** An American would be likely not to distinguish
between **Bann, Bahn,** and **Bonn,** but the three sounds are clearly different.

LONG o	VS.	SHORT o	
wohne		Wonne	*gonna*
Schote		Schotter	
Ton		Tonne	
Lote		Lotte	

PRONUNCI-ATION DRILL 15

SHORT o	VS.	LONG a	VS.	SHORT a
Bonn		Bahn		Bann
komm		kam		Kamm
Sonne		Sahne		Susanne
hoffen		Hafen		haften
Schollen		Schalen		schallen
locken		Laken		Schlacken
ob		gab		ab

strohout a

PRONUNCI-ATION DRILL 16

LONG e	VS.	LONG ö
redlich		rötlich
heben		höben
bete		böte
lege		löge

PRONUNCI-ATION DRILL 17

LONG o	VS.	LONG ö
Ton		Töne
Lohn		Löhne
Hof		Höfe
Not		Nöte
Bogen		Bögen

PRONUNCI-ATION DRILL 18

SHORT e	VS.	SHORT ö
stecken		Stöcken
Recke		Röcke
westlich		östlich
helle		Hölle

PRONUNCI-ATION DRILL 19

PRONUNCIATION DRILL 20

LONG ö	vs.	SHORT ö
Goethe		Götter
Schöße		schösse
Öfen		öffnen
Höhle		Hölle

PRONUNCIATION DRILL 21

LONG ö	vs.	LONG ü	vs.	LONG i
Söhne		Sühne		Kusine
löge		Lüge		liege
Öl		kühl		Kiel
schöbe		Schübe		schiebe

PRONUNCIATION DRILL 22

SHORT ö	vs.	SHORT ü
Stöcke		Stücke
schösse		Schüsse
Röcken		Rücken
Hölle		Hülle

PRONUNCIATION DRILL 23

SHORT u	vs.	SHORT ü	vs.	SHORT i
mußte		müßte		mißte
Stuck		Stück		Stickstoff
Kummer		Kümmel		Kimme
Kunde		künde		Kinder

Diphthongs

There are three German diphthongs, two of which can be spelled in two different ways: **ei** (**ai**), **eu** (**äu**), and **au**. They will not present much of a problem. They are similar to *i* in English *light, oi* in English *foible*, and *ou* in English *mouse*, but, like all German vowels, they are more precise, more clearly defined, and not as drawn-out as their English counterparts.

PRONUNCIATION DRILL 24

ei (ai)	eu (äu)	au
leiten	läuten	lauten
freien	freuen	Frauen
zeigen	zeugen	saugen
leise	Läuse	Laus
Meise	Mäuse	Maus

dabei
sogar
ng — g silent

You will be bothered by the fact that the combination **ei** represents a diphthong, but the combination **ie** is simply a long **i**. The following drill should help you overcome this difficulty. To keep the two sounds straight, think of the English phrase *The hEIght of my nIEce* or of the German phrase **wEIn und bIEr.**

ei	vs.	ie
meine		Miene
deine		diene
leider		Lieder
reimen		Riemen
Zeit		zieht
bereiten		berieten
keimen		Kiemen
verzeihen		verziehen

long ü — ie
short ü — i

Read the following words, distinguishing carefully between **ei** and **ie**:

short ä — e
long ä — a

Viel, Kleid, sieben, Liebe, Leib, leider, Lieder, Seife, siegen, zeigen, liegen, schieben, scheiden, Tier, einheitlich, einseifen, einfrieren, vierseitig, Bierseidel, Zeitspiegel, Spieglein, Meineid, Kleinigkeit.

German Consonants

In presenting the German vowel system, we have, of necessity, had to use almost all German consonant sounds. As you worked through the preceding section, you have doubtless noticed that some German consonants, such as **m** and **n**, differ hardly at all from their English equivalents. Others, such as **z**, have probably surprised you because they are not pronounced the way you expected them to sound. The combination of sounds represented by German **z**, however, does exist in English: if you can say *cats* in English, you should be able to say "**Tsoh**" in German, even though it is spelled **Zoo.**

There are only two consonant sounds in German which have no equivalent in English; they are both graphically represented by **ch.** The following notes and drills will introduce the German consonants and show you where you will encounter difficulties. We shall start with the two **ch**-sounds.

ch after **a, o, u, au**

This sound is relatively easy for Americans to produce; it corresponds to the **ch** in the Scottish word *loch*. To produce it, start with the sound **h**, let the air flow freely, and then, without diminishing the air flow, reduce the space between the back of your tongue and the roof of your mouth.

Most Americans tend to substitute a *k* for this **ch**-sound. The following drill will show you the difference. Note that the vowels preceding the **ch** are sometimes long and sometimes short.

	LONG VOWEL	SHORT VOWEL	DIPHTHONG
PRONUNCI- ATION DRILL 26	nach	Bach	auch
	hoch	noch	Lauch
	Buch	Bruch	Bauch

PRONUNCI- ATION DRILL 27	k̲	vs.	c̲h̲
	nackt		Nacht
	Akt		acht
	Laken		lachen
	lockt		locht
	dockt		Docht
	Kokken		kochen
	Pocken		pochen
	zuckt		Zucht
	pauken		brauchen

ch in combination with other letters; **chs**

For most Americans, this is the most difficult German consonant to produce. There are several ways of learning how to produce it. Say the English word *you* with an extended *y: y-y-y-you*. This *y* is a voiced sound; if you take the voice out of it, you'll produce something very close to this second **ch**-sound. (You can figure out the difference between a voiced and an unvoiced consonant by comparing the *s*-sounds in English *see* and *zee* (the letter *z*) or *Sioux* and *Zoo*.) Another way of getting at this second German **ch** is by starting with a word like *Hubert* or *huge*. Strongly aspirate the *h* and stretch it out: *h-h-huge;* the result will be quite similar to the **ch**-sound. Try the following combinations:

PRONUNCI- ATION DRILL 28	a human
	say Hugh
	the hue
	see Hubert

Again, you must be careful not to substitute *k* for **ch**:

k	vs.	ch
Bäcker		Becher
Leck		Lech
schleckt		schlecht
häkeln		hecheln
siegt		Sicht
nickt		nicht
Brücke		Brüche

PRONUNCI-
ATION
DRILL 29

The following drill contrasts the two **ch**-sounds. The words in the second column are the plurals of the words in the first column.

Dach	Dächer
Bach	Bäche
Loch	Löcher
Buch	Bücher
Bruch	Brüche
Brauch	Bräuche

PRONUNCI-
ATION
DRILL 30

In the following drill, the **ich**-sound occurs after consonants:

München
mancher
welcher
solcher
Milch
Furcht

PRONUNCI-
ATION
DRILL 31

Another difficulty arises when the **ich**-sound appears initially, as in the suffix **-chen**. Note that if the preceding consonant is an **s** or **sch**-sound, the **ch** in **-chen** is pronounced almost like an English *y*.

Männchen
Frauchen
Säckchen
bißchen
Häuschen
Tischchen

PRONUNCI-
ATION
DRILL 32

Finally, the combination **chs** is pronounced like English *x*.

sechs
Luchs
Lachs
Sachsen
wachsen
Büchse

b, d, g and p, t, k; pf, ps, ng, kn

You will have no trouble pronouncing these sounds, but there is one area where you must watch out: if **b, d, g** appear at the end of a syllable or in front of **t**, they are pronounced like **p, t, k**. In the following drill, the German words are not translations of the English words.

ENGLISH *b, d, g*	vs.	GERMAN b, d, g
glib		gib
glide		Kleid
lied		Leid
lead		Lied
bug		Bug

Compare the pronunciation of **b, d, g** in the following two columns:

b, d, g	vs.	p, t, k
lieben		lieb, liebt
heben		hob, hebt
sieben		Sieb, siebt
Abend		ab
loben		Lob, lobt
leiden		Leid
Lieder		Lied
baden		Bad
Süden		Süd
kriegen		Krieg, kriegt
fliegen		flog, fliegt
lügen		log, lügt

<u>b, d, g</u>	vs.	<u>p, t, k</u> (cont.)
beobachten		Obdach
aber		abfahren
radeln		Radfahrer
Tage		täglich
sagen		unsagbar

Now read the following words.

Bad Soden, Abendland, wegheben, abheben, Aberglaube, Staubwedel, Abwege, Feldweg, Feldwege, Waldwege, Laubwald, Laubwälder.

The **p** in the combinations **pf** and initial **ps** is always pronounced; the latter occurs only in foreign words:

Pfeife	Psychologie	PRONUNCI-ATION DRILL 36
Pfarrer	Psychiater	
hüpfen	Psalm	
Köpfe	Pseudonym	
Topf		
Napf		

The combination **ng** is pronounced as in English *singer*, not as in *finger*.

Finger	PRONUNCI-ATION DRILL 37
Sänger	
Ringe	
lange	
England	

The **k** in **kn** must be pronounced.

ENGLISH	GERMAN	
knave	Knabe	PRONUNCI-ATION DRILL 38
knack	knacken	
knead	kneten	
knee	Knie	
knight	Knecht	
knob	Knopf	

z

The German letter **z** represents the combination **ts,** which, in English, does not occur at the beginning of words. To learn to produce it in initial position start with the English word *cats;* say it again, but make a break between *ca-* and *-ts.* Then do the same with *Betsy: Be/tsy.* If you only say *tsy,* you almost have the first syllable of the German word **Ziege.**

PRONUNCI-ATION DRILL 39

INITIAL	MEDIAL	FINAL
ziehen	heizen	Kranz
zog	duzen	Pfalz
gezogen	geizig	Salz
zu	Lanze	Kreuz
Zug	Kanzel	Malz
Züge	Kerze	Pelz
Zahn	Kreuzung	stolz

However, if it occurs in the middle or at the end of a word, the *ts-* sound is usually represented by **tz.**

PRONUNCI-ATION DRILL 40

Katze
putzen
sitzen
Platz
Fritz

s, ß, sp, st, sch

German **s** does not present much of a problem. It is neither as strongly voiceless as the English *s*-sound as in *see* nor as strongly voiced as the *s*-sound as in *zoo.*

PRONUNCI-ATION DRILL 41

INITIAL	MEDIAL	FINAL
so	lesen	das
sie	blasen	los
sagen	gewesen	Glas
sicher	Käse	Mus

The *s*-sound may be represented by the symbol **ß** (instead of **ss**). It is called an **s-z** (**ess-zet**) and is used:

(a) between two vowels of which the first is long:

LONG VOWEL + ß	SHORT VOWEL + ss
Maße	Masse
Buße	Busse
Straße	Rasse
große	Rosse

PRONUNCI-ATION DRILL 42

(b) after a vowel or a diphthong before a consonant (mostly in verbs whose stem ends in -ss):

weißt
mußt
paßt
heißt

(c) in final position:

Fuß
Roß
weiß
daß

Many Germans no longer use the ß symbol, but write ss instead.

The s in German sp and st at the beginning is pronounced like English *sh:*

Spaß	Start	Strand
Sport	stehen	Strom
spät	still	streng
Spinne	Stock	streichen
Spule	Stück	streuen

PRONUNCI-ATION DRILL 43

German sch is pronounced like English *sh.*

schön
waschen
Busch

PRONUNCI-ATION DRILL 44

sch	vs.	ch
Tisch		dich
mischen		mich
Esche		Echo
Büsche		Bücher

w, v, f

There is no German equivalent of the English *w*-sound as in *water*. German w is pronounced like English *v*.

wann

wer

wo

wie

warum

German v is usually pronounced like English *f*.

Vater

verliebt

viel

voll

von

In some foreign words, German v corresponds to English *v*.

Vase

Villa

German f always corresponds to English *f*, as does the *ph*-sound in foreign words.

fallen

Fell

fliegen

fünf

Philosophie

Physik

w	vs.	f
Wein		fein
Wand		fand
winden		finden
Wort		fort
Wunde		Funde

l and r

These two consonants are mispronounced by most Americans. Such mispronunciations will not normally lead to a misunderstanding, but they do in large measure contribute to a "typical American accent." Constant practice with these two consonants is therefore essential.

The English *l* is a "dark," back *l,* and the German l s a "clear," front l. Listen to the difference:

ENGLISH *l*	vs.	GERMAN l
feel		viel
stool		Stuhl
mall		Mal
fall		Fall
toll		toll
still		still
hell		hell
lewd		lud
light		Leid
long		lang
bald		bald
built		Bild

PRONUNCIATION DRILL 46

In some parts of Germany, the **r** is trilled, but the preferred sound is a uvular **r.** To produce it, say **Buchen,** with the **ch**-sound as far back as possible. Then add voice to it and you should be saying **Buren.**

ENGLISH *r*	vs.	GERMAN **r**
run		ran
rudder		Ruder
reef		rief
rest		Rest
ray		Reh
row		roh
brown		braun
dry		drei
fry		frei
fresh		frisch
creek		Krieg
warn		warnen
start		Start
stork		Storch
worst		Wurst

PRONUNCIATION DRILL 47

We introduced the **er**-sound (ʌ) under the vowels. Many Germans use
this same sound for **r** before **t**.

**PRONUNCI-
ATION
DRILL 48**

er fährt

er lehrt

er bohrt

er irrt

er knurrt

**PRONUNCI-
ATION
DRILL 49**

INITIAL r	r AFTER CONSONANT	MEDIAL r	r BEFORE t	FINAL r (ʌ)
raffen	graben	fahren	fahrt	fahr'
Rebe	Bregenz	Beeren	fährt	Bär
riefen	Friesen	vieren	viert	vier
rot	Thron*	Toren	bohrt	Tor
Ruhe	Bruder	Uhren	fuhrt	Uhr

**PRONUNCI-
ATION
DRILL 50**

ch	vs.	r
Buchen		Buren
suchen		Suren
fachen		fahren
Acht		Art
Docht		dort
Sucht		surrt
Dach		dar
Loch		Lohr
Tuch		Tour

**PRONUNCI-
ATION
DRILL 51**

l	vs.	r
wild		wird
Geld		Gert
halt		hart
hold		Hort
bald		Bart
Spalt		spart
spülen		spüren
fühlen		führen
fallen		fahren
tollen		Toren

* The combination **th**, which occurs in a few German words, is always pronounced as **t:**
English *throne*, German **Thron.**

h

At the beginning of a word or syllable, **h** is pronounced as in English *house*. It is never silent as in English *honor*. The symbol **h**, however, is also used to indicate that the preceding vowel is long.

sehen	seht	steh'
fehlen	fehlt	geh'
Lehrer	lehrt	Reh

PRONUNCI-
ATION
DRILL 52

q

As in English, **q** appears only with a following **u,** but it is pronounced like English *kv*, not *kw*.

ENGLISH	GERMAN
quicksilver	Quecksilber
quadrant	Quadrant
Quaker	Quäker
qualify	qualifizieren
quality	Qualität
quarter	Quartier

PRONUNCI-
ATION
DRILL 53

j

This letter is pronounced like English *y*.

ENGLISH	GERMAN
yes	ja
year	Jahr
young	jung
youth	Jugend
yacht	Jacht
yoke	Joch

PRONUNCI-
ATION
DRILL 54

The Glottal Stop

The glottal stop is a phenomenon much more common in German than in English. In certain parts of the eastern United States, the word *bottle* is pronounced *bo-'l* with a very short open *o*, after which the glottis is closed and then suddenly reopened. This sudden release of air occurs in German in front of all initial vowels: **ein alter Affe.** Most Americans tend to run these words together: **[einalteraffe]**; this is another contributory factor in a "typical American accent." If you neglect to use the glottal stop, you may get yourself into embarrassing situations. For instance, if you don't use the stop in front of **-'au,** you will interpret the name of the village of **Himmelsau** as *Celestial Pig* instead of *Heavenly Meadow.*

ein alter Affe

Himmelsau

der erste Akt

ein alter Omnibus

er aber aß Austern

alle anderen Uhren

es erübrigt sich

es ist aber veraltet

eine alte Eule sitzt unter einer alten Ulme

Note the difference in

vereisen (to get covered with ice)   and   **verreisen** (to go on a trip)

verengen (to narrow)   **verrenken** (to sprain)

Sentence Intonation

Since sentence intonation is closely connected with syntax, it is dealt with in various units of this book, as new syntactical patterns are introduced. A few prefatory remarks, however, are in order, to explain the symbols used in the intonation graphs.

Like English, German is spoken on three basic levels of pitch; these levels are indicated by three horiontal lines:

Unstressed syllables are indicated by dots (**.**), stressed syllables by short lines with a stress mark (∠). Thus the English sentence *He lives in Munich* would be diagramed as follows:

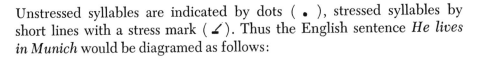

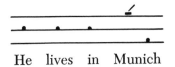

He   lives   in   Munich

If this same sentence is spoken as a question, the last syllable, though unstressed, shows a rise in pitch. This rise is indicated by the symbol (♪). If the last syllable is stressed, rising pitch is indicated by (∠) and falling pitch by (∠).

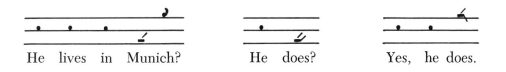

He lives in Munich?   He does?   Yes, he does.

Syllabication

German syllabication is considerably simpler than English syllabication. A few basic rules will suffice to see you through this book.

German words are divided before single consonants and between double consonants:

Va - ter   kom - men
Da - me   reg - nen
Te - le - fon   Mün - chen

The only exception to this rule is **st,** which is never separated:

fe - ster
mei - stens
Fen - ster

Unlike English, German does not consider suffixes independent units; thus it is **Woh - nung,** not [**Wohn - ung**].

Compound words are divided according to their individual parts:

Brief - trä - ger
Glas - au - ge
Sams - tag

Punctuation

Generally speaking, most German punctuation marks are used as in English. Only the use of the comma is different. The comma may be used to separate main clauses if the second clause contains a new subject, especially in front of coordinating conjunctions. The comma *must* be used to separate dependent clauses from main clauses. Relative clauses are dependent clauses, and German does not distinguish between restrictive and nonrestrictive relative clauses. In contrast to English, the comma is not used in front of **und** in series: **Männer, Frauen und Kinder.**

The first of a pair of quotation marks in German appears below the base line in writing or printing, the second appears at the top: "Be quiet!" **„Sei ruhig!"**

GERMAN

A Structural Approach

SHORTER EDITION

UNIT 1: The Present Tense—**sein** and **haben**—Gender—Verb-Second Position—Intonation Patterns—**auch** and **denn**

Practice and read aloud the following sentences until you have mastered the intonation pattern.

[1] Assertions: Basic Intonation Pattern

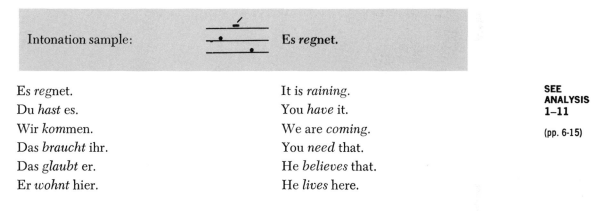

| Intonation sample: | Es *reg*net. |

Es *reg*net.	It is *raining*.	**SEE ANALYSIS 1–11**
Du *hast* es.	You *have* it.	
Wir *kom*men.	We are *coming*.	(pp. 6-15)
Das *braucht* ihr.	You *need* that.	
Das *glaubt* er.	He *believes* that.	
Er *wohnt* hier.	He *lives* here.	

[2] Assertions: Enlarged Pattern

| Intonation sample: | **Wir brauchen *alle* Geld.** |

Wir brauchen *alle* Geld.	We *all* need money.	**SEE ANALYSIS 1–11**
Sie hat *Hunger.*	She is *hungry*.	
Ich bin *hung*rig.	I am *hungry*.	(pp. 6-15)
Das ist Frau *Mey*er.	That's Mrs. *Meyer*.	
Das ist *Herr* Meyer.	That's *Mr*. Meyer.	
Wir brauchen *Re*gen.	We need *rain*.	
Wir *ar*beiten heute.	We are *working* today.	
Wir bleiben heute zu *Hau*se.	We are staying *home* today.	

1

[3] Assertions: Syntactical Stress on Last Syllable

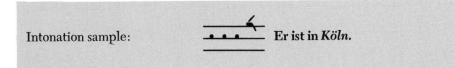

Intonation sample: Er ist in *Köln.*

SEE
ANALYSIS
1–11
(pp. 6-15)

Er ist in *Köln.*	He is in *Cologne.*
Sie *kommt.*	She is *coming.*
Das sagst *du.*	That's what *you* say.
Er hat *Geld.*	He has *money.*
Sie lernen *Deutsch.*	They are learning *German.*
Er wohnt in Ber*lin.*	He is living in *Berlin.*
Das glaube ich *auch.*	I believe that, *too.*
Ich studiere Medi*zin.*	I am studying *medicine.*
Ich glaube, er wohnt in *Köln.*	I believe he lives in *Cologne.*

[4] Assertions: Syntactical Stress on First Syllable

Intonation sample: *Fritz* ist schon hier.

SEE
ANALYSIS
1–11
(pp. 6-15)

Fritz ist schon hier!	*Fritz* is already here!
Du bist's!	It is *you!*
Geld hat sie!	She has *money!*

[5] Syntactical Stress on More than One Syllable

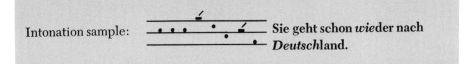

Intonation sample: Sie geht schon *wieder* nach *Deutsch*land.

SEE
ANALYSIS
1–11
(pp. 6-15)

Sie geht schon *wieder* nach *Deutsch*land.	She is going to *Germany again.*
Übrigens gehen wir *nächs*tes Jahr nach *Deutsch*land.	By the way, we are going to *Germany next* year.
Na*tür*lich gehen wir sonntags in die *Kirche.*	Of *course* we go to *church* on Sundays.

[6] Word Questions

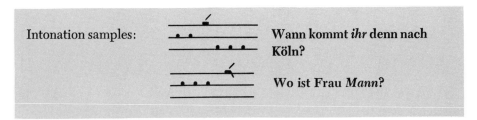

| Intonation samples: | Wann kommt *ihr* denn nach Köln? |
| | Wo ist Frau *Mann?* |

SEE
ANALYSIS
12–13

(pp. 15-17)

Wann kommt *ihr* denn nach Köln?	When are *you* coming to Cologne?
Wo *bist* du denn?	Where *are* you?
Was *hast* du denn?	What do you *have?*
Wo *wohnt* er denn?	Where does he *live?*
Wann *kommt* er denn?	When is he *coming?*
Wo *wohnt* ihr denn?	Where do you *live?*
Wo *ar*beiten Sie?	Where do you *work?*
Wann kommst du nach *Hause?*	When are you coming *home?*
Wo ist denn die *Zei*tung?	Where is the *newspaper?*
Wo ist Frau *Mann?*	Where is Mrs. *Mann?*
Wer ist denn *das?*	Who is *that?*

[7] Yes-or-No Questions

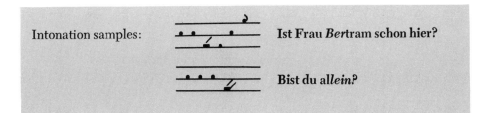

| Intonation samples: | Ist Frau *Ber*tram schon hier? |
| | Bist du al*lein?* |

SEE
ANALYSIS
12–13

(pp. 15-17)

Ist Frau *Ber*tram schon hier?	Is Mrs. *Bertram* already here?
Hast du *Hunger?*	Are you *hungry?*
Ist die *Zei*tung schon hier?	Is the *newspaper* already here?
Lernst du *auch* Deutsch?	Are *you* learning German, *too?*
Lernst du auch *Deutsch?*	Are you learning *German, too?*
*Reg*net es in Köln?	Is it *raining* in Cologne?
Kommst du *morgen* abend?	Are you coming *tomorrow* evening?
Geht ihr Sonntag in die *Kir*che?	Are you going to *church* Sunday?

[8] Assertions Intonated as Questions

Intonation sample: Du wohnst *auch* in München?

SEE
ANALYSIS
12–13
(pp. 15-17)

Du wohnst *auch* in München?	You live in Munich, *too?*
Er arbeitet jetzt in *M*ünchen?	He works in *Munich* now?
Ihr arbeitet *heute?*	You are working *today?*
Ihr *a*rbeitet heute?	You are *working* today?
Ihr braucht *Geld?*	You need *money?*
Erika ist hier?	*Erika* is here?
Erika ist hier in *Köln?*	Erika is here in *Cologne?*
Nein?	*No?*

''Pedestrian crossing''

Practice reading these conversations aloud until you have memorized them.

A: Sie kommen al*lein*, Inge? Wo ist denn Hans?

You've come *alone*, Inge? Where is *Hans?*

B: *Hans* kommt *auch.* Er kommt *später.*

Hans is coming, *too.* He will come *later.*

A: Hier in *Köln* re*g*net es. Regnet es in Hamburg *auch?*

Here in *Cologne* it is *raining.* Is it raining in *Hamburg, too?*

B: *Ja,* hier in Hamburg regnet es *auch.*

Yes, here in *Hamburg* it is raining, *too.*

A: Was tust *du* denn hier in Köln?

What are *you* doing here in Cologne?

B: Ich studiere Medi*z*in. Hans ist übrigens *auch* hier.

I am studying *medicine.* Hans, by the way, is here, *too.*

A: Studiert er *auch* Medizin?

Is he *also* studying medicine?

A: Hm! Sie arbeiten hier in *Köln?* Wo*h*nen Sie auch hier?

Well! You are working here in *Cologne?* Do you *live* here, too?

B: Ja, ich *woh*ne auch hier.

Yes, I also *live* here.

READING

Practice reading these sentences until you can read them rapidly and with correct intonation.

Natürlich	**bleibe**	ich morgen abend zu Hause.
Ich	**bleibe**	morgen abend natürlich zu Hause.
Morgen abend	**bleibe**	ich natürlich zu Hause.

Wir	**gehen**	natürlich Sonntag morgen in die Kirche.
Natürlich	**gehen**	wir Sonntag morgen in die Kirche.
Sonntag morgen	**gehen**	wir natürlich in die Kirche.

Übrigens	**gehen**	wir Sonntag abend ins Kino.
Wir	**gehen**	übrigens Sonntag abend ins Kino.
Sonntag abend	**gehen**	wir übrigens ins Kino.

Typical street signs: "Straight ahead and right turn only." "Begin. No parking from 7 p.m. to 7 a.m. and no stopping from 7 a.m. to 7 p.m."

ANALYSIS

1 The Infinitive

The infinitive is that form of the verb which is used as a dictionary entry. Thus the English forms *am, is,* and *was* are found in the dictionary under *be; bought* is found under *buy;* and *does* is found under *do.*

Most German infinitives end in **-en: arbeiten, bleiben, brauchen.** The infinitives **sein, tun,** and certain others to be introduced later end in **-n.** That part of the verb which precedes the infinitive ending **-en** or **-n** is called the stem. Thus:

STEM	+	INFINITIVE ENDING	=	INFINITIVE
arbeit-		-en		arbeiten
bleib-		-en		bleiben
brauch-		-en		brauchen
tu-		-n		tun

2 Personal Pronouns

SINGULAR		PLURAL	
ich	I	wir	we
du	you	ihr	you
er	he	sie	they
sie	she		
es	it	Sie	you

English "you": du, ihr, Sie

Modern English alone among all the Indo-European languages has just one form (*you*) for the second person. English *you* is both singular and plural, formal and informal. In German, there are three mutually exclusive forms:

1. **du** (corresponding to the archaic English *thou*) is the familiar singular. It expresses intimacy and is therefore used in the family, with close friends, and in prayer. It is also used with *all* children up to the age of about fourteen and with animals (pets).

2. **ihr** is the plural of **du.**

3. **Sie,** on the other hand, implies a certain formality and the recognition of social considerations. It is always used with **Herr, Frau, Fräulein,** or other titles. This polite **Sie,** which is both singular and plural, sounds like the plural **sie** (they) and it takes the same verb form. When written, it is always capitalized.

Brauchst du Geld, Maria?	Do you need money, Mary?
Brauchst du Geld, Karl?	Do you need money, Karl?
Braucht ihr Geld, Kinder?	Do you need money, children?
Du bist mein Gott.	Thou art my God. (Ps. 31:14)
Brauchen Sie Geld, Herr Meyer?	Do you need money, Mr. Meyer?
Wohnen Sie in München, Herr Doktor?	Do you live in Munich, Dr. Meyer?

Beware!	[Brauchst du Geld, Herr Meyer?]	DO NOT USE!
Americanism!	[Brauchst du Geld, Frau Meyer?]*	

NOTE: Germans love titles. If **Herr Meyer** has earned any kind of doctorate, he is addressed as **Herr Doktor** (no last name), and he is referred to as **Herr Dr. Meyer** or as **Dr. Meyer.**

---

* Brackets are used in this book to indicate unacceptable forms—either Germanisms in English or Americanisms in German.

The polite **Sie**, which maintains a certain distance between the speaker and the person spoken to, can be used together with the first name under specific social conditions. For instance, among sophisticated people of the upper class who are good acquaintances but not close personal friends, the polite **Sie** is often used with the first name.

3   Inflected Verb Forms

The predicate verb of a sentence or a clause is always an "inflected" form —that is, a form modified by a personal ending. (With the exception of *-s*, as in *he lives*, all personal endings have been dropped in English.)

The present tense of regular verbs is formed as follows:

PRONOUN	STEM	+	PERSONAL ENDING	=	INFLECTED FORM	
ich	glaub-		e		ich glaube	I believe
du	glaub-		st		du glaubst	you believe
er					er	he
sie	glaub-		t		sie } glaubt	she } believes
es					es	it
wir	glaub-		en		wir glauben	we believe
ihr	glaub-		t		ihr glaubt	you believe
sie	glaub-		en		sie glauben	they believe
Sie	glaub-		en		Sie glauben	you believe

4   Absence of Progressive and Emphatic Forms in German

A native speaker of English will always differentiate between the "simple present" and the "progressive form." The "simple present" usually expresses either a timeless fact:

Water boils at 100° C.

or some habitual attitude or activity:

He is usually nasty.
He smokes only cigars.
I just love our new house.

Use of the progressive form, on the other hand, expresses the idea of "being in the middle of it." Thus, it would make no sense to say *I am just loving our new house,* but it is possible to say:

He is being nasty again.
The water is boiling.
This week we are reading Emerson.
Dad is working in the garden.

Standard German does not express the difference between *boils* and *is boiling* by verb forms. Instead, German relies on syntax (**Wasser kocht** = *water boils;* **das Wasser kocht** = *the water is boiling*), and on context. One should not "translate" *he is having, he is being, he is working* into German. Otherwise one will start by saying **er ist . . .** and end up with an Americanism. **Er arbeitet** means both *he works* and *he is working*, and **es regnet** means both *it rains* and *it is raining*.

German also has no emphatic form. It cannot express the difference between *I go* and *I do go* by different verb forms. Instead, German relies on intonation and on certain particles. The unaccented **ja,** for instance, adds the flavor of *indeed,* implied in *we do go.*

Wir gehen jeden Sonntag in die Kirche.	We go to church *every* Sunday.
Aber Vater, wir gehen ja jeden Sonntag in die Kirche.	But, Father, we *do* go to church every Sunday.

5 Future Meaning of Present-Tense Forms

Just as the progressive form *I am going* has a future meaning in *I am going to Germany next year,* so the present tense of German verbs frequently assumes a future meaning:

Morgen abend gehen wir ins Kino.   We are going to the movies tomorrow night.

6 Variations in Personal Endings

In the case of **er glaubt** or **er kommt,** the ending **-t** is easily pronounced and heard. However, in the case of such verbs as **arbeiten** and of all other verbs whose stems end in **-d** or **-t,** the vowel **-e-** is inserted between the stem and the endings **-st** and **-t** to make these endings clearly audible. For similar reasons, it is **es regnet,** not [es regnt].

ORDINARY VERBS		VERBS WITH STEMS IN -d OR -t	
du	glaubst	du	arbeitest
er ⎫		er ⎫	
sie ⎬	glaubt	sie ⎬	arbeitet
es ⎭		es ⎭	
ihr	glaubt	ihr	arbeitet

Since the infinitive **tun** ends in **-n** and not in **-en,** the **wir**-form and the **sie**-form also end in **-n: wir tun, sie tun.**

7   sein and haben

A few of the most frequently used German verbs are quite irregular. In this lesson, we introduce **sein** (*to be*) and **haben** (*to have*). In the present tense, they are inflected as follows:

ich	bin		wir	sind
du	bist		ihr	seid
er			sie	sind
sie	ist		Sie	sind
es				

ich	habe		wir	haben
du	hast		ihr	habt
er			sie	haben
sie	hat		Sie	haben
es				

8   Gender of Nouns

Indo-European, the ancestor of most modern European languages, including English, distinguished between three classes of nouns, which we call masculines, feminines, and neuters. All Indo-European languages, including Old English, inherited this distinction. Modern English is the only Indo-European language which has given up the difference almost completely. All nouns in French and Spanish are either feminine or masculine. German, Russian, and some other languages have kept all three classes alive. Usually, the German nouns themselves can no longer be recognized as masculine, feminine, or neuter just by looking at their dictionary forms: **Winter** (masculine), **Butter** (feminine), and **Wetter** (neuter) all end in **-er.** However, the articles (and also the pronouns and the adjectives) used with nouns still show the old difference:

masculine	*der* **Winter**	(*the* winter)	*der* **Löffel**	(*the* spoon)
feminine	*die* **Butter**	(*the* butter)	*die* **Gabel**	(*the* fork)
neuter	*das* **Wetter**	(*the* weather)	*das* **Messer**	(*the* knife)

"Gender" is a linguistic, not a biological, term. There is obviously nothing "masculine" about a spoon, nothing "feminine" about a fork, and nothing "neuter" about a knife, though the genders of the German nouns are masculine, feminine, and neuter respectively. To be sure, it is **der Mann** (*the man*), **die Frau** (*the woman*), and **das Kind** (*the infant*), and this is the reason why the term "masculine" came to be applied to *all* nouns used with **der,** the term "feminine" to *all* nouns used with **die,** and the term "neuter" to *all* nouns used with **das.** German children are not conscious of gender, and they never hear the term until they go to school. But they always hear their elders and the other children say **der Löffel, die Gabel,** and **das Messer.** They imitate what they hear and thus learn gender without effort. For the English-speaking student there is only one thing to do: learn the article together with the noun.

9 Position of the Inflected Verb

The "inflected verb form" is that form of a verb which by its ending and by its position belongs to a particular grammatical person. Thus, the forms **bin, habe,** and **gehe** can only belong to **ich,** and the forms **bist, hast,** and **gehst** can only belong to **du.** To be sure, the forms **gehen** or **brauchen,** which belong to **wir** and **sie** (they), are identical with the infinitives **gehen** and **brauchen.** However, when a German hears the words

> **Morgen   gehen**   . . . . . .

he knows right away that the next syntactical unit will be either **wir, Sie,** or **sie** (or a plural noun, the equivalent of **sie**); *for in every assertion the inflected verb is the second syntactical unit.* In the phrase "**Morgen gehen . . . ,**" **gehen** can therefore not be an infinitive. It must be either the **wir**-form or the **sie**-form.

The place in front of the inflected verb is occupied by only one unit—that is, by the answer to only one possible question:

Er hat Geld.	**Wer hat Geld?—Er!**
Heute bleibe ich zu Hause.	**Wann bleibst du zu Hause?—Heute!**
Geld hat sie.	**Was hat sie?—Geld!**

The student should therefore never imitate English sentences like

> Tomorrow night we're going to the movies,

for the verbal element *are going* is here preceded both by *tomorrow night* and by *we*—that is, by the answer to two possible questions. In German this English sentence is expressed either by

Morgen abend   gehen   wir ins Kino

or by

Wir   gehen   morgen abend ins Kino.

10 Word Stress

Almost all simple (non-compound) German words stress the first syllable:
A'bend (*evening*), **ar'beiten** (*to work*), **heu'te** (*today*). Words composed
of two nouns stress the first noun much more strongly than the second:
Haus'frau (*housewife*), **Haus'hund** (*house dog*), **Hun'dehaus** (*dog-house*).

Words of non-German origin frequently do not stress the first syllable:
natür'lich, die Natur', studie'ren. Our vocabulary will indicate which
syllable is stressed in these cases.

11 Syntactical Stress and Intonation of Assertions

Word Stress versus Syntactical Stress

If one analyzes the stress situation in a short sentence like

August wohnt in Berlin.   Gus lives in Berlin.

one can either look at the individual words as words, or one can look at
the sentence as a whole.

Looking at the words **Au'gust** and **Berlin'** as words, one can say that
Au'gust is stressed on the first and **Berlin'** on the second syllable. This is
a question of word stress. Word stress is fixed, and it is simply a mistake
to say **August'** or **Ber'lin.** In fact, **Au'gust** is a personal name and **August'**
is the name of a month.

Looking at the sentence as a whole—that is, as one single unit of thought
—we find it ambiguous in its written form. The speaker may want to say:

1. *August* **wohnt in Berlin.**   *Gus* lives in Berlin.
2. **August** *wohnt* **in Berlin.**   Gus *lives* in Berlin.
3. **August wohnt in Ber***lin.*   Gus lives in *Berlin.*

The one written sentence turns out to be at least three spoken sentences,
which are not interchangeable. Each of them has a specific meaning. Each
of them is used in situations where the other two cannot be used.

In all three sentences, **August** is stressed on the first, and **Berlin** on the second syllable. But the stress on **Au′gust** in the first sentence above is so strong that, in comparison, the stress on **Berlin′** becomes insignificant. For in each sentence the speaker singles out at least one word into which he packs the major news value and upon which he therefore places such a strong emphasis that, as far as the sentence as a whole is concerned, all other syllables can be regarded as unstressed. Syntactical stress, by which the speaker distinguishes between important and unimportant words, overshadows word stress; and whereas word stress is fixed, syntactical stress can shift from one word to another, depending on which word is chosen by the speaker to be the important one in a certain situation. The stressed syllable of this important word is called the "stress point" of a sentence.

The Basic Intonation Pattern for Assertions

As long as only one syllable of an assertion receives syntactical stress, this one syllable (the stress point) is also the syllable with the highest pitch.

Pitch in German (and English) is usually distributed over three levels, symbolized by the three lines below.* An assertion usually starts on level 2, moves up to level 3 for the stress point, and then falls to level 1. By using dots for the syllables without syntactical stress, and a short line with an accent over it for the stress point, the pitch distribution can be diagramed as follows:

Sie *wohnt* **hier**   She *lives* here

Intonation of Assertions: The Enlarged Pattern

Depending on which syllable is selected by the speaker to assume the role of the stress point, the sentence **Maria wohnt in München,** as pointed out above, can be pronounced with the following three intonations:

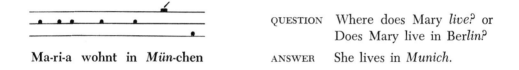

Ma-ri-a wohnt in Mün-chen

QUESTION Where does Mary *live?* or Does Mary live in Ber*lin?*

ANSWER She lives in *Munich.*

---

* For a full explanation of the symbols used in the intonation diagrams, see the introductory section on the sounds of German.

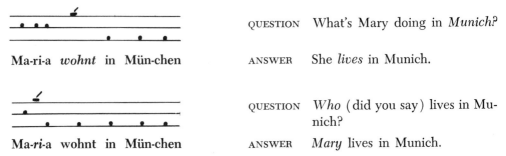

| | QUESTION | What's Mary doing in *Munich?* |
| Ma-ri-a *wohnt* in Mün-chen | ANSWER | She *lives* in Munich. |

| | QUESTION | *Who* (did you say) lives in Munich? |
| Ma-*ri*-a wohnt in Mün-chen | ANSWER | *Mary* lives in Munich. |

Observe that all the unstressed syllables preceding the stress point may be spoken with even level-2 pitch, and that all the unstressed syllables following the stress point show level-1 pitch.

Syntactical Stress on the Last Syllable

The drop from level 3 to level 1 at the end of a sentence functions as a signal. The drop in level means, "This is the end of the sentence." This drop must therefore be maintained, even if the last syllable is the stress point. The last syllable itself must then show a downward glide:

Er wohnt in Ber-*lin*

Compare the difference between *No!* (⌐) as an answer and *No?* (⌐) as a question.

Assertions with More than One Stressed Syllable

Many German sentences contain more than one syllable which carries a strong syntactical stress. The sentence **Wir arbeiten alle in München,** for instance, may be pronounced in the following ways:

ONE STRESSED SYLLABLE

Wir *ar*-bei-ten al-le in Mün-chen

We all *work* in Munich.
(Question: What are you all doing in *Munich?*)

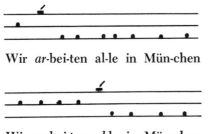

Wir ar-bei-ten *al*-le in Mün-chen

We *all* work in Munich.
(Question: How *many* of you work in Munich?)

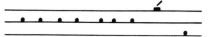

Wir ar·bei·ten al·le in *Mün*·chen

We all work in *Munich*.
(Question: Where do you all *work?*)

TWO STRESSED SYLLABLES

Sie ar·bei·ten *al*·le in *Mün*·chen

They *all* work in *Munich*.
(This stress pattern is probably not the answer to any question.)

As the last example shows, if a German sentence contains more than one stressed syllable, the first one has level-3 pitch, and the ones following are lower than the first. The end of the sentence provides the usual signal: the intonation falls to level 1 and thereby indicates the end of the assertion. All stressed syllables express items which have significant news value for the specific situation in which the sentence is spoken.

12 The Grammatical Structure of German Questions

As far as grammatical structure is concerned, German, like English, uses three types of questions.

Yes-or-No Questions

Questions which can be answered by **ja** (*yes*) or **nein** (*no*) may start with an inflected verb in both English and German. However, there is an important difference. The opening verb in English can only be (1) a form of *to be* (*Is Bob in?*), (2) a form of *to have* (*Has he gone?*), (3) a modal (*Can he play?*), or (4) a form of *to do* (*Does he want to play?*). In German, *any* verb can open a yes-or-no question, and the use of **tun** as an auxiliary is impossible. The German questions

> **Regnet es heute?**
> **Arbeitet er in Berlin?**
> **Brauchst du Geld?**

correspond in English to the unacceptable Germanisms

> [Rains it today?]
> [Works he in Berlin?]
> [Need you money?]

Conversely, the English questions

> Does he work?
> Do you need money?

correspond in German to the unacceptable Americanisms

Beware!	**[Tut er arbeiten?]**	DO NOT USE!
Americanism!	**[Tust du brauchen Geld?]**	

Word Questions

Questions which start with interrogatives (question words) such as **wer** (*who*), **wann** (*when*), **wo** (*where*), or **wie** (*how*) we shall call word questions. In word questions, the inflected verb follows immediately after the interrogative:

Wann kommt ihr?	When are you coming?
Wer ist das?	Who is that?
Wo wohnt sie?	Where does she live?

NOTE: Any German verb can follow the interrogative, and the use of **tun** as an auxiliary is again impossible.

Beware!	**[Wann tust du kommen?]**
Americanism!	**[Wo tut sie wohnen?]** DO NOT USE!

Questions Structured Like Assertions

German assertions, as we pointed out in **9**, are characterized by the fact that the inflected verb is always the second unit in the sentence. Any such assertion can be changed into a yes-or-no question by changing its intonation (see **13.**)

13 The Intonation of German Questions

Word Questions

Normally, German word questions follow the intonation pattern of assertions:

Wo *wohnst* **du?**	**Wo ist** *Fritz?*
Where do you *live?*	Where is *Fritz?*

Wann kom-men *Sie* **nach Köln?**
When will *you* come to Cologne?

Yes-or-No Questions

Yes-or-no questions, including assertions changed by intonation into questions, show an upward movement after the last stressed syllable. Although there are several other possibilities, the beginner, after starting as usual on level 2, should place the last stressed syllable on level 1 and then move upward.

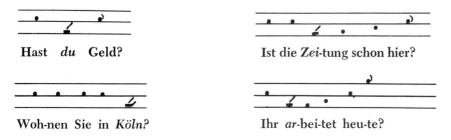

Hast *du* Geld?   Ist die *Zei*-tung schon hier?

Woh-nen Sie in *Köln?*   Ihr *ar*-bei-tet heu-te?

Note that after a stressed syllable on level 1 no other stressed syllables can follow.

14 auch

German **auch,** meaning *also* or *too,* is one of the most frequently used words. The stressed **auch** refers *back* to a preceding unit, regardless of whether this unit is stressed or not. The unstressed **auch** refers forward to a *stressed* unit, except in one case: Since the inflected verb is always the second unit in a German sentence, one cannot imitate the English sentence *He also likes money,* or *He also lives in Munich.* Instead, the stressed verb precedes the unstressed **auch.**

Er *wohnt* auch in München.   He also *lives* in Munich.
                                         He *lives* in Munich, too.

Here are some further examples:
  Sie ist *auch* intelligent.   *She, too,* is intelligent.
  Sie ist auch intelli*gent.*   She is also *intelligent.*
  Er hat *auch* ein Büro in Köln.   *He, too,* has an office in Cologne.
  Er hat auch ein *Büro* in Köln.   He also has an *office* in Cologne.
  Er hat auch ein Büro in *Köln.*   He also has an office in *Cologne.*

15 denn

Idiomatic German is characterized by the very frequent use of "particles" which, in addition to their definable dictionary meaning, have a psychological meaning sometimes hard to define. English occasionally uses such particles, too. Thus, *there* has a definable dictionary meaning in *She is there*. However, when a mother runs up to her crying baby, pats it on the back, and says, "There, there!" *there* is no longer the same word as in *She is there*.

The particles used most frequently in German will be introduced one by one; use them as often as possible in spoken German. We shall start with **denn.**

The unstressed German **denn** occurs most frequently in questions. It expresses either impatience or interest.

IMPATIENCE A: **Ist Meyer hier?**
Is Meyer here?

B: **Nein, Meyer ist noch nicht hier.**
No, Meyer is not here yet.

A: **Wo bleibt er denn?**
Well, where is he?
(I have been waiting long enough.)

INTEREST A: **Fritz ist hier!**

B: **Wo ist er denn?**
Where is he?
(I am interested in finding out.)

The use of this **denn** is so frequent in spoken German that about half of all questions contain it. It follows the inflected verb and personal pronouns, and it may even follow nouns.

Wann *brauchst* du es denn?
Wo *ist* das Büro denn?

In yes-or-no questions, **denn** usually implies a feeling of surprise or incredulity.

Arbeitet ihr denn heute?—   You are working today? (I can't believe it.)

EXERCISES

A. Using the pattern *I study and you do not study, you study and he does not study,* write out, and say aloud, the following German sentences. (In Unit 1, **nicht** should be used only in the patterns of this exercise.) Be prepared to go through these sentences in class without your book.

> **Ich studiere, und du studierst nicht.**
> **Du studierst, und er studiert nicht.**
> **Er studiert, und wir studieren nicht.**
> **Wir studieren, und ihr studiert nicht.**
> **Ihr studiert, und sie studieren nicht.**

1. Ich arbeite, und du _____ nicht.
   Du _____, und er _____ nicht.
   Er _____, und wir _____ nicht.
   Wir _____, und ihr _____ nicht.
   Ihr _____, und sie _____ nicht.

2. Ich wohne in Berlin, und du _____ nicht in Berlin.
   Du _____ in Berlin, und er _____ nicht in Berlin.
   Er _____ in Berlin, und wir _____ nicht in Berlin.
   Wir _____ in Berlin, und ihr _____ nicht in Berlin.
   Ihr _____ in Berlin, und sie _____ nicht in Berlin.

3. Ich tue es nicht, und du _____ es auch nicht.
   Du _____ es nicht, und er _____ es auch nicht.
   Er _____ es nicht, und wir _____ es auch nicht.
   Wir _____ es nicht, und ihr _____ es auch nicht.
   Ihr _____ es nicht, und sie _____ es auch nicht.

4. Ich bin hungrig, und du _____ nicht hungrig.
   Du _____ hungrig, und er _____ nicht hungrig.
   Er _____ hungrig, und wir _____ nicht hungrig.
   Wir _____ hungrig, und ihr _____ nicht hungrig.
   Ihr _____ hungrig, und sie _____ nicht hungrig.

B. Write down *one* possible answer to the following questions. To answer a yes-or-no question, start your answer with **ja** or **nein** followed by a comma and an affirmative statement. To answer a word question, put the words expressing the information requested at the end of the sentence. Be prepared to answer these questions in class, orally and at normal speed, without looking at your book or paper.

> **Wohnen Sie in Berlin?**   **Ja, ich wohne in Berlin.**
>   **Nein, ich wohne in München.**
> **Wo ist Fritz?**   **Fritz ist zu Hause.**
>   **Er ist in Bonn.**

1. Ist Fritz zu Hause?
2. Wer ist das?
3. Arbeiten Sie in Köln?
4. Wo arbeiten Sie?
5. Bleibst du heute abend zu Hause?
6. Studiert sie in Heidelberg?
7. Wann kommt ihr denn?
8. Wohnen Schmidts *auch* in Köln?

C. Write down one *yes-or-no* question which could be answered by the assertions printed. Copy the assertions also. Be prepared to ask these questions orally in class.

Haben wir (habt ihr, haben Sie) Geld?	Ja, wir haben Geld.
1.	Ja, wir wohnen in Berlin.
2.	Ja, sie arbeiten heute.
3.	Ja, das ist Frau Meyer.
4.	Natürlich ist Meyer intelligent.
5.	Ja, sie (die Zeitung) ist schon hier.
6.	Ja, sie (Erika) wohnt *auch* in München.
7.	Nein!
8.	Ja!

D. Write down the *word* questions which could be answered by the statements printed. Be prepared to ask these questions in class at normal speed, when you hear the statement.

Wo arbeitet Herr Meyer?	Er arbeitet in Berlin.
1.	Wir wohnen in Berlin.
2.	Zu Hause!
3.	Ich bin in Köln.
4.	Herr Meyer.
5.	In Berlin.
6.	Er studiert Psychologie.
7.	Herr Meyer kommt heute.
8.	Ich bin Anna Meyer.

E. Express in German. Be prepared to give the German equivalents instantly without using book or paper.

1. I am hungry.   2. We need money.

3. Hans will come later.
4. The newspaper is here.
5. Where does Dr. Meyer live?
6. We are studying psychology.
7. Hans is here, too.
8. Tomorrow night we are staying home.

9. She, too, is intelligent.
10. Does Meyer *also* live here?
11. Meyer also *lives* here.
12. We are also going to *Munich*.
13. Is it raining in Hamburg?
14. When are you coming to Munich, Mr. Meyer?

VOCABULARY

der Abend evening
 abends evenings
 Guten Abend! Good evening!
alle all, all of us
allein alone
arbeiten to work
auch also, too
bleiben to stay, to remain
brauchen to need
das Büro' office
die Butter butter
das that (*demonstrative*)
denn (*see* 15)
Deutsch German (language)
 Deutschland Germany
der Doktor doctor
die Frau woman, wife
 Frau Meyer Mrs. Meyer
gehen to go, to walk
das Geld money
glauben to think, to believe
der Gott god
 Gott God
gut good
haben to have
das Haus house
 ich gehe nach Hause I go home
 ich bin zu Hause I am at home
der Herr gentleman
 Herr Meyer Mr. Meyer
heute today
 heute abend this evening, tonight
 heute morgen this morning
hier here
der Hund dog

der Hunger hunger
 ich habe Hunger I am hungry
 hungrig hungry
in in
intelligent' intelligent
ja yes; indeed
das Jahr year
jetzt now
das Kind child
das Kino moviehouse
 ich gehe ins Kino I go to the movies
die Kirche church
 ich gehe in die Kirche I go to church
kochen to cook, to boil
kommen to come
lernen to learn
der Mann man, husband
die Medizin' medicine
 Medizin' (the science of) medicine
der Morgen morning
 morgen tomorrow
 morgen abend tomorrow evening
 Guten Morgen! Good morning!
nach to, toward; after
nächst next
 nächstes Jahr next year
die Natur' nature
 natür'lich naturally, of course
nein no
nicht not
noch still
 noch nicht not yet

die Psychologie' psychology
regnen to rain
 der Regen rain
sagen to say
schon already
sein to be
der Sonntag Sunday
 Sonntag abend Sunday evening
 Sonntag morgen Sunday morning
 jeden Sonntag every Sunday
 sonntags on Sundays, every Sunday
spät late
 später later
studie'ren to study
die Tochter daughter
tun to do
übrigens by the way, incidentally
und and
Wann? When? (*interrogative*)
Was? What?
Wer? Who?
das Wetter weather
wieder again (second or third time); back (to the place of origin)
der Winter winter
 im Winter in the winter
Wo? Where?
wohnen to reside, to live (in a place)
die Zeitung newspaper
zu to; at

UNIT 2: Plural of Nouns—Nominative and Accusative of Personal Pronouns and of **ein**-Words and **der**-Words— Adverbs and Predicate Adjectives—Sentence Structure—**doch**

[1] Accusative of Personal Pronouns

Find out the system by which this exercise is constructed. Then practice the sentences aloud until you can say them rapidly, without having to pause for the correct pronoun.

SEE
ANALYSIS
20–21

(pp. 31-33)

du brauchst *mich,* und *ich* brauche *dich*
er braucht *mich,* und *ich* brauche *ihn*
sie braucht *mich,* und *ich* brauche *sie*
ihr braucht *mich,* und *ich* brauche *euch*
sie brauchen *mich,* und *ich* brauche *sie*
Sie brauchen *mich,* und *ich* brauche *Sie*

ich brauche *dich,* und *du* brauchst *mich*
er braucht *dich,* und *du* brauchst *ihn*
sie braucht *dich,* und *du* brauchst *sie*
wir brauchen *dich,* und *du* brauchst *uns*
sie brauchen *dich,* und *du* brauchst *sie*

ich brauche *ihn,* und *er* braucht *mich*
du brauchst *ihn,* und *er* braucht *dich*
sie braucht *ihn,* und *er* braucht *sie*
wir brauchen *ihn,* und *er* braucht *uns*
ihr braucht *ihn,* und *er* braucht *euch*
sie brauchen *ihn,* und *er* braucht *sie*
Sie brauchen *ihn,* und *er* braucht *Sie*

ich brauche *sie,* und *sie* braucht *mich*
du brauchst *sie,* und *sie* braucht *dich*
er braucht *sie,* und *sie* braucht *ihn*
wir brauchen *sie,* und *sie* braucht *uns*
ihr braucht *sie,* und *sie* braucht *euch*

(Facing) **Policeman in Frankfurt**

du brauchst *uns,* und *wir* brauchen *dich*
er braucht *uns,* und *wir* brauchen *ihn*
sie braucht *uns,* und *wir* brauchen *sie*
ihr braucht *uns,* und *wir* brauchen *euch*
sie brauchen *uns,* und *wir* brauchen *sie*
Sie brauchen *uns,* und *wir* brauchen *Sie*

ich brauche *euch,* und *ihr* braucht *mich*
er braucht *euch,* und *ihr* braucht *ihn*
sie braucht *euch,* und *ihr* braucht *sie*
wir brauchen *euch,* und *ihr* braucht *uns*
sie brauchen *euch,* und *ihr* braucht *sie*

ich brauche *sie,* und *sie* brauchen *mich*
du brauchst *sie,* und *sie* brauchen *dich*
er braucht *sie,* und *sie* brauchen *ihn*
wir brauchen *sie,* und *sie* brauchen *uns*
ihr braucht *sie,* und *sie* brauchen *euch*

[2] Accusative of Personal Pronouns in Context

Practice these short conversations until you are ready to assume the role of either of the two speakers. After these conversations have been drilled in class, try to invent some variations of your own.

SEE
ANALYSIS
16–21

(pp. 30-33)

A: Erikas Mann heißt Max.
   Kennst du ihn?

B: Nein, ich kenne ihn nicht.

A: Aber ich weiß, er kennt dich.

B: Nein, er kennt mich nicht. Er weiß nur, wer ich bin.

Erika's husband's name is Max.
Do you know him?

No, I don't know him.

But I know that he knows you.

No, he does not know me. He just knows who I am.

A: Wagners Frau heißt Irene.
   Kennst du sie?

B: Nein, ich kenne sie nicht.

A: Aber sie sagt, sie kennt dich.

B: Nein, sie kennt mich nicht.
   Sie weiß nur, wer ich bin.

Wagner's wife's name is Irene.
Do you know her?

No, I don't know her.

But she says she knows you.

No, she does not know me. She only knows who I am.

A: Irene ist jetzt Frau Wagner.

B: Liebt Wagner sie denn?

A: Ich glaube, ja.

B: Liebt *sie* ihn *auch?*

Irene is now Mrs. Wagner.

Does Wagner love her?

I think so.

Does *she* love him, *too?*

A: Ich weiß nicht. Ich glaube, sie liebt   I don't think so. I think she loves Wagner's
Wagners Geld.   money.

[3] Nominative and Accusative of Possessive Adjectives—**wissen**

Ich *weiß* nicht, wo meine *Mut*ter ist.
Du *weißt* nicht, wo deine *Mut*ter ist?
Er *weiß* nicht, wo seine *Mut*ter ist.
Sie *weiß* nicht, wo ihre *Mut*ter ist.

SEE
ANALYSIS
18, 22

(pp. 30, 33-34)

Wir *wissen* nicht, *wo* unser Vater *ar*beitet.
Ihr *wißt* nicht, *wo* euer Vater *ar*beitet?
Sie *wissen* nicht, *wo* ihr Vater *ar*beitet.
Sie *wissen* nicht, *wo* Ihr Vater *ar*beitet?

Ich zahle für *mei*nen Kaffee, und *du* für *dei*nen Kaffee.
Du zahlst für *dei*nen Kaffee, und *er* für *sei*nen Kaffee.
Er zahlt für *sei*nen Kaffee, und *sie* für *ih*ren Kaffee.

Ich lese *mein* Buch, und *du* liest *dein* Buch.
Du liest *dein* Buch, und *er* liest *sein* Buch.
Er liest *sein* Buch, und *sie* liest *ihr* Buch.
Sie liest *ihr* Buch, und *wir* lesen *unsere* Bücher.
Wir lesen *unsere* Bücher, und *ihr* lest *eure* Bücher.
Ihr lest *eure* Bücher, und *sie* lesen *ihre* Bücher.

[4] **ein**-Words and Personal Pronouns in Context

Practice these brief conversations with another student.

A: Hast du einen *Freund* hier in München?   Do you have a friend here in Munich?
B: Na*tür*lich habe ich einen *Freund* hier in München, und eine *Freund*in habe ich *auch*.   Of course, I have a friend here in Munich, and I also have a girl.

SEE
ANALYSIS
22

(pp. 33-34)

A: Frau *Schmidt,* Sie kennen doch Frau *Hoff*mann! Kennen Sie auch ihren *Mann?*   Mrs. Smith, you know Mrs. Hoffmann, don't you? Do you also know her husband?
B: Ja, ihr Mann arbeitet für *mei*nen Mann.   Yes, her husband works for my husband.

ER: Was liest *du* denn da, Erika?   HE: What are you reading there, Erika?
SIE: Ein Buch!   SHE: A book!
ER: Ist es interes*sant?*   HE: Is it interesting?
SIE: Ja! Ein Stu*dent* liebt eine Stu*dent*in.   SHE: Yes, a student loves a coed.

ER:	Und *sie?* Liebt *sie* ihn *auch?*	HE:	And does *she* love him *too?*
SIE:	Nein, diese Stu*den*tin liebt ihren Pro*fes*sor.	SHE:	No, this coed loves her professor.
ER:	Und *er,* der Pro*fes*sor?	HE:	And the professor?
SIE:	Der Pro*fes*sor ist ein Dummkopf und liebt nur seine *Bü*cher!	SHE:	The professor is a fool and loves only his books.

[5] Numbers; Plural of Nouns

Invent your own variations:

SEE ANALYSIS 23 (p. 35)

Wir haben nur *ein* Haus. Werners haben *drei* Häuser.—Meyers haben jetzt *ei*nen Sohn und *zwei* Töchter, aber *Schmidts* haben nur einen *Sohn.*—Ich glaube, *Holl*manns haben zwei *Töch*ter. Oder haben sie nur *ei*ne Tochter?—Ich glaube, *Holl*manns haben *zwei* Söhne und *vier* Töchter. Oder haben sie nur *ei*nen Sohn und vier Töchter?

We have only one house. The Werners have three houses.—The Meyers now have one son and two daughters, but the Schmidts have only a son.—I think the Hollmanns have two daughters. Or do they have only one daughter?—I think the Hollmanns have two sons and four daughters. Or do they have only one son and four daughters?

[6] The Second Prong of the Predicate—The Front Field

Study these sentences carefully. Practice them until you can develop all variations without having to look at your book.

SEE ANALYSIS 26–35 (pp. 36-46)

IRREDUCIBLE VERBAL PATTERN: *fahren lernen*

Sie	lernt	doch jetzt	fahren.
Jetzt	lernt	sie *doch*	fahren.
Wann	lernt	sie denn	fahren?
Hoffentlich	lernt	sie jetzt	fahren.
Sie	lernt	jetzt hoffentlich	fahren.
Jetzt	lernt	sie hoffentlich	fahren.

IRREDUCIBLE VERBAL PATTERN: *abfahren*

Der Zug	fährt	um 6 Uhr 5 (sechs Uhr fünf)	ab.
Um 6 Uhr 5	fahren	wir	ab.
Wo	fährt	denn der Zug nach Köln	ab?
Wann	fährst	du denn	ab?
	Fährt	der Zug jetzt	ab?
Meyers	fahren	schon um sechs Uhr	ab.

,,Sie lernt jetzt hoffentlich fahren''

IRREDUCIBLE VERBAL PATTERN: *nach Berlin fahren*

Morgen	**fahre**	ich doch	nach Berlin.
Leider	**fahre**	ich morgen *doch*	nach Berlin.
Ich	**fahre**	morgen leider	nach Berlin.

IRREDUCIBLE VERBAL PATTERN: *ein Dummkopf sein*

Meyer	**ist**	leider	ein Dummkopf.
Leider	**ist**	Meyer	ein Dummkopf.
Wie du weißt,	**ist**	Meyer leider	ein Dummkopf.
Meyer	**ist,**	wie du weißt, leider	ein Dummkopf.
Leider	**ist**	Meyer, wie du weißt,	ein Dummkopf.

IRREDUCIBLE VERBAL PATTERN: *wieder gesund werden*

Nächstes Jahr	**wird**	Mutter hoffentlich	wieder gesund.
Mutter	**wird**	nächstes Jahr hoffentlich	wieder gesund.
Mutter	**wird**	hoffentlich nächstes Jahr	wieder gesund.
Hoffentlich	**wird**	Mutter nächstes Jahr	wieder gesund.

IRREDUCIBLE VERBAL PATTERN: *gut sein*

Das Bier	**ist**	doch	**gut**	in München.
In München	**ist**	das Bier	**gut.**	
	Ist	das Bier	**gut**	in München?
	Ist	das Bier in München	**gut?**	
Warum	**ist**	das Bier in München	**so gut?**	

CONVERSATION

Memorize this conversation and be ready to recite it in class.

ER: Weißt du *was,* Inge? Erika ist hier in Frankfurt!

You know what, Inge? Erika is here in Frankfurt!

SIE: Erika? Was tut denn Erika hier in Frankfurt?

Erika? What's Erika doing here in Frankfurt?

ER: Sie sagt, sie braucht einen *Sport*wagen!

She says she needs a sports car!

SIE: Einen *Sport*wagen! *E*inen Wagen *hat* sie schon, und *jetzt* braucht sie einen *Sport*wagen! Ja, ja, *sie* hat *al*les, und *wir* haben *nichts!*

A sports car! She already has *one* car, and now she needs a sports car. I tell you, she has everything, and we have nothing.

ER: Aber *Inge! Wer* hat denn *al*les? Du glaubst, Erika hat *al*les. Aber *ich* weiß, Erika ist *un*glücklich. Erika weiß es *auch! Sie* glaubt, sie hat *nichts.*

But Inge! Who does have everything? You think Erika has everything. But I know she is unhappy. Erika knows it too. She thinks she has nothing.

SIE: Aber *Geld* hat sie! Ist *Geld* „nichts"?

But she has money! Is money "nothing"?

ER: *Geld* ist *viel.* Aber Geld ist nicht *al*les. *Wir* sind Stu*den*ten. Stu*den*ten haben doch *nie* Geld! Aber ich bin *glück*lich, und *du* bist hoffentlich *auch* glücklich. Na*tür*lich hat Erika *Geld.* Sie ist doch jetzt Frau *Fischer. Frau Dr. Anton Fischer!* Warum bist *du* übrigens nicht Frau *Fischer?* Du weißt doch, Anton—

Money is a great deal. But money is not everything. We are students. Students, after all, never have any money. But I am happy, and I hope you are happy too. Of course Erika has money. She is now Mrs. Fischer, the wife of Dr. Anton Fischer. By the way, why aren't you Mrs. Fischer? You know, don't you, Anton . . .

SIE: *Ich? Frau Fischer? Antons Frau? Nein! Nie!*

I? Mrs. Fischer? Anton's wife? No! Never!

READING

Eine Frau lügt nicht

Frau Lenz kommt zu Frau Bertram:

FRAU B: Guten Morgen, Frau *Lenz! Gut,* daß Sie *kom*men! Was machen Sie denn heute *a*bend? Ich glaube, *ich* gehe ins *Ki*no.

Good morning, Mrs. Lenz. I'm glad you came! What are you doing tonight? I think I'll go to the movies.

FRAU L: Ins *Ki*no!   To the movies!

FRAU B: *Ja,* ich brauche heute abend nicht zu   Yes, I don't have to work tonight. And
*ar*beiten, und da bleibe ich natürlich   so, of course, I'm not staying home.
nicht zu *Hau*se.

FRAU L: *So!* Sie gehen ins *Ki*no! *Ich* gehe *nie* ins ⁵   Well! So you're going to the movies! I
Kino.   never go to the movies.

FRAU B: Warum kommen Sie nicht *mit* ins Kino!   Why don't you come along to the
Frau *Hoff*mann—*ken*nen Sie Frau *Hoff-*   movies too! Mrs. Hoffmann—do you
mann?—Frau Hoffmann kommt *auch*   know Mrs. Hoffmann?—Mrs. Hoff-
mit.   ¹⁰ mann is coming along too.

FRAU L: Ja, Frau *Hoff*mann *ken*ne ich. Aber ins   Yes, I know Mrs. Hoffmann. But to the
Kino? Ich *weiß* nicht. *Her*mann und *ich,*   movies? I don't know! Hermann and I,
wir gehen *nie* ins Kino. Er sagt, wir   we never go to a movie. He says we
haben kein *Geld.* Aber ich *glau*be, er   can't afford it. But I think he'd rather
bleibt lieber zu *Hau*se und liest die *Zei-*¹⁵ stay home and read the paper.
tung.

FRAU B: Wo *ist* er denn heute? Wann kommt er   Where is he today? When is he coming
denn heute nach *Hau*se?   home today?

FRAU L: *Heu*te kommt er *spät* nach Hause. Er   Today he is coming home late. He is
arbeitet heute in *Bonn.*   working in Bonn today.

FRAU B: In *Bonn! Das* ist doch *gut. Wir drei,* Sie,²⁰ In Bonn! That's just fine! The three of
Frau *Hoff*mann und *ich,* gehen ins *Ki*no;   us, you, Mrs. Hoffmann, and I, will go
und *er* arbeitet in *Bonn*—und *glaubt*   to a show; and he is working in Bonn
natürlich, seine *Frau* ist zu *Hau*se.   —and thinks, of course, that his wife is
at home.

FRAU L: *Gut,* Frau Bertram. Wir gehen alle *drei* ²⁵ Fine! All three of us will go to the
ins Kino. Und *Her*mann sage ich *nichts.*   movies. And I shall say nothing to
—Übrigens, Frau Bertram, wie *heißt*   Hermann. By the way, Mrs. Bertram,
denn der Film?   what's the name of the movie?

FRAU B: Der *Film?* Ach *ja!* Der Film heißt: „Eine The picture? Oh, yes! The picture is
Frau lügt nicht".   ₃₀ called: "A Woman Does Not Lie."

16   Verbs with Vowel Change

Certain verbs change the stem vowel in the **du**-form and **er**-form. In these cases, the vocabulary at the end of the unit will show in parentheses the correct **du**- and **er**-form. Example: **fahren** (**du fährst, er fährt**); **lesen** (**du liest, er liest**). Note that if there is a change of vowel, it occurs both with **du** and with **er**, but nowhere else.

ich	fahre	I	go		ich	lese	I	read
du	fährst	you	go		du	liest	you	read
er		he			er		he	
sie	fährt	she	goes		sie	liest	she	reads
es		it			es		it	
wir	fahren	we	go		wir	lesen	we	read
ihr	fahrt	you	go		ihr	lest	you	read
sie	fahren	they	go		sie	lesen	they	read
Sie	fahren	you	go		Sie	lesen	you	read

17   Stems Ending in -s

After a stem which ends in -s, like **lesen**, the **du**-form adds -t, not -st, to the stem. As a result, the **du**-form becomes identical with the **er**-form:

ich lese
du liest
er liest

18   werden and wissen

Like **sein** and **haben**, **werden** (*to become*) and **wissen** (*to know facts*) are irregular. In the present tense, they are inflected as follows:

ich	werde		ich	weiß
du	wirst		du	weißt
er			er	
sie	wird		sie	weiß
es			es	
wir	werden		wir	wissen
ihr	werdet		ihr	wißt
sie	werden		sie	wissen
Sie	werden		Sie	wissen

19 Singular and Plural Forms of Nouns

With a few exceptions, English nouns form the plural by adding -s or -es to the singular: *house, houses; glass, glasses;* but *foot, feet.*

In German, the plural form of a noun usually does not end in -s. It may be the same as the singular form, as in the case of English *sheep,* or it may be different from the singular form, as in the case of English *mouse, mice* or *child, children.*

Since there are no rules by which to tell the plural form of a given singular, there is only one safe way to learn the plural: memorize it together with the singular.

From Unit 2 on, the plural forms are indicated in the vocabulary as follows:

der Vater, ⸚ means that the plural of **der Vater** is **die Väter;**

| das Kind, –er | das Kind | die Kinder; |
| der Hund, –e | der Hund | die Hunde. |

The articles preceding plural nouns are the same for all three genders.

The nouns used in Unit 1 have the following plurals:

der Abend, –e	das Kind, –er
die Frau, –en	die Kirche, –n
der Gott, ⸚er	der Mann, ⸚er
das Haus, ⸚er	der Student, –en
der Herr, –en	die Tochter, ⸚er
der Hund, –e	der Winter, –
das Jahr, –e	die Zeitung, –en

Nouns of non-German origin may end in -s:

das Auto	die Autos
das Büro	die Büros
das Kino	die Kinos

20 The Nominative and Accusative Cases

In English we don't talk much about "cases" of nouns and pronouns, because the function of a noun in a sentence is ordinarily determined by its position. For instance, how do we know who bites whom in the sentence *The dog bit the cat?* Position alone indicates that *dog* is the subject and that *cat* is the object. By reversing position, the functions of *cat* and *dog* are *also* reversed.

However, in English sentences such as *I love him* the situation is quite different. Here, function is indicated by position *and* by form. Form alone would be sufficient, and, at least in theory, one could say *Him love I* without being misunderstood.

In German, the term "nominative case," or simply "nominative," is used whenever a noun or a pronoun, *by virtue of either its form or its position,* is marked as the subject or as the predicate noun. The term "accusative case," or simply "accusative," is used whenever a word, *by form or position,* is marked as the direct object of a verb or of certain prepositions such as **für.**

Whenever function is not indicated by form, German, like English, relies on position. In

    Meine Mutter kennt diese Frau   My mother knows this woman

meine Mutter and **diese Frau** can both be either nominative or accusative as far as form is concerned, but position makes **meine Mutter** the subject. In

    Diese Frau kennt meine Mutter   This woman knows my mother

position makes **diese Frau** the subject and **meine Mutter** the object.

On the other hand, the two German sentences

    Er liebt seinen Sohn

and

    Seinen Sohn liebt er

both mean *He loves his son.* The **er** indicates by its form that it is the subject, and **seinen** indicates by its form that **seinen Sohn** must be the object. In this case, therefore, form alone is sufficient to indicate function.

21 The Nominative and Accusative Forms of Personal Pronouns

NOMINATIVE	ich	du	er	sie	es	wir	ihr	sie	(Sie)
ACCUSATIVE	mich	dich	ihn	sie	es	uns	euch	sie	(Sie)

There is no difference in form between the nominative and the accusative of **sie, Sie,** and **es.**

Agreement between Nouns and Pronouns

Since **der Kaffee** is a masculine noun, the thing denoted by **dieser Kaffee** (this coffee) is, from a German point of view, a "he" and must be referred to by using the masculine pronouns **er** and **ihn:**

    Er (dieser Kaffee) ist gut. Wo kaufst du ihn?

Similarly, **die Zeitung** is a "she" and must be referred to by using the feminine pronoun **sie:**

> **Sie (die Zeitung) ist uninteressant. Ich lese sie nie.**

On the other hand, **das Geld** and **das Kind** are both neuter nouns. If these nouns are replaced by pronouns, one must use **es:**

> **Ich brauche es (das Geld).**
> **Ist es (das Kind) gesund?**

22 The Nominative and Accusative of **der**-Words, **ein**-Words, and Nouns

The term "**der**-words" is used for all words which indicate gender, case, and number in the same way in which the definite article **der,** by changing its form, indicates gender, case, and number. For instance, **dieser, jeder,** and **wer** are **der**-words. The term "**ein**-word" is used for all words which indicate case and number in the same way in which the indefinite article **ein** shows case and number. **Kein** (*no, not a*) and the possessive adjectives are **ein**-words.

The possessive adjectives are:

mein	my		**unser**	our
dein	your		**euer**	your
sein	his		**ihr**	their
ihr	her		**Ihr**	your (polite)
sein	its			

The Nominative and Accusative of **der**-Words

	MASC.	FEM.	NEUTER	MASC.	FEM.	NEUTER
NOM. SING.	**der**	**die**	**das**	**dieser**	**diese**	**dieses**
ACC. SING.	**den**	**die**	**das**	**diesen**	**diese**	**dieses**
NOM. PLUR.		**die**			**diese**	
ACC. PLUR.		**die**			**diese**	

EXAMPLES:

Der Vater kennt diese Frau.	Father knows this woman.
Diese Frau kennt der Vater.	(Function indicated by form; **der Vater** can only be nominative.)

NOTE:

1. Only the masculine singular of the **der**-words distinguishes the nominative from the accusative.

2. In the plural, all three genders have the same forms.

The Nominative and Accusative of **ein**-Words

	MASC.	FEM.	NEUTER	MASC.	FEM.	NEUTER	MASC.	FEM.	NEUTER
NOM. SING.	ein	eine	ein	mein	meine	mein	kein	keine	kein
ACC. SING.	einen	eine	ein	meinen	meine	mein	keinen	keine	kein
NOM. PLUR.	*(no plural)*				meine			keine	
ACC. PLUR.					meine			keine	

EXAMPLES:

Mein Vater kennt diese Frau.

Diese Frau kennt mein Vater.

My father knows this woman.

(Function indicated by form; **mein Vater** can only be nominative.)

However:

Frau Schmitz, meine Freundin versteht Ihre Tochter.

Mrs. Schmitz, my friend understands your daughter.

(Function indicated by position.)

NOTE:

1. Only the masculine singular of the **ein**-words distinguishes the nominative from the accusative.

2. Remember: The plural of **ein Kind** is **Kinder.**

3. In the accusative of **unser** and **euer,** the **-e-** before the **-r-** is frequently dropped.

unseren or unsren   unsere or unsre.

4. In the plural, all three genders have the same forms.

The Accusative of Nouns

Only very few nouns distinguish between nominative and accusative—for example, **der Mensch** and **der Student,** which add **-en** in all cases but the nominative singular. **Der Herr** adds an **-n** in all singular forms and an **-en** in all plural forms.

NOM. SING.	der Mensch	der Student	der Herr
ACC. SING.	den Menschen	den Studenten	den Herrn
NOM. PLUR.	die Menschen	die Studenten	die Herren
ACC. PLUR.	die Menschen	die Studenten	die Herren

23 Cardinal Numbers

The cardinal numbers from 1 to 6 are:

1	eins	4	vier
2	zwei	5	fünf
3	drei	6	sechs

The numeral **eins** is used only for counting, for telephone numbers, in arithmetic, etc; it is never used together with a following noun. In front of a noun, the numeral looks like the indefinite article **ein** and is declined the same way. In the sentence **wir haben eine Tochter, eine** means *one*, if it is stressed, and *a*, if it is not stressed.

NUMERAL	**Ich glaube, Meyers haben zwei Söhne.—Nein, sie haben nur *einen* Sohn.**	I believe the Meyers have two sons. —No, they have only *one* son.
INDEFINITE ARTICLE	**Ich glaube, Meyers haben jetzt auch eine *Tochter*.—Nein, sie haben nur einen *Sohn*.**	I believe the Meyers now have a *daughter*, too.—No, they have only a *son*.

If the other numbers are followed by a noun, they are not changed:

Wir haben drei Kinder, zwei Autos und einen Hund.

24 Adverbs and Predicate Adjectives

In the English sentences

He lived happily ever after
He was happy as long as he lived

the word *happily* is an adverb and characterizes the verbal act, the mode of living. The word *happy* is a predicate adjective. It characterizes the subject, not the verbal act.

German normally makes no distinction in form between a predicate adjective and an adverb.

PREDICATE ADJECTIVE	**Der Mensch ist gut.**	Man is good.
ADVERB	**Er fährt gut.**	He drives well.

NOTE: For the time being, do not use adjectives attributively—that is, in front of the noun to which they belong.

25   Sentence Adverbs

In most cases, adverbs modify

a verb:	He lived *happily* ever after.
an adjective:	He is *unusually* intelligent.
another adverb:	It happened *very* suddenly.

However, in order to use German adverbs correctly, it should be noted that certain adverbs, called "sentence adverbs," express the attitude of the speaker toward the content of the whole sentence.

Thus, *unfortunately, naturally,* and *obviously* are used as sentence adverbs in

Unfortunately he died.
(It is, in my opinion, unfortunate that he died.)

Naturally, he was not at home.
(As I had expected, he was not at home.)

He was obviously not stupid.
(It was clear to all of us that he wasn't stupid.)

Three German sentence adverbs were used in Unit 1: **denn, natürlich,** and **übrigens.** Four more—**doch, gottseidank, hoffentlich,** and **leider**—are introduced in this unit. In both English and German, these sentence adverbs count as *independent syntactical units* as far as word order is concerned, but **denn** and **doch** cannot appear in the front field. **Gottseidank,** which literally means *thanks be to God,* can also function as an independent sentence as in

Gottseidank, er ist wieder zu Hause.

26   German Word Order

To the native speaker of English, German word order often appears outrageously capricious and illogical. It seems strange that a German, disregarding the "logical" order of the English sentence

During the winter the street lights go on here at four,

will insist on saying

Im Winter gehen hier um vier die Laternen an,

which, literally imitated, would read in English

[During the winter go here at four the street lights on.]

Why is it that what is "unnatural" to the native speaker of English is so "natural" to a German—and vice versa?

The explanation is that position is used as a "signal" to express meaning—as anybody can see who looks at the three sentences:

> He looked over the fence.
> He overlooked the fence.
> He looked the fence over.

Word order—the arrangement of words within a sentence—is comparable to the Morse Code: it is established by convention. Once a specific system has been adopted, and once both speaker and listener are used to the "code," the position of a word becomes a semantic signal conveying to the listener a very specific message. That is why the three English clauses

> When I had that trained dog
> When I had that dog trained
> When I had trained that dog

are not interchangeable, for the meaning and function of *trained* depends just as much on its position as on its form.

If the student is willing to learn a new system "from scratch," German word order ceases to be a major problem, for the German system, though not at all like the English system, is really quite simple and logical.

27   The Over-all Structure of German Assertions

The structure of the simple statement

> **Das Bier ist übrigens gut hier in München**

exemplifies the structure of all German assertions. This unvarying structure can be represented by the following schematic diagram:

FRONT FIELD	First Part of Predicate	INNER FIELD	Second Part of Predicate	END FIELD
Das Bier	ist	übrigens	gut	hier in München

Not all German assertions use this pattern in its entirety, but *no German assertion will disregard it,* and all German assertions have at least a front field and a first part of the predicate. The following statements use the pattern

FRONT FIELD	First Part of Predicate
Ich	lese
Es	regnet
Sie	kommen

The following statements use the pattern

FRONT FIELD	First Part of Predicate	INNER FIELD
Das	weiß	ich
Da	ist	Frau Meyer
Hier in München	wohnt	auch Professor Dübel

The following statements use the pattern

FRONT FIELD	First Part of Predicate	INNER FIELD	Second Part of Predicate
Ich	bleibe	natürlich	zu Hause
Wir	fahren	morgen	nach Berlin
Das Bier	ist	übrigens	gut

The structural features most alien to the American student are the two "slots" reserved for the first and the second part of the predicate. We shall discuss this problem in the following two sections.

28 Compound Verbs

If one compares the English sentences
> He carried this for half an hour

and
> He carried this on for half an hour

it becomes apparent that the addition of *on* in the second sentence influences the meaning of *carried* to such an extent that, while the *this* in the first sentence must be an object, the *this* in the second sentence must be some activity. In a dictionary, one must therefore recognize that *to carry on* is a verb different in meaning from the simple verb *to carry*.

We shall call *to carry on* a "compound verb"—that is, a verb whose full meaning is the compound effect of two parts: of a simple verb such as *to carry*, and of a complement like *on*.

German has literally hundreds of verbs comparable to English *to carry on*. One such verb was used in the sentence
> **Hier gehen um vier die Laternen an**
> Here the street lights go on at four.

The verbs **gehen** and *go* are fused with the prepositions **an** and *on* into a new unit of meaning: **gehen an** and *go on* mean "are turned on."

That **gehen an** and *go on* have become one single semantic unit can also be shown in the following way: By leaving out **hier,** *here* and **um vier,** *at four,* the sentence
> **Hier gehen um vier die Laternen an**
> Here the street lights go on at four

can be reduced to
> **Die Laternen gehen an.**
> The street lights go on.

However, a further reduction is impossible; for leaving out **an** or *on* would result in
> **Die Laternen gehen.**
> The street lights go.

It is easy to see that the result of this further shortening would be not merely a reduction, but a completely different sentence, applicable only in a completely different situation. This proves that **gehen an** and *go on* are *irreducible verbal patterns;* and from the point of view of German sentence structure *all such irreducible verbal patterns are compound verbs.*

The sentence

> **Natürlich bin ich heute abend zu Hause**
> Of course I shall be at home tonight

also contains an irreducible verbal pattern. If a good friend of mine tells me over the phone, "I just heard that Mr. Bigwig is flying in at six, and it is important that you see him right away," I might say to him:

> **Gut, ich bin heute abend zu Hause.**
> Fine, I shall be at home tonight.

I might leave out **heute abend** and say

> **Gut, ich bin zu Hause.**
> Fine, I shall be at home.

But I cannot make a further reduction and say

> **Gut, ich bin.**
> Fine, I am.

That simply would not make any sense. The **bin zu Hause,** in other words, is an "irreducible verbal pattern"—that is, from the German point of view, a compound verb; and **zu Hause** is the complement of **bin.**

For our purposes, then,

and

are parallel cases: Both statements contain an irreducible verbal pattern consisting of a simple verb and a complement. In one case, the complement is the preposition **an;** in the other case, it is the idiom **zu Hause.** Adjectives, adverbs, infinitives, and other words may also be used as verbal complements.

The feeling of the "togetherness" of **bin** and **zu Hause** is, by the way, so strong in German that the question **Bist du zu Hause?** can be answered by **Ja!** or by **Ja, ich bin zu Hause,** but not by

Beware: [**Bist du zu Hause?—Ja, ich bin.**]   DO NOT USE!
Americanism:

If one wants to use the infinitive of a compound verb—and one frequently has to—the complement is always placed in front of the simple infinitive. Thus the infinitive belonging to the sentence **Ich fahre morgen wieder nach Hause** is **wieder nach Hause fahren,** and the infinitive belonging to **Der Zug fährt jetzt ab** is **ab'fahren.**

The case of **abfahren** shows that if the complement is a preposition like **an** or **aus,** or a one-word adverb like **ab, zurück,** or **wieder,** it is always joined to the simple infinitive and carries the main word stress. In dictionaries **abfahren** is listed under **ab,** not under **fahren.**

*an*gehen	to go on	**Die Laternen gehen an.** The street lights go on.
*aus*gehen	to go out	**Die Laternen gehen aus.** The street lights go out.
*an*machen	to turn on	**Wir machen das Licht an.** We turn on the light.
*aus*machen	to turn off	**Wir machen das Licht aus.** We turn off the light.
*ab*fahren	to depart	**Der Zug fährt sofort ab.** The train will depart at once.
*zurück*fahren	to return	**Ich fahre morgen zurück.** I shall return tomorrow.
*wieder*kommen	to come back	**Ich komme nächstes Jahr wieder.** I will come back next year.
*fah*ren lernen	to learn how to drive	**Sie lernt jetzt fahren.** She is now taking driving lessons.
zu *Hause* bleiben	to stay home	**Ich bleibe heute zu Hause.** I am staying home today.
nach *Hause* kommen	to come home	**Er kommt heute nach Hause.** He is coming home today.

29 The Two-Pronged Predicate

If one realizes that **angehen** and **zu Hause sein** are compound verbs, one can say that in the sentences

Hier gehen um vier die Laternen an

and

Natürlich bin ich heute abend zu Hause

the inflected verb forms **gehen** and **bin** are the first, and the complements **an** and **zu Hause** the second part of the predicate. Schematically, the patterns used in English and German would look as follows:

Here the street lights   go   on   at four.

Hier   gehen   um vier die Laternen   an.

Of course I   am   at home   tonight.

Natürlich   bin   ich heute abend   zu Hause.

In the German sentences, the two parts of the predicate are separated by the inner field. *This pulling apart of all compound verbs is the most characteristic feature of German syntax.* Any student set upon acquiring idiomatic habits of speech must, therefore, master this principle from the very beginning. For the sentence

[Hier die Laternen   gehen   an   um vier.]

is just as unacceptable as the Germanism

[Here   go   the street lights at four   on   .]

The two parts of the German predicate embrace the inner field like a pair of parentheses, or like the prongs that hold the jewel of a ring in place. And since it is inconvenient to speak of "the first part of the predicate" and "the second part of the predicate," we shall call them "the first prong" and "the second prong."

As was pointed out in **9**, the first prong—that is, the inflected verb—is position-fixed. *The second prong is also position-fixed:* it follows the inner field.

**,,Im Winter gehen hier um vier die Laternen
an.''**

30 The Front Field and Its Function

As was pointed out in **9**, the front field is always occupied by only *one*
unit—that is, by the answer to only *one* possible question

Das Bier		ist	übrigens	gut
Das Bier hier		ist	übrigens	gut
Sonntag morgen		fahre	ich	wieder nach Hause

One of the main functions of the front field is to mention an element
already known to the listener about which the speaker wants to say something not yet known to the listener. Usually, the element in the front field
has, therefore, no news value at all. (It contains the answer to a *possible*
question, not the answer to an *actual* question.) Rather, the front field
picks up an element already mentioned and thus connects one statement
with a preceding statement.

QUESTION **Wann regnet es denn in *Deutsch*land?**
ANSWER **Im *Winter*.** or: **In Deutschland regnet es im *Winter*.**
NOT **[Im *Winter* regnet es in Deutschland.]**

QUESTION	Wer ist denn *das?*
ANSWER	Frau *Meyer.* or: Das ist Frau *Meyer.*
NOT	[Frau *Meyer* ist das.]
QUESTION	Wo wohnt denn Dr. *Meyer?*
ANSWER	In *Köln.* or: Dr. Meyer wohnt in *Köln.*
NOT	[In *Köln* wohnt Dr. Meyer.]

Only after questions of the type *Who did you say lives in Munich?* or *What did you say her name was?* is the answering unit frequently found in the front field.

QUESTION	Wie *heißt* er denn?
ANSWER	*Hans.* or: Er heißt *Hans.*
QUESTION	*Wie* heißt er?
ANSWER	*Hans* heißt er.

If the subject does not occupy the front field—and very often it does not—it is part of the inner field. *Personal pronoun subjects stand at the very beginning of the inner field.* The position of noun subjects varies.

31 Directives as Verbal Complements

The question **Wohin?** (Where to?) is frequently answered by a prepositional phrase:

Wohin fährt er denn?—Er fährt nach Köln.

We shall call such prepositional phrases *directives*. German directives are verbal complements—that is, they form a second prong and are, therefore, just as position-fixed as **zu Hause** in **zu Hause sein.**

Morgen	**fahre**	ich leider	nach Berlin.
Ich	**fahre**	leider morgen	nach Berlin.
Leider	**fahre**	ich morgen	nach Berlin.

32 Predicate Adjectives and Predicate Nouns as Verbal Complements

German predicate adjectives and predicate nouns are verbal complements; they form a second prong and follow the inner field:

| Erika | ist, | wie du weißt, | intelligent. |
| Wie du weißt, | ist | Erika | intelligent. |

Meyer	ist,	wie du weißt, leider	ein Dummkopf
Leider	ist	Meyer, wie du weißt,	ein Dummkopf
Wie du weißt,	ist	Meyer leider	ein Dummkopf

33 Shift of Position

It has already been pointed out several times that a speaker does not necessarily have to start the assertion **Ich bleibe heute abend natürlich zu Hause** with the subject **ich.** Depending upon the specific situation, he can choose any of four possible positions.

Ich	bleibe	heute abend natürlich	zu Hause.
Ich	bleibe	natürlich heute abend	zu Hause.
Natürlich	bleibe	ich heute abend	zu Hause.
Heute abend	bleibe	ich natürlich	zu Hause.

These four variations show that any unit in the inner field can be brought into the front field, thereby forcing the unit already in the front field into the inner field. The second prong, however, stays in its position. For the time being, do not change the position of the second prong. In the sentence [**Zu Hause bleibe ich heute abend natürlich**], natürlich would mean *natural*, not *naturally*.

34 The End Field

Most German assertions end with the second prong and have, therefore, no end field. The end field *may* be used for afterthoughts—that is, for syntactical units added *after* the assertion has been completed by the second prong. If the speaker thinks of these afterthoughts in time, he places them in the inner field or in the front field. If sentence adverbs appear in the end field, they are set off by a comma.

Heute	ist	er	zu Hause	, gottseidank.
Heute	ist	er gottseidank	zu Hause	
Er	ist	heute gottseidank	zu Hause	
Er	ist	heute	zu Hause	, gottseidank.
Gottseidank	ist	er heute	zu Hause	

Sometimes the end field is used to clarify, by way of an afterthought, one of the units already mentioned. Thus **hier in München** in the following sentence clarifies **das Bier:**

| Das Bier | | ist | übrigens | *gut* | hier in München. |

35 Word Order in German Questions

German questions follow the pattern of word order found in assertions.

In word questions, the front field is *always* occupied by an interrogative, and personal pronoun subjects are always placed at the beginning of the inner field.

FRONT FIELD	1st Prong	INNER FIELD	2nd Prong
Warum	bleibst	du heute abend	zu Hause?
Warum	fahren	Sie morgen	nach Köln?

Yes-or-no questions have no front field, and again pronoun subjects are placed immediately after the opening verb—that is, at the beginning of the inner field.

Bleiben	Sie heute abend	zu Hause?
Fahren	Sie morgen	nach Köln?

36 doch

The word **doch** may be stressed or unstressed. The stressed **doch** implies that the fact reported is contrary to expectations. This stressed **doch** is frequently preceded by **also**, which adds the flavor of "so" when used at the beginning of English sentences.

Er kommt *doch!*	He's coming after all!
Es regnet also *doch!*	So it's raining after all.
	(That's what I was afraid of.)

Sie wird also *doch* wieder gesund.	So she is regaining her health after all. (Nobody had expected it.)
Er ist also *doch* ein Dummkopf.	So he really *is* a dumbbell. (There is no longer any doubt about it.)

The unstressed **doch** appears with great frequency in questions and assertions. It expresses the hope of the speaker that the opposite is not true or that the statement made cannot be contradicted.

Du bist doch ge*sund!*	You're healthy, aren't you?
Erika hat doch *Geld!*	Erika has money, doesn't she?
Sie *kommen* doch heute abend?	You are coming tonight, I hope?

EXERCISES

A. Complete the following conjugation samples. Be prepared to go through these sentences in class without your book.

1. Ich bin zu Hause. _____ du zu Hause?
   Du _____ zu Hause. _____ er zu Hause?
   Er _____ zu Hause. _____ wir zu Hause?
   Wir _____ zu Hause. _____ ihr zu Hause?
   Ihr _____ zu Hause. _____ sie zu Hause?

2. Ich weiß es. _____ du es *auch?*
   Du _____ es. _____ er es *auch?*
   Wir _____ es. _____ ihr es *auch?*
   Ihr _____ es. _____ sie es *auch?*

3. Ich fahre morgen nach Berlin. _____ du morgen *auch* nach Berlin?
   Du _____ morgen nach Berlin. _____ er morgen *auch* nach Berlin?
   Er _____ morgen nach Berlin. _____ wir morgen *auch* nach Berlin?
   Wir _____ morgen nach Berlin. _____ ihr morgen *auch* nach Berlin?
   Ihr _____ morgen nach Berlin. _____ sie morgen *auch* nach Berlin?

4. Ich lese keine Zeitung. _____ du auch keine Zeitung?
   Du _____ keine Zeitung. _____ er auch keine Zeitung?
   Er _____ keine Zeitung. _____ wir auch keine Zeitung?
   Wir _____ keine Zeitung. _____ ihr auch keine Zeitung?
   Ihr _____ keine Zeitung. _____ sie auch keine Zeitung?

NOTE: **kein** is an **ein**-word (see **22**); use it only in the pattern of this exercise.

B. Express in German:

1. We have a dog.
2. Our dog's name is Susi.
3. My father is well again.
4. I need a car.
5. Is that your son, Mrs. Meyer?
6. Is that your daughter, Mrs. Meyer?
7. He loves his son.
8. She loves this student.
9. Does your wife work in Cologne?
10. Do you know my girl friend?
11. Do you know this woman?
12. Do you know this child?
13. That is her father.
14. She loves her father.
15. He loves his daughters.

C. In the following sentences, replace the subject by a pronoun.

1. Erika ist jetzt meine Frau.
2. Unser Hund ist eine „sie“.
3. Dieses Buch ist uninteressant.
4. Der Zug fährt nach Frankfurt.
5. Seine Frau hat Geld.
6. Herr Meyer ist mein Freund.

D. Replace the object by a pronoun.

1. Ich kenne Herrn Lenz nicht.
2. Er liest diese Zeitung nicht.
3. Liebst du Inge?
4. Ich verstehe Hans und Erika gut.
5. Kennen Sie seine Kinder?
6. Ich brauche das Buch.

E. Formulate affirmative answers to the following questions, using personal pronouns.

> **Kennen Sie Frau Bertram?**   **Ja, ich kenne sie.**

1. Kennen Sie Fritz Bertram?
2. Kennen Sie mich?
3. Kennst du die drei Frauen da?

4. Hast du das Geld schon?
5. Arbeitet dein Vater da?
6. Verstehst du deine Mutter?
7. Liebst du deine Mutter?
8. Liebt Erika ihren Vater?
9. Brauchst du heute den Wagen?
10. Fährt der Zug sofort ab?
11. Machst du das Licht aus?
12. Ist das Bier gut hier?

VOCABULARY

aber but; however
ab off
alles everything
also therefore; well; in other words
an on; at
  angehen to go on
aus out
  ausgehen to go out
das Auto, –s car
das Bier, –e beer
das Buch, ¨er book
da there; then; under these circumstances
die Dame, –n lady, woman
dieser, diese, dieses this
doch (*see 36*)
drei three
der Dummkopf (*plural:* **die Dummköpfe**) dumbbell, fool
eins one (*cardinal number*)
fahren (**du fährst, er fährt**) to drive, to go (by train, boat, plane, car)
  abfahren to depart, to leave
  fahren lernen to learn how to drive
der Film, –e movie, film
der Freund, –e friend (*masculine*)
  die Freundin, –nen friend (*feminine*)
fünf five
für for (*governs accusative*)

gesund well, healthy
glücklich happy
  un'glücklich unhappy
gottseidank thank heavens, thank goodness
heißen to be called; to mean
hoffen to hope
  hoffentlich I hope (*sentence adverb*)
interessant' interesting
  un'interessant uninteresting
jeder, jede, jedes each, every
der Kaffee coffee
kaufen to buy
kein no (not any)
kennen to know (to be acquainted with)
die Laterne, –n street light
leider unfortunately (*sentence adverb*)
lesen (**du liest, er liest**) to read
das Licht, –er light
lieben to love
lieber rather
lügen to tell a lie
machen to make; to do
  anmachen to turn on
  ausmachen to turn off
der Mensch, –en man, human being
mit with; along
die Mutter, ¨ mother
nichts nothing

nie never
nur only
oder or
der Profes'sor, die Professo'ren professor
sechs six
so so
sofort immediately
der Sohn, ¨e son
der Student', –en student (masculine)
  die Studen'tin, –nen student (*feminine*)
die Uhr, –en clock, watch
  um ein Uhr at one o'clock
um around; about; at
der Vater, ¨ father
verstehen to understand
viel much
  soviel so much, as much
vier four
der Wagen, – car; wagon
warum why
werden to become
wie as; like; how
wissen to know (as a fact)
wohin? where, where to? (asks for a goal, not a location)
zahlen to pay (as in a restaurant)
der Zug, ¨e train
zurück back
  wieder zurück back, back again
zwei two

UNIT 3: aber, oder, denn, und—Negation by **kein** and **nicht**—The Modals—Contrast Intonation—The Imperative

PATTERNS

[1] aber, oder, denn, und

*Dies*es Jahr bleiben wir zu *Hause.*	*This* year we'll stay at *home.*	SEE ANALYSIS 37 (p. 64)
Aber *nächs*tes Jahr fahren wir nach *Deutsch*-land.	But *next* year we are going to *Germany.*	
*Nächs*tes Jahr fahren wir aber nach *Deutsch*-land.		
Kommst du *heu*te, oder kommst du *mor*-gen?	Are you coming *today,* or will you come *tomorrow?*	
Alle Menschen sind egoistisch; denn *jeder* Mensch will *glück*lich werden.	*All* humans are *egoistic,* for every human being wants to be *happy.*	
Meyers fahren nach *Köln,* und *wir* fahren nach *Mün*chen.	The Meyers are going to *Cologne,* and *we* are going to *Munich.*	

[2] nicht, nicht wahr

Wohnen Sie in *Köln?*	Do you live in *Cologne?*	SEE ANALYSIS 38-39 (p. 65)
Sie wohnen doch in *Köln,* nicht *wahr?*	You live in *Cologne,* don't you?	
Sie wohnen doch in *Köln, nicht?*	You live in *Cologne,* don't you?	

[3] nicht ein

Ich kenne hier auch nicht *ein*en Menschen.	I really don't know a *single* soul here.	SEE ANALYSIS 40 (p. 65)
Meyers haben *fünf* Töchter, aber auch nicht *ein*en Sohn.	The Meyers have *five daughters,* but not *one* son.	

[4] kein

The following sentences demonstrate the use of **kein.** Study these sentences first; then practice until you can say the sentences with **kein** when you hear the sentences without **kein,** and vice versa.

SEE
ANALYSIS
41–42

(pp. 66-67)

Hildegard hat *Geld*.   Hildegard hat *kein* Geld.

Ich trinke *Wein*.   Ich trinke *keinen* Wein.

Wir haben ein *Haus*.   Wir haben *kein* Haus.

Ich habe eine *Frau*.   Ich habe *keine* Frau.

Du bist ein *Kind*.   Du bist *kein* Kind.

Sie haben einen *Sohn*, Frau Meyer?   Nein, wir *haben* keinen Sohn. Wir haben auch keine *Tochter*.

Trinken Sie *Bier?*   Nein, ich *trinke* kein Bier.

Von Köln nach Bonn braucht der Zug zwei *Stunden*.   Von Köln nach Bonn braucht der Zug doch keine zwei *Stunden*.

[5] Negation by **nicht**

Be prepared to produce orally the sentences in one column when you hear the sentences in the other column.

SEE
ANALYSIS
43–44

(pp. 67-69)

Er *braucht* mich.   Er braucht mich *nicht*.

Hast du mein *Buch?*   Nein, ich *habe* dein Buch nicht.

Das *Wasser* kocht.   Das Wasser kocht *nicht*.

Vater ist gottseidank wieder ge*sund*.   *Vater* ist leider nicht ge*sund*.

Soviel ich *weiß*, ist *Inge* seine *Tochter*.   Soviel ich *weiß*, ist *Inge nicht* seine Tochter.

Sonntags gehen wir ins *Kino*.   *Sonntags* gehen wir *nicht* ins Kino.

Natürlich bleibe ich heute abend zu *Hause*.   Natürlich bleibe ich heute abend nicht zu *Hause*.

Hoffentlich kommt sie morgen *wie*der.   Hoffentlich kommt sie morgen nicht *wie*der.

[6] schon, noch, mehr

Be prepared to produce orally the sentences in one column when you hear the sentences in the other column.

SEE
ANALYSIS
45

(p. 69)

Regnet es *immer* noch?   Nein, es *regnet* nicht mehr.
  Is it *still* raining?   No, it isn't *raining* any more.

Er ist schon zu *Hause*.   Er ist noch *nicht* zu Hause.
  He is at *home* already.   He is *not* at home yet.

Er ist noch zu *Hause*.   Er ist nicht mehr zu *Hause*.
  He is still at *home*.   He isn't at *home* any more.

Wir wohnen noch *immer* in München.   Wir *wohnen* nicht mehr in München.
  We *still* live in Munich.   We don't *live* in Munich any more.

Ist er *immer* noch krank?   Nein, er ist *nicht* mehr krank.
  Is he *still* sick?   No, he *isn't* sick any more.

Ist er *imm*er noch dein Freund?
  Is he *still* your friend?

Nein, er *ist* nicht mehr mein Freund.
  No, he *isn't* my friend any more.

Haben wir noch *Bier?*
  Do we still have some *beer?*

Nein, wir *ha*ben kein Bier mehr.
  No, we don't *have* any more beer.

Haben wir kein *Bier* mehr?
  Don't we have any *beer* any more?

*Doch, Bier ha*ben wir noch.
  Yes, we still *have* some beer.

Sie ist noch ein *Kind.*
  She is still a *child.*

Sie ist kein *Kind* mehr.
  She is no longer a *child.*

Sie ist *imm*er noch ein Kind.
  She is *still* a child.

Sie ist noch *imm*er ein Kind.
  She is *still* a *child.*

Du bist doch noch ein *Kind,* Inge.
  You are still a *child,* Inge.

Nein, Mutter, ich bin *kein* Kind mehr.
  No, mother, I'm *not* a child any more.

Ich bin doch kein *Kind* mehr, Mutter.
  But I am not a *child* any more, mother.

Du *bist* noch ein Kind.
  You *are* still a child.

Er ist noch Stu*dent.*

  He is still a *student.*

Er ist noch kein *Arzt.*
Er ist noch nicht *Arzt.*
  He is not a *doctor* yet.

Er ist schon *Arzt.*
  He is already a *doctor.*

Er ist kein Stu*dent* mehr.
  He is no longer a *student.*

Ich habe noch einen *Bru*der.
  I still have a *brother.*

Ich *ha*be keinen *Bru*der mehr.
  I don't *have* a brother any more.

Ich habe *noch* einen Bruder.
  I have *another* brother.

[7] mehr, mehr als, nicht mehr als

Observe that in the following sentences **mehr** has a quantitative meaning and
not a temporal meaning as in [6] above.

SEE
ANALYSIS
45

(pp. 69-70)

Meine Frau sagt, sie braucht mehr Geld.
  My wife says she needs more money.

Meine Frau braucht mehr Geld als ich.
  My wife needs more money than I need.

Meyer braucht viel Geld, aber seine Frau braucht noch mehr Geld als er.
  Meyer needs much money, but his wife needs even more money than he does.

Er arbeitet mehr als ich.
  He works more than I do.

Er weiß mehr, als er sagt.
  He knows more than he says.

Er hat mehr Geld, als er braucht.
  He has more money than he needs.

Ich habe nur zehn Mark; ich habe leider nicht mehr.
> I only have ten marks; unfortunately, I don't have any more.

Das kostet nicht mehr als fünf Mark.
> That doesn't cost more than five marks.

Ich habe nicht mehr Geld als du.
> I don't have more money than you (have).

[8] **doch** as Answer to a Negative Question

Study these sentences as questions and answers. Be prepared to formulate the answers orally when you hear the questions, and vice versa.

SEE
ANALYSIS
46
(p. 70)

Fahren Sie heute nach *Köln?*	*Nein*, ich fahre erst *morg*en.
Fahren Sie *nicht* nach Köln?	*Doch*, natürlich fahre ich nach Köln.
Trinken Sie *Kaf*fee, Frau Schmidt?	*Nein*, ich *trin*ke keinen Kaffee.
Trinken Sie *kei*nen Kaffee?	*Doch*, natürlich trinke ich Kaffee.
Haben Meyers schon *Kin*der?	*Ja*, einen *Sohn* und eine *Toch*ter.
Haben Meyers noch keine *Kin*der?	*Doch*, einen *Sohn* und eine *Toch*ter.
Gehst du heute abend ins *Kino?*	*Ja*, mit *In*ge.
Gehst du heute abend *nicht* ins Kino?	*Doch*, aber *nicht* wieder mit *In*ge.

[9] **können**

Study the following sentences, which contain all the present tense forms of **können.** Then practice these forms by following the instruction under "Variations."

SEE
ANALYSIS
48–54
(pp. 71-74)

Ich kann heute *kom*men.	I can *come* today.
Ich kann heute *nicht* kommen.	I *cannot* come today.
Kannst du heute *kom*men?	Can you *come* today?
Kannst du heute nicht *kom*men?	Can't you *come* today?
Kann Herr Bauer heute *ar*beiten?	Will Mr. Bauer be able to *work* today?
Nein, er kann heute *nicht* arbeiten.	No, he will *not* be able to work today.
Wir können das Haus *kau*fen.	We can *buy* the house.
Wir können das Haus *nicht* kaufen.	We *cannot* buy the house.
Ihr könnt das Geld *mor*gen schon haben.	You can have the money *tomorrow.*
Ihr könnt das Geld morgen noch *nicht* haben.	Tomorrow you *can't* have the money yet.
Sie können jetzt das *Licht* ausmachen.	You can switch off the *light* now.
Sie können doch noch nicht das *Licht* ausmachen.	You can't switch off the *light* yet.

VARIATIONS

Ich kann heute kommen.

Er _____.

Er _____ nicht _____.

Sie _____ nicht _____.

_____ Sie _____?

Warum _____ du denn _____ nicht _____?

Warum _____ ihr denn _____ nicht _____?

Wir _____ leider nicht _____.

Könnt _____ nicht _____?

Doch, ich _____.

Nein, wir _____ nicht _____.

Heute _____ ich noch nicht _____.

Form the same variations using (1) **das Haus kaufen,** and (2) **nach München fahren**

[10] müssen

The following sentences contain all present-tense forms of **müssen**. Note that **brauchen zu** is used for the negative of **müssen**.

SEE ANALYSIS 48–54 (pp. 71-74)

Ich muß *ar*beiten.	I have to *work.*
Ich *brau*che nicht zu *ar*beiten.	I don't *have* to *work.*
Du mußt *kom*men.	You have to *come.*
Du *brauchst* nicht zu kommen.	You don't *have* to come.
Er muß morgen nach Ber*lin* fahren.	He has to go to *Berlin* tomorrow.
Er *braucht* morgen nicht nach Ber*lin* zu fahren.	He does not *have* to go to *Berlin* tomorrow.
Wir müssen morgen leider *ar*beiten.	Unfortunately, we have to *work* tomorow.
Wir *brau*chen morgen nicht zu arbeiten.	We don't *have* to work tomorow.
Ihr müßt Tante A*ma*lie besuchen.	You have to visit Aunt *Amalie.*
Ihr *braucht* sie nicht zu be*su*chen.	You don't *have* to visit her.
Sie müssen jetzt das *Licht* ausmachen.	You have to switch the *light* off now.
Sie brauchen das Licht noch nicht *aus*zu-machen.	You don't have to switch the light *off* yet.
Mein Mann und ich haben *mehr* Geld als wir *brau*chen. Wir *brau*chen nicht mehr zu *ar*beiten.	My husband and I have *more* money than we *need.* We don't *have* to work any longer.
Warum wollen Sie denn bei dem Regen nach *Ham*burg fahren?—Ich *muß!*	Why do you want to drive to *Hamburg* in this rain?—I *have* to!

Sie sagen, Sie arbeiten auch *sonn*tags?—Das *brauch*en Sie aber nicht.

You say you work also on *Sundays?*—You don't *have* to do that.

Sie *ar*beiten heute? *Müss*en Sie das?

You are *working* today? Do you *have* to?

VARIATIONS

Mußt du morgen arbeiten?

Nein, morgen _____ ich nicht zu arbeiten.

Ich hoffe, du brauchst morgen nicht zu arbeiten.

Doch, leider _____ ich auch *morgen* arbeiten.

Braucht er heute nicht zu arbeiten?

Nein, heute _____.

Müßt ihr heute arbeiten?

Ja, wir _____.

Muß Erika immer noch arbeiten?

Nein, sie _____ nicht mehr _____.

Form the same variations with (1) **nach Berlin fahren,** (2) **zu Hause bleiben,** and (3) **mit Tante Amalie ins Museum gehen.**

[11] wollen

Be prepared to produce orally the negative sentences when you hear the affirmative sentences and vice versa.

SEE
ANALYSIS
48–54

(pp. 71-74)

Ich will *hei*raten.
   I want to *marry.*

Ich *will* noch nicht heiraten.
   I don't *want* to marry yet.

Willst du jetzt *schla*fen?
   You want to *sleep* now?

Willst du jetzt *nicht* schlafen?
   Don't you want to sleep now?

Sie will *immer* Kaffee trinken.
   She *always* wants to drink coffee.

Sie *will* keinen Kaffee mehr trinken.
   She doesn't *want* to drink coffee any more.

Wir wollen heute abend ins *Ki*no gehen.
   We want to go to the *movies* tonight.

Wir wollen heute abend *nicht* ins Kino.
   We *don't* want to go to the movies tonight.

Wann wollt ihr denn *hei*raten?
　When do you intend to get married?
Sie wollen *ar*beiten.
　They want to *work*.

Warum *wollt* ihr denn noch nicht heiraten?
　Why don't you *want* to get married yet?
Sie wollen nicht mehr soviel *ar*beiten.
　They no longer want to *work* so much.

VARIATIONS

Hans und Erika wollen heiraten.
Hans _____ heiraten.
Ich _____ noch nicht _____.
Wir _____ erst nächstes Jahr _____.
So, du _____?
Wann _____ ihr denn _____?

[12] sollen

For each sentence, form a parallel example according to the translation on the right.

Ich soll heute abend zu *Hau*se bleiben.

_____

Aber *Hans!* Du *sollst* doch keinen Kaffee trinken.

_____

Sie *soll* sonntags nicht mehr arbeiten.

_____

Was sollen wir denn *tun?*

_____

Warum sollt ihr ihn denn schon wieder be*su*chen?

_____

Herr Meyer, Sie sollen morgen nach *Ber*lin fahren.

_____

I am supposed to stay *home* tonight.
I am supposed to visit Aunt *Amalie* tonight.

But Hans, you're not *supposed* to drink coffee.

But Hans, you're not *supposed* to work so much.

She's not *supposed* to work on Sundays any more.

She's not *supposed* to go to the movies with Hans any more.

What are we supposed to *do?*
When are we supposed to *visit* them?

Why are you supposed to *visit* him again?

Why aren't you supposed to *read* this book?

Mr. Meyer, you are supposed to go to *Ber*lin tomorrow.

Mr. Meyer, you are supposed to stay *here* tomorrow.

SEE
ANALYSIS
48–54

(pp. 71-74)

[13] möchte

After studying these sentences, practice the forms of **möchte** as indicated below.

SEE
ANALYSIS
48-54
(pp. 71-74)

Ich *möch*te jetzt nichts essen; ich möchte *schla*fen.

I don't *want* to eat anything now; I want to *sleep.*

Möchtest du Frau *Mey*er kennenlernen?—Er möchte *Arzt* werden.—Sie möchte nächstes Jahr *hei*raten.—Wir möchten nächstes Jahr *hei*raten.—Wann möchtet ihr denn *hei*raten?—Alle Menschen möchten *glück*lich werden.

Would you like to meet Mrs. *Meyer?*—He would like to become a *doctor.*—She would like to *marry* next year.—We would like to *marry* next year.—When would you like to get *married?*—All men want to become *happy.*

Ich möchte eine Tasse *Kaf*fee trinken.—Möchten Sie *auch* eine Tasse Kaffee?

I should like to have (drink) a cup of *coffee.*—Would you *also* like to have a cup of coffee?

Möchtest du heute abend *nicht* ins Kino gehen?—*Nein,* ich möchte *wirk*lich zu *Hau*se bleiben.

Would you rather *not* go to the movies tonight?—*No,* I *really* want to stay at *home.*

Sie *brau*chen das Buch nicht zu *le*sen, wenn Sie nicht *wol*len.—Aber ich *möch*te es lesen.

You *need* not *read* the book if you don't *want* to.—But I would *like* to read it.

VARIATIONS

Ich schlafe.

Ich möchte schlafen.

Ich fahre nächstes Jahr nach Italien.

_____

Morgen gehe ich nicht ins Kino.

_____

Gehst du nach Hause?

_____

Meyer kauft unser Haus.

_____

Wir essen heute abend im "Regina."

_____

,,Er möchte Arzt werden"

[14] dürfen

After studying these sentences, go through the variations below.

Ich darf ihn nicht besuchen.—Ich darf ihn noch nicht besuchen.—Ich darf ihn nicht mehr besuchen.	I am not permitted to *visit* him.—I am not yet permitted to *visit* him.—I am no longer permitted to *visit* him.	SEE ANALYSIS 48-54 (pp. 71-74)
Darfst du *Kaff*ee trinken?—Darf er jetzt wieder *Kaff*ee trinken?	Can you drink *coffee*?—Can he drink *coffee* again (now)?	
Dürfen wir euch morgen besuchen?—Dürft ihr uns besuchen?	May we *visit* you tomorrow?—May you *visit* us?	
Sie dürfen uns nicht besuchen.	They may not *visit* us.	

VARIATIONS

Vary each sentence with the new subjects indicated.

Ich darf morgen meinen Mann besuchen.   Du _____
                                         Frau Meyer _____

Wir dürfen keinen Kaffee mehr trinken.   Er _____
                                         Erika _____

Ich darf sonntags nicht ins Kino gehen. Inge _____
                                         Wir _____

,,Darf man hier nicht rauchen?''

,,Hier darf man rauchen''

[15] Second Prong

FRONT FIELD	1ST PRONG	INNER FIELD	NICHT	1ST BOX	2ND BOX	
Ich	möchte	das Buch			lesen	SEE ANALYSIS 52-53 (pp. 73-74)
Ich	möchte	das Buch	nicht		lesen	
Ich	darf	Kaffee			trinken	
Ich	darf	keinen Kaffee			trinken	

FRONT FIELD	1ST PRONG	INNER FIELD	NICHT	1ST BOX	2ND BOX
Morgen	kann	sie ihren Mann	noch nicht		besuchen
Wir	dürfen	sonntags	nicht mehr		arbeiten
Er	scheint	jetzt			zu schlafen
Er	scheint	jetzt	nicht		zu schlafen
Er	kann		nicht mehr		schlafen
Er	scheint		noch nicht		zu schlafen
Warum	brauchst	du morgen	nicht		zu arbeiten?
Seine Frau	scheint	wirklich	nicht	intelligent	zu sein
Das	muß			seine Frau	sein
Das	kann	doch	nicht	seine Frau	sein
Das	scheint			seine Frau	zu sein
Das	scheint		nicht	seine Frau	zu sein
Erika	möchte	heute abend	nicht	zu Hause	bleiben
Ich	möchte	sie		wieder-	sehen
Ich	möchte	sie	nicht	wieder-	sehen
Ich	möchte	sie wirklich		kennen-	lernen
Ich	brauche	sie	nicht	kennen-	zu-lernen

SEE
ANALYSIS
55–56

(pp. 75-76)

[16] Contrast Intonation

Read these sentences aloud until you have thoroughly mastered this intonation
pattern.

Du fährst morgen nach It*a*lien? *Ich* kann
nicht nach Italien fahren.

You are going to *Italy* tomorrow? *I* can*not*
go to Italy.

Hast *du Geld? Ich* habe *kein* Geld.

Do *you* have *money? I don't* have any
money.

Trinken Meyers *Kaf*fee?—*Sie ja,* aber *er
nicht.*

Do the Meyers drink *coffee?*—She does, but
he does *not.*

Ist er intelli*gent* oder interes*sant?*—Intelli-
gent ist er, aber interes*sant* ist er *nicht.*

Is he *intelligent* or *interesting?*—He is in-
telligent all right. But *interesting?* No!

Ich höre, dein Bruder studiert Psycholo*gie.*
Was studierst *du?*—Ich studiere Medi*zin.*

I hear your brother is majoring in *psychology.* What are *you* majoring in?—*I*
am in Med. School.

Kennen Sie Fritz *En*ders, Frau *Holl*mann?
—Nein, seine *Mutter* kenne ich *gut,* aber
ihn kenne ich *nicht.*

Do you know Fritz *Enders,* Mrs. *Hollmann?*
—No, I know his *mother well,* but I do
not know *him.*

Warum gehst du nie mit *In*ge ins *Ki*no? Sie
ist doch *so* intelli*gent.*—*Ja,* intelli*gent ist*
sie.

Why don't you ever go to the *movies* with
Inge? She is *so intelligent!*—*Yes,* she is
intelligent all right.

Warum gehst du so oft mit *Inge* ins *Kino*? Ist sie intelli*gent*?—*Nein,* intelli*gent* ist sie *nicht.*

Why do you take *Inge* to the *movies* so often? Is she *intelligent*?—*No,* she's not *intelligent.*

[17] Contrast Intonation

Das ist *Wasser.* Das ist *kein* Wasser. *Wasser* ist das *nicht.*

This is *water.* This is *not* water. This is *no* water.

Wir trinken *Wein.* Wir trinken *kei*nen Wein. *Wein* trinken wir *nicht.*

We drink *wine.* We do *not* drink wine. *Wine* we do *not* drink.

Meyers haben einen *Sohn.* Meyers haben *kei*nen Sohn. Einen *Sohn* haben Meyers *nicht.*

The Meyers have a *son.* The Meyers do *not* have a son. The Meyers have *no son.*

SEE ANALYSIS 56 (p. 76)

Vary the following sentences in the same manner as above:

> Sie haben eine Tochter.
>
> Wir trinken Bier.
>
> Hans hat eine Freundin.
>
> Ich kenne hier einen Arzt.

[18] Imperative

Arbeiten Sie nicht soviel!   Don't work so much.

Bleiben Sie doch hier!   Why don't you stay here?

Gehen Sie doch nach Hause!   Why don't you go home?

Kommen Sie doch morgen!   Why don't you come tomorrow?

Lernen Sie Deutsch!   Learn German.

Sagen Sie doch etwas!   Say something.

Seien Sie nicht so egoistisch!   Don't be so selfish.

Tun Sie das doch bitte nicht!   Please don't do that.

Machen Sie bitte das Licht an!   Please turn on the light.

Kaufen Sie doch einen Volkswagen!   Why don't you buy a VW?

Schlafen Sie gut!   Sleep well!

Lassen Sie mich allein!   Leave me alone.

SEE ANALYSIS 57 (p. 76-77)

CONVERSATION

I

TANTE AMALIE: Was willst *du* denn studieren, Erika?

What do *you* intend to study, Erika?

ERIKA:	Ich *will* nicht studieren. Hans und ich wollen *hei*raten.	I don't *intend* to go to a university. Hans and I intend to *marry*.
TANTE AMALIE:	Und Hans will *auch* nicht studieren?	And Hans does not intend to go to the university *either?*
ERIKA:	Nein!	No!
TANTE AMALIE:	Will *er* heiraten, oder willst *du* heiraten?	Does *he* want to marry, or do *you* want to marry?
ERIKA:	*Hans* will immer, was *ich* will.	*Hans* always wants what *I* want.
TANTE AMALIE:	Ach *so!* Er möchte also *doch* studieren!	Is that *right?* So he wants to go to a university *after* all!
ERIKA:	Na*tür*lich möchte er. Ich möchte *auch*. Aber kann man heiraten *und* studieren?	Of *course* he would like to. I would like to, *too*. But can one marry *and* be a (university) student?
TANTE AMALIE:	Das *kann* man. Aber dann muß man *Geld* haben, *viel* Geld. Aber man kann auch *erst* studieren und *dann* heiraten, nicht wahr?	One *can* do that. But then one must have *money*, a good *deal* of money. But one can also *first* go to a university and *then* marry.
ERIKA:	Ich *weiß!* Das *kann* man. Aber das *wol*len wir nicht.	I *know*. One *can* do that. But we don't *want* to do that.
TANTE AMALIE:	Ich glaube, das willst *du* nicht. Ich kann dich *wirk*lich nicht ver*ste*hen, Erika. Ich hoffe nur, *Hans* versteht dich.	I believe *you* don't want that. *Really*. I can't understand you, Erika. I only hope *Hans* understands you.

II

INGE:	Du, Hans, wir haben nicht viel *Zeit*. Sollen wir nicht ein *Taxi* nehmen?
HANS:	Nein, ein Taxi nehmen wir heute *nicht*. Aber wir *fah*ren *doch*. Ich habe einen *Wa*gen!
INGE:	Einen *Wa*gen? Du hast einen *Wa*gen? Das ist aber *prima*. Ist es *dein* Wagen?
HANS:	Nein, nein, es ist nicht *mein* Wagen. Ich habe keinen Wagen. Es ist *Otto*s Wagen, aber er *braucht* ihn heute nicht. Also brauchen wir heute nicht ins Theater zu *ge*hen, wir können ins Theater *fah*ren.
INGE:	Du, das ist *gut*. Jetzt haben wir noch *so* viel Zeit. Es ist ja erst sechs *Uhr*. Jetzt können wir *erst* essen und *dann* ins Theater fahren.
HANS:	*Essen will* ich jetzt nichts; ich habe keinen *Hun*ger. Ich möchte jetzt nur eine Tasse *Kaf*fee. Aber *du* sollst natürlich *essen*, wenn du *willst*.

INGE: *Nein,* du mußt *auch* essen. Weißt du, was die Leute *den*ken, wenn *ich* esse und *du* trinkst nur Kaffee? Das ist ein Stu*dent,* denken sie, er hat also kein *Geld* und sagt, er hat keinen *Hun*ger.

HANS: Aber ich habe *wirk*lich keinen Hunger.

INGE: Also gut, dann *esse* ich etwas und *du* trinkst *Kaff*ee, und die *Leu*te sollen *den*ken, was sie *wol*len.

READING

Der Mensch, das kann man schon bei Aristoteles lesen, ist ein Tier. Aber dieses Tier, sagt Aristoteles, hat Vernunft.

Man, one can read already in Aristotle, is an animal. But this animal, says Arisotle, has reason.

Und was ist Vernunft? Vernunft ist nicht Intelligenz. Vernunft ist mehr als Intelligenz. 5

And what is reason? Reason is not intelligence. Reason is more than intelligence.

Wer nur intelligent ist, glaubt: „Alle Menschen sind egoistisch. Ja, sie müssen egoistisch sein. Denn jeder Mensch will glücklich werden. Das heißt aber, der Emil möchte haben, was Fritz hat; und der Fritz 10 möchte sein, was Emil ist. Aber der Emil kann nicht immer alles haben, was er möchte; und Fritz kann nicht sein, was Emil ist. Und darum haßt der Fritz den Emil, und der Emil den Fritz. Darum haßt ein 15 Sohn seinen Vater, und darum haßt Nation A Nation B. Der Krieg zwischen Fritz und Emil, zwischen Sohn und Vater und zwischen Nation A und Nation B ist also natürlich. So ist es, und so bleibt es. Leider!" 20

Whoever is merely intelligent believes: "All human beings are egoistic. Indeed, they have to be egoistic. For every human being desires to become happy. But this means: Emil would like to have what Fritz has; and Fritz would like to be what Emil is. But Emil cannot always have what he would like (to have); and Fritz cannot be what Emil is. And for this reason Fritz hates Emil, and Emil hates Fritz. Therefore, a son will hate his father, and Nation A will hate Nation B. War between Fritz and Emil, between father and son, and between Nation A and Nation B is therefore natural. That's the way it is, and that's the way it will remain, unfortunately."

Aber warum „leider"? Was ist, ist, und es kann nur so sein, wie es ist. Warum also „leider"?

But why "unfortunately"? Whatever is, is, and it can only be as it is. Why, therefore, "unfortunately"?

Hier spricht nicht unsere Intelligenz. Hier 25 spricht unsere Vernunft. Unsere Intelligenz sieht nur, was ist. Unsere Vernunft sieht mehr. Sie sieht: Das, was ist, soll und darf nicht sein.

Here (through this "unfortunately") speaks not our intelligence, but our reason. Our intelligence sees only what exists. Our reason sees more. It sees that what is, should not and must not be.

Natürlich will jeder Mensch glücklich werden. Er will es instinktiv. Er muß es wollen. 30

Naturally every human being desires to become happy. He desires it instinctively. He

Der Hans will *sein* Glück, und ich will *mein* Glück. Er will also nur, was ich auch will. Ich habe ein Haus und bin glücklich. Hans hat kein Haus und ist unglücklich. Aber, so sagt meine Vernunft, ich kann nicht glück- 5 lich sein, wenn Hans unglücklich ist. Denn wenn Hans sagt: „Du hast ein Haus und ich habe kein Haus", dann sagt er auch bald: „Warum sollst du ein Haus haben, und ich habe kein Haus?" Und so beginnen 10 alle Kriege. Aber ich will keinen Krieg; Hans will auch keinen Krieg, er will ein Haus. Ich muß also etwas für ihn tun. Er braucht mich und kann ohne mich nicht glücklich werden; und ich brauche ihn und 15 kann ohne ihn nicht glücklich bleiben. Also muß ich für ihn tun, was ich kann.

Das heißt aber: Ich muß ihn lieben. Denn „lieben" heißt ja „für den Mitmenschen das tun, was gut für ihn ist". Der Krieg, so sagt 20 meine Vernunft, ist nicht natürlich. Natürlich ist nur die Liebe.

Aber leider zwingt mich meine Vernunft nicht. Ich weiß jetzt, was ich soll, aber meine Vernunft läßt mich frei, zu tun oder 25 nicht zu tun, was ich soll. Und das ist unsere Tragik. Wir wollen oft nicht, was wir sollen; und wir können, wenn wir wollen, auch tun, was wir nicht sollen.

Aber wir müssen lernen zu wollen, was wir 30 sollen. Ja, der Mensch ist nur dann wirklich frei—frei zu tun, was er will—wenn er will, was er soll.

must desire it. Hans wants *his* happiness and I want *my* happiness. Thus he only wants what I want too. I have a house and am happy. Hans does not have a house and is unhappy. But, my reason tells me, I cannot be happy if Hans is unhappy. For if Hans says, "You have a house and I have no house," then he will soon say also, "Why should (shall) you have a house, and I don't have a house?" And thus begin all wars. But I don't want a war; Hans wants no war either, he wants a house. Therefore I have to do something for him. He needs me and cannot become happy without me; and I need him and cannot remain happy without him. Therefore I must do for him what I can.

But this means: I must love him. For "to love" means, after all, "to do that for a fellow man which is good for him." War, says my reason, is not natural. Only love is natural.

But unfortunately my reason does not force me. I now know what I ought to do, but my reason leaves me free to do or not to do what I ought (to do). And that is our tragic fate. We often do not want to do what we ought to do; and we can, if we want to, also do what we ought not to do.

However, we must learn to want to do what we ought to do. Indeed, man is only then really free—free to do what he wants to do —when he wants to do what he ought to do.

ANALYSIS

37 aber, oder, denn, und

aber, oder, denn, and **und** are coordinating conjunctions—that is, conjunctions that connect two main clauses. They precede the front field and are not counted as syntactical units. Of these four conjunctions, only

aber can also be placed in the inner field. It then follows pronoun subjects and pronoun objects. If **denn** stands in the inner field, it is not the coordinating conjunction **denn,** *for,* but the particle **denn** discussed in **15.**

38 kein, nicht, and nichts

In English, most negative statements contain either *no* or *not.* The most frequently used German words of negation (besides **Nein!**) are **kein** and **nicht.** However, the use of **kein** and **nicht** does not parallel the use of *no* and *not.* To speak socially acceptable German, the student must therefore learn from the very beginning how and when to use **kein,** and how and when to use **nicht.**

German **nichts** means **nothing** or **not anything;** it is the antonym of **etwas,** *something.*

> **Hast du etwas gegen Erika?**
> Do you have anything against Erika?
> **Nein, ich habe nichts gegen Erika.**
> No, I have nothing against Erika.

39 Nicht wahr? and Nicht? as Complete Questions

Nicht wahr? (an abbreviation of **Ist das nicht wahr?**—*Isn't that true?*) corresponds to English *Isn't that so?, don't you?, haven't you?, weren't you?* etc. This **nicht wahr?** is frequently shortened to **nicht?** Since **nicht?** or **nicht wahr?** asks for confirmation, the preceding sentence usually contains **doch** (see **36**).

> **Sie *kom*men doch heute abend, nicht *wahr?***
> **Sie *kom*men doch heute abend, *nicht?***
> (You are coming tonight, aren't you?)

40 nicht ein

German **nicht ein** does not correspond to English *not a.* The **ein** in **nicht ein** is the numeral *one* and is always stressed. German *nicht ein* therefore means *not one* or *not a single:*

> **Ich habe nicht *ei*ne Frau.**
> I don't have a *single* wife. (Though I am a Mohammedan and could have three or four.)

This **nicht ein** is frequently strengthened by a preceding unstressed **auch** which may be translated by *even:*

Ich kenne hier auch nicht *ei*nen Menschen
I don't know even *one* person around here.

41 Negation by **kein**

German **kein** is declined like the indefinite article **ein.** For the time being, the student should not use **kein** without a following noun. When used with a following noun,

$$\textbf{kein} + \text{noun equals} \begin{cases} \textit{no} & + \text{noun} \\ \textit{not any} + \text{noun} \\ \textit{not a} & + \text{noun} \end{cases}$$

Ich habe kein Geld
I have no money
I don't have any money

Ich habe keine Frau
I have no wife
I don't have a wife

Ich habe keinen Wagen
I have no car
I don't have a car

kein after the Inflected Verb

To make a negative statement, **kein** *must* be used in front of a noun object or in front of a predicate noun, *if* in the corresponding affirmative statement the noun would be used *either* with the indefinite article **ein** *or* all by itself without any article or possessive adjective.

POSITIVE	NEGATIVE
Das ist Wasser	Das ist kein Wasser
Meyers haben einen Sohn	Meyers haben keinen Sohn
Meyers haben Kinder	Meyers haben keine Kinder
Meyers haben Geld	Meyers haben kein Geld

NOTE: The plural of **ein Kind** is **Kinder**, the plural of **kein Kind** is **keine Kinder.** The negation of **zwei Kinder** is **keine zwei Kinder**; of **zwei Jahre**, **keine zwei Jahre.**

kein in the Front Field

Occasionally, **kein** plus noun is found in front of the inflected verb: **Kein Mensch weiß, wo Meyer wohnt**—*Nobody knows where Meyer lives.* However, such usage is very restricted. To be safe, *do not use **kein** in front of the inflected verb.*

42 Intonation of **kein**

The difference in stress distribution between **sie ist** *kein* **Kind** and **sie ist kein** *Kind* parallels the difference between *she is* not *a child* and *she isn't a child:* **kein** is stressed if it strongly contradicts a preceding affirmative statement; if no strong contradiction is intended or if the noun is mentioned for the first time, the noun itself is stressed.

Mutter:	**Deine Tochter geht heute abend schon *wieder* mit Fritz ins Kino.**	Mother:	Your daughter is going to the *movies* tonight, and *again* with *Fritz.*
Vater:	**Na *und?* Sie ist doch noch ein Kind!**	Father:	So what? She is still a *child,* isn't she?
Mutter:	**Sie ist *kein* Kind mehr.**	Mother:	She is *not* a child any longer.

43 Negation by **nicht**

To form a negative statement, **nicht** is used whenever **kein** does not have to be used. For instance, the sentence

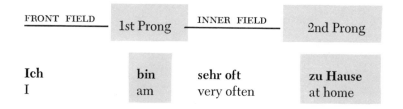

FRONT FIELD	1st Prong	INNER FIELD	2nd Prong
Ich I	**bin** am	**sehr oft** very often	**zu Hause** at home

does not contain a predicate noun or a noun object and therefore cannot be negated by **kein**; it has to be negated by **nicht.** The problem is where this **nicht** should be placed.

Placed at the end of the inner field, i.e., in front of the second prong, **nicht** *negates the entire predicate.* The sentence

Ich	**bin**	**sehr oft nicht**	**zu Hause**

therefore means basically: *I am not at home;* and the **sehr oft** expresses the idea that this not-being-at-home happens *very often.*

If **nicht** is placed in the inner field, the validity of the predicate is left untouched. The sentence

Ich	**bin**	**nicht sehr oft**	**zu Hause**

means basically: *I am at home;* however, this being-at-home happens *not very often.*

Usually, the speaker wants to negate the predicate (and thereby the entire sentence); and for the time being we will use **nicht** mainly in this function. *This means that the student must develop the habit of placing **nicht** behind the inner field,—that is, right in front of the second prong, if the sentence has a second prong.*

Sentences without a Second Prong

Meyer	arbeitet		nicht
Heute	regnet	es	nicht
Ich	verstehe	Meyer	nicht
Warum	kommt	er heute	nicht?
	Kennst	du mich	nicht?

Sentences with a Second Prong

nicht PRECEDES A PREDICATE ADJECTIVE

Er	ist	leider	nicht	gesund
Leider	ist	er	nicht	gesund
Warum	ist	er denn	nicht	glücklich?
	Ist	sie wirklich	nicht	glücklich?

nicht PRECEDES A PREDICATE NOUN

Sie	ist	doch	nicht	meine Mutter
Soviel ich weiß,	ist	Inge	nicht	seine Tochter
Warum	werden	Sie	nicht	Arzt?
	Sind	Sie	nicht	Frau Meyer?

nicht PRECEDES A DIRECTIVE—THAT IS, THE ANSWER TO A *wohin*-QUESTION*

Nächstes Jahr	fahren	wir	nicht	nach Deutschland
Wir	gehen	sonntags	nicht	ins Kino
Warum	geht	ihr sonntags	nicht	in die Kirche?

---

* Both **wo** and **wohin** correspond to English *where*. **Wo** asks for the place at which an entire action takes place; **wohin** asks for a goal toward which an action is directed and at which it ends.

nicht PRECEDES OTHER VERBAL COMPLEMENTS

Morgen abend	bleibe	ich natürlich	nicht	zu Hause
Warum	bleibst	du morgen abend	nicht	zu Hause?
Warum	fährt	denn der Zug	nicht	ab?
Warum	lernt	sie denn	nicht	fahren?

44 Intonation of **nicht**

The intonation of **nicht** corresponds to the intonation of English *not:* If the sentence containing **nicht** is an intentional and somewhat curt contradiction to an immediately preceding statement, **nicht** is stressed and functions as the stress point of the sentence:

| **Sie sind Frau Schmidt, nicht *wahr?*** | You are Mrs. Schmidt, *aren't you?* |
| *Nein,* ich bin *nicht* **Frau Schmidt.** | *No,* I am *not* Mrs. Schmidt. |

In all other cases, **nicht** is completely unstressed.

| **Sie sind Frau *Schmidt,* nicht *wahr?*** | You are Mrs. *Schmidt, aren't you?* |
| *Nein,* **ich bin nicht Frau *Schmidt,* ich bin Frau *Döring.*** | *No,* I am not Mrs. *Schmidt,* I am Mrs. *Döring.* |

45 **noch, schon,** and **mehr**

Noch means *still* or *yet* and signifies that a state of affairs continues to exist.

| **Sie ist noch ein *Kind.*** | She is still a *child.* |
| **Er *schläft* noch.** | He's still *asleep.* |

This **noch** can be emphasized by a preceding or following **immer** (which, when used without **noch,** means *always*).

| **Sie ist *immer* noch ein Kind.** | She is *still* a child. |
| **Sie ist noch *immer* ein Kind.** | |

If a negative state continues to exist, **noch** (**noch immer, immer noch**) precedes **nicht** or **kein:**

Er *schläft* noch nicht.	He isn't *asleep* yet.
Er schläft *immer* noch nicht.	He *still* isn't asleep.
Sie *haben* noch keine Kinder.	They don't *have* any children yet.

NOTE: **noch ein** frequently means *another:*

Trinken Sie noch eine Tasse Kaffee?
Would you like another cup of coffee?

Schon signifies that a state of affairs exists already, perhaps earlier than expected. **Schon** is therefore the opposite of **noch nicht** and **noch kein.**

Er ist schon zu Hause.	**Er ist noch nicht zu Hause.**
He's already at home.	He isn't home yet.
Sie haben schon zwei Kinder.	**Sie haben noch keine Kinder.**
They have two children already.	They don't have any children yet.

To express that a state or an action has come to an end, German uses either **kein . . . mehr** (with a noun between **kein** and **mehr**) or **nicht mehr**. In this context, **kein . . . mehr** and **nicht mehr** have the same (temporal!) meaning as *no more* in *He is no more.* The usage of **kein . . . mehr** and **nicht mehr** parallels that of **kein** and **nicht**.

Ich brauche das Geld nicht mehr.	I don't need the money any more.
Sie ist kein Kind mehr.	She is no longer a child.
Wir wohnen nicht mehr in München.	We don't live in Munich any more.

German **mehr** and English *more,* either by themselves or together with an immediately following noun, can also have a *quantitative* meaning, which always involves a comparison. This comparison may be merely implied. English *more than* is expressed by **mehr als.**

Er arbeitet mehr als ich.	He works more than I do.
Ich brauche mehr Geld.	I need more money (than I have).
Er hat mehr Geld als ich.	He has more money than I have.
Er hat nicht mehr Geld als ich.	He doesn't have more money than I have.
Hier sind fünf Mark; mehr (Geld) habe ich nicht.	Here are five marks; I don't have any more.

46   **doch** to Answer a Negative Question

If a negative question is answered in the affirmative, **doch** with a strong stress is used instead of **ja.**

Fährst du nicht nach Köln?	*Doch,* natürlich fahre ich nach Köln.
Fährst du nicht nach Köln?	*Doch,* aber nicht *heute.*

doch is also used to contradict a negative statement with an affirmative statement.

Ich bin doch kein Kind mehr.	*Doch,* du *bist* noch ein Kind.

47   Professional Status

Certain nouns, such as **Arzt, Schriftsteller, Soldat, Student,** and **Studentin** can be used to express legal or professional status, and in this function they are used all by themselves without any article.

It is perfectly normal to say

Wir brauchen einen Arzt.	We need a doctor.

However, the question *What is your profession?* can only be answered by:

> **Ich bin Arzt.**
> **Mein Sohn wird Arzt.**

If these sentences are negated, either **kein** or **nicht** may be used.

> **Ich bin kein Arzt.**   or   **Ich bin nicht Arzt.**

48 Infinitives with and without **zu**

The infinitive of a verb is not merely used as a dictionary entry. Both in English and in German, infinitives are frequently used in connection with other verbs. The infinitive is used sometimes with, and sometimes without, *to* or **zu:**

Infinitive with **zu:**

Er hat nichts zu tun.	He has nothing to do.
Er scheint zu schlafen.	He seems to be asleep.
Warum brauchst du heute nicht zu arbeiten?	Why don't you have to work today?

Infinitive without **zu:**

Er kann arbeiten.	He can work.
Du mußt kommen.	You must come.
Soll ich gehen?	Shall I go?

49 Modal Auxiliaries

The most important verbs used with a following infinitive without **zu** are the modal auxiliaries, or simply the modals.

They usually express, by themselves, not a specific action, but an attitude toward the action expressed by the infinitive. Thus English *shalt* and *must* in *Thou shalt not steal* and *I must go home* view the action expressed by *steal* and *go home* as forbidden or necessary.

These modals are conjugated irregularly both in English and in German: *he must,* not *he musts;* **er kann,** not **er kannt.**

The English modals are incomplete: they have, for instance, no infinitive and no compound tenses. The German system, though grammatically complete, has peculiarities of its own. For instance, **müssen** is primarily used in positive statements. In negative statements, **müssen** is usually replaced by **brauchen zu:**

Ich muß arbeiten.	I have to work.
Ich brauche nicht zu arbeiten.	I don't have to work.

50   The Six German Modals and Their Meaning

It is definitely unwise to attempt to equate each form of a modal with a corresponding English modal. Instead, the student should master the basic meaning of each modal.

können	to be able to	*expresses ability*
Ich kann lesen	I can read	
müssen	to have to	*expresses necessity*
Ich muß nach Hause gehen	I have to go home	
dürfen	to be allowed to	*expresses permission*
Ich darf hierbleiben	I have permission to stay here	
Das darfst du nicht tun.	You mustn't do that.	
mögen	would like to	*expresses desire*
Ich möchte hierbleiben	I would like to stay here	
wollen	to want to	*expresses intention*
Ich will ins Kino gehen	I intend to go to the movies	
sollen	to be (supposed) to	*expresses imposed obligation; in questions it may express a suggestion*
Ich soll nach Bonn fahren.	I am (supposed) to go to Bonn.	
Sollen wir ins Theater gehen?	Shall we go to the theater?	

51   The Forms of the German Modals

	KÖNNEN	WOLLEN	MÜSSEN	MÖGEN*	SOLLEN	DÜRFEN
ich	kann	will	muß	möchte	soll	darf
du	kannst	willst	mußt	möchtest	sollst	darfst
er sie es	kann	will	muß	möchte	soll	darf
wir	können	wollen	müssen	möchten	sollen	dürfen
ihr	könnt	wollt	müßt	möchtet	sollt	dürft
sie	können	wollen	müssen	möchten	sollen	dürfen
Sie	können	wollen	müssen	möchten	sollen	dürfen

* These forms of **mögen** will be explained in Unit 9.

52 Position of Dependent Infinitives

When infinitives like **arbeiten** or **zu arbeiten** depend on modals or on verbs like **brauchen**, they form a second prong, follow the inner field, and are preceded by **nicht.**

MODAL IN FIRST PRONG, INFINITIVE IN SECOND PRONG

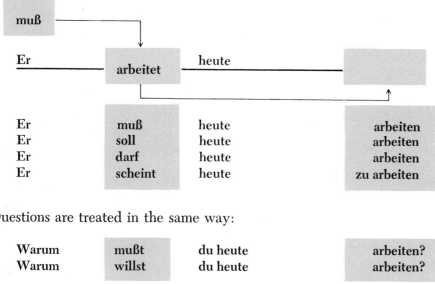

Er	muß	heute	arbeiten
Er	soll	heute	arbeiten
Er	darf	heute	arbeiten
Er	scheint	heute	zu arbeiten

Questions are treated in the same way:

| Warum | mußt | du heute | arbeiten? |
| Warum | willst | du heute | arbeiten? |

| Arbeitet | er heute? | |

| Muß | er heute | arbeiten? |
| Kann | er heute | arbeiten? |

The procedure is the same if **nicht** stands at the end of the inner field:

Er	möchte	heute	nicht	arbeiten
Er	kann	heute	nicht	arbeiten
Er	braucht	heute	nicht	zu arbeiten
Er	scheint	heute	nicht	zu arbeiten
Warum	will	er denn heute	nicht	arbeiten?
Warum	braucht	er denn heute	nicht	zu arbeiten?

53 The Two-Box Second Prong

If a simple verb like **arbeiten** is pushed by a modal out of the slot for the first prong, it moves into the slot for the second prong. But what happens if the verb displaced by the modal or by an auxiliary such as **brauchen** and **scheinen** is a compound verb with some complement already filling the slot for the second prong?—The second prong has two boxes, so to speak, and the infinitive dependent on an auxiliary verb always goes into the second box, whereas all complements go into the first box. The following diagram shows what happens:

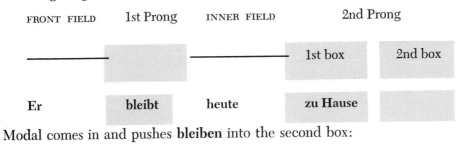

Modal comes in and pushes **bleiben** into the second box:

This two-box second-prong pattern, in which the verbal complement precedes the infinitive without **zu,** is used so frequently in German that German dictionaries list many compound verbs, especially if the complement is a preposition or an adverb, in the form in which they appear in this two-box sequence (see 28). Thus the **fahre zurück** in **Ich fahre morgen zurück** is listed under **zurückfahren,** because it occurs so frequently in such sentences as **Ich will morgen zurückfahren.**

If an infinitive with **zu** is required, this **zu** is inserted between complement and infinitive, and the whole thing is written as one word.

> **Er braucht nicht zurückzufahren.**
> **Er braucht das Licht nicht auszumachen.**

But:

> **Er braucht nicht zu Hause zu bleiben.**

54 Replacement or Omission of the Dependent Infinitive

An infinitive can be replaced by **das,** if the verb was mentioned in the sentence immediately preceding:

> **Sie arbeiten heute? Dürfen Sie das?**

The infinitives **gehen, fahren,** and others, if clearly understood, are frequently omitted. Compare English *He wants out.*

> **Ich muß nach Hause.**   (**gehen** omitted)
> **Ich will heute nach Köln.**   (**fahren** omitted)
> **Du brauchst nicht zu arbeiten, wenn**
> **du nicht willst.**   (**arbeiten** omitted)

55 Contrast Intonation

Imagine the following situation: Mr. and Mrs. Baker have had a serious traffic accident. A friend calls the hospital and asks "How are Mr. and Mrs. Baker?" The doctor answers, "Mrs. Baker is alive." Can this be the answer to the question, "How are Mr. *and* Mrs. Baker?" It can be, but only if the doctor uses the intonation pattern

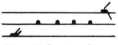

Mrs. Baker is alive

By using this intonation pattern, the doctor clearly implies that Mr. Baker is dead. A German doctor, in the same situation, will answer

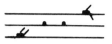

Frau Meyer lebt

No German will fail to register the implication that Herr Meyer is dead.

This "contrast-intonation" pattern is not the same pattern as in sentences with two stressed syllables such as

Sie wohnt noch im-mer in Köln

Contrast intonation is characterized by the fact that the first stressed syllable has a rising pitch starting on level 1, and the second stressed syllable has a falling pitch starting on level 3.

CONTRAST INTONATION

IMPLICATION

Geld hat sie

A-ber in-tel-li-gent ist sie nicht
(contrast intonation)

or:

A-ber sie ist nicht in-tel-li-gent
(normal intonation)

56 Word Order under Contrast Intonation

Under contrast intonation, the second prong frequently appears in the front field. The two sentences:

Sie ist in-tel-li-gent   and   In-tel-li-gent ist sie

are not interchangeable. The first one is a remark of praise, the second is a sophisticated insult. Likewise,

Er ist nicht zu Hau-se   and   Zu Hau-se ist er nicht

are not interchangeable; for only the second contains some implication like "Let's try to reach him somewhere else!"

Under contrast intonation, **kein** is replaced by (**ein**) . . . **nicht.**

    Meyer ist kein *Dummkopf.*
    Ein *Dummkopf* ist Meyer *nicht.*
    Ich habe kein *Geld.*
    Geld habe ich *nicht,*   or: *Geld habe* ich nicht.

57 The Imperative

The English imperative is identical with the infinitive. One can say *Be my guest* no matter whether one calls the person addressed *Jack* or *Dr. Able.* German distinguishes between the **du**-form, the **ihr**-form, and the **Sie**-form of the imperative. At this point, we introduce only the **Sie**-form, which looks like the infinitive plus an immediately following **Sie: Kommen Sie! Gehen Sie! Sehen Sie!** The imperative of **sein** is **Seien Sie.**

Imperatives, like yes-or-no questions, have verb-first position; they are distinguished by intonation.

IMPERATIVE   QUESTION

Kom-men Sie doch heu-te!

Kom-men Sie heu-te?

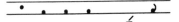

Fah-ren Sie nach Mün-chen!   Fah-ren Sie nach Mün-chen?

In a polite request, the stress-point of an imperative sentence is placed on level 2, as in the examples above. If **bitte** (*please*) is used, it must be placed either at the very beginning, or after the unstressed elements following the first prong.

> **Bitte besuchen Sie uns doch!**
> **Besuchen Sie uns doch bitte!**

If the stress point is raised to level 3, the request, in spite of the use of **bitte**, is changed into a command:

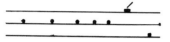

Kom-men Sie bit-te heu-te!

A. Express in German:

1. He is intelligent, isn't he?
2. He lives in Munich, doesn't he?
3. She has a house in Cologne, doesn't she?
4. You are a doctor, aren't you?
5. They have a son, don't they?

B. Transform the following sentences by substituting **kein** for **nicht ein**. Say each pair of sentences aloud to practice the shift in intonation.

> **Ich kenne hier nicht *einen* Menschen.**
> **Ich *kenne* hier keinen Menschen.**

1. Er hat auch nicht einen Freund.
2. Wir haben hier nicht einen Arzt.
3. Heute abend fährt auch nicht ein Zug nach Köln.
4. Heute trinke ich nicht ein Glas Wein.

C. Negate the following sentences by using **kein**.

1. Er ist Arzt.
2. Haben Sie einen Wagen?
3. Sie hat eine Tochter.
4. Brauchst du Geld?
5. Trinken Sie Kaffee, Frau Meyer?

D. Negate the following sentences by using **nicht**; use **noch nicht** and **nicht mehr** only where necessary.

1. Du bist doch meine Mutter.
2. Er liebt mich aber.
3. Sie wohnen noch in Köln.
4. Ihr seid intelligent.
5. Das glaube ich heute immer noch.

E. Write replies to the following negative statements or questions by using **doch.**

> **Wohnt er nicht mehr in München?**
> **Doch, er wohnt immer noch in München.**

1. Ich bin doch kein Kind mehr.
2. Fährst du heute nicht nach Köln?
3. Sind Sie heute abend nicht allein?
4. Haben wir keine Butter mehr?
5. Lebt denn Tante Amalie nicht mehr?

F. For each of the following sentences, invent a preceding sentence with contrast intonation.

> _____, und _ich_ bleibe zu _Hause._
> _Du_ kannst ins _Ki_no gehen, und _ich_ bleibe zu _Hause._

1. _____, und _ich_ muß _ar_beiten.
2. _____, aber intelli_gent_ ist sie _nicht._
3. _____, aber eine _Tochter ha_ben sie nicht.
4. _____, aber ihr _Freund hat_ Geld.
5. _____, aber _ich_ studiere _Deutsch._
6. _____, aber _ar_beiten _will_ er nicht.

G. Express in German:

1. I do not know one single person (human being) here.
2. Would you still like to live in Berlin, Erika?
3. I know he is not home yet.
4. Money is not everything, but can one be happy without money?
5. We do not intend to buy a house yet.
6. I know she can't be happy.
7. He is not permitted to drink wine.
8. Can't he drink coffee either?
9. We are supposed to go to America next year.

ach so oh, I see
als than
der Arzt, ⸚e physician, doctor
bald soon
bei at, at the home of; near
beginnen to begin, to start
besuchen to visit
bitte please
der Bruder, ⸚ brother
dann then; in that case
darum for that reason
denken to think
denn for (conjunction)
der Dok'tor, die Dokto'ren
　doctor
dürfen (see 49 ff.)
egoi'stisch egoistic, selfish
erst first; not until, only
　erst dann not until (or
　only) then
essen (du ißt, er ißt) to eat
　das Essen food, meal
etwas something, somewhat
frei free
gegen against
das Glas, ⸚er glass
das Glück happiness; luck
hassen to hate
heiraten to marry, to get
　married
hören to hear
immer always
　immer noch, noch immer
　still
die Intelligenz' intelligence,
　intellect
Ita'lien Italy
　italie'nisch Italian

kalt cold
kennenlernen to meet, to be-
　come acquainted with
können (see 49 ff.)
kosten to cost
krank sick
der Krieg, –e war
lassen (du läßt, er läßt) to
　let, to leave
　die Kinder zu Hause las-
　sen* to leave the chil-
　dren at home
leben to live, to be alive
die Leute people (plural
　only)
die Liebe love
man one (pronoun); accusa-
　tive: einen
die Mark mark
　zwei Mark two marks
mehr more
　mehr als more than
　nicht mehr no longer
mögen (see 49 ff.)
das Muse'um (pl. die Muse'-
　en) the museum
müssen (see 49 ff.)
na und? so what?
nehmen (du nimmst, er
　nimmt) to take
oft often
ohne without (with accusa-
　tive)
prima wonderful (colloquial)
rauchen to smoke
scheinen to seem; to shine
　er scheint zu schlafen he
　seems to be asleep

schlafen (du schläfst, er
　schläft) to sleep
sehen (du siehst, er sieht) to
　see
sollen (see 49 ff.)
sprechen (du sprichst, er
　spricht) to speak, to talk
die Stunde, –n hour
die Tante, –n aunt
die Tasse, –n cup
das Taxi, –s, or die Taxe, –n
　taxi
das Thea'ter, – theater
das Tier, –e animal
trinken to drink
die Uhr, –en clock, watch
　sechs Uhr six o'clock
　wieviel Uhr what time
　um wieviel Uhr at what
　time
die Vernunft reason (intel-
　lect)
von from
wahr true
das Wasser water
der Wein, –e wine
wenn when; whenever; if
wiedersehen to see again
　auf Wiedersehen good-bye
wieviel how much
wirklich really
wollen (see 49 ff.)
zehn ten
die Zeit, –en time
zu to, too
　zuviel too much
zwingen to force
zwischen between

---

* Do not confuse this with
　abfahren to depart; to leave (intransitive)
　der Zug fährt ab the train is leaving

UNIT 4: The Dative—Prepositions with Dative and Accusative —**lange** versus **schon lange**—The Perfect

[1] The Dative of the Personal Pronouns

This pattern drill contains all the dative forms of the personal pronouns (with the exception of the polite **Ihnen**). After memorizing these pronouns, follow the system used in this drill and recite these sentences until you can do them automatically.

Heute helfe ich dir, und morgen hilfst du mir.
Heute helfe ich ihm, und morgen hilft er mir.
Heute helfe ich ihr, und morgen hilft sie mir.
Heute helfe ich euch, und morgen helft ihr mir.
Heute helfe ich ihnen, und morgen helfen sie mir.

Heute hilfst du mir, und morgen helfe ich dir.
Heute hilfst du ihm, und morgen hilft er dir.
Heute hilfst du ihr, und morgen hilft sie dir.
Heute hilfst du uns, und morgen helfen wir dir.
Heute hilfst du ihnen, und morgen helfen sie dir.

Heute helfen wir dir, und morgen hilfst du uns.
Heute helfen wir ihm, und morgen hilft er uns.
Heute helfen wir ihr, und morgen hilft sie uns.
Heute helfen wir euch, und morgen helft ihr uns.
Heute helfen wir ihnen, und morgen helfen sie uns.

SEE
ANALYSIS
58–59

(pp. 92-95)

[2] The Dative with **glauben** and **helfen**

Follow the instructions for [1]. Do not change intonation.

Wenn du mir nicht *glaubst*, kann ich dir nicht *helf*en.
Wenn er mir nicht *glaubt*, kann ich ihm nicht *helf*en.
Wenn sie mir nicht *glaubt*, kann ich ihr nicht *helf*en.
Wenn sie mir nicht *glau*ben, kann ich ihnen nicht *helf*en.

SEE
ANALYSIS
58–59

(pp. 92-95)

(Facing) **Fahrkartenkontrolle [ticket checking] auf dem Bahnhof**

Wenn du uns nicht *glaubst,* können wir dir nicht *hel*fen.

Wenn er uns nicht *glaubt,* können wir ihm nicht *hel*fen.

Wenn sie uns nicht *glaubt,* können wir ihr nicht *hel*fen.

Wenn ihr uns nicht *glaubt,* können wir euch nicht *hel*fen.

Wenn sie uns nicht *glau*ben, können wir ihnen nicht *hel*fen.

[3] The Dative with **danken**

Follow the instructions for [1]. Do not change intonation.

SEE
ANALYSIS
58-59

(pp. 92-95)

Ich *weiß,* du hilfst mir *gern.* Aber wie kann ich dir *dan*ken?

Ich *weiß,* er hilft mir *gern.* Aber wie kann ich ihm *dan*ken?

Ich *weiß,* sie hilft mir *gern.* Aber wie kann ich ihr *dan*ken?

Ich *weiß,* ihr helft mir *gern.* Aber wie kann ich euch *dan*ken?

Ich *weiß,* sie helfen mir *gern.* Aber wie kann ich ihnen *dan*ken?

[4] The Dative with **antworten**

Follow the instructions for [1]. Do not change intonation.

SEE
ANALYSIS
58-59

(pp. 92-95)

Na*tür*lich kannst du mich fragen! Aber ich brauche dir nicht zu *ant*worten!

Na*tür*lich kann er mich fragen! Aber ich brauche ihm nicht zu *ant*worten!

Na*tür*lich kann sie mich fragen! Aber ich brauche ihr nicht zu *ant*worten!

Na*tür*lich könnt ihr mich fragen! Aber ich brauche euch nicht zu *ant*worten!

Na*tür*lich können sie mich fragen! Aber ich brauche ihnen nicht zu *ant*worten!

[5] The Dative with **gehören**—Replacement of **er, sie, es** by **der, die, das**

Practice these pairs of sentences until you can produce the second sentence orally when you hear the first.

SEE
ANALYSIS
58-59, 72

(pp. 92-95, 114)

Das ist mein Wagen. Der gehört mir.

Das ist deine Uhr. Die gehört dir.

Das ist sein Auto. Das gehört ihm.

Das ist ihr Hut. Der gehört ihr.

Das ist unsere Zeitung. Die gehört uns.

Das ist euer Haus. Das gehört euch.

Das ist Ihr Hund. Der gehört Ihnen.

Das sind meine Zeitungen. Die gehören mir.

Das sind deine Häuser. Die gehören dir.

Das sind seine Hüte. Die gehören ihm.

Das sind unsere Zeitungen. Die gehören uns.

Das sind eure Häuser? Die gehören euch?

Das sind ihre Hüte. Die gehören ihnen.

After you have mastered the pattern above, be prepared to produce orally **Das ist mein Wagen** when you hear **Der Wagen gehört mir.**

[6] The Dative with **gehören**

Formulate similar questions and answers. Do not place the word containing the answer in the front field. Be prepared to do this orally in class.

SEE
ANALYSIS
58-59, 72

(pp. 92-95, 114)

Wem	gehört	das *Haus* da?
Das	gehört	Frau *Schulz.*
Wem	gehören	denn diese *Häus*er hier?
Das da	gehört	*mir.*
So? Das	gehört	*dir?*
Frau *Schmidt* sagt, das Auto	gehört	*ihr.*
Nein, es	gehört	*uns.*
	Gehört	dieses Auto *euch?*
Nein, es	gehört	Frau *Ber*tram.
Was? Dieses Auto	gehört	*Ih*nen, Frau Bertram?

[7] Variations—Plural Verb Forms after **es** and **das**

Practice these sentences until, when hearing one, you can produce the other four.

SEE
ANALYSIS
58-59,
72-73

(pp. 92-95, 114)

Das Haus gehört dem *Vater.*—Das Haus gehört meinem *Vater.*—Das Haus gehört *ihm.*—Es ist *sein* Haus.—Das ist *sein* Haus.

Der Wagen gehört der *Tante.*—Er gehört meiner *Tante.*—Er gehört *ihr.*—Es ist *ihr* Wagen.—Das ist *ihr* Wagen.

Die Bücher gehören den *Kindern.*—Sie gehören unseren *Kindern.*—Sie gehören *ihnen.*—Es sind *ih*re Bücher.—Das sind *ih*re Bücher.

[8] Word Order in the Inner Field

Study the following sentences and observe the word order. Note that if you answer with a complete sentence, the element containing the answer always stands at the end of the inner field unless the verb itself is the answer.

SEE
ANALYSIS
58-60, 64

(pp. 92-95,
97-99)

Ich gebe meiner Frau eine *Uhr.*

Ich gebe ihr eine *Uhr.*

Ich gebe die Uhr meiner *Frau.*

Ich gebe sie meiner *Frau.*

Ich gebe ihr die *Uhr.*

Ich *gebe* sie ihr.

Was willst du denn deiner Mutter *schicken?*

Ich glaube, ich schicke ihr *Blu*men.

Was willst du denn mit diesen *Blu*men hier machen?

Die schicke ich meiner *Mut*ter.

Ich glaube, ich schicke sie meiner *Mut*ter.

Ich glaube, ich schicke diese Blumen meiner *Mut*ter.

Fritz möchte seiner Freundin ein *Buch* schicken.

Was will Fritz seiner Freundin schicken?

Ein *Buch!*

Er will ihr ein *Buch* schicken!

Wem will Fritz das Buch schicken?

Seiner *Freun*din!

Er will das Buch seiner *Freun*din schicken.

Er will es seiner *Freun*din schicken.

Warum will Fritz seiner Freundin denn ein *Buch* schicken?

Warum will er seiner Freundin denn ein *Buch* schicken?

Warum will er ihr denn ein *Buch* schicken?

Willst du das Buch deiner *Freun*din schicken?

Willst du es deiner *Freun*din schicken?

Willst du es ihr *schic*ken?

Willst du deiner Freundin ein *Buch* schicken?

Willst du ihr ein *Buch* schicken?

Nein, ich will ihr *Geld* schicken.

Wann willst du ihr das Geld denn *schic*ken?

Wann willst du es ihr denn *schic*ken?

[9] Adjectives with the Dative

Form variations by changing the pronouns.

SEE
ANALYSIS
61
(p. 96)

Das ist interessant.	That's interesting.
Das ist mir interessant.	I think that's interesting.
Er ist böse.	He is angry.
Er ist mir böse.	He is angry with me.
Sie ist zu jung.	She is too young.
Sie ist mir zu jung.	She is too young as far as I'm concerned.
Ist Ihnen das recht, Frau Meyer?	Is that all right with you, Mrs. Meyer?
Natürlich ist mir das recht.	Of course that's all right with me.
Ist das Ihrem Mann recht, Frau Meyer?	Is that all right with your husband, Mrs. Meyer?

Natürlich ist ihm das recht. Of course that's all right with him.

[10] Prepositions with the Accusative

Form variations of your own, but do not replace nouns by pronouns.

Wir müssen	durch	die Stadt fahren.	SEE ANALYSIS **62** (p. 96)
Herr Lenz arbeitet	für	meinen Vater.	
Hast du etwas	gegen	mich?	
Ich muß	ohne	ihn abfahren.	
Ich kann	ohne	dich nicht leben.	

[11] Prepositions with the Dative

Woher *kommst* du?—

Aus dem *Kino!*
Aus der *Stadt!*

SEE ANALYSIS **63** (pp. 96-97)

Wir sind *alle* hier

außer meinem *Vater.*
außer *ihm.*
außer *Ih*nen, Herr Lenz.

Hans ist heute

bei seinem *Vater.*
bei seiner *Mut*ter.
bei *uns.*

Mit wem gehst du ins Kino?

Mit Frau *Hoff*mann!
Mit *ihr!*
Mit *der?*

Wann dürft *ihr* denn heiraten?—

Nach dem *Kriege!*

Er geht

nach Ber*lin.*
nach *Hause.*
nach *Ame*rika.

Ich komme heute sehr spät nach *Hause.*—*Wann?*—Um *neun.*
Wie *spät* ist es jetzt?—*Zehn* nach *sechs.*

Seit wann bist *du* denn hier?—

Seit einer *Stunde!*
Seit drei *Wochen!*
Seit einem *Jahr!*

Von wem hast du das *Buch?*

Von meinem *Bruder!*
Von meiner *Tante!*
Ich habe es von meinem *Vater!*

,,Wohin gehst du?''—,,Zum Postamt''

Wohin *gehst* du?

Zu meinem V*ater!*
Zu *ihm!*
Zur Universi*tät!*
Zu meiner T*ante!*
Zum *Essen!*

[12] The Perfect

SEE
ANALYSIS
65–68

(pp. 100–103)

Read these sentences aloud to get used to this pattern, in which the participle appears at the end of the sentence.

FRONT FIELD	1st Prong	INNER FIELD	nicht	1st box	2nd box
Ich	habe	Physik			studiert.
Was	haben	Sie			studiert?
Ich	habe	ihren Vater	nicht		gekannt.
Er	hat	sie	nie		geliebt.
Wir	haben	Frau Meyer			gesehen.
Wir	haben	Sie	nicht		verstanden.
Warum	haben	Sie mich	nicht		verstanden?
Er	ist	heute morgen			gestorben.
Wir	sind	gestern abend			gekommen.
Der Zug	ist	schon		ab-	gefahren.
Warum	seid	ihr heute		zu Hause	geblieben?
Sie	ist	schon		nach Hause	gegangen.
Meyer	ist	schon immer		ein Idiot	gewesen.
Ich	habe	gestern			arbeiten müssen.
Ich	habe	gestern	nicht		zu arbeiten brauchen.
Er	hat	noch nie			arbeiten wollen.
Ich	habe	ihn leider	nicht		besuchen dürfen.
Ich	habe	gestern	nicht	zu Hause	bleiben wollen.

[13] The Inner Field—The Perfect

Find substitutions for the elements in the inner field of each group of sentences. Leave the perfect verb forms unchanged.

SEE ANALYSIS 64–68

(pp. 97-103)

Wer hat denn gestern Tante Amalie zum *Bahn*hof gebracht?
Wer hat denn Tante Amalie *ges*tern zum Bahnhof gebracht?
Wer hat sie denn gestern zum *Bahn*hof gebracht?
Warum hast *du* sie denn nicht zum Bahnhof gebracht?

Herr Kunz hat seiner Frau in Frankfurt ein *Auto* gekauft.
Er hat seiner Frau das Auto in *Frank*furt gekauft.
Er hat ihr das Auto in *Frank*furt gekauft.
Er hat es ihr in *Frank*furt gekauft.
Nein, in Ber*lin* hat er es ihr *nicht* gekauft.

[14] The Meaning of the German Perfect—Time Phrases

The following conversational sentences contain time expressions which denote a date or a point in time. Observe that English always uses the past tense. Get used to the "all-past" meaning of the German perfect.

SEE ANALYSIS 69-71

(pp. 103-113)

Meyer ist heute morgen nach P*aris* gefahren?—*Nein,* er ist schon *ges*tern gefahren.

Did Meyer go to *Paris* this morning?—*No,* he went *yesterday.*

Wie hast du denn heute nacht *geschla*fen? —Heute nacht habe ich *gut* geschlafen.

How did you *sleep* last night?—Last night I slept *well.*

Kennen Sie Frau *Leh*mann?—Ja, die habe ich vor einem Jahr in *Mün*chen kennengelernt.

Do you know Mrs. *Lehmann?*—Yes, I met (was introduced to) her a year ago in *Munich.*

Was habt *ihr* denn gestern abend *ge*macht? *Wir* sind gestern abend ins *Ki*no gegangen.

What did *you* do last night? *We* went to the *movies* last night.

Sie wollen nach *Mün*chen fahren? *Da* kommen Sie zu *spät.* Der Zug nach München ist schon vor einer *Stun*de *ab*gefahren.

You want to go to *Munich?* Then you are too *late.* The train to Munich *left* an *hour* ago.

Hast du gut *geschla*fen, Tante Amalie?— *Nein!* Die Laterne vor eurem Hause ist erst heute *mor*gen *aus*gegangen. Und bei *Licht* kann ich nicht *schla*fen. Außer*dem* habe ich gestern abend zuviel *Kaf*fee getrunken.

Did you *sleep* well, Aunt *Amalie?*—*No!* The street lamp in front of your house didn't go *out* until this *morning.* And I can't sleep when there is a light on. *Besides,* I drank too much *coffee* last evening.

[15] Stretch-of-Time Phrases

The following sentences contain stretch-of-time phrases. Note the difference between "all-past" and "up-to-now" situations.

Kennen Sie *München?*—Ja, ich habe zwei Jahre lang in München ge*wohnt,* vor dem *Kriege.*

Do you know *Munich?*—Yes, I *lived* in Munich for two years before the *war.*

Hast du Erika schon besucht?—*Ja,* aber erst *gest*ern. Ich habe lange nicht gewußt, wo sie *wohnt.*

Have you seen *Erika?*—Yes, but only *yesterday.* I didn't know for a long time where she is *living.*

Ich bin damals Athe*ist* gewesen und habe *lange* nicht an Gott ge*glaubt.* Aber *heute* weiß ich: ohne *Gott* kann man nicht *le*ben.

At that time, I was an *atheist,* and for a *long* time I did not *believe* in God. But *now* I *know:* One cannot *live* without *God!*

Wie geht's denn Herrn *Meyer?*—Oh, *jetzt* geht's ihm wieder *gut.* Aber *letzt*es Jahr ist er monatelang *krank* gewesen und hat *lange* nicht *arbeiten* können.—Und wie geht's seinem *Bruder?*—*Dem* geht's noch immer *gut. Der* hat noch *nie* zu arbeiten brauchen.

How is Mr. *Meyer?*—Oh, *now* he's *all right* again. But *last* year he was *sick* for *months,* and for *quite* some time he wasn't able to *work.*—And how is his *brother?*—He is still doing *fine. He* has never had to work *yet!*

Ich *weiß,* Erika wohnt seit drei Wochen hier in *Köln,* aber bis *heute* habe ich sie noch *nicht* be*suchen* können. Ich habe *wirk*lich noch keine *Zeit* gehabt, sie zu be*suchen.*

I *know* Erika has been living here in *Cologne* for three weeks. But up to *now* I have not yet been able to *visit* her. I *really* haven't had the *time* yet to *visit* her.

Na*türlich* muß mein Sohn in Tübingen viel *arbeiten.* Und warum auch *nicht! Ich* habe *auch* vier Jahre in *Tü*bingen studiert, und *ich* habe *auch* viel arbeiten müssen.

Of *course,* my son has to *work* hard in Tübingen. And why *not!* I, *too,* went to the University of *Tübingen* for four years, and *I, too,* had to work hard.

Ist Schmidt ge*sund* aus Afrika zurückgekommen?—*Nein,* seine Frau hat *jahre*lang auf ihn ge*war*tet. Aber *letzt*es Jahr hat sie gehört, daß er nicht mehr *lebt.*

Did Schmidt get home *safe* from Africa?—No, his wife *waited* for him for *years,* but *last* year she heard that he is no longer *alive.*

Seit wann wohnt denn seine Frau schon bei ihrer *Toch*ter?—Oh, schon *lange,* schon seit *vier* oder fünf *Jah*ren.

Since when has his wife been living with her *daughter?*—Oh, for *quite* some time, it must be *four* or *five years* by now.

Wo ist denn *Ihr* Sohn, Frau Meyer?— *Mein* Sohn ist seit Anfang Mai in Be*r*lin. Er studiert Medi*z*in. Sie *wiss*en ja, er hat schon *immer* Arzt werden wollen.

And where is *your* son, Mrs. Meyer?—*My* son has been in *Berlin* since the beginning of May. He is studying *medicine.* As you *know,* he has *always* wanted to become a *doctor.*

Wie lange sitzt du denn schon hier und *war*test?—Seit einer *Stun*de!

How long have you been sitting here *waiting*?—For an *hour!*

Nein, hier hat es gestern *nicht* geregnet. Hier hat es schon *wochen*lang nicht mehr geregnet. Wir warten schon *lange* auf *Re*gen.

No, it did not rain *here* yesterday. It hasn't rained here for *weeks*. We have been waiting for rain for quite some *time*.

CONVERSATION

I

HERR LORENZ: So, jetzt muß ich aber *wirk*lich gehen, Herr Kunz.

HERR KUNZ: Aber wa*rum* denn? Es ist doch erst fünf *Uhr.*

HERR LORENZ: *Ja,* aber ich will nach dem Essen noch mit meiner Frau ins *Ki*no.

HERR KUNZ: Mit dem *Wa*gen sind Sie doch in zehn Mi*nu*ten zu Hause.

HERR LORENZ: Mit dem *Wa*gen, *ja.* Ich *ha*be aber heute keinen Wagen.

HERR KUNZ: Sie haben keinen *Wa*gen? Bei *dem Re*gen?

HERR LORENZ: Nein, den *Wa*gen hat heute meine *Frau.* Bei dem Regen wollte sie nicht mit dem *Zug* in die Stadt fahren.

HERR KUNZ: Aha, also sind *Sie* mit dem Zug gefahren.

II

FRAU KUNZ: Herr Lorenz, glauben Sie, Ihre Frau ist schon aus der Stadt zu*rück*?

HERR LORENZ: Na*tür*lich, Sie hat doch den *Wa*gen.

FRAU KUNZ: Dann rufen Sie sie doch *an*; sie soll mit dem Wagen zu *uns* kommen. Ich habe Ihre Frau schon *so* lange nicht ge*se*hen.

HERR LORENZ: Das ist eine I*dee.*

FRAU KUNZ: Na*tür*lich, und *Sie* können mit meinem Mann noch ein Glas *Bier* trinken.

HERR LORENZ: Vielen *Dank*, Frau Kunz. Und meine *Frau* rufe ich so*fort an.*

FRAU KUNZ: Darf *ich* mit Ihrer Frau sprechen, Herr Lorenz?

HERR LORENZ: Aber na*tür*lich.

III

FRAU KUNZ: Frau *Lo*renz? Guten Abend, hier ist Gertrud *Kunz.*

FRAU LORENZ: Ah, Frau *Kunz,* guten Abend. Wie *geht's* Ihnen denn?

FRAU KUNZ: *Dan*ke, mir geht's *gut. Ih*nen hoffentlich *auch.*

FRAU LORENZ: *Dan*ke, *ja.* Ich komme gerade aus der *Stadt,*—es hat ja *so* geregnet.

FRAU KUNZ: Ja, *hier* regnet es *im*mer noch.

FRAU LORENZ: Gottseidank habe ich heute den *Wagen*. Mein Mann ist mit dem *Zug* in die Stadt gefahren.

FRAU KUNZ: Ich *weiß*. Ihr Mann ist *hier* bei *uns*. Er hat seit zwei Uhr mit meinem Mann hier ge*ar*beitet.

FRAU LORENZ: Das ist *gut*. Dann kann ich doch mit dem Wagen kommen und ihn *ab*holen.

FRAU KUNZ: Ich höre, Sie wollen heute abend noch ins *Kino*.

FRAU LORENZ: *Ja*, nach dem *Essen*.

FRAU KUNZ: *Hören* Sie, Frau Lorenz, möchten Sie nicht zum Essen zu *uns* kommen?

FRAU LORENZ: Aber *gerne*, vielen *Dank*, Frau Kunz. Ich habe Sie ja schon *so* lange nicht mehr gesehen.

FRAU KUNZ: *Ja*, und wenn es Ihnen *recht* ist, können wir nach dem Essen alle *vier* ins Kino gehen.

**„Willst du mit dem Taxi ins Museum, Tante Amalie?
Die Nummer ist sechs-sechs, null-null, zwo-zwo."**

TAXI-FUNK
Berlin e.G.m.b.H.
66 00 22
Berlin 61
Mehringdamm 107

**TAG
UND
NACHT
BEREIT**

66 00 22

Vorbestellung
jederzeit

READING

Viel Lärm um nichts?

KAPITEL EINS: A News Item

New York Star. International Edition. Paris, April 30.—According to a report from Konstanz, Germany, the famous German novelist Johannes Schmidt–Ingelheim has been missing since April 8. Schmidt–Ingelheim had gone to Africa to collect material for a new novel which is to deal with the fate of General Rommel, the famous 5

Viel Lärm um nichts the German translation of *Much Ado about Nothing.*

commander of the German Afrika Korps. In a letter from Cairo, dated April 8, Schmidt–Ingelheim promised to call his wife on April 12, her birthday, from Casablanca. Since then he has not been heard from. Schmidt–Ingelheim's novel *Wie das Gesetz es befahl* (*As the Law Demanded*) is the literary sensation of the year. Even ⁵ here in Paris, critics praise his objectivity and the penetrating realism of the scenes dealing with the battle on the Normandy beaches. Everybody here feels that this book was written by a man who, "as the law demanded," did his best as a soldier, but who nevertheless remained a human being. Just a few weeks ago Schmidt–Ingelheim ¹⁰ was awarded the *Grand Prix Littéraire de l'Europe*.

KAPITEL ZWEI: Frau Schmidt–Ingelheim am Telefon

Hier Frau Schmidt–*In*gelheim! . . .
*Meh*rens?—*Bit*te, ich kann Sie nicht ver*ste*hen. . . .
Ach *so*, Behrens, B wie *Ber*ta. . . .   ₁₅
Und Sie sind ein Freund von meinem *Mann*, Herr Behrens? . . .

Ach *so*, Sie haben den Artikel im *New York Star* gelesen. Und *Sie* sind von der *Bild*-Zeitung? . . .

Nein, nein, ich bin *nicht* mit meinem Mann nach *Kai*ro gefahren. Er hat mir nur aus Kairo ge*schrie*ben! „Ich fahre morgen nach ₂₀ Casa*blan*ca", hat er geschrieben. . . .

Nein, nein, nicht mit einer *Jacht!* Mit der *Luft*hansa! . . .

So, Sie kennen Herrn Thistlethwaite? Ja, Herr Thistlethwaite ist ein *Freund* von meinem Mann. . . .

Und Sie sagen, Herr Thistlethwaite hat am 9. April [am *neun*ten ₂₅ April] auf seiner Jacht in Alexandria von *den In*gelheims geredet? . . .

„Die Ingelheims sind auf meiner Jacht", hat er gesagt? . . .

Nein, da haben Sie Herrn Thistlethwaite nicht richtig ver*stan*den. Ich *sa*ge Ihnen doch, ich bin *nicht* mit meinem Mann nach *Ägyp*ten gefahren. Ich bin zu *Hau*se geblieben. . . .   ₃₀

Nein, unsere Tochter ist es *auch* nicht ge*we*sen. Unsere *Toch*ter ist doch erst *acht*. Wir haben ja erst vor *neun* Jahren ge*hei*ratet, in Berlin! . . .

Bin ich *glück*lich mit Johannes? Aber na*tür*lich bin ich *glück*lich! . . .

Warum *Kä*the nicht glücklich mit ihm gewesen ist? Aber wo haben ₃₅ *Sie* denn von *Kä*the gehört? . . . .

So, *so*, die Zeitung weiß alles! *Ja*, mein Mann hat von seiner ersten Frau eine *Toch*ter. Erika heißt sie. . . .

ersten first (disregard the ending **–en**)

Nein, sie muß jetzt *zwan*zig sein. Ich *ken*ne sie nicht. Ich habe sie *nie* gesehen. . . .   ₄₀

Ja, mein Mann redet *viel* von seiner *Toch*ter. Aber be*sucht* hat sie uns *nie*. . . .

Na*tür*lich möchte ich die Erika *kennen*lernen. Aber sie *darf* uns nicht be*suchen*, die Mutter *will* das nicht. . . .

Nein, die Tochter ist *nicht* mit ihrem Vater nach Alexandria ge- ₅ fahren. . . .

Was die Tochter *tut?* Ich *glaube*, sie studiert Arch*äologie*.—Aber hier kommt der *Brief*träger. Vielleicht bringt er einen Brief von meinem *Mann*. . . .

Gut, Sie rufen mich später wieder *an*.   ₁₀

Fortsetzung folgt (To be continued)

ANALYSIS

58   The Dative Case

The term "case" was explained in **20.** There are four cases in German: nominative, genitive, dative, and accusative.

In this lesson, the dative case is introduced. The dative is the case of the indirect object, or—to use the German term—of the dative object. This dative object answers the question *To whom*—**Wem?** It is usually a person.

> She gave the money to Charlie.
> She gave the money to him.
> To whom did she give it?—To Charlie, to him.

Note that, whenever you have a genuine dative object in English, you can, by rearranging the sentence, force the form with *to* to appear or to disappear:

> She gave him the book.
> She gave the book to him.

The *him* in *She gave him the book* is therefore syntactically not the same kind of *him* as that in

> She loves him

for only the first *him* can be changed into a *to him*. The *him* which can be replaced by *to him* corresponds to the German dative. Note also that the *to* in

> He took Charlie to the station

cannot be eliminated, since *to the station* is not an object but a directive. It is important that you remember this distinction when dealing with the German dative (indirect) object, which *never* uses the preposition *zu*.

The Forms of the Dative Case

INTERROGATIVE PRONOUNS

NOM.	**wer**	who
DAT.	*wem*	to whom
ACC.	**wen**	whom

NOTE: The interrogative pronouns **wer, wem,** and **wen** have the same endings as the corresponding forms of the masculine definite article **der, dem, den.**

der-WORDS

	MASC.	FEM.	NEUT.	PLURAL
NOM.	der	die	das	die
DAT.	*dem*	*der*	*dem*	*den*
ACC.	den	die	das	die

ein-WORDS

	MASC.	FEM.	NEUT.	PLURAL
NOM.	kein	keine	kein	keine
DAT.	*keinem*	*keiner*	*keinem*	*keinen*
ACC.	keinen	keine	kein	keine

NOTE: There is no difference between the dative endings of the **ein**-words and those of the **der**-words.

PERSONAL PRONOUNS

SINGULAR:	NOM.	ich	du	er	sie	es	Sie
	DAT.	*mir*	*dir*	*ihm*	*ihr*	*ihm*	*Ihnen*
	ACC.	mich	dich	ihn	sie	es	Sie

PLURAL:	NOM.	wir	ihr	sie	Sie
	DAT.	*uns*	*euch*	*ihnen*	*Ihnen*
	ACC.	uns	euch	sie	Sie

NOUNS

In the singular, nouns have no special ending for the dative. Occasionally, masculine and neuter nouns of one syllable use **-e** (**dem Manne**), but this ending is obsolescent and no longer required, except in such idiomatic expressions as **zu Hause** or **nach Hause.**

A number of masculine German nouns have the ending **-en** in all cases except the nominative singular—e.g., **der Student, dem Studenten, den**

Studenten, plural **die Studenten; der Mensch, dem Menschen, den Menschen,** plural **die Menschen.**

The noun **Herr** is declined as follows:

SINGULAR	NOM.	**der Herr**
	DAT.	**dem Herrn**
	ACC.	**den Herrn**
PLURAL	NOM.	**die Herren**
	DAT.	**den Herren**
	ACC.	**die Herren**

In the dative plural, all German nouns must end in **-n,** except those foreign words the plural of which ends in **-s.** If the nominative plural already ends in **-n,** no additional **-n** is required.

NOM. SING.	NOM. PLURAL	DATIVE PLURAL
der Mann	**die Männer**	**den Männern**
die Frau	**die Frauen**	**den Frauen**
die Freundin	**die Freundinnen**	**den Freundinnen**
das Auto	**die Autos**	**den Autos**

NOTE: Nouns ending in **-in** double the **n** in the plural in order to keep the **i** short: **die Freundin, die Freundinnen.**

59 Verbs with Only a Dative Object

For the English-speaking student, the *him* in

> They helped him

is clearly a direct object. For a native German, the verb **helfen** means *to give help to.* For this reason, **helfen,** and a number of other verbs, take a dative object, *not* an accusative object, in German.

We are introducing five of these verbs in this lesson. They are

gehören	to belong to (ownership)
helfen	to help, give help to
danken	to thank, give thanks to
glauben	to believe (someone), give credence to
antworten	to answer, give an answer (to someone)

Note that of the five corresponding English verbs, only *belong* must be used with the preposition *to.* You can only say *The book belongs to me,* not *The book belongs me.* English, unlike German, does not distinguish between ownership and membership. German **gehören zu** expresses membership only:

| Der Hund gehört uns. | The dog belongs to us. |
| Maria gehört zu uns. | Mary is one of us, belongs to our group. |

The indispensable *to* (when *to belong to* expresses ownership) is one important case where an English verb cannot get rid of the *to*, and where German nevertheless cannot use **zu**.

60 Verbs Governing the Dative and Accusative

In English there are a number of verbs that can be used with both an indirect and a direct object:

Mr. Jones gave his wife a hat.

The German sentence

Er schenkt seiner Frau einen Hut

The most important verbs in this group are

geben	to give
schenken	to give (a present)
bringen	to bring, to take
zeigen	to show
glauben	to believe
sagen	to tell, to say
antworten	to (give an) answer (to)

NOTE:

1. The English phrases *to take something to somebody* and *to take somebody home* are expressed in German by using **bringen**:

| Er bringt ihr eine Tasse Kaffee. | He is taking her a cup of coffee. |
| Er bringt sie nach Hause. | He is taking her home. |

2. **glauben** sometimes takes only a dative object and sometimes only an accusative object:

| Ich glaube dir. | I believe you. |
| Das glaube ich nicht. | I don't believe that. |

But, unlike English, German can combine these two sentences into one:

| Das glaube ich dir nicht. | I don't believe what you say. |

Observe that the dative object represents the person and the accusative object represents the facts.

3. **antworten** and **sagen** can also be used with two objects:

| Was hat er dir geantwortet? | What answer did he give you? |
| Was hat er dir gesagt? | What did he tell you? |

But:

| Was hat er dich gefragt? | What did he ask you? |

61 Adjectives Governing the Dative

Certain adjectives like **interessant, böse,** and **recht,** as well as most adjectives preceded by **zu,** can be used with the dative to point out the person for whom the grammatical subject has the quality denoted by the adjective.

Das ist interessant.	That's interesting.
Das ist mir interessant.	I think that's interesting.
Er ist böse.	He is angry.
Er ist mir böse.	He is angry with me.
Sie ist zu jung.	She is too young.
Sie ist mir zu jung.	She is too young as far as I'm concerned.

62 Prepositions Governing the Accusative

A small group of prepositions is *always* used with the accusative. This group includes: **durch** (*through*), **für** (*for*), **gegen** (*against*), and **ohne** (*without*).

63 Prepositions Governing the Dative

Some prepositions are *always* used with the dative case. All the important prepositions of this group are introduced in this unit: **aus** (*out of*), **außer** (*except*), **bei** (*with*), **mit** (*with*), **nach** (*after*), **seit** (*since*), **von** (*from*), **zu** (*to*).

NOTE:

1. A third group of prepositions, which includes **in** and **vor,** is used with either dative or accusative. These prepositions will be introduced later.

2. **Bei** does not normally correspond to English *by;* it expresses the idea of close proximity, and frequently means *at the house of.*

Er wohnt in Potsdam bei Berlin.
Er wohnt bei seiner Tante.

3. Some prepositions are normally contracted with the following article into a single word, as long as the article is not stressed. (See **72.**)

von dem:	Ich komme vom Bahnhof.	I am coming from the station.
zu dem:	Ich gehe zum Bahnhof.	I am on my way to the station.
zu der:	Ich gehe zur Universität.	I am on my way to the University.
durch das:	Er geht durchs Haus.	He is going through the house.
für das:	Er hat kein Geld fürs Kino.	He has no money for the show.
bei dem:	Meine Frau ist beim Arzt.	My wife is at the doctor's.

But

Bei *dem* Regen kommt er nicht.   He won't come in *this* rain.

4. **Nach** is used to indicate time:

Nach dem Abendessen gehen wir ins   After supper, we'll go to the movies.
   Kino.
Er kommt nach acht Uhr.   He will arrive after eight o'clock.

Nach indicates *place,* if a geographical proper name is mentioned:

Er geht nach Amerika.
        nach Deutschland.
        nach Alabama.
        nach Berlin.

and in the idiom:

Er geht nach Hause.

5. If no geographical proper name is used, **zu** is normally used to express direction:

Er geht zum Bahnhof.   He goes to the station.
Er geht zur Universität.   He is walking to the University.

Zu must be used with persons:

Er geht zu Karl.   He goes to Karl.
Ich gehe zu meinem Vater.   I go to my father.

and in the idiom:

Er ist zu Hause.   He is at home.

64 Word Order within the Inner Field

Word order within the inner field is governed by *one* principle: The various elements are arranged in the order of increasing news value. The following rules govern most normal situations and are therefore safe to use.

The Position of the Subject

If a pronoun subject like **er, sie,** or **wir** stands in the inner field, it follows the verb immediately:

Gestern hat er es ihm gesagt.   He told it to him yesterday.

Since nouns generally have more news value than pronouns, noun subjects in the inner field are usually preceded by pronoun objects.

Heute ge*hört* ihm das Haus.

However,

Heute gehört das Haus *ihm.*

is also possible.

Accusative Pronouns Precede Dative Pronouns

The dative pronouns **mir, ihm, ihr** are longer in sound than most accusative pronouns. The accusative personal pronouns therefore always precede the dative personal pronouns.

Warum will er es ihm nicht sagen?	Why doesn't he want to tell him that?
Leider kann ich es Ihnen nicht schenken.	Unfortunately, I can't give it to you.
Ich habe es ihm geschickt.	I have sent it to him.

Pronoun objects stand at the beginning of the inner field and can be preceded only by a subject.

Nouns and Pronouns

Nouns have more weight and more news value than pronouns. A noun object therefore follows a pronoun object.

Ich habe es meinem Vater schon gesagt.	I've already told it to my father.
Ich kaufe mir morgen einen Hut.	I am going to buy myself a hat tomorrow.

Dative and Accusative Nouns

Nouns preceded by definite articles usually refer to something already known or mentioned before. Nouns preceded by indefinite articles (**ein Buch**, plural **Bücher**), on the other hand, usually introduce something not mentioned before—something, therefore, of news value.

Since the sequence of elements in the inner field is determined by increasing news value, noun objects preceded by definite articles are usually placed before nouns preceded by indefinite articles.

Ich habe dem Studenten ein *Buch* gegeben.
Ich habe das Buch einem *Studenten* gegeben.

If both nouns are preceded by a definite article, the sequence is also determined by news value. In the sentence

Hast du dem Kind die Medi*zin* gegeben?

the topic under discussion is the child; in the sentence

Hast du die Medizin dem *Kind* gegeben?

the question is raised of what has happened to the medicine.

Time Phrases

The position of time phrases in the inner field is again determined by news value, but they must precede **ein**-objects which are position-fixed at the end of the inner field.

> Ich habe ihm gestern das *Buch* gegeben.
> Ich habe ihm das Buch *gestern* gegeben.
> Ich habe ihm *gestern* ein Buch gegeben.

Several time phrases follow each other in the order of greater specificity:

> Er ist gestern morgen um 10 Uhr 5 gestorben.   He died at 10:05 yesterday morning.
>
> Er ist gestern abend um neun nach München gefahren.   Last evening at nine he went to Munich.

Place Phrases

Sentences of the type

> Ich kaufe mir morgen in Berlin einen Hut.

are so frequent that one can say: Usually, place follows time.

On the whole, place phrases which are neither directives (which belong in the second prong) nor used in connection with a preceding time phrase are comparatively rare. Their position within the inner field depends on their news value:

> Ich habe meine Frau in der Sonntags-schule kennengelernt.   I met my wife in Sunday school. (when the topic "wives" is under discussion)
>
> Ich habe in der Sonntagsschule meine Frau kennengelernt.   (when the topic "Sunday school" is under discussion)

Quite often place phrases which are not directives occur in "irreducible verbal patterns," and therefore belong in the second prong. Thus

> Ich wohne   and   Er ist

make no sense unless complemented. This is the reason why one must say:

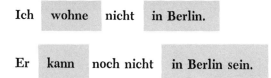

> Ich   wohne   nicht   in Berlin.
>
> Er   kann   noch nicht   in Berlin sein.

Sentence Adverbs

Sentence adverbs, if used in the inner field, follow items of no news value and precede items with news value:

> Morgen kann ich ihn leider nicht *sehen.*
> Das sage ich natürlich meinem V*a*ter.
> Wann hast du ihm das Buch denn gegeben?

65   The German Perfect

By now you have become accustomed to the fact that German does not have as many verb forms as English. English *I see, I am seeing,* and *I do see* are all expressed in German by **Ich sehe.**

This is also true in regard to the past tenses. While English has the forms

PAST   I did   PRESENT PERFECT   I have done
         I was doing   I have been doing

German must get along with

PAST   **Ich tat**   PERFECT   **Ich habe getan**

66   Formation of the German Participle

German verbs form their participles in either a "regular" or an "irregular" way.

Regular Verbs

All *regular* verbs place the *unchanged* stem in the frame

     ge———t

Thus the participle of **lieben** is **ge-lieb-t,** the participle of **glauben** is **ge-glaub-t.**

All verbs with the **ge**———t frame are called "weak" verbs.

INFINITIVE	STEM	PARTICIPLE
hassen	hass-	gehaßt
machen	mach-	gemacht
regnen	regn-	geregnet
sagen	sag-	gesagt
wohnen	wohn-	gewohnt

The **ge-** prefix is never stressed. Since the **-t** of the frame must be audible, verbs like **heiraten** insert **-e-** before the **-t.**

INFINITIVE	STEM	PARTICIPLE
arbeiten	arbeit-	gearbeitet
heiraten	heirat-	geheiratet

A participle cannot have more than one unstressed prefix. Therefore all verbs formed with the unstressed prefixes **be-, emp-, ent-, er-, ge-, ver-** and **zer-** form their participle without the **ge-** prefix. Verbs ending in **-ieren** like **studieren**, which always begin with at least one unstressed syllable, also form their participles without **ge-**.

INFINITIVE	PARTICIPLE
gehören	gehört
studieren	studiert
telefonieren	telefoniert

Irregular Verbs

Most irregular verbs place either the unchanged stem, or a changed form of the stem, or even an entirely different stem in the frame

ge_____en

Thus the participle of **bleiben** is **ge-blieb-en**, that of **fahren** is **ge-fahr-en**, and that of **sein** is **ge-wes-en.**° Verbs using the frame **ge_____en** are called "strong" verbs.

A few irregular verbs place a changed form of the stem in the frame **ge_____t**. Thus the participle of **kennen** is **ge-kann-t**.

Since the irregular verbs are used with great frequency in everyday German, you should memorize the following participles together with their auxiliaries.

INFINITIVE	PARTICIPLE	INFINITIVE	PARTICIPLE
beginnen	hat begonnen	scheinen	hat geschienen
bleiben	ist geblieben	schlafen	hat geschlafen
denken	hat gedacht	schreiben	hat geschrieben
essen	hat gegessen	sehen	hat gesehen
fahren	ist gefahren	sein	ist gewesen
gehen	ist gegangen	sprechen	hat gesprochen
haben	hat gehabt	trinken	hat getrunken
heißen	hat geheißen	tun	hat getan
kennen	hat gekannt	verstehen	hat verstanden
kommen	ist gekommen	werden	ist geworden
lassen	hat gelassen	wissen	hat gewußt
lesen	hat gelesen	zwingen	hat gezwungen
lügen	hat gelogen		

Modal Auxiliaries

Whenever the modal auxiliaries and **brauchen** are used with a dependent infinitive, their participles are identical with their infinitives.

° Beginning with Unit 5 the participles of all newly introduced irregular verbs will appear in the list of irregular verbs at the end of each unit.

Er hat gestern arbeiten müssen.
Er hat gestern nicht zu arbeiten brauchen.

If the modals are used without a dependent infinitive, their participles are "normal"; that is, **gemußt, gewollt, gekonnt, gesollt, gedurft, gebraucht.**

67 The Use of **sein** and **haben** as Auxiliaries

Certain English verbs used to form their compound tenses with *to be*. Thus the older versions of the King James version of the Bible, translated in the seventeenth century, had *Christ is risen*. But now even the Bible translations have changed from *Christ is risen* to *Christ has risen,* so that *to have* is today the only auxiliary still used. In contrast, the use of **sein** as an auxiliary is still very common in German.

The German verbs using **sein** instead of **haben** are all intransitive; that is, they do not govern an accusative object. Usually, though not in the case of **sein** and **bleiben,** they indicate a change in the position or the condition of the grammatical subject. Since it is most inconvenient to constantly ask oneself, "Should I use **haben** or should I use **sein?**" it is best simply to memorize the participles together with their auxiliaries. See the list in **66.**

68 Position of the Participle

The participle has a reserved "slot": the second box of the second prong. This means that it is preceded by **nicht** and by the verbal complements (if any) in the first box.

FRONT FIELD	1st Prong	INNER FIELD	nicht	1st Box	2nd Box
Er	kommt	heute.			
Er	ist	gestern	nicht		gekommen.
Der Zug	fährt		noch nicht	ab.	
Der Zug	ist		noch nicht	ab-	gefahren.
Sie	ist	leider	nicht	glücklich.	
Sie	ist	leider	nie	glücklich	gewesen.
Ich	bleibe	natürlich	nicht	zu Hause.	
Ich	bin	natürlich	nicht	zu Hause	geblieben.

NOTE: Verb complements like **aus, ab,** and **wieder** are written with the participle as one word: **abgefahren, ausgemacht, wiedergekommen.**

When a modal is used with an infinitive, the participle of the modal (which looks like an infinitive) goes into the second box behind the dependent infinitive.

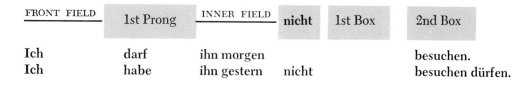

FRONT FIELD	1st Prong	INNER FIELD	nicht	1st Box	2nd Box
Ich	darf	ihn morgen			besuchen.
Ich	habe	ihn gestern	nicht		besuchen dürfen.

69 The Use of the German Perfect

Take a look at the following English and German sentences and compare the verb tenses.

1. **Ich glaube, er wohnt in Berlin.** (present)
   I think he lives in Berlin. (present)
2. **Nein, er wohnt jetzt nicht mehr in Berlin.** (present)
   No, he is no longer living in Berlin. (present progressive)
3. **Mein Vater hat nie in Berlin gewohnt.** (perfect)
   My (late) father never lived in Berlin. (past)
4. **Vor drei Jahren habe ich noch in Berlin gewohnt.** (perfect)
   Three years ago I was still living in Berlin. (past progressive)
5. **Haben Sie schon einmal in Berlin gewohnt?** (perfect)
   Have you ever lived in Berlin? (present perfect)
6. **Wir wohnen seit Jahren in Berlin.** (present)
   We have been living in Berlin for years. (perfect progressive)
7. **In zwei Jahren wohnen wir schon in Berlin.** (present)
   Two years from now, we'll be living in Berlin. (future)

You can see that in conversational sentences of this type English uses seven different tenses where German can get along with two, the present and the perfect.

Leaving out the German future (which will be introduced later), it can be stated that German, which has no progressive forms at all, has only four major tenses: the present, the perfect, the past, and the pluperfect. The past and the pluperfect are the major tenses for story telling. The present and the perfect are the set used for conversation. For this reason we introduce the perfect first, and then the past and the pluperfect.

In conversational situations the present is used to refer to what is happening at the moment of speaking or what will happen later. The perfect is used to refer to what happened prior to the moment of speaking. This is why **er wohnt** and **wir wohnen**, in sentences 1, 2, 6, and 7 above, mean *he lives, he is living, we have been living,* and *we will be living.* The meaning of 6 is most alien to native speakers of English. However, you will agree that the sentence *Fritz has been living in Berlin since 1960* implies that Fritz is living in Berlin at the moment of speaking. So German, which uses the present to refer to everything that is happening at the moment of speaking or later, remains consistent by using the present tense: **Fritz wohnt seit 1960 in Berlin.** Similarly, **hat gewohnt,** in sentences 3, 4, and 5 above, means *lived, was living,* and *has lived,* for in all these cases the verbs refer to something that happened prior to the moment of speaking. You should acquire the habit of expressing *all* actions which happened before the moment of speaking by using the perfect.

Let us take an example. The verb **fahren** *does* have a past tense—**fuhr.** One of its forms is **wir fuhren,** *we went.* However, the conversational sentence, *We drove downtown last night,* cannot be expressed by

> [Wir fuhren gestern abend in die Stadt.]

The sentence **Wir fuhren in die Stadt** can only be used in a narration, in "telling a story." In reply to a question like **Was habt ihr denn gestern abend gemacht?**, one can only say

> Wir sind gestern abend in die Stadt gefahren.

The rule "Use the perfect to express what came to an end before the moment of speaking" is not without exceptions. We shall learn in Unit 5 that the past tense of **haben,** of **sein,** and of the modals is very frequently used to replace the perfect. Thus **ich wollte** (the past tense of **wollen**) is used to replace **ich habe wollen.** It is therefore idiomatic to say

> Gestern abend wollte meine Frau nicht kochen. Also sind wir in die Stadt gefahren und haben im Hotel Regina gegessen.

But we must say **sind gefahren** and **haben gegessen,** since **fahren** and **essen** are not modals. Therefore, **sind gefahren** and **haben gegessen** are the only forms we can use in a conversation to express that the driving and the dining happened prior to the moment of speaking.

In a way, then, the German conversational system of tenses is simple. If we leave out **haben, sein,** and the modals, we can get along with two tenses, present and perfect.

However, this simplicity also creates a difficulty. For instance: As long as Aunt Betty is alive, her American nephew can say, "I *have never asked* her how much money she has." But after she is dead, he can only say, "I *never asked* her how much money she had." The choice between *have never asked* and *never asked* is obligatory. If someone were to state after her death *I have never asked her,* this would indicate either that the speaker has established regular contact with Aunt Betty's departed soul, or—much more likely—that he is one of her *German* nephews who has not yet mastered the English system of tenses.

The trouble is that both *I never asked her* and *I have never asked her* refer to actions which, if they had occurred, would have preceded the moment of speaking. So the German system of tenses provides the nephew from Cologne with only one verbal form:

Ich habe sie . . . gefragt,

and this one form means both *I have asked* and *I asked.* It is therefore no wonder that, misled by his speech habits, the poor fellow will state after the funeral: *I have never asked her* when he should say *I never asked her.* If he does, forgive him until you have mastered **71.** For you will have to learn how to express the difference in German before and after the funeral of Tante Amalie.

70 Point-of-Time Phrases

Sometimes phrases like *now, tomorrow, last week, next year,* and others denote a point rather than a stretch of time. Of course, it can be taken for granted that next year will be at least 365 days long. However, when I say **Wir fahren nächstes Jahr nach Deutschland,** I do not mean that the trip to Germany will take a whole year. I mean that I expect to get there at some point during the coming year.

Point-of-time phrases present no syntactical problem. They refer to a point prior to the moment of speaking (**gestern abend**), or to the moment of speaking (**jetzt**), or to a point following the moment of speaking (**nächstes Jahr**). If a point prior to the moment of speaking is involved, the perfect is used. If the moment of speaking or a point following the moment of speaking is involved, one uses the present tense:

Er ist gestern abend nach Köln gefahren.
Er ist jetzt in Köln.
Er fährt nächstes Jahr nach Köln.

Sometimes, it is the tense used which determines whether a point or date precedes or follows the moment of speaking. In **Wir sind Sonntag in die Kirche gegangen, Sonntag** can only mean *last Sunday.* In **Wir gehen Sonntag in die Kirche, Sonntag** can only mean *next Sunday.*

All English and German time phrases are either adverbs, prepositional phrases, or time nouns like **Sonntag** used without a preposition. Some of these are:

ADVERBS **oft, gestern, heute, morgen, heute morgen, gestern abend, jetzt.**

PREPOSITIONAL PHRASES *nach einem Jahr* (*after one year*), **um drei Uhr** (*at three o'clock*), **vor einem Jahr** (*a year ago*).

TIME NOUNS **Sonntag, jeden Sonntag, nächsten Sonntag, jede Woche, dieses Jahr, letztes Jahr, nächstes Jahr, jedes Jahr, alle drei Jahre** (*every three years*).

NOTE:

1. Time nouns used without a preposition show the accusative case (**jeden Sonntag**). If a preposition is used, this preposition determines the case: **nach einem Jahr** (**nach** always governs the dative); **für einen Monat** (**für** always governs the accusative).

2. Phrases with **vor** (plus dative) may be misleading to the beginner. German **vor** is not equivalent to English *for;* **vor** means *in front of.* Therefore, **vor einem Jahr** means "at a point just in front of one year," or, simply, *a year ago.*

3. Time phrases with **in** (plus dative) pose no problem. German **in einer Stunde** means either *within one hour,* or *in one hour.* If it is a future hour, use the present:

> **Ich fliege in einer Stunde nach Frankfurt.**
> I'll be on my way to Frankfurt in one hour.

If it is a past hour, use the German perfect:

> **Wir sind in sechs Stunden nach Frankfurt geflogen.**
> We completed the flight to Frankfurt within six hours.

71 Stretch-of-Time Phrases

Some English time phrases like *for three years* clearly denote a stretch rather than a point of time. For a German learning English, such phrases are difficult to handle. The trouble with them is that they do not, by their own strength, contain any hint as to where the end point of the stretch is located. The location of the end point depends entirely on the verbal tense used.

If I use the past tense, the end point precedes the moment of speaking:

> For three years he *was not able* to drive.   (He is driving again.)

If I use the present perfect, the time stretch extends into (and perhaps beyond) the moment of speaking:

> He *has not been able* to drive for three years.   (He cannot drive at the moment of speaking.)

If I use the present tense, the three-year period will definitely end at some time after the moment of speaking:

The judge was hard on him. He *can't* drive for three years.

German, which has only two tenses reserved for conversation, cannot fix the end point of time stretches by using three tenses. To make up for this deficiency, German has invented an ingenious and, to native English speakers, a totally alien system for locating the end point of stretches of time: German uses two distinct sets of stretch-of-time phrases. One set— for lack of a better name, let us call them up-to-now phrases—is used to refer to periods of time which begin somewhere in the past and continue up to (and perhaps beyond) the moment of speaking. Such up-to-now phrases usually start with **schon** or **seit.** A second set—let us call them end-in-past-or-future phrases—refers to stretches of time which end *either* in the past (when used with the perfect) *or* in the future (when used with the present tense). These phrases do *not* start with **schon** or **seit.**

UP-TO-NOW	END-IN-PAST-OR-FUTURE	
schon lange	lange	for a long time
seit langem		
schon seit langem		
	noch lange	for a long time thereafter
seitdem		ever since
schon drei Jahre	drei Jahre	for three years
seit drei Jahren		
schon seit drei Jahren		
schon tagelang	tagelang	for days
schon wochenlang	wochenlang	for weeks
schon jahrelang	jahrelang	for years
noch nicht	nicht	
noch nie	nie	never
schon einmal	einmal, je	ever
schon oft	oft	often
schon immer	immer	always

Let us see how this system works.
A. How to express things that were but are no longer.

Ich habe lange an Gott geglaubt.
Ich habe lange nicht an Gott geglaubt.

Both sentences are misleading to English-speaking people. They know that **lange** means *for a long time,* and they believe that **habe geglaubt** means *have believed.* So they "translate" the first sentence by *I have* *believed in God for a long time.* And that's exactly what this sentence does *not* mean. German **habe geglaubt** denotes a past act of believing. How long did this act last? Well, **lange!** But **lange** is an end-in-past-or-future phrase. In connection with the perfect it refers to a period which came to an end before the moment of speaking. The sentence means *For a long time I believed in God,* that is, the speaker once believed in God, but at some point in the past had a change of heart, stopped believing in God and is consequently now an atheist.

In the second sentence, **habe nicht geglaubt** refers to a past act of not believing. How long did this disbelief last? Again, **lange,** that is, for a long period which came to an end in the past. The speaker no longer "disbelieves" that God exists. He now believes. He is a theist.

German **noch lange** is also an end-in-past-or-future phrase. In connection with the perfect, it also expresses "something which was but is no longer."

Now try to figure out what is meant by:

Ich habe lange auf ihn gewartet.	(Is the speaker still waiting?)
Ich habe lange nicht arbeiten können.	(Is the speaker still unable to work?)
Er hat zwei Jahre nicht fahren dürfen.	(Is he permitted to drive again?)
Wie lange hat sie in Bonn gewohnt?	(Is she still living in Bonn?)
Ich habe drei Jahre in Bonn gewohnt.	(Is the speaker living in Bonn?)
Meyer hat noch drei Jahre gelebt.	(Is Meyer still alive?)
Meyers sind noch lange geblieben.	(Are they still there?)

B. How to express what has been and still is (or what has not been and still is not).

> **Wir wohnen schon seit drei Jahren in München.**
> **Seit drei Jahren wohnen wir nicht mehr in München.**

Both sentences use the present tense. The first sentence describes a positive action (**wohnen**) which is still going on; the second sentence describes the absence of an action (**nicht mehr wohnen**) which is still in effect at the moment of speaking. **Seit drei Jahren** is an up-to-now phrase denoting a stretch of time which started three years ago and continues up to (and beyond) the moment of speaking. The English phrase corresponding to **seit drei Jahren** is *these last three years* or *for three years.* The first sentence therefore means *These last three years we have been living in Munich* or *We have been living in Munich for three years.* Note that *these last three years* is actually an English up-to-now phrase, whereas *for three years* can be either an up-to-now or an end-in-past-or-future phrase.

The second sentence contains **nicht mehr,** *no longer.* It can be translated clumsily by *During these last three years we have not been living in*

Munich any more, or, better, *We left Munich three years ago.*

Remember: If you want to express what *has been* and still *is* (or what *has not been* and still *is not*), use the present tense and an up-to-now phrase starting with **schon** or **seit**.

Now figure out what is meant by:

> Er kann seit drei Jahren nicht arbeiten.
> Ich kenne Herrn Meyer schon seit Jahren.
> Das weiß ich schon lange.
> Wie lange wartest du denn schon?

C. How to express what will end after the moment of speaking.

> Wir bleiben zwei Tage in München.
> Keinen Kaffee mehr, bitte. Sonst schlafe ich die ganze Nacht nicht.

Both sentences show the present tense. **Zwei Tage** and **die ganze Nacht** (containing no **schon** or **seit**) are end-in-past-or-future phrases which, when used with a present tense, refer to a stretch of time which will end in the future. It makes really no difference whether the speaker already is in Munich or whether he intends to go to Munich. What is important is that the end of the **zwei Tage** must follow the moment of speaking. The first sentence means *We shall stay in Munich for two days* or *We are staying in Munich for two days.*

If used together with the present tense, **die ganze Nacht** must also refer to a period of time which will end in the future. The sentence means *Or else I won't be able to sleep all night.*

What is meant by:

> Wie lange kannst du hier bleiben?
> Ich kann nicht lange bleiben.
> Gut, ich warte eine Stunde, aber nicht länger.
> Das kann noch lange dauern.
> Wir bleiben zwei Jahre in Deutschland.
> Wir bleiben noch zwei Jahre in Deutschland.

D. How to express what had been going on, and then broke off at the very moment of speaking.

> Ich habe schon lange auf dich gewartet.

The sentence contains the up-to-now **schon lange** denoting a stretch of time reaching up to the moment of speaking. This time the up-to-now

Darauf haben Sie schon lange gewartet:
Eine Suppe für den großen Hunger.

phrase is used with the perfect. The use of the perfect means that the verbal activity (**warten**) is no longer going on at the moment of speaking. The two ideas, "reaching up to the moment of speaking (**schon lange**)" and "no longer going on at the moment of speaking (the perfect tense)," add up to the notion "ending just at the moment of speaking."

The sentence means *I have been waiting for you for a long time.* The anxiously awaited husband has just arrived. The waiting is over.

Perhaps you can now understand the following "true-to-life" report: Mrs. Meyer is expecting a baby. The Meyers have two boys; now they want a girl. Two months before the blessed event they say,

   Wir wünschen uns schon lange ein Mädchen.

They use the present tense to make it clear that they do desire a girl at the moment of speaking. They use the up-to-now phrase **schon lange** to make it clear that the desire is not new. They have had it for a long time, they still have it, and they will continue to have it until they have a girl. The sentence means *We've been wanting a girl for a long time.*

Two months later a smiling nurse shows the father the new baby. It is, indeed, a girl, and she says,

   Darauf (*for this event*) **haben Sie schon lange gewartet.**

She uses the perfect **haben gewartet** to indicate that the waiting is now a thing of the past. She uses the up-to-now phrase **schon lange** to indicate that the waiting continued right up to the moment of speaking before it stopped and did become a thing of the past. The sentence means *This is just what you've been waiting for all this time.*

But maybe the new baby is another boy. What then? Well, they try again. After five boys in a row, they give up. Years later, when the five boys come home to help their parents celebrate their wedding anniversary, Mrs. Meyer says wistfully,

> **Wir haben uns ja lange ein Mädchen gewünscht.**

She again uses the perfect to indicate that the hoping and waiting for a girl is a thing of the past. But now she uses the end-in-past-or-future phrase **lange,** which, when used with the perfect, means that the period of hoping came to an end at some time before the moment of speaking. The third sentence means *For a long time we wanted a girl.*

Now try to match the following sentences with the right answers. This time Mrs. Meyer is expecting Mr. Meyer. She is waiting at the Cologne airport. He is to fly in from Hamburg. Somebody says:

> a. **Wie lange wartest du denn schon hier?**
> b. **Wie lange hast du denn schon gewartet?**
> c. **Wie lange hast du denn gewartet?**

1. This is Mr. Meyer speaking to Mrs. Meyer from Hamburg. He missed the plane, could not get her paged, and finally reaches her at home.
2. This is a friend who bumps into Mrs. Meyer while she is still waiting at the airport.
3. This is Mr. Meyer. Mrs. Meyer knew he was coming, but not which plane he was on. So she met several planes in a row.

E. How to look backward scanning the past.

Some verbal actions are punctual rather than continuous. Thus **nach Deutschland fahren** has an end point, that is, the arrival in Germany, built into it, and it is *getting there* rather than *being on the way* which we have in mind when we say

> **Wir fahren nächstes Jahr nach Deutschland.**

Punctual events like arriving cannot fill a stretch of time from beginning to end. Rather, they happen at a point *within* a stretch of time.

Very frequently, a speaker looks backward from the moment of speaking into the past, scanning the line point by point and then stating that something happened at no point (**nie, noch nie**), once at one point (**je** or **einmal, schon einmal**), frequently (**oft, schon oft**), or at all points (**immer, schon immer**). If the speaker views the stretch as not reaching up to the

moment of speaking, he uses the phrases without **noch** or **schon.** If he
views it as reaching up to the moment of speaking, he uses the phrases
with **noch** or **schon.** In both cases, he uses the perfect.

Examples:

NEVER HAPPENED

Washington hat *nie* **gelogen.**
Washington never told a lie.

Fritz hat *noch nie* **gelogen.**
Fritz has never yet told a lie.   (The period
for telling lies has not ended.)

Er hat *nie* **zu arbeiten brauchen.**
He never had to work.

Er hat *noch nie* **zu arbeiten brauchen.**
He has never had to work.

HAPPENED ONCE

Hast du Tante Amalie *je* (*einmal*) **ge-**
fragt, wieviel Geld sie hat?
Answer: *Nie!*
Did you ever ask Aunt Amalie how
much money she had?

Hast du Tante Amalie *schon einmal* **ge-**
fragt, wieviel Geld sie hat?
Answer: *Noch nie!*
Have you ever asked Aunt Amalie how
much money she has?

HAPPENED OFTEN

Sie hat uns *oft* **besucht.**
She visited us quite often (but she can't
do it any longer).

Sie hat uns *schon oft* **besucht.**
She has called on us often.   (She might
continue.)

Wir sind *dreimal* **nach Paris gefahren.**
We went to Paris three times.   (Now
we have given up traveling.)

Wir sind *schon dreimal* **nach Paris gefahren.**
We have gone to Paris three times.   (Maybe
we'll go again.)

HAPPENED AT ALL POINTS

So? Fritz will nicht Medizin studieren?
Er hat doch *immer* **Arzt werden**
wollen!
He always wanted to become a doctor.
(Has he changed his mind?)

Natürlich studiert Fritz Medizin. Er hat
doch *schon immer* **Arzt werden wollen.**

He has always wanted to become a doctor.
(He still does.)

Früher habe ich *immer* **gerne Wein ge-**
trunken.
I used to enjoy drinking wine.   (I
don't like it anymore now.)

Ich habe doch *schon immer* **gerne Wein**
getrunken.
I have always enjoyed wine.   (I still do.)

Compare the two sentences:

Er ist *schon immer* **ein Genie gewesen.**
Seitdem **ist er schwachsinnig.**

He has always been a genius.
He has been feeble-minded ever since (he
got the flu and had a temperature of 105°).

In both cases we are talking about "what has been and still is." (See B
above.) However, in the second sentence, I am reporting a continuous,

uninterrupted condition, just as in **Wir wohnen seit drei Jahren in München.** In the first sentence, I let my mind rove from the moment of speaking to the distant past, scanning the line point by point, and then coming to the conclusion: It has always been that way, it has never been different.

Now try to find out what the following sentences mean:

> Ich habe noch nie geraucht.
> So gut habe ich schon lange nicht gegessen.
> Bist du schon mal ins Museum gegangen?
> Ich habe sie nie kennengelernt.
> Ich habe sie noch nicht kennengelernt.
> Ich bin auch einmal jung gewesen.
> Sie ist noch nie glücklich gewesen.
> Ich habe schon oft im Hotel Berlin gegessen.
> Wir haben auch oft im Hotel Berlin gegessen.
> So ist es schon immer gewesen.

F. für-phrases.

It is one thing to say *I want to rest for a few minutes* and another to say *I want to sit down for a few minutes*. English *to rest* is one of those "stretchable" verbs (the technical term is "durative") which have no end built into them, and *for a few minutes*, used in connection with such a verb, actually measures the length of the verbal activity. In contrast, *to sit down* is a "punctual" verb (the technical term is "perfective") that does have an end built in. The phrase *for a few minutes*, if used together with *to sit down*, does not measure the length of the verbal activity. The few minutes start when the verbal act has been completed.

German **für**-phrases like **für eine Woche** should only be used in connection with "punctual" verbs. It is idiomatic to say

> Ich fahre morgen für eine Woche nach Rom.
> Er ist gestern für eine Woche nach Rom gefahren.

It would not be idiomatic to say

> [Ich will für zwei Jahre in Köln studieren.]
> [Ich habe für zwei Jahre in Köln studiert.]

One can only say

> Ich will zwei Jahre in Köln studieren.
> Ich habe zwei Jahre in Köln studiert.

In other words, if a stretch of time is "filled out" by an uninterrupted activity (durative verb), it is not safe to use a **für**-phrase.

72 Replacement of **er, sie, es** by **der, die, das**

In informal but perfectly acceptable German, nouns and names are frequently replaced by **der, die, das** instead of by **er, sie, es.** When used in this function, **der, die,** and **das** are not articles, but demonstrative pronouns, and the dative plural is **denen,** not **den.** These demonstrative pronouns may be stressed or unstressed.

Wem gehört denn der Wagen?	Der Wagen gehört mir.
	Er gehört mir.
	Der gehört mir.
Wo hast du denn den *Hut* gekauft?	Den habe ich in *Mün*chen gekauft.
Wo hast du denn *den* gekauft?	*Den* habe ich in *Mün*chen gekauft, aber *den* hier habe ich in Ber*lin* gekauft.
Kennen Sie Frau Dr. Walter?	Ja, die habe ich in Ber*lin* kennengelernt.
	Ja, mit *der* gehe ich heute abend ins Theater.

Note that if stressed, these demonstrative pronouns may mean *this one* and *that one.*

For the time being, do not use either the personal pronouns or the demonstrative pronouns after a preposition, unless they refer to persons.

73 **es** and **das,** Followed by Plural Verb Forms

A daughter recognizing that a certain lady on the TV screen is her mother, can say

    It's my mother!
    That's my mother!

This impersonal *it* or *that* is used in sentences identifying somebody or something for the first time. *She is my mother,* on the other hand, is used when *she* has already been talked about and a further statement is being made about her. German makes the same distinction:

    Es ist meine Mutter!
    Das ist meine Mutter!

But:

    Kennen Sie Frau Bertram?
    Natürlich! Sie ist meine Mutter!

In contrast to English *it* and *that,* German **es** and **das** are followed by plural verb forms when the identifying nouns are in the plural:

Es sind die Kinder.	It's the children.
Das sind die Kinder.	That's the children.

EXERCISES

A. Give negative answers to the following questions.

1. Bist du glücklich mit ihm?
2. Wohnt ihr noch in Berlin?
3. Mußt du denn morgen nach Paris fahren?
4. Hast du noch Geld?
5. Redet Frau Müller noch immer soviel?
6. Ist Erika intelligent?
7. Geht Fritz schon in die Schule?
8. Lebt Meyer noch?
9. Brauchst du *auch* einen Hut? (Use contrast intonation.)
10. Brauchst du auch einen *Hut?* (Use contrast intonation.)

B. Replace the dative or accusative pronouns in italics by the proper form of the nouns in parentheses.

1. Ich will *es* nicht lesen. (Buch)
2. Kennst du *ihn?* (mein Vater)
3. Ich kann *ihn* schon sehen. (Zug)
4. Kennt er *sie?* (deine Frau)
5. Tante Amalie will mit *ihr* nach Italien fahren. (unsere Tochter)
6. Die Uhr gehört *ihr.* (meine Frau)
7. Liebt sie *ihn* denn nicht? (ihr Mann)
8. Liebt er *sie* denn nicht? (seine Frau)
9. Ich will nicht für *ihn* arbeiten. (Herr Meyer)
10. Bei *der* möchte ich nicht wohnen. (deine Tante)

C. Express the following sentences in German. This is not meant to be a translation exercise; the English sentences should "trigger" their German equivalents. Practice the sentences orally, until you can produce them without hesitation. Only then should you try to write them down.

1. That is my house.
2. It (the house) belongs to me.
3. It (the house) belongs to you?
4. Yes, to me.
5. This house belongs to Hans.
6. It (the house) belongs to him.
7. It (the house) belongs to her.
8. The car belongs to her.
9. It (the car) belongs to her.
10. It is her car.

D. Replace nouns and names by personal pronouns.

Ich fahre mit meinem Freund Fritz.
Ich fahre mit ihm.

1. Er wohnt bei seiner Tante.
2. Er will zu seinem Vater.
3. Er hilft seiner Mutter.
4. Er hilft seiner Freundin.
5. Er hilft seinem Freund.

6. Er kommt von seinem Freund Hans.
7. Er arbeitet für seinen Bruder.
8. Er arbeitet heute ohne seinen Freund.
9. Außer Erika sind wir alle hier.
10. Bei meiner Tante bin ich gern.

E. Complete the following sentences by using either **nach, zu,** or **bei.**

1. Ich gehe _____ Bahnhof.
2. Er wohnt _____ seiner Tante.
3. Wir gehen _____ Meyers.
4. Sie sind _____ Hans.
5. Wir fahren _____ Europa.

6. Wir fahren _____ Universität.
7. Wir fahren _____ Bahnhof.
8. Wir fahren _____ München.
9. Man spricht nicht _____ Essen.
10. Oskar wohnt _____ Schmidts.

F. In the following sentences, the inner field is left empty. Fill the inner field with each of the several series of words by rearranging them in the correct word order.

1. Ich habe _____ geschenkt.
   (a) es, gestern, ihm
   (b) das Buch, gestern, ihm
   (c) ein Buch, gestern, meinem Vater
   (d) es, gestern, meinem Vater

2. Willst du _____ schenken?
   (a) einen Hund, deiner Freundin
   (b) den Hund, deiner Freundin
   (c) deiner Freundin, ihn
   (d) einen Hund, ihr
   (e) ihn, ihr

3. Wollen Sie _____ schicken?
   (a) Ihrem Vater, das Buch
   (b) ein Buch, ihm (Ihrem Vater)
   (c) es, ihm
   (d) Ihrem Vater, es
   (e) das Buch, ihm

4. Ich habe _____ mitgebracht.
   (a) ein Buch, meiner Freundin, aus Berlin
   (b) aus Berlin, ein Buch, ihr
   (c) das Buch, ihr, aus Berlin
   (d) ihr, es, aus Berlin

5. Darf ich _____ ins Haus schicken, Herr Doktor?
   (a) morgen, Ihnen, den Wein
   (b) die Blumen, morgen, Ihrer Frau
   (c) sie (die Blumen), ihr (Ihrer Frau), morgen
   (d) sie (die Blumen), morgen, Ihrer Frau
   (e) Blumen, Ihrer Frau, morgen
   (f) Blumen, ihr, morgen
   (g) die Blumen, ihr, morgen

G. Restate the following sentences by using the perfect tense.

1. Er arbeitet auch sonntags.
2. Sie bleibt Sonntag zu Hause.
3. Wieviel Geld brauchst du?
4. Inge fährt heute nach München.
5. Ich gehe mit Tante Amalie ins Museum.
6. Außer mir glaubt dir das kein Mensch.
7. Wir haben in München ein Haus.
8. Seine Kinder hassen ihn.
9. Ihr Mann kommt zurück.
10. Ich kenne ihn.
11. Das Wasser kocht schon.
12. Er kommt heute spät nach Hause.

13. Was sagt er denn?—Nichts! Er lacht!
14. Bei Meyer lerne ich nichts.
15. Liebt sie ihren Mann denn nicht?
16. Was machst du denn Sonntag?
17. Regnet es in Hamburg?
18. Er studiert Medizin.
19. Ich verstehe ihn nicht.
20. Er wird Arzt.
21. Das wissen wir nicht.
22. Wo wohnt ihr denn?
23. Zahlst du für den Wein?
24. Wann rufst du sie an?
25. Du antwortest ihm?
26. Wann machst du das Licht aus?
27. Ich bringe Erika nach Hause.
28. Natürlich danke ich ihm.
29. Dich frage ich nicht.
30. Warum gibst du mir kein Geld?
31. Dieses Haus gehört meinem Vater.
32. Warum helft ihr ihm denn nicht?
33. Ich kaufe mir eine Zeitung.
34. Er will nicht arbeiten.
35. Ich rauche nie.
36. Meine Frau redet wieder viel zuviel.
37. Was schenkst du ihr denn?
38. Wem schicken Sie denn das Buch?
39. Er schreibt mir nicht.
40. Wo sitzt sie denn?

H. Complete the following sentences:

1. Wir haben das Haus gesehen, aber gekauft (haben wir es nicht).
2. Seine Freundin ist intelligent, aber interessant _____.
3. Ich gehe oft ins Theater, aber ins Kino _____.
4. Er hat den Professor gehört, aber verstanden _____.
5. Ich fahre mit dir nach Hamburg, aber nach Casablanca _____.

I. Express in German:

1. He gave his girl friend a watch.
2. He gave the watch to his girl friend.
3. He gave it (the watch) to her.
4. He is coming from the movies.
5. Are you living with your aunt, Erika?
6. Were you living with your aunt at that time?
7. Why did you come home so late?
8. Meyer bought a car in Berlin.
9. Meyer bought a house (which stands) in Berlin.
10. (While) in Berlin, he bought a house.
11. For a long time I did not know that.
12. I have known that for a long time.
13. Last year I didn't smoke one (single) cigarette. But now I smoke ten each (*accusative*) day.
14. Since the beginning of May I have not smoked one (single) cigarette.
15. I did not smoke for two years.
16. Two years ago, I smoked too much.
17. You are still smoking too much.
18. Yes, I believe in God. But for a long time I did not believe in God.
19. Meyer died three years ago.
20. Meyer died a year ago.

BASIC VOCABULARY*

das Abendessen supper
abholen to pick up, to call for
acht eight
anfangen (fängt an, hat angefangen) to begin, to
start
    der Anfang, ⁻e beginning,
    start
anrufen (hat angerufen) to
call up (on the telephone)
antworten (*plus dative of
person*) to answer
der April' April
aus out of
außer besides, except for
    außerdem moreover
der Bahnhof, ⁻e railway station
    zum Bahnhof to the station
    im Bahnhof within the sta-
    tion
    auf dem Bahnhof on the
    platform
befehlen (befiehlt, hat befohlen) (*plus dative of
person*) to command, to
order
bei at, with, near
    bei Schmidts at the
    Schmidts
    beim Essen while eating
das Bild, -er picture
bis until, up until; up to, as
far as
    bis gestern until yester-
    day
    bis Köln as far as Cologne
    bis zum Winter (up) until
    winter
    bis zum Bahnhof as far as
    the station
    zwei bis drei two to three
böse mad, angry at; bad,
evil

der Brief, -e letter
    der Briefträger, – mailman
bringen (hat gebracht) to
bring
    ich bringe dich nach Hause
    I'll take you home
damals at that time
danken (*plus personal dative*)
to thank
    danke! thank you, thanks
    vielen Dank! thank you
    very much
durch through
einmal (*colloquial* mal) once,
at some time
    zweimal twice
    dreimal three times
    viermal, etc.
    (noch) *nicht* einmal not
    even
    nicht *ein*mal not once
fragen to ask
    die Frage, -n question
früh early
    früher earlier; formerly
geben (gibt, hat gegeben) to
give
gehören (*plus personal dative*)
to belong to (property)
    gehören zu to belong to
    (membership)
gern(e) gladly
    ich esse gern(e) I like to
    eat
    ich möchte gern(e) etwas
    essen I'd like to eat
    something
gestern yesterday
glauben an (*with acc.*) to
believe in
helfen (hilft, hat geholfen)
(*plus personal dative*)
to help
das Hotel, -s hotel

der Hut, ⁻e hat
die Idee', die Ide'en idea
je, jemals ever
jung young
lachen to laugh
lang long
    lange for a long time
    jahrelang for years
    fünf Jahre lang for five
    years
letzt last
    letzten Mai last May
    letzte Woche last week
    letztes Jahr last year
der Mai May
die Minu'te, -n minute
der Mo'nat, -e month
der Montag, -e Monday
die Nacht, ⁻e night
    heute nacht this coming
    night; last night
    but: gestern abend last
    night (before going to
    bed), yesterday evening
neun nine
der Onkel uncle
recht right
    rechts to the right
    das ist mir recht that's all
    right with me
reden to talk, to speak
richtig correct, accurate
schenken to give (as a present)
schicken to send
schreiben (hat geschrieben)
to write
die Schule, -n school
sehr very
seit since
    seitdem since (*conj.*);
    since then, since that
    time (*adv.*)
    seit langem for a long time

---

* From this unit on, some of the new words introduced in each unit will appear under the heading "Additional Vocabulary." Most of these words appear primarily in the Reading sections and occur less frequently throughout the text than those in the main vocabulary sections.

seit Anfang Mai since the beginning of May
sieben seven
sitzen (**hat gesessen**) to sit
der Sommer, – summer
die Stadt, ⸚e town, city
sterben (**stirbt, ist gestorben**) to die
der Tag, –e day

das Telefon, –e telephone
am Telefon on the telephone
telefonieren (**mit**) to talk on the phone (with); to make a phone call
die Universität', –en university

vor before; in front of; ago
vor einem Jahr a year ago
warten auf (*with acc.*) to wait for
die Woche, –n week
woher from where
zeigen to show
zwanzig twenty

ADDITIONAL VOCABULARY

Ägypten Egypt
die Blume, –n flower
das Gesetz, –e law

der Lärm (*no plural*) noise; din
die Nummer, –n number

die Physik' (*no pl.*) physics
die Zigar're, –n cigar
die Zigaret'te, –n cigarette

UNIT 5: Numbers—The Past—The Pluperfect—Verb-Last Position—Open Conditions—um . . . zu—mit—Word Formation

[1] Cardinal Numbers

Learn the numbers; then go through the drills as indicated.

Null, eins, zwei, drei, vier, fünf, sechs, sieben, acht, neun, zehn, elf, zwölf, dreizehn, vierzehn, fünfzehn, sechzehn, siebzehn, achtzehn, neunzehn, zwanzig.

SEE ANALYSIS 74 (p. 130)

eins und eins ist zwei	eins plus eins ist zwei
eins und zwei ist . . .	eins plus zwei ist . . .
eins . . .	eins . . . . .
zwanzig weniger eins ist neunzehn	zwanzig minus eins ist neunzehn
neunzehn weniger eins . . .	zwanzig minus zwei ist . . .
achtzehn . . .	zwanzig . . .
Wieviel Uhr ist es?	Es ist zehn Uhr dreizehn.
Wie spät ist es?	Es ist zehn Uhr dreizehn.
Wann kommt der Zug an?	Um sechs Uhr siebzehn.
Um wieviel Uhr kommt der Zug an?	Um sechs Uhr siebzehn.
Wann fährt der Zug ab?	Um sieben Uhr sechzehn.
Um wieviel Uhr fährt der Zug ab?	Um sieben Uhr sechzehn.
Wann fängt das Theater an?	Um acht Uhr funfzehn.

[2] Past Tense of Weak Verbs

In order to practice the forms of the past tense, vary these sentences by substituting the subjects in parentheses.

SEE ANALYSIS 75-76, 79 (pp. 130-132 133-135)

Leider glaubte sie mir nicht.   Unfortunately, she did not believe me. (you)

(Facing) **Schlafwagenschaffner**

Nach dem Krieg heiratete er ein Mädchen aus Berlin.	After the war he married a girl from Berlin. (I)
Damals brauchte ich nicht so oft nach Berlin zu fahren.	At that time I didn't have to go to Berlin so often. (we)
Die Tochter lachte gerade wie ihr Vater.	The daughter laughed just like her father. (the daughters)
Wir machten damals oft Reisen.	At that time we often went on trips. (I)
Vor dem Krieg lebte Ingelheim in Berlin.	Before the war Ingelheim lived in Berlin. (we)
Rosemarie studierte damals in München.	At that time Rosemarie studied in Munich. (Rosemarie and I)

[3] The Past Forms of the Modals

Vary these sentences by substituting the subjects in parentheses.

SEE
ANALYSIS
76

(pp. 131-132)

Ich konnte gestern leider nicht kommen; ich mußte zu Hause bleiben.	Unfortunately, I couldn't come yesterday; I had to stay home. (we)
Er wollte nicht mit Tante Amalie ins Museum gehen.	He didn't want to go to the museum with Aunt Amalie. (I)
Warum wolltest du denn nicht ins Theater gehen?	Why didn't you want to go to the theater? (they)
Warum mußtet ihr denn nach Berlin fahren?	Why did you have to go to Berlin? (you, sing.)
Hans sollte mir helfen, aber er wollte nicht.	Hans was supposed to help me, but he didn't want to. (Hans and Inge)
Wir wollten mitgehen, aber wir durften nicht.	We wanted to go along, but we weren't allowed to. (they)

[4] Past Tense of **haben**

Form your own variations.

SEE
ANALYSIS
77

(pp. 132-133)

Ich fahre *heute* nach Bonn; *ge*stern hatte ich keine *Zeit.*	I am going to Bonn today; yesterday I didn't have time.
Warum *hat*test du denn keine Zeit?	Why didn't you have any time?
Herr Lenz hatte *auch* keine Zeit. Wir hatten *al*le zu viel zu tun.	Herr Lenz had no time either. We all had too much to do.
Was, ihr hattet keine *Zeit?*	What, you had no time?
Sie hatten *al*le zu viel zu tun.	They all had too much to do.
Hatten Sie gestern *auch* so viel zu tun, Herr Lohmann?	Did you also have so much to do yesterday, Mr. Lohmann?

[5] Past Tense of **sein**

Form your own variations.

Herr Lenz ist heute in *Bonn.—Ge*stern war er in *Köln.*	Herr Lenz is in Bonn today.—Yesterday he was in Cologne.	SEE ANALYSIS 77 (pp. 132-133)
Wo warst *du* gestern, Inge?—*Ich* war in *Frank*furt.	Where were you yesterday, Inge?—I was in Frankfurt.	
Ist Fritz heute *auch* hier?—Nein, er war *ge*stern hier; *heu*te ist er in *Frank*furt.	Is Fritz here too today?—No, he was here yesterday; today he is in Frankfurt.	
Wir waren gestern *auch* in Frankfurt.—Wo wart *ihr* gestern?	We were in Frankfurt, too, yesterday.— Where were you yesterday?	
Wo waren *Sie* denn, Herr Lenz?	Where were you, Herr Lenz?	

[6] Past Tense of Strong Verbs

Vary these sentences by substituting the subjects in parentheses.

Ich rief sie damals jede Woche an.	I called her every week then. (she)	SEE ANALYSIS 77 (pp. 132-133)
Ich bekam jede Woche drei Briefe von ihr.	I got three letters from her every week. (she)	
Sonntags blieb er immer zu Hause.	On Sundays he always stayed home. (they)	
Damals brachte ich sie jeden Abend nach Hause.	At that time, I took her home every night. (he)	
Sie luden uns oft zum Essen ein.	They often invited us to dinner. (she)	
Wir aßen damals oft im Regina.	We often ate at the Regina then. (I)	
Er fuhr jeden Sommer nach Italien.	He went to Italy every summer. (we)	
Wir fanden ihn in der Regina-Bar.	We found him in the Regina Bar. (they)	
Ich gab ihm jede Woche zwanzig Mark. ,	I gave him twenty marks every week. (we)	
Sonntags gingen wir nie ins Kino.	On Sundays we never went to the movies. (he)	
Wir halfen ihm damals oft bei seiner Arbeit.	We often helped him with his work. (she)	
Damals hieß sie noch Schmidt.	At that time, her name was still Schmidt. (my)	
Ich kannte sie gut.	I knew her well. (we)	
Er kam immer spät nach Hause.	He always came home late. (they)	
Wir ließen unsere Kinder zu Hause.	We left our children at home. (they)	
Er lief nach Hause.	He ran home. (she)	
Ich dachte damals oft an sie.	I often thought of her then. (we)	
Er schien mich nicht zu kennen.	He didn't seem to know me. (they)	
Er schlief oft bis elf Uhr.	He often slept until eleven o'clock. (I)	
Sie schrieb ihm jede Woche drei Briefe.	She wrote him three letters every week. (he)	
Ich saß im Garten und las ein Buch.	I was sitting in the garden reading a book. (he)	

Von Erika sprach er nie.	He never talked about Erika. (she)
Er stand vor dem Kino und wartete auf mich.	He was standing in front of the movie house waiting for me. (she)
Leider trank er.	Unfortunately he drank. (she)
Und dann tat er jahrelang nichts.	Then he didn't do a thing for years. (she)
Er starb drei Jahre später.	He died three years later. (she)
Jeden Sommer verschwand er auf eine Woche.	Every summer he disappeared for a week. (they)
Sie verstand ihn einfach nicht.	She simply didn't understand him. (they)
Sie wurde Ärztin.	She became a doctor. (he)
Sie wußte nichts von seiner Reise.	She didn't know anything about his trip. (we)

[7] Two Past Forms in One Sentence

Read these sentences carefully and note their narrative character.

SEE ANALYSIS 75–79 (pp. 130-135)

Er kaufte ein Buch und schenkte es seiner Freundin.	He bought a book and gave it to his friend.
Hans kam um zehn Uhr aus dem Theater und fuhr nach Hause.	At ten o'clock, Hans got out of the theater and drove home.
Hans ging mit Inge ins Kino; dann brachte er sie nach Hause.	Hans went to the movies with Inge; then he took her home.
Herr Kunz trank ein Glas Wein und las die Zeitung.	Herr Kunz drank a glass of wine and read the paper.
Er hörte, was ich sagte, aber er glaubte mir nicht.	He heard what I said, but he did not believe me.
In Hamburg regnete es, aber in Casablanca schien die Sonne.	It was raining in Hamburg, but in Casablanca the sun was shining.

[8] Verb-Last Position in Dependent Clauses

By leaving out the main clauses, change the dependent clauses into assertions or questions.

SEE ANALYSIS 84–88 (pp. 136-141)

Ich weiß, daß er Geld   hat.
Ich weiß, daß er Geld   hatte.
Ich weiß, daß er Geld   gehabt hat.

Ich weiß nicht, ob Fritz mit dem Auto zum Bahnhof   fährt.
Ich wußte, daß er immer mit dem Auto zur Arbeit   fuhr.
Ich glaube nicht, daß er mit dem Auto zum Bahnhof   gefahren ist.

Ich möchte, daß du morgen vernünftig   bist.
Ich hoffe, daß du gestern vernünftig   warst.
Ich weiß, daß du immer vernünftig   gewesen bist.

Wissen Sie, ob Meyers hier   wohnen?
Wir wußten, daß Meyers da   wohnten.
Wie soll ich wissen, wo Meyers   gewohnt haben?

Weiß er, daß er dir helfen   soll?
Er wußte, daß er mir helfen   sollte.

[9] The Pluperfect

Form your own variations.

Als ich ihn kennenlernte, war er gerade aus Afrika zurückgekommen.	When I met him, he had just come back from Africa.	**SEE ANALYSIS 82–83**
Er bekam die Gelbsucht, weil er zuviel gegessen hatte.	He got jaundice because he had eaten too much.	(pp. 135-136)
Wir wußten nicht, daß er Soldat geworden war.	We didn't know that he had become a soldier.	
Er war zwei Jahre lang in Norwegen gewesen, als man ihn an die Westfront schickte.	He had been in Norway for two years when he was sent to the Western Front.	
Als ich Hans nach dem Krieg wiedersah, war er Schriftsteller geworden.	When I saw Hans again after the war, he had become a writer.	

[10] Open Conditions

Try to reverse the order of conditions and conclusions. You may have to make some logical changes.

SEE ANALYSIS 89

(pp. 141-143)

Wenn es morgen nicht regnet, können wir arbeiten.
Wir können morgen nur arbeiten, wenn es nicht regnet.
Wenn ich kann, komme ich.
Ich fahre nur nach Casablanca, wenn du auch fährst.
Wenn du nach Casablanca fährst, fahre ich auch.
Wenn Herr Büttner hier ist, soll er zu mir kommen.
Wenn du kein Geld hast, helfe ich dir gerne.
Ich trinke nie Wein, wenn ich Auto fahren muß.

[11] um . . . zu

After studying **90,** replace the **um . . . zu** clauses by either **weil** clauses or open conditions.

SEE
ANALYSIS
90
(p. 143)

Inge fuhr nach Frankfurt, um ins Theater zu gehen.

Er fuhr nach Kairo, um dort einen Roman zu schreiben.

Sie ging ins Theater, um *Hamlet* zu sehen.

Er studierte Englisch, um Shakespeare lesen zu können.

Herr Lenz ging in die Stadt, um seiner Frau ein Buch zu kaufen.

Um nach Casablanca fahren zu können, muß man viel Geld haben.

Um eine Frau verstehen zu können, muß man sie lieben.

CONVERSATION

FRAU A: Weißt du, ob Hans und Maria das Haus hier in Bonn ge*kauft* haben?

FRAU B: Das *weiß* ich nicht; aber warum *fragst* du?

FRAU A: Weil *wir* es gerne kaufen möchten, wenn Hans und Maria es nicht wollen.

FRAU B: Das ist mir *neu.* Ich dachte, ihr wollt ein Haus in *Köln* kaufen.

FRAU A: Das *woll*ten wir auch. Gestern sind wir nach Köln gefahren und haben das Haus noch einmal gesehen. Es war wirklich sehr schön.

FRAU B: Aber ge*kauft* habt ihr es *nicht?* War es denn zu teuer?

FRAU A: Nein, zu *teu*er war es *nicht,* aber wir wollen doch lieber hier in Bonn bleiben. —Übrigens habe ich in Bonn einen *Hut* gekauft.

FRAU B: *Wirk*lich? Den mußt du mir *zeig*en.

READING

Viel Lärm um nichts?

KAPITEL DREI: Ein Interview mit Schmidt-Ingelheim

REPORTER: Wie lange sind Sie schon in Kairo, Herr Schmidt-Ingelheim?

SCHMIDT-INGELHEIM: Seit vierzehn Tagen*—seit Anfang April.

REPORTER: Und wie lange wollen Sie noch hierbleiben?

* **vierzehn Tage** in German, the usual way of expressing *two weeks.*

SCHMIDT-INGELHEIM: Das kann ich Ihnen noch nicht sagen; ich wollte noch zwei, drei Wochen hier arbeiten, aber gerade hat mich ein Freund angerufen und wollte wissen, ob ich mit nach Casablanca fahren will. Er hat eine Jacht, wissen Sie, und weil ich schon lange nicht mehr auf einem Schiff gewesen bin, dachte ich, ich fahre vielleicht mit. 5

REPORTER: Das kann nur Mr. Thistlethwaite gewesen sein, oder?

SCHMIDT-INGELHEIM: Sie haben recht—aber wie wußten Sie denn, . . . ?

REPORTER: Ich habe ihn vor drei oder vier Wochen zufällig kennengelernt und habe ihn seitdem zwei- oder dreimal besucht. Von ihm weiß ich auch, daß Sie hier sind. Er hat viel von Ihnen und von Ihrer Frau 10 gesprochen—wie schön Ihre Frau ist, und wie intelligent—und er hat mir auch erzählt, daß Sie wieder an einem Roman arbeiten.

SCHMIDT-INGELHEIM: Ja, mein Roman! Um diesen Roman zu schreiben, bin ich nach Kairo gekommen, wissen Sie—ich mußte ein paar† Wochen allein sein, um arbeiten zu können. Und außerdem wollte ich Afrika wiedersehen, 15 —der Roman hat viel mit Afrika zu tun.

REPORTER: Es ist also wieder ein Kriegsroman, Herr Schmidt-Ingelheim?

SCHMIDT-INGELHEIM: Ja, ja,—*Ende bei Karthago* heißt er. Ich arbeite jetzt schon seit zwei Jahren an diesem Roman, aber wissen Sie, wenn man immer so zu Hause sitzt, dann . . . 20

REPORTER: Das kann ich gut verstehen, Herr Schmidt-Ingelheim.—Sie mußten eine Reise machen; Sie mußten nach Afrika kommen, um über ihren Roman nachdenken zu können; Sie mußten einmal verschwinden . . .

SCHMIDT-INGELHEIM: Richtig! Kein Telefon, kein Briefträger, keine Reporter—verstehen Sie, ich möchte wirklich einmal verschwinden, spurlos verschwinden. 25 Nur so für vierzehn Tage oder drei Wochen. Aber so ist das Leben leider nicht. Und der Briefträger kommt auch; heute morgen zum Beispiel habe ich einen Brief von meiner Tochter bekommen—sie schreibt, sie will nach Kairo kommen.

REPORTER: Von Ihrer Tochter? Das habe ich nicht gewußt, daß Sie eine Tochter 30 haben.

SCHMIDT-INGELHEIM: Oh, doch,—von meiner ersten* Frau; sie wird Ende Mai zwanzig und studiert in Mainz Archäologie. Ich habe sie seit zehn Jahren nicht gesehen.

REPORTER: Das ist ja interessant.—Aber ich möchte Sie noch etwas fragen, 35 Herr Ingelheim. Ihr Roman—können Sie mir nicht noch etwas von Ihrem Roman erzählen?

† **ein paar** a few
* **ersten** first

SCHMIDT-INGELHEIM: Möchte ich ja gern, aber ich muß jetzt wirklich gehen; man erwartet mich zum Frühstück;—und wissen Sie, ohne meinen Frühstückskaffee ist das Leben nur halb so schön.

KAPITEL VIER: Ein Brief an Frau Schmidt–Ingelheim

Katharina Schmidt   65 Mainz/Rhein
                                                     Riedbachstraße 4
                                                     den 12. Mai

Sehr geehrte Frau Schmidt-Ingelheim!

Gerade habe ich in der† Zeitung gelesen, daß Ihr Mann seit drei 5
Wochen in Afrika spurlos verschwunden ist.

Ich weiß, was Sie durchmachen. Mein Mann war auch einmal drei
Wochen spurlos verschwunden. Aber wenn Sie diesen Brief bekommen, ist Hans vielleicht schon wieder zu Hause und sagt Ihnen beim Frühstück: „Ohne deinen Kaffee, Ingrid, wäre das Leben nur 10
halb so schön."

Woher ich weiß, daß er das sagt? Ich bin Frau Schmidt Nummer eins, und ich glaube, Sie sind Frau Schmidt Nummer zwei oder drei. Ich weiß nicht, wie oft Hans geheiratet hat, und ich möchte es auch nicht wissen. Ich möchte aber, daß Sie warten, bis Hans 15
wiederkommt, und daß e rnicht mehr in die Zeitung kommt. Sie brauchen nicht zu fürchten, daß ihm etwas passiert ist. Ihrem Hans passiert nie etwas; ich kenne ihn. Ich habe ihn einmal geliebt, wissen Sie; und oft, wenn ich sehe, wie seine Tochter mit einem Lachen in den Augen zum Frühstück kommt, gerade wie früher 20
ihr Vater, dann frage ich mich, ob ich ihn nicht vielleicht doch noch liebe.

Nein, passiert ist ihm nichts. Wie habe ich Angst gehabt, als er 1939 Soldat wurde. Damals wußte ich noch nicht, daß ich keine Angst zu haben brauchte. Man schickte ihn in ein Städtchen hinter 25
der Westfront, und da hat er ein Jahr lang Brieftauben gefüttert. Gerade als es 1940 im Westen gefährlich wurde, schickte man ihn nach Hause, weil er Hepatitis bekam.

Wir heirateten.

Hans hatte aber keine Hepatitis. Er hatte nur Gelbsucht, weil er 30
zu gut gegessen und zu viel getrunken hatte; und so wurde er 1941
wieder Soldat. Man schickte ihn, wieder mit Brieftauben, nach Norwegen. Seine Briefe sprachen im Sommer vom Fischen, und im Winter vom Schilaufen. Bei Kriegsende war er zufällig in Ingelheim, und die Amerikaner nahmen ihn gefangen. Jetzt bekam er wirklich 35

Marginal glosses:

Sehr geehrte Standard form of address: literally "very honored Mrs. Schmidt-Ingelheim"

wäre would be

1939: neunzehnhundertneununddreißig

1940: neunzehnhundertvierzig

Gelbsucht jaundice

1941: neunzehnhunderteinundvierzig

---

† The use of dative or accusative after prepositions like *an* and *in* will be discussed in Unit 7.

Hepatitis, und man schickte ihn nach Hause. Dreiundzwanzig
Schüler haben 1931 mit ihm das Abitur gemacht. Von den dreiundzwanzig leben heute noch sechs, und ihm allein ist im Krieg
nichts passiert.

Hans wurde Schriftsteller. Seinen Kriegsroman *Wie das Gesetz es* 5
befahl habe ich auf der Maschine geschrieben. Er machte damals oft
Reisen, ohne mich, und wohin, weiß ich nicht. Ich habe ihn auch
nie gefragt. Er mußte, so sagte er, zwei oder drei Wochen allein sein,
um seine Romane schreiben zu können. Aber er kam immer wieder,
mit seinem Lachen in den Augen, und trank seinen Kaffee, wie man 10
Rheinwein trinkt. Aber dann passierte ihm doch etwas. Als er von
einer Reise zurückkam, sagte er beim Frühstück: „Ohne deinen
Kaffee, Gisela, wäre das Leben nur halb so schön." Ich weiß nicht,
wer Gisela war, aber ich fuhr mit meiner Tochter zu meiner Mutter.

Noch einmal, sehr geehrte Frau Schmidt, Ihrem Hans ist nichts 15
passiert. Ich weiß, er lebt und ist gesund. Seit Sie geheiratet haben,
war er wohl noch nie so lange „spurlos verschwunden". Ich gratuliere Ihnen; Sie müssen interessant sein, interessanter als ich. Aber
wenn er wieder zu Hause ist, dann fragen Sie ihn doch beim
Frühstück: „Wie war Giselas Kaffee? Oder hieß sie diesmal nicht 20
Gisela?" Vielleicht verschwindet er dann drei Wochen mit Ihnen.
Auf keinen Fall aber dürfen Sie mit Ihren Kindern zu Ihrer Mutter
fahren. Ich habe damals einen Fehler gemacht; ich hoffe, Sie machen
diesen Fehler nicht.

Ihre
Katharina Schmidt

KAPITEL FÜNF: Frau Schmidt-Ingelheim wieder am Telefon

Ah, Herr Behrens; gut, daß Sie wieder anrufen. Wissen Sie was? 25
Der Briefträger hatte wirklich zwei Briefe von meinem Mann. Und
seine Tochter, die Erika, war *doch* in Kairo. . . .

Nein, Johannes wußte es auch nicht. Sie studiert doch Archäologie
und war gerade in Ägypten, und zufällig war sie in Kairo, als mein
Mann in Kairo war. Die Welt ist doch wirklich klein, nicht? . . .   30

Und diese Männer! Er hatte mir geschrieben, daß er nicht mit der
Lufthansa nach Casablanca wollte. Thistlethwaite hatte ihn eingeladen, mit ihm auf seiner Jacht nach Casablanca zu fahren. Und
dann nimmt der Mann den Brief mit aufs Schiff, und gefunden hat
er ihn erst in Casablanca im Hotel. . . .   35

Nein, nein, alles ist OK; ich fahre morgen nach Zürich und hole ihn
ab. . . .

Ja, so sind die Männer, aber ich bin ja so glücklich, daß er gesund
ist. . . .

Margin notes:

**1931: neunzehnhun-
derteinunddreißig
Abitur** comprehensive
examination at the end
of German secondary
school

Auf . . . Fall under no
circumstances.

Ja, mit dem Nekrolog müssen Sie jetzt natürlich noch warten. . . .

Natürlich, ich sage ihm morgen, daß Sie angerufen haben. Ich danke Ihnen, Herr Behrens. Auf Wiederhören!

ANALYSIS

74 Cardinal Numbers

The numbers from 0 to 20 are:

null	sieben	vierzehn
eins	acht	fünfzehn
zwei	neun	sechzehn
drei	zehn	siebzehn
vier	elf	achtzehn
fünf	zwölf	neunzehn
sechs	dreizehn	zwanzig

Note the difference in spelling:

sech*s,*	but	sechzehn
sieb*en,*	but	siebzehn

One can say either

zwei und zwei ist vier   or   zwei plus zwei ist vier,

and

vier weniger zwei ist zwei   or   vier minus zwei ist zwei.

Plus and **minus** are mathematical terms; **und** and **weniger** are used in non-mathematical everyday language.

75 The Past Tense of Weak Verbs

Just as the present-tense form **ich gehe** may mean both *I go* and *I am going,* the past-tense form **ich ging** may mean both *I went* and *I was going;* in other words, German does not have progressive forms in any tense.

It was pointed out in Unit 4 that "weak" verbs form their participles by prefixing **ge-** and adding **-t** to the stem, whereas "strong" verbs form their participles by prefixing **ge-** and adding **-en** to the stem:

WEAK	STRONG
lieben, geliebt	bleiben, geblieben
lachen, gelacht	lesen, gelesen
kennen, gekannt	sein, gewesen

There is also a difference in the way "weak" and "strong" verbs form the past tense.

Weak verbs form the past tense by adding a personal ending starting with -t- to the unchanged (or only slightly changed) stem:

INFINITIVE	STEM	PERSONAL ENDING	PAST TENSE
		-te	ich liebte
		-test	du liebtest
		-te	er liebte
lieben	lieb-		
		-ten	wir liebten
		-tet	ihr liebtet
		-ten	sie liebten

Thousands of verbs follow the pattern of **lieben** without any deviation. Some deviations are regular and will be discussed in the next paragraph. The few irregular deviations will be found in the tables of irregular verbs which, from now on, will follow the vocabulary of each unit.

76   Regular Deviations in the Past of Weak Verbs

Three slight deviations will not appear in the tables of irregular verbs:

Modals

The modals lose the umlaut found in the infinitive:

dürfen	ich durfte
können	ich konnte
müssen	ich mußte
sollen	ich sollte
wollen	ich wollte

We will not use, for a while, the past tense forms belonging to **ich möchte.** Note the difference between **ich konnte,** *I was able to,* and **ich kannte,** *I knew.*

Verbs with an -e- before the Ending -te

The endings -te, -test, -te, -ten, -tet, and -ten must be clearly audible. Therefore, verbs with a stem ending in -d or -t, like **arbeiten** and **reden**, insert an -e- between the stem and the ending.

ich arbeitete	ich redete
du arbeitetest	du redetest
er arbeitete	er redete
wir arbeiteten	wir redeten
ihr arbeitetet	ihr redetet
sie arbeiteten	sie redeten

For similar reasons, an -e- before the ending -t is also found in the past forms of verbs like **regnen, atmen** (*to breathe*), and **rechnen** (*to figure, to calculate*):

es regnete
er atmete
er rechnete

The Verb **haben**

ich hatte	wir hatten
du hattest	ihr hattet
er hatte	sie hatten

NOTE: In the past tense, the third person singular of a weak verb *never* ends in -t.

77 Past Tense of Strong Verbs

To form the past, strong verbs add the following endings to the changed stem:

ich:	—		wir:	-en
du:	-st		ihr:	-t
er:	—		sie:	-en

The change in the stem is unpredictable, and the best way to master these forms is to memorize them as they appear in the tables of irregular verbs.

INFINITIVE	CHANGED STEM	ENDING	PAST TENSE
		-	ich ging
		-st	du gingst
		-	er ging
gehen	ging-	-en	wir gingen
		-t	ihr gingt
		-en	sie gingen

Like the weak verbs whose stems end in **-d** or **-t**, strong verbs ending in **-d** or **-t** insert an **-e-** between the stem and the ending in the **du**-form and the **ihr**-form.

INFINITIVE	CHANGED STEM	ENDING	PAST TENSE
		-	ich fand
		-est	du fandest
		-	er fand
finden	fand-		
		-en	wir fanden
		-et	ihr fandet
		-en	sie fanden

NOTE: In the past tense, the first and third persons singular of a strong verb *never* have an ending.

78 The Principal Parts of Strong and Irregular German Verbs

One can form all the tenses of an English verb like *to sing* if one knows the three forms

sing   sang   sung.

These three forms are called the "principal parts" of *to sing*.

The student learning German must learn two additional forms:

1. the **er**-form of verbs like **fahren**—that is, of strong verbs with a vowel change in the second and third persons singular. (Weak verbs never change their stem vowel in the present tense.)

2. the auxiliary (**haben** or **sein**) used to form the perfect.

Thus the principal parts of **kennen, schreiben,** and **fahren,** arranged in the traditional way, are:

kennen	kannte	hat gekannt	kennt
schreiben	schrieb	hat geschrieben	schreibt
fahren	fuhr	ist gefahren	fährt

The verb **kennen** is a weak verb. However, it changes the vowel in the past and in the perfect in an unpredictable way and therefore appears in the table of irregular verbs.

79 The Difference in the Use of the Perfect and the Past

A native speaker of English is tempted to express the ideas
    Did you eat at the Regina last night?
    Did you sleep well last night?

by the Anglicisms

Beware!   [Aßt ihr gestern abend im Regina?]   DO NOT USE!
Americanism!   [Schliefst du heute nacht gut?]

The native speaker of English talks about "all-in-the-past" events (see **71**) by using the simple past tense, and he quite naturally transfers this habit to German. However, a German will ask only

Habt ihr gestern abend im Regina gegessen?
Hast du gut geschlafen?

The forms

ich aß   and   ich habe gegessen
ich schlief   and   ich habe geschlafen

are not interchangeable. As long as people are engaged in a conversation, (and telling a story is *not* conversation), they use the German perfect:

A: **Wohnt Dr. Müller noch hier?**
B: **Nein, Dr. Müller ist vor einem Jahr gestorben, und seine Frau ist nach München gezogen.** (ist gezogen—*has moved*)
   Not: [**Dr. Müller starb vor einem Jahr, und seine Frau zog nach München.**]

However, the sentence

Dr. Müller starb, und seine Frau zog nach München

is possible when the speaker turns into an author, when the conversational partner becomes a passive reader or listener, when two-way conversation changes to one-way storytelling. For then the storyteller uses the simple past tense to enumerate step by step those events, and only those events, which are part of the progressing story.

Hans wurde Schriftsteller. Seinen Kriegsroman *Wie das Gesetz es befahl* habe ich auf der Maschine geschrieben. Er machte damals oft Reisen, ohne mich, und wohin, weiß ich nicht. Ich habe ihn auch nie gefragt. Er mußte, so sagte er, zwei oder drei Wochen allein sein, um seine Romane schreiben zu können. Aber er kam immer wieder, mit seinem Lachen in den Augen, und trank seinen Kaffee, wie man Rheinwein trinkt. Aber dann passierte ihm doch etwas. Als er von einer Reise zurückkam, sagte er beim Frühstück: „Ohne deinen Kaffee, Gisela, wäre das Leben nur halb so schön." Ich weiß nicht, wer Gisela war, aber ich fuhr mit meiner Tochter zu meiner Mutter.

Most of the verb forms in this passage are past-tense forms. These forms narrate, step by step, the events of the story. The perfect forms **habe ich auf der Maschine geschrieben** and **Ich habe ihn auch nie gefragt** are parenthetical remarks which interrupt the story. The two present forms **ich weiß nicht** refer to the time of writing the letter, not to what the author knew while the past was going on. Such shifts from the narrative past to a present or to a perfect are quite normal. The present or perfect forms in such cases interrupt the story and reestablish a connection with the present.

80   The Use of the Past Tense of **haben, sein,** and the Modals

What has been said about the difference between the past and the perfect is not applicable to **haben, sein,** and the modals. The perfect tense of these verbs is used primarily in up-to-now situations. In all-past situations, the simple past is preferred. This means that, as far as **haben, sein,** and the modals are concerned, the German use of tenses is parallel to English usage.

A: **Wo warst du denn gestern? Ich habe dich überall gesucht.**

Where were you yesterday? I looked for you everywhere.

B: **Ich hatte gestern Kopfschmerzen und bin zu Hause geblieben** (*or* **. . . und konnte nicht kommen** *or* **. . . und mußte zu Hause bleiben**).

I had a headache yesterday and stayed at home (*or* . . . and I couldn't come *or* . . . and I had to stay at home).

81   The Use of the Past in Dependent Clauses

Frequently a perfect form in the main clause is accompanied by a past form in the dependent clause (see 84–87). This is virtually obligatory in **als**-clauses and in other dependent clauses which fix the time of an event or describe the circumstances that brought the event about:

Ich habe bis elf gewartet. Aber als er dann immer noch nicht kam, bin ich ins Bett gegangen.

I waited until eleven. But when he still did not come, I went to bed.

Warum hat sie ihn denn geheiratet, wenn sie ihn nicht liebte?—Weil sie wußte, daß er Geld hatte.

Why did she marry him if she didn't love him?—Because she knew he had money.

NOTE: If the action of the dependent clause occurs while the action of the main clause is in progress, the past tense may be used in both clauses.

Als ich meine Frau kennenlernte, wohnte sie in München.

82   The Formation of the Pluperfect

The German pluperfect is formed by combining the simple past of **haben** or **sein** with the participle of the main verb. Verbs which use **sein** for the perfect, like

    bleiben   **blieb**   **ist geblieben**   **bleibt,**

also form their pluperfect with **sein: ich war geblieben** (*I had stayed*). Verbs which, like

    schreiben   **schrieb**   **hat geschrieben**   **schreibt,**

use **haben** for the perfect, also use **haben** for the pluperfect: **ich hatte geschrieben** (*I had written*).

83 The Use of the Pluperfect

Like the English past perfect, the German pluperfect is the tense used to describe events or situations which precede events or situations that occurred in the past.

Hans hatte die Gelbsucht, weil er monatelang zu gut gegessen und zu viel getrunken hatte.	Hans had jaundice, because for months he had been eating and drinking too much.
Es war Abend geworden, und es regnete.	Night had come and it was raining.

When the sentence

    Erich wohnt jetzt schon drei Jahre in München und geht jede Woche einmal ins Theater

becomes part of a narrative, it will appear as

    Erich wohnte damals schon drei Jahre in München und ging jede Woche einmal ins Theater.

The "up-to-now" situation of the first sentence has become an "up-to-then" situation in the second sentence.

84 Dependent Clauses

Dependent clauses are syntactical units of main clauses. They can function as any part of the main clause: as subject, predicate noun, object, adverb, etc.

SUBJECT	*The winner* gets the prize.
	Whoever wins gets the prize.
PREDICATE NOUN	This is not *the expected result*.
	This is not *what I had expected*.

OBJECT	I'll never know *your thoughts.*
	I'll never know *what you think.*
ADVERB	He met John *during his stay in New York.*
	He met John *while he stayed in New York.*

Dependent clauses are usually introduced by a connecting word: a subordinating conjunction (*while, because, if,* etc.), a relative pronoun (*who, whom, what,* etc.), or an interrogative pronoun (*who, what, when, why,* etc.).

After certain introductory phrases containing a verb of thought, the connecting word can be left out:

I am sure (that) he'll come.

In English, the word order in both introduced and unintroduced dependent clauses is usually the same as the word order of a main clause.

She took him to the airport.
I know she took him to the airport.
I know that she took him to the airport.

In German, *only unintroduced dependent clauses have the same structure as main clauses.* We have had many examples of this type.

Meyer arbeitet heute in Bonn.
Ich glaube, Meyer arbeitet heute in Bonn.

All unintroduced dependent clauses in German have verb-second position. They normally start with the subject, and the introductory main clause is never negated. If the main clause is negated, a major change takes place which has no parallel in English (see **85**).

85 Verb-Last Position

By now you are familiar with the most characteristic feature of German syntax—the tendency to separate a semantic unit into two parts and to use these parts as brackets to establish a larger unit. Thus the two prongs of the predicate enclose the inner field.

A similar bracket principle is used in all dependent clauses which are introduced by a subordinating conjunction, a relative pronoun, or an interrogative. The introductory word is used as the first bracket and, of all things, the first prong is moved out of its usual position and is used as the second bracket. The rest of the sentence, including the second prong, remains unchanged. This means that the first prong now follows the second prong and stands at the end of the clause if there is no end field. We therefore speak of "verb-last position."

	FRONT FIELD	1st Prong	INNER FIELD	2nd Prong
MAIN CLAUSE	Er	ist	heute	hier
UNINTRODUCED DEPENDENT CLAUSE	Ich glaube, er	ist	heute	hier
INTRODUCED DEPENDENT CLAUSE	Ich glaube, daß er		heute	hier	ist

NOTE: Verbal complements like **an, aus, ab,** and any others that are written as one word with an infinitive, must also be connected in verb-last position.

> Die Laternen gehen an.—Wenn die Laternen angehen, . . .
> Er macht das Licht aus.—Daß er das Licht ausmacht, . . .
> Er lernte sie in Bonn kennen.—Als er sie in Bonn kennenlernte, . . .

All introduced dependent clauses follow this pattern of verb-last position. In this unit, three groups of connecting words are used:

Subordinating Conjunctions

Ich weiß,	*daß*	er seit drei Wochen	verschwunden	*ist.*
Er will erst schreiben,	*wenn*	er wieder	zu Hause	*ist.*
Ich mußte warten,	*bis*	Herr Behrens mich	angerufen	*hatte.*
Er schrieb erst,	*als*	er von seiner Reise	zurückgekommen	*war.*
Er blieb zu Hause,	*weil*	er nicht	ins Kino gehen	*wollte.*
Er redet nicht viel,	*seit*	er aus Afrika	zurückgekommen	*ist.*

Interrogative Conjunctions

Sie wußte nicht mehr,	*wer*	ihr das Buch	gegeben	*hatte.*
Ich weiß nicht,	*was*	er in Norwegen	gemacht	*hat.*
Wissen Sie,	*wo*	er bei Kriegsende		*war?*

NOTE: Any German word question can be changed into a dependent clause by changing word order:

> Wann ist er nach Hause gekommen?
> Ich weiß nicht, wann er nach Hause gekommen ist.

The Conjunction **ob**

Any German yes-or-no question can be changed into a dependent **ob**-clause by changing word order:

> **Hat Meyer Geld?**
> **Weißt du, ob Meyer Geld hat?**
>
> **Hat sie geheiratet?**
> **Weißt du, ob sie geheiratet hat?**

NOTE: In English, yes-or-no questions can be changed into dependent clauses by using either *whether* or *if*:

	Is he here?
Do you know whether	he is here?
Do you know if	he is here?

Every English *if* which can be replaced by *whether* must be expressed by **ob** in German. This **ob** cannot be replaced by **wenn.**

86 Dependent Clauses in the Front Field

In all the above examples, the dependent clause follows the main clause. *If the dependent clause precedes the main clause, it is considered the first element of the main clause; that is, it occupies the front field of the main clause—and must therefore be followed by the first prong of the main clause* to conform to the principle of verb-second position. This means that, separated by a comma, the finite verb of the main clause immediately follows the finite verb of the dependent clause.

In Hamburg	**bin**	ich jeden Abend	**ins Kino**	**gegangen.**

Als ich in Hamburg war,	**bin**	ich jeden Abend	**ins Kino**	**gegangen.**

Frequently, especially after **wenn**-clauses, the dependent clause—that is, the first element of the main clause—is repeated and summed up at the beginning of the main clause by either **dann** or **so**. This **dann** or **so** immediately precedes the first prong—that is, the second element of the main clause.

> *Wenn ich seine Tochter sehe,*
> 1
>
>   *dann* | *weiß* ich, daß ich ihn immer noch liebe.
>   1a | 2

English uses a similar construction in such sentences as

> Well, if you won't sell, then there's nothing more to be said.

87   Position of the Subject in Dependent Clauses

In most dependent clauses, the subject follows the connecting word. (See all the above examples). However, a noun subject may be preceded by pronoun objects:

Ich weiß, daß *Herr Meyer seiner Frau* einen Sportwagen geschenkt hat.
Ich weiß, daß *Herr Meyer ihr* einen Sportwagen geschenkt hat.
Ich weiß, daß *ihr Herr Meyer* einen Sportwagen geschenkt hat.

In order to increase the news value of a noun subject, it may be moved toward the end of the inner field. Thus, in the following sentences, the news value is shifted from the time element to the subject:

Ich kann nicht glauben, daß *die Laternen* hier schon um vier Uhr angehen.
Ich kann nicht glauben, daß hier schon um vier Uhr *die Laternen* angehen.

88   Intonation of Dependent Clauses

It was pointed out in Unit 1 that when a German assertion sinks down at the end to level 1 of the three intonation levels, as it does in

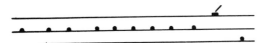

Wir blei·ben heu·te na·tür·lich zu Hau·se,

the fall to level 1 means "this is the end of the sentence."

Whenever an assertion is followed by a dependent clause, the speaker has several possibilities.

1. He may want to indicate that everything important has already been said in the main clause. In that case the entire dependent clause may have level 1 intonation, and the preceding main clause shows the usual 2–3–1 intonation pattern.

Ich war schon im Bett, als er nach Hau·se kam.

2. He may pack *all* the news value into the dependent clause and speak the preceding main clause entirely on level 2.

Ich war doch schon hier, als er kam.

3. He may want to distribute the news value over the main clause and the dependent clause by placing (at least) *one* stressed syllable in the main clause and (at least) *one* stressed syllable in the dependent clause.

Er will warten , bis du kommst.

The intonation patterns in (1) and (2) contain nothing new (they simply represent a "long-breath" variation of **Es regnet**), but the intonation pattern under (3) illustrates a new principle:

The main clause and the dependent clause are usually separated by a slight pause; and at the end of the main clause the pitch of the unstressed syllables does not sink to level 1 (which would signal the end of the sentence), but is spoken on level 3. This lack of a drop in pitch is a signal meaning: "This is not the end of the sentence; wait for the next clause."

The high-pitch last-syllable intonation is also characteristic for dependent clauses which precede a main clause.

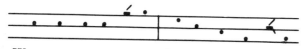

Wenn es morgen regnet , bleiben wir zu Hause.

89 Open Conditions

A condition is an event or a situation without which another event or situation cannot take place. Thus, in the statement *If the weather is good tomorrow, we can go to the beach,* good weather is the prerequisite for the trip to the beach. The *if*-clause (the grammatical "condition") does not indicate whether or not the weather will be good; it simply states that unless the weather is good, the second part of the statement (the grammatical "conclusion") will not become a reality.

Similarly, if someone says, *I haven't seen my old teacher for years. If he is still alive he was fifty years old last Monday,* this means that the speaker does not know whether the teacher is still alive, and that consequently he doesn't know whether the teacher was able to celebrate his fiftieth birthday. *The question as to the reality of the facts is left open.* However, this question *is not left open* if someone says, *If my teacher were still alive, he would have turned fifty last Monday.* The speaker now implies that the teacher is dead. In other words: The situation described in the condition is known to be unreal and to exist only in the speaker's thought and imagination.

The difference in meaning between "if he is alive" and "if he were alive" depends entirely on verb forms. The *is* leaves the question of the actual facts open; the *were* expresses the unreality of the situation imagined.

From now on, we shall use the terms "open conditions" and "irreal" or "contrary-to-fact conditions" to indicate whether the question of the facts is open or whether these facts are contrary to reality and merely assumed in imagination.

In Unit 5, only open conditions are introduced. Irreal conditions, which require the use of the subjunctive, will be discussed in Unit 6. German *if*-clauses are introduced by the subordinating conjunction **wenn.** As dependent clauses, they require verb-last position.

>   **Wenn Inge kommen kann, gehe ich mit ihr ins Museum.**
>   **Wenn ihm nichts passiert ist, muß er schon zu Hause sein.**
>   **Ich schenke dir den Roman gern, wenn du ihn haben möchtest.**
>   **Wenn Sie diesen Brief bekommen, müssen Sie mir sofort antworten.**
>   **Ich habe keine Angst, wenn mein Mann nach Afrika fährt.**

NOTE: Without context, some of these sentences, especially the last two,

Wenn es in Europa regnet...

...scheint im Libanon die Sonne

are ambiguous, since **wenn** means both *when* and *if*. Thus the last sentence may mean

> I won't be afraid if my husband goes to Africa

or

> I am not afraid when my husband goes to Africa.

90 um . . . zu, in order to

We have introduced a number of situations in which an infinitive must be used with the preposition **zu**:

> **Er braucht heute nicht zu arbeiten.**
> **Er scheint zu glauben, daß Meyer intelligent ist.**

There is another type of infinitive construction, as, for example, in the English sentence

> We eat to stay alive,

which can be expanded into

> We eat in order to stay alive.

Whenever this English expansion is possible, German *must* introduce the infinitive phrase with the preposition **um**:

> **Wir essen, um zu leben.**

This construction with **um . . . zu** must be separated from the main clause by a comma. When it is expanded by other syntactical units, **um** stands at the beginning and the infinitive stands at the end of the phrase:

> **Er fuhr nach Kairo,** *um* **dort einen Roman** *zu schreiben.*
> **Sie ging nach Mainz,** *um* **dort Archäologie** *zu studieren.*
> *Um* **das Haus kaufen** *zu können,* **braucht er Geld.**

Usually, the **um . . . zu** phrase occupies either the end field or the front field.

Note: If the **um . . . zu** clause follows the main clause, it can be replaced by a clause of the type **weil . . . er will** (**wollte**); if it precedes the main clause, it can be replaced by an open condition.

> **Er braucht Geld, um nach Berlin zu fahren.**
> **Er braucht Geld, weil er nach Berlin fahren will.**

> **Um nach Berlin fahren zu können, braucht man Geld.**
> **Wenn man nach Berlin fahren will, braucht man Geld.**

91 **mit** as a Verbal Complement

The preposition **mit** is frequently used as a verbal complement, meaning *along*. It forms the second prong of the predicate:

Rosemarie geht *auch* mit.
Rosemarie is coming along too.

If the sentence is negated, **mit** is preceded by **nicht**:

Rosemarie geht diesmal leider nicht mit.

Mit is often used with, and always precedes, directives:

Sie geht wieder mit nach Deutschland.

Mit alone can never occupy the front field:

IMPOSSIBLE: [**Mit geht sie diesmal nicht.**]

If used with an infinitive, **mit** and the infinitive are written as one word.

Sie möchte wieder mitgehen.

If the sentence contains a prepositional phrase with **mit**, the verbal complement **mit** is not used.

Ich gehe mit ihr nach Deutschland.

92 Word Formation

The native speaker of any language not only has an active and a passive vocabulary at his disposal, but also knows how to construct new words from known stems. Thus, by adding the suffix *-ing* to the stem of "love," English derives the form "loving"; by adding the suffix *-er*, English forms the agent noun "lover," and by adding the prefix *be-* plus the suffix *-ed*, the adjective "beloved" is formed. The suffix *-er* can not only be added to the stem *lov-*; it also appears in "worker," "reader," "listener," "drinker," "driver," and many other agent nouns. The suffix *-er* is a very important part of our active vocabulary. We know how to use it, we know its semantic function, and anyone who doesn't know how to use the suffix *-er* cannot use English properly.

In German, even more frequently than in English, prefixes and suffixes are used to form derivatives. It is therefore important to learn when and how to apply the German prefixes and suffixes. From now on we shall present in most lessons a section on word formation.

93   The Suffixes -chen and -lein

These suffixes are added to nouns to form diminutive nouns, all of which
are neuter. Thus the nouns **Vater, Mutter, Bruder, Haus, Stadt,** and **Mann**
are the base for the diminutives

Väterchen	Väterlein
Mütterchen	Mütterlein
Brüderchen	Brüderlein
Häuschen	Häuslein
Städtchen	Städtlein
Männchen	Männlein

Diminutives umlaut the stem vowel and remain unchanged in the plural.
The suffix -**chen** is standard, -**lein** is rather poetic.

If added to nouns referring to persons, diminutives express either smallness or affection; if added to nouns designating things they express either
smallness or polite "belittling":

ein Täßchen Kaffee	ein Städtchen
ein Gläschen Wein	ein Häuschen

NOTE: The noun **Fräulein** now means *Miss;* the nouns **Männchen** and
Weibchen are zoological terms meaning the male and the female (of the
species).

94   The Suffix -er

The German suffix -**er** corresponds to the English suffixes -*er* and -*or*. It is
added to verb stems to form agent nouns, which denote the person or
instrument that performs the action implied.

denken	der Denker	the thinker
lesen	der Leser	the reader
zeigen	der Zeiger	the hand (of a clock)

In some cases, the agent noun shows a vowel change from **a** to **ä**.

schlafen	der Schläfer	the sleeper (sleeping person).

If agent nouns refer to human beings, the suffix -**in** is added to the suffix
-**er** to form feminine agent nouns.

lesen	der Leser, -	die Leserin, -nen

NOTE: The suffix -**in** may also be added to other nouns:

der Student, -en	die Studentin, -nen
der Freund, -e	die Freundin, -nen

95 Infinitives as Neuter Nouns

German infinitives can be used as neuter nouns.

Das Leben ist schön.	Life is beautiful.
mit einem **Lachen**	with a laugh

These neuter nouns denote the activity expressed by the verb. **Beim** (**bei dem**), followed by such a verbal noun, always means "in the process (or act) of" or "while."

beim **Fahren**	in the act of driving
beim **Essen**	while eating
beim **Trinken**	while drinking

96 Compound Nouns

Both in English and in German two nouns can be combined to form a compound noun. For example, *house* and *dog* can form two combinations—*house dog* and *doghouse*, a house dog being a kind of dog and a doghouse being a kind of house. The second part of the compound is always the basic form, which is modified by the first part. For this reason, German compounds derive their gender from the second part. Thus:

das **Haus**	der **Hund**	der **Haushund**
der **Hund**	das **Haus**	das **Hundehaus.**

Other examples found in Unit 5 include:

der **Krieg**	der **Roman**	der **Kriegsroman**
der **Brief**	die **Taube**	die **Brieftaube**
der **Brief**	der **Träger**	der **Briefträger**
der **Westen**	die **Front**	die **Westfront**
das **Militär**	der **Arzt**	der **Militärarzt**
der **Rhein**	der **Wein**	der **Rheinwein**

NOTE: In many such compounds, a letter is inserted between the two parts—for example, **Kriegsroman, Damenhut, Liebesbrief.** While there are some historical grammatical explanations for these formations, there are no general rules. It is best, therefore, to memorize these compounds as they occur.

A. Read the following problems:

$2 + 4 = 6$	$1 + 14 = 15$	$19 - 12 = 7$
$12 + 4 = 16$	$9 + 11 = 20$	$16 - 10 = 6$
$7 + 3 = 10$	$18 + 1 = 19$	$8 - 5 = 3$
$7 + 10 = 17$	$16 + 2 = 18$	$20 - 3 = 17$
$5 + 8 = 13$	$17 + 2 = 19$	$11 - 11 = 0$

B. The following is an excerpt from a railroad timetable. Form questions and statements using the information given.

Wann fährt der Zug nach München in Köln ab?—Um 2 Uhr.
Der Zug kommt um 8 Uhr 16 in Ulm an.
Wie lange ist der Zug in Frankfurt?—12 Minuten.

Köln	ab	2.00		München	ab	1.20
Bonn	an	2.18		Ulm	an	4.04
	ab	2.20			ab	4.05
Frankfurt	an	4.15		Stuttgart	an	5.08
	ab	4.20			ab	5.14
Heidelberg	an	5.12		Heidelberg	an	8.02
	ab	5.17			ab	8.06
Stuttgart	an	7.01		Frankfurt	an	9.08
	ab	7.06			ab	9.20
Ulm	an	8.16		Bonn	an	11.17
	ab	8.17			ab	11.20
München	an	10.03		Köln	an	12.00

C. This exercise is meant as a quick drill of the present, past, and perfect forms of weak verbs. Transform according to the following pattern:

antworten   —   er antwortet, er antwortete, er hat geantwortet

arbeiten	—	ich	heiraten	—	wir
brauchen	—	wir	hoffen	—	ich
danken	—	er	kochen	—	sie
fragen	—	sie	lachen	—	er
gehören	—	es	leben	—	wir
glauben	—	du	lernen	—	wir
hassen	—	er	lieben	—	ich

D. Restate the following sentences in the past tense. In each sentence, add **damals,** as in the following example:

> **Erika studiert in München.—Erika studierte damals in München.**

1. Hans hat nie Hunger.
2. Er besucht seinen Vater in Berlin.
3. Wir kaufen ein Haus in München.
4. Dieses Haus gehört meinem Vater.
5. Er antwortet mir nicht.
6. Ist deine Mutter nicht in Berlin?
7. Wir können leider nicht kommen.
8. Ich will ihm die Stadt zeigen.
9. Er soll zu Hause bleiben.
10. Ich darf es ihm nicht sagen.
11. Wir müssen leider nach Hause fahren.
12. Er braucht nicht zu arbeiten.

E. Form the present, past, and perfect. All verbs in this exercise are irregular.

> **bleiben   —   wir bleiben, wir blieben, wir sind geblieben**

anfangen	—	ich	scheinen	—	es
anrufen	—	er	schlafen	—	er
bringen	—	er	schreiben	—	ich
essen	—	er	sehen	—	er
fahren	—	du	sein	—	ihr
geben	—	er	sitzen	—	wir
gehen	—	wir	sprechen	—	ich
helfen	—	er	sterben	—	er
heißen	—	sie	trinken	—	wir
kennen	—	ich	tun	—	ich
kommen	—	wir	verstehen	—	er
lassen	—	er	werden	—	er
lesen	—	er	wissen	—	du

F. Restate the following sentences in the past tense:

1. Inge geht zum Bahnhof.
2. Er versteht Professor Hansen sehr gut.
3. Hans hört mich nicht.
4. Erika hilft mir bei der Arbeit.
5. Ingelheim antwortet nicht.
6. Herr Bergmann kommt um 9 Uhr aus dem Kino.

7. Herr Lenz fährt mit seinem Freund durch die Stadt.
8. Ich sehe meine Mutter in Berlin.
9. Er trinkt keinen Wein.
10. Ich hole ihn in Köln ab.
11. Er bekommt jeden Tag einen Brief von seiner Freundin.
12. Hans lädt mich oft zum Essen ein.
13. Er denkt lange nach.
14. So etwas passiert nicht oft.
15. Hans und Inge stehen vor dem Theater.

G. Transform the ten sentences of this exercise according to the following pattern:

> **Er wohnt in Berlin.**
> **a. Ich glaube, er wohnt in Berlin.**
> **b. Ich glaube nicht, daß er in Berlin wohnt.**
> **c. Ich möchte wissen, ob er in Berlin wohnt.**

1. Hans studiert Mathematik.
2. Der Wagen gehört Frau Lenz.
3. Sie kann sie sehen.
4. Er will mir die Stadt zeigen.
5. Frau Lenz geht mit Frau Hoffmann ins Kino.
6. Er muß heute nach Hamburg.
7. Hans will ohne Inge ins Theater gehen.
8. Herr Meyer hat zu viel Wein getrunken.
9. Sie sind gestern in Berlin gewesen.
10. Er hat in Berlin einen Freund besucht.

H. Ask correct questions for the following answers. Your questions should ask for the italicized parts of the answers.

> **Er geht *heute abend* ins Kino.**
> **Wann geht er ins Kino?**

Then restate the question, starting with **Ich möchte wissen:**

> **Ich möchte wissen, wann er ins Kino geht.**

1. Ihr Mann ist *gestern* nach Köln gefahren.
2. Erika war gestern *in Berlin*.
3. Es (das Buch) gehört *meinem Vater*.
4. Er hat ihr *ein Buch* geschenkt.
5. Er heißt *Fritz*.

6. *Mein Vater* hat das gesagt.
7. Er geht *mit Inge* ins Kino.

I. Join the following pairs of sentences to form open conditions. The first sentence should always become the **wenn**-clause.

> **Es regnet morgen. Wir gehen ins Kino.**
> **Wenn es morgen regnet, gehen wir ins Kino.**

1. Du hast Geld. Du kannst ein Haus kaufen.
2. Du hast kein Geld. Du kannst das Haus nicht kaufen.
3. Er studiert Mathematik. Er muß intelligent sein.
4. Nancy ist intelligent. Sie lernt Deutsch.
5. Morgen regnet es nicht. Wir besuchen euch.
6. Ihr wollt ins Kino gehen. Wir gehen mit.
7. Herr Meyer wohnt in Berlin. Ich kann ihn besuchen.
8. Er ist dein Freund. Er hilft dir bestimmt.
9. Du liebst mich. Du fährst nicht nach Casablanca.
10. Man hat kein Geld. Man kann nicht an die Riviera fahren.

J. Of the following pairs of sentences, change the second to an infinitive with **um . . . zu.**

> **Inge fuhr nach Frankfurt. Sie wollte ins Theater gehen.**
> **Inge fuhr nach Frankfurt, um ins Theater zu gehen.**

1. Ingelheim fuhr nach Afrika. Er wollte einen Roman schreiben.
2. Er kam nach Frankfurt. Er wollte seinen Vater besuchen.
3. Seine Tochter ging nach Mainz. Sie wollte Archäologie studieren.
4. John fuhr nach Deutschland. Er wollte Deutsch lernen.
5. Hans ging zum Telefon. Er wollte Inge anrufen.

K. Express in German. Where appropriate, defend your choice of the German past or perfect.

1. Are you taking her along?
2. Hans went along to Cologne.
3. Does he want to go along to Berlin, too?
4. At that time the house belonged to my father.
5. I simply couldn't believe it.
6. I'd like to know why you couldn't believe it.
7. If you want to, you may go.
8. I don't know where he was.
9. I don't know whether he was in Berlin.
10. At that time I didn't know that he was in Berlin, too.

11. It is ten after eleven, and I must go home.
12. At that time he was visiting his friend in Berlin.
13. Today he visited his friend.
14. They went to Berlin today.
15. I bought the book yesterday, but I haven't read it yet.
16. Unfortunately, I didn't understand him.
17. He never needed much money.
18. Why didn't you stay home yesterday, Karl?
19. The train left at 8:11.
20. I didn't understand why she didn't want to come.
21. How am I supposed to know whether he went to Casablanca?
22. We would like to know why she does not drink wine.
23. I hope I'll never see him again.
24. Do you believe that Karl is very intelligent?
25. *That* he is intelligent I know.
26. But that he is *very* intelligent, I cannot believe.
27. Whether Meyer really went to Casablanca (that) I cannot tell you. (*Use* **sagen.**)
28. Why he wanted to go to the movies with Inge, I don't know.
29. I cannot believe that you only do what you want to do.
30. If you are home tomorrow, I would like to visit you.
31. I'd like to visit Ingrid, but I don't know whether she is at home.
32. If you want (me to), I'll come along to the movies.
33. Before the war he was a writer.
34. Then he became a soldier.
35. I married him because I loved him.
36. I didn't meet him at that time, for he was in Norway.
37. I know he is here, but I haven't seen him yet.
38. She has never been afraid yet.
39. Not until three weeks later did he tell us his story.
40. He had not visited us for years when I accidentally saw him in Berlin.
41. I have known her for a long time, but I don't know who she is.
42. When he met her in Berlin she was still a child.
43. He only wants to go if I go too.
44. He didn't want to tell us where he wanted to go.
45. I'd like to know when he'll come home.
46. I've just read in the paper that her friend has been in Africa for three months.
47. You don't need to tell me how often he goes to the theater.
48. If I see him, I'll tell him that you were here and that you wanted to speak with him.
49. I wanted to visit him (in order) to thank him, but unfortunately he wasn't home.
50. I can't visit you tomorrow, because tomorrow I have to be in Munich.

BASIC VOCABULARY

achtzehn eighteen
als when; than; as
  als er kam when he came
    (single event in the past)
  mehr als more than
  ich als dein Vater I as your
    father
der Amerika′ner, – American
die Angst, ⁻e fear, anxiety
  Angst haben vor to be
    afraid of
ankommen to arrive
die Arbeit, –en work
das Auge, –n eye
das Beispiel, –e example
  zum Beispiel for example
bekommen to get, to receive
daß that (*conjunction*)
diesmal this time
dort there
dreizehn thirteen
einfach easy, simple
einladen to invite
elf eleven
das Ende, –n end
erwarten to expect
erzählen to tell, to relate
der Fehler, – mistake
finden to find
das Fräulein, – Miss, young
  lady
das Frühstück, –e breakfast
  frühstücken to eat break-
    fast

fünfzehn fifteen
fürchten to fear
der Garten, ⁻ garden
gerade just; straight
gratulieren to congratulate
halb half
hinter behind
klein little
der Kopf, ⁻e head
  die Kopfschmerzen (*pl.*)
    headache
das Lachen laughter
laufen to run
das Leben, – life
das Mädchen, – girl
nachdenken to reflect, to
  meditate
nehmen to take; to seize
  gefangennehmen to cap-
    ture, to take prisoner
neu new
  das ist mir neu that's news
    to me
neunzehn nineteen
null zero
ob whether
passie′ren (*aux.:* **sein**) to
  happen
plus plus
recht haben to be right
die Reise, –n trip
  eine Reise machen to take
    a trip

schön beautiful, pretty; good,
  OK
der Schüler, – pupil, student
  (in a secondary school)
sechzehn sixteen
siebzehn seventeen
der Soldat′, –en soldier (*declined like* **der Mensch**)
die Sonne, –n sun
die Spur, –en trace
  spurlos without a trace
stehen to stand
die Straße, –n street
suchen to look for, to seek, to
  search
tragen to carry
über over
überall everywhere
um . . . zu in order to
vernünftig reasonable
verschwinden to disappear
  verschwunden (*adj.*) lost
vielleicht′ perhaps
vierzehn fourteen
weil (*conj.*) because
die Welt, –en world
weniger minus, less
Auf Wiederhören! Good-by!
  (telephone)
Auf Wiedersehen! Good-by!
  (in person)
wohl well; probably
zwölf twelve

ADDITIONAL VOCABULARY

das Abitur′ final comprehensive examination in the
  secondary school
das Bett, –en bed
die Brieftaube, –n carrier
  pigeon
durchmachen to go through,
  to suffer
der Fisch, –e fish

fischen to fish
füttern to feed
gefährlich dangerous
das Kapi′tel, – chapter
die Maschi′ne, –n machine,
  typewriter
die Mathematik′ mathematics
Norwegen Norway

der Roman′, –e novel
das Schiff, –e ship, boat
schilaufen to ski
der Schriftsteller, – writer
der Westen the West
  die Westfront the Western
    Front
zufällig by coincidence, by
  chance, accidentally

LIST OF STRONG AND IRREGULAR VERBS

abfahren to depart, to leave
fuhr ab, ist abgefahren, er fährt ab

anfangen to begin, to start
fing an, hat angefangen, er fängt an

angehen to go on
ging an, ist angegangen, er geht an

ankommen to arrive
kam an, ist angekommen, er kommt an

anrufen to call up (on the telephone)
rief an, hat angerufen, er ruft an

ausgehen to go out
ging aus, ist ausgegangen, er geht aus

befehlen to order, to command
befahl, hat befohlen, er befiehlt

beginnen to begin, to start
begann, hat begonnen, er beginnt

bekommen to get, to receive
bekam, hat bekommen, er bekommt

bleiben to stay, to remain
blieb, ist geblieben, er bleibt

bringen to bring
brachte, hat gebracht, er bringt

denken to think
dachte, hat gedacht, er denkt

einladen to invite
lud ein, hat eingeladen, er lädt ein

essen to eat
aß, hat gegessen, er ißt

fahren to drive, to go (by train, boat, plane, car)
fuhr, ist gefahren, er fährt

finden to find
fand, hat gefunden, er findet

geben to give
gab, hat gegeben, er gibt

gefangennehmen to capture, to take prisoner
nahm gefangen, hat gefangengenommen, er nimmt gefangen

gehen to go, to walk
ging, ist gegangen, er geht

haben to have
hatte, hat gehabt, er hat

heißen to be called; to mean
hieß, hat geheißen, er heißt

helfen to help
half, hat geholfen, er hilft

kennen to know, to be acquainted with
kannte, hat gekannt, er kennt

kommen to come
kam, ist gekommen, er kommt

lassen to let, to leave
ließ, hat gelassen, er läßt

laufen to run
lief, ist gelaufen, er läuft

lesen to read
las, hat gelesen, er liest

lügen to tell a lie
log, hat gelogen, er lügt

nachdenken to reflect, to meditate
dachte nach, hat nachgedacht, er denkt nach

nehmen to take, to seize
nahm, hat genommen, er nimmt

scheinen to seem; to shine
schien, hat geschienen, er scheint

schilaufen to ski
lief Schi, ist schigelaufen, er läuft Schi

schlafen to sleep
schlief, hat geschlafen, er schläft

schreiben to write
schrieb, hat geschrieben, er schreibt

sehen to see
sah, hat gesehen, er sieht

sein to be
war, ist gewesen, er ist

sitzen to sit
saß, hat gesessen, er sitzt

sprechen to speak, to talk
sprach, hat gesprochen, er spricht

stehen to stand
stand, hat gestanden, er steht

sterben to die
starb, ist gestorben, er stirbt

tragen to carry
trug, hat getragen, er trägt

trinken to drink
trank, hat getrunken, er trinkt

tun to do
tat, hat getan, er tut

verschwinden to disappear
verschwand, ist verschwunden, er verschwindet

verstehen to understand
verstand, hat verstanden, er versteht

werden to become
wurde, ist geworden, er wird

wiedersehen to see again
sah wieder, hat wiedergesehen, er sieht wieder

wissen to know
wußte, hat gewußt, er weiß

zwingen to force
zwang, hat gezwungen, er zwingt

UNIT 6: The Future Tense—The Subjunctive

[1] The Future Tense

Ich glaube, ich werde sie nie wiedersehen.	I believe I will never see them (her) again.	SEE ANALYSIS 97
Diesen Sonntag werde ich nie vergessen.	I shall never forget this Sunday.	
Diesen Sonntag werde ich leider nie vergessen können.	Unfortunately, I shall never be able to forget this Sunday.	(pp. 168-169)
Nein, Herr Behrens, ich werde es nicht vergessen. Ich werde Sie morgen um 9 Uhr 10 anrufen.	No, Mr. Behrens, I shall not forget it. I'll give you a ring at 9:10 tomorrow.	
Inge ist schon vor einer Stunde abgefahren, also wird sie jetzt schon lange zu Hause sein.	Inge left an hour ago, so she has probably been home for a long time now.	
Ich möchte wissen, warum Hans mich immer noch nicht angerufen hat; ob er mir böse ist?—Warum soll er dir böse sein? Er wird (wohl) noch schlafen.	I'd like to know why Hans hasn't called me up yet. I wonder whether he's mad at me.—Why should he be mad at you? He's probably still asleep.	
Den Emil habe ich schon wochenlang nicht gesehen. Wo kann der denn nur sein?—Er wird wieder in Bonn arbeiten müssen.	I haven't seen Emil in weeks. Where could he be?—He probably has to work in Bonn again.	

[2] The Subjunctive—Wishes with **Ich wollte** or **Ich wünschte** (Present Time)

Be prepared to produce orally the subjunctive statement when you hear the indicative statement, and vice versa.

Ich wollte, wir wären in Italien, aber wir sind nicht in Italien.	I wish we were in Italy, but we are not in Italy.	SEE ANALYSIS 98–102
Ich wünschte, sie hätte Geld, aber sie hat kein Geld.	I wish she had money, but she doesn't have any money.	(pp. 169-177)

(Facing) **Kleiner Mann bei großem Einkauf**

Ich wollte, mein Vater kaufte mir ein Auto (würde mir ein Auto kaufen), aber er kauft mir kein Auto (wird mir kein Auto kaufen).

I wish my father would buy me a car, but he won't buy me a car.

Ich wünschte, wir brauchten nicht nach Köln zu fahren, aber wir müssen.

I wish we didn't have to go to Cologne, but we have to.

Ich wollte, er bliebe noch eine Woche hier (würde noch eine Woche hierbleiben), aber er bleibt nicht hier.

I wish he'd stay here for another week, but he isn't going to.

Ich wünschte, er brächte Monika mit (würde Monika mitbringen), aber er bringt sie nicht mit.

I wish he'd bring Monika along, but he won't.

Ich wünschte, wir könnten jedes Jahr nach Italien fahren; Meyers können jedes Jahr fahren.

I wish we could go to Italy every year; the Meyers can go every year.

[3] Wishes with **Ich wollte** or **Ich wünschte** (Past Time)

Be prepared to produce orally the subjunctive statement when you hear the indicative statement, and vice versa.

SEE
ANALYSIS
102
(p. 177)

Ich wünschte, ich hätte nicht soviel gegessen; aber ich habe leider zuviel gegessen.

I wish I hadn't eaten so much. However, I have eaten too much.

Ich wollte, du hättest mir mehr Geld geschickt, aber du hast mir nur zehn Mark geschickt.

I wish you had sent me more money, but you sent me only ten marks.

Ich wünschte, ich hätte sie nie kennengelernt, aber leider habe ich sie kennengelernt.

I wish I had never met her, but unfortunately I did.

Ich wollte, er wäre zu Hause geblieben, aber leider ist er nicht zu Hause geblieben.

I wish he'd stayed home, but unfortunately he didn't.

Ich wünschte, ich hätte *auch* einen Monat in Casablanca bleiben können, aber ich konnte nicht.

I wish I, too, had been able to stay in Casablanca for a month, but I couldn't.

Ich wollte, ich hätte letzten Sommer nicht nach Casablanca zu fahren brauchen, aber ich mußte.

I wish I hadn't had to go to Casablanca last summer, but I had to.

[4] Wishes Introduced by **Es wäre nett, wenn . . .**

After studying these sentences, complete the variations at the end of the section.

Ich hoffe, wir finden sofort eine Wohnung. Es wäre nett, wenn wir sofort eine Wohnung fänden (finden würden).

I hope we'll find an apartment right away. It would be nice if we found a place to live immediately.

SEE ANALYSIS 102 (p. 177)

Ich hoffe, du fliegst. Dann bist du in zwei Stunden in Hamburg, nicht wahr? Es wäre nett, wenn du fliegen würdest (flögst). Dann wärst du in zwei Stunden in Hamburg, nicht?

I hope you'll take a plane. Then you'll be in Hamburg in two hours, won't you? It would be nice if you went by plane. Then you would be in Hamburg in two hours, wouldn't you?

Letztes Jahr hast du meinen Geburtstag vergessen. Es wäre nett, wenn du ihn dieses Jahr einmal nicht vergäßest (vergessen würdest).

Last year you forgot my birthday. It would be nice if this year you would not forget it for a change.

VARIATIONS

Ich hoffe, du kommst morgen. Es wäre nett, wenn _____.

Ich hoffe, du kannst morgen kommen. _____.

Ich hoffe, du besuchst uns bald. _____.

Ich hoffe, er braucht morgen nicht zu arbeiten. _____.

Ich hoffe, du bringst mir etwas mit. _____.

Invent further variations of your own.

[5] Irreal Conditions

SEE ANALYSIS 98, 103 (pp. 169-170, 177-179)

Sie schreibt mir nicht. Ich schreibe ihr auch nicht.

Wenn sie mir schriebe, schriebe ich ihr auch.

Wenn sie mir schriebe, würde ich ihr auch schreiben.

If she wrote to me, I'd write to her, too.

Sie hat mir nicht geschrieben. Ich habe ihr auch nicht geschrieben.

Wenn sie mir geschrieben hätte, hätte ich ihr auch geschrieben.

If she had written to me, I would have written to her, too.

Das Essen ist schlecht. Ich bleibe nicht hier.

Wenn das Essen nicht so schlecht wäre, bliebe ich hier.

Wenn das Essen nicht so schlecht wäre, würde ich hierbleiben.

If the food weren't so bad, I would stay here.

Das Essen war schlecht. Ich bin nicht dageblieben.

    Wenn das Essen nicht so schlecht gewesen wäre, wäre ich dageblieben.

    If the food hadn't been so bad, I would have stayed.

Es regnet. Wir können nicht arbeiten.

    Wenn es nicht regnete, könnten wir arbeiten.

    If it weren't raining, we could work.

Gestern hat es geregnet, und wir konnten nicht arbeiten.

    Wenn es gestern nicht geregnet hätte, hätten wir arbeiten können.

    If it hadn't rained yesterday, we could have worked.

[6] Irreal Conditions in Context

SEE
ANALYSIS
103
(pp. 177-179)

Inges Vater hat Geld. Sie kann jede Woche ins Theater gehen, und ich muß zu Hause bleiben. Wenn mein Vater mehr Geld hätte, könnte ich auch jede Woche ins Theater gehen und brauchte nicht zu Hause zu bleiben.—Inges Vater hatte Geld. Inge konnte jede Woche ins Theater gehen, und ich mußte zu Hause bleiben. Wenn mein Vater mehr Geld gehabt hätte, hätte ich auch jede Woche ins Theater gehen können und hätte nicht zu Hause zu bleiben brauchen.

Inge's father has money. She can go to the theater every week, and I have to stay at home. If my father had more money, I, too, could go to the theater every week and would not have to stay at home.—Inge's father had a lot of money. Inge could go to the theater every week, and I had to stay at home. If my father had had more money, I, too, could have gone to the theater every week and would not have had to stay at home.

[7] hätte in Dependent Clauses with Double Infinitive

SEE
ANALYSIS
103, 108
(pp. 177-179,
184-185)

Wenn Inge nicht hätte nach München fahren müssen, hätte Meyer sie nie kennengelernt.*

If Inge hadn't had to go to Munich, Meyer would never have met her.

Wenn du nicht hättest kommen können, wäre ich sehr unglücklich gewesen.

If you had not been able to come, I would have been very unhappy.

Wenn er gestern abend nicht hätte zu Hause bleiben müssen, hätte er mit uns ins Kino gehen können.

If he had not had to stay home last night, he could have gone to a show with us.

VARIATIONS

    Hans konnte nicht kommen. Es wäre nett gewesen, wenn ⎯⎯⎯⎯⎯⎯⎯⎯⎯⎯.

    Erika durfte nicht mitgehen. Es wäre nett gewesen, wenn ⎯⎯⎯⎯⎯⎯⎯⎯⎯.

    Fritz mußte zu Hause bleiben. Es wäre nett gewesen, wenn ⎯⎯⎯⎯⎯⎯⎯⎯.

    Sie hat nie zu kochen brauchen. Es wäre nett gewesen, wenn sie auch einmal ⎯⎯⎯.

⎯⎯⎯⎯⎯⎯

* In irreal **wenn**-clauses, **nicht müssen** is used rather than **nicht brauchen zu**.

[8] Irreal *If*-Clauses to Express Desires

Be prepared to formulate subjective statements when you hear indicative statements, and vice versa.

> **Ich kann nicht gut schlafen.**
> **Wenn ich nur gut schlafen könnte!**

Wenn ich doch nur einmal gut schlafen könnte! Aber ich kann einfach nicht mehr so schlafen wie früher.

If only I could sleep well for once! But I simply can't sleep the way I used to.

SEE ANALYSIS 104 (pp. 179-180)

Wenn Meyers doch nur endlich nach Hause gehen wollten! Aber sie gehen nicht nach Hause. Sie bleiben hier.

If the Meyers would only go home! But they won't. They are staying here.

Wenn doch nur endlich wieder einmal die Sonne schiene! Aber es regnet, und die Sonne scheint nicht.

If only the sun would shine again! But it is raining, and the sun isn't shining.

[9] Irreal Conclusions without *If*-Clauses (Wishes)

After studying these sentences, express the variations at the end of this section in German.

Meyers fahren jedes Jahr nach Italien. Ich führe *auch* gerne einmal mit dir nach Italien (würde *auch* gerne einmal mit dir nach Italien fahren).

The Meyers go to Italy every year. Some day I'd like to go to Italy with you, *too.*

SEE ANALYSIS 105 (pp. 180-181)

Meine Freunde haben alle einen Wagen. Ich hätte *auch* gerne einen Wagen.

My friends all have a car. I'd like to have a car, *too.*

Ich weiß, Meyers wohnen jetzt in München. Natürlich wohnten wir *auch* lieber in München (würden wir *auch* lieber in München wohnen).

I know Meyers live in Munich now. Of course, we, too, would rather live in Munich.

Was willst *du* denn werden, Fritz?—Am liebsten würde ich Arzt (werden). Mein Bruder wird *auch* Arzt.

What are you going to be, Fritz?—I'd like very much to become a doctor. My brother is also going to be (become) a doctor.

Meyers sind heute morgen nach Italien gefahren. Ich wäre auch gerne mit dir nach Italien gefahren.

The Meyers went to Italy this morning. I would have liked to go to Italy with you, too.

Wir wohnten damals in Augsburg. Natürlich hätten wir lieber in München gewohnt.

At that time we lived in Augsburg. Of course, we would have preferred to live in Munich.

VARIATIONS

I'd like to go to Italy next summer.
I'd like to have a car.
I'd like to live in Munich.
I'd rather live in Berlin.
I'd like best of all to live in Cologne.
I would have liked to go to the theater.
I would rather have read the newspaper.

[10] Irreal Conclusions without *If*-Clauses (Polite Requests)

Invent variations of your own.

SEE
ANALYSIS
105
(pp. 180-181)

Könnte (Kann) ich noch eine Tasse Kaffee haben?

Could I have another cup of coffee?

Guten Abend! Hätten (Haben) Sie vielleicht noch ein Zimmer frei?

Good evening! Do you by any chance still have a room available?

Könnten (können) Sie mir vielleicht sagen, ob die Maschine aus Hamburg schon angekommen ist?

Could you perhaps tell me whether the flight from Hamburg has arrived yet?

Dürfte ich Sie bitten, mir den Wein ins Haus zu schicken?

Could I ask you to deliver the wine to my house?

,,Ich weiß, Meyers wohnen jetzt in München. Wir wohnten natürlich auch lieber in München.''

**Warum jeder,
der im
Wirtschaftsleben
steht, eine
American Express Karte
haben sollte**

Guten Morgen! Könnten Sie mir bitte Zimmer 6 geben? Danke schön!	Good morning! Would you connect me with Room 6, please? Thank you.
Könnten (Würden) Sie mich morgen um zehn anrufen?	Could you call me up at ten tomorrow?
Ich hätte gerne einen Kriminalroman.	I would like to have a detective story.
Haben Sie noch ein Zimmer frei? Ich hätte gern ein Zimmer mit Bad.	Do you still have a room available? I would like to have a room with bath.

[11] Indirect Discourse: Present and Future Time

Be prepared to change orally all statements in direct discourse to indirect discourse, and vice versa.

SEE
ANALYSIS
106
(pp. 181-183)

Hans sagte: „Mein Vater bleibt noch in Berlin."
    Hans sagte, sein Vater bliebe noch in Berlin.
    Hans sagte, sein Vater würde noch in Berlin bleiben.

Frau Lenz sagte: „Erika wohnt nicht mehr in Köln."
    Frau Lenz sagte, du wohntest nicht mehr in Köln.
    Frau Lenz glaubte, du würdest wohl nicht mehr in Köln wohnen.

Er sagte: „Mein Freund will morgen abend doch nicht mitgehen."
    Er sagte, sein Freund wollte morgen abend doch nicht mitgehen.
    Er meinte, sein Freund würde morgen abend doch nicht mitgehen wollen.

Inge sagte: „Erika fährt morgen nach Frankfurt."
    Inge sagte, Erika führe morgen nach Frankfurt.
    Inge sagte, Erika würde morgen nach Frankfurt fahren.
    Inge sagte, daß Erika morgen nach Frankfurt führe.
    Inge sagte, daß Erika morgen nach Frankfurt fahren würde.

Er sagte, seine Frau lernte jetzt fahren.
Er sagte, er studierte Medizin.

Er sagte, er wollte seinen Vater besuchen.

Er sagte, er müßte morgen arbeiten.
Er sagte, er brauchte nicht nach Köln zu fahren.

Er sagte, der Film wäre sehr gut.

Er sagte, das wäre ihm recht.

Er sagte, ich hätte sein Buch.
Er sagte, Erika hätte heute keine Zeit.

Er sagte, er ginge mit Inge ins Kino.
Er sagte, sie kämen heute sehr spät nach Hause.

Er sagte, er würde mich nie wieder küssen.

[12] Indirect Questions: Present and Future Time

Be prepared to transform orally all direct questions into indirect questions, and
vice versa.

SEE
ANALYSIS
106

(pp. 181-183)

Er fragte: „Ist dein Vater heute abend zu Hause?"
Er fragte, ob mein Vater heute abend zu Hause wäre.

Er fragte: „Wohin geht ihr heute abend zum Essen?"
Er fragte, wohin wir heute abend zum Essen gingen.

Er fragte: „Wo studiert Fritz denn jetzt?"
Er wollte wissen, wo Fritz denn jetzt studierte.

Er fragte, ob ich krank wäre.
Er fragte, ob ich kein Geld hätte.

Er fragte, ob wir das Haus in Köln kaufen wollten.
Er fragte, ob er mich zum Bahnhof bringen dürfte.

Er fragte mich, warum ich denn nicht mit nach Köln führe.
Er fragte Fritz, wann sein Vater nach Hause käme.
Er fragte sie, wie sie hieße.

Er wollte wissen, ob Maria zu Hause wäre.
Er wollte wissen, warum Hans nicht mitgehen könnte.
Er wollte wissen, ob ich Angst hätte.

[13] Indirect Discourse: Past Time

Be prepared to transform direct statements into indirect statements, and vice
versa.

SEE
ANALYSIS
106

(pp. 181-183)

Er sagte: „Ich arbeitete damals in Hamburg."
Er sagte, daß er damals in Hamburg gearbeitet hätte.

Er sagte: „Ich habe damals in Hamburg gearbeitet."
Er sagte, daß er damals in Hamburg gearbeitet hätte.

Er sagte: „Ich hatte gerade eine Woche in Hamburg gearbeitet."
Er sagte, daß er gerade eine Woche in Hamburg gearbeitet hätte.

Er sagte, außer Ernst und seiner Frau wäre niemand da gewesen.
Er sagte, kein Mensch hätte ihm geglaubt.
Er sagte, er hätte ihm sein Büro gezeigt.

Er sagte, sie hätte das Buch meiner Mutter geschickt.
Er sagte, seine Frau hätte ihm das Buch geschenkt.

Frau Schmidt sagte, ihr Mann hätte nach Afrika fahren wollen.
Frau Schmidt sagte, sie hätten erst nach dem Kriege heiraten können.
Frau Schmidt sagte, Johannes hätte nach Kairo fahren müssen.

[14] Indirect Questions: Past Time

Be prepared to transform direct questions into indirect questions, and vice versa.

Er fragte: „Warum sind Sie denn gestern nicht nach Köln gefahren?"
Er fragte, warum ich denn gestern nicht nach Köln gefahren wäre.

Er fragte: „Mit wem warst du denn gestern abend im Theater?"
Er wollte wissen, mit wem ich gestern abend im Theater gewesen wäre.

Er wollte wissen, wieviel die Zigarren gekostet hätten.
Er wollte wissen, wie lange ich für die Lufthansa gearbeitet hätte.

SEE
ANALYSIS
106

(pp. 181-183)

[15] Position of **hätte** with Double Infinitive in Indirect Discourse

Be prepared to produce orally the other two sentences of each group when you hear one.

Er sagte: „Ich wollte gestern eigentlich hierbleiben."
Er sagte, er hätte gestern eigentlich hierbleiben wollen.
Er sagte, daß er gestern eigentlich hätte hierbleiben wollen.

Er sagte: „Leider mußte ich gestern abend zu Hause bleiben."
Er sagte, er hätte leider gestern abend zu Hause bleiben müssen.
Er sagte, daß er leider gestern abend hätte zu Hause bleiben müssen.

Er sagte: „Kurz vor dem Kriege mußte ich Soldat werden."
Er sagte, kurz vor dem Krieg hätte er Soldat werden müssen.
Er sagte, daß er kurz vor dem Krieg hätte Soldat werden müssen.

SEE
ANALYSIS
108

(pp. 184-185)

I

ERIKA: Du Hans, Tante Amalie hat angerufen.

HANS: Was wollte sie denn?

ERIKA: Sie wollte wissen, ob du heute nachmittag mit ihr ins Museum gehen könntest.

HANS: Du hast ihr doch hoffentlich gesagt, ich wäre heute nicht zu Hause.

ERIKA: Nein, ich dachte, du würdest gerne mit ihr gehen.

HANS: Das hättest du nicht tun sollen.

ERIKA: Ja, wenn ich gewusst hätte, daß du nicht willst, dann hätte ich ihr natürlich gesagt, du könntest heute nicht. Aber ich dachte, . . .

HANS: Du solltest nicht immer so viel denken.

II

TANTE AMALIE: Das war wirklich nett von dir, daß du mit mir ins Museum gegangen bist. Und jetzt würde ich gerne noch eine Tasse Kaffee trinken.

HANS: Das ist mir recht. Wo möchtest du denn hin?

TANTE AMALIE: Ich ginge gerne mal ins Café Schneider; da war ich schon lange nicht mehr.

HANS: Gut, und dann könnten wir Erika anrufen. Sie käme sicher auch gerne.

TANTE AMALIE: Ja, und wie wäre es, wenn ihr dann zum Abendessen zu mir kommen würdet?

HANS: Das wäre sehr nett, Tante Amalie, aber ich kann leider nicht; ich habe zu viel zu tun.

TANTE AMALIE: Wenn du nur nicht immer so viel arbeiten müßtest!

HANS: Ja, aber ohne meine Arbeit wäre das Leben nur halb so schön.

III

ERIKA: Na, Hans, wie war's denn?

HANS: Ach, weißt du, Tante Amalie ist ja eigentlich sehr nett. Wenn sie nur nicht immer so viel reden würde.

ERIKA: Dann wäre sie nicht Tante Amalie.

HANS: Weißt du, sie hat mir erzählt, daß sie gestern bei Overhoffs den Museumsdirektor kennengelernt hat. Sie sagte, er wäre sehr interessant und hätte ihr sehr viel über Picasso erzählt.

ERIKA: Nun, wenn sie jetzt den Direktor kennt, brauchst du vielleicht nicht mehr so oft mit ihr ins Museum zu gehen.

HANS: Ja, und wenn sie den Direktor heiraten würde, brauchte ich nie mehr mit ihr ins Museum zu gehen. Dann könnte sie im Museum wohnen.

ERIKA: Hans, das ist nicht sehr nett von dir.

Viel Lärm um nichts? (**Schluß**)*

KAPITEL SECHS: Frau Ingelheim has just met her husband at the airport upon his return from Africa.

FRAU SCHMIDT-INGELHEIM:	Und dann hat der Herr Behrens angerufen und wollte wissen, ob du wirklich spurlos verschwunden wärst.
SCHMIDT-INGELHEIM:	Behrens? Den kenne ich nicht.
FRAU SCHMIDT-INGELHEIM:	Doch, du kennst ihn. Er hat mir gesagt, er hätte dich in Afrika kennengelernt. 5
SCHMIDT-INGELHEIM:	Ach, der Reporter. Du hast ihm doch hoffentlich gesagt, daß du von mir gehört hättest,—daß ich dir geschrieben hätte, ich käme heute.
FRAU SCHMIDT-INGELHEIM:	Ja, aber erst, als er mich wieder anrief. Denn als er das erste Mal† anrief, wußte ich noch nicht, daß du in Casablanca 10 warst; der Briefträger kam gerade, als ich mit ihm sprach. Und ich hatte doch Angst, verstehst du; vierzehn Tage hatte ich nichts von dir gehört.
SCHMIDT-INGELHEIM:	Du hast ihm also nicht gesagt, ich wäre *nicht* verschwunden. Das war unvernünftig. Das hättest du nicht tun sollen. 15
FRAU SCHMIDT-INGELHEIM:	Aber Hans, ich dachte doch nur . . .
SCHMIDT-INGELHEIM:	Du solltest nicht immer denken. Es wäre mir viel lieber, wenn du nicht immer so viel reden würdest. Du kanntest doch diesen Behrens gar nicht.
FRAU SCHMIDT-INGELHEIM:	Er war aber sehr nett zu mir. Hätte ich ihm vielleicht sagen 20 sollen, ich wüßte, wo du bist? Ich wußte es doch nicht.
SCHMIDT-INGELHEIM:	Du hättest ihm aber *sagen* sollen, daß du es wüßtest.
FRAU SCHMIDT-INGELHEIM:	Und dann hätte er mich gefragt, *wo* du wärst. Ich war ja so glücklich, als er mir sagte, er hätte dich gesehen. Ich dachte, er wäre vielleicht ein Freund von dir. Er sagte, er wollte 25 auch Käthe anrufen . . .
SCHMIDT-INGELHEIM:	Käthe! Woher wußte denn dieser Mensch, daß ich schon einmal verheiratet war? Hast *du* ihm das gesagt?

* conclusion
† the first time

FRAU SCHMIDT-INGELHEIM: Nein, ich habe es ihm *nicht* gesagt, aber er sagte, die Zeitung
                          wüßte alles.

SCHMIDT-INGELHEIM: „Alles?" Was heißt „alles"! Wenn du nur nicht immer so viel
                          erzählen würdest, Inge.

FRAU SCHMIDT-INGELHEIM: Nun, alles hat er doch nicht gewußt. Zum Beispiel, daß du   5
                          eine Tochter hast und daß diese Tochter in Mainz Archä-
                          ologie studiert. Ich habe ihm gesagt, daß deine Tochter zu-
                          fällig auch in Kairo gewesen wäre und zufällig auch in
                          deinem Hotel gewohnt hätte.

SCHMIDT-INGELHEIM: Das hättest du ihm nicht sagen sollen! Das kommt morgen   10
                          bestimmt in die Zeitung, und es wäre viel besser, wenn es
                          nicht in die Zeitung käme.

FRAU SCHMIDT-INGELHEIM: Ja, Hans.

SCHMIDT-INGELHEIM: Und du hättest ihm sagen können, du wüßtest gar nichts, und
                          er sollte warten, bis ich zurückkäme. Du weißt doch, daß ich   15
                          nicht einfach spurlos verschwinde. Ich muß nur allein sein,
                          wenn ich arbeite. Aber das braucht die Zeitung doch nicht
                          zu wissen. Ich bin doch schon so oft allein zum Arbeiten
                          weggefahren, daß du eigentlich wissen müßtest, was du tun
                          sollst.   20

FRAU SCHMIDT-INGELHEIM: Ja, Hans.
                          (Pause)
                          Du, Hans!

SCHMIDT-INGELHEIM: Ja?

FRAU SCHMIDT-INGELHEIM: Hans,—wie war denn Giselas Kaffee?   25

Zwei und zwei ist fünf

EINE UNMÖGLICHE GESCHICHTE

von Johannes Schmidt-Ingelheim

**eine unmögliche Ge-
schichte** an impos-
sible story

Hinter unserem Haus haben wir eine Terrasse. Sie ist fünf Meter
breit und zehn Meter lang. Ich habe die Platten für diese Terrasse
letzten Winter in Italien gekauft; sie sind alle ein Meter breit und
ein Meter lang.

Ich bin nie auf den Gedanken gekommen, diese Platten zu zählen.   30
Ich weiß, es müssen fünfzig sein. Und als meine Frau vor einem
Monat doch auf den Gedanken kam, die Platten zu zählen, und mir
dann sagte, es wären einundfünfzig (51), da wußte ich, daß sie
beim Zählen einen Fehler gemacht hatte. Denn wenn es wirklich

einundfünfzig wären, dann—nun, man kann den Gedanken einfach nicht zu Ende denken; man würde den Verstand verlieren, wenn man es versuchte.

Aber nach diesem Wochenende weiß ich nicht mehr, ob fünf mal zehn wirklich immer fünfzig ist. Natürlich wird mir kein Mensch ⁵ glauben, was ich dieses Wochenende erlebt habe. Aber wahr ist es doch.

Die Geschichte fing Freitag morgen in Tripolis an, das heißt, eigentlich hat sie schon angefangen, als wir noch mit Rommel in Afrika gegen die Amerikaner kämpften. ₁₀

Mein Schulfreund Hermann Schneider, Erich Karsten und ich wohnten damals in Tripolis bei dem Ägypter Ali und seiner Frau Busuq. Ali war ungefähr sechzig; Busuq war mindestens achtzig. Vor Busuq hatten wir alle Angst. Wenn wir mit ihr sprachen, hatten wir das Gefühl: sie sieht dich nicht nur an, sie sieht durch dich durch. Nur ₁₅ Erich hatte keine Angst vor ihr. Für ihn war diese Frau eine Königin. Er brachte ihr immer etwas mit, wenn er ins Haus kam, und man sah, es machte ihn glücklich, wenn sie seine Geschenke annahm.

Einmal, als wir nicht weit von der Stadt an unserem Wagen ar- ₂₀ beiteten, erschienen plötzlich ein paar englische Tiefflieger. Wir warfen uns zu Boden, aber nicht schnell genug. Als wir wieder aufstanden, blieb Erich mit einer Kopfwunde wie tot liegen.

Wir warfen uns zu Boden we threw ourselves on the ground

Wir fuhren mit ihm nach Tripolis zurück. Als Busuq Erichs Wunde sah, befahl sie uns, ihn ins Haus zu bringen. Wir hatten, wie immer, ₂₅ Angst vor ihr. Darum gehorchten wir und brachten ihn ins Haus. Wir konnten aber nicht bei ihm bleiben und kamen erst nach vierzehn Tagen wieder zurück. Erich war noch schwach, aber die Wunde war gottseidank geheilt.

Doch Erich war nicht mehr unser Erich. Er redete nicht mehr so viel ₃₀ wie früher, und seine Augen schienen sagen zu wollen: Ich weiß etwas, was ihr nicht wißt. Außerdem sah er oft stundenlang irgendwohin in die Ferne und war sozusagen einfach nicht da.

Nun, Hermann und ich hatten keine Zeit, Erich zu analysieren. Die Situation in Afrika war damals schon gefährlich, und wir fragten uns ₃₅ oft: Wie kommt ihr nur zurück nach Deutschland?

Zwei oder drei Wochen später saßen Hermann und ich in Alis Haus und schrieben Briefe. Erich saß bei uns und war wieder einmal sozusagen nicht da. Aber plötzlich sah er mich mit seinem Ich-weiß-etwas-was-du-nicht-weißt Blick an und sagte: „Weißt du, daß deine ₄₀

Frau dir gerade einen Brief schreibt, um dir zu erzählen, daß deine Tochter schon bis fünf zählen kann?" Niemand lachte. Ich wußte nicht, was ich denken sollte.

Ungefähr zehn Tage später flog man Hermann und mich nach Deutschland. Erich blieb in Afrika zurück. Wie lange er noch bei 5 der Ägypterin gewesen ist, weiß ich nicht. Ich habe ihn erst dieses Wochenende wiedergesehen.

Kurz vor dem Abflug nach Deutschland aber bekam ich damals noch einen Brief von meiner Frau. Was sie schrieb, machte mich unruhig. „Es wäre wirklich nett," schrieb sie, „wenn Du* hier wärst. Du 10 hättest sehen sollen, wie Dein Töchterchen heute morgen an den Fingern bis fünf gezählt . . . Du, Hans, was ich gerade erlebt habe, ist wirklich unglaublich, und ich muß mich zwingen, ruhig zu bleiben. Ich hatte beim Schreiben plötzlich das Gefühl, daß jemand hinter mir stand. Ich fühlte es. Ich wußte einfach, daß jemand 15 hinter mir stand. Ich saß eine Zeitlang still, dann sprang ich auf. Niemand war im Zimmer. Aber Hans, auf dem Boden waren Fußabdrücke, wie Du sie machst, wenn Du mit Deinen Militärschuhen nach Hause kommst. Du darfst nicht lachen. Ich weiß, was ich Dir schreibe, kann einfach nicht passieren. Aber es *ist* passiert!—Oder 20 ist es doch nicht passiert? Hans, ich bin einfach zu viel allein."

(Fortsetzung folgt)

* In letters, all pronouns of direct address must be capitalized (**Du, Dich, Dein, Ihr,** etc.).

ANALYSIS

97 The Future

Formation

The German future is formed by using **werden** as an auxiliary in the first prong and any infinitive in the second prong.

Ich werde	. . . sein	ich werde	. . . haben	ich werde	. . . fahren
du wirst	. . . sein	du wirst	. . . haben	du wirst	. . . fahren
er wird	. . . sein	er wird	. . . haben	er wird	. . . fahren
wir werden	. . . sein	wir werden	. . . haben	wir werden	. . . fahren
ihr werdet	. . . sein	ihr werdet	. . . haben	ihr werdet	. . . fahren
sie werden	. . . sein	sie werden	. . . haben	sie werden	. . . fahren

Use

Since the present tense can refer to future time, the future tense is comparatively rare. One usually hears

Ich fahre morgen nach Berlin,

not

Ich werde morgen nach Berlin fahren.

However, if a sentence contains no time phrase, the future is used more frequently:

Ihr werdet ja sehen, wie es ist.   You'll see how it is.

Very frequently, future forms express not futurity but present probability. Such a probability statement often contains adverbs such as **wohl** (probably), **sicher** (certainly), **vielleicht** (perhaps), and **wahrscheinlich** (probably).

Es ist jetzt sieben. Inge wird wohl (sicher, wahrscheinlich) schon zu Hause sein.   It's seven o'clock now. Inge is probably at home by now.

98   Irreal (Contrary-to-Fact) Conditions in English

It was pointed out in Unit 5 that the open condition

If his parents *are* still alive, they *are* now fifty

leaves the question of whether or not the parents are alive entirely unanswered. *If they are still alive* means "they may or may not be alive." By substituting *were* for *are* in the *if*-clause, and *would be* for *are* in the conclusion, the open condition changes into the irreal or contrary-to-fact condition

If his parents *were* still alive, they *would* be fifty now.

Now the question as to whether or not the parents are alive is no longer left undecided. *If his parents were alive* contains the unmistakable implication "they are dead," and *they would be fifty now* implies that they did not live to be fifty.

A similar change from an open condition to an irreal condition can occur when reference is made not to present time, but to past or future time:

PAST TIME, OPEN CONDITION:

John always did things in a big way. I therefore suspect that *if he stole, he stole* at least a million.

PAST TIME, IRREAL CONDITION:

John always did things in a big way. *If he had stolen, he would have stolen* at least a million.

FUTURE TIME, OPEN CONDITION:

I will not forget this, even *if I live* to be a hundred.

FUTURE TIME, IRREAL CONDITION:

I would not forget this, even *if I lived* to be a thousand years old.

As can be seen from the sentences quoted, the change from an open condition to an irreal condition is accomplished in English by changing the verb forms

(a) in the *if-clause* from the indicative to the subjunctive, and

(b) in the *conclusion* from the indicative to the conditional.

The question now is: Does German also shift from the indicative to the subjunctive in the *if*-clause and from the indicative to the conditional in the conclusion? Before we can answer this question, we have to analyze the English subjunctive in greater detail.

99   The English Subjunctive

The subjunctive found in English irreal *if*-clauses (and in wishes of the type "I wish they were here") consists of a very interesting set of forms. If the speaker refers to *past time*, he always uses a form which looks as if it were the past perfect.

REALITY	IRREALITY
(Past Perfect Indicative)	(Past Subjunctive)
I suddenly realized that *I had lost* my wallet.	If *I had lost* my wallet I'd really be upset now.

If the speaker refers to *present* or *future time*, he uses forms like *had, lost,* or *loved,* that is, forms which look as if they were past indicatives:

REALITY	IRREALITY
(Past Indicative)	(Present Subjunctive)
When I was a child, *we had* a mountain cabin.	If *we had* a mountain cabin, we could spend our vacations there.
I know *he loved* me as long as he lived.	If *he loved* me he would marry me.
We lost the last game.	It would be too bad if *we lost* this game.

It is perhaps surprising, but nevertheless a fact, that forms like *had, lost,* and *loved,* if taken out of context, have no time reference built into them at all. The time reference depends entirely on context.

If these forms are used in a context of reality to express real events or open possibilities, they refer to past time:

We *lost* the last game.

They are then used in the indicative (reality) mood, and they are in the past tense.

However, if these forms are used in a context of irreality to describe something which exists only in thought, imagination, or desire, they refer to present or future time:

It would be too bad if we *lost* this game.

Although *had, lost,* and *loved* still remind us by their "looks" of the past indicative, they are now used in the subjunctive (irreality) mood, and we shall call them the present tense of the subjunctive. Like all present tenses, the present tense of the subjunctive may, as it does in the case of *lost,* take on a future meaning.

For the sake of convenience, let us call this the *had : had* pattern, the first *had* referring to the indicative and the second to the subjunctive. The past indicative *had* of *I know he had a cabin* is identical with the present subjunctive *had* of *I wish he had a cabin,* and it is the same with other verbs.

There is only one verb which does not follow the *had : had* pattern; this is the verb *to be.*

Although one hears people say (systematically following the *had : had* pattern)

If she was only a little older, I'd like her better

this is generally considered substandard English; the accepted form is

If she were only a little older, . . .

Because the past indicative *was* is, in this case, not identical with the present subjunctive *were,* we shall call this arrangement the *was : were* pattern. It is an exception in English and occurs only in the singular of one verb: *if I were* and *if he were.* In German, however, the *was : were* pattern is very common.

An interesting fact about the *had : had* pattern form is that it makes *if-*clauses ambiguous. The sentence

> *If he had money,* he must have squandered it

is an open condition. But the sentence

> *If he had money,* he would surely squander it

is an irreal condition.

This means that the irreal *if-*clause *if he had money* has its subjunctive (irreality) flavor not by virtue of its own linguistic character, but through the character of the following conclusion *he would surely squander it.*

Similarly, in English *if-*clauses referring to past time, phrases like *if he had done it* are also "neutral," that is, by themselves they are neither indicatives nor subjunctives. They acquire subjunctive character if they are followed (or preceded) by a conditional:

> I was curious to find out *if he had done it.* (Indicative)
> *If he had done it,* he would have told me about it. (Subjunctive)

On the other hand, the *if-*clause *If she were only a little older* is never ambiguous; for *if she were,* which follows the *was : were* model, can only be a present subjunctive; and therefore it can only be followed by a conditional.

Summary of the English Subjunctive in Irreal *If*-Clauses

1. Without context, all *had : had* pattern forms are ambiguous and have no time reference built into them.

2. The *was : were* pattern forms are never ambiguous.

3. The ambiguous *had : had* pattern forms in *if-*clauses acquire an unmistakable irreality (subjunctive) character

 (a) when they are followed by a conditional verb form in the conclusion: *If he had money, he would surely squander it.*

 (b) when they appear in a fixed "if-only" frame, as in *If I only had some money.*

This summary is valid not only for English but also for German. Let us see now how German derives its conditional, its *had : had* pattern, and its *was : were* pattern forms.

100 The Forms of the Conditional and of the Present Subjunctive

The Conditional

The German conditional is derived from the future indicative.

FUTURE INDICATIVE	CONDITIONAL
ich werde gehen	ich würde gehen
du wirst gehen	du würdest gehen
er wird gehen	er würde gehen
wir werden gehen	wir würden gehen
ihr werdet gehen	ihr würdet gehen
sie werden gehen	sie würden gehen

There are—gottseidank—no deviations from this pattern. These **würde**-forms are definitely subjunctives; they cannot be anything else.

The use of **würde**-forms in **wenn**-clauses is still rare; however, they are frequently found in the conclusion. They can refer either to present or to future time.

PRESENT TIME

Wenn ich Geld hätte, würde ich jetzt auch an der Riviera wohnen.
   If I had money, I'd live on the Riviera, too, now.

FUTURE TIME

Wenn wir Geld hätten, würden wir diesen Sommer heiraten.
   If we had money, we'd get married this summer.

The Present Subjunctive of Weak Verbs

Weak verbs use the same forms for the past indicative and the present subjunctive; in other words, they are parallel to the English *had : had* pattern.

PAST INDICATIVE	PRESENT SUBJUNCTIVE
ich lebte	ich lebte
du lebtest	du lebtest
er lebte	er lebte
wir lebten	wir lebten
ihr lebtet	ihr lebtet
sie lebten	sie lebten

This means that **wenn**-clauses like

> **Wenn es regnete, ...**
> **Wenn wir lachten, ...**

are intolerably ambiguous. One doesn't know whether the forms **regnete** and **lachten** are past indicatives meaning

> Whenever it rained, ...
> Whenever we laughed, ...

or whether they are present subjunctives meaning

> If it were raining ...
> If we were to laugh ...

These forms can therefore be used only in contexts which resolve this ambiguity (see **102, 103**).

The Present Subjunctive of the Modals

The present subjunctive of the modals is formed by adding the endings of the past tense to the *unchanged* stem.

PAST INDICATIVE	PRESENT SUBJUNCTIVE
ich wollte	ich wollte
ich sollte	ich sollte
ich mußte	ich müßte
ich konnte	ich könnte
ich durfte	ich dürfte

This table shows that **wollen** and **sollen** have ambiguous *had : had* pattern forms, whereas **müssen**, **können**, and **dürfen** have unambiguous *was : were* pattern forms. The form **ich möchte**, which we have been using since Unit 3, is a polite subjunctive which is now used as if it were an indicative. The indicative form **ich mag** is discussed in Unit 9.

Sentences with **wollte** and **sollte** are therefore ambiguous unless they are clarified by context (see **102** and **107.**)

The Present Subjunctive of Strong Verbs

Strong verbs form the present subjunctive by adding **-e, -est, -e, -en, -et, -en** (that is, the endings of **leb-te** minus **-t-**) to the stem of the past, which is umlauted whenever possible—that is, whenever the stem vowel is *a*, *o*, *u*, or *au*. The endings **-est** and **-et** are often shortened to **-st** and **-t**.

PAST INDICATIVE	PRESENT SUBJUNCTIVE
ich war	ich wär-e
du war-st	du wär-est, wär-st
er war	er wär-e
wir war-en	wir wär-en
ihr war-t	ihr wär-et, wär-t
sie war-en	sie wär-en
ich ging	ich ging-e
du ging-st	du ging-est, ging-st
er ging	er ging-e
wir ging-en	wir ging-en
ihr ging-t	ihr ging-et, ging-t
sie ging-en	sie ging-en

This system leads to both *had : had* and *was : were* pattern forms. Thus, a **wenn**-clause like

Wenn wir nach Hause gingen, . . .

is again ambiguous. It may mean

Whenever we went home, . . .

or:

If we were to go home (should go home).

Context will resolve this ambiguity (see **102, 103**).

Irregular Forms

A few weak verbs umlaut their subjunctive forms, and occasionally a strong verb changes the stem vowel in an irregular way. The following forms must therefore be memorized.

PAST INDICATIVE	PRESENT SUBJUNCTIVE
ich hatt-e	ich hätt-e
du hatt-est	du hätt-est
er hatt-e	er hätt-e
wir hatt-en	wir hätt-en
ihr hatt-et	ihr hätt-et
sie hatt-en	sie hätt-en
ich wußt-e	ich wüßt-e

PAST INDICATIVE	PRESENT SUBJUNCTIVE
ich bracht-e	ich brächt-e
ich kannt-e	ich kennt-e
ich half	ich hülfe
ich wurde	ich würde
ich starb	ich stürbe

All these irregular forms are *was : were* forms; they can clearly be recognized as subjunctives.

NOTE:

1. Distinguish between the following forms:

ich konnte	I was able to
wenn ich könnte	If I were able to
ich kannte	I knew
wenn ich kennte	If I knew

2. The present subjunctive of **sein** (**wäre**) and **haben** (**hätte**) occurs more frequently than the corresponding conditional forms **würde sein** and **würde haben.** The conditional of the modals (**würde müssen, würde können**) is hardly ever used.

101 The Past Subjunctive

The German past subjunctive is formed from the pluperfect indicative as illustrated by the following table.

PLUPERFECT INDICATIVE	PAST SUBJUNCTIVE
ich war gegangen	**ich wäre gegangen**
du warst gegangen	**du wär(e)st gegangen**
er war gegangen	**er wäre gegangen**
wir waren gegangen	**wir wären gegangen**
ihr wart gegangen	**ihr wär(e)t gegangen**
sie waren gegangen	**sie wären gegangen**
ich hatte gehabt	**ich hätte gehabt**
du hattest gehabt	**du hättest gehabt**
er hatte gehabt	**er hätte gehabt**
wir hatten gehabt	**wir hätten gehabt**
ihr hattet gehabt	**ihr hättet gehabt**
sie hatten gehabt	**sie hätten gehabt.**

As this table shows, all German past subjunctive forms follow the *was : were* pattern and can be clearly recognized as subjunctives. Modals follow the same pattern:

ich hatte gekonnt	**ich hätte gekonnt**
ich hatte gehen können	**ich hätte gehen können**

NOTE: The past subjunctives of modals usually correspond to English statements starting with *could have, should have,* and *would have.*

Ich hätte gehen können.	I could have gone.
Ich hätte gehen sollen.	I should have gone.
Ich hätte gehen müssen.	I would have had to go.

102 Wishes Starting with **Ich wollte** or **Ich wünschte**

The easiest way to start practicing German subjunctives is by means of the patterns

> **Ich wollte, es regnete morgen.**
> **Ich wollte, es würde morgen regnen.**

The short introductory clauses **ich wollte** or **ich wünschte**, which are interchangeable, are present subjunctives and follow the obsolescent English pattern

> Oh, would I were a boy again,

where *would* is also a subjunctive referring to present time.

Ich wollte, wir wohnten in München.	I wish we were living in Munich.
Ich wollte, es wäre schon Frühling.	I wish it were already spring.
Ich wollte, es regnete morgen (würde morgen regnen).	I wish it would rain tomorrow.
Ich wollte, es hätte gestern geregnet.	I wish it had rained yesterday.

Note that the structure of these sentences is fixed: they always start with **ich wollte** or **ich wünschte**, which are then followed by an unintroduced dependent clause. The subjunctive flavor (and thereby reference to present or future time) depends on this fixed structure. That is why **Ich wollte, es regnete** (*I wish it were raining*) is always unambiguous, although **regnete** by itself is a *had : had* pattern form which could also be indicative. The subjunctive flavor disappears if **ich wollte** or **ich wünschte** is followed by a **daß**-clause:

Ich wollte, er heiratete.	I wish he would get married.
Ich wollte, daß er heiratete.	I wanted him to get married.

Wishes are also expressed by using the introductory phrase **Es wäre nett, wenn . . .** followed by a subjunctive.

Es wäre nett, wenn du morgen kommen könntest.	It would be nice if you could come tomorrow.
Es wäre nett, wenn wir nächstes Jahr nach Deutschland führen (fahren würden).	It would be nice if we went to Germany next year.
Es wäre nett gewesen, wenn du meinen Geburtstag nicht wieder vergessen hättest.	It would have been nice if you had not forgotten my birthday again.

103 Irreal (Contrary-to-Fact) Conditions

Irreal conditions refer either to present and future time or to past time.

Present and Future Time

We have seen (**99**) that, with the exception of some forms of the verb *to be* (the *was : were* pattern), all the verb forms which appear in irreal *if*-clauses in present-day English speech are ambiguous *had : had* pattern

forms which, in a different context, could just as well be indicatives. For this reason, any *if*-clause like *if they lost this game* hangs in the air until it is rescued by a preceding or following conclusion.

If this conclusion is *it was their own fault*, then the *lost* of the *if*-clause is a past indicative; but in *It would be too bad if they lost this game*, the *lost* of the *if*-clause is a subjunctive.

The necessity to rescue the otherwise ambiguous *if*-clauses of contrary-to-fact conditions has forced English to use only conditional forms with *would* or *should* in the conclusion. For when used with *if*-clauses, these conditional forms are unambiguous subjunctives which guarantee that the ambiguous *had : had* forms in the *if*-clauses will also be interpreted as subjunctives.

German, too, prefers to use only unambiguous subjunctive forms in the conclusions belonging to contrary-to-fact **wenn**-clauses. But the conditional **würde**-forms, which English-speaking students are tempted to prefer, are not the only unambiguous subjunctives:

ich könnte		**ich würde können**
ich hätte	are just as unambiguous as	**ich würde haben**
ich wäre		**ich würde sein**
ich ginge		**ich würde gehen**

On the whole, the shorter forms, especially the shorter forms of **haben, sein,** and the modals, are preferred. Thus, one will usually hear

> **Wenn ich Geld hätte, könnte ich heiraten.**
> **   , wäre ich schon lange nicht mehr hier.**
> **   , führe ich auch nach Deutschland.**

However, it is also very common to say

> **Wenn ich Geld hätte, würde ich auch nach Deutschland fahren.**

Even such ambiguous forms as **brauchte** and **wohnte**, which can be either past indicatives or present subjunctives, can appear in contrary-to-fact conclusions as long as the **wenn**-clause contains an unambiguous subjunctive:

> **Wenn ich Geld hätte, brauchte ich nicht zu arbeiten.**
> **   , wohnte ich auch an der Riviera.**

The **würde**-forms are mandatory only
1. if a weak verb refers to the future:
   Wenn ich Geld hätte, würde ich heiraten.
   (not: **heiratete ich.**)

2. if two ambiguous weak verbs would otherwise follow each other:
   Wenn es regnete, würden wir nicht arbeiten.
   (Not: **arbeiteten wir nicht.**)

As a matter of fact, the sentence
   Wenn es regnete, arbeiteten wir nicht

would be interpreted to mean
   Whenever it rained, we didn't work.

Past Time

To express past time, use only the past subjunctive (**hätte** or **wäre** plus participle) for both the *if*-clause and the conclusion. Do not try to imitate English conditionals like *would have died,* which refer to past time. If you want to express English *would have* plus a participle, you must use **hätte** or **wäre** plus a participle in German. Since all these forms are un-ambiguous *was : were* forms, no complications will arise.

Wenn es gestern geregnet hätte, wären wir zu Hause geblieben.	If it had rained yesterday, we would have stayed at home.
Wenn du hier gewesen wärst, wäre mein Bruder nicht gestorben.	If you had been here, my brother would not have died (John 11:21). (King James Version: If thou hadst been here, my brother had not died.)

104 *If*-Clauses to Express Desires

If a speaker is dissatisfied with the situation as it actually exists, he may express what he would like the facts to be or to have been. Such wishes-contrary-to-fact may assume the form of an irreal *if-clause* used by itself without a conclusion, as in English *If he would only come!*

If German *if*-clauses of this type refer to present or future time, either the present subjunctive or the conditional may be used, but remember that the conditional of **sein, haben,** and the modals is rare. If they refer to past time, only the past subjunctive (**hätte** or **wäre** plus participle) should be used. *If*-clauses that express wishes must contain at least a **nur** or **doch nur;** if the speaker is anxiously looking forward to something, he uses **nur endlich, doch endlich,** or **doch nur endlich.** (This **endlich** does not mean *finally;* it merely expresses impatience.) As sentence adverbs, these little inserts stand between elements without news value and elements with news value.

Wenn es doch nur endlich regnen würde!	If it would only rain!
Wenn ich doch nur mehr Geld hätte!	If only I had more money!
Wenn ich nur nicht soviel Kaffee getrunken hätte!	If only I had not had so much coffee!

105   Irreal Conclusions without *If*-Clause

The English sentence

> I would like to have a cup of coffee

is an irreal conclusion. The irreal *if*-clause is not expressed, but the use of the subjunctive implies "if this should be possible."

Such irreal conclusions express a wish or a polite request. In German, they frequently contain the adverbs **gerne** (*with pleasure*), **lieber** (*rather, preferably*), or **am liebsten** (*what I would like most of all . . .*). If these irreal conclusions express something the speaker would look forward to, they frequently contain **einmal,** which, literally, means *at some time* or *once,* but which usually adds the flavor of "if this were possible" and replaces the suppressed *if*-clause. Polite requests, in the form of a question, frequently contain **vielleicht.** Examples:

Wishes

Ich führe auch gerne einmal nach Italien (würde auch gerne einmal nach Italien fahren).	I would like to go to Italy too, sometime.
Wir wohnten auch lieber in München (würden auch lieber in München wohnen).	We too would rather live in Munich.
Am liebsten wäre ich nach Köln gefahren.	Most of all, I would have liked to go to Cologne.
Wir hätten auch lieber in München gewohnt.	We, too, would rather have lived in Munich.

Polite Requests

Ich hätte gerne ein Zimmer mit Bad.	I should like to have a room with bath.
Könnte ich noch eine Tasse Kaffee haben?	Could I have another cup of coffee?
Hätten Sie vielleicht noch ein Zimmer frei?	Would you perhaps still have a room?
Würdest du mich bitte morgen zum Flughafen bringen?	Would you please drive me to the airport tomorrow?

106 The Subjunctive in Indirect Discourse

The English System

When I, the speaker, want to report to one person, my wife for instance, what another person, for instance my father, has just told me over the phone, I can freely choose between two syntactical patterns:

I can use quotation marks and repeat verbatim what my father said. If he said, "Fred, I am sick," I can report, *Father just called and said, "Fred, I am sick."* Such "direct discourse" presents no problems. One simply quotes verbatim what one hears.

I may also use the "indirect discourse" pattern—that is, I may change the original statement into a dependent clause: *Father just called and said he was sick.* In this case the original words *I am sick* change into *he was sick.* If the original is "I was sick last week," I may report: *Father just called and said he had been sick last week.*

The rule governing English indirect discourse is usually formulated as follows: If the opening verb (*said, told, reported, maintained, read*) is in the past tense, then any *present tense* in the words to be reported is normally changed to *past tense* and any *past tense* (simple past, present perfect, past perfect) is normally changed to *past perfect.*

Schematically, this English system can be represented as follows:

	DIRECT DISCOURSE	INDIRECT DISCOURSE
PRESENT TENSE	I am sick	He said he was sick
	I have money	He said he had money
ANY PAST TENSE	I was sick	He said he had been sick
	I have broken my arm	He said he had broken his arm
	I had not thought of it	He said he had not thought of it.

In learning German, you will find it helpful to regard this shift in verb forms not as a shift in tense but as a shift from the indicative to the subjunctive, a shift which in English follows the *had : had* pattern all the way through. You will then automatically do what you ought to do: shift from the German indicative to the German subjunctive.

The German System

AFTER AN OPENING VERB IN ONE OF THE PAST TENSES

If the original statement (that is, the statement in quotation marks) referred to the present time, the present subjunctive is used, and such *had : had* forms as **wohnte** and **liebte** do not have to be replaced by **würde**-forms.

If the original statement referred to the future, one can use either the present subjunctive or the future subjunctive; *had : had* pattern forms like **heiratete**—that is, weak verbs with a future meaning—are usually replaced by a **würde** form.

„Ich bin krank."	Er sagte, er wäre krank.
„Ich wohne in München."	Er sagte, er wohnte in München.
„Ich kann kommen."	Er sagte, er könnte kommen.
„Ich werde zu Hause bleiben."	Er sagte, er würde zu Hause bleiben (bliebe zu Hause).
„Ich komme morgen."	Er sagte, er käme morgen (würde morgen kommen).
„Ich heirate sie bestimmt."	Er sagte, er würde sie bestimmt heiraten.
„Fährst du morgen nach Köln?"	Er wollte wissen, ob ich morgen nach Köln führe.

If the original statement was made in any past tense, one shifts to the past subjunctive (**wäre** or **hätte** plus participle).

„Ich war krank."	Er sagte, er wäre krank gewesen.
„Ich bin krank gewesen."	Er sagte, er wäre krank gewesen.
„Bei uns schien die Sonne."	Er sagte, bei ihnen hätte die Sonne geschienen.
„Eva ist schon nach Hause gegangen."	Er sagte, Eva wäre schon nach Hause gegangen.

If the original statement contained a subjunctive, no change is possible:

„Wenn wir Geld hätten, würden wir   Er sagte, wenn sie Geld hätten, würden sie
sofort heiraten.“   sofort heiraten.

AFTER AN OPENING VERB IN THE PRESENT TENSE

If the opening verb is in the present tense, a change from indicative to subjunctive is possible though not as frequent in spoken German as in literary German. However, after an **ich**-form in the present tense, the subjunctive is apt to indicate deceit.

„Meyer ist intelligent.“   Fritz meint, Meyer ist intelligent.
                                     Fritz meint, Meyer wäre intelligent.
                                     Ich sage, Meyer ist intelligent.
                                     Ich sage ihm einfach, Meyer wäre intelli-
                                     gent.

„Meyer ist nicht gekommen.“   Fritz sagt, Meyer ist nicht gekommen.
                                     Fritz sagt, Meyer wäre nicht gekommen.
                                     Ich sage, Meyer ist nicht gekommen.

NOTE:

1. If the speaker wants to emphasize that the words reported refer to a fact, he uses the indicative:

Er wollte wissen, warum Erika so oft nach Berlin fährt.

But:

Er wollte wissen, ob Erika immer noch so oft nach Berlin führe.

Wer hat Ihnen denn gesagt, daß mein Mann in Afrika ist?

But:

Wer hat Ihnen denn gesagt, mein Mann wäre in Afrika?

2. In most of the examples above, indirect discourse appears in the form of unintroduced clauses with verb-second position. These clauses can, however, be introduced by **daß** and then show verb-last position:

Er sagte, daß in Hamburg die Sonne schiene.

107 sollte

German **sollte** is one of the ambiguous *had : had* pattern forms which can be used either as a past indicative or as a present subjunctive.

Past Indicative

> **Jedes Mal, wenn du mit mir ins The-ater gehen solltest, hattest du Kopf-schmerzen.**

Every time you were supposed (Every time I wanted you) to go to the theater with me, you had a headache.

> **Wir sollten schon um acht in Köln sein. Jetzt ist es neun, und wir sind immer noch in Bonn.**

We were supposed to be in Cologne at eight. Now it is nine, and we are still in Bonn.

Present Subjunctive

In the *if*-clause, the present subjunctive denotes a future possibility which the speaker does not expect to materialize. The conclusion shows the indicative.

> **Wenn es morgen regnen sollte, bleiben wir zu Hause.**

If it should rain tomorrow, we'll stay at home.

In the conclusion, the present subjunctive denotes an as yet unfulfilled obligation. The *if*-clause shows the indicative.

> **Wenn du kannst, solltest du ihm helfen.**

If you can, you should (ought to) help him.

> **Du solltest nicht soviel rauchen.**

You should not (ought not to) smoke so much.

Sentences with the modal subjunctives **sollte, müßte, könnte** frequently contain the word **eigentlich;** such sentences express the notion *I ought to (should, could), but I guess I won't.*

> **Morgen sollte ich eigentlich nach Köln fahren.**

I really ought to go to Cologne tomorrow. (But I probably won't.)

> **Ich hätte gestern eigentlich nach Köln fahren sollen.**

I really ought to have gone to Cologne yesterday. (But I didn't.)

108 Position of **hätte** in Connection with "Double Infinitives"

It was pointed out before that when the modals and **brauchen** are used with a dependent infinitive, the participles look like infinitives: **Ich habe sie noch nicht besuchen können.** As a result, **besuchen können** looks like a double infinitive. If subjunctive sentences like

> **Er hätte zu Hause bleiben können,**   or
> **Er hätte nicht zu Hause bleiben sollen,**

are changed into dependent clauses which should show verb-last position, the **hätte** does not go to the end, but follows **nicht** and precedes the second prong.

Wenn ich doch nur hätte zu Hause bleiben können.

Es wäre nett gewesen, wenn ich gestern nicht hätte zurückfahren müssen.

NOTE: This exception to the principle of verb-last position occurs also in those rare cases when the indicative is used:

Sie war mir böse, weil ich sie noch nie hatte besuchen können.

109   The Prefix **un-**

The prefix un- is added to many adjectives and a few nouns to form antonyms.

glücklich	unglücklich
interessant	uninteressant
vernünftig	unvernünftig
das Wissen (knowledge)	das Unwissen (ignorance)
das Glück (happiness, good luck)	das Unglück (misfortune, accident)

110   The Suffix **-lich** Added to Nouns

Like the English suffix -ly, the German suffix -lich is added to nouns. It forms adjectives with the meaning of "having the qualities one associates with things or people of such a nature." The stem vowel of the noun is usually umlauted.

der Freund	friend	freundlich	friendly
die Mutter	mother	mütterlich	motherly
das Kind	child	kindlich	childlike
die Welt	world	weltlich	worldly, secular
die Natur	nature	natürlich	naturally

111   The Suffixes **-lich** and **-bar** Added to Verb Stems

Added to verb stems, -bar and -lich form passive adjectives corresponding to English adjectives in -able and -ible.

glauben	to believe	unglaublich	unbelievable
brauchen	to use	brauchbar	usable
vergessen	to forget	unvergeßlich	unforgettable

Some of the adjectives formed by -lich have an active meaning. (Compare English durable.)

sterben	to die	sterblich	mortal, apt to die
vergessen	to forget	vergeßlich	forgetful

EXERCISES

A. Change the following sentences to wishes starting with **Ich wollte.** Change from affirmative to negative, and from negative to affirmative.

> **Wir haben noch kein Haus an der Riviera.**
> **Ich wollte, wir hätten schon ein Haus an der Riviera.**

1. Sie hat mich nicht angerufen.
2. Er fährt morgen leider nach Kairo.
3. Ich habe mein Buch zu Hause gelassen.
4. Ich bin zu meiner Mutter gefahren.
5. Wir haben das Haus gekauft.

B. Change the following short statements into irreal *if*-clauses. Change negative statements to affirmative *if*-clauses, and affirmative statements to negative *if*-clauses. Add **nur.** Use the **würde**-form only if you want to stress future meaning.

> **Ich habe kein Geld.—Wenn ich nur Geld hätte.**
> **Ich hatte kein Geld.—Wenn ich nur Geld gehabt hätte.**

1. Er kommt nicht.
2. Sie ist nicht intelligent.
3. Sie haben keine Kinder.
4. Wir haben ihn gestern besucht.
5. Wir müssen zu Hause bleiben.

C. Change the following statements to wishes or requests in the subjunctive. Add **gerne, auch gerne einmal, am liebsten, bitte,** or **vielleicht,** as indicated. Whenever the wishes demand the present subjunctive, use the **würde**-form as well.

> **Ich fahre nach Italien.—Ich führe auch gerne einmal nach Italien.**
> **Ich würde gerne nach Italien fahren.**
> **Kann ich morgen nach Bonn fahren?—Könnte ich vielleicht morgen nach Bonn fahren?**
> **Ich habe eine Tasse Kaffee.—Ich hätte gerne eine Tasse Kaffee.**

1. Darf ich ein Glas Wein haben?   (bitte)
2. Ich bin nach Bonn gefahren.   (auch gerne)
3. Hans blieb zu Hause.   (gerne)
4. Ich habe meine Mutter besucht.   (am liebsten)
5. Haben Sie ein Zimmer für mich?   (vielleicht)

6. Ich esse im Hotel Regina.   (auch gerne einmal)
7. Darf ich auf meinem Zimmer frühstücken?   (vielleicht)
8. Können Sie mir jetzt das Frühstück bringen?   (bitte)

D. Change the following pairs of sentences to irreal conditions. Affirmative statements must then appear in negative form and negative statements in affirmative form. Use the first statements for the **wenn**-clause. In the conclusion, use either the subjunctive or, if possible, the **würde**-form.

> **Ich habe kein Geld. Ich kann nicht nach Paris fahren.**
> **Wenn ich Geld hätte, könnte ich nach Paris fahren.**

1. Es regnet. Wir können jetzt nicht arbeiten.
2. Es regnet nicht. Wir können jetzt arbeiten.
3. Wir haben keine Zeit. Wir fahren morgen nicht an den Rhein.
4. Ich kann nicht arbeiten. Ich bin unglücklich.
5. Ich wohne nicht in München. Ich gehe nicht jeden Tag ins Theater.
6. Wir haben viel zu tun. Wir können nicht in die Stadt fahren.
7. Ingelheim ist nicht glücklich verheiratet. Er fährt allein nach Kairo.
8. Ich liebe dich. Ich habe dich geheiratet.

E. The following sentences contain a dependent clause introduced by **weil**. Changing the **weil**-clause into a **wenn**-clause, transform the sentences into irreal conditions.

> **Ich kann nicht arbeiten, weil ich krank bin.**
> **Ich könnte arbeiten, wenn ich nicht krank wäre.**

1. Weil ich nicht soviel Geld habe wie Meyer, kann ich nicht an der Riviera wohnen.
2. Weil in Hamburg die Sonne nicht schien, bin ich nach Afrika gefahren.
3. Er kam so spät nach Hause, weil er im Kino war.
4. Weil er Geld hatte, hat sie ihn geheiratet.
5. Weil Frau Meyer Frau Meyer ist, kann man nicht mit ihr sprechen.
6. Weil das Essen nicht gut war, fuhren wir nach Hause.
7. Weil er Hepatitis bekam, schickte man ihn nach Hause.
8. Wir wohnen in der Stadt, weil wir keine Kinder haben.

F. Restate the following sentences in the past subjunctive, starting with **Es wäre nett gewesen, wenn . . .**

1. Ich kann ihn besuchen.
2. Ich darf nach Köln fahren.
3. Ich kann arbeiten.

4. Ich brauche das Buch nicht zu lesen.
5. Ich darf mit nach Casablanca fahren.

G. Change the following sentences to indirect discourse, starting with **Er sagte, daß** . . . Change
   pronouns as appropriate.

1. Meyer wohnt in Köln.
2. Ich brauche kein Geld.
3. Wir arbeiten heute nicht.
4. Ich brauche nicht nach Bonn zu fahren.
5. Ich bleibe heute abend zu Hause.
6. Das kann ich Ihnen nicht glauben.
7. Ich will ihn in Berlin besuchen.
8. Ich möchte mit dir ins Kino gehen.
9. Ich muß Ingelheims Roman lesen.
10. Ich darf mit meinem Vater nach Afrika fahren.

H. Change the following sentences to indirect discourse, starting with **Er sagte,** . . . Change pronouns as appropriate.

1. Man hat ihn nach Norwegen geschickt.
2. Leider war sie viel zu intelligent.
3. Leider hatte sie zuviel Geld.
4. Er ist nicht mit uns nach Berlin gefahren.
5. Ich mußte nach Casablanca fliegen.
6. Wir konnten das Haus in Köln nicht kaufen.
7. Ich habe zuviel Kaffee getrunken.
8. Er konnte uns gestern nicht besuchen.
9. Leider mußte ich damals Brieftauben füttern.
10. Den Roman von Ingelheim habe ich noch nicht gelesen.

I. Change the following questions to indirect yes-or-no questions. First start with **Ich wüßte gerne,
   ob** . . . (indicative), and then with **Er fragte mich, ob** . . . (subjunctive).

1. Fährt Erika morgen bestimmt nach Berlin?
2. Sind Sie verheiratet?
3. Wohnen Sie in München?
4. Haben Sie noch ein Zimmer frei?
5. Kennst du meine Freundin?
6. Kannst du mich morgen anrufen?

J. Change to direct questions. Change pronouns as appropriate.

1. Er wollte wissen, ob ich nach Berlin kommen könnte.
2. Er wollte wissen, ob mein Vater Schriftsteller wäre.
3. Er wollte wissen, was er mir schenken sollte.

4. Er wollte wissen, ob mein Vater bald nach Hause käme.
5. Er wollte wissen, ob ich ihm vielleicht zwanzig Mark geben könnte.
6. Er wollte wissen, warum ich Angst vor ihm hätte.

K. Change to indirect questions (past time). Start with **Er fragte mich, . . .** Change pronouns as appropriate.

1. Waren Sie damals auch Student?
2. Warst du gestern abend in der Universität?
3. Hattest du kein Geld bei dir?
4. Stand da drüben nicht früher ein Hotel?
5. Wa*rum* hattest du eigentlich nie Geld?
6. Wie lange war Hans denn in Afrika?
7. Warum konntest du nicht nach Hause kommen?
8. Warum ist Inge nicht mitgegangen?
9. Wen wolltest du denn in Berlin besuchen?
10. Mußtest du gestern abend schon wieder arbeiten?

L. Change to direct questions:

1. Er fragte, ob viele Leute dagewesen wären.
2. Er fragte, ob ich gestern krank gewesen wäre.
3. Er fragte, ob es wahr wäre, daß es im Winter hier immer so kalt ist.
4. Er fragte, ob ich auch Hepatitis gehabt hätte.
5. Er fragte, wie lange ich in Afrika gewesen wäre.
6. Er fragte, warum ich um neun Uhr noch im Bett gelegen hätte.
7. Er fragte, warum Inge nicht hätte mit nach Italien fahren dürfen.
8. Er fragte, warum Erika gestern abend hätte zu Hause bleiben müssen.
9. Er fragte, warum ich ihr nicht hätte schreiben können.
10. Er fragte, ob sein Sohn nicht hätte zu Hause bleiben können.

M. Express in German:

1. When it began to rain, we couldn't work any more.
2. If it begins to rain now, we can't work any more.
3. If it began to rain now, we wouldn't be able to work any more.
4. I was often unhappy; but when I saw her, I was always happy.
5. I'd like to know whether he is really a writer.
6. I wish he weren't a writer.
7. I don't understand why you always want to eat here.
8. I wish we could always eat here.
9. I wish we'd eat at home tonight.
10. It would have been nice if you had stayed at home.
11. Why did Ingelheim go to Africa alone?
12. It was not against the law.
13. I really should (ought to) invite him, but I have no time.

14. I really should have invited him, but I had no time.
15. Not until yesterday did I hear from him.
16. Not until yesterday did he ask me whether I could go to Bonn with him.
17. She told me she would go to Bonn with me.
18. If only we could go to Bonn again!
19. Thank goodness I've always been healthy.
20. He said he had never been in Berlin.
21. I'd like to have a cup of coffee.
22. When Ingelheim became twenty, he got hepatitis.
23. You should have seen him three years ago.
24. If only she had learned to drive.
25. Has he found the mistake yet?—No, not yet.
26. He told us that Ingelheim had disappeared in Africa without a trace.
27. I shall never be able to forget you.
28. I wish he didn't always forget my birthday.
29. I wish you hadn't forgotten my birthday again.
30. Whenever I needed her, she came immediately.
31. I know Aunt Amalie is unreasonable.
32. In three weeks they saw sixteen cities; now they believe they know Europe.
33. He knows he should have stayed at home.
34. If he hadn't lived in Munich at that time, he would never have met her.

BASIC VOCABULARY

achtzig eighty
anfangen to begin
  es fängt an zu regnen it is beginning to rain
baden to bathe
das Bad, ⸚er bath
begleiten to accompany
besser better
bestimmt definitely
bitten um to request, to ask for
breit broad, wide
danke schön thank you very much
drüben over there
eigentlich actually, really
das Ende, –n end
  zu Ende to an end, to a conclusion
endlich at last, finally
erleben to experience
erscheinen to appear
fern far away, distant

die Ferne distance
der Finger, – finger
fliegen to fly
  der Flieger, – flyer
  der Tiefflieger, – strafing plane
  der Flug, ⸚e flight
  der Abflug, ⸚e departure
  der Flughafen, ⸚ airport
frei unoccupied, free
der Freitag, –e Friday
fühlen to feel
  das Gefühl, –e feeling
fünfzig fifty
gar nicht not at all
geboren born
  ich bin geboren I was born
die Geburt, –en birth
  der Geburtstag, –e the birthday
der Gedanke, –n thought, idea

  auf den Gedanken kommen to hit upon the idea
genug enough
die Geschichte, –n story, history
heiraten to marry
  verheiratet married
  ich bin verheiratet I am married
hinter behind, beyond, on the other side of
irgendwohin somewhere
jemand somebody, someone (*dat.:* jemand, jemandem; *acc.:* jemand, jemanden)
kurz short
küssen to kiss
lieber (*adverb*) rather
  am liebsten (to like) most of all
liegen to lie (flat); to be situated

dieses Mal this time
  noch einmal once more
  manchmal sometimes
  jedesmal every time
  diesmal this time
  zwei mal zwei two times two
mindestens at least
möglich possible
der Montag, –e Monday
nett nice
niemand nobody, no one (*dat.:* **niemand, niemandem**; *acc.:* **niemand, niemanden**)
nun now
das Paar, –e pair, couple
  ein paar a few
plötzlich suddenly
der Rhein the Rhine

ruhig quiet, restful
  unruhig restless
der Samstag, –e Saturday
  samstags on Saturdays
schenken to present, to give
  das Geschenk, –e present, gift
schlecht bad
schnell fast, rapid
der Schuh, –e shoe
schwach weak
sechzig sixty
sicher certain, sure; probably
springen to jump
  aufspringen to jump up
stehen to stand
  aufstehen to arise, to get up, to rise
still quiet, still
tot dead

ungefähr approximate(ly), about
vergessen to forget
verlieren to lose
der Verstand (*no pl.*) mind, reason
versuchen to try, to attempt
wahrschein'lich probably
weg away
  wegfahren to drive away, to leave
weit far
werfen to throw
das Wissen knowledge
die Wohnung, –en apartment
wünschen to wish
zählen to count
eine Zeitlang for a while (*not:* for a long time)
das Zimmer, – room

ADDITIONAL VOCABULARY

annehmen to accept; to assume, to take on
ansehen to look at
blicken to look, to glance
der Blick, –e look, glance; view
der Boden, ÷ ground; floor

der Fußabdruck, ÷e footprint
gehorchen to obey
heilen to heal
  geheilt healed, well
kämpfen to fight
der König, –e king

das Meter, – meter (measure of length)
die Platte, –n (phonograph) record; flagstone
die Situation, –en* situation
die Terras'se, –n terrace
die Wunde, –n wound

* All foreign nouns in **-tion** are feminine and are declined like **Situation**.

STRONG VERBS

anfangen to begin
  fing an, hat angefangen, er fängt an
annehmen to accept; to assume, to take on
  nahm an, hat angenommen, er nimmt an
ansehen to look at
  sah an, hat angesehen, er sieht an
bitten to ask for, to request
  bat, hat gebeten, er bittet
erscheinen to appear
  erschien, ist erschienen, er erscheint
fliegen to fly

  flog, ist geflogen, er fliegt
liegen to lie (flat); to be situated
  lag, hat gelegen, er liegt
springen to jump
  sprang, ist gesprungen, er springt
  aufspringen to jump up
  sprang auf, ist aufgesprungen, er springt auf
stehen to stand
  stand, hat gestanden, er steht
  aufstehen to get up, to rise, to arise

  stand auf, ist aufgestanden, er steht auf
vergessen to forget
  vergaß, hat vergessen, er vergißt
verlieren to lose
  verlor, hat verloren, er verliert
wegfahren to drive away, to leave
  fuhr weg, ist weggefahren, er fährt weg
werfen to throw
  warf, hat geworfen, er wirft

UNIT 7: Prepositions with Dative or Accusative—
The Genitive Case— **ein**–Words without Nouns—
The Indirect–Discourse Subjunctive

PATTERNS

[1] Prepositions with either Dative or Accusative

Analyze the use of case after the prepositions. Be prepared to produce the answers orally in class when you hear the questions.

Wo fahrt *ihr* denn hin?—*Wir* fahren an den *Rhein.*
  Where are *you* going?—*We* are going to the *Rhine.*

SEE
ANALYSIS
112–114
(pp. 204-207)

Wo *wart* ihr denn gestern?—Wir waren gestern am *Rhein.*
  Where *were* you yesterday?—We were at the *Rhine* yesterday.

Wohin fuhr er denn mit seiner Frau?—Er fuhr mit ihr an die Riviera.
  Where did he go with his wife?—He went to the Riviera with her.

Wo wohnt er denn?—Er wohnt an der Riviera.
  Where does he live?—He lives on the Riviera.

Wo hat er sie denn hingefahren?—Er hat sie ans Theater gebracht.
  Where did he take her?—He took her to the theater.

Wo wartete ihr Freund?—Er wartete am Theater.
  Where was her friend waiting?—He was waiting at the theater.

Wo hat er denn seinen Hut hingelegt?—Er hat ihn aufs Bett gelegt.

Wo lag denn sein Hut?—Er lag auf dem Bett.

Was hat er denn mit seinem Geld gemacht?—Er hat es auf die Bank gebracht.

Wo hast *du* dein Geld?—*Ich* habe mein Geld *auch* auf der Bank.

Wo hast du den Wagen denn hingestellt?—Hinter das Haus.

Wo steht denn dein Wagen?—Hinter dem Haus.

(Facing) **Universität München**

Was habt *ihr* denn gestern gemacht?—*Wir* sind gestern ins Theater gegangen.

Wo wart ihr denn gestern abend?—Im Theater.

Was hast du denn mit meiner Zeitung gemacht?—Ich habe sie neben deinen Hut gelegt.

Neben meinem Hut liegt sie aber nicht.—Wo kann sie denn sein?

Wie seid ihr nach Deutschland geflogen?—Wir sind nonstop über den Atlantik geflogen.

Und wo habt ihr gefrühstückt?—Über dem Atlantik.

Es regnete, und wir hielten unter der Brücke.

Es regnete, und wir liefen unter die Brücke.

Wo hast du Rosemarie denn gesehen?—Vor dem Hotel.

Bringst du mir bitte den Wagen?—Ja, ich bringe ihn dir vor das Hotel.

Ich war schon vor dem Krieg in Afrika.

Vor zehn Jahren stand hier ein Haus.

Sollen wir vor oder nach dem Theater essen?

Vor einem Jahr kam Ingelheim nach Hause.

Ich möchte vor dem Essen noch einen Brief schreiben.

Wo lag denn der Brief?—Er lag zwischen den Zeitungen, und ich konnte ihn nicht finden.

Er konnte den Brief lange nicht finden; seine Frau hatte ihn zwischen die Zeitungen gelegt.

[2] Prepositions with the Genitive

SEE
ANALYSIS
115, 116
(pp. 208-212)

Während des Krieges war Schmidt in Frankreich.
  During the war Schmidt was in France.

Während der Woche kannst du mich nicht besuchen.
  During the week you can't visit me.

Ihr könnt doch wegen des Regens nicht zu Hause bleiben.
  You can't stay at home because of the rain.

Wir haben trotz des Regens gestern gearbeitet.
  We worked yesterday in spite of the rain.

Wir haben trotz dem Regen gestern gearbeitet.
  We worked yesterday in spite of the rain.

Try to form sentences of your own using **während, wegen,** and **trotz.**

[3] The Attributive Genitive

Rephrase the German sentences by using the elements indicated in parentheses.

Am Abend ihres Geburtstages ging er mit ihr ins Theater.
  On the evening of her birthday he went to the theater with her.
  (on the evening of his birthday)

SEE
ANALYSIS
116
(pp. 210-212)

Gegen Ende des Jahres kam er aus Afrika zurück.
  Toward the end of the year he came back from Africa.
  (toward the end of the week)

Die Integrität des Menschen ist das Thema dieses Buches.
  The theme of this book is the integrity of man.
  (the intelligence of our children)

Herr Behrens ist ein Freund meines Mannes.
  Herr Behrens is a friend of my husband.
  (the son of my friend)

Werners Freundin kenne ich nicht.
  I don't know Werner's girl friend.
  (Ingrid's aunt)

Schmidt-Ingelheims Roman habe ich nicht gelesen.
  I haven't read Schmidt-Ingelheim's novel.
  (father's books)

Hast du Mutters Hut gesehen?
  Have you seen mother's hat?
  (Karl's car)

Den Vater dieses Mädchens kenne ich sehr gut.
  I know this girl's father very well.
  (his friend's mother)

Dr. Schmidt ist ein Schüler meines Mannes.
  Dr. Schmidt is a student of my husband's.
  (a friend of my father's)

Von dem Geld meines Vaters habe ich nie etwas gesehen.
    I've never seen anything of my father's money.
    (my wife's money)

Hannelore? Das ist doch die Freundin von Werner Schlosser!
    Hannelore? She's Werner Schlosser's friend, isn't she?
    (Hans Wagner's wife)

Herr Behrens ist ein Freund von meinem Mann.
    Herr Behrens is a friend of my husband's.
    (Frau Behrens; of my wife's)

Herr Behrens ist ein Freund von Johannes.
    Herr Behrens is a friend of Johannes'.
    (Frau Behrens; a friend of Inge's)

Und die Tochter von *die*sen Leuten willst du heiraten?—Na und?
    And you want to marry the daughter of *those* people?—Well, so what?
    (the son of *that* man?)

Maria ist eine von Dieters Freundinnen.
    Maria is one of Dieter's girl friends.
    (Fritz; Karl's friends)

[4] von plus Dative as a Genitive Substitute

Note the difference in the use of the genitive and of **von** plus dative in the following sentences. When is the **von**-phrase obligatory?

SEE
ANALYSIS
116
(pp. 210-212)

Ingelheims Kinder sind noch klein.

Die Kinder von Ingelheim sind noch klein.

Die Kinder von Ingelheims sind noch sehr klein.

Ingrids Kinder sind noch sehr klein.

Die Kinder von Ingrid sind noch sehr klein.

Sie war eine Freundin von Overhoffs Frau.

Er war der Vater von dreizehn Kindern.

Ich bin kein Freund von Rheinwein.

Jeder Leser von Kriegsromanen weiß, wer Schmidt-Ingelheim ist.

[5] Special Constructions

Er ist ein Freund von mir.

SEE
ANALYSIS
116
(pp. 210-212)

                    von _____ (du)
                    von _____ (er)
                    von _____ (sie)
                    von _____ (wir)
                    von _____ (ihr)
                    von _____ (Sie)
                    von _____ (meine Mutter)
                    von _____ (mein Vater)

Möchten Sie noch eine Tasse Tee?
   Would you like another cup of tea?

Haben Sie schon gewählt?—Ja, ich hätte gerne ein Glas Mosel.
   Have you decided yet?—Yes, I'd like a glass of Moselle.

Meine Frau würde gerne ein Glas Wasser trinken.
   My wife would like to drink a glass of water.

[6] ein-Words without Nouns

Form variations of your own.

Ich habe leider kein Buch mitgebracht. Hast du eins bei dir?
   Unfortunately, I didn't bring a book along. Do you have one with you?

SEE
ANALYSIS
117
(p. 212)

Keiner von seinen Freunden hat ihn besucht.
   None of his friends visited him.

Hier ist das Buch von Fritz.—Nein, das ist meins.
   Here is Fritz's book.—No, that's mine.

Mir gehört das Buch nicht; es muß deins sein.
   That book doesn't belong to me. It must be yours.

Wem gehört denn der Mercedes? Ist das Ihrer, Frau Ingelheim?
   Who owns that Mercedes? Is it yours, Frau Ingelheim?

Einen Ihrer Romane habe ich gelesen.
   I have read one of your novels.

Einen von Ihren Romanen habe ich gelesen.
   I have read one of your novels.

Eine seiner Töchter studiert jetzt Medizin.

   One of his daughters is studying medicine now.

Eine von seinen Töchtern studiert jetzt Medizin.

   One of his daughters is studying medicine now.

[7] The Indirect-Discourse Subjunctive

After studying these sentences, form statements in indirect discourse using the assertions printed below the pattern sentences. If possible, use both forms of the subjunctive.

SEE
ANALYSIS
118, 119

(pp. 212-214)

„Ich bin nur zwei Tage in München."

Sie sagte, sie wäre nur zwei Tage in München.

Sie sagte, sie sei nur zwei Tage in München.

„Ich habe ein Zimmer im Regina."

Sie sagte, sie hätte ein Zimmer im Regina.

Sie sagte, sie habe ein Zimmer im Regina.

München. Ludwigstraße von der Feldherrnhalle

„Wann bist du denn gestern abend nach Hause gekommen?"
Er fragte mich, wann ich gestern abend nach Hause gekommen wäre.
Er fragte mich, wann ich gestern abend nach Hause gekommen sei.

„Dann können wir zusammen frühstücken."
Er sagte, wir könnten dann zusammen frühstücken.

„Kannst du mit mir frühstücken?"
Er fragte, ob ich mit ihm frühstücken könnte.
Er fragte, ob ich mit ihm frühstücken könne.

„Ich mußte gestern nach Berlin fahren."
Er sagte, er hätte gestern nach Berlin fahren müssen.
Er sagte, er habe gestern nach Berlin fahren müssen.

„Ihr braucht nicht auf mich zu warten; ich komme erst morgen."
Er sagte, wir brauchten nicht auf ihn zu warten; er käme erst morgen.
Er sagte, wir brauchten nicht auf ihn zu warten; er komme erst morgen.

Transform the following statements into indirect discourse in accordance with the examples above:

„Er ist seit langem wieder zu Hause."
„Morgen habe ich keine Zeit."
„Ich kann dich morgen leider nicht besuchen."
„Leider muß ich morgen nach Berlin fahren."
„Fahren *Sie* doch morgen nach Köln, Herr Müller."
„Ich darf meinen Mann noch nicht besuchen."
„Ich will nicht studieren."
„Liebst du mich, und findest du mich schön?"
„Wann fährst du nach Berlin?"
„Du rauchst zuviel."
„Der Mantel ist ganz neu."
„Ich muß mal telefonieren."

CONVERSATION

The following is one continuous conversation in typical, everyday German. The first two sections may be used for class drill and memorization. The third section is meant for listening and reading practice. The entire conversation, as well as an additional section, also appears on tape and in the lab manual.

I

TELEFONISTIN: Hotel Regina, guten Morgen.

KLAUS: Guten Morgen. Ich hätte gerne Zimmer 641 (sechseinundvierzig).

TELEFONISTIN: Einen Augenblick, bitte.

II

ROSEMARIE: Ja, bitte?

KLAUS: Rosemarie? Guten Morgen.

ROSEMARIE: Klaus? Guten Morgen. Du hättest aber wirklich nicht so früh anzurufen brauchen. Ich schlafe ja noch.

KLAUS: Das höre ich.

ROSEMARIE: Wieviel Uhr ist es denn? Sieben? Oder ist es schon acht?

KLAUS: Acht? Es ist zwanzig nach zehn.

ROSEMARIE: Nein, das ist nicht möglich—zwanzig nach zehn?

KLAUS: Doch, das *ist* möglich. Wenn es *nicht* schon so spät wäre, hätte ich dich nicht angerufen.

ROSEMARIE: Ja, und wenn wir gestern abend nicht so lange getanzt hätten, wäre ich auch schon lange auf.

KLAUS: Aber wer wollte denn gestern so lange tanzen, du oder ich?

ROSEMARIE: Ich, natürlich. Wenn ich nur zwei Tage in München bin, will ich doch auch etwas sehen.

KLAUS: Na, *so* interessant ist die Regina-Bar ja *auch* nicht!

III

ROSEMARIE: Du, Klaus, wo bist du denn eigentlich? Hier im Hotel?

KLAUS: Nein, ich bin noch zu Hause. Aber wenn du willst, komme ich um elf ins Hotel. Dann können wir zusammen frühstücken. Du könntest natürlich auch auf deinem Zimmer frühstücken, und ich komme erst um zwölf,— wie du willst.

ROSEMARIE: Nein, das möchte ich nicht. Wenn ich nur drei Nächte in München bin, will ich mit *dir* frühstücken.

KLAUS: Gut, Rosemarie,—ich bin um elf in der Hotelhalle,—und es wäre schön, wenn du nicht erst um zwölf kämst: ich habe Hunger, ich bin schon seit acht Uhr auf.

ROSEMARIE: Aber Klaus, du weißt doch, daß du nie auf mich zu warten brauchst. Gestern hast du auch gesagt, daß ich um acht Uhr da sein müßte oder wir kämen nicht mehr in das Restaurant—wie hieß es doch?

KLAUS: Feldherrnkeller.

ROSEMARIE: Ja richtig,—wir kämen nicht mehr in den Feldherrnkeller, weil dort
                immer so viele Leute seien. Na, und wann war ich da? Um zehn vor acht.
                —Übrigens, Klaus, wie ist denn das Wetter? Ich habe noch nicht aus dem
                Fenster gesehen, aber es wäre schön, wenn heute die Sonne schiene.

KLAUS: Das Wetter könnte nicht besser sein. Heute morgen sah es ja aus, als
                ob es wieder regnen würde,—und wenn du nicht hier wärst, hätte es
                heute bestimmt geregnet.

ROSEMARIE: Vielen Dank für das Kompliment, Klaus. Aber wenn es geregnet hätte,
                das hätte auch nichts gemacht. Wir hätten ja in ein Museum gehen
                können. Aber weißt du was? Ich ginge nach dem Frühstück gerne durch
                die Stadt; ich möchte mir doch einen Mantel kaufen, und es wäre nett,
                wenn wir das zusammen machen könnten.

KLAUS: Gut;—und was machen wir, wenn wir den Mantel gekauft haben?

ROSEMARIE: Dann können wir eine Stunde auf einer Bank in der Sonne sitzen.

KLAUS: Im Hofgarten:* Das wäre prima. Wir gehen eine Stunde in den Hof-
                garten, und dann gehen wir essen.

* The Royal Gardens, a public park in the center of Munich.

Zwei und zwei ist fünf (Fortsetzung)

Ich wußte sofort, daß meine Frau diesen Brief an dem Tag geschrieben hatte, als ich mit Erich und Hermann bei Ali gesessen
hatte und Erich plötzlich sagte: „Du Hans, deine Frau schreibt
dir bestimmt gerade einen Brief." Aber wie gesagt, ich wußte damals
nicht, wo Erich war, und habe ihn erst letzten Freitag in Tripolis   5
wiedergesehen.

Ich arbeitete gerade an meinem Roman *Das Ende bei Karthago* und
war nach Afrika geflogen, um noch einmal die Gegend zu besuchen,
wo wir damals gegen die Amerikaner gekämpft haben. Es war darum
ganz natürlich, daß ich, sofort nachdem ich in Tripolis angekommen   10
war, zu Busuqs Haus gehen wollte. Es steht tatsächlich noch. Ich
wollte gerade mit meiner Leica eine Aufnahme machen (hätte ich
diese Aufnahme doch nur gemacht!), als jemand aus dem Haus
kam. Es war Erich.

Erich, der mich jahrelang immer nur in Uniform gesehen hatte,   15 **der** (*relative pro-*
erkannte mich nicht. Er sah nur einen Mann mit einer Kamera—   *noun*) who. (Relative
und war auf einmal verschwunden. Verschwunden, sage ich: er ging   pronouns will be dis-
nicht um die Ecke, er ging nicht ins Haus zurück, er war plötzlich   cussed in Unit 8.)
einfach nicht mehr da. „Diese Sonne", dachte ich, „die macht einen
noch ganz verrückt." Dann ging ich ins Haus. Ali saß im Garten. Er   20
war jetzt über achtzig. Er erzählte mir, daß seine Frau kurz nach dem   **achtzig** eighty
Ende des Krieges gestorben sei und daß mein Freund Erich ihn jedes
Jahr einmal besucht habe. Ja, Erich wäre gerade vor ein paar
Minuten im Haus gewesen und habe ihm, wie jedes Jahr um diese
Zeit, fünf Goldstücke dagelassen. Tatsächlich stand Ali auf, nahm   25
einen Stein aus der Wand des Hauses, griff in ein Loch hinter dem
Stein und zeigte mir fünf Goldstücke, fünf Zwanzigmarkstücke.
„Also war es wirklich Erich, den du gesehen hast und der dann   **den** whom
einfach nicht mehr da war", sagte ich mir; und plötzlich wußte ich:
hier ist etwas nicht in Ordnung.   30

Ich ging ins Hotel zurück, um nachzudenken. Im Hotel wartete ein
Brief von Hermann Schneider aus Hamburg auf mich. „Lieber   **Lieber Hans** Dear
Hans," schrieb Hermann, „ich habe Dich zwar seit Ende des Krieges   Hans
nicht mehr gesehen, aber ich habe alle Deine Bücher gelesen. Ich
gratuliere Dir zu Deinen Detektivromanen, die ich viel besser finde   35 **die** which
als Deine Kriegsromane. Dein Verleger ist ein Freund von mir und   **Verleger** publisher
hat mir versprochen, Dir diesen Brief nachzuschicken. Aber da er

mir nicht sagen wollte, wo Du bist, weiß ich nicht, wo und wann
Dich mein Brief erreichen wird. Ich habe eine Bitte an den Detektiv
in Dir.

Wie Du vielleicht weißt, bin ich in Hamburg Direktor der Hansa-
Bank. In unserer Bank verschwinden seit zehn Jahren jedes Jahr um 5
diese Zeit fünf Zwanzigmarkstücke. Natürlich sind hundert Mark
in Gold nicht viel Geld. Aber es ist doch seltsam, daß jemand in
unserer Bank jedes Jahr fünf Goldstücke stiehlt. Ich will noch nicht
die Polizei anrufen, denn ich habe das Gefühl, ich stehe hier vor
irgendeinem Geheimnis. Ich bitte Dich daher, die Sache zu unter- 10 **irgendein**   some kind
suchen. Du könntest ein paar Wochen lang in der Bank ‚arbeiten‘   of
und versuchen, den Dieb zu finden. Mein Privatsekretär ist übrigens
unser Freund Erich Karsten.“

Erich Karsten!

Erich Karsten! Gerade vor einer Stunde war er bei Ali gewesen und 15
hatte ihm, „wie jedes Jahr um diese Zeit“, fünf Goldstücke gegeben.
Und damals hatte er mit seinen Militärschuhen hinter meiner Frau
gestanden und den Brief gelesen.

Es wäre nicht gerade intelligent gewesen, Hermann Schneider von   **nicht gerade**   not
Tripolis aus anzurufen. Wenn Erich der Dieb war—und er mußte 20 exactly
es sein—durfte er auf keinen Fall wissen, daß ich gerade heute in
Tripolis war, als er Ali fünf Goldstücke ins Haus getragen hatte.

Ich nahm daher ein Taxi zum Flughafen, bekam auf der Maschine
nach Paris noch einen Platz und rief Hermann Schneider von Paris
aus an. Da ich nicht wußte, ob Erich bei Hermann war oder nicht, 25
erzählte ich Hermann, ich sei ein paar Tage in der Normandie
gewesen, hätte gerade seinen Brief bekommen und werde gegen
sechs in Hamburg ankommen. Ich gab meinem Freund die Flug-
nummer und bat ihn, mich abzuholen. „Natürlich hole ich dich ab“,
sagte Hermann. „Ich wohne nicht weit vom Hamburger Flughafen. 30 **Hamburger**   When
Es ist zwar sehr heiß hier in Hamburg, aber gottseidank habe ich   city names are used
hinter dem Haus ein Schwimmbecken.“   attributively, they
                                                                      have the ending **–er.**

Es war ungefähr sieben Uhr, als wir vor Hermanns Haus hielten.
Vor dem Haus stand ein Volkswagen. „Das ist Gerdas Wagen“, sagte
Hermann. „Sie hat deine Romane gelesen und wollte dich gerne 35
kennenlernen; übrigens werden wir nächste Woche heiraten. Ich—“

Hinter dem Haus schrie eine Frau. Sie schrie, daß mir fast das Herz
stillstand. Bevor ich wußte, was geschah, hatte Hermann einen
Revolver aus dem Wagen geholt und lief hinter das Haus. Ich folgte
ihm. Am Schwimmbecken stand ein Mädchen, blond, schön, und 40

mit einer Figur, wie man sie sonst nur im Film sieht. Auf dem Wasser schwamm ein Hut. Sie zitterte, zeigte auf den Hut und sagte: „Er ist weg,—oh, ich hasse diesen Menschen.“

(Fortsetzung folgt)

ANALYSIS

112   Prepositions with either Dative or Accusative

Nouns or pronouns following the prepositions **aus, außer, bei, mit, nach, seit, von, zu** must always be in the dative case:

> **Ich komme von meiner Tante.**
> **Ich komme von ihr.**

Nouns or pronouns following **durch, für, gegen, ohne** must always be in the accusative:

> **Ich gehe ohne meinen Freund.**
> **Ich gehe ohne ihn.**

In both groups, it is the preposition alone that determines the case of the following noun or pronoun.

There is, however, a group of prepositions which can be used with either dative or accusative, and the case of the noun or pronoun following these prepositions depends on the particular situation.

These prepositions are:

> **an, auf, hinter, in, neben, über, unter, vor, zwischen.**

These nine prepositions are used to describe local areas in relation to some fixed point of reference. Thus, the English phrases *under the sofa* and *behind the sofa* describe different areas in relation to a stationary object.

To a native speaker of English, the phrase *under the sofa* is not ambiguous; it can be used without danger of confusion in such sentences as

> The dog slept under the sofa.

and

> The dog crawled under the sofa.

However, the same speaker of English will usually distinguish between *in* and *into* in such sentences as

The dog slept in the house.—The dog ran into the house.
He moved in high circles.—He moved into high circles.
He slipped in his slippers.—He slipped into his slippers.

The areas designated by *into* are the goals toward which the actions of running, moving, and slipping are directed; and in each case, the action stops when that goal has been reached. On the other hand, the area *in the house* is not reached by sleeping there. The dog was in the house when he started to sleep; and the poor fellow who slipped in his slippers had already slipped into his slippers and was in his slippers when he started to slip in his slippers.

A German will argue that the difference between

sleeping in the house

and

running into the house

is exactly parallel to the difference between

sleeping under the sofa

and

crawling under the sofa.

Germans are very conscious of this difference because their language forces them to distinguish not only between *in*-situations and *into*-situations, but also between the two kinds of *under*-situations. The distinction is made in German not by the use of different prepositions like *in* and *into* but by the use of different cases following one and the same preposition.

If the area described by one of the nine prepositions above functions as the end-point or goal reached by the action (of crawling under the sofa), the noun following this preposition shows the accusative case.

If the area is the place where the entire action (of sleeping under the sofa) goes on from beginning to end, the noun following the preposition shows the dative.

This means that a German will always distinguish between **unter das Sofa** and **unter dem Sofa:**

Der Hund schläft unter dem Sofa.	**Der Hund springt unter das Sofa.**
Der Hund schläft hinter dem Sofa.	**Der Hund springt hinter das Sofa.**
Der Hund schläft auf dem Sofa.	**Der Hund springt auf das Sofa.**

It is important to realize that the distinction between dative and accusative after these nine prepositions is not one of rest versus motion. In both situations there may be motion (*He walked in the garden* and *He walked into the garden*). The determining factor is whether or not, in the course of the verbal action, a borderline is crossed by either the subject or the object. If such a borderline is crossed, the accusative must be used; if not, the dative must be used. This "borderline" may be real or imagined. Thus, the area **vor dem Haus** does not have a clearly defined border, but there is nevertheless common consent as to the meaning of **vor dem Haus.** If this area **vor dem Haus** is entered in the course of the verbal action, the accusative must be used: **Er fuhr vor das Haus** (*He drove up to the house*). If the entire verbal action takes place within the area **vor dem Haus,** the dative must be used: **Er hielt vor dem Haus** (*He stopped in front of the house*).

On the other hand, after verbs which cannot imply motion, such as **sein** and **bleiben,** the dative is always required with these nine prepositions.

> **Er ist schon im Bett.**
> **Er muß im Haus sein.**

NOTE:

1. The preposition corresponding to English *on* is **auf,** not **an.** German **an** describes an area "leaning against and touching" the point of reference. Thus it is **Frankfurt am Main** and **Köln am Rhein** (cf. *Stratford-on-Avon*). One speaks of a bed which stands **an der Wand** (**an** plus dative) after it has been pushed **an die Wand** (**an** plus accusative).

2. Unless the article is stressed, the following contractions are customary: **an dem = am; an das = ans; in dem = im; in das = ins.** The contractions **aufs, hinterm, übers, unterm** also occur in colloquial German.

3. If used with the accusative, **über** means either *over* with the implication "into the territory across," or it means *via* or *by way of.*

Er sprang über *den* Zaun.	He jumped over the fence (into the neighbor's garden).
Er ist über *die* Schweiz nach Italien gefahren.	He went to Italy via Switzerland.

When **über** means *via,* the corresponding interrogative is **wie?,** not **wohin?**

Wie seid ihr nach Italien gefahren, über Österreich oder über die Schweiz?	How did you go to Italy, via Austria or via Switzerland?

but

Wohin seid ihr gefahren?	Where did you go?
Nach Italien! Und zwar über die Schweiz!	To Italy—and by way of Switzerland.

(Note that the article *must* be used with **Schweiz**, but is not used with the names of most other countries.)

4. As you already know, the preposition **vor** frequently means *ago*. If so used, it must be followed by the dative: **vor drei Jahren** (*three years ago*).

113   wo and wohin

The difference between **unter dem Sofa** and **unter das Sofa** reappears in the difference between **wo** and **wohin**. If you ask a **wo**-question, chances are that the answer will contain one of the nine "local area" prepositions with the dative; if you ask a **wohin**-question, chances are that the answer will contain one of those prepositions with the accusative:

> **Wo warst du denn?—In der Stadt.**
> **Wohin willst du denn?—In die Stadt.**

114   The Splitting of wohin, woher, dahin, and daher

In spoken German, the interrogatives **wohin** (*to which place*) and **woher** (*from which place*) and the demonstratives **dahin** (*to that place*) and **daher** (*from that place*) are usually split in such a way that **hin** and **her** become part of the second prong. They are then treated as if they were complements like **ab** or **an** and thus join a following verb form.

UNSPLIT POSITION	SPLIT POSITION
Wohin *gehst* du?	Wo gehst du *hin*?
Wohin willst du gehen?	Wo willst du denn *hingehen*?
Woher *kommst* du?	Wo kommst du *her*?
Woher ist der Brief ge*kommen*?	Wo ist denn der Brief *hergekommen*?
Dahin *will* ich nicht.	Da will ich gar nicht *hin*.
Daher komme ich *auch*.	Da komme ich *auch* her.

This splitting is colloquial, but not substandard. In the Lutheran translation of the Bible, Ruth 1:16 still reads:

> **Wo du hingehst, da will ich auch hin; wo du bleibst, da bleibe ich auch. Dein Volk ist mein Volk, und dein Gott ist mein Gott.**

These "split" forms are very commonly used. When a German unexpectedly meets a friend, he asks,

> **Wo kommst *du* denn her?**

not:

> **Woher kommst du?**

115 The Genitive Case

The English phrases *John Miller's house* and *the house of John Miller* are interchangeable. Both forms are "possessives" and answer the question *whose?* But *John Miller's* is called a genitive form, and *of John Miller* is a prepositional phrase used as a substitute for that genitive form. Forms like *John's* are normally used when referring to persons or to personifications; phrases with *of* are used in English when referring to things or ideas. It is normal to say *the purpose of the experiment,* not *the experiment's purpose.* Phrases with *of* are much more prevalent than forms with *'s.*

In this unit the German genitive case is introduced. It is important to recognize from the very beginning two areas where German differs from English:

1. Phrases like *John's father* as well as phrases like *the purpose of the experiment* can be expressed in German by genuine genitive forms—that is, without the use of a preposition. German, in other words, does not make any distinction between persons and things. For example, **das Haus meines Vaters** and **der Titel meines Romans** correspond structurally to *my father's house* and *my novel's title.*

2. There is a growing tendency in German, especially in the spoken language, to avoid the genitive and to replace it with a prepositional phrase with **von,** again without any distinction between persons and things. It is very important, therefore, that you memorize thoroughly the patterns demonstrating these constructions, and that you keep in mind the fact that quite often the same English phrase can be expressed in two different ways in German.

ein Freund meines Mannes	or	**ein Freund von meinem Mann**
das Ende dieses Romans	or	**das Ende von diesem Roman**

Forms of the Genitive Case

INTERROGATIVE PRONOUNS

NOM.	**wer**	**was**
GEN.	*wessen*	
DAT.	**wem**	**was**
ACC.	**wen**	**was**

NOTE: **Was** has no genitive of its own. The dative **was** is used only after prepositions governing the dative, for example, **Von *was* habt ihr geredet?**

DEFINITE AND INDEFINITE ARTICLES

	MASC.	FEM.	NEUT.	PLUR.
NOM.	der	die	das	die
	ein	eine	ein	(keine)
GEN.	*des*	*der*	*des*	*der*
	eines	*einer*	*eines*	*(keiner)*
DAT.	dem	der	dem	den
	einem	einer	einem	(keinen)
ACC.	den	die	das	die
	einen	eine	ein	(keine)

GENITIVE OF NOUNS

Feminine nouns have the same form throughout the singular; there is no special ending for the genitive.

NOM.	die Frau	die Zeitung
GEN.	der Frau	der Zeitung
DAT.	der Frau	der Zeitung
ACC.	die Frau	die Zeitung

The majority of masculine and neuter nouns add the ending **-es,** if their stem consists of one syllable, and **-s,** if their stem consists of two or more syllables.

NOM.	der Mann	der Bahnhof	das Buch
GEN.	des Mannes	des Bahnhofs	des Buches
DAT.	dem Mann	dem Bahnhof	dem Buch
ACC.	den Mann	den Bahnhof	das Buch

Some masculine nouns, for example, **der Student, der Mensch, der Polizist'** (the policeman) have the ending **-en** in the genitive; this ending **-en** in such nouns occurs in all forms but the nominative singular.

	SINGULAR	PLURAL
NOM.	der Student	die Studenten
GEN.	des Studenten	der Studenten
DAT.	dem Studenten	den Studenten
ACC.	den Studenten	die Studenten

There are a few nouns that are irregular in the singular, for example, **das Herz** (the heart).

	SINGULAR	PLURAL
NOM.	das Herz	die Herzen
GEN.	des Herzens	der Herzen
DAT.	dem Herz(en)	den Herzen
ACC.	das Herz	die Herzen

The genitive plural of nouns has the same form as the nominative plural and the accusative plural. Remember that the dative plural of most German nouns ends in **-n** (see **58**).

NOM.	die Männer	die Frauen	die Bücher
GEN.	der Männer	der Frauen	der Bücher
DAT.	den Männern	den Frauen	den Büchern
ACC.	die Männer	die Frauen	die Bücher

116 Use of the Genitive

Prepositions Governing the Genitive

There are a number of prepositions which must be used with the genitive, but only three of these are of importance to the beginner: **während** (during); **wegen** (because of); and **trotz** (in spite of).

> **Während des Krieges war Schmidt in Norwegen.**
> **Wegen des Regens bleiben wir zu Hause.**
> **Trotz des Regens fahren wir nach Köln.**

With **trotz** and **wegen,** there is a tendency to replace the genitive with the dative, but this is still considered colloquial (**trotz dem Regen**). The compound **trotzdem** (in spite of that, nevertheless) has become standard.

We have now introduced all the major German prepositions. Remember that they *must* be used with specific cases. There are four different groups:

WITH THE GENITIVE:	während, wegen, trotz
WITH THE DATIVE:	aus, außer, bei, mit, nach, seit, von, zu
WITH THE ACCUSATIVE:	durch, für, gegen, ohne
WITH EITHER DATIVE OR ACCUSATIVE:	an, auf, hinter, in, neben, über, unter, vor, zwischen

The Genitive of Time

Occasionally, the genitive is used to express indefinite time. In contrast to English *one day* (past) and *some day* (future), **eines Tages** can be used for both past and future. Similarly: **eines Morgens, eines Abends,** and, by analogy, **eines Nachts** (and not **einer Nacht**).

The Attributive Genitive

By far the most common occurrence of the genitive is its use as an attribute. It then modifies a noun in the same way that an adjective does.

The government's decision did not come unexpectedly.
(*government's* is an attribute of the subject *the decision*)
The Thurbers expected Joan's cousin to arrive momentarily.
(*Joan's:* attribute of the direct object *cousin*)

In these sentences, the "possessive" attributes can be eliminated without impairing the basic structure of the sentence; in other words, even without the attributes, the sentences are complete units of thought.

The decision did not come unexpectedly.
The Thurbers expected (the) cousin momentarily.

In German, the use of the attributive genitive is considered standard in the written language. It is used in two positions:

1. If the genitive form is a proper name, it *precedes* the noun it modifies:
   Schmidt-Ingelheims Roman war eine Sensation.
   Werners Freundin kannte er nicht.

Note that German does not use an apostrophe with this personal genitive.

2. If the genitive form is a common noun, it *follows* the noun it modifies.
   Am Abend ihres Geburtstages ging er mit ihr ins Theater.
   Die Integrität des Menschen ist das Thema seines Romans.

This means that *the woman's husband* must be rendered by **der Mann der Frau** and *the girl's father* by **der Vater des Mädchens.**

In the spoken language, the situation is far more complicated. While the attributive genitive is still considered standard German by most educated speakers, there is a steady erosion of these forms. The genitive most frequently replaced is the real possessive genitive in such forms as *my father's house* (expressing ownership: *My father owns the house.*) The German equivalent is **das Hause meines Vaters,** but the variant **das Haus von meinem Vater** also occurs and is used even by many well-educated Germans.

Von plus dative is always used when the genitive would not be recognizable—that is, primarily in the absence of an article or of a **der-** or **ein-** word.

die Bücher von Studenten	students' books
der Vater von zehn Kindern	the father of ten children
eine Freundin von Müllers Frau	a friend of Müller's wife

With **Freund** and other nouns expressing similar relationships, **von** plus dative is used as the equivalent of the English phrases

> *He is a friend of mine.*
> **Er ist ein Freund von mir.**
> *He is a friend of Karl's.*
> **Er ist ein Freund von Karl.**

The idea *one of* in such sentences as *He is one of my friends* is expressed by **einer** (**eine, eins**) **von** (see **117**).

> **Er ist einer von meinen Freunden.**
> **Sie ist eine von Karls Freundinnen.**

In such phrases as *a cup of coffee, a glass of wine, a pound of butter,* where the first noun denotes a measure and the second something measured, the second German noun shows no case.

> **eine Tasse Kaffee**
> **ein Glas Wein**
> **ein Pfund Butter**

If more than one measured unit is involved, only feminine nouns are used in the plural; masculines and neuters retain the singular form.

> **zwei Tassen Kaffee**
> **zwei Glas Wein**
> **zwei Pfund Butter**

Compounding of nouns is another means by which German very frequently expresses the equivalent of English phrases with *of,* for example, *the production of leather goods:* **die Produktion von Lederwaren** or **die Lederwarenproduktion.** English, of course, uses the same device, but usually without spelling the compound as one word: *wheat production, book publishing,* etc.

117   ein-Words without Nouns

When **ein**-words are not followed by nouns, their declension is exactly the same as that of the **der**-words. The neuter ending is usually **-s** instead of **-es.**

> **Inges Freund heißt Hans, und *meiner* heißt Werner.**
> **Ich habe leider kein Buch. Hast du *eins?***

118   The Indirect-Discourse Subjunctive

In addition to the subjunctive forms introduced in Unit 6, German has a second set of subjunctive forms which we shall call the indirect-discourse subjunctive. This set is not complete. It is sufficient to know the following forms:

PRESENT INDIRECT-DISCOURSE SUBJUNCTIVE

	sein	All other verbs						
		haben	werden	können	wollen	lieben	nehmen	fahren
ich	sei	habe	werde	könne	wolle	liebe	nehme	fahre
du	—	—	—	—	—	—	—	—
er	sei	habe	werde	könne	wolle	liebe	nehme	fahre
wir	seien	—	—	—	—	—	—	—
ihr	—	—	—	—	—	—	—	—
sie	seien	—	—	—	—	—	—	—

PAST INDIRECT-DISCOURSE SUBJUNCTIVE

ich sei gekommen   ich habe gegessen
er sei gekommen   er habe gegessen
wir seien gekommen   _____
sie seien gekommen   _____

NOTE:

1. The **ich**-form is always identical with the **er**-form.

2. The past indirect-discourse subjunctive replaces the past and the perfect of the indicative.

119 The Use of the Indirect-Discourse Subjunctive

As stated in Unit 6, the forms of the regular subjunctive can *always* be used in indirect discourse. It is not possible to formulate any definite rule stating when the indirect-discourse subjunctive should be used. It simply exists as an alternative preferred by some and almost completely avoided by others. In spoken German, the regular subjunctive is constantly gaining ground. Of the **ich**-forms listed above, the forms of **sein** and the modals are clearly recognizable as subjunctive forms; all other **ich**-forms are indistinguishable from the present-tense indicative (**ich liebe** can be either subjunctive or indicative).

Those who do use the indirect-discourse subjunctive usually follow this rule: the forms not recognizable as subjunctive occur only in indirect questions.

    Sie fragte mich, ob ich sie liebe.

In an indirect assertion, the unrecognizable **ich liebe** is replaced by the regular subjunctive **ich liebte**:

    Ich sagte ihr, daß ich sie liebte.

To illustrate the range of choice, let us assume that somebody asks the following question:

Liebst du mich denn, und findest du mich schön?

By using the regular subjunctive only, this question could be reported in the form:

Sie fragte mich, ob ich sie denn liebte und schön fände.

By using the new set only, one could write:

Sie fragte mich, ob ich sie denn liebe und schön finde.

Most probably, one will find a mixture: thus (in Heinrich Böll, *Ansichten eines Clowns*):

Sie fragte mich, ob ich sie denn liebe und schön fände,

is followed, at the end of the same paragraph, by:

Ich murmelte [mumbled], **ja, ja, ich fände sie schön und liebte sie.**

NOTE:

1. If the original statement was made in the regular subjunctive, it cannot be changed.

„Es wäre schön, wenn heute die Sonne schiene.“
Er sagte, es wäre schön, wenn heute die Sonne schiene.

2. To put an imperative into indirect discourse, **sollen** is used.

„Seien Sie mir nicht böse.“
Er sagte, ich sollte ihm nicht böse sein.
Er sagte, ich solle ihm nicht böse sein.

120 The Suffix **-ung**

The suffix **-ung** is added to many verb stems. It forms feminine nouns, the plural form being **-ungen**. Comparable to English derivatives in *-tion*, these nouns designate the verbal act as such (cf. English *the foundation of Rome*) or the result of a verbal act (*the foundations of the cathedral*).

die Einladung	invitation
die Erwartung	expectation
die Erzählung	story, narration
die Hoffnung	hope
die Untersuchung	investigation
die Versuchung	temptation

A special case is

die Wohnung	living quarters, apartment.

EXERCISES

A. Read aloud, then write out the numbers.

$$1 + 10 = 11 \qquad\qquad 11 - 4 = 7$$
$$6 + 10 = 16 \qquad\qquad 10 - 2 = 8$$
$$12 + 5 = 17 \qquad\qquad 9 - 0 = 9$$
$$14 + 6 = 20 \qquad\qquad 16 - 6 = 10$$

Es ist jetzt 7 Uhr 20. (7^{20} Uhr)
Es ist jetzt 8 Uhr 19.
Es ist jetzt 9 Uhr 18.
Es ist jetzt 10 Uhr 17.
Es ist jetzt 11 Uhr 16.
Es ist jetzt 12 Uhr 15.

B. Form questions for the following statements, using either **wo** or **wohin.**

1. Ich habe den Tisch an die Wand gestellt.
2. Gestern habe ich im Theater Frau Lenz gesehen.
3. Ich wollte mir auf dem Bahnhof eine Zeitung kaufen.
4. Im Sommer war er mit Rosemarie an der Mosel.
5. Morgen fährt er mit Rosemarie nach Bonn.
6. Seine Tochter ist in Mainz in die Schule gegangen.
7. Seine Tochter war in Mainz.
8. Meine Frau liest die Zeitung immer im Bett.
9. Zu Hause trinkt Anton immer Tee.
10. Meyer hat uns zum Bahnhof gefahren.

C. Answer the following questions, using in your answers one of the prepositions that can take either the dative or the accusative.

1. Wohin hat er seinen Hut gelegt?
2. Wo hast du sie gesehen?
3. Wo waren Sie während des Krieges, Herr Schmidt?
4. Wo steht denn euer Wagen?
5. Wo geht ihr heute abend hin?
6. Wo wohnen Sie in München, Herr Schneider?
7. Was tut Anton Meyer denn mit seinem Geld?
8. Wie seid ihr nach Italien gefahren?
9. Was hast du denn mit meinem Hut getan?
10. Wo hast du heute gefrühstückt?

D. Express in German:

1. He is my friend.
2. He is Karl's friend.
3. He is my sister's friend.
4. He is a friend of my sister's.
5. He is one of my sister's friends.
6. He is my father.
7. He is Mary's father.
8. He is my wife's father.
9. He is her son.
10. He is Inge's son.
11. He is my brother's son.
12. Karl is one of my brother's sons.
13. Ernst is one of the sons of Mr. Bertram.
14. Fritz is her friend.
15. Fritz is a friend of hers.
16. Fritz is one of her friends.
17. Her daughters are very intelligent.
18. Ingrid's daughter is also very intelligent.
19. Ingelheim's daughters are intelligent.
20. The Ingelheims' daughters are intelligent.

E. Give appropriate answers to the following questions, using either the genitive or **von** plus dative:

1. Wessen Buch ist das?
2. Mit wessen Wagen bist du denn nach Köln gefahren?
3. Mit *wes*sen Freundin warst du im Theater?
4. Von wessen Roman sprecht ihr denn?
5. Wessen Haus habt ihr gekauft?
6. Wessen Tochter hat er geheiratet?
7. Wessen Freundin ist das?
8. Wessen Vater hast du besucht?
9. Für wessen Haus willst du so viel Geld bezahlen?
10. Durch wessen Freundin hast du ihn kennengelernt?

F. Fill the blanks with appropriate **ein**-words.

1. Ich habe leider kein Buch. Hast du _____?
2. Ich habe meinen Wagen nicht hier, Hans. Wo ist denn _____?
3. Habt ihr schon ein Haus? Nein, wir haben noch _____.
4. Hast du Zeit? Ich habe _____.

5. Das ist _____ von den Büchern, die mein Vater mir geschickt hat.
6. Er ist auch _____ von den Soldaten, die nicht über den Krieg sprechen wollen.
7. Ich habe nicht _____ von seinen Büchern gelesen.
8. _____ seiner Romane habe ich mir gekauft.
9. Mein Hut ist das nicht; es muß _____ sein, Frau Bertram.

G. Supply the missing words:

1. Ich habe heute morgen meine Frau _____ Bahnhof gebracht.
2. Woher wissen Sie denn, daß Johannes schon _____ verheiratet war?
3. Mein Mann spricht oft _____ seiner Tochter.
4. In Frankreich war Ingelheim nur während _____ Krieges.
5. Ich habe gerade gelesen, daß Sie _____ drei Wochen in München wohnen.
6. Liegt er immer noch _____ Bett?
7. Von Ingelheims Kriegsroman spricht heute _____ Mensch mehr.
8. Ich bin nicht Soldat geworden, um Brieftauben _____ füttern.
9. Der Arzt glaubte, Ingelheim _____ Hepatitis, aber er _____ nur zu viel getrunken.
10. Ich weiß, daß Anton nach Berlin gefahren _____.
11. Kannst du mir sagen, _____ Ingelheims Kinder haben?
12. Er ist einer _____ Ingelheims Söhnen.
13. Ich möchte wissen, _____ du mich eigentlich geheiratet hast.
14. Können Sie mir sagen, _____ der Zug nach Köln fährt?
15. _____ der Krieg anfing, studierte Schmidt in Frankfurt Medizin.
16. Man kann doch nicht im Garten arbeiten, _____ es regnet.
17. Er fragte mich, ob ich heute abend auch ins Kino _____.
18. Ich wollte, ich _____ dich nie gesehen.
19. Wenn er nicht nach Deutschland gefahren _____, hätte ich ihn nie kennengelernt.
20. Ich habe das Haus nicht kaufen _____.

H. Rewrite Hermann Schneider's letter to Ingelheim (page 202) in indirect discourse, using either the normal subjunctive or, when possible, the indirect-discourse subjunctive.

I. Express in German:

1. We really ought to put (**stellen**) that little table (**-chen**) between our beds.
2. I don't believe that they sit here because they have no money in the bank.
3. Do you always have to put your books on the breakfast table?
4. Why can't they lie on the breakfast table?
5. During the war Ingelheim was on the Western Front.
6. At that time he was happy that he did not have to go to Africa.
7. It is cold tonight; I wish you hadn't forgotten your overcoat.

8. One of them asked Ingelheim if he had been in Cairo during the war.

9. If only that woman hadn't been so unfriendly!

10. If only I hadn't accepted the money!

11. You should have given him more money.

12. I wish I weren't so far away from you.

J. Write a brief paragraph in German containing the following ideas; use the past tense.
Do *not* translate the passage; just use it as an outline. Use your own words, but do not attempt to use any construction or any vocabulary that you haven't had yet.

Hermann Schneider drove to the Hansa-Bank at 7 A.M. It was hot, and he would much rather have stayed at home by his swimming pool. But he had to go to the bank, because Karsten had just called to tell him that five gold pieces had disappeared again. Schneider didn't understand why this could happen every year. The thief had to be somebody who worked in the bank, but Schneider did not want to call the police yet. He would rather discuss the matter with Karsten first, he thought.

K. Now write a brief dialogue between Schneider and his fiancée Gerda, taking place in the evening of the same day.

Hermann tells Gerda about the theft of the gold pieces. She wants to know whether he has told Karsten about it, and whether Karsten had any ideas. Yes, he has, and Karsten thought it was somebody who works in the bank, but he was very much against calling the police. Gerda has an idea: What about Hermann's friend Ingelheim? He has written detective stories, and perhaps he can help Hermann. But Hermann hasn't seen Ingelheim since the war and doesn't know where he is. Gerda suggests that he call Ingelheim's publisher, which Hermann promises to do the next morning. Gerda is pleased, because she has wanted to meet Ingelheim for a long time.

BASIC VOCABULARY

ach oh

auf on, on top of; up; open
 auf sein to be up (out of bed)

der Augenblick, –e moment

aussehen to look, give the appearance

die Bank, ⸚e bench

die Bank, –en bank

bevor (*conj.*) before

die Bitte, –n request

da (*conj.*) since

daher therefore; from there, from that place

dahin there, toward that place

erreichen to reach, attain

der Fall, ⸚e case; fall
 auf jeden Fall in any case, at any rate
 auf keinen Fall in no case, under no circumstances

fast almost

das Fenster, – window

folgen (*with dative*) to follow

fort away

Frankreich France

ganz whole, entire

gegen sechs Uhr around six o'clock

geschehen to happen, occur

halten to hold; stop

heiß hot

her toward the speaker (in the sense of "hither")
 herauskommen to come out
 herkommen to come here

das Herz, –en heart
 (*gen.*: **des Herzens;** *dat.*: **dem Herzen**)

hin away from the speaker
 hineingehen to go in
 hinfahren to go there

der Hof, ⸚e (royal) court; yard
 der Hofgarten the Royal Gardens

der Bahnhof, ⸚e station

holen to get, fetch
hundert hundred, a hundred
kaum (*adverb*) hardly
legen to lay, place
es macht nichts it doesn't
    matter
möglich possible
    unmöglich impossible;
    (*sentence adverb*) not
    possibly
na! well! (*interj.*)
nachdem' (*conj.*) after
nachschicken to forward
    (mail)
neben next to, beside
die Ordnung, –en order
    in Ordnung in order, all

right, O.K.
der Platz, –̈e place, seat
die Polizei' police
    der Polizist', –en policeman
rufen to call
die Sache, –n thing, matter
die Schweiz Switzerland
schwimmen to swim
    das Schwimmbecken, –
    swimming pool
selten rare, seldom
seltsam strange, peculiar
sonst otherwise
stehlen to steal
stellen to place, put (up-
    right)
das Stück, –e piece

das Goldstück, –e gold coin
tanzen to dance
tatsächlich actual(ly)
der Tee, –s tea
der Tisch, –e table
trotz in spite of
unter under
verrückt crazy
versprechen to promise
das Volk, –̈er people
von (Paris) aus from (Paris)
wählen to choose; to dial
während during
die Wand, –̈e wall
wegen because of
zusammen together
zwar to be sure

ADDITIONAL VOCABULARY

die Aufnahme, –n picture,
    photo
die Brücke, –n bridge
der Dieb, –e thief
die Ecke, –n corner
erkennen (an) to recognize
    (by)
die Gegend, –en area

geheim secret
    das Geheimnis, –se secret
greifen to grasp, reach out
    (for something)
die Halle, –n hall, lobby
das Loch, –̈er hole
der Mantel, –̈ coat, overcoat
das Pfund, –e pound

schreien to scream, cry out
der Sekretär', –e secretary
der Stein, –e stone
untersu'chen to investigate
der Verleger, – publisher
wie gesagt as I said
zittern to tremble, shake

IRREGULAR VERBS

backen to bake
    backte, hat gebacken, er
    backt
erkennen to recognize
    erkannte, hat erkannt, er
    erkennt
    ertrank, ist ertrunken, er
    ertrinkt
geschehen to happen, occur
    geschah, ist geschehen, es
    geschieht
greifen to grasp

griff, hat gegriffen, er
    greift
halten to hold, stop
    hielt, hat gehalten, er hält
rufen to call
    rief, hat gerufen, er ruft
schneiden to cut
    schnitt, hat geschnitten, er
    schneidet
schreien to scream, cry out
    schrie, hat geschrie(e)n, er
    schreit

schwimmen to swim
    schwamm, ist geschwom-
    men, er schwimmt
stehlen to steal
    stahl, hat gestohlen, er
    stiehlt
versprechen to promise
    versprach, hat ver-
    sprochen, er verspricht
werfen to throw
    warf, hat geworfen, er
    wirft

UNIT 8: Relative Pronouns—wann, ob, als, wenn—
gar—da–Compounds—wo–Compounds—
Prepositional Objects

[1] Definite Relative Pronouns

Analyze carefully the relative clauses contained in these sentences.

Mein Vater, der nicht studiert hatte, konnte nicht verstehen, warum ich
Schriftsteller werden wollte.

> My father, who had not gone to the university, could not understand why
> I wanted to become a writer.

Maria ist auch eine von den Frauen, die ihren Mann nicht verstehen.

> Maria is also one of those women who don't understand their husbands.

Sein Vater, dessen Frau aus Leningrad kam, sprach gut Russisch.

> His father, whose wife came from Leningrad, spoke Russian well.

Seine Frau, deren Vater aus Leningrad kam, sprach gut Russisch.

> His wife, whose father came from Leningrad, spoke Russian well.

Kennen Sie meinen Freund Müller?—Meinen Sie den Müller, dem das Corona-
Hotel gehört?

> Do you know my friend Müller?—Do you mean the Müller who owns the
> Corona Hotel?

Ist das· der Hut, den dir dein Mann aus Paris mitgebracht hat?

> Is that the hat your husband brought you from Paris?

Habe ich dir schon die Omega gezeigt, die ich in Zürich gekauft habe?

> Have I shown you the Omega (that) I bought in Zurich?

Das Essen, das wir hier bekommen, ist so gut, daß wir noch eine Woche
bleiben wollen.

> The food we get here is so good that we want to stay another week.

SEE
ANALYSIS
121

(pp. 235-236)

(Facing) **In einem schwäbischen Gasthof**

Ich wußte natürlich, woher die Goldstücke kamen, die bei Ali in einem Loch
in der Wand lagen.

> I knew, of course, where the gold pieces came from that were lying in a
> hole in the wall at Ali's.

Ich wollte Ali und Busuq wiedersehen, deren Gast ich während des Krieges
gewesen war.

> I wanted to see Ali and Busuq again, whose guest I had been during the
> war.

Ist das der Wagen, mit dem du nach Italien gefahren bist?

> Is that the car you went to Italy in?

Hermann, durch den ich meine Frau kennengelernt habe, ist jetzt Bankdirektor
in Hamburg.

> Hermann, through whom I met my wife, is now director of a bank in
> Hamburg.

Wer waren denn die drei Herren, Ingrid, mit denen ich Sie gestern abend
gesehen habe?

> Who were the three gentlemen with whom I saw you last night, Ingrid?

Wer sind eigentlich diese Schmidts, von denen du immer redest?

> Who are those Schmidts, anyway, that you always talk about?

Ihre Töchter, für die sie so schwer gearbeitet hat, wollen heute nichts mehr
von ihr wissen.

> Today her daughters, for whom she worked so hard, don't want to have
> anything to do with her any more.

Der Mann, ohne dessen Hilfe ich heute nicht Arzt wäre, ist Professor Schmidt.

> The man without whose help I wouldn't be a doctor today is Professor
> Schmidt.

[2] Indefinite Relative Pronouns

SEE
ANALYSIS
121
(pp. 235-236)

Wer Geld hat, hat auch Freunde.
Wer Geld hat, der hat auch Freunde.

> (He) who has money has friends, too.

Was Ingelheim gestern abend zu erzählen hatte, war wirklich nicht viel.
Was Ingelheim gestern abend zu erzählen hatte, das war wirklich nicht viel.

> What Ingelheim had to say last night really wasn't very much.

Hans hat mich zum Essen eingeladen, was ich sehr nett finde.

> Hans has invited me to dinner, which I think is very nice.

Ich habe leider nicht alles verstanden, was sie gesagt hat.

Unfortunately, I did not understand everything she said.

Professor Schmidt hat wirklich nichts gesagt, was ich nicht schon wußte.

Professor Schmidt really didn't say anything that I didn't already know.

Ich habe dieses Wochenende in Afrika etwas erlebt, was man eigentlich nicht erleben kann.

This weekend I experienced something in Africa that one really cannot experience.

[3] wann

Form other questions with **wann** and transform them into dependent clauses.

„Wann ist Fritz denn gestern abend nach Hause gekommen?"
Fritz, Vater möchte wissen, wann du gestern abend nach Hause gekommen bist.

„Wann will Heidi denn heiraten?"
Ich weiß nicht, wann sie heiraten will.

SEE
ANALYSIS
122

(pp. 237-238)

[4] ob

Form other yes-or-no questions and transform them into dependent clauses.

„Fährst du nach Berlin?"
Mutter will wissen, ob du nach Berlin fährst.

„War Erich wirklich in Tripolis?"
Ich habe nie erfahren können, ob Erich wirklich in Tripolis war.

SEE
ANALYSIS
122

(pp. 237-238)

[5] als ob, als wenn, als

Form parallel examples. Be prepared to produce orally **Er tut, als ob er schliefe,** when you hear **Er schläft.**

Er tut, als ob er schliefe.	He acts as if he were asleep.
Er tut, als schliefe er.	
Er tat, als ob er schliefe.	He acted as if he were asleep.
Er tat, als schliefe er.	
Er tut, als ob er geschlafen hätte.	He acts as if he had been alseep.
Er tut, als hätte er geschlafen.	

SEE
ANALYSIS
122

(pp. 237-238)

Er tat, als ob er geschlafen hätte.	He acted as if he had been asleep.
Er tat, als hätte er geschlafen.	
Er tat, als wenn er schliefe.	He acted as if he were asleep.
Er tat, als wenn er geschlafen hätte.	He acted as if he had been asleep.
Gerda sah aus, als wäre sie krank.	Gerda looked as if she were sick.

[6] **als** with the Comparative

Form parallel sentences with **besser als** and **mehr als.**

SEE
ANALYSIS
122

(pp. 237-238)

Du bist auch nicht besser als er.	You are no better than he is.
Das ist besser als nichts.	That is better than nothing.
In New York wohnen mehr Menschen als in Berlin.	More people live in New York than in Berlin.
Frau Behrens hat in Casablanca mehr Geld verloren, als sie wollte.	Frau Behrens lost more money in Casablanca than she intended to.
Er wußte bestimmt mehr, als er uns gesagt hat.	I'm sure he knew more than he told us.

[7] The Conjunction **als**

SEE
ANALYSIS
122

(pp. 237-238)

Als Ingelheim ins Hotel kam, wartete ein Brief auf ihn.

Als wir in Tripolis waren, wohnten wir bei Ali und Busuq.

Hermann und ich saßen bei Ali, als Erich von meiner Frau sprach.

Wir wollten gerade ins Haus gehen, als eine Frau laut schrie.

[8] **wenn**

Form parallel sentences with **wenn,** in the meaning of both *if* and *whenever.*

SEE
ANALYSIS
122

(pp. 237-238)

Wenn es morgen regnet, bleiben wir zu Hause.

Wenn er wirklich in Köln gewesen wäre, hätte er auch den Dom sehen müssen.

Wenn er schon hier wäre, könnten wir ihn besuchen.

Wenn der Sommer kam, fuhren unsere Eltern immer mit uns an den Rhein.

Jedesmal, wenn Tante Amalie uns besuchte, mußte ich mit ihr ins Museum gehen.

Wenn ich in München bin, gehe ich abends immer ins Theater.

[9] **gar nicht, gar kein, gar nichts**

Study these sentences carefully. Note that whenever **gar** is stressed, it denies an immediately preceding idea. Be prepared to form your own examples.

SEE
ANALYSIS
123

(p. 239)

Meyer ist gar nicht *dumm;* er weiß immer, was er will.

Meyer isn't at all stupid; he always knows what he wants.

Was, Heidi will heiraten? Das habe ich gar nicht ge*wußt*.

> What? Heidi wants to get married? I didn't have any idea of that.

Er spricht so leise, daß man ihn gar nicht ver*st*ehen kann.

> He speaks so softly that you can't understand him at all.

Wie hast du denn geschlafen?—Ich habe *gar* nicht geschlafen.

> How did you sleep?—I didn't sleep at all.

Was habt ihr denn heute gelernt?—*Gar* nichts, wir haben nur gespielt.

> What did you learn today?—Nothing at all, we only played.

Ingelheim *war* gar kein General; er war nur Leutnant.

> Ingelheim wasn't a general at all; he was only a lieutenant.

[10] da-Compounds with unstressed da-

Wo ist denn mein Kugelschreiber?—Ich schreibe gerade damit.

> Where is my ballpoint pen?—I'm writing with it.

Wir haben *auch* ein Haus mit einer Garage dahinter.

> We, too, have a house with a garage behind it.

Das ist die Marienkirche, und in dem Haus da*n*eben hat früher mein Bruder gewohnt.

> That's St. Mary's, and my brother used to live in the house next to it.

Haben Sie Ingelheims Roman gelesen?—Nur den Anfang davon.

> Have you read Ingelheim's novel?—Only the beginning of it.

SEE
ANALYSIS
124

(pp. 239-240)

[11] Stressed and unstressed da-Compounds—Split da-Compounds —der hier, der da

Be prepared to produce orally the statements containing **da**-compounds when you hear the initial statements or questions of each group.

(a) *Den* Kugelschreiber kannst du zurückbringen.
   Damit (mit *dem*) kann ich nicht schreiben.
   Da kann ich nicht mit schreiben.

(b) Was soll ich denn mit einem *Ku*gelschreiber?
   Damit kann man doch nicht *schrei*ben!
   Da kann man doch nicht mit *schrei*ben!

(c) Dieser Kugelschreiber hier ist mir zu schwer. Darf ich mal *den* da versuchen?

(a) In die *O*per brauchst du mit Tante Amalie *nicht* zu gehen.
   *Da*bei schläft sie immer ein.
   Da schläft sie immer bei *ein*.

SEE
ANALYSIS
124-128

(pp. 239-242)

(b) Für eine *Wagner*-Oper ist Tante Amalie doch zu alt.
Das dauert doch sechs Stunden; dabei muß sie ja *ein*schlafen.
Da muß sie ja bei *ein*schlafen.

(c) Sonntag im Kino ist sie *auch* eingeschlafen.—Aber im Gloria-Palast läuft
heute abend ein Hitchcock-Film. Bei *dem* schläft sie be*stimmt* nicht ein.

[12] wo-Compounds

Wofür brauchst du denn so viel Geld? Was willst du denn kaufen?
What do you need so much money for? What do you want to buy?

Für was brauchst du denn das Geld?
What do you need the money for?

SEE
ANALYSIS
129
(pp. 242-243)

Ich weiß nicht, wofür er das Geld ausgegeben hat.
I don't know what he spent the money for.

War der Briefträger immer noch nicht da?—Warum fragst du denn schon
wieder? Auf was (worauf) wartest du denn eigentlich, auf einen Brief von
deiner Freundin?

Hasn't the mailman been here yet?—Why are you asking again? What are
you waiting for anyway, a letter from your girl friend?

[13] Prepositional Objects

After memorizing these verbs with their prepositions, form variations of your
own.

SEE
ANALYSIS
130–132
(pp. 243-247)

Angst haben vor

Hast du Angst vor ihm?—Nein, nicht vor ihm, aber vor seiner Intelligenz.
Are you afraid of him?—No, not of him, but of his intelligence.

antworten auf

Sie hat immer noch nicht auf meinen Brief geantwortet.
She still hasn't answered my letter.

bitten um

Dürfte ich Sie um eine Tasse Kaffee bitten?
Could I ask you for a cup of coffee?

danken für

Ich hätte ihm natürlich schon längst für die Blumen danken sollen.
Of course I should have thanked him for the flowers long ago.

denken an   and   nachdenken über

Weißt du, daß ich noch oft an unsre Reise denke?
Do you know that I still think about our trip very often?

Über *dies*es Problem habe ich *auch* schon nachgedacht.
I've thought about this problem, too.

einladen zu

Darf ich Sie zu einem Glas Wein einladen?
May I invite you to (have) a glass of wine (with me)?

fragen nach

Hat jemand nach mir gefragt?—Du kannst dir doch denken, daß sie alle nach dir gefragt haben.
Did anybody ask about me?—Don't you know that they all asked about you?

gehören zu

Diese Schlüssel gehören zu unserem VW.
These keys belong to our VW.

Weißt du, daß Meyer jetzt zur Antivivisektionsliga gehört?
Do you know that Meyer belongs to the Anti-Vivisection League now?

glauben an

Ein Athe*ist* glaubt nicht an Gott.
An atheist doesn't believe in God.

halten von, halten für

Was halten Sie von Meyer? Ich halte ihn für sehr intelligent.—Ich nicht, ich halte ihn gar nicht für intelligent.
What do you think of Meyer? I think he is very intelligent.—I don't; I don't think he's intelligent at all.

hoffen auf

Ich weiß, ihr Touristen hofft, daß morgen wieder die Sonne scheint. Aber die Leute hier hoffen auf Regen.
I know you tourists hope that the sun is going to shine again tomorrow. But the people here are hoping for rain.

hören von

Seit dem Kriege habe ich nichts mehr von Meyer gehört.
Since the war, I haven't heard anything from Meyer (of Meyer, about Meyer).

lachen über   (to laugh at, about)

Ich lache gar nicht über dich; ich lache nur über deinen Akzent.
But I'm not laughing at you; I'm only laughing at your accent.

auslachen   (to laugh at, jeer at, make fun of)

Sie haben ihn einfach ausgelacht.
>   They simply laughed at him.

Wenn ein Humorist gut ist, lacht man über ihn; wenn er schlecht ist, lacht
   man ihn aus.
>   If a humorist is good, you laugh at him; if he is bad, you jeer at him.

reagieren auf

Wie reagieren denn Ihre Leser auf diesen Kriegsroman?
>   How do your readers react to this war novel?

Wie hat er denn auf dich reagiert?
>   How did he react to you?

sein für, sein gegen

Wer nicht für mich ist, ist gegen mich.
>   Whoever is not for me, is against me.

sprechen von

Von seiner Frau hat er nicht gesprochen.
>   He didn't talk about his wife.

Ich weiß nicht, warum er nie von seinen Romanen spricht.
>   I don't know why he never talks about his novels.

sprechen über

Heute abend spricht Professor Leid über Psychoanalyse.
>   Tonight Professor Leid will speak about psychoanalysis.

verstehen von

Du weißt doch, daß ich nichts von Archäologie verstehe.
>   You know, don't you, that I know nothing about archeology.

warten auf

Wie lange wartest du denn schon auf Fritz?
>   How long have you been waiting for Fritz?

wissen von

Leider weiß ich gar nichts von Ingelheim.
>   Unfortunately I know nothing about Ingelheim.

Was weißt *du* denn von den Kämpfen in der Normandie?
>   What do *you* know about the fighting in Normandy?

CONVERSATION

Snatches of Conversation Overheard by the Hat-Check Girl at the
Regina Bar

FRAUENSTIMME 1: Und als er dann endlich erschienen ist, ·habe ich gesagt: „Jetzt hättest du aber wirklich nicht mehr zu kommen brauchen." Und weißt du, was er mir darauf geantwortet hat? Ich hätte ja nicht auf ihn zu warten brauchen!

FRAUENSTIMME 2: Na so was! Wenn er *mir* das gesagt hätte, dann hätte ich ihm aber ...

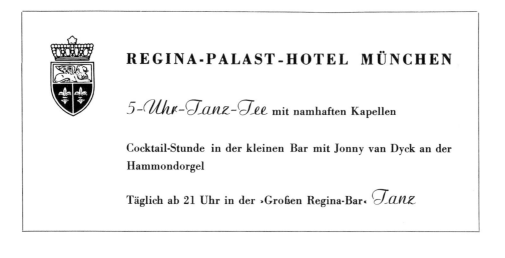

REGINA-PALAST-HOTEL MÜNCHEN

5-Uhr-Tanz-Tee mit namhaften Kapellen

Cocktail-Stunde in der kleinen Bar mit Jonny van Dyck an der Hammondorgel

Täglich ab 21 Uhr in der ›Großen Regina-Bar‹ *Tanz*

FRAU A: Wer? Der mit dem Hut? Das soll Schmidt-Ingelheim sein?

FRAU B: Nein, nicht *der.* Der da, mit dem Mantel über dem Arm.

FRAU A: Glaubst du wirklich, daß er das ist?

FRAU B: Ganz bestimmt. Gestern war doch sein Bild in der Zeitung. Er ist gerade aus Afrika zurückgekommen.

FRAU A: *Der* sieht aber gut aus, den möchte ich kennenlernen.

FRAU B: Du, ob das wohl seine Frau ist, die da neben ihm steht?

FRAU A: Nein, bestimmt nicht, die ist doch viel zu jung für ihn;—vielleicht seine Tochter.

MANN: . . . mir viel zu heiß war! Im Theater ist es mir immer zu heiß, und dann auch noch Wagner. Da schläft man ja bei ein. Fünf Stunden hab' ich da gesessen, und am liebsten wär' ich schon nach zehn Minuten aufgestanden und nach Hause gegangen. Acht Stunden im Büro sitzen und dann noch Wagner! Nee, da mach' ich nicht mehr mit. Das nächste Mal bleibe ich zu Hause und lese meine Zeitung.

FRAU: Von mir aus kannst du ruhig zu Hause bleiben. Dann gehe ich eben allein. Ach, ich liebe doch Wagner so sehr . . .

MÄDCHEN A: Niemand weiß etwas davon—kein Mensch. Außer dir habe ich das noch niemandem erzählt, und du mußt mir versprechen, daß du mit keinem darüber redest, auch mit Fritz nicht.

MÄDCHEN B: Natürlich nicht! Mit wem könnte ich über so etwas reden? Du kennst mich doch. Übrigens, weißt du, daß die Erika den Hans jetzt *doch* heiraten will?

MÄDCHEN A: Ach was! Wirklich? Das hätte ich nicht gedacht.

MÄDCHEN B: Ja, doch! Sie hat mir's gestern erzählt, es soll aber noch niemand etwas davon wissen.

MÄNNERSTIMME I: Plötzlich waren schon wieder ein paar Tiefflieger da. Ich denke, ich werde verrückt. Ich drücke mich auf den Boden, einer von den Tieffliegern sieht mich und kommt herunter. . . . Hier ist mein Hut, Fräulein. Was bekommen Sie dafür? Ach so, erst wenn wir weggehen. . . . Ja, wo war ich, also der kommt herunter, und ich denke, jetzt ist alles zu Ende, aber da fliegt er plötzlich nach rechts weg und. . . .

MÄNNERSTIMME II: Müssen Sie hier stehenbleiben und mit den Händen reden? Fräulein, meinen Mantel, bitte. . . .

MÄNNERSTIMME I: Ja, also, das hätten Sie erleben sollen, damals in Afrika. Dagegen war die Westfront gar nichts. Und dann war da noch dieser Erich Karsten, das müßte ich Ihnen wirklich noch erzählen. Also, wir haben nämlich damals bei einem Ägypter gewohnt, wissen Sie, Ali hieß. . . .

EIN MANN: Ingelheim, Ingelheim, Ingelheim, müßt ihr denn den ganzen Abend von Ingelheim reden? Als ob es sonst keine Schriftsteller mehr in Deutschland gäbe! Also, wenn ich den Namen Ingelheim noch einmal höre, könnt ihr allein Wein trinken gehen, ohne mich, ich kann den Namen nicht mehr hören. Ingelheim, Ingelheim, Ingelheim. . . .

Zwei und zwei ist fünf (**Schluß**)

„Wer ist weg?" fragte Hermann. „Herr Karsten", antwortete das
Mädchen. Hermann führte sie zu einem der Gartenstühle, versuchte,
ganz ruhig zu sein, und sagte: „Gerda, dies ist mein Freund Schmidt-
Ingelheim. Ich habe ihn gerade am Flugplatz abgeholt", und als sie
nicht auf seine Worte reagierte, sagte er: „Gerda, könntest du dich 5
zwingen, mir und Hans jetzt zu erzählen, was hier geschehen ist?"

Es dauerte doch noch ein paar Minuten, bis Gerda ruhig sprechen
konnte. Dann erzählte sie: „Ich bin kurz nach fünf mit meiner
Mutter hier angekommen. Wir sahen, daß du noch nicht zurück
warst. Mutter ist spazierengegangen, und ich wollte schwimmen, 10
bis du kamst. Als ich ins Wasser sprang, war niemand hier, das
weiß ich bestimmt. Aber als ich aus dem Wasser wollte, stand Herr
Karsten oben und hielt mir die Hand hin, um mir zu helfen. Ich   **hielt . . . hin** held
erschrak, schrie laut und sprang zurück. Herr Karsten fiel ins   out his hand
Wasser. Als ich auf dieser Seite aus dem Wasser kam, war Herr 15
Karsten weg. Aber da schwimmt sein Hut."

Hermann, dem ich auf dem Weg vom Flughafen erzählt hatte, was
in Tripolis geschehen war, sah mich an, dann ging er ins Wohnzimmer, holte ein Telefon, stellte es auf den Gartentisch beim
Schwimmbecken, wählte eine Nummer und wartete. Gerda und ich
hörten, wie es am anderen Ende klingelte. Dann gab mir Hermann   5
den Hörer. „Hier Karsten", sagte eine Männerstimme. Und obwohl
ich seit dem Kriege nicht mit Erich gesprochen hatte, erkannte ich
seine Stimme sofort. Ich log und sagte ihm, ich riefe vom Flughafen
aus an.

Ich hätte gehofft, Hermann könnte mich abholen, er sei aber nir- 10
gends zu sehen, und zu Hause sei er auch nicht. „Er wollte dich
auch abholen", sagte Erich, „aber vielleicht ist er nicht so schnell
durch die Stadt gekommen, wie er wollte. Ich rufe ihn trotzdem
sofort noch einmal an und sage ihm, daß du da bist. Aber er ist
bestimmt nicht mehr zu Hause."   15

Einen Augenblick später klingelte das Telefon. Wir antworteten
nicht. „Wie weit ist es von hier bis zu Erichs Wohnung?" fragte ich
Hermann. „Mit dem Wagen mindestens eine Stunde", war die
Antwort. Ich sagte nichts, auch Gerda schwieg; aber ich glaube,
sie fühlte, daß Hermann und ich mehr wußten, als wir sagten.   20

Endlich meinte Hermann: „Gerda, die Geschichte, die du uns da
erzählt hast, ist einfach unmöglich. Wem der Hut auf dem Wasser
gehört, weiß ich nicht. Aber Erich kann er nicht gehören, Erich kann
nicht hier gewesen sein. Wenn er hier gewesen wäre, könnte er
jetzt nicht zu Hause sein. Weißt du was, wir warten, bis deine   25
Mutter zurückkommt, und dann fahre ich euch beide in meinem
Wagen nach Hamburg zurück. Hans kann mit deinem VW hinter   **hinter uns herfahren**
uns herfahren."   follow us

Es war schon ungefähr neun, als wir Gerda und ihrer Mutter gute
Nacht sagten. Gerda hatte versprochen, ein Bad zu nehmen, eine   30
Tasse Tee mit Kognak zu trinken und dann ins Bett zu gehen. Um   **um halb zehn** at half-
halb zehn saßen wir bei Hermann, tranken einen Whisky und re-   past nine
deten von den Fußabdrücken hinter dem Stuhl meiner Frau, von
den fünf Goldstücken hinter dem Stein in Alis Haus und von Erichs
Hut in Hermanns Schwimmbecken. Wir versuchten, etwas zu er-   35
klären, was man einfach nicht erklären kann.

Da klingelte das Telefon; Hermann nahm den Hörer ab. Lange
sagte er nichts, und ich wußte nicht, mit wem er sprach. „Wir
kommen sofort, Gerda", sagte er dann, legte den Hörer auf und
sprang auf. „Aber so etwas ist doch einfach unmöglich!" rief er. 40
„Was ist unmöglich?" fragte ich und versuchte, ruhig zu bleiben.
Das Telefon klingelte wieder. Diesmal ging ich in Hermanns Ar-

beitszimmer, wo noch ein Telefon stand, und hörte mit.

„Hier ist Elisabeth Meyer", hörte ich eine Frauenstimme sagen. „Bei mir in der Wohnung wohnt ein Herr Karsten. Soviel ich weiß, ist er Ihr Privatsekretär. Herr Direktor, Ihrem Sekretär muß irgendetwas passiert sein. Er ist heute noch gar nicht weggewesen. Seit dem Frühstück sitzt er auf seinem Zimmer. Vor ein paar Minuten habe ich an seine Tür geklopft, um ihn zu fragen, ob er nicht etwas essen wollte. Während ich klopfte, hörte ich einen lauten Schrei, und dann war es still im Zimmer. Ich habe die Polizei schon angerufen, aber es wäre vielleicht gut, wenn Sie auch kämen. Er ist doch ein Freund von Ihnen." „Ich komme sofort, Frau Meyer", sagte Hermann und legte auf. Dann sagte er zu mir: „Hans, das ist zum Verrücktwerden. Du mußt sofort zu Gerda fahren. Die zwei Frauen dürfen heute abend nicht allein in ihrer Wohnung sein. Du kannst meinen Wagen nehmen, und ich fahre mit einer Taxe zu Erichs Wohnung. Ich sehe dich dann später bei Gerda. Sie soll dir erzählen, was dort passiert ist." „OK", sagte ich. Dann liefen wir aus dem Haus.

Gerda und ihre Mutter waren erstaunt, mich allein zu sehen. „Hermann ist zu Erich gefahren", sagte ich. „Erichs Wirtin hat ihn vor einer halben Stunde laut schreien hören, und sie meint, ihm sei etwas passiert."

„Aber Erich war doch vor einer halben Stunde hier", sagte Gerda. „Hat Ihnen Hermann denn nichts davon erzählt?"—„Unmöglich! Wie kann er vor einer halben Stunde hier gewesen sein, wenn er vor einer halben Stunde in seinem Zimmer laut geschrien hat? Gerda, ich glaube, Sie hätten keinen Kognak trinken sollen."

Aber Gerda lachte nicht. „Hans, Sie wissen mehr als Sie sagen", meinte sie, und dann erzählte sie mir, was passiert war. „Nachdem Sie beide heute abend weggegangen waren, nahm ich, wie ich versprochen hatte, ein Bad. Als ich nach zehn Minuten aus der Badewanne stieg, stand plötzlich der Karsten wieder vor mir. Wie er ins Badezimmer gekommen ist, weiß ich nicht. Niemand hat geklingelt, und meine Mutter hat niemand hereingelassen. Auch durch den Garten kann er nicht gekommen sein, sonst hätte bestimmt der Hund gebellt. Fitzi schläft nämlich auf der Terrasse, wissen Sie. Aber trotzdem stand Karsten in der Badezimmertür und fragte: ‚Wo haben Sie meinen Hut?' Ich wurde wütend, nahm meinen Schuh und schlug ihm damit auf den Kopf. Und dann war er plötzlich weg, gerade wie heute nachmittag im Schwimmbecken. Und mein Schuh ist auch weg."—„Ich glaube, wir sollten jetzt wirklich eine Tasse Tee mit Kognak trinken", sagte ich zu den Frauen, „oder noch besser einen Kognak ohne Tee." Dann warteten wir auf Hermann.

vor einer halben Stunde half an hour ago

Es war schon eins, als er kam. „Eine unglaubliche Geschichte", fing
er an, „einfach unmöglich. Als ich vor Erichs Wohnung hielt, war
die Polizei gerade angekommen. ‚Aber ich sage Ihnen doch, er hat
laut geschrien', hörte ich die Wirtin sagen, ‚gerade als ich an die
Tür klopfte, um ihn zu fragen, ob ich ihm etwas zu essen bringen ₅
könnte. Als er mir dann nicht antwortete, habe ich Sie sofort angerufen, und ich habe hier vor der Tür gestanden, bis Sie kamen.'—
Es dauerte fast zehn Minuten, bis die Polizisten endlich die Tür
aufmachen konnten. Dann gingen wir alle ins Zimmer. Erich war
weg; kein Mensch war im Zimmer, aber auf dem Tisch stand eine ₁₀
Tasse Kaffee, der noch warm war. Die Polizisten wußten nicht, was
sie von der Sache halten sollten. Ich konnte ihnen nicht helfen, denn
wenn ich ihnen erzählt hätte, was seit gestern geschehen ist, hätten
sie bestimmt gedacht, ich wäre verrückt."

Ich wäre nicht erstaunt gewesen, wenn Gerda jetzt hysterisch ge- ₁₅
worden wäre, aber sie blieb ruhig, erzählte noch einmal, daß Erich
in der Tür zum Badezimmer gestanden und sie nach seinem Hut
gefragt habe, daß sie ihm mit einem Schuh auf den Kopf geschlagen
hätte, und daß Erich plötzlich einfach nicht mehr dagewesen sei.

Hermann, die zwei Frauen und ich redeten, bis es Tag wurde.   ₂₀

Dann frühstückten wir zusammen—Gerdas Kaffee war übrigens unglaublich gut—und fuhren nach Hause.

Gestern abend waren Gerda und ihre Mutter wieder bei uns. Wir
saßen gerade beim Abendessen, als das Telefon klingelte. Ich hörte
wieder mit. Es war die Polizei, aber nicht die Hamburger Polizei. ₂₅
Es war Interpol in Tripolis. Vor dem Haus eines Ägypters habe*
man am Morgen einen Mann gefunden, tot und mit einer Wunde
im Kopf. Die Untersuchung durch die Polizei hätte bis jetzt zu
nichts geführt. Einen Paß habe der Mann nicht gehabt; in seiner
Tasche wäre ein Brief gewesen, adressiert an Hermann, aber ₃₀
außer hundert Mark wäre in dem Brief nichts gewesen. Niemand
wisse, wer der Mann sei; in keinem der Hotels in Tripolis kenne
man ihn, und so sei nur die eine Spur da, die zu Hermann führe,
und ob er wüßte, wer der Mann sein könnte. Übrigens habe man
neben ihm—wie seltsam—einen Damenschuh gefunden, und sonst ₃₅
gar nichts.

Hermann zitterte. „Das könnte mein Privatsekretär Erich Karsten
sein", sagte er, „er ist seit gestern abend spurlos verschwunden. Ich
werde sofort die Polizei hier in Hamburg anrufen." Dann legte er
auf. Er zitterte noch immer.   ₄₀

---

* Note that the use of the subjunctive is sufficient to indicate indirect discourse;
no introductory statement such as **Man sagte uns,** . . . is necessary.

Heute nachmittag fliege ich nach Hause. Meine Frau holt mich, wie immer, am Flughafen ab. Und morgen, noch vor dem Frühstück, werde ich etwas tun, was ich vor einem Monat nicht tun wollte: Ich werde die Steinplatten auf unserer Terrasse zählen.

Und was tue ich, wenn es wirklich einundfünfzig sind?

ANALYSIS

121 Relative Pronouns

The Definite Relative Pronoun

The German relative pronouns are **der, die, das.** Their forms are the same as those of the definite article, except that the singular genitive and the plural genitive and dative add the ending **-en.** This **-en** necessitates doubling the **-s-** in the masculine and neuter forms in order to keep the preceding **-e-** short.

	MASC.	FEM.	NEUT.	PLURAL
NOM.	der	die	das	die
GEN.	dessen	deren	dessen	deren
DAT.	dem	der	dem	denen
ACC.	den	die	das	die

Relative pronouns must agree in gender and number with their antecedent; but their case depends on their function within the relative clause. The German relative pronouns are never omitted. All relative clauses are thus introduced dependent clauses and therefore have verb-last position.

Kennst du den Mann, *der* gestern hier war?
Do you know the man who was here yesterday?
Kennst du die Frau, *die* gestern hier war?
Kennst du das Mädchen, *das* gestern hier war?

Sein Vater, *dessen* Frau aus Leningrad kam, sprach gut Russisch.
His father, whose wife came from Leningrad, spoke Russian well.
Seine Frau, *deren* Vater aus Leningrad kam, sprach gut Russisch.

Wer war denn der Junge, mit *dem* ich dich gestern gesehen habe?
Who was the boy I saw you with (with whom I saw you) yesterday?
Wer war denn die Dame, mit *der* ich dich gestern gesehen habe?
Wer war denn das Mädchen, mit *dem* ich dich gestern gesehen habe?

Der Junge, *den* **du gestern gesehen hast, ist mein Sohn.**
The boy (whom) you saw yesterday is my son.

Die Dame, *die* **du gestern gesehen hast, ist meine Tante.**

Das Mädchen, *das* **du gestern gesehen hast, ist meine Schwester.**

Kennst du die Leute, *die* **gestern hier waren?**
Do you know the people who were here yesterday?

Wer waren denn die Mädchen, mit *denen* **ich dich gestern gesehen habe?**
Who were the girls I saw you with (with whom I saw you) yesterday?

Die Mädchen, *die* **du gesehen hast, waren meine Schwestern.**
The girls (whom) you saw were my sisters.

Relative clauses do not always follow their antecedents immediately. If only the second prong is needed to complete the main clause, this clause is not interrupted by a relative clause.

Ich wollte Hermann Schneider besuchen, mit dem ich während des Krieges in Afrika gewesen war.

I wanted to visit Hermann Schneider, with whom I had been in Africa during the war.

(*Not:* **Ich wollte Hermann Schneider, mit dem ich während des Krieges in Afrika gewesen war, besuchen.**)

The Indefinite Relative Pronoun

The German indefinite relative pronouns are **wer** and **was**. They are always used if there is no antecedent:

Wer **Geld hat, hat auch Freunde.**
Whoever (He who) has money has friends too.

Wer **nicht für mich ist, ist gegen mich.**
Whoever is not for me is against me.

Was **er zu erzählen hatte, war nicht viel.**
What he had to tell was not much.

Was er zu erzählen hatte, das war nicht viel.
Wer Geld hat, der hat auch Freunde.
Wer mich liebt, den liebe ich auch.

In the last three examples, **das, der,** and **den** repeat the relative clause.

Was is also used to refer to an entire clause or to **alles, nichts,** or **etwas.**

Hans hat mich zum Essen eingeladen, was ich sehr nett finde.
Ich habe nicht alles verstanden, was er gesagt hat.
Er hat nichts gesagt, was ich nicht schon wußte.
Ich habe etwas erlebt, was man eigentlich nicht erleben kann.

122 wann, ob, als, wenn

Wann is an interrogative, meaning *when*. It is used

1. to introduce a question:

> **Wann fährst du nach Köln?**
> When are you going to Cologne?

2. as an interrogative conjunction when a **wann**-question is changed into a dependent clause:

> **Mutter will wissen, wann du nach Köln fährst.**
> Mother wants to know (the answer to the question) when you are going to Cologne.

Ob is a conjunction used to change a yes-or-no question into a dependent clause:

> **Fährst du nach Berlin?**
> **Mutter will wissen, ob du nach Berlin fährst.**

Als is used in the following ways:

1. As a particle in comparisons, it means *than* and is used only to compare what is *not* equal:

> **Er trinkt mehr als du.**
> He drinks more than you (drink).
> **Ich habe nicht mehr als hundert Mark.**
> I don't have more than a hundred marks.

2. As a conjunction, **als** means *when* and introduces dependent clauses referring to *one single event or situation in the past* (English *when* has a much wider usage):

> **Als mein Mann noch lebte, gingen wir oft ins Theater.**
> When my husband was still alive, we often went to the theater.

3. **Als** may be the short version of **als ob** or **als wenn,** both meaning *as if*. When so used, **als** or **als ob** is followed either by the normal subjunctive or, less frequently, by the indirect-discourse subjunctive.

If **als** is equivalent to **als ob** (**als wenn**), the verb of the dependent clause follows immediately after **als**.

> **Er tat, als ob er schliefe.**   He acted as if he were asleep.
> **Er tat, als schliefe er.**
> **Er tat, als schlafe er.**
>
> **Er tat, als wenn er alles wüßte.**   He acted as if he knew everything.
> **Er tat, als wüßte er alles.**

Wenn is troublesome to the beginner, because it introduces both conditional and time clauses.

1. In conditional clauses, **wenn** always corresponds to English *if;* and any *if* which cannot be replaced by *whether* must be rendered by **wenn.**

2. In time clauses, **wenn** basically means *whenever* and presents no difficulties as long as it is used with this meaning.

3. Trouble arises because English *when* is apt to be a source of interference. English *when* is used as an interrogative and then corresponds to German **wann.** English *when* can also be a time conjunction meaning "at the time when." In this latter function, *when* corresponds to **als** if the clause refers to one single event in the past, and it corresponds to **wenn** if the clause refers to present or future time. The following table summarizes the situation:

	IF (condition)	IF (whether)	WHENEVER	WHEN (interrogative)	WHEN (conjunction)
PAST	wenn	ob	wenn	wann	als
PRESENT	wenn	ob	wenn	wann	wenn
FUTURE	wenn	ob	wenn	wann	wenn

NOTE. The student can eliminate all interference caused by his own speech habits if he realizes that

(a) in the sentence *I'd like to know when he came home*, the *when* is an interrogative replaceable by "the answer to the question when"; *when* therefore corresponds to German **wann:**

> **Ich möchte wissen, wann er nach Hause gekommen ist.**

(b) in *When my husband was still alive, we often went to the theater,* *when* is a conjunction replaceable by "at the time when"; *when* therefore corresponds to German **als,** because it refers to a single event or situation in the past:

> **Als mein Mann noch lebte, sind wir oft ins Theater gegangen.**

(c) in *When he comes home from the war, we will get married, when* is also a conjunction replaceable by "at the time when." But this time it refers to the future and corresponds to German **wenn.**

> **Wenn er aus dem Krieg nach Hause kommt, heiraten wir.**
> When he comes home from the war, we will get married.

Since **wenn** also corresponds to English *if,* this last sentence is ambiguous from an English point of view; only the context makes the meaning clear. There are no linguistic means in German of distinguishing between *when* and *if* as long as *when* refers to the future.

123 gar nicht, gar kein, gar nichts

The particle **gar** is used in connection with a following **nicht, kein,** or **nichts** either to add the idea "contrary to expectation" or to strengthen the negative particle in the same way in which *at all* strengthens the *not* in *not at all*.

> **Meyer ist gar nicht so dumm, wie du denkst.**
> Meyer isn't as stupid as you think.

> **Ich habe heute nacht gar nicht geschlafen.**
> I didn't sleep at all last night.

124 da-Compounds

You should by now be thoroughly familiar with the forms of the personal pronouns and of the demonstrative pronouns.

	SINGULAR			PLURAL
NOM.	er	sie	es	sie
DAT.	ihm	ihr	ihm	ihnen
ACC.	ihn	sie	es	sie

	SINGULAR			PLURAL
NOM.	der	die	das	die
DAT.	dem	der	dem	denen
ACC.	den	die	das	die

We have used both personal and demonstrative pronouns as substitutes for names and nouns.

However, when these pronouns referred to things or ideas, we have tried to avoid using them after prepositions.

The reason is this: The demonstrative pronouns (**der, die, das,** etc.) frequently function as the stressed forms of the personal pronouns (**er, sie, es,** etc.), just as English changes from *it* to *that* if

> He won't be *sát*isfied with it

is changed to

> He won't be satisfied with *thát.*

In English, the difference between *with it* and *with that* is only one of stress. Both the unstressed *with it* and the stressed *with that* can refer to a thing like a hat or a car. In German, there is no structural equivalent of the unstressed *with it*. German prepositional phrases like **mit ihm** or **für ihn** (which look as though they might refer to **dieser Hut** or **dieser Wagen**) can refer only to persons, not to things. The **ihm** in

> **Ich kann nicht mehr mit ihm nach Paris fahren**

can only refer to my friend, not to my rickety jalopy. To express the un-stressed *with it*, German uses a "**da**-compound," comparable to English *therewith:* The unstressed personal pronoun is replaced by **da-**, preceding and compounded with the preposition. Thus,

Kannst du mit dem Wagen nach Paris fahren?

becomes

Kannst du damit nach Paris fahren?

This **da-** can be a substitute for any noun in the dative or accusative case. Therefore, the questions

Was soll *ich* denn	**mit diesem Schlüssel?**
	mit dieser Uhr?
	mit diesem Buch?
	mit diesen Büchern?

all become

Was soll *ich* denn   damit?

Similarly, the questions

Was hast du denn	**für diesen Wein**	**bezahlt?**
	für diese Uhr	
	für dieses Haus	
	für diese Blumen	

all become

Was hast du denn   dafür   bezahlt?

The **da-** of the above examples is unstressed, just as the nouns replaced by **da-** are unstressed. The preposition is usually unstressed, too, but occasionally it may become the stress point of the sentence:

Ich habe nichts dagegen, aber ich bin auch nicht dafür.

125 **da**-Compounds with Stressed **da-**

The preceding section dealt with the replacement by **da-** of unstressed nouns denoting things. If stressed nouns denoting things and preceded by a preposition are to be replaced, one has a choice. One can use either the stressed demonstrative pronoun *after* a preposition or a stressed **da-** *preceding* the preposition.

Thus

Was soll ich denn	mit *dem* Schlüssel?
	mit *der* Uhr?
	mit *dem* Buch?
	mit *den* Büchern?

may become either

Was soll ich denn	mit *dem?*
	mit *der?*
	mit *dem?*
	mit *denen?*

or

Was soll ich denn	*da*mit?

In assertions, **da**-compounds with a stressed **da-** usually occupy the front field and carry contrast intonation:

Was soll ich denn mit *dem* Hut? *Da*mit gehe ich *nicht* in die Kirche.
So, Jutta hat ge*hei*ratet? *Da*von habe ich nichts ge*wußt*.

NOTE:

1. The second example above shows that **da**-compounds are used not only to refer to things, but also to refer to entire sentences.

2. Do not replace directives like **ins Haus, zum Bahnhof, nach Berlin** with **da**-compounds. Such directives are sometimes replaced by **hin** or **dahin**.

Mußt du zum Bahnhof? Ich bringe dich gerne *hin*.
Ich soll nach Kairo fahren? Nein, *da*hin fahre ich nicht.
Sie fahren nach Berlin? Da möchte ich *auch* gerne mal hinfahren.

126 Table of **da**-Compounds

If the preposition starts with a vowel, **dar-** is used instead of **da-**.

dadurch	dabei	dahinter
dafür	damit	daneben
dagegen	danach	daran
	daraus	darauf

davon   darin
dazu   darüber
               darunter
               davor
               dazwischen

Note that **ohne, außer, seit** and the prepositions governing the genitive (**während, wegen, trotz**) do not form **da**-compounds. **Außer** forms **außerdem** (*besides*), **seit** forms **seitdem** (*since then,* conj. *since*), and **trotz** forms **trotzdem** (*in spite of that, nevertheless*).

127 Split **da**-Compounds

In the spoken language, **da**-compounds may be split. The **da-** (stressed or unstressed) then stands in the front field, and the preposition becomes the first part of the second prong. This pattern, however, is quite colloquial.

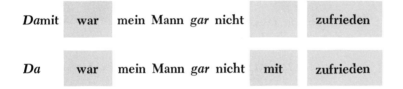

If the preposition begins with a vowel, **daraus** does not become **da . . . aus**, but **da . . . draus; daran: da . . . dran; darauf: da . . . drauf;** etc.

128 **der hier** and **der da**

In spoken German, the contrast *this one: that one* is expressed by **der hier** (or **dieser hier**): **der da** (or **dieser da**).

> **Dieses Haus hier möchte ich nicht, aber das da hätte ich gerne.**
> **Dieser Kugelschreiber hier ist mir zu schwer. Mit dem kann ich nicht schreiben. Kann ich den da mal versuchen?**
> **Die hier (diese Uhr hier) kostet mir zu viel. Darf ich die da mal sehen?**

129 **wo**-Compounds

If the question word **was** is preceded by a preposition, it may be replaced by **wo** (**wor-** in front of vowels) compounded with and followed by the preposition in question. One may ask

EITHER	OR
An was glaubst du?	Woran glaubst du?
An was denkst du?	Woran denkst du?
Auf was wartest du?	Worauf wartest du?

Also the indefinite relative pronoun **was** may be replaced by **wo-**:

Ich möchte wissen, auf was du noch wartest.
Ich möchte wissen, worauf du noch wartest.

130 Prepositional Objects

It was pointed out in Unit 2 that prepositions can be used to form compound verbs—that is, irreducible verbal patterns which constitute separate dictionary entries.

You have to turn off the light.
Du mußt das Licht ausmachen.

We now have to introduce a number of semantic units which consist of a verb plus a whole prepositional phrase rather than of a verb and just a preposition.

We are not thinking of time phrases like **vor einem Jahr,** of directives like **ins Kino,** or of place phrases like **zu Hause.** To be sure, directives and phrases like **zu Hause** are second-prong complements; however, **zu Hause bleiben, im Bett bleiben,** and **bei Schmidts bleiben** are not separate dictionary entries; they are examples of the use of **bleiben,** which, when used without such complements, is almost as devoid of independent meaning as **sein.**

What we are thinking of is the type of prepositional phrase occurring in such sentences as

She waited for him.
She waited on him.

where *to wait for somebody* and *to wait on somebody* are clearly separate dictionary entries: A woman may be willing to wait *for* a man, but that does not necessarily mean that she is also willing to wait *on* him. The phrase *on him* forces a meaning on the verb *to wait* which is clearly different from the meaning of the same verb in *to wait for somebody:*

| *She waited on him* | means | *She served him;* |
| *She waited for him* | means | *She expected him.* |

Now, if we call *him* the object of *expected,* we can call *on him* or *for him* the object of *waited.* We shall call phrases like *on him* and *for him,* when they occur in such semantic units as *to wait on somebody* and *to wait for somebody,* "prepositional objects."

Both English and German have literally hundreds of such fixed combinations of verbs plus prepositional objects. Unfortunately, however, the prepositions used with the German verbs hardly ever correspond to the prepositions used with the English verbs. Compare the following sentences:

Ich bin *in* sie verliebt.	I'm in love *with* her.
Ich bin *mit* ihr verlobt.	I'm engaged *to* her.
Ich warte *auf* sie.	I'm waiting *for* her.
Ich lache *über* sie.	I'm laughing *at* her.
Ich glaube *an* sie.	I believe *in* her.
Ich habe Angst *vor* ihr.	I'm afraid *of* her.
Ich bin stolz *auf* sie.	I'm proud *of* her.

Note that the prepositional objects sometimes belong to such compound verbs as **Angst haben** or **stolz sein.**

131 Frequent Prepositional Objects

Memorize the following verbs with their prepositions:

Angst haben vor (*dat.*)	to be afraid of
antworten auf (*acc.*)	to reply to (something)
bitten um (*acc.*)	to ask for (something)
danken für	to thank (someone) for
denken an (*acc.*)	to think of, to remember
nachdenken über (*acc.*)	to think, meditate about
einladen zu	to invite to
fragen nach	to ask about, inquire about
gehören zu	to be part or a member of, to belong to
glauben an (*acc.*)	to believe in
halten von	to have an opinion about; to think (highly, a great deal, not much, etc.) of (somebody or something)
halten für	to think that something (or somebody) is (something)
hoffen auf (*acc.*)	to hope for, to trust in, to look forward to
hören von	to hear from somebody or about something
lachen über (*acc.*)	to laugh about
jemanden auslachen	to laugh at (make fun of) somebody
reagieren auf (*acc.*)	to react to (something or somebody)

sein für or **sein gegen**	to be for or against
sprechen von	to talk of, to mention
sprechen über (*acc.*)	to talk in detail about a topic
verstehen von	to understand about
warten auf (*acc.*)	to wait for
wissen von	to know about

NOTE: A number of these prepositional objects use the prepositions **an, auf, über.** In all cases listed, **an, auf,** and **über** are used with the accusative, even though these phrases are not directives answering the question **wohin.** There are other cases where the dative *must* be used—for example, with **Angst haben vor.** From now on, the correct case will be indicated in the vocabulary. How important it is to use the correct case can be seen from the following example:

Ich warte auf *die* Straßenbahn

means

I am waiting for the streetcar,

whereas

Ich warte auf *der* Straßenbahn

could only mean

I am waiting on top of the streetcar.

132 The Syntax of Prepositional Objects

Preposition plus Noun or Personal Pronoun

The prepositional object constitutes the second prong. Under contrast intonation, it can be placed in the front field.

Ich glaube nicht an Gott.
Ich warte auf sie.
Auf Fritz brauchst du heute abend nicht zu warten.
Auf mich brauchst du nach dem Theater nicht zu warten.
An meinen Geburtstag hast du natürlich nicht gedacht.

Replacement of Nouns and Pronouns by Demonstratives

The stressed demonstratives used to replace nouns or names are usually placed in the front field.

Erika? Von der hat kein Mensch gesprochen.
Erika? Auf die brauchst du nicht zu warten.
Meyers? Von denen haben wir lange nichts gehört.
Meyers? Auf die brauchst du nicht zu warten.

Das ist ein *Wein!* Mit *dem* werden Sie be*stimmt* zufrieden sein! Gegen *den* kann auch ein *Kenner* nichts sagen.

Prepositional **da**-Compounds

The **da**-compounds with an unstressed **da-** appear in the first box of the second prong. The compounds with a stressed **da-** appear in the front field, with contrast intonation.

> *Daran glaube* ich nicht.
> Ich *glaube* noch nicht daran.
> *Darauf* kann ich nicht *warten.*
> Ich hoffe, ich brauche nicht darauf zu *warten.*

Prepositional **wo**-Compounds

Like all questions, questions introduced by a **wo**-compound can be changed into dependent clauses.

> **Auf was wartet er denn?**
> **Worauf wartet er denn?**
> **Ich weiß nicht, auf was er wartet.**
> **Ich weiß nicht, worauf er wartet.**

da-Compounds with an Anticipatory Function

The prepositional object may be replaced by a dependent clause or an infinitive phrase. If this is the case, a **da**-compound anticipating or repeating this dependent clause frequently appears in the main clause:

> **Ich habe gar nicht daran gedacht, daß**   It had slipped my mind that you too live in
> **du ja auch in Köln wohnst.**   Cologne.

or

> **Daran, daß du ja auch in Köln wohnst,**
> **habe ich gar nicht gedacht.**

or

> **Daran habe ich gar nicht gedacht, daß**
> **du ja auch in Köln wohnst.**

> **Ich möchte Ihnen noch einmal dafür**   I would like to thank you once more (for
> **danken, daß Sie gekommen sind.**   the fact that you came) for your coming.

> **Ich hoffe immer noch darauf, sie wie-**   I still hope to see her again.
> **derzusehen.**

These anticipatory **da**-compounds are especially frequent if the ideas contained in the dependent clause or in the infinitive phrase have, in some form, existed before and are not news either for the speaker or for the listener.

133 Feminine Nouns Ending in **-in**

Masculine nouns denoting persons (and a few animals), especially agent nouns in **-er,** form corresponding feminines ending in **-in** (plural **-innen**).

der Freund	die Freundin
der Lehrer	die Lehrerin
der Student	die Studentin

EXERCISES

A. Each of the following incomplete sentences contains a blank for a relative pronoun. Fill in the correct forms.

1. das Haus, aus _____ er kam
2. die Betten, zwischen _____ der Tisch stand
3. der Blick, mit _____ er mich ansah
4. die vielen Aufnahmen, _____ ich von ihm gemacht habe
5. die Leute, _____ zu uns kamen
6. der Herr, nach _____ Sie fragen
7. der Materialismus, gegen _____ wir kämpfen
8. das Haus, in _____ wir wohnen
9. das Theater, vor _____ ich sie treffen wollte
10. die Familie, bei _____ du wohnst
11. das Haus, vor _____ wir unseren Wagen stellten
12. seine Frau, _____ Vater in Berlin Architekt war
13. meine Bücher, ohne _____ ich nicht leben kann
14. der Zug, mit _____ du fahren willst
15. die Blicke, _____ sie mir zuwarf
16. die Ecke, an _____ er stand
17. die Stadt, von _____ wir sprachen
18. das Fenster, aus _____ sie heraussah
19. ihr Mann, _____ Vater in Berlin Architekt war
20. die zwei Fußabdrücke, _____ wir neben dem Haus fanden

B. Join the following pairs of sentences by changing one of them into a relative clause.

1. Werners Vater sprach gut Englisch. Er hatte lange in Amerika gelebt.
2. Werners Vater sprach gut Englisch. Seine Frau kam aus London.
3. Ich habe dich gestern abend im Theater mit einem jungen Mann gesehen. Wer war denn der junge Mann?

4. In Mainz besuchte ich meinen Freund Emil. Ich bin mit ihm in die Schule gegangen.
5. Ich fuhr nach Hamburg, um Hermann wiederzusehen. Während des Krieges war ich mit Hermann in Afrika.
6. Wer ist denn eigentlich dieser Schmidt? Du redest schon seit Tagen von ihm.
7. Der Brief lag vor ihr auf dem Tisch. Ihr Mann hatte ihn aus Kairo geschickt.
8. Ich kann diese Vase doch nicht wegwerfen. Tante Amalie hat sie mir geschickt.

C. Restate the following sentences by starting with **Er sah aus, als ob** . . . and **Er sah aus, als.** . . .

1. Er hat die Gelbsucht.
2. Er hat nicht gut geschlafen.
3. Er hat viel erlebt.
4. Er ist unglücklich.
5. Er war krank.

D. Restate the following sentences in the past tense. Note that with the change from present tense to past tense, **wenn** must be in some cases changed to **als.**

1. Wir können erst ins Theater gehen, wenn Else kommt.
2. Jedesmal, wenn Tante Amalie hier ist, muß ich mich zwingen, nett zu ihr zu sein.
3. Wenn mein Zug in München ankommt, bist du schon in Chicago.
4. Wenn meine Wohnung groß genug wäre, könnte ich auch fünfundzwanzig Leute einladen.
5. Wenn Hans geht, gehe ich auch.

E. In the following sentences, supply **als, als ob, ob, wann,** or **wenn.**

1. Ich weiß, jemand hat hinter mir gestanden, _____ ich den Brief schrieb.
2. _____ ich gewußt hätte, daß sie nicht schwimmen konnte, wäre ich natürlich nicht mit ihr fischen gegangen.
3. Können Sie mir sagen, _____ der Zug aus Köln ankommt?
4. Können Sie mir sagen, _____ der Zug aus Köln schon angekommen ist?
5. Ich wußte nicht, _____ Erich mich erkannt hatte; jedenfalls tat er, _____ hätte er mich nicht gesehen.
6. Ich bin so müde. _____ ich nur endlich einmal lange schlafen könnte!
7. Ich bin nicht sicher, _____ ich das Geschenk annehmen soll oder nicht.
8. Was? Tante Amalie will uns schon wieder besuchen? _____ kommt sie denn?
9. Aber Inge, du tust ja, _____ *du* immer mit ihr ins Museum gehen müßtest.
10. Du weißt doch, ich komme erst um 7 Uhr nach Hause. _____ soll ich denn essen, _____ das Theater schon um 7 Uhr 30 anfängt?

F. Read the following sentences and supply either **nicht** or **nichts,** or the correct form of **kein.**

1. Ich habe seit gestern morgen gar _____ gegessen.
2. Daß du in Italien warst, habe ich gar _____ gewußt.
3. Hast du denn mit deiner neuen Kamera noch gar _____ Aufnahmen gemacht?
4. Es ist doch dumm, daß er uns gar _____ geschrieben hat, wann er ankommt.
5. Aber der Hund hat doch gar _____ gebellt.

G. Fill in each blank by using a form of the demonstrative **der, die, das.**

1. Sollen Inge und Gerda auch kommen?—Nein, _____ brauchst du nicht einzuladen; _____ können zu Hause bleiben; mit _____ will ich nichts mehr zu tun haben.
2. Kennen Sie _____ Friedrich Bertram?—Aber natürlich; mit _____ war ich doch in Mainz auf der Schule.
3. Diese Schuhe hier möchten Sie also doch nicht, gnädige Frau?—Nein, ich nehme lieber _____ da.
4. Nein, Maria; mit _____ Hut kannst du dich in Paris nicht sehen lassen. _____ läßt du besser zu Hause.—Aber Paul, _____ kommt doch aus Paris. _____ hast du mir doch letztes Jahr aus Paris mitgebracht.
5. Dieser Kaffee ist aber gut. Wo hast du _____ denn gekauft?—_____ hat mein Mann gekauft.—Dein Mann? Versteht _____ was von Kaffee?

H. In the following sentences, substitute a **da**-compound for the italicized prepositional phrases.

1. Der Garten *hinter dem Haus* braucht viel Wasser.
2. *Mit dem Hut* kannst du dich nicht sehen lassen.
3. Und *vor dem Wohnzimmer* ist eine grosse Terrasse.
4. Er hat viel Geld *für das Haus* bezahlt.
5. Aber den Namen *unter dem Bild* kann ich nicht lesen.

I. In the following sentences, substitute for the prepositional phrase in the front field (a) a stressed **da**-compound, and (b) the preposition plus demonstrative article.

Für *den* Wein hast du zuviel bezahlt.
(a) ***Da*für hast du zuviel bezahlt.**
(b) **Für *den* hast du zuviel bezahlt.**

1. Mit *dem* Wagen fahre ich nicht.
2. Mit *diesem* Hut kann ich nichts anfangen.
3. In *diesem* Bett kann ich nicht schlafen.

4. Für *den* Wagen bezahle ich keine zweitausend Mark.
5. Mit *mei*ner Leica kann ich auch bei Nacht Aufnahmen machen.

J. Write down the questions to which the following sentences would be the answers. Start each question with (a) a **wo**-compound and (b) the preposition plus demonstrative article.

Meine Tochter hat Angst vor der Schule.
(a) **Wovor hat sie denn Angst?**
(b) **Vor was hat sie denn Angst?**

1. Wir warten auf schönes Wetter.
2. Ich brauche das Geld für einen neuen Wagen.
3. Wir haben gerade von dem neuen Hitchcock-Film gesprochen.
4. Ich denke gerade daran, daß Vater morgen Geburtstag hat.
5. Ich habe ihn an seiner Stimme erkannt.

K. Read the following sentences aloud and supply the missing prepositions.

1. Ich glaube _____ Gott.
2. Wir haben _____ unserer Reise gesprochen.
3. Denkst du auch noch _____ mich?
4. Hast du schon _____ den Brief geantwortet?
5. Hast du auch nicht vergessen, ihn _____ seiner Frau zu fragen?
6. Ich danke Ihnen _____ Ihre Hilfe.
7. Meyer hat mich _____ einem Glas Wein eingeladen.
8. Dürfte ich Sie _____ eine Zigarette bitten?
9. Er spricht nie _____ seiner Frau.
10. _____ wen warten Sie denn?

L. Read the following sentences aloud and supply the missing articles or possessives.

1. Wir warten auf _____ Zug aus Köln.
2. Wir warten auf _____ Bahnhof.
3. Meyer hat Angst vor _____ Frau.
4. Ingelheim hat viel über _____ Krieg geschrieben.
5. Erich stand an _____ Ecke und wartete auf _____ Freundin.
6. Ich muß in _____ Universität über _____ Krieg zwischen Rom und Karthago sprechen.
7. Ich halte nicht viel von _____ Film.
8. Wir hoffen sehr auf _____ Mitarbeit Ihres Mannes, Frau Becker.
9. Frau Direktor, als Sie an die Tür kamen, habe ich Sie für _____ Tochter gehalten.
10. Sie hat den ganzen Abend nicht von _____ Mann gesprochen.

M. Using the verbs in parentheses, form main clauses containing a **da**-compound anticipating the dependent clause.

> (schon lange nachdenken), wo ich dieses Jahr hinfahren soll.
> **Ich denke schon lange darüber nach, wo ich dieses Jahr hinfahren soll.**

1. (sehr hoffen), daß er morgen kommen kann.
2. (gerade sprechen), daß er im Sommer nach Italien fahren will.
3. (warten), daß mein Mann endlich nach Hause kommt.
4. (nicht viel halten), daß meine Tochter Psychologie studieren will.
5. (wohl bitten dürfen), daß Sie um acht Uhr im Büro sind.

N. Expand the prepositional objects in the following sentences into dependent clauses.

> **Ich warte auf einen Brief von ihr.**
> **Ich warte darauf, daß sie mir schreibt.**

1. Ich möchte Ihnen noch einmal für Ihre Hilfe danken.
2. An seinen Geburtstag gestern habe ich gar nicht gedacht.
3. Ich glaube an Gottes Liebe zu den Menschen.
4. Wir sind sehr unglücklich über die Heirat unserer Tochter.
5. Lacht sie immer noch über seinen Akzent?

O. Expand the prepositional objects in the following sentences into infinitive phrases.

> **Erika denkt gar nicht an eine Italienreise.**
> **Erika denkt gar nicht daran, nach Italien zu fahren.**

1. Darf ich Sie zu einem Glas Wein einladen, Herr Müller?
2. Ich habe meinen Freund um Ingelheims Romane gebeten.
3. Hoffst du immer noch auf ein Wiedersehen mit ihr?
4. Ich hoffe auf ein Wiedersehen mit Ihnen.
5. Ich habe wochenlang auf einen Brief von ihr gewartet.

P. Read the following sentences starting with each of the italicized words and rearrange the syntax accordingly.

1. Daran, *daß* wir heute vor zehn Jahren geheiratet haben, hast *du natürlich* nicht gedacht.
2. Natürlich bin *ich* nicht *glücklich darüber*, *daß* Heidi so jung heiraten will.
3. Mir hat *er gestern* nichts *davon* gesagt, *daß* er bald heiraten will.

Q. Express in German:

1. Not until yesterday did he ask me whether I wanted to marry him.
2. The man with whom Mrs. Ingelheim is talking is called Behrens.
3. If the walls in this room could talk, we would never have to read a novel again.
4. Hans wanted to know whether I could pick him up at the station.
5. When did you pick him up?
6. Can you tell me when you picked him up? (indicative)
7. When I arrived, she was not there yet.
8. He acted as if the house belonged to him.
9. He looked as if he hadn't slept well.
10. You know him better than her, don't you?
11. That was more than I had expected.
12. If it hadn't been so hot in Cairo, we would not have flown back to Germany.
13. That was a moment I shall not forget.
14. The man I saw in front of the house was Erich.
15. Behind the stone was a hole in which Ali had five goldpieces.
16. He said that he had seen nothing at all.
17. If I'm not there at three o'clock, you'll simply have to wait for me.
18. When I knocked at the door, Erich didn't answer.
19. And this is a picture of our house.—And where is your swimming pool?— That's behind it.
20. In front of the house stood a Mercedes; next to it stood a Volkswagen.

BASIC VOCABULARY

alt old
die Antwort, –en answer, reply
der Arm, –e arm
aufmachen to open
bauen to build
beide both
bezahlen to pay
dauern to last, to take (time)
der Dom, –e cathedral
dreißig thirty
dumm stupid, dumb
eben just
einschlafen to fall asleep
die Eltern parents
erfahren to find out, learn
erklären to explain
erschrecken to be frightened
erstaunt astonished

fallen to fall, drop
die Fami'lie, –n family
führen to lead, guide
ganz gut pretty good, not bad
der Gast, ⁼e guest
groß big, great, tall
halten für to consider
halten von to have an opinion about; to think (highly, a great deal, not much, etc.) of
die Hand, ⁼e hand
die Hilfe help
irgendetwas something, anything
der Junge, –n boy
der Juni June
kämpfen to fight
der Kampf, ⁼ fight, battle

klingeln to ring (said of a bell)
klopfen to knock
anklopfen to knock (at the door)
längst, schon längst for a long time, a long time ago
laut loud
leise soft, without noise
meinen to mean, to have an opinion; to say
der Mittag, –e noon
der Nachmittag, –e afternoon
müde tired
na so was! (expression of astonishment) You don't mean it! What do you think of that!

der Name, –n name
(*gen.:* **des Namens;** *dat.:*
dem Namen; *acc.:* **den
Namen**)
nämlich namely; that is to
say; you know
nee (*colloquial*) = **nein** no
nirgends nowhere
oben up (above); upstairs;
on top
obwohl' although
das Problem', –e problem
reagieren auf to react to
reich rich
ruhig quiet, calm; (*sentence
adverb*) it won't bother
me, I'll stay calm about it
russisch Russian
schlagen to beat, hit
der Schluß end; conclusion

schweigen to be silent, say
nothing
schwer heavy; hard (difficult)
die Schwester, –n sister
die Seite, –n page; side
singen to sing
der Sänger singer
so etwas something like this
soviel (*conjunction*) as far as
spazierengehen to go for a
walk
spielen to play
statt (*with genitive*) instead
of
statt zu (**kaufen**) instead
of (buying)
stehenbleiben to stop (walking or moving)
steigen to climb
die Stimme, –n voice
der Stolz (*no pl.*) pride

stolz proud
die Straßenbahn, –en streetcar
der Stuhl, ¨e chair
die Tasche, –n pocket; handbag; briefcase
tausend thousand, a thousand
trotzdem in spite of that;
nevertheless
die Tür, –en door
verliebt in love
verlobt engaged
von (**mir**) **aus** as far as I am
concerned
während (*conjunction*) while
warm warm
der Weg, –e way; path
das Wort, ¨er (or **–e**) word
zufrie'den satisfied, content
zu'hören (*with dative*) to
listen to

ADDITIONAL VOCABULARY

die Adres'se, –n address
adressieren to address
auslachen to laugh at, make
fun of
die Badewanne, –n bathtub
bellen to bark
drücken to push, press
der General', ¨e general
der Hörer, – (telephone) receiver; listener

die Kugel, –n ball, globe;
bullet
der Kugelschreiber, –
ball-point pen
der Leutnant, –e lieutenant
mitmachen to go along, to
cooperate
die O'per, –n opera; opera
house

der Paß, die Pässe passport;
pass
der Plan, ¨e plan
der Schrei, –e scream
die Vase, –n vase (*v* pronounced similar to
English *v*)
der Wirt, –e innkeeper, landlord
wütend mad, angry

IRREGULAR VERBS

einschlafen to fall asleep
**schlief ein, ist einge-
schlafen, er schläft ein**
erfahren to find out, learn
**erfuhr, hat erfahren, er
erfährt**
erschrecken to be frightened
**erschrak, ist erschrocken, er
erschrickt**
fallen to fall

fiel, ist gefallen, er fällt
schlagen to beat, hit
**schlug, hat geschlagen, er
schlägt**
schweigen to be silent, say
nothing
**schwieg, hat geschwiegen,
er schweigt**
singen to sing
sang, hat gesungen, er singt

spazierengehen to go for a
walk
**ging spazieren, ist spazie-
rengegangen, er geht
spazieren**
stehenbleiben to stop (walking or moving)
**blieb stehen, ist stehenge-
blieben, er bleibt stehen**
steigen to climb
stieg, ist gestiegen, er steigt

UNIT 9: nicht in the Inner Field—nicht A, sondern B—
Present and Past Infinitives—Subjective and Objective
Use of Modals—The Reflexive Pronoun sich—
Contrary-to-Fact Conditions without wenn

[1] nicht in the Inner Field

Study these sentences carefully; then follow the instructions at the end of this
section.

SEE
ANALYSIS
134

(pp. 273-274)

Aber du kannst doch nicht den ganzen Tag schlafen!
But you can't sleep all day!

Warum denn nicht? Ich habe die ganze Nacht nicht geschlafen.
Why not? I didn't sleep all night.

Meyer war krank und hat lange nicht arbeiten können.
Meyer was sick, and for a long time he couldn't work.

Heute haben wir nicht lange arbeiten können.
Today we couldn't work very long.

Du brauchst nicht auf dem Sofa zu schlafen. Wir haben ein Bett für dich.
You don't have to sleep on the sofa. We have a bed for you.

Ich kann in diesem Bett einfach nicht schlafen. Es ist zu kurz.
I simply can't sleep in this bed. It is too short.

Geschlafen habe ich. Aber ich habe nicht gut geschlafen.

Ingelheim war in Kairo. Aber! War er allein in Kairo, oder war er nicht allein
in Kairo?

(Facing) **München. Leopoldstraße**

[2] nicht A, sondern B

Study these sentences; then follow the instructions below.

SEE
ANALYSIS
134
(pp. 273-274)

Ich wartete nicht auf Inge. Ich wartete auf Erika.
Ich wartete damals nicht auf Inge, sondern auf Erika.
Ich habe nicht auf Inge, sondern auf Erika gewartet.
Ich habe nicht auf Inge gewartet, sondern auf Erika.
Nicht auf Inge, sondern auf Erika habe ich gewartet.
Du weißt doch, daß ich nicht auf Inge, sondern auf Erika gewartet habe.
Du weißt doch, daß ich nicht auf Inge gewartet habe, sondern auf Erika.

Er ist nicht *ges*tern, sondern erst *heu*te nach Berlin gefahren.
Er ist nicht *ges*tern nach Berlin gefahren, sondern erst *heu*te.

Er ist gestern nicht nach Ber*lin*, sondern nach *Ham*burg gefahren.
Er ist gestern nicht nach Ber*lin* gefahren, sondern nach *Ham*burg.

Wir sind gestern nicht nach Hamburg ge*flo*gen, sondern ge*fah*ren.

Inge ist nicht nur schön, sondern auch intelligent.
Weißt du, daß Inge nicht nur schön, sondern auch intelligent ist?
Weißt du, daß Inge nicht nur schön ist, sondern auch intelligent?

Be prepared to produce orally sentences of your own.

[3] Numbers from 1 to 100

zwanzig, einundzwanzig, zweiundzwanzig, dreiundzwanzig, vierundzwanzig, fünfundzwanzig, sechsundzwanzig, siebenundzwanzig, achtundzwanzig, neunundzwanzig, dreißig, einunddreißig, zweiunddreißig, vierzig, dreiundvierzig, vierundvierzig, fünfundvierzig, fünfzig, fünfundfünfzig, sechsundfünfzig, sechzig, sechsundsechzig, siebenundsechzig, siebzig, siebenundsiebzig, achtundsiebzig, achtzig, achtundachtzig, neunundachtzig, neunzig, hundert (einhundert)

SEE
ANALYSIS
135
(p. 274)

ein mal zwei ist zwei	hundert (geteilt) durch zehn ist zehn
zwei mal zwei ist vier	neunzig (geteilt) durch zehn ist neun
drei mal zwei ist sechs	achtzig (geteilt) durch zehn ist acht
vier mal zwei ist acht	siebzig (geteilt) durch zehn ist sieben
fünf mal zwei ist zehn	sechzig (geteilt) durch zehn ist sechs

[4] Past Infinitives

SEE
ANALYSIS
136
(pp. 274-275)

Er scheint zu schlafen.
Er scheint gut geschlafen zu haben.

Er schien in Paris zu sein.
Er schien in Paris gewesen zu sein.

Sie scheint Geld zu haben.
Sie scheint Geld gehabt zu haben.

Meyer schien sehr glücklich zu sein.
Meyer scheint sehr glücklich gewesen zu sein.

Wer Arzt werden will, muß sechs Jahre studieren.
Wer Arzt ist, muß sechs Jahre studiert haben.

Ich muß um sechs Uhr meine Brieftauben füttern.
Ich muß um sechs Uhr meine Brieftauben gefüttert haben.

[5] The Objective Use of müssen (Review)

Read these sentences carefully and review the forms of müssen. Then go through the variations below. You should be able to do these and similar variations without hesitation.

SEE
ANALYSIS
137

(pp. 275-280)

Jetzt habe ich keine Zeit. Ich muß erst die Kinder in die Schule schicken und dann noch die Betten machen.

> I have no time now. First I have to send the children off to school, and then I still have to make the beds.

Sie sagte, sie hätte keine Zeit. Sie müßte erst die Kinder in die Schule schicken und dann noch die Betten machen.

> She said she didn't have time. She had to send the children off to school first, and then she still had to make the beds.

Sie sagte, sie hätte erst die Kinder in die Schule schicken müssen.

> She said she had had to send the children off to school first.

Die Erika hat's gut. Sie hat eine Hilfe und hat noch nie ein Bett zu machen brauchen.

> Erika is well off. She has a maid and hasn't ever had to make a bed.

Um eins kommt mein Mann nach Hause. Bis dahin muß ich in der Stadt gewesen sein und das Mittagessen gekocht haben.

> My husband is coming home at one. By then I must be back from downtown and have dinner ready.

Wenn Meyer morgens um neun ins Büro kam, mußte seine Sekretärin schon die Post gelesen haben.

> When Meyer got to the office at nine in the morning his secretary had to have read the mail already. (= he expected his secretary to have read the mail already.)

[6] The Subjective Use of **müssen**

Study the subjective use in these sentences; then follow the instructions below.

SEE
ANALYSIS
137
(pp. 275-280)

Diesen Brief habe ich heute von einem Herrn Brandt bekommen. Er muß Amerikaner sein. Er schreibt: „Gestern ich war in Berlin und habe gekauft Ihren Roman."

> I got this letter from a Mr. Brandt today. He must be an American. He writes, "Yesterday I was in Berlin and bought your novel."

Ich hörte sofort, daß Herr Brandt trotz seines Namens Amerikaner sein mußte, denn er sagte: „Morgen ich kann nicht kommen, weil ich muß fahren nach Berlin."

> I heard immediately that Mr. Brandt had to be an American in spite of his name, for he said, "Tomorrow I can't come because I have to go to Berlin."

Sie ist doch in Stuttgart aufs Gymnasium gegangen. Sie muß also Englisch können und Faulkner gelesen haben.

> But she went to the Gymnasium in Stuttgart. So she must know English and must have read Faulkner.

Sie ist doch in Stuttgart aufs Gymnasium gegangen. Sie müßte eigentlich Englisch können und Faulkner gelesen haben.

> But she went to the Gymnasium in Stuttgart. So she ought to know English and ought to have read Faulkner.

Ich wußte, sie war in Stuttgart aufs Gymnasium gegangen. Sie mußte also Englisch können und Faulkner gelesen haben.

> I knew she had gone to the Gymnasium in Stuttgart. So she had to know English and had to have read Faulkner.

Ich wußte, sie war in Stuttgart aufs Gymnasium gegangen, und sie hätte eigentlich Englisch können müssen.

> I knew she had gone to the Gymnasium in Stuttgart and should have known English.

VARIATIONS

Following the pattern of the examples below, answer the questions by using a subjective form of **müssen**; try to support your conclusion with a sentence starting with **denn.**

> (a) **Ist sie wirklich schon achtzehn?—**
> **Sie muß achtzehn sein, denn sie will nächste Woche heiraten.**
>
> (b) **Waren Meyers wirklich an der Riviera?—**
> **Sie müssen an der Riviera gewesen sein, denn sie sind so braun wie Kaffee.**

1. Hat Meyer wirklich so viel Geld?
2. Ist Inge wirklich intelligent?
3. War Ingelheim schon einmal verheiratet?
4. Woher wußtest du, daß er Amerikaner war?

[7] wollen

Study these sentences carefully and determine whether **wollen** is used subjectively or objectively; then follow the instructions below.

SEE
ANALYSIS
137

(pp. 275-280)

Tante Amalie will uns nächste Woche besuchen.
>Tante Amalie wants to visit us next week.

Ich habe dich noch nie gebeten, mir zu helfen. Und jetzt, wo ich dich brauche,
sagst du nein. Und du willst mein Freund sein!
>I have never asked you to help me, and now that I need you, you say no.
>And you claim to be my friend!

Er will in der Normandie gekämpft haben? Das glaube ich nicht.
>He says he has fought in Normandy? I don't believe that.

Hast du nicht gesagt, du wolltest morgen nach Hamburg fahren?
>Didn't you say you wanted to go to Hamburg tomorrow?

Um acht wollte ich schon gefrühstückt haben. Und jetzt ist es zehn, und ich
liege immer noch im Bett.
>I wanted to have finished my breakfast by eight. Now it's ten, and I'm
>still in bed.

**Geht Tante Amalie
wirklich allein ins
Museum?**

Als Ingelheim den Preis bekam, wollte natürlich jeder seinen Roman schon gelesen haben. *Ich* hatte ihn *wirk*lich gelesen.—So?—Und ich wollte, ich hätte ihn *nicht* gelesen.

When Ingelheim got the prize, everybody pretended to have read his novel already, of course. I really *had* read it.—Really?—And I wish I *hadn't* read it.

VARIATIONS

Change the following sentences according to the pattern of the example.

> **Er behauptet, ein Freund des Direktors zu sein.**
> **Er will ein Freund des Direktors sein.**

1. Er behauptet, ein Freund des Direktors gewesen zu sein.
2. Er behauptete, ein Freund des Direktors zu sein.
3. Er behauptete, ein Freund des Direktors gewesen zu sein.
4. Er behauptet, ein Haus an der Riviera zu haben.
5. Er behauptet, ein Haus an der Riviera gehabt zu haben.
6. Er behauptete, ein Haus an der Riviera zu haben.
7. Er behauptete, ein Haus an der Riviera gehabt zu haben.

[8] sollen

Reread Analysis **107**; then read the following sentences carefully and decide which express "hearsay about the grammatical subject." Then follow the instructions below.

**SEE
ANALYSIS
137**

(pp. 275-280)

Du sollst nicht stehlen.
> Thou shalt not steal.

Wir sollen morgen um acht auf dem Bahnhof sein.
> We are supposed to be at the station at eight tomorrow.

Er sagte, wir sollten morgen um acht Uhr auf dem Bahnhof sein.
> He said we were to be at the station at eight tomorrow.

Ich weiß, ich sollte nicht soviel rauchen.
> I know I shouldn't smoke so much.

Das werde ich nie vergessen! Und wenn ich hundert Jahre alt werden sollte!
> I'll never forget that, even if I should live to be a hundred.

Die Brücke sollte schon letztes Jahr fertig sein, aber sie ist immer noch nicht fertig.

> The bridge was supposed to be finished last year, but it still isn't finished.

Damals suchte IBM zwanzig Ingenieure. Alle sollten Deutsch können und mindestens vier Semester Elektronik studiert haben.

> At that time, IBM was looking for twenty engineers. They all were supposed to know German and to have had four semesters of electronics.

Wo ist denn der Erich?—Der soll schon wieder an der Riviera sein.

> Where is Erich?—Supposedly he is on the Riviera again.

Hast du etwas von Inge gehört?—Die soll im Juni geheiratet haben. Ihr Mann soll Ingenieur sein.

> Have you heard anything about Inge?—I've heard that she got married last June. I understand her husband is an engineer.

VARIATIONS

Change the following sentences according to the pattern of the example.

> **Ich höre, Meyer wohnt in Berlin.—Meyer soll in Berlin wohnen.**

Ich höre, er ist schon wieder in Afrika.

Ich höre, er ist noch nie in Afrika gewesen.

Ich höre, seine Frau war krank.

Ich höre, Erika hat geheiratet.

Ich höre, er muß schon wieder nach Amerika fahren.

[9] können

Read the following sentences and determine whether **können** is used objectively or subjectively; then follow the instructions below.

Meyer ist krank und kann leider nicht kommen.

> Meyer is sick and unfortunately can't come.

Heute ist ja schon Donnerstag. Bis Samstag kann ich den Roman nicht gelesen haben.

> But today is Thursday already. I can't possibly have read the novel by Saturday.

Intelligent kann sie nicht sein. Wenn sie intelligent wäre, würde sie nicht für Meyer arbeiten.

SEE ANALYSIS 137 (pp. 275-280)

She can't be intelligent. If she were intelligent, she wouldn't work for Meyer.

Sie war fast noch ein Kind und konnte nicht älter sein als siebzehn.

She was still almost a child and couldn't have been any older than seventeen.

Wenn Meyer kein Geld hätte, könnte er keinen Mercedes 300 fahren.

If Meyer didn't have any money, he couldn't drive a Mercedes 300.

Seine Frau sagte, er sei krank und könne leider nicht kommen.

His wife said he was sick and unfortunately wouldn't be able to come.

Könnte ich vielleicht ein Zimmer mit Bad haben?

Could I have a room with bath?

Und der Herr, der mich sprechen wollte, hat nicht gesagt, wie er heißt? Wer kann das nur gewesen sein? Er sprach mit einem Akzent, sagen Sie? Hm, das könnte Mr. Taylor gewesen sein.

And the gentleman who wanted to talk to me didn't tell you his name? Who could that have been? You say he had an accent? Hm, that could have been Mr. Taylor.

Ich glaube, wir sollten heute im Garten arbeiten. Morgen könnte es regnen.

I think we should work in the garden today. It could (might) rain tomorrow.

Die Zimmer sind *gut*. Aber das *Essen* könnte *bess*er sein.

The rooms are OK. But the food could be better.

VARIATIONS

Change the following sentences according to the pattern of the example.

> **Ist er schon hier?**
> **Nein, er kann noch nicht hier sein. Es ist doch erst acht.**

Ist sie schon verheiratet?
Nein, _____ Sie ist doch erst sechzehn.

War er gestern abend im Kino?
Nein, _____ Er war gestern abend bei Meyers.

Bist du sicher, daß es Erich war?
Nein, sicher bin ich nicht, aber _____

[10] dürfen

Study the use of **dürfen** in these sentences and determine whether it is used objectively or subjectively.

SEE
ANALYSIS
137
(pp. 275-280)

Darf ich heute abend ins Kino gehen, Mutti?
Kann ich heute abend ins Kino gehen, Mutti?
    May I go to the movies tonight, Mom?

Ich fragte sie, ob ich sie nach Hause bringen dürfte.
    I asked her whether I could (might) take her home.

Rauchen darf man hier leider nicht.
    Unfortunately smoking is not permitted here.

Sie dürfen nicht mehr so viel Kaffee trinken, Frau Emmerich.
    You mustn't (shouldn't) drink so much coffee any more, Frau Emmerich.

Wann ist er denn weggefahren?—Vor zwei Stunden.—Dann dürfte er jetzt schon in Frankfurt sein.
    When did he leave?—Over two hours ago.—Then we can assume that he is in Frankfurt by now.

Ich möchte wissen, wer mich gestern abend um elf noch angerufen hat.—Das dürfte Erich gewesen sein; der ruft doch immer so spät an.
    I wonder who called me last night at eleven.—I suppose that was Erich; he always calls that late, doesn't he?

[11] mögen

Acquaint yourself with the indicative use of **mögen,** both as a non-modal and as a subjective modal. Then follow the instructions below.

SEE
ANALYSIS
137
(pp. 275-280)

Ingelheims Romane sind ja ganz gut, aber als Mensch mag ich ihn gar nicht.
    Ingelheim's novels aren't bad, but as a person I don't care for him at all.

Ich mochte ihn schon nicht, als wir während des Krieges in Afrika waren.
    I disliked him already when we were in Africa during the war.

Meine Frau hat ihn auch nie gemocht.
    My wife never liked him either.

Danke, Schweinefleisch mag ich nicht; ich esse lieber ein Steak.
    Thanks, I don't care for pork; I'd rather have a steak.

Wie alt ist seine Tochter eigentlich?—Oh, ich weiß nicht. Sie mag achtzehn oder neunzehn sein.
    How old is his daughter?—Oh, I don't know, maybe eighteen or nineteen.

Er mochte damals etwa dreißig sein.

    At that time, he was probably about thirty.

Was mag ihm nur passiert sein?

    I wonder what has happened to him?

Er mag gedacht haben, ich hätte ihn nicht gesehen.

    He may have thought that I hadn't seen him.

VARIATIONS

Change the following sentences according to the pattern of the example.

> **Ich glaube, sie ist etwa zwanzig.—Sie mag etwa zwanzig sein.**

Ich glaubte, sie war zwanzig.—Sie _____.

Ich glaube, sie war damals etwa zwanzig.—Sie _____.

Ich glaube, er hat mich nicht gesehen.—Er _____.

Ich glaube, das ist Zufall.—Das _____.

Ich glaube, das war Zufall.—Das _____.

[12] hätte fliehen können vs. könnte geflohen sein

After studying **138** carefully, try to find the various ways in which these sentences can be expressed in English.

SEE
ANALYSIS
138

(pp. 280-283)

Meyer hätte fliehen können, aber er wollte nicht.

Wahrscheinlich ist er noch im Lande, aber er könnte natürlich auch geflohen sein.

Natürlich hätte ich das Geld stehlen können, aber ich bin doch kein Dieb.

Sie können doch gar nicht wissen, ob mir das Geld wirklich gehört; ich könnte es ja auch gestohlen haben.

Du willst Anglist sein und hast nie Chaucer gelesen? Als Anglist müßtest du doch Chaucer gelesen haben.

Da hast du ganz recht; wir hätten ihn schon auf dem Gymnasium lesen müssen.

Wir waren dumm; wir hätten uns einen Volkswagen kaufen sollen.

Meyers sollen schon wieder einen Mercedes gekauft haben.

Ich habe schon immer Deutsch lernen wollen, aber ich habe nie genug Zeit dazu gehabt.

Er will in drei Wochen Deutsch gelernt haben. Glaubst du das?

[13] The Reflexive Pronoun **sich**

Er hat mir ein Auto gekauft.
Er hat sich ein Auto gekauft. (He bought himself a car.)

Ich wasche mir die Hände.
Er wäscht sich die Hände.

Wir haben uns ein Haus gebaut.
Sie haben sich ein Haus gebaut.

Ich konnte es mir einfach nicht erklären.
Er konnte es sich einfach nicht erklären.

Ich will mich noch baden.
Hat sie sich schon gebadet?

Ich lege mich bald ins Bett.
Er hat sich schon ins Bett gelegt.

Ich halte ihn für dumm,
aber er hält sich für sehr intelligent.

SEE
ANALYSIS
139

(pp. 283-284)

VARIATIONS

> **Er hat sich ein Auto gekauft.—Ich habe mir ein Auto gekauft.**

Er hat sich schon gebadet?—Du _____?
Er hat sich schon gebadet?—Ihr _____?

Er hat sich ins Bett gelegt.—Ich _____.
Er hat sich ins Bett gelegt.—Wir _____.

Sie haben sich ein Haus gebaut.—Wir _____.

Using the phrase **ein Haus bauen,** form sentences, with and without modals, negative and affirmative, using the reflexive **sich.**

[14] Contrary-to-Fact Conditions without **wenn**

Wäre Ingelheim nicht Soldat gewesen, so hätte er keine Kriegsromane schreiben
  können.
  If Ingelheim hadn't been a soldier, he couldn't have written war novels.

SEE
ANALYSIS
140

(pp. 284-285)

Hätte Erich seinen Hut nicht verloren, so hätte niemand geglaubt, was Gerda erzählte.

> If Erich hadn't lost his hat, nobody would have believed what Gerda was saying.

Hätten wir uns dieses Wochenendhaus nicht gekauft, dann könnten wir jetzt jeden Sommer nach Italien fahren.

> If only we hadn't bought this weekend house, we could go to Italy every summer now.

Wenn Otto nur nicht so *dumm* wäre!

> If only Otto weren't so *stupid!*

Wenn nur *Ot*to nicht so dumm wäre!

> If only *Otto* weren't so stupid!

Wenn meine Frau nur nicht so viel Geld brauchte!

> If only my wife didn't need so much money!

Wenn du wenigstens Kaffee kochen könntest!

> If only you could at least make coffee!

Wenn sie nur nicht so oft ins Kino gehen wollte!

> If only she didn't want to go to the movies so often!

Wenn ich damals nur *Geld* gehabt hätte!

> If only I had had *money* then!

Wenn ich das Geld nur *damals* gehabt hätte!

> If only I had had the money *then!*

Hättest du mir doch nur geschrieben, daß du Geld brauchtest! Du weißt doch, daß ich dir gerne geholfen hätte.

> If only you had written that you needed money! You know that I would have been glad to help you.

Hätte ich doch nur gewußt, daß Meyer krank war! Ich hätte ihn gerne besucht.

> Had I only known that Meyer was sick! I would have been glad to visit him.

VARIATIONS

Transform the following sentences into wishes. Shift the position of **nur** or **wenigstens**.

> Er hat meine Freundin nicht eingeladen.
> Wenn er nur meine *Freun*din eingeladen hätte!
> Wenn er meine Freundin nur *ein*geladen hätte!
> Hätte er doch nur meine *Freun*din eingeladen!
> Hätte er meine Freundin doch nur *ein*geladen!

1. Er war gestern nicht hier.
2. Er ist mit seiner Frau nach München gefahren.
3. Er hat meiner Frau Blumen geschickt.

CONVERSATION

We took a tape recorder to a German university and listened to students talking
between lectures and in the university cafeteria. Here are some of the results,
slightly edited.

I

STUDENT A: Kennst du die Gisela Wiesner? Das ist so 'ne Blonde; die macht jetzt Examen.[1]

STUDENT B: Ja, die kenne ich; die hab' ich auf einer Party kennengelernt; die muß doch mindestens zwölftes Semester sein.

STUDENT A: Ist sie auch; es ist Zeit, daß die endlich mal Examen macht.—Und Peter Lemmert, kennst du den? Aus München.

STUDENT B: Ach der—ich dachte früher immer, das wär' ein Engländer.

STUDENT A: Ja, ich dachte auch, das wäre ein Engländer—der rollte das „r" am Ende so—ich hör' manchmal englische Sender—daher weiß ich das. Aber dann war ich mit ihm zusammen bei Hornemann im Seminar, und als er das erste Mal den Mund aufgemacht hat, wußte ich, der kommt aus München.

II

STUDENT: Wie geht's?

STUDENTIN: Ach, ganz gut. Das war vielleicht eine Arbeit mit dem Referat![2] Ich hab' vier Nächte dran gearbeitet. Das hat was gekostet, diese ganze Literatur durchzuarbeiten. Aber ich hab' doch viel dabei gelernt.

STUDENT: Ja, aber man kann nur eins: entweder Referat schreiben oder Vorlesungen[3]

---

[1] **Examen machen**   to take a (final) examination
[2] **Referat**   term paper
[3] **Vorlesung**   university lecture

besuchen. Und wenn man am Proseminar teilnimmt,[4] *muß* man ein Referat schreiben, oder man bekommt keinen Seminarschein.[5] Ich werd' mir wohl noch einen holen, wenn ich auch nicht weiß, wie ich das machen soll.— Übrigens, was hat denn der Burkhardt zu deinem Referat gesagt?

STUDENTIN: Zum Referat? Also, er hat gesagt, ich brauchte keine Angst zu haben; die Arbeit sei gut, und ich könne ruhig an mein Referat für das Romantik-Seminar gehen. Er sagte, das und das sei ganz richtig gesehen, aber—na ja, dann kamen die „Aber".

STUDENT: Ist ja eigentlich alles Unsinn,—so zu arbeiten. Die Hannelore Schneider, die hat doch jetzt ein Semester lang Latein gepaukt,[6] und dann hat sie am Tag der Prüfung[7] so gezittert, daß sie nicht hingehen konnte. „Jetzt werd' ich nicht Studienrätin,[8] jetzt werd' ich Mittelschullehrerin", hat sie gesagt.

III

STUDENT: Kommen Sie, wir wollen uns weiter vorne hinsetzen—dann schlaf' ich wenigstens nicht ein. An der Vorlesung hab' ich wirklich keine Freude.

STUDENTIN: Ich kriege gottseidank immer die Notizen[9] für alle Vorlesungen von Kurt Müller—das ist schick,[10] da brauche ich nie mitzuschreiben. Übrigens, wo ist denn Ihre Freundin heute?

[4] **teil'nehmen** to take part
[5] **Seminarschein** certificate of participation in a seminar
[6] **pauken** to cram
[7] **prüfen** to test, to examine
[8] **der Studienrat** teacher at a Gymnasium
[9] **Notizen** (lecture) notes
[10] **schick** (*colloq.*) great, fine, sharp

Universität Frankfurt

STUDENT: Ach, das ist eigentlich gar nicht meine Freundin, das ist eine Bekannte.[11]— Ich muß mir doch mal Ihren Namen aufschreiben; fünf Buchstaben, genau wie meiner. Und wie war noch Ihr Vorname? Ich vergesse das immer.

STUDENTIN: Helga.

STUDENT: Wollen Sie jetzt hier wirklich zuhören? Wollen wir nicht lieber Kaffee trinken gehen?

STUDENTIN: Warum eigentlich nicht? So interessant ist der Paulsen ja nun auch nicht.

IV

STUDENT: Ich muß abends um halb elf zu Hause sein, sonst meckert[12] meine Wirtin. Aber gestern habe ich gekündigt.[13] Ich habe gesagt, das wäre besser für sie und für mich,—dann brauchte sie keine Anfälle[14] mehr zu haben über mich. Es war ihr ja nicht ganz recht, daß ich kündigte,—weil sie dann vielleicht keine Miete[15] kriegt für einen Monat—und die hundert Mark will sie natürlich haben.

STUDENTIN: Warum mußt du denn so früh zu Hause sein?

STUDENT: Wegen ihrer Tochter, die bekommt sonst nicht genug Schlaf. Und die wacht schon auf, wenn ich den Schlüssel ins Schlüsselloch stecke.

STUDENTIN: Wie alt ist die denn?

STUDENT: Och, die ist wohl so fünfunddreißig oder achtunddreißig—schon uralt.[16] Aber lieber schlaf' ich irgendwo auf dem Fußboden[17] als *da* bleiben.

STUDENTIN: Ich hab' jetzt Forsythien in der Vase. Du mußt mich mal besuchen.

[11] **Bekannte** acquaintance
[12] **meckern** here: to complain
[13] **kündigen** to give notice
[14] **der Anfall** seizure, attack; fit
[15] **die Miete** rent
[16] **uralt** ancient
[17] **der Fußboden** floor

READING

"Dear Abby" auf Deutsch

The following exchange of letters was taken, with only minor changes, from the "Dear Abby" column of a German newspaper.

Liebe Frau Erika,

als Max (mein Mann) und ich uns vor drei Jahren verlobten, kauften wir uns zwei Goldringe. Ich war stolz auf meinen, und er war stolz auf seinen Ring.

wir verlobten uns we got engaged

Nun sind wir seit zwei Jahren verheiratet. Als wir in die Kirche gingen, trugen wir die Ringe an der linken Hand. Und als wir dann s freudestrahlend aus der Kirche kamen, trug jeder seinen Ring an der rechten Hand.

an der linken Hand on the left hand
strahlen to beam

Wir waren glücklich und sind auch heute noch glücklich. Aber, mein Mann legte seinen Ring kurz nach der Hochzeit in seine Schublade, in dieselbe Schublade, in der auch sein Rasierapparat liegt. „Der Ring", meinte er, „hindert mich beim Arbeiten." Er ist nämlich Automechaniker, wissen Sie, und ich kann es verstehen, daß er den Ring nicht gerne bei der Arbeit trägt. Aber auch samstags und sonntags, wenn er nicht arbeitet, will er ihn nicht mehr tragen. Ich habe ihm den Ring auf den Frühstückstisch gelegt, aber er schiebt ihn einfach auf die Seite und liest die Zeitung.

die **Hochzeit** wedding
die **Schublade** drawer
dieselbe the same
der **Rasierapparat** razor
hindern to hinder, be in the way

Vor einem Monat habe ich meinen Ring auch in die Schublade gelegt. Wenn er seinen Ring nicht tragen will, brauche ich auch keinen Ring zu tragen, habe ich mir gesagt. Und wissen Sie was, liebe Frau Erika? Max hat es gar nicht gemerkt, daß ich seit einem Monat keinen Ring mehr trage. Meine Freundinnen haben es natürlich sofort gemerkt und fragen immer, was denn mit uns los wäre.

Was ist los? What's the matter?

Was soll ich tun? Es wäre doch *so* nett, wenn Max und ich beide unsere Ringe trügen! Bitte geben Sie mir Ihren Rat.

raten to advise; der **Rat** advice

Annemarie S., Dortmund

Liebe Frau Annemarie,

Ich bin auch seit Jahren glücklich verheiratet, und mein Mann trägt auch keinen Ring. Nicht weil der Ring ihn beim Arbeiten hindert, sondern weil seine Finger nicht mehr so schlank sind wie

schlank slender

Guten Morgen! Was möchten Sie gern zum Frühstück, bitte?

Portion Kaffee — Nescafé — Tee — Schokolade
mit Butter, Konfitüre, Marmelade, Honig, Brot,
Brötchen, Hörnchen, Zwieback 3,50

Eierspeisen

1 weichgekochtes Ei .... —,60
2 Eier im Glas 1,20
2 Stück Rührei oder Spiegeleier 1,50
2 Spiegeleier mit Schinken oder Speck 2,50

Diverses

Käse nach Wahl 1,30
Porridge mit Sahne und Zucker 1,50
Cornflakes mit Sahne oder Milch 1,50
Joghurt mit Zucker .... 1,—

Kleine Fleischbeilage

Wurstaufschnitt 1,30
Spezial-Frühstücksteller (unser Titelfoto) 1,50
Gekochter Schinken 1,80
Roher Räucherschinken .... 2,—
Roastbeef .... 2,—

Fruchtsäfte und Früchte

Orangensaft, frisch gepreßt 1,50
Grapefruitsaft 1,25
Tomatensaft 1,25
Karottensaft, frisch 1,50
Frische halbe Pampelmuse .... 1,—
Geeiste Melone .... nach Jahreszeit
Gemischtes Kompott oder Backpflaumen mit Sahne 2,—
Frisches Obst .... zum Tagespreis

15 % Etage · Etagenaufschlag pro Person DM 0,50 · 10 % Service

früher. Aber das macht mir gar nichts aus. Legen Sie Ihrem Mann   **macht ... aus** doesn't
den Ring sonntags nicht wieder auf den Frühstückstisch. Aber   bother me at all

machen Sie den Kaffee besonders gut und fahren Sie mit ihm übers
Wochenende in die Berge. Und wenn Sie mit Ihrem Max in ein
Restaurant gehen, dann stecken Sie Ihren Ring vorher an den Finger. 5
Oder sind Ihre Finger nicht mehr schlank genug für Ihren Ring?
Das wäre schade.

Woher wußten Sie denn, daß ich Amerikanerin bin?

Ich weiß, mein Deutsch ist gut und fast akzentfrei; und wenn ich
nach Deutschland fahre, glaubt man oft, daß ich in Deutschland
geboren bin. Aber letztes Jahr habe ich gelernt, daß man mehr als 10
die Sprache können muß, wenn man nicht will, daß jeder sofort
weiß, daß man Amerikaner ist.

Ich war mit meinem Mann in Hamburg, und wir wohnten in den
„Vier Jahreszeiten". Morgens im Frühstückszimmer saßen wir kaum   **Vier Jahreszeiten**
an unserem Tisch, als der Kellner kam und uns fragte: „And what 15   Four Seasons
would you like for breakfast?" Woher wußte er, daß wir Amerikaner
waren?

Mein Kleid hatte ich am Tage vorher in Hamburg gekauft; ich hatte

---

Good morning!
What would you like for breakfast, please?

Coffee — Nescafé — tea — chocolate
compl. with butter, jam, marmelade, honey,
rolls, recent-rolls, bread, biscuits   3,50

Egg - dishes

1 soft boiled egg	—,60
2 boiled eggs in a glass	1,20
Scrambled eggs or fried eggs	1,50
2 fried eggs with ham or bacon	2,50

Sundries

Assorted cheese	1,30
Porridge with cream and sugar	1,50
Cornflakes with cream or milk	1,50
Yoghurt with sugar	1,—

Small meat supplements

Sausages cold meat	1,30
Assorted cold meat	1,50
Boiled ham	1,80
Smoked ham	2,—
Roastbeef	2,—

Fruit and fruit-juices

Orange juice, fresh	1,50
Grapefruit juice	1,25
Tomato juice	1,25
Carrots juice, fresh	1,50
Fresh half grapefruit	1,—
Mixed fruits or stewed prunes with cream	2,—
Fresh fruit	price of day

15 % room-service · room-tax per person DM 0,50 · 10 % service

keinen Lippenstift an, und meine Dauerwelle hatte ich mir in Köln
machen lassen. Außerdem las mein Mann eine Hamburger Zeitung.
Und trotzdem sagte der Kellner: „What would you like for breakfast?" Ich war neugierig und fragte: „Herr Ober, woher wissen
Sie, daß wir Amerikaner sind?"   5

„Wenn man seit dreißig Jahren Kellner ist, dann sieht man das
sofort, gnädige Frau", sagte er auf Deutsch. „Als Sie Platz nahmen,
hat Ihnen Ihr Mann den Stuhl gehalten,—und das tut man in
Deutschland nicht. Und als ich an Ihren Tisch kam, habe ich sofort
gesehen, daß Sie Ihren Ring an der linken Hand tragen,—und das 10
tut man in Deutschland nur, solange man verlobt ist."

„Und woher wußten Sie, daß wir verheiratet sind?"

„Gnädige Frau, das darf ich Ihnen wirklich nicht sagen."

„Das brauchen Sie auch nicht", sagte mein Mann, der bis jetzt
hinter seiner Zeitung gesessen und nichts gesagt hatte. Er grinste, 15
faltete die Zeitung zusammen, gab sie dem Kellner und sagte:
„Herr Ober, Sie sind ein Menschenkenner.—Also: zwei Orangensaft, Spiegeleier mit Schinken, Toast und Kaffee."

„In other words, an American breakfast", sagte der Ober und verschwand.   20

der Lippenstift lip-
stick
die Dauerwelle per-
manent
neugierig curious

grinsen to grin
zusammenfalten to
fold
der Saft juice
das Ei, -er egg; das
Spiegelei fried egg,
sunny side up
der Schinken ham

134 The Use of **nicht**

nicht in the Inner Field

As was pointed out in **43, nicht,** if placed at the end of the inner field in front of the second prong, negates the predicate.

Ich	**bin**	sehr oft	**nicht**	**zu Hause**

I am very often not at home

means basically *I am not at home,* and this *not being at home* happens *very often.*

It was also pointed out that if **nicht** is placed within the inner field, the validity of the predicate is untouched. The sentence

Ich	**bin**	**nicht**	sehr oft	**zu Hause**

I am not very often at home

means basically *I am at home,* but this *being at home* happens *not very often.*

The difference in meaning between the two positions of **nicht** is sometimes rather startling. Compare

Er wollte Priester werden. Und darum hat er freiwillig nicht geheiratet.
He wanted to become a priest. For this reason he voluntarily did not marry.

Ihre Eltern haben sie gezwungen, einen Mann zu heiraten, den sie nicht liebte. Sie hat nicht freiwillig geheiratet.
Her parents forced her to marry a man she did not love. She did not marry voluntarily.

nicht Followed by **sondern**

The English pattern "not A, but B," which occurs in such sentences as

You are not my friend, but my enemy

is expressed in German by **nicht A, sondern B.**

Das war nicht gestern, sondern vorgestern.
That was not yesterday, but the day before yesterday.

Such sentences use contrast intonation. The element introduced by **nicht** (or **kein**) has a rising stress ($\underline{/}$), and the element introduced by **sondern** has a falling stress ($\overline{}\backslash$). The **nicht** (or **kein**) and the **sondern** are normally unstressed.

The element introduced by **sondern** can either stand behind the second prong in the end field, or it can follow immediately upon the **nicht A** element:

> **Ich war nicht gestern in Berlin, sondern vorgestern.**
> **Ich war nicht gestern, sondern vorgestern in Berlin.**

135   Numbers from 1 to 100

The German system is quite similar to English. From 0 to 12, each number has its own name; from 13 on, and with the exception of 100, the numbers are either compounded or are derived from the basic set 1–9. Note that from 21 to 29, 31 to 39, etc. German reverses the English pattern: *twenty-one* becomes **einundzwanzig.**

null		zwanzig	
eins		einundzwanzig	
zwei		zweiundzwanzig	*zwanzig*
drei	dreizehn	dreiundzwanzig	*dreißig*
vier	vierzehn	vierundzwanzig	vierzig
fünf	fünfzehn	fünfundzwanzig	fünfzig
sechs	*sechzehn*	sechsundzwanzig	*sechzig*
sieben	*siebzehn*	siebenundzwanzig	*siebzig*
acht	achtzehn	achtundzwanzig	achtzig
neun	neunzehn	neunundzwanzig	neunzig
zehn			(ein)hundert
elf			
zwölf			

Particular attention must be paid to the spelling and pronunciation of the italicized numbers in the table.

136   Present and Past Infinitives

In any sentence containing an infinitive, there is always a time relation between this infinitive and the inflected verb. Consider the sentences

Er scheint zu schlafen.	He seems to be asleep.
Er schien zu schlafen.	He seemed to be asleep.

In both sentences the infinitive (**schlafen**) refers to the same time as the inflected verbs (**scheint** and **schien**).

If the infinitives, compared to the time of the inflected verb, refer to the same time, they are called present infinitives, *even if* (as in **er schien zu schlafen**) both the inflected verb and the infinitive refer to past time compared to the moment of speaking. Up to now, only such present infinitives have been used in this book.

The situation is quite different in sentences such as

Er scheint gut geschlafen zu haben.
He seems to have slept well.
Er behauptet, General gewesen zu sein.
He claims to have been a general.

Here the infinitives **geschlafen zu haben** (to have slept) and **gewesen zu sein** (to have been) refer to a point in time which precedes the time of the inflected verb. The compound infinitives used in such cases are called past infinitives.

In German past infinitives, the participle (**geschlafen; gewesen**) precedes the infinitive of the auxiliary, which is always either **haben** or **sein**. The **zu** stands between the participle and **sein** or **haben**. **Zu** is, of course, not used after modals.

PRESENT INFINITIVE	PAST INFINITIVE
haben	gehabt (zu) haben
sein	gewesen (zu) sein
essen	gegessen (zu) haben
abfahren	abgefahren (zu) sein
kennenlernen	kennengelernt (zu) haben
glücklich sein	glücklich gewesen (zu) sein.

137 The Subjective Use of Modals

In such sentences as

| **Alle Menschen müssen sterben.** | All humans must die. |
| **Ich muß morgen arbeiten.** | I must (have to) work tomorrow. |

both English *must* and German **müssen** express an unavoidable necessity. It is important to point out that this necessity exists for the grammatical subject (which is sometimes the speaker himself). The speaker, in such cases, reports in an objective way what exists in the world of facts and objects. He is using the modals *must* and **müssen** "objectively."

The situation is quite different in sentences like

> See the smoke coming out of the Meyers' chimney?
> They must be home!
> **Meyer fährt jetzt einen Mercedes 300.**
> **Er muß Geld haben.**

The *must* and the **muß** in these sentences do not mean that the Meyers are compelled to be at home or that Herr Meyer is compelled to have money. Rather, the modal expresses inferences: the speaker has analyzed the visible facts and arrived at an unavoidable conclusion. The *must* and the **muß** express the speaker's subjective judgment. He is now using the modal "subjectively."

In spite of the fact that the subjective use of **müssen** is usually parallel to the use of English *must*, we have until now carefully avoided the subjective use of the German modals. For very good reasons. First of all, German modals, when used subjectively, are frequently followed by a past infinitive, and past infinitives are used for the first time in this unit. Second, some of the German modals have subjective meanings which do not occur in English. We shall therefore have to look systematically into the subjective use of all the German modals.

müssen

When used subjectively, **müssen** and all other modals occur only in the present and past tenses.

The present indicative

> **Er muß schon angekommen sein.**
> He must have arrived by now.

can be changed to the subjunctive to express the notion that, though the inference *He must have arrived* is logical, it is nevertheless uncertain. The use of **eigentlich** underscores the uncertainty of the inference:

> **Er müßte eigentlich schon angekommen sein.**
> He really ought to have arrived by now.

This subjunctive **müßte** is very frequent in German and has no structural parallel in English.

wollen

When used subjectively, **wollen** assumes the meaning *to claim:*

> **Er will Arzt sein und in Wien studiert haben.**
> He claims to be a doctor and to have studied in Vienna.

Eine Reise um die Welt muß nicht ein Vermögen kosten und nicht ewig dauern.

It is only context, not structure, that will show whether **wollen** is used subjectively or objectively. Thus

Sie wollen alle dabei gewesen sein

may mean, subjectively,

They all claim to have been there.

It may also mean, objectively,

They all want to have been there.

sollen

The basic meaning of **sollen** can be defined as "a plan of operation not made by the grammatical subject."

Er soll morgen nach Berlin fahren.
He is supposed to go to Berlin tomorrow.
Die Brücke soll nächstes Jahr fertig sein.
The bridge is supposed to be finished by next year.

The sentences quoted denote a plan of operation and therefore may contain a connotation of hearsay:

I understand that he is going to Berlin tomorrow.
I have heard that the bridge is to be finished by next year.

This suggestion of hearsay—both for German **sollen** and for English *to be supposed to*—may become the predominant meaning:

Meyer soll viel Geld haben.
Meyer is supposed to have a lot of money.
(It is common gossip that he has a lot of money.)

Meyer soll früher viel Geld gehabt haben.
Meyer is said to have had a lot of money.

On the other hand, since plans of operation are often made by authorities, **sollen** frequently expresses obligation.

Wir sollen um elf zu Hause sein.
We are to be home at eleven.

können

When used objectively, **können** expresses the ability of the grammatical subject to do something.

Leider konnte sie nicht schwimmen.
Unfortunately she couldn't (wasn't able to) swim.

When used subjectively, **können** expresses a possibility inferred by the speaker on the basis of observable facts. English expresses such inferred possibility by using *can* or *may* in the present and by using *could* or *might* in the past or in the subjunctive.

Das kann nicht Frau Müller sein; die ist doch in München.
That can't be Mrs. Müller; she's in Munich, you know.

Sie war noch so jung; sie konnte höchstens siebzehn sein.
She was so young; she could have been seventeen at the most.

The subjunctive is used to express an inference which is not so certain.

Es könnte Erich gewesen sein.
It might have been Erich.

dürfen

Of the six modals, **dürfen** has the lowest frequency. When used objectively, it expresses the idea that the grammatical subject has been given permission. Since nobody wants to be bossy or be bossed around, **dürfen,** like **erlauben,** is not used very often. Even a child prefers

Kann ich heute abend ins Kino gehen?

to the obedient

Darf ich heute abend ins Kino gehen?

The real "live" use of **dürfen** therefore tends to be restricted to situations where no person giving permission is involved:

Darf man hier rauchen?   Is smoking permitted here?

or where **dürfen** really means "it would be wise":

> **Sie dürfen abends keinen Kaffee mehr**   You mustn't drink coffee at night any more.
> **trinken.**

The only subjective meaning of **dürfen** is the use of the subjunctive **dürfte** to express probability:

> **Erika dürfte jetzt schon in Frankfurt**   Erika is probably already in Frankfurt by
> **sein.**   now.

mögen

Up to this point, we have used only the forms **ich möchte, du möchtest,** etc. But although these **möchte**-forms are the ones used most frequently, **mögen**, like the other modals, has a complete set of forms:

PRESENT INDICATIVE	PRESENT SUBJUNCTIVE
ich mag	ich möchte
du magst	du möchtest
er mag	er möchte
wir mögen	wir möchten
ihr mögt	ihr möchtet
sie mögen	sie möchten

PAST INDICATIVE	PAST SUBJUNCTIVE
ich mochte	Ich hätte . . . (infinitive) mögen
du mochtest	du hättest " "
er mochte	er hätte " "
wir mochten	wir hätten " "
ihr mochtet	ihr hättet " "
sie mochten	sie hätten " "

PERFECT WITH DEPENDENT INFINITIVE	PERFECT WITHOUT INFINITIVE
ich habe . . . mögen	ich habe gemocht
du hast . . . mögen	du hast gemocht
etc.	etc.

The verb **mögen** can be used without a following infinitive. If so used, it means *to like* and takes an accusative object:

> **Sie mag ihn nicht.**   She doesn't like him.
> **Wir mögen kein Schweinefleisch.** We don't like pork.
> **Wir mochten ihn nicht.**   We did not like him.
> **Ich habe sie nie gemocht.**   I never liked her.

When used as a modal—that is, with a dependent infinitive, **mögen** has an objective and a subjective meaning.

Used objectively, **mögen** plus infinitive expresses the fact that the grammatical subject has a desire. This use, for all practical purposes, is restricted to the **möchte**-forms.

When used subjectively, as in **Das mag sein** (*That may be*), **mögen** means *may* and denotes that the speaker presents his statement with the reservation that what he reports "may be" the case. As a matter of fact, **Mag sein!**, used as a sentence by itself, does mean *Maybe!*

This subjective use of **mögen** occurs quite frequently in modern literature. The present indicative **mag** denotes a present possibility, and **mochte**, the past indicative, a past possibility. The use of the past infinitive is frequent. The following examples are taken from modern literature:

Man mag es nicht glauben wollen.	You may not want to believe it.
Das mag einer der Punkte gewesen sein.	That may have been one of the points.
Das mochte wirklich Zufall gewesen sein.	Perhaps that was really a coincidence.
Er mag geglaubt haben, ich verstände ihn.	He may have thought that I understood him.

138 The Use of Past Infinitives after Modals

You are by now familiar with such sentences as

Meyer konnte fliehen, aber er wollte nicht.
Meyer could (was able to) escape, but he didn't want to (wouldn't).

By using the past-tense forms **konnte** and *could* and the present infinitives **fliehen** and *escape*—infinitives that express simultaneity, just as in **Er schien zu schlafen**—both English and German refer to a chance in the past to do something (to escape) while this chance was good. The chance involved can be defined as "a past chance for somebody to do something."

The parallelism between

Er konnte fliehen

and

He could escape

disappears if the sentence above is expressed as a contrary-to-fact condition:

Er hätte fliehen können, wenn er gewollt hätte.
He could have escaped if he had wanted to.

Note that

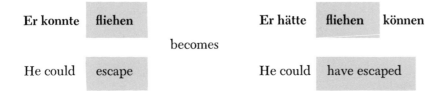

Er konnte	fliehen		Er hätte	fliehen	können
		becomes			
He could	escape		He could	have escaped	

In German, the past indicative **konnte** is replaced by the past subjunctive **hätte können** while the present infinitive **fliehen** is retained; English, on the other hand, changes from the present infinitive *escape* to the past infinitive *have escaped*.

Since the chance involved in the sentence

Er hätte fliehen können, wenn er gewollt hätte

must still be defined as "a past chance for somebody to do something," the use of the past infinitive *have escaped* in English seems utterly illogical to a German; and your German teacher might point out with glee that

He could   have escaped

can be replaced by the "more logical"

He would have been able to   escape

which actually shows a present infinitive.

For the English-speaking student, the pattern *could have escaped* constitutes a serious source of interference. He is always tempted to say

Er könnte   geflohen sein.

This is a perfectly good German sentence without a single grammatical mistake, but, unfortunately, it doesn't mean *He would have been able to flee,* although it may mean—and we are not being facetious—*He could have fled.* The fact is that *could have fled* is an ambiguous phrase and can refer to two entirely different situations.

Situation A. Imagine the following news item: "The police are still looking for the elegantly dressed young woman who shot the Prime Minister last night. Of course, she *could* conceivably *have fled* the country, but since all airports were alerted immediately, it is assumed that she is still in the country." German, in this situation, would use a structural pattern parallel to English:

Sie könnte   geflohen sein

She could (might)   have fled

The subjunctives **könnte,** *could (might)*—all used subjectively—suggest that the possibility (a *present* possibility) is slim and almost imaginary. The past infinitives are used, because the chance involved must here be defined as "a chance that somebody has already done something." The sentences mean "It is at present considered unlikely that the assassin has fled."

The subjunctive sentences
> **Sie könnte geflohen sein**
> She might have fled

belong to the present indicative sentences
> **Sie kann geflohen sein**
> She may have fled.

In all four of these sentences, the modals are used subjectively; that is, they express an inference.

The difference between the subjunctive and the indicative is mainly a difference in degree, not in meaning. **Kann** and *may* are more positive than **könnte** and *might.*

Situation B. The news item above could have read: "The young lady who shot the Prime Minister was arrested as she tried to board a small private plane. If the police had not been tipped off, she could have fled the country."

Here we are back to the past chance to do something, to the objective use of **können,** and to the difference between the past indicative

Sie konnte fliehen

She could (was able to) escape

and the past subjunctive

Sie hätte fliehen **können**

She could have escaped

which was discussed above.

You will now realize, we hope, that you must learn to distinguish between a chance to do something and a chance that somebody has done something. Subjunctive sentences involving modals are apt to confuse you unless you clearly understand the following table:

CHANCE TO DO SOMETHING

INDICATIVE	SUBJUNCTIVE (irreality)
Sie konnte fliehen	**Sie hätte** fliehen **können**

CHANCE THAT SOMEBODY HAS DONE SOMETHING

INDICATIVE	SUBJUNCTIVE (uncertainty)
Sie kann geflohen sein	**Sie könnte** geflohen sein

139 The Reflexive Pronoun **sich**

Very often the subject and the object of a verb are one and the same person or thing:

He hated himself.
History never repeats itself.
I bought myself a car.

In all these cases, English uses reflexive pronouns for the object. In a way, this is linguistic luxury. "I bought me a car," though considered substandard, is just as clear as "I bought myself a car." German gets along without reflexive pronouns for all first and second persons:

Ich habe mich gebadet.	Ich kaufe mir ein Auto.
Du hast dich gebadet.	Du kaufst dir ein Auto.
Wir haben uns gebadet.	Wir kaufen uns ein Auto.
Ihr habt euch gebadet.	Ihr kauft euch ein Auto.

The situation is different in all third persons. Whereas the difference between *me* and *myself* is luxury, the difference between *him* and *himself* may be the difference between murder and suicide: *he killed him; he killed himself.*

German has only the one reflexive pronoun **sich** for all third-person cases. This **sich** serves both as a dative and as an accusative, both as a singular and as a plural.

Er hat sie vergiftet.	He poisoned her.
Sie hat ihn vergiftet.	She poisoned him.
Er hat sich vergiftet.	He poisoned himself.
Sie hat sich vergiftet.	She poisoned herself.
Sie haben sich vergiftet.	They poisoned themselves.
Er hat ihr ein Auto gekauft.	He bought her a car.
Sie hat ihm ein Auto gekauft.	She bought him a car.
Er hat sich ein Auto gekauft.	He bought himself a car.
Sie hat sich ein Auto gekauft.	She bought herself a car.
Sie haben sich ein Auto gekauft.	They bought themselves a car.

140 Contrary-to-Fact Conditions without **wenn**

In contrary-to-fact conditions, the conjunction **wenn** may be omitted. In contemporary German, and particularly in the spoken language, this pattern occurs almost exclusively in past time.

> Wenn Ingelheim nicht Soldat gewesen wäre, hätte er keine Kriegs-
> romane schreiben können.

> Wäre Ingelheim nicht Soldat gewesen, dann hätte er keine Kriegs-
> romane schreiben können.

The clause with the omitted **wenn** always shows verb-first position and usually precedes the conclusion. The conclusion is usually introduced by **dann** or **so**.

If the condition stands alone to express a wish or desire, the **wenn** can also be omitted, but again primarily in past time.

> **Wenn er mir nur geschrieben hätte!**
> **Hätte er mir doch nur geschrieben!**

NOTE: These wishful **wenn**-clauses are independent syntactical units and almost always contain a **nur** or **doch nur** or a **wenigstens**. Like all sentence adverbs, this **nur** or **wenigstens** shifts position as follows: The elements preceding *nur, doch nur,* or *wenigstens* are unstressed and include all those things which have already been talked about; the elements following *nur, doch nur,* or *wenigstens* are all news items.

> **Ich wollte ja studieren. Wenn ich nur das Geld dazu gehabt hätte!**
> **Jetzt habe ich das Geld. Wenn ich das Geld nur früher gehabt hätte!**

141   ja

The most obvious use of **ja,** of course, is to answer a question. Frequently, however, it is used in the same position and with the same affirmative function, even if there is no question or previous conversation. Similar to English *well,* this **ja** can precede any reaction.

> **Ja, das ist aber schön, daß ihr doch noch gekommen seid.**
> Well, how nice that you came after all.

> **Ja, was machen wir denn jetzt?**
> Well, what are we going to do now?

As an unstressed sentence adverb, **ja** occurs very frequently. It has two functions:

1. The speaker wants to express the idea that the facts asserted are well known and accepted by both speaker and listener.

> **Bei uns regnet es im Sommer ja sehr oft.**
> As you know, we have lots of rain during the summer.

> **Wir müssen ja alle einmal sterben.**
> We've all got to die, you know.

2. In sentences spoken with emphatic stress, **ja** heightens the emotional flavor.

> **Das ist ja himmlisch.**
> **Ich komme ja schon.**
> **Ich bin ja so glücklich.**
> **Das ist ja nicht möglich.**

When used as a sentence adverb, **ja** follows items of no news value and precedes items with news value, unless the verb itself is stressed.

142 Adverbs in **-erweise**

These sentence adverbs are formed from adjectives and express a judgment.

glücklicherweise	fortunately, it is fortunate that
möglicherweise	possibly, it is possible that
normalerweise	normally, as a rule, it is normal that

143 Adverbs in **-ens**

The following derivatives are frequently used:

frühstens	at the earliest
spätestens	at the latest
höchstens	at most
meistens	in most cases, mostly
nächstens	in the near future

EXERCISES

A. Without changing word order, negate the following sentences by using **nicht** in at least two different positions.

1. Ich möchte mit Rosemarie ins Theater gehen.
2. Meyer hat lange arbeiten können.
3. Ich bin oft ins Kino gegangen.
4. Ich kann aber auf dem Sofa schlafen.
5. Sie wollte aber den Meyer heiraten.

B. Using the **nicht A, sondern B** pattern, combine the following pairs of sentences.

> **Wir fahren nicht im Juli nach Berlin. Wir fahren im August.**
> (a) **Wir fahren nicht im Juli, sondern im August nach Berlin.**
> (b) **Wir fahren nicht im Juli nach Berlin, sondern im August.**

1. Ich habe nicht meine Mutter besucht. Ich habe meinen Vater besucht.
2. Er hat nicht acht Stunden gearbeitet. Er hat nur zwei Stunden gearbeitet.
3. Gestern abend hat Erich keinen Wein getrunken. Er hat nur Bier getrunken.
4. Er hat mir kein Buch geschenkt. Er hat mir einen Hut geschenkt.

C. Read and write down the following:

1, 2, 3, 7, 11, 13, 17, 19, 23, 31, 37, 41, 43, 47, 53, 59, 61, 67, 71, 73, 79, 83, 87, 89, 93, 97.

D. In the following sentences, change the present infinitives to past infinitives.

> **Maria muß schon aufstehen.**
> **Maria muß schon aufgestanden sein.**

1. Meyer muß nach Berlin fahren.
2. Er scheint sehr freundlich zu sein.
3. Mein Vater scheint sehr viel von ihm zu halten.
4. Sie kann doch nicht schon wieder spazierengehen.
5. Ihr Mann muß sehr viel Geld haben.

E. Change the following sentences, all containing objective modals, from present indicative to present subjunctive and add **eigentlich** in the place indicated by /. (**Eigentlich** follows the pronouns and elements of no news value.) Then translate these sentences into English.

1. Ich soll / um sechs Uhr zu Hause sein.
2. Hans muß / hierbleiben.
3. Wir müssen heute abend / schon wieder ausgehen.
4. Wir können / auch einmal ins Theater gehen.
5. Ich kann ja / auch mit *Inge* spazierengehen.

F. Change the following sentences to the past.

1. Ich kann es ihm noch nicht sagen.
2. Wir müssen auch schwer arbeiten.
3. Ich darf ihn nie wieder besuchen.
4. Ich will nie wieder nach Berlin fahren.
5. Und trotzdem muß ich immer wieder freundlich zu ihr sein.

G. Connect the following pairs of sentences by means of the words in parentheses. Which of the connecting words are adverbs, which are coordinating conjunctions, and which are subordinating conjunctions?

1. Ich habe nichts davon gewußt. Er hat mir nicht geschrieben. (weil)
2. Er stand lange vor der Tür. Er klopfte endlich an. (dann)
3. Er wollte nicht mit Prof. Müller sprechen. Er hatte Angst vor ihm. (denn)
4. Er war krank. Ich konnte ihn nicht besuchen. (daher)
5. Ich konnte ihn nicht besuchen. Er war krank. (da)
6. Ich rief von Paris aus an. Erich sollte nicht wissen, daß ich in Afrika gewesen war. (weil)
7. Er fuhr sofort nach Hamburg. Er hatte meinen Brief bekommen. (nachdem)
8. Sollen wir ins Kino gehen? Sollen wir zu Hause bleiben? (oder)
9. Tante Amalie kommt morgen. Wir gehen bestimmt wieder ins Museum. (Wenn . . . , dann)

10. Erich hat die Goldstücke gestohlen. Ich kann es nicht glauben. (Daß . . . , das)
11. Ich habe Erich nicht mehr gesehen. Wir waren zusammen in Afrika. (seit)
12. Ich war mit Erich zusammen in Afrika. Ich habe ihn nicht mehr gesehen. (seitdem)
13. Er ist nicht mit ins Kino gegangen. Er hat seiner Frau einen Brief geschrieben. (sondern)
14. Der Meyer will mich heiraten. Ich kann nur lachen. (Daß . . . , darüber)
15. Er hätte eigentlich um zehn nach Hause gehen sollen. Er blieb bis elf. (trotzdem)
16. Er blieb bis elf. Er sollte um zehn zu Hause sein. (obwohl)
17. Ich habe ihn lange gesucht. Ich habe ihn nicht finden können. (aber)
18. Er hat mir nicht geschrieben. Ich habe ihm auch nicht mehr geschrieben. (darum)
19. Gestern bei Meyers habe ich eine Frau kennengelernt. Ihr Mann soll Arabisch sprechen. (deren)

H. Change the following sentences in two ways: (a) Change the modal to the perfect; (b) keep the modal in the present and change the infinitive to a past infinitive. Then translate the two resulting sentences so as to show the difference in meaning.

> **Er soll um acht Uhr zu Hause sein.**
> (a) **Er hat um acht Uhr zu Hause sein sollen.**
>   He had to be at home at eight.
> (b) **Er soll um acht Uhr zu Hause gewesen sein.**
>   He is said to have been at home at eight.

1. Er kann nicht in Berlin arbeiten.
2. Ingelheim muß Soldat werden.
3. Ingeborg muß heiraten.
4. Meyer will ein Haus an der Riviera kaufen.
5. Ingelheim soll Arabisch lernen.

I. By using the proper forms of modals, express in one sentence each of the following ideas:

1. There is a rumor that five gold pieces have disappeared.
2. Ingelheim claims that he fought in Africa.
3. I came to the conclusion that he was living in Berlin.
4. I have arrived at the conclusion that he has been in America.
5. You should have gone to Berlin two years ago.
6. There was a rumor that she had gone to Berlin.
7. It is possible that he is still here.
8. It is not possible that he was in Berlin.
9. It has never been possible for him to go to Berlin.
10. He tries to give the impression that he was a friend of my father.

J. Change the following sentences from the past indicative to the past subjunctive. Add **eigentlich** in the place indicated by /.

> **Ich mußte gestern nach Berlin fahren.**
> **Ich hätte gestern eigentlich nach Berlin fahren müssen.**

1. Ich sollte gestern / meine Mutter besuchen.
2. Ich durfte es Ihnen / nicht sagen.
3. Ich brauchte / gar nichts zu sagen.
4. Ich konnte damals / auch nach Casablanca fliegen.
5. Mir konntest du das ja / erzählen.

K. In the following sentences, change the modals from indicative to subjunctive. Add **eigentlich** when appropriate.

1. Er kann, wenn er will.
2. Ich kann auch mitgehen.
3. Ich muß auch einmal nach Italien fahren.
4. Sie sollen nicht so viel rauchen.
5. Sein Sohn sollte in Heidelberg studieren.

L. The following sentences contain a dependent clause introduced by **weil**. By changing the **weil**-clause, first into a conditional clause with **wenn** and then without **wenn**, transform the sentences into contrary-to-fact conditions. Start all sentences with the conditional clause.

> **Weil er krank war, konnte er nicht arbeiten.**
> (a) **Wenn er nicht krank gewesen wäre, hätte er arbeiten können.**
> (b) **Wäre er nicht krank gewesen, dann hätte er arbeiten können.**

1. Weil ich nicht so viel Geld hatte wie Meyer, konnte ich nicht an der Riviera wohnen.
2. Weil es mir in Hamburg zu kalt war, bin ich nach Afrika gefahren.
3. Er kam spät nach Hause, weil er ins Kino gegangen war.
4. Er hat sie geheiratet, weil sie Geld hatte.
5. Weil das Essen so schlecht war, fuhren wir nach Hause.

M. Change the following statements to wishes contrary to fact, using either **doch nur** or **doch nur nicht** and starting with **wenn** and then without **wenn**. (Like **eigentlich**, **doch nur** follows the pronouns and elements of no news value.)

> **Er ist nach Italien gefahren.**
> (a) **Wenn er doch nur nicht nach Italien gefahren wäre.**
> (b) **Wäre er doch nur nicht nach Italien gefahren.**

1. Er kam so oft.
2. Er hat mir nicht geschrieben, daß er Geld braucht.
3. Sie hat mir gesagt, daß sie Thusnelda heißt.
4. Die Desdemona konnte ich leider nicht spielen.
5. Ich habe nicht gewußt, daß du auch in Berlin warst.

N. Express in German:

1. He must have waited for me for three hours.
2. He had to wait for me for three hours.
3. He can't have slept long. I called him up at seven o'clock, but I couldn't reach him any more.
4. Had he sent the letter to me, I could have answered him immediately.
5. His letter must have arrived when I had already gone to Munich.
6. What you claim to have experienced cannot have happened.
7. He has always wanted to go to Africa.
8. He cannot have been in Africa.
9. Erich must have recognized me.
10. Erika seems to have arrived already.
11. I don't think much of him.
12. I often think of you.
13. He ought to have arrived an hour ago.
14. Dr. Schmidt was at the Meyers' too; you must have met him there.
15. It could not have been Erich, for I knew that Erich had gone to the airport to pick up Ingelheim.
16. Could I have another cup of coffee, please?
17. Could you work in the garden yesterday?
18. Of course we could have gone to the movies, but we didn't want to.
19. She claims to be thirty; she looks as if she were thirty-five; but she is said to be forty.
20. She may have thought that Erich wanted to help her.

O. Write a conversation between two students, Doris Weise and Günter Hartmann, using the following outline:

Doris has just seen Professor Niemann to talk to him about a term paper she has just written for his seminar. Günter wants to know what Professor Niemann told her; he has heard that Niemann is very nice and likes to talk to students. But Doris doesn't agree with him; she was so nervous that she trembled when she talked to Niemann. It turns out, however, that her paper was really very good, and she didn't need to be afraid at all. Günter congratulates her and suggests that they go and have a cup of coffee. Doris thinks that she ought to go to Professor Neuhof's lecture, but Günter thinks that she can easily get somebody else's lecture notes; after all, that lecture isn't all that interesting. Doris agrees, and Günter uses the occasion to invite her to a party that he and some friends are giving the following week.

BASIC VOCABULARY

die Ankunft arrival
aufschreiben to write down, note
der August' August
behaupten to maintain, claim
bemerken to notice, mention, note, say
der Berg, –e mountain
besonders especially
braun brown
der Donnerstag, –e Thursday
entweder... oder either... or
   weder... noch neither... nor
etwa about; by any chance
fertig ready, complete
fliehen to escape, flee
froh glad, gay
frühstens at the earliest
genau exact(ly)
glücklicherweise fortunately, happily
der Himmel heaven, sky
   himmlisch heavenly
höchstens at the most

irgendwo somewhere
der Juli July
der Kellner, – waiter
   der Oberkellner, – headwaiter
   Herr Ober (usual way of addressing a waiter)
das Kleid, –er dress
das Land, ¨er the land, country
meistens usually, mostly
merken to notice
das Mittagessen, – dinner (noon meal, the main meal in Germany)
möglicherweise possibly
Mutti Mom, Mommy
nächstens in the near future
der Name, –n name
   der Vorname, –n first name
   der Nachname, –n last name
Platz nehmen to sit down, have a seat

die Post mail; post office
der Preis, –e price; prize
der Ring, –e ring
schade too bad
schieben to push, shove
der Schlüssel, – key
senden to send; broadcast
   der Sender, – sender; broadcasting station
sondern (nicht A, sondern B) but (not A but B)
spätestens at the latest
teilen to divide
   geteilt durch divided by
umziehen to move (change residence)
verkaufen to sell
vorgestern day before yesterday
vorher (adv.) before, earlier
vorne (adv.) in front
waschen to wash
wenigstens at least
Wien Vienna

ADDITIONAL VOCABULARY

der Anglist', –en anglicist
der Buchstabe, –n letter (of the alphabet)
freiwillig voluntary
das Gymnasium, die Gymnasien (German secondary school, grades 5–13)
der Ingenieur', –e engineer

kriegen (colloquial) = bekommen to get
der Mond, –e moon
normalerweise normally
der Punkt, –e point; period (in punctuation)
rollen to roll
das Schwein, –e pig

das Schweinefleisch (no pl.) pork
   das Fleisch (no pl.) meat
der Unsinn nonsense
vergiften to poison
der Zufall, ¨e accident, coincidence
   durch Zufall by accident

IRREGULAR VERBS

fliehen to flee, escape
   floh, ist geflohen, er flieht
schieben to push, shove
   schob, hat geschoben, er schiebt

senden to send; broadcast
   sandte, hat gesandt, er sendet
umziehen to move (change residence)

   zog um, ist umgezogen, er zieht um
waschen to wash
   wusch, hat gewaschen, er wäscht

UNIT 10: Adjectives

[1] Attributive Adjectives, Nominative Singular

Read the analysis first; then try to visualize the slots while you read these examples:

Der alte Mann kam aus der Tür.	The old man came out of the door.
Ein junger Mann wartete auf ihn.	A young man was waiting for him.
Die junge Frau hieß Barbara.	The young woman's name was Barbara.
Eine junge Frau stand neben ihm.	A young woman was standing next to him.
Das kleine Mädchen hieß auch Barbara.	The little girl's name was also Barbara.
Barbara war noch ein kleines Mädchen, als Paul sie kennenlernte.	Barbara was still a little girl when Paul met her.
Mein lieber Vater!	My dear Father: (Salutation)
Meine liebe Mutter!	My dear Mother:
Mein liebes Kind!	My dear Child:
Lieber Vater!	Dear Father:
Liebe Mutter!	Dear Mother:
Liebes Kind!	Dear Child:
Das ist wirklich ein guter Wein!	That is really a good wine!
Guter Wein ist teuer.	Good wine is expensive.
Klare Fleischsuppe ist eine Spezialität unseres Hauses.	Clear broth is a specialty of the house.
Eine gute Suppe gehört zu jeder Mahlzeit.	A good soup belongs with every meal.
Unsere italienische Gemüsesuppe ist auch nicht schlecht.	Our Italian vegetable soup isn't bad either.
Frisches Obst ist immer gut.	Fresh fruit is always good.
Das italienische Obst ist nicht mehr so teuer wie früher.	Italian fruit is no longer as expensive as it used to be.
Ich empfehle Ihnen Dortmunder Union; das ist ein gutes Bier.	I recommend Dortmunder Union; that's a good beer.

SEE ANALYSIS 144–149 (pp. 310-314)

(Facing) **Bischofsheim in der Rhön**

VARIATIONS

Der Mann war sehr alt. Es war ein sehr _____.

Sie ist intelligent. Sie ist _____ Mädchen.

Der Wein ist wirklich gut. Das ist wirklich ein _____.

Sie ist immer noch schön. Sie ist immer noch _____ Frau.

Das Wasser ist aber kalt. Das ist aber _____.

Das Bier hier ist gut. Das ist wirklich ein _____.

So klein ist eure Barbara nicht mehr. Sie ist kein _____ Kind mehr.

Gestern war es kalt. Gestern war _____ Tag.

[2] Attributive Adjectives, Accusative Singular

SEE
ANALYSIS
144–149

(pp. 310-314)

Hast du den alten Mann gesehen?	Did you see the old man?
Nein, einen alten Mann habe ich nicht gesehen.	No, I haven't seen an old man.
Ich kenne die junge Dame leider nicht.	I don't know the young lady, unfortunately.
Paul hatte das junge Mädchen lange nicht gesehen.	Paul hadn't seen the young girl for a long time.
Schmidts haben gestern ein kleines Mädchen bekommen.	The Schmidts had a little girl yesterday.
Nehmen Sie ein heißes Bad und gehen Sie früh ins Bett.	Take a hot bath and go to bed early.

VARIATIONS

Gestern war das Wetter schlecht. Gestern hatten wir _____.

Gestern war es kalt. Gestern hatten wir einen _____ Tag.

Der Wein war gut. Wir haben einen _____ getrunken.

Das Bier ist wirklich gut. Wo habt ihr denn dieses _____ Bier gekauft?

Meyers Frau ist jung. Meyer hat _____.

[3] Attributive Adjectives, Dative Singular

SEE
ANALYSIS
144–149

(pp. 310-314)

Mit *dem* alten Wagen fahre ich aber nicht in die Schweiz.	I won't drive to Switzerland with *that* old car.
Was soll ich denn mit einem alten Wagen?	What am I supposed to do with an old car?
Wir wohnten damals in einer kleinen Stadt.	At that time we lived in a small town.
Ingrid ist aus guter Familie.	Ingrid comes from a good family.
Wir wohnten damals in einem kleinen Städtchen am Rhein.	We then lived in a small town on the Rhine.

VARIATIONS

Gibt es hier warmes Wasser?—Ja, wir haben nur Zimmer mit _____.

Das Haus ist alt. Wir wohnen in einem _____ Haus.

Die Stadt ist klein. Wir wohnen in _____.

Das Wetter ist schlecht. Bei dem _____ Wetter bleibe ich zu Hause.

Seit wann ist Inge denn blond?—Sie meint, mit _____ Haar sieht sie besser
aus.

[4] Attributive Adjectives, Genitive Singular

Während des letzten Krieges mußte Ingelheim Brieftauben füttern.	During the last war, Ingelheim had to feed carrier pigeons.	**SEE ANALYSIS 144–149** (pp. 310-314)
Ingrid war die Tochter eines bekannten Architekten in Berlin.	Ingrid was the daughter of a well-known architect in Berlin.	
Der Besuch der alten Dame ist ein Stück von Dürrenmatt.	*The Visit of the Old Lady* is a play by Dürrenmatt.	
Wegen des schlechten Wetters konnten wir in Frankfurt nicht landen.	Because of the bad weather we couldn't land in Frankfurt.	

VARIATIONS

Die Reise war lang, aber trotz _____ war ich gar nicht müde.

Ein intelligenter Mann raucht PRIVAT. PRIVAT, die Zigarette des _____ Mannes.

Denken Sie modern? Der Preis eines _____ Hauses ist nicht so hoch, wie
Sie denken.

[5] Attributive Adjectives, Plural

Die ersten Fluggäste kamen aus dem Zoll.	The first passengers were coming out of customs.	**SEE ANALYSIS 144–149** (pp. 310-314)
Meine amerikanischen Freunde wohnen in Chicago.	My American friends live in Chicago.	
Liebe Eltern!	Dear Parents:	
Barbara war die Mutter der beiden Kinder.	Barbara was the mother of the two children.	
Eines der kleinen Mädchen hieß Barbara.	One of the little girls was called Barbara.	
Sie wußten nicht, was sie von den amerikanischen Soldaten zu erwarten hatten.	They didn't know what to expect of the American soldiers.	
Für die deutschen Soldaten war der Krieg im Mai zu Ende.	For the German soldiers the war was over in May.	
Niemand liest seine letzten Romane.	Nobody reads his last novels.	
Er brachte ihr rote Rosen.	He brought her red roses.	
Sie hat zwei intelligente Kinder.	She has two intelligent children.	

VARIATIONS

Meyers Kinder sind intelligent. Meyer hat _____.

Rot ist meine Lieblingsfarbe; daher bringt er mir immer _____ Rosen.

Ich habe Freunde in Amerika. Ich fliege morgen zu meinen _____ Freunden.

Sie kennen doch Amerika, nicht wahr? Was halten Sie denn von den _____ Schulen?

Bei uns wohnten damals Amerikaner. Einer _____ Soldaten hieß Paul Suhl.

[6] Series of Attributive Adjectives

SEE
ANALYSIS
150–151
(pp. 315-316)

Der blonde junge Mann da drüben heißt Suhl.

The name of the blond young man over there is Suhl.

Zuerst kam ein blonder junger Mann aus dem Zoll.

First a blond young man came out of customs.

Die blonde junge Dame ist seine Frau.

The blond young lady is his wife.

Zuerst kam eine blonde junge Dame aus dem Zoll.

First a blond young lady came out of customs.

Das kleine blonde Mädchen hieß Barbara.

The name of the blond little girl was Barbara.

Vor dem Hause saß ein blondes kleines Mädchen.

A blond little girl was sitting in front of the house.

Die Eltern des netten jungen Mannes kamen aus Leningrad.

The parents of the nice young man came from Leningrad.

Mit deinem alten grauen Mantel kannst du dich in Berlin nicht sehen lassen.

With your old gray coat you can't let yourself be seen in Berlin.

Ich nehme an, Sie kennen den netten jungen Mann da drüben.

I assume you know the nice young man over there.

Die hellen, kurzen Sommernächte Norwegens hat er nie vergessen können.

He has never been able to forget the bright, short summer nights of Norway.

Helle kurze Sommernächte wie in Norwegen gibt es in Afrika nicht.

In Africa, there are no bright, short summer nights as in Norway.

Mit seinen langen, sentimentalen Romanen hat er viel Geld verdient.

He has made a lot of money with his long, sentimental novels.

Zimmer mit fließendem warmen und kalten Wasser.

Rooms with running hot and cold water.

VARIATIONS

Insert the adjectives **neu** and **automatisch** in the following sentences:

Ich wollte, ich hätte eine Waschmaschine.

Der Preis einer Waschmaschine ist gar nicht so hoch.

Die Preise unserer Waschmaschinen sind gar nicht so hoch.

Mit dieser Waschmaschine ist Ihre Frau bestimmt zufrieden.

Ist das eure Waschmaschine?

Diese Waschmaschinen sind gar nicht teuer.

Waschmaschinen sind gar nicht teuer.

Wir können nur noch Waschmaschinen verkaufen.

[7] der-Words

Bei diesem schlechten Wetter bleibe ich zu Hause.	In this bad weather I'll stay home.	**SEE ANALYSIS 152**
Ohne dieses kleine Stückchen Papier hätte ich euch nie gefunden.	Without this little piece of paper I would never have found you.	(p. 316)
Bei welcher amerikanischen Division waren Sie denn?	With which American division were you?	
Welche deutschen Städte haben Sie denn gesehen?	Which German cities did you see?	
Jeder junge Mensch sollte einmal ein Jahr lang im Ausland leben.	Every young person ought to live abroad for a year.	
Von hier aus fährt jede halbe Stunde ein Zug nach Stuttgart.	From here, a train goes to Stuttgart every half-hour.	
Dort haben wir schon manchen schönen Tag verbracht.	We've spent many a beautiful day there.	
Mancher von den jungen Soldaten wußte gar nicht, wofür er kämpfte.	Many a young soldier didn't know at all what he was fighting for.	

VARIATIONS

Express in German:

Who is this young man?

Which young man? (*nom.*)

Who are these young men?

Which young men?

In which hotel does he live?

He always lives in this old hotel.

These old hotels are not expensive.

Every good hotel should have rooms with running water.

[8] solcher, solch, so

So einen guten Freund finde ich so bald nicht wieder.	Such a good friend I will not find again soon.	**SEE ANALYSIS 153**
		(p. 317)

Wie kann ein so intelligenter Mensch nur so dumm sein!	How can a man who is that intelligent be so stupid!
Für einen so alten Wagen bekommst du bestimmt keine tausend Mark.	I'm sure you won't get a thousand marks for a car as old as that.
Für solch einen Wagen bezahlen Sie mindestens zwanzigtausend Mark.	For such a (fancy) car you'll have to pay at least twenty thousand marks.
Ich wußte gar nicht, daß er noch so kleine Kinder hat.	I didn't know that his children are still that little.
Solche Kinder wie die möchte ich auch haben.	I'd like to have children like that too.

Using such combinations as **gute Freundin, schönes Haus, hübsche Kinder,** form your own variations.

[9] all, ganz

SEE
ANALYSIS
154

(pp. 317-319)

Alles Gute zum neuen Jahr wünscht Dir Deine Luise.	All good wishes for the New Year. Yours, Louise.
Was hilft ihm jetzt all sein schönes Geld? Er muß doch sterben.	What good does all his lovely money do him now? He's got to die anyway.
Was hilft ihm denn jetzt das ganze Geld?	What good does all that money do him now?
Was sollen wir denn mit all dem Brot?	What are we going to do with all that bread?
Ich habe alle meine alten Freunde besucht.	I visited all my old friends.
All meine Freunde sind im Krieg gefallen.	All my friends were killed in the war.
Ich habe alle seine Romane gelesen.	I have read all his novels.
Ich habe seine Romane alle gelesen.	I have read all his novels.
Kannst du für uns alle *Kar*ten kaufen?	Can you buy tickets for all of us?
Kannst du Karten für uns *al*le kaufen?	Can you buy tickets for all of us?
Ich habe alle Karten gekauft, die noch zu haben waren.	I've bought all the tickets that were still to be had.
Alle guten Karten waren schon ausverkauft.	All the good tickets were sold out already.
Das Geld ist alle.	The money is all gone.
Der Wein ist alle.	The wine is all gone.
Die Dummen werden nicht alle.	There'll always be some stupid people.
Wir alle sind dir dankbar.	We are all grateful to you.
Wir sind dir alle dankbar.	We are all grateful to you.
Er hat den ganzen Tag auf mich gewartet.	He waited for me all day.
Fritzchen hat einen ganzen Apfel gegessen.	Fritzchen has eaten a whole apple.
Sie war ganz allein.	She was all alone.

Wie geht's dir denn?—Danke, ganz gut.   How are you?—Thanks, pretty well.
Wir sind durch ganz Deutschland gefahren.   We drove through all of Germany.

Form variations of your own on all but the first two examples above.

[10] Adjectives Used as Nouns

In dem Zimmer lag ein Toter.	A dead man was lying in the room.	SEE ANALYSIS 155

In dem Zimmer lag ein Toter.   A dead man was lying in the room.
Die Polizei fand einen Toten im Zimmer.   The police found a dead man in the room.
Kein Mensch wußte, wer der Tote war.   Nobody knew who the dead man was.
Wer ist denn die Blonde da drüben?   Who is the blonde over there?
Der junge Deutsche auf Zimmer Eins ist   The young German in Room 1 arrived only
erst gestern angekommen.   yesterday.
Auf Zimmer Eins wohnt ein junger Deut-   A young German lives in Room 1.
scher.
John wohnt mit einem jungen Deutschen   John lives in Room 1 with a young German.
auf Zimmer Eins.
Den jungen Deutschen habe ich noch nicht   I haven't met the young German yet.
kennengelernt.
Auf Zimmer Eins wohnen zwei junge Deut-   Two young Germans are living in Room 1.
sche.
Die beiden jungen Deutschen habe ich noch   I haven't met the two young Germans yet.
nicht kennengelernt.
Er spricht ein gutes Deutsch.   He speaks good German.
Sie haben recht, er spricht wirklich gut   You are right, he really does speak German
Deutsch.   well.
Auf Wiedersehen, und alles Gute.   Good-bye and good luck.
Er hat viel Gutes getan.   He has done much good.
Könnte ich noch etwas Warmes zu essen   Could I still get something warm to eat?
bekommen?
Ich habe gestern etwas sehr Schönes erlebt. Yesterday I experienced something very
                                                 beautiful.
Ich hoffe, ich habe nichts Wichtiges ver-   I hope I haven't forgotten anything im-
gessen.   portant.

By changing gender, number, or case, form variations on all those examples
above that refer to persons.

[11] Participles Used as Adjectives and Nouns

Es war nicht leicht, in einer zerstörten   It was not easy to live in a destroyed city.
Stadt zu leben.

SEE
ANALYSIS
156

(p. 320)

Er kam mit einem gebrochenen Bein vom Schilaufen zurück.

He returned from skiing with a broken leg.

Sie kam mit gebrochenem Herzen vom Schilaufen zurück.

She returned from skiing with a broken heart.

Er war bei uns immer ein gern gesehener Gast.

He was always a welcome guest at our house. (Literally: he was a gladly seen guest.)

Meyer ist ein guter Bekannter von uns.

Meyer is a close acquaintance of ours.

Frau Meyer ist eine gute Bekannte von meiner Frau.

Mrs. Meyer is a close acquaintance of my wife's.

Haben Sie Bekannte hier in der Stadt?

Do you have acquaintances here in town?

Haben Sie Verwandte in Deutschland?

Do you have relatives in Germany?

Otto Müller ist ein Verwandter von mir.

Otto Müller is a relative of mine.

Heidi ist eine entfernte Verwandte von mir.

Heidi is a distant relative of mine.

Das ist der amerikanische Gesandte.

That is the American ambassador.

Sein Vater war ein hoher Beamter bei der Bundesregierung.

His father was a high official in the Federal Government.

Alle deutschen Lehrer sind Beamte.

All German teachers are civil servants.

Hier auf der Post arbeiten über hundert Beamtinnen.

More than a hundred women civil servants work here at the post office.

Auch Frau Meyer ist eine Beamtin.

Mrs. Meyer is a civil servant too.

Form variations of your own.

[12] -d Adjectives

SEE ANALYSIS 157 (p. 321)

Wer war denn der gut aussehende junge Mann gestern abend?

Who was the good-looking young man last night?

Er hatte so ein gewinnendes Lächeln.

He had such a winning smile.

Alles um sich her vergessend, saßen sie mit klopfendem Herzen unter der blühenden Linde; und ihre vielsagenden Blicke aus leuchtenden Augen sagten mehr als ihre zurückhaltenden Worte.
(from: Schmidt-Ingelheim, *Die Frau mit dem Flamingo*, p. 97)

Forgetting everything around them, they sat under the blooming linden tree, with their hearts pounding, and the meaningful glances of their shining eyes said more than their reserved words.

[13] derselbe

SEE ANALYSIS 158 (p. 321)

Ist das derselbe Wein, den wir gestern abend getrunken haben?

Is that the same wine that we drank last night?

Wir wohnen in demselben Hotel, in dem Schmidts gewohnt haben.

We are staying in the same hotel in which the Schmidts stayed.

Seit Jahren trägt sie jeden Sonntag dasselbe Kleid.

For years she's been wearing the same dress every Sunday.

Wir saßen gestern mit Meyers am selben Tisch.

Yesterday we sat at the same table with the Meyers.

Form variations of your own.

[14] was für

Was ist denn das für ein Wagen?
Was für ein Wagen ist das?

} What kind of car is that?

Was hast du dir denn für einen Wagen gekauft?
Was für einen Wagen hast du dir denn gekauft?

} What kind of car did you buy?

Mit was für einem Wagen bist du denn gefahren?

What kind of car did you go in?

Ich muß noch immer daran denken, was für wunderbare Tage wir an der See verbracht haben.

I still remember what wonderful days we spent at the seashore.

Ich muß noch immer daran denken, was für einen unvergeßlichen Tag wir an der Mosel verbracht haben.

I still remember what an unforgettable day we spent by the Mosel.

Hast du gesehen, was für einen unmöglichen Hut die Anita schon wieder aufhat?

Did you see what an impossible hat Anita has on again?

Weißt du noch, mit was für einem unmöglichen Hut sie damals im Theater war?

Do you remember with what an impossible hat she came to the theater?

By changing nouns, form variations on each of the examples above.

SEE ANALYSIS 159

(pp. 321-322)

,,Mit was für einem Wagen bist du denn gefahren?''

,,. . . was für einen unvergeßlichen Tag wir an der Mosel verbracht haben!''

[15] viel, wenig

SEE
ANALYSIS
160
(pp. 322-323)

Meyer hat viel Geld.	Meyer has a lot of money.
Ja, aber das viele Geld macht ihn auch nicht glücklich.	Yes, but all that money doesn't make him happy either.
Sein vieles Geld macht ihn nicht glücklich.	All his money doesn't make him happy.
Heute ist Sonntag, und viele Leute fahren heute spazieren.	Today is Sunday, and many people go for a ride today.
Was haben Sie denn während der vielen langen Winternächte in Norwegen gemacht?	What did you do during the many long winter nights in Norway?
Ich habe viel zu wenig Geld, um jedes Jahr in die Schweiz fahren zu können.	I have far too little money to be able to go to Switzerland every year.
Mit dem wenigen Geld, das du mir schickst, kann ich nicht viel kaufen.	With the little money you send me I can't buy much.
Wir haben dieses Wochenende nur wenige Gäste im Hause. Bei dem Wetter bleiben die Leute zu Hause.	We have only a few guests here this weekend. In this weather, people stay at home.

VARIATIONS

Insert the correct form of **viel**.

Ich habe nicht _____ Geld.

Was tut sie denn mit ihrem _____ Geld?

Wie _____ Kinder habt ihr denn?
Wie _____ Bier habt ihr denn getrunken?
Was machst du denn jetzt mit deinen _____ Büchern?
Er hat schon immer _____ gelesen.

[16] ander-

So geht das nicht; das mußt du anders machen.	It won't work that way; you'll have to do it differently.	**SEE ANALYSIS 161** (pp. 323-324)

Aber Erich, du bist ja ganz anders als früher.

But Erich, you are so different from the way you used to be.

Erich soll ein ganz anderer Mensch geworden sein.

Erich supposedly has become a completely different person.

Er spricht von nichts anderem als von seiner Amerikareise.

He talks about nothing (else) but his trip to America.

Den einen Herrn kannte ich, aber wer war denn der andere?

One of the gentlemen I knew, but who was the other one?

Den anderen Herrn kenne ich auch nicht.

I don't know the other gentleman either.

Das muß jemand anders gewesen sein.

That must have been somebody else.

Das kann niemand anders gewesen sein als Meyer.

That can have been nobody (else) but Meyer.

Anderen hat er geholfen; sich selbst kann er nicht helfen.

Others he has helped; himself he cannot help.

Keiner will es getan haben; es sind immer die anderen gewesen.

Nobody will admit having done it; it was always "the others."

VARIATIONS

Insert the correct form of **ander-**.

Es war ganz _____ als ich gedacht hatte.
Wer waren denn die _____ Herren?
Sie wohnen in einem _____ Hotel.
Ich war es nicht; es war jemand _____.
Dieses Buch war es nicht; es war ein _____.
Ich habe leider keinen _____ Mantel.
Alle _____ gingen nach Hause.
Wir blieben noch da, aber viele _____ gingen nach Hause.
Ich hätte lieber etwas _____.

[17] ein paar, einige, mehrere

SEE
ANALYSIS
162
(pp. 324-325)

„In ein paar Tagen bin ich wieder hier", hatte er gesagt. Aber dann wurden aus den paar Tagen ein paar Jahre.

"I'll be back in a few days," he had said. But then the few days turned into a few years.

Es waren nur ein paar Leute da.

Only a few people were there.

Mit den paar Mark kannst du doch nicht nach Italien fahren.

You can't go to Italy with those few marks.

Ein paar schöne Tage haben wir ja gehabt, aber die meiste Zeit hat es geregnet.

We did have a few nice days, but most of the time it rained.

Ich hätte gerne ein paar kleine Würstchen zum Frühstück.

I'd like to have a few sausages for breakfast.

Bringen Sie mir doch bitte ein Paar Würstchen.

Could I have a couple of sausages (frankfurters), please?

Ich habe nur zwei Paar gute Schuhe mitgebracht.

I've only brought two pairs of good shoes.

Anton und Emma waren ein schönes Paar.

Anton and Emma were a lovely couple.

Einige von unseren Lesern möchten wissen, ob Ingelheim noch in Konstanz wohnt.

Some of our readers would like to know whether Ingelheim still lives in Constance.

Wir kamen durch mehrere zerstörte Dörfer.

We came through several destroyed villages.

Einige der Soldaten wohnten im Hause des Pfarrers.

Some of the soldiers lived in the pastor's house.

Im Löwen kann man für ein paar Mark gut essen.

At the Lion Inn one can eat well for a few marks.

Ich habe auch schon einige Male da gegessen.

I've eaten there several times, too.

Letzte Woche habe ich mehrere Male im Löwen gegessen.

Last week I ate at the Lion several times.

Form variations of your own.

READING

Ankunft in Deutschland

Wir wollen annehmen, daß Sie während der Nacht über den Atlantik geflogen sind und morgens auf dem Rhein-Main Flughafen bei Frankfurt ankommen, vielleicht nach einer Zwischenlandung in Paris oder London.

Wenn Sie non-stop fliegen, ist die Flugzeit von New York etwa
sieben Stunden, von Chicago neun Stunden und von San Franzisko
etwa dreizehn Stunden. Dazu kommt aber der Zeitunterschied
zwischen Amerika und Europa. Wenn Sie in New York abfliegen,
ist es vielleicht 7 P.M. EST oder EDST, und wenn Sie in Frankfurt 5
ankommen, ist es 8 oder 7 Uhr MEZ. MEZ heißt Mitteleuropäische
Zeit. Wenn es in Frankfurt Mitternacht ist, ist es im Sommer in New
York erst 7 Uhr abends, und um 7 Uhr abends sind Sie ja abgeflogen.
Das heißt, Sie kommen in Frankfurt um 2 Uhr nachts an, aber nach
New Yorker Zeit EST, und in Frankfurt ist es dann schon 8 Uhr 10
morgens, oder, im Sommer, 7 Uhr morgens, weil es in Deutschland
keine Sommerzeit (Daylight Saving Time) mehr gibt.

Vielleicht bleiben Sie oft bis zwei Uhr morgens auf, aber es ist doch
spät und eigentlich Zeit, schlafen zu gehen. Aber die Nacht ist vorbei, für immer verloren. Sie haben im Flugzeug ein amerikanisches 15
Dinner gegessen, von acht bis zehn Uhr abends, und dann tat man,
als käme jetzt eine lange Nacht. Alle Lichter gingen aus, und weil
es dunkel war, haben Sie versucht zu schlafen. Vielleicht haben Sie
auch eine Stunde geschlafen, aber dann hielt Ihnen die Stewardess
plötzlich ein Glas Orangensaft unter die Nase und tat, als ob es 20 **der Saft, ⸚e** juice
sechs Uhr morgens wäre. Frühstück um Mitternacht ist eigentlich
verrückt, aber es war ja in Wirklichkeit sechs Uhr morgens, nur
war es nicht 6 A.M. EDST, sondern 6 Uhr MEZ.

Und jetzt landen Sie also in Frankfurt. „Bitte anschnallen", lesen   **anschnallen** to fasten
Sie über Ihrem Sitz und „Nicht rauchen", und über den Laut- 25 the seat belt
sprecher hören Sie: „Wir möchten Sie bitten sitzenzubleiben, bis
die Maschine völlig zum Stillstand gekommen ist." Gottseidank wie-   **völlig** completely
derholt die Stewardess das auf Englisch: „Please remain seated
until the plane has come to a complete stop."

Dann hält die Maschine, aber vom Flugzeug zum Empfangsgebäude 30 **der Empfang, ⸚e** re-
ist es mindestens eine halbe Meile,—nein, Sie denken jetzt schon   ception; **das Gebäude**
ganz europäisch und sagen zu Ihrer netten Nachbarin: „Das ist ja   building

fast ein Kilometer! Müssen wir denn jetzt dahin laufen?" „Nein, nein", lacht die Nachbarin, die gerade ein Jahr als Austauschstudentin in Amerika studiert hat, „da kommen schon die Busse." **der Austausch** exchange

Auf vielen europäischen Flughäfen holen Busse die Fluggäste direkt am Flugzeug ab und bringen sie zum Empfangsgebäude. Man hat 5 dann nur noch ein paar Meter zu gehen und ist schon an der Paßkontrolle. Die Formalitäten sind schnell erledigt; der Beamte **erledigen** to take care of, to settle sieht Ihren Paß kaum an. Dann kommt der Zoll. Die deutsche Studentin ist vor Ihnen an der Reihe. „Haben Sie etwas zu verzollen?" **verzollen** to pay duty on „Nein, gar nichts." „Dann machen Sie doch bitte einmal Ihren 10 Koffer auf." Eine halbe Minute, und die Studentin ist fertig; sie hatte wirklich nichts zu verzollen. Jetzt kommen Sie an die Reihe. Der Zollbeamte sieht schon, daß Sie Amerikaner sind. (Die meisten Amerikaner in Europa sehen aus, als ob sie Amerikaner wären.) "Anything to declare?" fragt er. "Coffee, tea, cigarettes?" Aber 15 weil Sie nicht rauchen und auch keinen Kaffee trinken, können Sie ruhig sagen: „Nein, gar nichts". "OK", sagt der Beamte, „danke schön", und dann sagt er noch: „Viel Spaß", was so viel heißt wie **Spaß** fun, pleasure "Have fun."

Dann gehen Sie durch eine große Glastür, und da steht Ihre Kusine 20 Emma und sagt: „Da bist du ja endlich." Und Sie sind froh, daß Sie eine Kusine Emma haben, die jetzt alles für Sie tun wird, weil sie ein praktisches Mädchen ist und weiß, daß man um drei Uhr morgens sehr müde ist.

Aber nicht alle haben eine Emma.   25

Wenn Sie nun keine Kusine in Frankfurt haben, dann haben Sie noch viel zu tun, bevor Sie sich schlafen legen können. Zunächst brauchen Sie deutsches Geld. Sie gehen also zu einer Wechselstube. **die Stube, –n** room; **wechseln** to change, exchange Solche Wechselstuben gibt es auf allen deutschen Flughäfen und in den großen Bahnhöfen. Der Dollarkurs ist nicht ganz 1:4 (eins 30 **der Kurs, –e** rate of exchange zu vier); für einen Reisescheck über $20 bekommen Sie DM 78,80. **der Scheck, –s** check (DM heißt „ Deutsche Mark".) Der Bankbeamte sagt „Achtundsiebzig Mark achtzig" und gibt Ihnen einen Fünfzigmarkschein, einen **der Schein, –e** bill Zwanzigmarkschein, ein Fünfmarkstück, ein Zweimarkstück, ein Markstück, ein Fünfzigpfennigstück und drei Zehnpfennigstücke. 35 Sie haben also jetzt statt Ihres amerikanischen Reisescheck deutsches Bargeld in der Hand. **das Bargeld** cash

Es gibt nun drei Möglichkeiten: Erstens—und das ist die vernünftigste Möglichkeit—Sie haben schon von Amerika aus in Frankfurt ein Zimmer bestellt und schlafen sich zunächst aus. Zweitens: Sie 40 wollen vielleicht mit der Bahn weiterfahren, sagen wir nach Koblenz, **die Bahn = Eisenbahn** weil Sie am nächsten Tag mit dem Schiff den Rhein hinunter fahren wollen. Drittens, wenn *Ihre* Kusine Emma in *München* wohnt, dann müssen Sie natürlich noch am gleichen Tag nach München weiterfliegen.

Sie gehen also zum Lufthansaschalter und geben einer der jungen Damen Ihren Flugschein.

der Schalter, – ticket window, counter
der Schein, –e ticket

„Ich komme gerade aus New York und möchte nach München weiterfliegen."

„Haben Sie schon einen Platz gebucht?"

„Ja, für heute nachmittag."

„Das ist Flug Nummer 604, Abflug 13.45 Uhr (dreizehn Uhr fünfundvierzig), Ankunft in München um 14.30 Uhr. Warteraum B bitte,—der Flug wird um 13.15 Uhr aufgerufen."

der Raum, ⁻e room

Die junge Dame wiegt Ihren Koffer, dann gibt sie Ihnen Ihr Ticket zurück, und Sie können nun in aller Ruhe etwas essen, eine Zeitung lesen (vielleicht die *Frankfurter Rundschau*, die *Frankfurter Allgemeine* oder einen Artikel im *Spiegel*) und die Leute beobachten. Um halb zwei gehen Sie zum Ausgang B 6, dann fahren Sie wieder mit dem Bus zum Flugzeug, und pünktlich um dreiviertel zwei startet Ihre Maschine zum Flug nach München.

pünktlich prompt(ly), punctual(ly)
dreiviertel zwei a quarter of two

Der Wolf und die sieben Geißlein*

Es war einmal eine alte Geiß, die hatte sieben junge Geißlein, und hatte sie lieb, wie eine Mutter ihre Kinder lieb hat. Eines Tages wollte sie in den Wald gehen und etwas zu essen holen. Da rief sie alle sieben ins Haus und sprach: „Liebe Kinder, ich will in den Wald. Wenn der Wolf kommt, dürft ihr ihn nicht ins Haus lassen. 5 Wenn er hereinkommt, so frißt er euch alle. Der Bösewicht verstellt sich oft, aber an seiner Stimme und an seinen schwarzen Füßen werdet ihr ihn gleich erkennen." Die Geißlein sagten: „Liebe Mutter, du brauchst keine Angst zu haben." Da meckerte die Alte und ging in den Wald. 10

Es dauerte nicht lange, so klopfte jemand an die Haustür und rief: „Macht auf, ihr lieben Kinder, eure Mutter ist da und hat jedem von euch etwas mitgebracht." Aber die Geißlein hörten an der

eine alte Geiß an old goat.

Der Bösewicht . . . oft the rascal often disguises himself

meckern to bleat

---

* This story is taken, with very few changes, from the famous collection of fairy tales by the brothers Grimm. The German of these fairy tales is highly sophisticated and yet of classic simplicity. Every German child grows up with Grimm.

Stimme, daß es der Wolf war. „Wir machen nicht auf," riefen sie,
„du bist nicht unsere Mutter, die hat eine feine und liebliche
Stimme, aber deine Stimme ist rauh; du bist der Wolf." Da ging der
Wolf fort und kaufte ein Stück Kreide; die aß er und machte damit
seine Stimme fein. Dann kam er zurück, klopfte an die Haustür und ₅
rief: „Macht auf, ihr lieben Kinder, eure Mutter ist da und hat
jedem von euch etwas mitgebracht." Aber der Wolf hatte seinen
schwarzen Fuß in das Fenster gelegt; das sahen die Kinder und
riefen: „Wir machen nicht auf, unsere Mutter hat keinen schwarzen
Fuß, wie du; du bist der Wolf." Da lief der Wolf zu einem Bäcker ₁₀
und sprach: „Ich habe etwas an meinem Fuß, kannst du etwas Teig
auf meinen Fuß streichen?" Und als der Bäcker den Teig auf seinen
Fuß gestrichen hatte, so lief er zum Müller und sprach: „Kannst du
etwas Mehl auf meinen Fuß streuen?" Der Müller dachte: „Der
Wolf will einen betrügen", und wollte es nicht tun; aber der Wolf ₁₅
sprach: „Wenn du es nicht tust, so fresse ich dich." Da bekam der
Müller Angst und machte ihm den Fuß weiß. Ja, so sind die
Menschen.

Nun ging der Bösewicht wieder zu der Haustür, klopfte an und
sprach: „Macht auf, Kinder, euer liebes Mütterchen ist zurück und ₂₀
hat jedem von euch etwas aus dem Wald mitgebracht." Die Geißlein
riefen: „Du mußt uns erst deinen Fuß zeigen, sonst wissen wir
nicht, ob du unser liebes Mütterchen bist." Da legte er den Fuß
ins Fenster, und als sie sahen, daß er weiß war, so glaubten sie,
es wäre alles wahr, was er sagte, und machten die Tür auf. Wer ₂₅
aber hereinkam, das war der Wolf.

Da bekamen sie alle Angst. Das eine sprang unter den Tisch, das
zweite ins Bett, das dritte in den Ofen, das vierte in die Küche, das
fünfte in den Schrank, das sechste unter die Waschschüssel, das
siebte in den Kasten der Wanduhr. Aber der Wolf fand sie alle und ₃₀
fraß sie eins nach dem andern; nur das jüngste in dem Uhrkasten
fand er nicht. Als der Wolf die Sechs gefressen hatte, ging er fort,
legte sich draußen vor dem Haus unter einen Baum und fing an
zu schlafen.

Es dauerte nicht lange, da kam die alte Geiß aus dem Wald wieder ₃₅
nach Hause. Ach, was mußte sie da sehen! Die Haustür stand auf,
Tisch, Stühle und Bänke waren umgeworfen. Sie suchte ihre Kinder,
aber sie konnte sie nicht finden. Sie rief sie alle bei Namen, aber
niemand antwortete. Endlich, als sie an das jüngste kam, da rief
eine feine Stimme: „Liebe Mutter, ich bin im Uhrkasten." Sie holte ₄₀
es heraus, und es erzählte ihr, daß der Wolf gekommen wäre und
die anderen alle gefressen hätte. Da könnt ihr denken, wie sie über
ihre armen Kinder geweint hat.°

Glossary (margin):

rauh rough
damit with it
Teig dough
streuen sprinkle
betrügen deceive
Waschschüssel wash-bowl

° Observe the change of tense: this sentence is not part of the story.

Endlich ging sie hinaus, und das jüngste Geißlein lief mit. Als sie
vor das Haus kam, so lag da der Wolf unter dem Baum und
schnarchte, daß die Äste zitterten. „Ach Gott," dachte sie, „vielleicht
leben meine Kinder doch noch." Da mußte das Geißlein ins Haus
laufen und Schere, Nadel und Zwirn holen. Dann schnitt sie dem 5 **Schere, . . . Zwirn**
Bösewicht den Bauch auf, und kaum hatte sie einen Schnitt getan,   scissors, needle, and
so steckte schon ein Geißlein den Kopf heraus, und als sie weiter   thread
schnitt, so sprangen sie alle sechs heraus, und waren noch alle am
Leben. Das war eine Freude! Die Alte aber sagte: „Jetzt wollen
wir Steine suchen, mit denen füllen wir dem Bösewicht den Bauch, 10
solange er noch schläft." Da brachten die sieben Geißlein Steine
herbei und steckten sie ihm in den Bauch. Dann nähte ihn die Alte
wieder zu.

Als der Wolf endlich ausgeschlafen hatte, stand er auf, und weil
ihn die Steine in seinem Bauch durstig machten, so wollte er zu 15
einem Brunnen gehen und trinken. Als er aber an den Brunnen kam
und trinken wollte, da zogen ihn die Steine in den Brunnen hinein,
und er mußte ertrinken. Als die sieben Geißlein das sahen, da kamen   **da . . . herbeigelaufen**
sie herbeigelaufen, riefen laut: „Der Wolf ist tot! der Wolf ist tot!"   they came running
und lachten und tanzten mit ihrer Mutter um den Brunnen.   20

The first three sections of the story by Mathias Koch, *Ein Mann kommt nach
San Franzisko,* which appears after Unit 13, may be read after Unit 10.

ANALYSIS

144 Predicate Adjectives and Adverbs

Most English adjectives can be transformed into adverbs by adding the
suffix -*ly,* for example, *high—highly, beautiful—beautifully;* for some
others, there is a separate adverbial form, for example, *good—well;* and
only a few have the same form both as adjectives and as adverbs, for
example, *fast.*

In German, there is no distinction between the predicate adjective and
the adverb.

> **Seine Frau soll *schön* sein.**
> His wife is supposed to be very *beautiful.*
> **Sie soll auch sehr *schön* singen können.**
> Supposedly she can also sing very *beautifully.*

145 Predicate Adjectives and Attributive Adjectives

The predicate adjective, as the name implies, is part of the predicate; it constitutes a verbal complement and thus forms the second prong of the predicate.

| Das Wetter | war | wochenlang | schlecht. |

The attributive adjective is an attribute of a following noun.

> Im Januar war wochenlang *schlechtes Wetter.*
> Bei diesem *schlechten Wetter* bleibe ich zu Hause.
> Der *junge Mann* hieß Suhl.

The German predicate adjective never has an ending; the German attributive adjective *must* take an ending. These endings are determined by a variety of factors: gender, number, case, and the presence or absence of a **der**-word or **ein**-word.

146 Strong Endings

The endings of the definite article, **der, die, das,** are most important. This set of endings is generally referred to as "strong" adjective endings.

| | Singular | | | Plural |
	MASCULINE	FEMININE	NEUTER	ALL GENDERS
NOM.	der	die	das	die
GEN.	des	der	des	der
DAT.	dem	der	dem	den
ACC.	den	die	das	die

You are already used to the fact that when these endings are unstressed, as in the forms of **dieser,** the long **-ie** of **die** becomes **-e** and the **-as** of **das** becomes **-es.**

| | Singular | | | Plural |
	MASCULINE	FEMININE	NEUTER	ALL GENDERS
	-er	-e	-es	-e
	-es	-er	-es	-er
	-em	-er	-em	-en
	-en	-e	-es	-e

147 Weak Endings

Attributive adjectives following a definite article must take what are generally referred to as "weak" endings. There are only two weak endings, **-e** and **-en.** The ending is **-en** in all cases except five: the three nominative singular forms, and the accusative feminine and neuter.

	Singular			Plural
	MASCULINE	FEMININE	NEUTER	ALL GENDERS
NOM.	-e	-e	-e	-en
GEN.	-en	-en	-en	-en
DAT.	-en	-en	-en	-en
ACC.	-en	-e	-e	-en

Note that there is a similarity between these weak endings and the strong endings: Only the masculine singular distinguishes between nominative and accusative.

If we assign definite positions (or slots) for each of the three words in the phrase **der alte Herr,** then slot 1 contains the **der**-word—that is, the strong ending—slot 2 contains the attributive adjective with the weak ending, and slot 3 contains the noun. Note again that only the masculine singular distinguishes between nominative and accusative.

	SLOT 1	SLOT 2	SLOT 3
MASC.			
NOM.	*der*	*alte*	Herr
GEN.	des	alten	Herrn
DAT.	dem	alten	Herrn
ACC.	*den*	*alten*	Herrn
FEM.			
NOM.	*die*	*alte*	Dame
GEN.	der	alten	Dame
DAT.	der	alten	Dame
ACC.	*die*	*alte*	Dame
NEUTER			
NOM.	*das*	*junge*	Mädchen
GEN.	des	jungen	Mädchens
DAT.	dem	jungen	Mädchen
ACC.	*das*	*junge*	Mädchen

	SLOT 1	SLOT 2	SLOT 3
PLURAL, ALL GENDERS			
NOM.	*die*	*alten*	**Herren**
GEN.	der	alten	**Herren**
DAT.	den	alten	**Herren**
ACC.	*die*	*alten*	**Herren**

148 Attributive Adjectives after **ein**-Words

The **ein**-words (**ein, kein, mein, dein, sein, ihr, unser, euer, ihr**) are declined like the definite article, that is, they have strong endings. However, in three forms they have no ending at all:, nominative masculine and nominative and accusative neuter.

	Singular		Plural
MASCULINE	FEMININE	NEUTER	ALL GENDERS
ein	eine	ein	keine
eines	einer	eines	keiner
einem	einer	einer	keinen
einen	eine	ein	keine

The basic rule governing phrases containing **der**- or **ein**- words followed by attributive adjectives is that *there must be a strong ending* in slot 1. With **der**-words, this is simple: since **der**-words have strong endings in all forms, they always occupy slot 1.

SLOT 1	SLOT 2	SLOT 3
der	**alte**	**Mann**

All **ein**-words *with* an ending follow the same pattern: they occupy slot 1.

SLOT 1	SLOT 2	SLOT 3
einem	**alten**	**Mann**

In the three forms, however, in which the **ein**-word does not have an ending, the following shift takes place:

The **ein**-word is moved forward, as it were, into slot 0 (reserved for introductory words without endings); thus, slot 1 is vacated, and the adjective moves into it and takes a strong ending. Slot 2 then remains empty.

SLOT 0	SLOT 1	SLOT 2	SLOT 3
	der	alte	Mann
ein	alter		Mann

If we compare the singular forms of phrases starting with **der**-words and of phrases starting with **ein**-words, this shift becomes quite clear:

	der-words				ein-words			
	SLOT 0	SLOT 1	SLOT 2	SLOT 3	SLOT 0	SLOT 1	SLOT 2	SLOT 3
MASC.								
NOM.		der	alte	Herr	ein	alter		Herr
GEN.		des	alten	Herrn		eines	alten	Herrn
DAT.		dem	alten	Herrn		einem	alten	Herrn
ACC.		den	alten	Herrn		einen	alten	Herrn
FEM.								
NOM.		die	alte	Dame		eine	alte	Dame
GEN.		der	alten	Dame		einer	alten	Dame
DAT.		der	alten	Dame		einer	alten	Dame
ACC.		die	alte	Dame		eine	alte	Dame
NEUTER								
NOM.		das	junge	Mädchen	ein	junges		Mädchen
GEN.		des	jungen	Mädchens		eines	jungen	Mädchens
DAT.		dem	jungen	Mädchen		einem	jungen	Mädchen
ACC.		das	junge	Mädchen	ein	junges		Mädchen

149 Attributive Adjectives without **der-** or **ein**-Words

If there is neither a **der**-word nor an **ein**- word to fill slot 1, the adjective must always occupy slot 1. Both slot 0 and slot 2 are then empty.

SLOT 0	SLOT 1	SLOT 2	SLOT 3
	Lieber		Vater!
	Liebe		Mutter!
	Liebes		Kind!

150 Series of Attributive Adjectives

If two or more attributive adjectives stand together, they all occupy the same slot and show the same endings.

SLOT 0	SLOT 1	SLOT 2	SLOT 3
	der	blonde junge	Mann
ein	blonder junger		Mann
	eine	kleine alte	Stadt
	das	beste deutsche	Bier
	gutes deutsches		Bier

NOTE: Adjectives in a series may be separated by a comma; such commas have the same function as **und** would have. Thus **ein blonder junger Mann** is a young man who happens to be blond, whereas **ein langer, sentimentaler Roman** is a novel which is both long and sentimental.

151 Variations

1. In the dative masculine and neuter, the sequence **-em -en** is so ingrained that of two or more adjectives not preceded by a strong ending only the first tends to take on the strong ending:

	SLOT 0	SLOT 1	SLOT 2	SLOT 3
Bei		diesem	nebligen kalten	Wetter
Bei		nebligem	kalten	Wetter

2. In the genitive masculine and neuter, with adjectives not preceded by a **der**-word or an **ein**-word, the strong endings have been replaced by weak endings. These forms, however, do not, as a rule, occur in the spoken language.

	SLOT 0	SLOT 1	SLOT 2	SLOT 3
Trotz			starken	Nebels
Trotz			schlechten	Wetters

The spoken language prefers the regular pattern with the dative:

	slot 0	slot 1	slot 2	slot 3
Trotz		starkem		Nebel
Trotz		schlechtem		Wetter

3. Adjectives ending in **-el** and **-er** drop the **-e-** if an attributive ending is added.

Das Zimmer war dunkel.
Sie saßen in einem dunklen Zimmer.

Die Zimmer hier sind aber sehr teuer.
Wir wohnten in einem teuren Zimmer.

4. The adjective **hoch** drops the **-c-** if an ending is added, and the **h** becomes silent.

Der Baum war sehr hoch.
The tree was very tall.

Vor dem Haus stand ein hoher Baum.
A tall tree stood in front of the house.

152 **der**-Words

The following are declined like the definite article; that is, they take strong endings:

dieser, this
jeder, each, every
welcher, which, what
mancher, many a; plural: some

(a) The neuter singular **dieses** may be used without an ending (**dies**) in the nominative and accusative.

Dies Buch hier ist wirklich gut.

In identifying or in introducing phrases, **dies** must be used:

Gerda, dies ist mein Freund Hans.
Und dies, meine Damen und Herren, war das Schlafzimmer des Königs.

(b) **Jeder** has no plural forms. The plural of **jeder Mensch** is **alle Menschen.**

(c) **Welcher** is normally used as an interrogative: **in welcher Stadt?** *in which (what) city?*

153 so, solch

In the singular, both **so ein** and **ein so** are usually followed by adjectives.

so ein intelligentes Mädchen	such an intelligent girl
ein so intelligentes Mädchen	a girl who is so intelligent
Sie ist doch so ein intelligentes Mädchen.	She is such an intelligent girl.
Ein so intelligentes Mädchen müßte doch einen Mann finden.	A girl who is that intelligent ought to be able to find a husband.

In the plural, **so** is immediately followed by an adjective.

so kleine Kinder	children who are that little
Ich wußte gar nicht, daß er noch so kleine Kinder hat.	I didn't know that his children are still so little.

It is advisable to use **solch** only with a strong ending and without a following adjective; it then means "such a degree of" (cf. English *with such force*) or "that kind of."

Warum hast du denn immer solche Angst? (so große Angst?)	Why are you always so afraid?
Mit solchen Menschen will ich nichts zu tun haben.	I don't want to have anything to do with that kind of people.

154 all, ganz

All is used with or without endings. When there is an ending, it is always strong.

SINGULAR

(a) Forms with an ending are not used very frequently. They occur, immediately followed by a noun, in stereotyped phrases:

Ich wünsche dir alles Gute

and in proverbial expressions:

Aller Anfang ist schwer.

(b) If used without an ending, **all** must be followed by a **der**-word or a possessive adjective:

all das schöne Geld
all mein Geld

Such phrases express bulk quantity, and **all** can be replaced by the attributive adjective **ganz:**

> das ganze schöne Geld
> mein ganzes Geld.

PLURAL

(a) **All** with an ending is the plural of **jeder** and means *every single one of them;* it precedes nouns and follows pronouns.

> **Alle meine Brüder sind im Krieg gefallen.**
> **Wir alle haben ihn gestern besucht.**

In the spoken language, it is usually separated from its noun or pronoun and placed in the inner field preceding the first item of news value:

> **Meine Brüder sind im Krieg alle gefallen.**
> **Wir haben ihn gestern alle besucht.**
> **Gestern haben wir ihn alle besucht.**

(b) **All** without an ending refers again to bulk quantity and means *the whole bunch of them.* Again, it must be followed by a **der-** or an **ein-**word.

> **Ich habe all meine Bücher verloren.**

Again, this "bulk" meaning of **all** can be replaced by the attributive adjective **ganz.**

> **Ich habe meine ganzen Bücher verloren.**

NOTE: **Alle** may be used predicatively to mean *all gone.*

> **Das Geld ist alle.**
> **Der Wein ist alle.**
> **Die Dummen werden nicht alle.**
> There will always be stupid people.

Ganz, if not used as a replacement for **all,** is used in the following ways:

(a) as an attributive adjective meaning *whole* or *entire.*

> **Er hat den ganzen Tag auf mich ge-**   He waited for me all day.
> **wartet.**

(b) as an adverb, meaning *completely,* modifying an adjective.

> **Sie war ganz allein.**   She was all alone.

(c) as an *unstressed* adverb, meaning *quite* or *rather,* modifying such "praising" adjectives as **gut, glücklich, intelligent.**

> **Das Wetter war ja ganz gut, aber es**   The weather wasn't bad, but it could have
> **hätte besser sein können.**   been better.

Do not thank your hostess by saying **Das Essen war ganz gut.** This would mean that the food wasn't bad, but certainly nothing to rave about.

(d) without an ending and preceding geographical names. It then means *all of.*

Wir sind durch ganz Deutschland gefahren.

155 Adjectives Used as Nouns

In such English phrases as

the idle rich	*Gentlemen Prefer Blondes*
he helped the poor	*The Naked and the Dead,*

the adjectives *rich, poor, blonde, naked,* and *dead* are used as plural nouns. In German, many more adjectives can be used as nouns than in English, and, unlike English, they very often occur in the singular. If so used, they are capitalized, but are otherwise treated like attributive adjectives.

SLOT 0	SLOT 1	SLOT 2	SLOT 3	
	der	Reiche		the rich man
	die	Alte		the old woman
	das	Gute		the good
mein	Alter			my old man
	die	Armen		the poor
	der	Tote		the dead man
	die	Tote		the dead woman
	die	Toten		the dead
ein	Toter			a dead man

When an adjective follows **nichts, etwas,** or **wenig,** as in the English *nothing new* or *something important,* the German adjective is capitalized and has a strong neuter singular ending.

Es gibt leider nichts Neues.
Ich habe etwas Wichtiges vergessen.
Das führt zu nichts Gutem.

NOTE: Of all nouns indicating nationality, **Deutsch** is the only one declined like an adjective.

der Deutsche, the German (man)
die Deutsche, the German (woman)

156 Participles Used as Adjectives

In German, as in English, participles can be used as attributive adjectives.

SLOT 0	SLOT 1	SLOT 2	SLOT 3
	die	zerstörte	Stadt
	eine	zerstörte	Stadt
	zerstörte		Städte
ein	gestohlenes		Goldstück
	das	gestohlene	Goldstück
mein	geliebter		Sohn

the destroyed city
a destroyed city
destroyed cities
a stolen gold coin
the stolen gold coin
my beloved son

Both German and English can use participles as plural nouns:

> **die Verwundeten**   the wounded
> **die Besiegten**   the conquered

Unlike English, however, German can also use participles as singular nouns:

SLOT 0	SLOT 1	SLOT 2	SLOT 3
	der	Verwundete	
ein	Verwundeter		
	die	Verwundeten	
	der	amerikanische Gesandte	
	der	Gekreuzigte*	
	der	Erwählte†	
	die	Betrogene‡	

Similarly:

> **der Bekannte,** acquaintance—from: **bekannt sein,** to be (well) known
> **die Bekannte**
> **der Verwandte,** relative—from: **verwandt sein,** to be related
> **die Verwandte**
> **der Beamte,** official, civil servant—from: **das Amt,** office
>   (originally: **der Beamtete,** one who is given an office)

but:

> **die Beamtin**

---

* The crucified one (Christ)
† The chosen one (title of Thomas Mann's novel *The Holy Sinner*)
‡ The deceived one (title of Thomas Mann's novel *The Black Swan*)

157 -d Adjectives

In principle, any German verb can form an adjective corresponding to English adjectives in *-ing* simply by adding the suffix **-d** to the infinitive. These **-d** derivatives can be used safely only as attributive adjectives.

	SLOT 0	SLOT 1	SLOT 2	SLOT 3
		das	lachende	Kind
	ein	lachendes		Kind
mit		klopfendem		Herzen
		ihre	leuchtenden	Augen

158 derselbe

There are two German adjectives to express English *the same:* **der gleiche** and **derselbe.** The forms of **derselbe** are written as one word unless the article is contracted with a preposition. Both **der** and **selb-** must be declined.

> **Ist das derselbe Wein wie gestern?**
> **Ist das der gleiche Wein wie gestern?**
> **Wir trinken heute wieder denselben Wein wie gestern.**
> **Wir wohnen in derselben Stadt.**
> **Wir wohnen im selben Hotel.**
> **Wir wohnen im gleichen Hotel.**
> **Wir wohnen in demselben Hotel.**

Strictly speaking, **der gleiche** expresses similarity (the same kind), and **derselbe** expresses identity (the very same). However, this distinction is rapidly disappearing.

159 was für

There is no English structural equivalent for the very frequently used construction with **was für.** It is not declined, nor does **für** have any influence on the case of the following adjective or noun. **Was für** means *what kind of* or *what.*

In the nominative and accusative, **was** occupies the front field; **für** plus the noun or pronoun may either follow the **was** immediately or stand in the inner field, usually right before the second prong.

Was für ein Wagen ist denn das da drüben?
Was ist denn das *für ein Wagen* da drüben?*
Was ist denn das da drüben *für ein Wagen?*

Was für einen Wagen hast du dir denn gekauft?
Was hast du dir denn *für einen Wagen* gekauft?

Was für Bücher hast du mir denn mitgebracht?
Was hast du mir denn *für Bücher* mitgebracht?

In the dative, the **was für** construction cannot be split. Nor can it be split if it is preceded by a preposition.

Was für einem Mann gehört denn der Wagen?
Mit was für einem Wagen bist du denn gefahren?
Durch was für Dörfer seid ihr denn gefahren?
Auf was für einen Mann wartest du denn?

160 viel, wenig

Viel (*much;* plural: *many*) and **wenig** (*little;* plural: *few*) have the same characteristics. Their use is in a state of flux, but it is safe to use them in the following ways.

(a) In the singular, **viel** and **wenig** express bulk and are usually used without endings.

Wieviel Fisch habt ihr gegessen? (**wieviel**—one word)
Wir haben damals viel Fisch und wenig Fleisch gegessen.

Adjectives used after these endingless forms have strong endings:

Ich habe noch viel deutsches Geld.
Ich habe nur noch wenig deutsches Geld.

After possessive adjectives and definite articles, **viel** and **wenig**, still indicating bulk, take attributive adjective endings: **sein vieles Geld, das viele Geld.**

NOTE: **Vielen Dank,** *thank you very much,* is an exception.

(b) In the plural, **viele** means *many* and **wenige** *few*. They are then treated as attributive adjectives.

	SLOT 1	SLOT 2	SLOT 3
	viele junge		Leute
	die	vielen jungen	Leute
mit	wenigen		Worten

---

* **da drüben** is end field; remember the sentence **Das Bier ist gut hier in München.**

(c) **Viel** and **wenig** may be used as adverbs preceding comparatives:

> Er war viel älter als sie.
> Er war nur wenig älter als sie.
> Er hatte viel mehr Geld als ich.

Viel must not be confused with the adverb **sehr** (*very*) which sometimes corresponds to an English *very much*.

Ich habe sie sehr geliebt.	I loved her very much.
Ich ginge sehr gerne mit nach Köln.	I'd like very much to go along to Cologne.
Er war sehr krank.	He was very sick.
Die Amerikaner essen sehr viel Fleisch.	Americans eat very much meat.
Ich war sehr dagegen.	I was very much against it.
Es waren sehr viele Leute dort.	There were very many people there.

Note that German and English are not always parallel:

geliebt	sehr geliebt	loved very much
gerne	sehr gerne	very gladly
krank	sehr krank	very sick
viel Fleisch	sehr viel Fleisch	very much (a lot of) meat
dagegen	sehr dagegen	very much against it
viele Leute	sehr viele Leute	very many people

English *very* always precedes *much, many,* or some other adjective or adverb. German **sehr,** on the other hand, is an independent adverb and does not have to be followed by anything: **Sie liebte ihn sehr.**

161 ander-

Ander- means *other, different,* or *else*. If used attributively or after **etwas** or **nichts,** it takes the same endings as any other attributive adjective and is often preceded by **ganz.**

> Das eine Buch kenne ich, aber das andere habe ich noch nicht gelesen.
> Erika kenne ich ja, aber wer war denn die andere Dame?
> Dieser Herr war es nicht, es muß ein anderer gewesen sein.
> Das ist natürlich etwas anderes. (something else)
> Das ist etwas ganz anderes. (something quite different)

NOTE: For some unfathomable reason, no form of **ander-** is ever capitalized.

If **ander-** is used as an adverb or a predicate adjective, it always has the form **anders.**

> Ich hätte das ganz anders gemacht. I would have done that quite differently.
> Es ist alles ganz anders gekommen, als wir dachten.
> Er ist anders, als er früher war.

Note also the following frequently used phrases:

> **Das kann nicht mein Bruder gewesen sein, das muß *jemand anders*** [somebody else] **gewesen sein.**

> **Das kann *niemand anders*** [nobody else] **gewesen sein als Anton Meyer.**

162 mehrere, einige, ein paar

All three of these terms mean *more than two, but not many.*

Mehrere and **einige** are never used with an article, as is possible with English *the several states.* They therefore take strong endings.

Mehrere means *several,* **einige** (literary) and **ein paar** mean *a few (some, a bunch).*

SLOT 0	SLOT 1	SLOT 2	SLOT 3
	mehrere junge		Leute
	einige deutsche		Bücher
ein paar	junge		Leute
ein paar	deutsche		Bücher

Do not confuse *few (not many),* **wenige,** with *a few (some),* **ein paar.**

> **Wenige Menschen wußten, wer er wirklich war.**
> **Ein paar Menschen wußten, wer er wirklich war.**

After the article or a possessive adjective, **ein paar** becomes **paar.**

Neither **paar** (*few*) nor **ein paar** (*a few*) is ever declined, nor does either of them have any influence on the ending of a following adjective.

	SLOT 0	SLOT 1	SLOT 2	SLOT 3
	(ein paar)	alte		Hemden
		die (paar)	alten	Hemden
mit	(ein paar)	alten		Hemden
mit		den (paar)	alten	Hemden
		meine (paar)	alten	Hemden
mit		meinen (paar)	alten	Hemden
mit	(ein paar)	alten		Hemden

> **Bring mir doch bitte ein paar Zigaretten mit.**
> **Ich komme in ein paar Minuten.**
> **Er wollte in Berlin ein paar Freunde besuchen.**
> **Er ist ein paar Tage in Berlin gewesen.**
> **Wir haben ein paar schöne Tage an der Riviera verbracht.**

Die paar schönen Tage an der Riviera waren viel zu kurz.
In den paar kurzen Tagen konnte ich nicht viel arbeiten.

Note the difference between **ein paar** (*a few*) and **ein Paar** (*a pair, a couple*):

Wir aßen Suppe mit ein paar Würstchen.
Wir aßen Suppe mit einem Paar Würstchen.
Anton und Emma waren ein schönes Paar.

163 Word Formation: Nouns of Action Derived from Weak Verbs

The stem of some weak verbs appears as a masculine noun of action—that is, a noun denoting the activity expressed by the verb. Feel free to use the nouns listed, but do not try to invent your own—they may not exist. Most of these nouns are masculine, but there are also a few feminines and neuters.

antworten	die Antwort, –en	das war eine gute Antwort
baden	das Bad, ⸚er	ein heißes Bad
besuchen	der Besuch, –e	Der Besuch der alten Dame (Dürrenmatt)
blicken	der Blick, –e	ein vielsagender Blick
danken	der Dank (*no pl.*)	vielen Dank
fragen	die Frage, –n	das kommt nicht in Frage (that's out of the question)
glauben	der Glaube *gen.* des Glaubens (*no pl.*)	Glaube, Liebe, Hoffnung
grüßen	der Gruß, ⸚e	viele Grüße aus den Bergen
hassen	der Haß (*no pl.*)	Ohne Liebe kein Haß (Ingelheim)
heiraten	die Heirat	ich bin gegen diese Heirat
kaufen	der Kauf, ⸚e	ein guter Kauf
küssen	der Kuß, die Küsse	mit Gruß und Kuß, Dein Julius
lieben	die Liebe (*no pl.*)	Liebe macht blind
reden	die Rede, –n	er hielt eine lange Rede
suchen	die Suche (*no pl.*)	die Suche nach dem Dieb
tanzen	der Tanz, ⸚e	der Tanz um das goldene Kalb
versuchen	der Versuch, –e	ein chemischer Versuch
wünschen	der Wunsch, ⸚e	alle guten Wünsche zum Neuen Jahr

The most common nouns of action are the feminine nouns in **-ung** (see **120**).

164 Nouns of Action Derived from Strong Verbs

Theoretically, any one of the various forms of the stem of a strong verb
can occur as a noun denoting the action of the verb, or the result of such
action, or the thing used for such action.

> Action: **der Schlaf** sleep
> Result of action: **der Fund** the find
> Thing used for action: **der Sitz** the seat

Again, it is safe to use the nouns listed, but do not invent your own. Note
that of the nouns ending in **-t** and **-e**, most are feminine.

abfahren	die Abfahrt, –en	departure
anfangen	der Anfang, ¨e	beginning
ankommen	die Ankunft, ¨e	arrival
annehmen	die Annahme, –n	reception; assumption
anrufen	der Anruf, –e	phone call
ansehen	die Ansicht, –en	view, sight
ausgeben	die Ausgabe, –n	expense, delivery
aufnehmen	die Aufnahme, –n	reception; photograph
ausgehen	der Ausgang, ¨e	exit
aussehen	die Aussicht, –en	expectation, view
befehlen	der Befehl, –e	order, command
beginnen	der Beginn (*no pl.*)	beginning
bitten	die Bitte, –n	request
brechen	der Bruch, ¨e	break, fracture, fraction
fahren	die Fahrt, –en	drive, trip
fallen	der Fall, ¨e	fall, case
geben	die Gabe, –n	gift
	das Gift, –e	poison
	die Mitgift (*no pl.*)	dowry
gehen	der Gang, ¨e	gait, corridor, gear (in a motor)
gewinnen	der Gewinn, –e	profit, gain
greifen	der Griff, –e	handle; grasp
helfen	die Hilfe	help
lesen (to read, to gather)	die Weinlese, –n	grape harvest
	„Spätlese"	a wine made from overripe grapes
liegen	die Lage, –n	situation
raten	der Rat	advice
scheinen	der Schein (*no pl.*)	appearance, light
	der (Geld)schein, –e	banknote
schlafen	der Schlaf (*no pl.*)	sleep
schlagen	der Schlag, ¨e	strike, stroke, hit

schneiden	der Schnitt, –e	cut
schreiben	die Schrift, –en	(hand)writing
	die Heilige Schrift	Bible, Holy Writ
sehen	das Gesicht, –er	face
sitzen	der Sitz, –e	seat
sprechen	die Sprache, –n	language, speech
springen	der Sprung, ⸚e	jump
stehen	der Stand, ⸚e	stand
trinken	das Getränk, –e	beverage
tun	die Tat, –en	deed
	die Tatsache, –n	(actual) fact
verbieten	das Verbot, –e	prohibition
verlieren	der Verlust, –e	loss
verstehen	der Verstand (*no pl.*)	reason, intelligence
ziehen	der Zug, ⸚e	train

165 The Suffix -ig

This suffix may be added to nouns to form adjectives corresponding to
English derivatives of the type *stone: stony, meat: meaty.*

der Stein	steinig	stony
die Güte	gütig	good, kind
die Ecke	eckig	angular
das Dreieck (triangle)	dreieckig	three-cornered, triangular
das Viereck (rectangle)	viereckig	four-cornered, rectangular
die Seite	-seitig	-sided
	einseitig	onesided
	ein gleichseitiges Dreieck	an equilateral triangle

Frequently, the suffix -ig is added to time expressions to form adjectives.
Most of these adjectives cannot be imitated in English.

die Zeit	zeitig	in (good) time
	rechtzeitig	on time, at the right time
das Jahr	-jährig	
	dreijährig	three years old, lasting for three years
	ein dreijähriges Kind	a three-year-old child
	eine dreitägige Wanderung	a three-day hike
heute	heutig	of today
	die heutige Zeitung	today's paper
jetzt	jetzig	of today, present, contemporary

	der jetzige Bürgermeister	the name of the present
	heißt Böttle	mayor is Böttle
damals	damalig	then
	der damalige Bürgermeister	the then mayor's name
	hieß Meyer	was Meyer

Note also:

| hier | hiesig | |
| | die hiesige Bevölkerung | the local population |

EXERCISES

A. Insert the adjectives given in parentheses into the following sentences:

1. Meyer ist mit einer Frau verheiratet. (sehr intelligent)
2. Eine Frau ist sie *nicht.* (intelli*gent*)
3. Er ist dumm, aber er hat eine Frau geheiratet. (intelligent)
4. Sie ist dumm, aber sie hat einen Mann geheiratet. (intelligent)
5. Er ist ein Mensch. (intelligent)
6. Wer *ist* denn der Mann, von dem ihr da sprecht? (intelligent)
7. Sie ist ein Kind. (intelligent)
8. Wer *ist* denn das Mädchen, von dem ihr da sprecht? (intelligent)
9. Von einem Mädchen hätte ich das nicht erwartet. (so intelligent)
10. Mein Sohn hat ein Mädchen geheiratet. (intelligent)
11. Meyers haben drei Kinder. (intelligent)
12. Frauen wissen immer, was sie wollen. (intelligent)
13. Mit Studenten kann man gut arbeiten. (intelligent)
14. Was machen Sie denn mit den Kindern in Ihrer Schule? (intelli*gent*)
15. Sie ist mit einem Mann verheiratet. (intelligent)

B. Restate the following sentences, leaving out the italicized **der-** or **ein**-words.

1. *Jeder* gute Wein ist teuer.
2. *Alle* intelligenten Frauen wissen, was sie wollen.
3. Das ist wirklich *ein* guter Wein.
4. *Dieses* deutsche Bier ist sehr gut.
5. *Mein* lieber Vater!
6. *Das* frische Obst ist jetzt zu teuer.
7. Bei *dem* starken Regen fahre ich nicht in die Stadt.

C. Place the word in parentheses in front of the adjective.

1. Für intelligente Kinder tun wir viel zu wenig. (unsere)
2. Automatische Uhren sind teuer. (diese)

3. Nach kurzer Pause fuhren wir weiter. (einer)
4. Beide Kinder gingen damals schon in die Schule. (seine)
5. Westfälischer Schinken ist eine Spezialität unseres Hauses. (dieser)

D. Restate the following sentences by changing the italicized nouns to the singular and by making the corresponding changes in the **der**-words and adjectives.

1. Siehst du *die jungen Mädchen* da drüben?
2. Woher hast du denn *die schönen Bücher?*
3. *Diese neuen Maschinen* fliegen tausend Kilometer in der Stunde.
4. *Die ersten Fluggäste* kamen aus dem Zoll.
5. Wir fragten *die jungen Männer,* wo sie herkämen.
6. *In den zerstörten Städten* gab es kein Wasser.
7. *Die kleinen Dörfer* lagen im Schwarzwald.

E. Restate the following sentences by changing the nouns to the singular. Change the adjective ending as required and place an **ein**-word before the adjective.

1. Ich habe Verwandte in Frankfurt.
2. Bei uns wohnen jetzt amerikanische Soldaten.
3. Vor ihm saßen zwei blonde Mädchen.
4. Er rauchte amerikanische Zigaretten.
5. Meyers sind gute Freunde von mir.

F. In the following sentences, insert an appropriate **der**- or **ein**-word (if necessary) and the correct form of the adjective in parentheses.

1. Mit _____ _____ Roman hat er viel Geld verdient. (letzt)
2. Wir wohnen in _____ _____ Haus. (neu)
3. Gestern abend habe ich _____ _____ Professor kennengelernt. (deutsch)
4. Ich freue mich auf _____ Sonntag. (nächst)
5. Mein Mann ist gerade von _____ _____ Reise zurückgekommen. (lang)
6. Mit _____ _____ Schreibmaschine kann ich nicht schreiben. (alt)
7. Wann soll _____ _____ Brücke denn fertig sein? (neu)
8. Mit _____ _____ Mantel kannst du nicht nach Paris fahren. (alt)
9. Bist du mit _____ _____ Sekretärin zufrieden? (neu)
10. Barbara war die Mutter _____ _____ Kinder. (beid)
11. Für _____ _____ Soldaten war der Krieg zu Ende. (deutsch)
12. Ich möchte ein Zimmer mit _____ Wasser. (fließend)
13. Haben Sie etwas _____ gehört? (neu)
14. Er hat viel _____ getan. (gut)
15. Er hat zwei _____ Romane geschrieben. (gut)

G. Express in German:

1. We have two small children.

2. He lived with his old mother.
3. I hope you'll marry an intelligent woman.
4. She wrote him a long letter.
5. She never read his long letters.
6. Good coffee is very expensive.
7. He is an old friend of mine.
8. She is a good friend of mine.
9. Is that the new hotel?
10. Last week I was in Berlin.
11. Last Monday I was in Berlin.
18. I am living with my German relatives.
19. I have a German aunt.
20. Do you know that we have a new director?
21. Dear Hans!
22. Our dear old Aunt Amalie died last week.
23. In which hotel did you live?
24. She really is a very interesting woman.
25. In this city we don't have one single good hotel.
26. We all went to the movies last night.
27. I have read all his novels.
28. This is really a good wine.
29. My old friends are all dead.
30. All my old friends are dead.
31. She has married a young German.
32. He married a young German.
33. In the room above me lives a young German (man).
34. I have forgotten something very important.
35. Today I experienced something very beautiful.
36. When a man is thirty-nine, he is no longer a young man in the eyes of a young girl.

H. Change singular nouns in the following sentences to plurals.

1. Was für einen herrlichen Tag wir gehabt haben!
2. Was für ein Buch möchtest du denn gerne haben?
3. Was für eine schöne Tochter Sie haben!
4. Was für ein Haus ist denn das?

I. Change the plural nouns in the following sentences to singulars.

1. Was für schöne Kinder das sind!
2. Was müssen das für Menschen sein!
3. Was für schöne Tage das waren!
4. Was für interessante Kleider die Anita anhat!

J. Insert the words italicized in the first sentence as adjectives into the second sentence.

1. Die Deutschen hatten die Brücke *zerstört*. Wir konnten nicht über die _____ Brücke fahren.
2. Dieses Wasser ist *kalt*. Trinken Sie gerne _____ Wasser?
3. Erich hatte fünf Goldstücke *gestohlen*. Mit den _____ Goldstücken fuhr er nach Afrika.
4. Die Maschine aus London ist gerade *gelandet*. Die gerade _____ Maschine hat 35 Minuten Verspätung.

K. Change the italicized inflected form of the verb into a **-d** adjective and insert it into the second sentence.

1. Der *sieht* aber gut *aus*. Er ist ein gut _____ junger Mann.
2. Die Linden *blühten* noch; sie saßen unter einer _____ Linde.
3. Das Kind *schlief*, als er abfuhr. Er sah noch einmal auf das _____ Kind und fuhr dann ab.
4. Die Kinder *spielten* auf der Straße, aber der alte Mann sah die _____ Kinder nicht.

L. Construct a conversation between yourself and your cousin Emma who has come to pick you up at the Frankfurt Airport. This is not an exercise in translation, but you should nevertheless follow the English outline. Use your imagination, but avoid using patterns that you are not thoroughly familiar with. Be prepared to produce a similar conversation orally in class.

Emma, of course, wants to know how you are, how the flight was, whether you are tired, and whether you would like to have breakfast before driving into town. You try to figure out what time it is in New York and you talk a bit about time differences. When Emma mentions MEZ, you are puzzled because you've never heard the term. Emma explains. Then you decide that you are really tired and ought to get to your hotel. She wants to know whether you have ordered a room, which, of course, you have done. Emma thinks it might be a good idea to call the hotel to be sure that you have the room. Since you have never made a phone call in Germany, you ask her whether she would please do that for you. While she telephones, you want to get some German money. She asks you to come to the exit in ten minutes, and she will get her car in the meantime.

Now, here is your first sentence: Emma: „Da bist du ja endlich."

BASIC VOCABULARY

ander– other
    eins nach dem anderen one after the other
anders different (See **161**)
arm poor

ausgeben to spend
ausschlafen to get enough sleep
    schlief aus, hat ausgeschlafen, er schläft aus

der Baum, ⸚e tree
das Bein, –e leg
bekannt well known
    der Bekannte, –n acquaintance (see **156**)

bestellen to order
der Besuch, –e visit
blühen to bloom, blossom, flower
brechen to break
das Brot, –e bread
der Bus, –se bus
da drüben over there
dankbar grateful, thankful
dauern to last, to take (time)
derselbe the same (see **158**)
das Dorf, ¨er village
draußen (*adverb*) outside
dunkel dark
durstig thirsty
einige some, several, a few
einsteigen to enter, board (a train or plane)
die Eisenbahn, –en railroad
entfernt distant
erstens first(ly)
  zweitens second(ly)
  drittens third(ly)
  etc.
ertrinken to drown
  ertrank, ist ertrunken, er ertrinkt
Euro′pa Europe
  europä′isch European
fein fine
das Fleisch (*no pl.*) meat
fließen to flow
das Flugzeug, –e airplane
fremd strange, alien
fressen to eat (said of animals)
  fraß, hat gefressen, er frißt
die Freude, –n joy
frisch fresh
der Frühling, –e spring
der Fuß, ¨e foot
gewinnen to win
gleich (*adjective*) same, like, equal; (*time adverb*) immediately, presently
der Großvater, ¨er grandfather
grüßen to greet
  der Gruß, ¨e greeting
das Haar, –e hair
hereinkommen to come in
herum around
hinunter down

den (Rhein) hinunter down the Rhine
hoch high
immer wieder again and again
  immer größer bigger and bigger
  immer schöner more and more beautiful
der Januar January
die Karte, –n map, ticket
klar clear
klopfen to knock
  anklopfen to knock (at the door)
die Kreide chalk
die Küche, –n kitchen
lächeln to smile
  das Lächeln smile
landen to land
laut loud
lehren to teach
  der Lehrer teacher
leicht easy, light (in weight)
lieb dear
  liebhaben to love
  lieblich lovely
der Liebling, –e darling, favorite
mancher many a (see **152**)
mehrere several
meist– most
Mitternacht midnight
modern′ modern
die Möglichkeit, –en possibility
der Nachbar, –n neighbor
die Nase, –n nose
öffnen to open
  offen (*adjective*) open
die Pause, –n pause, intermission
der Pfennig pfennig, penny (100 to a Mark)
raten to advise; give counsel; guess
  der Rat advice, counsel; council; councilor
  das Rathaus, ¨er town hall, city hall
rechtzeitig on time
die Regie′rung, –en government

die Bundesregierung the Federal Government (of Germany)
die Reihe, –n row; series
  ich bin an der Reihe it's my turn
  ich komme an die Reihe I'm next
rennen to run
die Rose, –n rose
rot red
die Ruhe (*no pl.*) rest; quietness
  in aller Ruhe at leisure
der Schinken, – ham
schneiden to cut
  der Schnitt, –e the cut
schwarz black
sentimental′ sentimental
solange (*conj.*) as long as
solcher such (see **153**)
der Staat, –en state
stark strong, heavy (as rain, wind, etc.)
stecken to stick, put
die Stimme, –n voice
der Stuhl, ¨e chair
die Suppe, –n soup
teuer expensive
treten to step
die Tür, –en door
unten down, down below, downstairs
der Unterschied, –e difference
verbieten to forbid, prohibit
verlassen to leave (somebody or something)
verbringen to spend (time)
die Verspätung, –en delay
  Verspätung haben to be late, not on schedule
verwandt related
  der Verwandte, –n relative (see **156**)
vorbei (*adverb*) gone, past
der Wald, ¨er woods, forest
was für what kind of (see **159**)
weinen to cry
weiß white
welcher which
wenig little (See **162**)

werfen to throw
   umwerfen to knock over
wichtig important
wiederho'len to repeat
wiegen to weigh

die Wirklichkeit, –en
   reality
wunderbar wonderful, marvelous
der Wunsch, ⸚e wish
die Wurst, ⸚e sausage

Wurst cold cuts
   das Würstchen, – sausage
zerstören to destroy
ziehen to pull; to move
der Zoll, ⸚e customs; duty
zunächst first, first of all

ADDITIONAL VOCABULARY

der Apfel, ⸚ apple
der Ast, ⸚e branch
das Ausland foreign countries
   er lebt im Ausland he lives abroad
backen to bake
   der Bäcker, – baker
der Bauch, ⸚e stomach, belly
der Beamte, –n civil servant, (government) official
   (gen.: des Beamten, dat.: dem Beamten)
   die Beamtin, –nen official (female)
der Brunnen, – well, fountain
eigen (adjective) own

empfehlen to recommend
die Farbe, –n color
   die Lieblingsfarbe, –n favorite color
der Fluggast, ⸚e airplane passenger
füllen to fill
die Geiß, –en goat
das Gemüse, – vegetable
der Gesandte, –n ambassador, envoy
das Hemd, –en shirt
der Kasten, ⸚ chest, box
der Koffer, – suitcase
die Kusi'ne, –n (female) cousin

leuchten to shine
die Mahlzeit, –en meal
das Mehl flour
die Meile, –n mile
der Müller, – miller
nähen to sew
der Nebel, – fog
   neblig foggy
das Obst (no pl.) fruit
der Pfarrer, – pastor
schnarchen to snore
der Schrank, ⸚e cupboard, wardrobe
streichen to spread (as paint), stroke
der Wolf, ⸚e wolf

IRREGULAR VERBS

ausschlafen to get enough sleep
   schlief aus, hat ausgeschlafen, er schläft aus
brechen to break
   brach, hat gebrochen, er bricht
empfehlen to recommend
   empfahl, hat empfohlen, er empfiehlt
ertrinken to drown
   ertrank, ist ertrunken, er ertrinkt
fließen to flow
   floß, ist geflossen, er fließt
fressen to eat (said of animals)
   fraß, hat gefressen, er

   frißt
frieren to freeze
   fror, hat gefroren, er friert
gewinnen to win
   gewann, hat gewonnen, er gewinnt
leid tun to be sorry
   tat ... leid, hat ... leid getan, es tut ... leid
raten to advise; to guess
   riet, hat geraten, er rät
rennen to run
   rannte, ist gerannt, er rennt
streichen to spread (as paint), stroke
   strich, hat gestrichen, er streicht
treten to step

   trat, ist getreten, er tritt
verbieten to forbid
   verbot, hat verboten, er verbietet
verbringen to spend (time)
   verbrachte, hat verbracht, er verbringt
verlassen to leave
   verließ, hat verlassen, er verläßt
werfen to throw
   warf, hat geworfen, er wirft
wiegen to weigh
   wog, hat gewogen, er wiegt
ziehen to pull, move
   zog, hat gezogen, er zieht

UNIT 11: Infinitive Constructions—**hin** and **her**—
Comparison of Adjectives—The Rhetorical **nicht**—Numbers

PATTERNS

[1] **lernen** plus Infinitive

Observe the position of the dependent infinitives; then complete the variations below.

Ingelheim kannte ich schon vor dem Kriege, aber seine Frau lernte ich erst kennen, als er mit ihr nach München zog.

SEE ANALYSIS 166, 167 (pp. 354-359)

Ingelheim kenne ich schon lange, aber seine Frau habe ich leider noch nicht kennengelernt. Ich möchte sie gerne kennenlernen.

Ali war sehr intelligent, aber er hatte nie lesen gelernt.

Viele Kinder lernen schon mit fünf Jahren lesen.

Bevor Sie nach Kalifornien gehen, müssen Sie unbedingt Auto fahren lernen.

Es wäre besser, wenn Sie Auto fahren gelernt hätten.
It would be better if you had learned to drive.

VARIATIONS

Complete the following sentences by using the infinitives in parentheses. Use more than one tense if possible.

Es wäre besser, wenn sie _____ (kochen lernen).
Ich möchte wissen, ob sie _____ (kochen lernen).
Ich dachte, du _____ (schwimmen lernen).
Sie soll tatsächlich _____ (Auto fahren lernen).
Ich hoffe, daß er hier jemanden _____ (kennenlernen).

(Facing) **Der ,,Römer''—das Rathaus in Frankfurt**

335

[2] **bleiben** plus Infinitive

Observe again the position of the dependent infinitives; then complete the variations below.

SEE
ANALYSIS
167

(pp. 355-359)

Bitte bleiben Sie doch sitzen, Herr Schmidt.

    Please stay seated (don't get up).

Warum hat sie denn den Meyer geheiratet? Um nicht sitzenzubleiben?—Ja, weil sie nicht sitzenbleiben wollte.

    Why did she marry Meyer? In order not to become an old maid?—Yes, because she didn't want to become an old maid.

Du brauchst noch nicht aufzustehen; du kannst noch liegen bleiben.

    You don't have to get up yet; you can still stay in bed.

Wem gehört denn das Buch da?—Das weiß ich nicht; es ist gestern abend hier liegengeblieben.

    To whom does that book belong?—I don't know; it was left here last night.

Meine Uhr ist gestern abend plötzlich stehengeblieben.

    My watch suddenly stopped last night.

Bitte gehen Sie weiter; Sie dürfen hier nicht stehenbleiben.

    Please go on, you mustn't stop here.

VARIATIONS

Complete the following sentences, using the infinitives in parentheses. Use more than one tense, if possible.

    Bitte _____, Herr Meyer! (sitzen bleiben).
    Ich hoffe, meine Uhr _____ (stehenbleiben).
    Ich glaube, meine Uhr _____ (stehenbleiben).
    Ich dachte, meine Uhr _____ (stehenbleiben).
    Er kommt heute nicht zum Frühstück. Er _____ (liegen bleiben).

[3] **gehen** and **fahren** plus Infinitive

Observe again the position of the dependent infinitives; then complete the variations that follow.

SEE
ANALYSIS
167

(pp. 355-359)

Wie wäre es, wenn wir jetzt essen gingen?

Fritz ist auch schon essen gegangen.

Können wir bald essen gehen?

Du brauchst doch nicht schon wieder essen zu gehen; du hast doch gerade erst gefrühstückt.

Wie wär's denn, wenn wir Sonntag baden gingen?

Was habt ihr denn heute gemacht?—Erst sind wir schwimmen gegangen, und dann sind
wir spazierengefahren.

VARIATIONS

Complete the following sentences by using the infinitives in parentheses. Use
more than one tense, if possible.

Es wäre nett, wenn wir morgen _____ (schwimmen gehen).
Er soll jeden Tag mit Erika _____ (schwimmen gehen).
Ist Hans schon im Bett?—Ja, er _____ (schlafen gehen).
Ich wollte, wir _____ (schlafen gehen).

[4] hören and sehen plus Infinitive

Observe how **hören** and **sehen** behave like modals in these sentences. Then follow the instructions below.

SEE
ANALYSIS
167

(pp. 355-359)

Ich hörte ihn gestern abend nach Hause kommen.
Ich habe ihn gestern abend nach Hause kommen hören.
Ich habe gehört, wie er gestern abend nach Hause kam.
    I heard him come home last night.

Wir sahen sie in Berlin die Desdemona spielen.
    We saw her play Desdemona in Berlin.

Wir haben sie die Desdemona spielen sehen.
    We've seen her play Desdemona.

VARIATIONS

Form sentences with the following phrases, using modals, subjunctives, and
various tenses:

Emma einmal (noch nie) lachen sehen
den Kleinen schreien hören
die Maria nach Hause kommen hören

[5] lassen

The various uses of **lassen** are shown below, each followed by a short exercise.

SEE
ANALYSIS
167

(pp. 355-359)

Heute regnet es bestimmt nicht. Deinen Regenmantel kannst du zu Hause lassen.
    I'm sure it won't rain today. You can leave your raincoat at home.

Heute regnet es bestimmt nicht. Du hättest deinen Mantel zu Hause lassen können.
    I'm sure it won't rain today. You could have left your raincoat at home.

Bitte lassen Sie mich jetzt allein.

> Please leave me alone now.

Ich wollte, er ließe mich in Ruhe.

> I wish he'd leave me alone (in peace).

Express in German:

> I've left my coat at home.
> I wish I hadn't left it at home.
> Why do you always leave your coat at home?

Jetzt habe ich schon wieder meinen Mantel im Hotel hängenlassen.

> Now I've left my coat at the hotel again.

Und wo ist deine Handtasche?—Die habe ich bei Tante Amalie auf dem Tisch stehen-lassen.

> Where is yourbag? —I left it on the table at Aunt Amalie's.

Und deine Handschuhe hast du wohl auch irgendwo liegenlassen?

> And I suppose you left your gloves somewhere too?

Express in German (note that the infinitives **hängen, stehen, liegen** behave like prefixes and do not change):

> I hope you won't leave your coat in the hotel again.
> I have left my gloves at Aunt Amalie's.
> You can't leave your car in front of the hotel.

Ich lasse dich nicht nach Berlin fahren.

Ich habe ihn doch nach Berlin fahren lassen.

Ich wollte, ich hätte ihn nicht nach Berlin fahren lassen.

Du kannst mich doch nicht ohne Geld nach Berlin fahren lassen.

Ich hätte ihn nicht allein nach Berlin fahren lassen sollen.

Warum darf *ich* nicht allein ins Kino gehen? *Müll*ers lassen ihre Tochter allein ins Kino gehen.

Express in German:

> Why don't you let me study medicine?
> I wish you'd let me study medicine.
> I wish we had let him study medicine.
> We can't let him study medicine.
> We shouldn't have let him study medicine.
> We shall let him study medicine.

Meyer mußte gestern abend den Arzt kommen lassen.
　Meyer had to have the doctor come last night.

Ich habe ihm sagen lassen, daß er mich morgen anrufen soll.
　I left word for him to call me tomorrow.

Ich wollte ihn nicht anrufen; ich habe ihm ein Telegramm schicken lassen.
　I didn't want to call him; I've had a telegram sent to him.

Wo hast du dir die Haare schneiden lassen?
　Where did you have your hair cut?

Frau Lenz hat sich schon wieder einen Mantel machen lassen.
　Frau Lenz has had another coat made.

Du, *der* Mantel ist aber todschick; in *dem* kannst du dich sehen lassen.
　Say, that coat is really something (great, fine); it really does something for you.

Der Wein ist gut; der läßt sich trinken.
　This wine is good; it's quite drinkable. (Understatement)

Meyer tut, was er will. Der läßt sich nie etwas sagen.
　Meyer does what he wants. You can't tell him a thing.

Ich lasse mir eine Tasse Kaffee aufs Zimmer bringen.
　I'm having a cup of coffee brought to my room.

Ich habe mir eine Tasse Kaffee aufs Zimmer bringen lassen.
　I've had a cup of coffee brought to my room.

Warum hast du dir denn nicht eine Tasse Kaffee aufs Zimmer bringen lassen?
　Why didn't you have a cup of coffee brought to your room?

Warum hat sie sich denn den Kaffee nicht aufs Zimmer bringen lassen?
　Why didn't she have the coffee brought to her room?

Hans ist doch Student; du kannst dir doch von ihm nicht immer das Essen bezahlen lassen.
　But Hans is a student; you can't always let him pay for your meals.

Using the phrase **die Haare schneiden,** express in German:

　I must get a haircut today.
　I got a haircut yesterday.
　I always have him cut my hair.
　Why didn't you get a haircut today?
　Yes, I'll get a haircut tomorrow.
　François? I'll never have *him* cut my hair again.
　　(Start with *Von dem* . . .)

[6] brauchen, scheinen, haben, sein

Observe the use of infinitives with **zu** depending on these verbs.

SEE
ANALYSIS
167

(pp. 355-359)

Du brauchst nicht auf mich zu warten; ich komme heute spät nach Hause.
> You don't need to wait for me; I'll come home late today.

Du hättest nicht auf mich zu warten brauchen.
> You needn't have waited for me.

Es scheint zu regnen.
Er scheint zu schlafen.
Er scheint nicht zu Hause zu sein.
Er scheint schon abgefahren zu sein.
Gut ge*schla*fen zu haben scheinst du *nicht*.
Er scheint heute nicht zu arbeiten zu brauchen.
Er scheint nichts zu sagen zu haben.

Ich kann leider nicht mitgehen; ich habe noch etwas zu tun.
> I'm sorry, but I can't come along; I still have something to do.

Ich hatte den ganzen Tag nichts zu tun.
> I didn't have anything to do all day.

Wenn ich nicht so viel zu tun gehabt hätte, hätte ich dir gerne geholfen.
> If I hadn't had so much to do, I would gladly have helped you.

Nur um etwas zu tun zu haben, ging er jeden Abend ins Kino.
> Just to have something to do, he went to the movies every night.

Da ist nichts zu machen.
> There's nothing to be done (about it).

Hans war einfach nicht zu finden.

>Hans was simply not to be found.

Professor Mertens ist immer gut zu verstehen.

>Professor Mertens is always easy to understand.

Er soll gut zu verstehen gewesen sein.

>He is supposed to have been easy to understand. (I hear he was easy to understand.)

VARIATIONS

Express in German:

>Don't you have anything to do?
>Don't you have anything to say?
>Why does he never have anything to say?
>It would be nice if I had nothing to do today.
>I wish I had something to do today.
>He seems to have nothing to do today.

[7] End-Field Infinitives (the Group **anfangen**)

In the following sentences, note that the clause to which the infinitive belongs has to be completed before the infinitive phrase can be started. Then complete the variations below.

Es fing an zu regnen.

Als es anfing zu regnen, gingen wir nach Hause.

Es hat angefangen zu regnen.

Es fing an, sehr stark zu regnen.

Als es anfing, sehr stark zu regnen, gingen wir nach Hause.

Kannst du nicht endlich aufhören zu arbeiten?

Ich finde es langweilig, jeden Abend stundenlang fernzusehen.

Weil ich vergessen hatte, ihm zu schreiben, kam er nicht zum Bahnhof.

Hast du denn nicht versucht, sie anzurufen?

>Didn't you try to call her?

SEE
ANALYSIS
168
(pp. 359-362)

VARIATIONS

Change the following sentences to infinitive clauses and use the verbs in parentheses to form introductory clauses.

Es regnet nicht mehr. (aufhören)
Es hat aufgehört zu regnen.

Er will in Paris gewesen sein. (behaupten)

Ich habe ihr nicht geschrieben. (vergessen)

Meyer will seiner Frau ein Auto schenken. (versprechen)

Ich möchte sie bald wiedersehen. (hoffen)

Ich wollte dich gestern abend anrufen (versuchen)

Ich muß jeden Tag zwei Stunden im Auto sitzen. (es dumm finden)

Ich kann meinen Vater nicht um Geld bitten. (es nicht wagen)

[8] End-Field Infinitives (the Group **befehlen**)

Observe the identity of the personal dative and the unmentioned subject of the end-field infinitive. Then complete the variations.

SEE
ANALYSIS
168

(pp. 359-362)

Er schlug mir vor, an die Nordsee zu fahren.

    He suggested that I go to the North Sea.

Wenn Sie mir nicht vorgeschlagen hätten, an die Nordsee zu fahren, hätte ich meinen Mann nie kennengelernt.

    If you hadn't suggested that I go to the North Sea, I would never have met my husband.

Ich rate dir, nicht mehr so viel zu rauchen.

    I advise you not to smoke so much any more.

Wir erlauben unseren Kindern nicht, jede Woche zweimal ins Kino zu gehen.

    We don't allow our children to go to the movies twice a week.

In Deutschland ist es verboten, im Kino zu rauchen.

    In Germany it is forbidden to smoke in the movie theater.

Niemand kann mir befehlen, einen Mann zu heiraten, den ich nicht liebe.

    Nobody can order me to marry a man I don't love.

Wir können Ihnen leider nicht gestatten, dieses Buch mitnach Hause zu nehmen.

    I'm sorry, but we can't permit you to take this book home.

VARIATIONS

Change the following sentences to infinitive clauses and use the verbs in parentheses to form introductory clauses. Use **Er** and the perfect tense throughout.

> **Fahren Sie doch mal an die See. (raten)**
> **Er hat mir geraten, einmal an die See zu fahren.**

Trinken Sie jeden Abend vor dem Schlafengehen ein Glas Wein. (empfehlen)

Bleiben Sie morgen zu Hause. (erlauben)

Ich wünsche nicht, daß Sie mit meiner Tochter ins Theater gehen. (verbieten)

Fahren Sie doch mit mir nach München. (vorschlagen)

[9] End-Field Infinitives after Adjectives

After studying these sentences, complete the variations.

Inge war froh, ihren Mann wiederzusehen.

    Inge was glad to see her husband again.

Ich wußte, Inge wäre froh gewesen, ihren Mann wiederzusehen.

    I knew Inge would have been glad to see her husband again.

Ich bin immer bereit gewesen, ihm zu helfen.

    I have always been ready to help him.

Ich war sehr erstaunt, Erich aus dem Haus des Ägypters kommen zu sehen.

    I was very astonished to see Erich come out of the Egyptian's house.

SEE ANALYSIS 168 (pp. 359-362)

VARIATIONS

Change the following sentences to infinitive clauses. Use the subjects of these sentences and the adjectives in parentheses to form introductory clauses.

> **Inge sah ihren Mann wieder. (froh)**
> **Inge war froh, ihren Mann wiederzusehen.**

Gottseidank sind wir wieder zu Hause. (glücklich)

Erich half uns immer. (bereit)

Das Kind kann schon bis zehn zählen. (fähig)

Ich sah ihn letztes Wochenende in Hamburg wieder. (erstaunt)

[10] End-Field Infinitives after da-Compounds

Note that the subject of the inflected verb is also the unmentioned subject of the infinitive.

Ich denke nicht daran, mit Inge schwimmen zu gehen.

Du weißt doch, daß ich gar nicht daran denke, mit Inge schwimmen zu gehen.

Ich habe ja gar nicht daran gedacht, mit Inge schwimmen zu gehen.

Ich hätte nie daran gedacht, mit Inge schwimmen zu gehen.

SEE ANALYSIS 168 (pp. 359-362)

Form similar sentences with **Angst haben vor, jemanden bitten um, hoffen auf.**

[11] End-Field Infinitives with um . . . zu, ohne . . . zu, statt . . . zu

Note how the German construction changes if the subject of the infinitive is not also the subject of the inflected verb.

SEE
ANALYSIS
168
(pp. 359-362)

Wir bleiben heute zu Hause, um endlich einmal arbeiten zu können.
> We're going to stay at home today in order to get some work done finally.

Wir bleiben heute zu Hause, damit mein Mann endlich einmal arbeiten kann.
> We're going to stay at home today in order that my husband can finally get some work done (so that my husband can finally get some work done).

Ohne auch nur einen Augenblick nachzudenken, lief Hermann hinter das Haus.
> Without a moment's thought, Hermann ran behind the house.

Mit Meyer kann man nie sprechen, ohne daß seine Frau dabei ist.
> You can never talk to Meyer without his wife being there too.

Hast du schon wieder die ganze Nacht gelesen, statt zu schlafen?
> Have you read all night again instead of going to sleep?

Statt daß man *Meyer* nach Berlin geschickt hätte, muß *ich* schon wieder fahren.
> Instead of their having sent Meyer to Berlin (which they should have done and didn't), I have to go again.

[12] hin and her

Be prepared to produce orally the sentences on the left when you hear the sentences on the right, and vice versa.

SEE ANALYSIS
169
(pp. 362-365)

Ich fahre sofort hin.	Er kommt sofort her.
Kannst du hinfahren?	Kannst du herkommen?
Ich bin sofort hingefahren.	Er ist sofort hergekommen.
Ich brauche nicht hinzufahren.	Er braucht nicht herzukommen.
Wer hat dich denn dahingebracht?	Wer hat dich denn hierhergebracht?
Wie bist du denn dahingekommen?	Wie bist du denn hierhergekommen?
Sie fahren nach Köln? Dahin fahre ich auch.	Sie kommen von Köln? Daher komme ich auch.

VARIATIONS

Form variations with the following pattern:

> **Den kenne ich noch von früher her.**
> (Literally: I've known him from an earlier time on.)

von der Schule	von der Tanzstunde
vom Kriege	von München

Form variations on the following situation with **vorher** and **nachher**:

> **Gestern abend waren wir im Theater. Vorher haben wir im Regina gegessen, und nachher waren wir bei Schmidts.**

Letzten Mittwoch war ich in Köln.
Um sieben haben wir zu Abend gegessen.
Morgen mittag besuche ich Tante Amalie.

Memorize the following sentences:

Weißt du was? Rosemarie hat vorhin angerufen.
Ich war vorhin bei Schmidts.

Diese Uhr hier ist hin,—die ist kaputt.
Meine Ruh' ist hin, mein Herz ist schwer. (Goethe)

Be prepared to produce the sentences on the left when you hear the sentences on the right, and vice versa:

Wohin gehst du denn?	Wo gehst du denn hin?
Woher kommst du denn?	Wo kommst du denn her?
Wohin ist er denn gegangen?	Wo ist er denn hingegangen?
Woher ist er denn gekommen?	Wo ist er denn hergekommen?
Dahin gehe ich auch.	Da gehe ich auch hin.
Daher komme ich auch.	Da komme ich auch her.

In the following examples, note the difference in meaning between the forms with **hin-** and **her-** and the forms without **hin-** and **her-**.

Die Titanic ist untergegangen.	Ich gehe ins Eßzimmer hinunter.
The Titanic sank.	I'm going down to the dining room.
Die Sonne geht unter.	Er kommt sofort herunter.
The sun sets.	He'll be down in a minute.
Wo seid ihr denn untergekommen?	Ist er schon heruntergekommen?
Where did you find a place to stay?	Has he come down yet?
Das Licht ist ausgegangen.	Er ist gerade hinausgegangen.
The light went out.	He just went out.
Die Sonne geht auf.	Herr Doktor Schmidt ist schon hinaufgegangen.
The sun rises.	Dr. Schmidt has already gone up.
Ich konnte ihn nicht mehr einholen.	Hast du die Zeitung schon hereingeholt?
I couldn't catch up with him any more.	Have you brought the paper in yet?

Mit zweihundert Mark im Monat kann ich   Ich habe ihn noch nicht herauskommen
  nicht auskommen.   sehen.

    I can't get along on two hundred marks   I haven't seen him come out yet.
    a month.

Note the "prepositional brackets" in the following sentences:

Er kam aus dem Haus heraus.
Er ging ins Haus hinein.
Wir fahren durch den Panamakanal hindurch.
Wir stiegen auf den Berg hinauf.
Er sprang über den Zaun hinüber.

[13] Comparative Forms of Adjectives

Be prepared to produce orally the sentences on the right when you hear the
sentences on the left.

SEE
ANALYSIS
170

(pp. 365-368)

Sie ist so alt wie ich.	Sie ist älter als ich.
Hier ist es so kalt wie in Hamburg.	Hier ist es kälter als in Hamburg.
Leider ist sie nicht so jung wie er.	Leider ist er jünger als sie.
Hier ist es nicht so warm wie bei euch.	Bei euch ist es viel wärmer als bei uns.
Die Alpen sind nicht so hoch wie die Sierras.	Die Sierras sind höher als die Alpen.
Ingelheim ist nicht ganz so interessant wie Thomas Mann.	Thomas Mann ist etwas interessanter als Ingelheim.
Du bist doch nicht so groß wie ich.	Doch, ich bin größer als du.
Das Bier hier ist wirklich gut.	Ja, aber das Bier in München ist noch besser.
Tante Dorothea redet genau so viel wie Tante Amalie.	Nee, nee, die redet noch mehr als Tante Amalie, noch viel mehr.
Hier ist das frische Obst nicht so teuer wie bei uns.	Bei uns ist das Obst viel teurer als bei euch.
Inges Haar war schon immer so dunkel wie meins.	Aber seit sie vierzig ist, wird es immer dunkler.
Möchtest du dir gern den Faustfilm ansehen?	Nein, ich ginge viel lieber in einen Wildwestfilm.

Form similar pairs with the following adjectives:

schnell, schneller	hart, härter	oft, öfter
freundlich, freundlicher	kurz, kürzer	stark, stärker
arm, ärmer	lang, länger	nah, näher

[14] Superlative Forms of Adjectives

Read the following sentences and complete the variations:

SEE
ANALYSIS
170

(pp. 365-368)

Die Frau mit dem Flamingo ist sein bester Roman.
Ich halte *Die Frau mit dem Flamingo* für _____.

Monika ist die interessanteste Frau, die ich kenne.
Von allen Frauen, die ich kenne, ist sie die _____.

Im Dezember sind die Tage am kürzesten.
Der 21. Dezember ist der _____ Tag des Jahres.

In dieser Show sehen Sie Giganto, den stärksten Mann der Welt.
Giganto ist von allen Männern der _____.

Was ist Ingelheims bester Roman?
Mir gefällt *Die Frau mit dem Flamingo* am _____.

Hier ist es ja das ganze Jahr sehr schön, aber im Mai ist es hier doch am _____.

Spieglein, Spieglein an der Wand,
Wer ist die Schönste im ganzen Land?
   Frau Königin, Ihr* seid die Schönste hier,
   aber Schneewittchen hinter den Bergen,
   bei den sieben Zwergen,
   ist noch tausendmal schöner als Ihr.

[15] Comparatives and Superlatives: Advertising Slogans

You can find advertisements like these in German magazines.

Sie können natürlich mehr Geld ausgeben, aber es ist nicht sicher, ob Sie einen besseren Waschautomaten bekommen.

Gesünder und darum besser ist ein Cottona-Hemd.

Sie sollten nicht weniger für ihr Geld verlangen.

Sie sollten mehr verlangen: Ein VW ist der beste Kauf.

Cinzano on the rocks: der beste Anfang einer guten Sache.

In der ganzen Welt kennt man den Namen Pall Mall als Garantie für teuerste Tabake. Die Pall Mall Filter ist eine mild-aromatische Blendcigarette im King-Size-Format. 20 Pall Mall Filter kosten DM 1,75.

Was trinken Sie am liebsten, wenn Sie mit Ihrer Frau abends fernsehen? Natürlich Löwenbräu.

Wie gern essen wir ein Steak. Noch lieber ist es uns mit einem Schuß Ketchup. Am liebsten essen wir es aber mit Thomy's Tomaten-Ketchup. Es gehört zu den neun Thomy's Delikatessen.

---

* **Ihr** is an obsolete polite form now replaced by **Sie.**

Statt für jeden etwas, etwas Besonderes für alle: Triumpf, die beste Schreibmaschine.

Jede moderne Frau weiß, wie man sich interessanter macht. Die interessantesten Frauen tragen Elastiform.

[16] The Rhetorical **nicht**

SEE
ANALYSIS
172

(pp. 370-371)

Haben Sie einen *Bru*der?	Do you have a brother?
Haben Sie keinen *Bru*der?	Don't you have a brother?
Haben Sie nicht *ei*nen *Bru*der?	Don't you have a single brother?
Haben Sie nicht einen *Bru*der?	You have a brother, haven't you?

Habe ich nicht einen intelligenten Sohn?

Ist sie nicht ein hübsches Mädchen?

Warst du nicht gestern abend mit Inge im Kino?

Haben Sie nicht früher bei der Hansa-Bank gearbeitet?

Bin ich nicht schon immer dagegen gewesen?

Hat nicht unsere Partei seit Jahren immer wieder bewiesen, daß sie allein den Weg weiß in eine bessere Zukunft?

Change the following statements into rhetorical questions:

Sie haben ihn schon vor dem Krieg kennengelernt, nicht wahr?

Seine Tochter hat den Fritz Müller geheiratet, nicht wahr?

Sie haben schon immer einmal nach Amerika fahren wollen, nicht wahr?

[17] Numbers

Read aloud and observe stress:

SEE
ANALYSIS
173

(pp. 371-373)

100 *hun*dert		100 *ein*hundert	
101 hundert*eins*		200 *zwei*hundert	
102 hundert*zwei*		300 *drei*hundert	
110 hundert*zehn*		900 *neun*hundert	
120 hundert*zwan*zig		1.000 *tau*send	
121 hundert*ein*undzwanzig			
122 hundert*zwei*undzwanzig		7.839 *sie*bentausend*acht*hundert*neun*undd*rei*ßig	
198 hundert*acht*undneunzig		1.000.000 eine Milli*on*	
199 hundert*neun*undneunzig		2.000.000 zwei Milli*o*nen	
200 *zwei*hundert		1.000.000.000 eine Milli*ar*de (one billion)	

Ich brauche zweihundert*ein*undvierzig *Mark*.

In unserer Stadt wohnen jetzt über *drei*hunderttausend *Men*schen.

Unsere Bibliothek hat mehrere Millionen *Mark* gekostet.

„Und Noah lebte nach der Flut *drei*hundertund*fünf*zig Jahre; alle Tage Noahs waren *neun*hundertund*fünf*zig Jahre, und er *starb*.“

0,7   *null* komma *sieben*

0,17 *null* komma *siebzehn* (*null* komma *eins sieben*)

3,14159 *drei* komma *eins vier eins fünf neun*

Read the following numbers:

758   75,8   7,58   2,718282   232.493,00   232,493

DM   4,20 vier Mark zwanzig

DM 121,00 hunderteinundzwanzig Mark

DM 100,21 hundert Mark einundzwanzig

DM   0,75 fünfundsiebzig Pfennig

$1.477,00 vierzehnhundertsiebenundsiebzig Dollar
            eintausendvierhundertsiebenundsiebzig Dollar

$ 18,37 achtzehn Dollar siebenunddreißig

Am ersten und zweiten Februar waren wir in Berlin, am dritten und vierten in Hamburg
und vom fünften bis zum zehnten in Bonn.

Berlin, den 1.2.1970 (den ersten Februar 1970)

Hamburg, 8.9.71 (den achten September 1971)

Read the following dates:

13.1.27   7.7.29   18.6.1962

8.2.25   20.8.54   22.2.1732

25.10.04   1.9.38   7.12.1941

Heinrich I. (Heinrich der Erste)

Friedrich Wilhelm IV. (Friedrich Wilhelm der Vierte)

Er war ein Sohn Friedrichs II. (Er war ein Sohn Friedrichs des Zweiten.)

Read the following:

Leo XIII. (1887–1903) (1887 bis 1903)

Pius X. (1903–1914)

Benedict XV. (1914–1922)

Pius XI. (1922–1939)

Pius XII. (1939–1958)

Johannes XXIII. (1958–1963) (der Dreiundzwanzigste)

Und hier, meine Damen und Herren, sehen Sie ein Bild von Herzog August III., der, wie
Sie wissen, der Vater Sigismunds II. war. Seine Frau Mechthild, eine Tochter Augusts
V. von Niederlohe-Schroffenstein, soll die schönste Frau ihrer Zeit gewesen sein.

Nein, nach Italien fahren will ich nicht. Erstens habe ich kein Geld, zweitens habe ich
keine Lust, drittens mag ich Meyers nicht und viertens: meine Frau ist dagegen.

Nein, soviel kann ich nicht essen. Die Hälfte davon ist mehr als genug.

Hat Tante Amalie schon ihr Testament gemacht?—Ja, und ein Drittel von ihrem Geld
bekommt das Museum.

Seine Frau erhielt zwei Drittel seines Vermögens, und das dritte Drittel ging an seine
beiden Söhne.

Ich hätte gerne ein halbes Pfund Butter.
Geben Sie mir bitte ein viertel Pfund Schinken.

Read aloud:

½   ⅓   ²⁄₇   ⁶⁄₈   ⁵⁄₁₂

[18] Time

SEE
ANALYSIS
174

(p. 373)

11.00 Uhr	elf Uhr	11.35 Uhr	fünf nach halb zwölf
11.05 Uhr	fünf nach elf	11.40 Uhr	zehn nach halb zwölf
11.10 Uhr	zehn nach elf	11.45 Uhr	dreiviertel zwölf; viertel vor zwölf
11.15 Uhr	viertel nach elf; viertel zwölf	11.50 Uhr	zehn vor zwölf
11.20 Uhr	zwanzig nach elf	11.55 Uhr	fünf vor zwölf
11.25 Uhr	fünf vor halb zwölf	12.00 Uhr	zwölf Uhr
11.30 Uhr	halb zwölf		

Read aloud and, where possible, in several ways:

9.05 (Uhr)	4.25 (Uhr)	12.45 (Uhr)
9.15	7.45	1.30
10.30	7.57	21.45

Eisenbahnterminologie

Es ist nicht leicht, einen deutschen Fahrplan zu lesen. Die folgende Tabelle (siehe Seite 480) ist eine Seite aus einem deutschen Kursbuch, und wir wollen versuchen, einen Zug von Frankfurt nach Koblenz zu finden.

Zunächst suchen wir Frankfurt (Zeile 11) und Koblenz (Zeile 23). 5 *Hbf.* steht für Hauptbahnhof. Der erste Zug hat die Nummer D 1269, d.h. es ist ein D-Zug oder Schnellzug, der nur auf größeren Bahnhöfen hält. Dieser Zug kommt um 13.57 Uhr in Koblenz an, aber er fährt nicht über Frankfurt, sondern direkt von Mannheim nach Mainz. Auch der nächste Zug, D 463, aus Basel in der Schweiz, 10 fährt nicht über Frankfurt. Jetzt kommt ein Eilzug (E 721), ab Frankfurt Hbf. um 12.32 Uhr und an Koblenz um 14.27 Uhr. Eilzüge halten öfter als Schnellzüge, aber nur Personenzüge halten auf allen Bahnhöfen. Außerdem gibt es noch F-Züge, d.h. Fernschnellzüge und TEE– (Trans-Europ-Express) Züge. TEE- und 15 F-Züge haben nur 1. Klasse, alle anderen Züge haben 1. und 2. Klasse. Fahrkarten für die 1. Klasse kosten 12 Pf. pro km, für die 2. Klasse 8 Pf./km. Außerdem gibt es Rückfahrkarten mit 10 bis

der Fahrplan, ⸚e timetable
die Tabelle, –n table
das Kursbuch, ⸚er complete book of timetables

die Zeile, –n line
das Haupt, ⸚er head; **Haupt–** (in compounds) main
d.h. = das heißt that is (i.e.)

eilen to hurry

Europ shortened form of **Europa**

AUS DEM FAHRPLAN DER BUNDESBAHN

10 KARLSRUHE und FRANKFURT (Main)—KÖLN—DORTMUND*

		D1269	D463	E721	E590	E297	D203	D1114	D455
1 München Hbf.	ab	....	....	....	....	....	9.00	....	8.42
2 Stuttgart Hbf.	ab	....	....	....	....	....	11.55	....	
3 Basel Bad. Bf.	ab	....	9.18	....	....	....		....	
ZUG NR.		D1269	D463	E721	E590	E297	D203	D1114	D455
4 Karlsruhe Hbf.	ab	11.30	11.36	....	....	....	|	....	von Athen
5 Heidelberg Hbf.		|	|	....	....	....	13.15	....	
6 Mannheim Hbf.		12.06	12.13	....	....	....	13.34	....	
7 Ludwigshafen (Rh.)				....	....	....	13.50	....	
8 Worms Hbf.	ab			....	....	....		....	
9 Nürnberg Hbf.	ab			....	....	....		....	10.59
10 Würzburg Hbf.	ab			10.09	....	....		....	12.10
11 Frankfurt Hbf.	ab			12.32	12.42	13.14		14.00	14.04
12 Rüsselsheim				12.51	13.01	↓		|	
13 Mainz Hbf.	ab	12.53	13.03	13.07	13.17	↓	14.37	14.29	
14 Mainz-Kastel	ab	von Freiburg	↓		von Hof	13.40	↓	an	|
15 Wiesbaden Hbf.						13.55		....	14.42
16 Eltville						14.07		....	|
17 Rüdesheim (Rh.)						14.20		....	15.06
18 Niederlahnstein	ab					15.10		....	Hellas-Express
19 Bingen (Rhein)	ab	13.12		13.30	13.41		↓	....	
20 Bingerbrück		|		13.33	13.43		14.58	....	
21 St. Goar				13.57	an			....	
22 Boppard		13.40		14.10	nach Saarbrücken			....	
23 Koblenz Hbf.		13.57	14.03	14.27			15.40	....	15.57
24 Andernach		|		14.40				....	
25 Remagen		|		14.58				....	|
26 Bad Godesberg		|		15.08				....	
27 Bonn	an	14.35	14.40	15.14			16.17	....	16.34
28 Neuwied	ab					15.29	↓	....	
29 Linz (Rhein)						15.48		....	
30 Königswinter						16.01		....	
31 Beuel					....	16.09		....	
32 Troisdorf					....	16.16		....	
33 KÖLN Hbf.	an	15.00	15.05	15.41	....	16.35	16.40	....	17.00
34 Aachen Hbf.	an	....	....	....	....	....	....	....	....
35 Mönchengladb. Hbf.	an	....	....	....	....	17.38	....	....	....
36 Krefeld Hbf.	an	....	....	....	....	....	....	....	....
ZUG NR.					E441			E315	
37 Köln Hbf.	ab	15.05	15.10	15.47	16.13	....	16.45	16.48	17.10
38 Solingen-Ohligs	an	15.23	|		16.38			17.15	
39 Wuppertal-Elberf.	an	15.38			16.55			17.32	
40 Hagen	an	16.03			17.20			18.03	
41 Münster (Westf.)	ab	....			....			....	

* Abbreviations
Hbf.—Hauptbahnhof
Bf.—Bahnhof
Bad. Bf.—Badischer Bahnhof
Nr.—Nummer
Rh.—am Rhein

St. Goar—Sankt Goar
Mönchengladb.—Mönchengladbach
Elberf.—Elberfeld
Westf.—Westfalen

40% (Prozent) Ermäßigung. In F-Zügen und D-Zügen bezahlt man zum Fahrpreis noch einen besonderen Zuschlag von 2 bis 4 Mark.

die Ermäßigung, –en reduction, reduced price
der Zuschlag, ⸚e surcharge

Zurück zum Fahrplan: Die nächsten beiden Züge sind wieder Eilzüge (E 590 und E 297), aber der erste fährt von Bingerbrück aus nach Saarbrücken, der zweite fährt rechtsrheinisch, d.h. auf der [5] östlichen Seite des Rheins, und Koblenz liegt auf der westlichen Rheinseite, wo die Mosel in den Rhein mündet. Der D 203 (von München nach Dortmund) fährt nicht über Frankfurt, aber der D 1114, ab Frankfurt um 14 Uhr, hat in Mainz Anschluß an diesen Zug. Allerdings muß man dabei umsteigen und hat zwischen den [10] beiden Zügen nur acht Minuten Zeit.

münden to flow into

der Anschluß, ⸚e connection
umsteigen to change (trains)

Der letzte Zug auf unserem Fahrplan ist die beste Verbindung von Frankfurt nach Koblenz und auch der interessanteste Zug. Es ist der Hellas-Expreß, und er kommt aus Athen.

die Verbindung, –en connection

Hellas Greece

Fahrkarten bekommt man am Fahrkartenschalter. Man sagt: „Eine [15] Fahrkarte erster Klasse nach Koblenz", oder als alter Eisenbahnfahrer: „Einmal erster Koblenz."

„Einfach oder hin und zurück?"

einfach (here) one way
hin und zurück round trip

„Einfach, bitte. Und einen D-Zug-Zuschlag."

„So, mein Herr, das macht 17,88 und 2 Mark für den Zuschlag: 19 [20] Mark 88, bitte."

In Deutschland kann man nicht ohne Fahrkarte auf den Bahnsteig, sondern man muß zuerst durch die Sperre, wo ein Eisenbahnbeamter die Fahrkarte locht. Der Zug soll um 13.47 auf Gleis 12 ankommen, aber kurz vorher hört man über den Lautsprecher: „Der Schnellzug [25] aus München, planmäßige Ankunft 13.47 Uhr, hat voraussichtlich 30 Minuten Verspätung." Aber es dauert etwas länger als eine halbe Stunde, und um halb drei heißt es endlich: „Der verspätete Schnellzug aus München läuft soeben auf Gleis 12 ein. Bitte von der Bahnsteigkante zurücktreten." Der Zug ist nicht stark besetzt, und es ist [30] leicht, in einem Nichtraucherabteil erster Klasse einen Fensterplatz zu bekommen. Der Zug hat eine elektrische Lokomotive; in großen Teilen Deutschlands ist die Eisenbahn elektrifiziert, aber man sieht auch Diesellokomotiven und noch Dampflokomotiven. Der Zug hat

der Bahnsteig, – platform
die Sperre, –n gate
das Gleis, –e track
planmäßig scheduled, according to plan
voraussichtlich probably
Verspätung haben to be late (not on schedule)
heißt es it is announced
die Kante, –n the edge
das Abteil, –e compartment
der Dampf steam

Nicht öffnen, bevor der Zug hält   Zu   Offen

Wagen erster und zweiter Klasse; in jedem Wagen gibt es zwölf   je (here) each, apiece
Abteile mit je sechs Sitzplätzen. In den meisten D-Zügen kann man
sich einen Platz reservieren lassen. Außerdem hat der Zug einen
Postwagen, einen Gepäckwagen und einen Speisewagen, aber keinen   das Gepäck baggage
Schlafwagen, denn er kommt schon um 19.06 in Dortmund an, fährt 5   speisen to dine
also nicht mehr über Nacht.

Sections IV–VII of *Ein Mann kommt nach San Franzisko* appear after Unit 13
but may be read in conjunction with this unit.

ANALYSIS

166   The Position of Dependent Infinitives

The two German sentences

> **Er brauchte sie heute nicht anzurufen.**
> (He did not have to call her up today.)
> **Er versprach, sie heute nicht anzurufen.**
> (He promised not to call her up today.)

seem to have the same structure. But they don't. After **brauchte,** there is
no pause. But after **versprach,** the speaker stops for a split second before
he goes on to **sie heute nicht anzurufen.** The pause creates the impression
that the infinitive phrase which follows is something like a dependent
clause—an "infinitive clause." If the two sentences above are changed
from the past tense to the perfect, the second one shows a syntactical pattern which we have tried to avoid until now.

This diagram shows: The infinitive depending on **brauchen** stands in the
first box of the second prong, but if this same infinitive depends on **versprechen** it stands in the end field, together with the syntactical units that
belong to it.

The difference between the old pattern and the new one is just as striking if we change from verb-second to verb-last position:

weil ich		sie nicht	**anzurufen**	**brauchte**	
FRONT FIELD	1st Prong	INNER FIELD	2nd Prong	verb-last slot	END FIELD
als ich		(ihr gestern)		**versprach**	, sie nicht anzurufen.

The diagram shows again: The infinitive depending on **versprechen** stands in the end field. *This end field cannot be started until the preceding clause has been completed.*

In the following paragraphs we shall discuss which infinitives belong in the second prong and which belong in the end field.

167 Second-Prong Infinitives

The most important group of verbs which are used together with an infinitive in the second prong are the modals and **brauchen**. Though **brauchen** has a dependent infinitive with **zu**, it behaves like the modals: the participle following the infinitive is **brauchen**, not **gebraucht**:

> Ich habe sie heute noch nicht anrufen können.
> Ich habe sie heute nicht anzurufen brauchen.

However, the modals and **brauchen** are not the only verbs which are used with a second-prong infinitive. There are others of which some govern an infinitive with **zu**, and some an infinitive without **zu**.

Second-Prong Infinitives without **zu**

LERNEN

The infinitives depending on **lernen** all take the second-prong position of **kennen** in **kennenlernen**, but only **kennenlernen** is spelled as one word:

lesen lernen	gehen lernen
schreiben lernen	fahren lernen
kochen lernen	Auto fahren lernen

Sie lernt jetzt fahren.	, weil sie jetzt fahren lernt.
Sie hat schon kochen gelernt.	, weil sie schon kochen gelernt hat.
Ich habe sie schon kennengelernt.	, weil ich sie schon kennengelernt habe.

NOTE: Though **lernen** is used with an infinitive without **zu**, it does not behave like a modal. If it did, **kochen gelernt hat** in the example above would have to be replaced by [**hat kochen lernen**].

BLEIBEN

The infinitives used most frequently with **bleiben** are **liegen, stehen,** and **sitzen.** As long as **liegen** means literally *lying,* **sitzen** *sitting,* and **stehen** *standing,* they are written separately.

Dieser Baum hier kann stehen bleiben.	This tree can stay here.
Du brauchst noch nicht aufzustehen, du kannst noch etwas liegen bleiben.	You don't have to get up yet; you can stay in bed for a while.
In Deutschland dürfen die Herren sitzen bleiben, wenn die Hausfrau aus dem Wohnzimmer in die Küche geht.	In Germany, the gentlemen may stay seated if the lady of the house goes from the livingroom to the kitchen.

Usually, however, these combinations are used with non-literal meanings and are spelled as one word. **Stehenbleiben** then means *to stop,* **liegenbleiben** means *to be left behind (forgotten),* and **sitzenbleiben** means *not to find a husband* or *not to be promoted into the next higher class in school.*

Der Hut ist gestern abend hier liegengeblieben.
Meine Uhr ist gestern abend stehengeblieben.
Kein Mädchen möchte gerne sitzenbleiben.
Fritz ist schon wieder sitzengeblieben.

GEHEN AND FAHREN

German **gehen** is frequently used with an infinitive which denotes some routine activity like **essen, schlafen, baden, schilaufen,** and others.

Wir gehen jetzt essen.
Wir wollen morgen schwimmen gehen.
Wir gehen jetzt schlafen.
Er ist schon schlafen gegangen.
Wir wollen morgen schilaufen gehen.

The verb **spazieren** can mean *to promenade.* Today it is mostly used in **spazierenfahren** (*to go for a ride*) and in **spazierengehen** (*to go for a walk*):

Wir sind gestern spazierengefahren.
Wir sind gestern spazierengegangen.
Warum gehen wir nicht etwas spazieren?

Observe again that **gehen** and **fahren** do not behave like modals. If they did, **gegangen** and **gefahren** in the above examples would have to be replaced by **gehen** and **fahren.**

HÖREN AND SEHEN

In the English sentence *I heard him come, him* is the object of the governing verb *heard* and at the same time the subject of the infinitive *come.* The corresponding German sentence **Ich hörte ihn kommen** shows the same relation: the **ihn** is at the same time the object of **hörte** and the subject of **kommen.** In both languages, the dependent infinitive is used without *to* or **zu.**

When used in this pattern, **hören** and **sehen** do behave like modals: their past participles are **sehen** and **hören,** not **gesehen** and **gehört.**

> **Ich habe ihn nie nach Hause kommen hören.**
> **Ich habe ihn kommen sehen.**
> **Das habe ich kommen sehen.**

LASSEN

The verb **lassen** is one of the most frequently used German verbs. It occurs with two different basic meanings: (1) *to leave* and (2) *to cause* or *to permit.*

1. **lassen** *to leave* (*behind*)

> **Ich habe meinen Mantel zu Hause gelassen.**
> **Ich hätte meinen Mantel nicht zu Hause lassen sollen.**

In combination with **hängen, liegen, stehen** (used like **kennen** in **kennenlernen**), **lassen** also means *to leave.* In this case the participle is either **lassen** or **gelassen,** but we advise you to use only **lassen.**

> **Ich habe meinen Mantel zu Hause hängenlassen.**
> **Ich habe mein Buch zu Hause liegenlassen.**
> **Ich habe meinen Schirm** (umbrella) **zu Hause stehenlassen.**

2. **lassen** *to cause* or *to permit*

When used (like **hören** and **sehen**) with a subject-infinitive construction, **lassen** means "to cause—*either* by permission *or* by request—somebody to do something."

> **Wir ließen ihn kommen.**
> We let (or had) him come.

When it means *to cause* or *to permit,* **lassen** behaves like a modal, that is, the participle is **lassen,** not **gelassen.**

>**Wir haben ihn kommen lassen.**
>We permitted (asked) him to come.

Compare also:

>**Ich lasse meinen Mann nicht allein nach Kairo fahren.**
>**Vater hat mich gestern abend nicht ins Kino gehen lassen.**
>**Meyers haben gestern den Arzt kommen lassen müssen.**

By *suppressing the subject* of the subject-infinitive construction, German arrives at a pattern which cannot be imitated in English:

>**Ich ließ mir eine Tasse Kaffee aufs Zimmer bringen.**
>I asked (somebody) to bring me a cup of coffee to my room.
>I had a cup of coffee brought to my room.

>**Ich ließ mir die Haare schneiden.**
>I asked (somebody) to give me a haircut.
>I had my hair cut.

>**Wir haben uns ein Haus bauen lassen.**
>We asked (somebody) to build a house for us.
>We had a house built.

The subject of the infinitive can also be expressed by **von** plus noun or pronoun. Again the result is a construction not possible in English:

>**Wir lassen uns von Meyer ein Haus bauen.**
>We're letting Meyer build our house.
>We are having our house built by Meyer.

If the **Ich** in

>**Ich habe mir das Frühstück aufs Zimmer bringen lassen**

is replaced by **er,** two different sentences are possible, both of which correspond to the ambiguous English sentence

>He had his breakfast brought up to his room.
>**Er hat ihm das Frühstück aufs Zimmer bringen lassen.**
>**Er hat sich das Frühstück aufs Zimmer bringen lassen.**

In the first sentence, **er** and **ihm** must be two different people (Jack had Joe's breakfast taken to Joe's room); in the second sentence, **er** and **sich** must be the same person (He had his own breakfast brought to his own room).

Second-Prong Infinitives with **zu**

SCHEINEN

The verb **scheinen,** when meaning *to seem,* is used, like **brauchen,** with a second-prong infinitive. It behaves like a subjective modal and occurs only in the present and in the past.

> **Er scheint zu schlafen.**
> **Er schien nicht gut geschlafen zu haben.**

HABEN

The verb **haben** must be mentioned in this context because it is frequently followed by an infinitive with **zu** which *looks* like a second-prong infinitive. Actually, these infinitives usually follow **etwas, nichts, viel,** and **wenig** and form one single syntactical unit with these words:

etwas zu tun	etwas zu essen
nichts zu tun	nichts zu essen
viel zu tun	viel zu essen
wenig zu tun	wenig zu essen

> **Wenn ich nur nicht soviel zu tun hätte!**
> **Gestern hatten wir kaum etwas zu tun.**
> **Hast du etwas zu trinken im Hause?**

This same construction is frequently found after verbs like **mitbringen** and **kaufen.**

> **Kannst du mir etwas zu lesen mitbringen?**
> **Kannst du mir etwas zu lesen kaufen?**

SEIN

The verb **sein** can be used with a second-prong infinitive provided that the subject of **sein** is the same as the object of the infinitive. English uses this construction in sentences like

> He was easy to find.
> **Er war leicht zu finden.**

The English use of the passive infinitive after *to be* cannot be imitated in German:

> He was not to be found.
> **Er war nicht zu finden.**

168 End-Field Infinitives

As can be seen from the following examples, the word order of the elements (objects, time phrases, place phrases, etc.) belonging to an end-field infinitive is the same as that found in the inner field preceding a second-prong infinitive.

Ich brauche ihn heute nicht anzurufen.

Ich habe versprochen, ihn heute nicht anzurufen.

All elements in the main clause preceding the infinitive clause take their usual position:

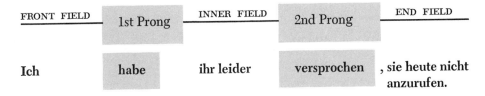

FRONT FIELD	1st Prong	INNER FIELD	2nd Prong	END FIELD
Ich	habe	ihr leider	versprochen	, sie heute nicht anzurufen.

As long as only the infinitive with **zu** occupies the end field, it is not separated by a comma.

> **Es fing an zu regnen.**

In all other cases, a comma is necessary, not only to indicate the pause which separates such infinitive clauses from the preceding part of the sentence, but also to avoid ambiguity.

> **Er behauptet schon wieder, in Paris gewesen zu sein.**
> **Er behauptet, schon wieder in Paris gewesen zu sein.**

The Group **anfangen**

The following verbs are frequently used with end-field infinitives:

anfangen	to begin
aufhören	to stop, cease
behaupten	to claim
es langweilig (dumm, etc.) finden	to find boring (stupid, etc.)
hoffen	to hope
vergessen	to forget
versprechen	to promise
versuchen	to try
es wagen	to dare

The Group **befehlen**

In the sentence

> **Ich habe ihr gestern versprochen, sie heute anzurufen**

the subject of **versprechen** is the same as the subject of the end-field infinitive.

The verbs

befehlen	to give an order to somebody
empfehlen	to make a recommendation to somebody
erlauben	to give permission to somebody
gestatten	to permit (social term)
helfen	to give help to someone in doing something
raten	to give somebody the advice
verbieten	to forbid someone to do something
vorschlagen	to make a suggestion to somebody

all take a personal *dative* object which is the same as the subject of the infinitive clause that follows it.

Mein Arzt riet mir, einmal an die See zu fahren.
Darf ich Ihnen vorschlagen, einmal einen Mosel zu versuchen?

The End-Field Infinitive after Predicate Adjectives

The following predicate adjectives are frequently used with end-field infinitives:

bereit	ready	froh	glad
erstaunt	astonished	schön	nice
glücklich	happy	nett	nice

Sie wissen doch, daß ich immer bereit gewesen bin, Ihrem Mann zu helfen.
Warum sind Sie denn so erstaunt, mich hier zu sehen?
Inge war froh, ihren Mann endlich wiedersehen zu dürfen.

Replacement of Prepositional Objects

Verbs which take a prepositional object frequently replace this complement with a **da**-compound which anticipates an infinitive phrase in the end field. (See **132.**)

Ich denke ja gar nicht daran,
Du weißt doch, daß ich gar nicht daran denke,
Ich habe ja nie daran gedacht,
Du weißt doch, daß ich nie daran gedacht habe, } **den Meyer zu heiraten.**

um . . . zu, ohne . . . zu, statt . . . zu

We have already used infinitives with **um . . . zu** in the end-field position. The same construction is possible with **ohne . . . zu** and **statt (anstatt) . . . zu.** All of these infinitives appear most frequently in either end-field or front-field position.

Er fuhr nach Afrika, um dort einen Roman zu schreiben.
Er fuhr nach München, ohne seine Frau mitzunehmen.
Er fuhr nach Afrika, statt zu Hause zu bleiben.

English uses an infinitive as the equivalent of the **um . . . zu** forms (*in order to write a novel*), but for the **ohne . . . zu** and **statt . . . zu** forms, English must use the gerund (*without taking his wife along; instead of staying at home*).

In the above examples, the subject of the infinitive clause is the same as the subject of the main clause. If there is a different subject, the infinitive constructions must be replaced by dependent clauses:

um . . . zu	damit
ohne . . . zu	ohne daß
statt . . . zu	statt daß

Wir bleiben zu Hause, um endlich einmal arbeiten zu können.
Wir bleiben zu Hause, damit mein Mann endlich einmal arbeiten kann.

169 hin and her

Hin and **her** are both directional adverbs denoting motion. **Hin** indicates motion away from the speaker or the speaker's position, **her** refers to motion toward the speaker.

hin and her as Verbal Complements

Hin and **her** can both be used by themselves as complements of certain verbs denoting various methods of traveling or change of location.

Thus a person told to visit his father immediately might say:

Ich fahre (gehe, reise) sofort hin.

or he might say:

Ich werde sofort hinfahren.
Ich bin sofort hingefahren.
Ich brauche nicht sofort hinzufahren.
Ich weiß nicht, ob ich sofort hinfahren kann.

The father might say:

Mein Sohn ist sofort hergekommen.
Kannst du sofort herkommen?

hin and her with Adverbs of Place and of Time

Since **hin** implies no specific goal and since **her** implies no specific point of origin, they are frequently found after **da, dort, hier,** and after prepositional phrases expressing goal or origin.

Wer hat dich denn hierhergebracht?
Du willst sofort zum Flughafen? Wer bringt dich denn dahin?

Im nächsten Dorf gibt es ein Hotel? Wie weit ist es denn bis dahin?—Zehn Kilometer. Wir kommen gerade daher. (dorther, von dorther)

Her may also be used with a temporal meaning.

Das ist ein alter Freund von mir. Den kenne ich noch *von der Schule her.* Den kenne ich noch *von früher her.*

Gestern abend waren wir im Theater. *Vor*her haben wir im Regina gegessen, und *nach*her waren wir bei Schmidts.

Hin may be used as a predicate adjective meaning *gone* or *beyond repair.* Alles ist hin.

Vorhin is an adverb of time meaning *just a little while ago.* Vorhin hat Rosemarie angerufen.

hin and her Following wo

In many cases, the use of **her** and **hin** stems from the "splitting" of **wohin** and **woher.**

Wohin *gehst* du denn?
Wo gehst du denn *hin?*
Wo willst du denn *hin?*
Wo ist er denn *hin*gegangen?
Wo *du* hingehst, da will ich *auch* hin.

Woher *kom*men Sie denn?
Wo kommen *Sie* denn her?
Wo kann *der* denn hergekommen sein?
Wo hast du denn den neuen *Man*tel her?

The unseparated **wohin** and **woher** are today slightly literary in character. They *may* be used in conversation, but the separated forms are heard much more frequently.

hin and her Preceding Another Verbal Prefix

Certain English compound verbs have developed special meanings which are apt to trap a foreigner. It is, for instance, a surprise to a German-speaking person to find out that *he threw in the towel* cannot always be replaced by *he threw the towel in.*

In German, the verbal prefixes **ein-, unter-, auf-,** and **aus-,** if used without **hin-** or **her-,** are apt to develop nonliteral meanings. To express a strictly *spatial* meaning **hinein-** or **herein-, hinunter-** or **herunter-, hinauf-** or **herauf-, hinaus-** or **heraus-** must be used.

For example, **untergehen** may mean not only *to sink,* but also *to come to* *an end, to vanish, to perish.* Note the difference between

> **Die Inkakultur ging unter.**   The Inca civilization vanished.

and

> **Er ist schon hinuntergegangen.**   He has already gone down.

Compare also:

> **Das Licht ging aus.**   The light went out.
> **Wir sind ausgegangen.**   We went out.
> **Wir sind hinausgegangen.**   We went out (of a room).

There are no definite rules governing the use of **hin-** and **her-** in these cases, but in general it can be said that verbs with **hin** and **her** in the complement have a strictly spatial meaning, whereas verbs with the simple complements **ein-, unter-, auf-,** and **aus-** tend to have figurative meanings:

> **Kommst du mit dem Geld aus?**
> Can you get along with the money you have?
>
> **Er kam heraus.**
> He came out (of a room).
>
> **Ich konnte mit meinem VW den Mercedes nicht einholen.**
> With my VW I could not catch up with the Mercedes.
>
> **Hast du die Zeitung schon hereingeholt?**
> Have you brought the paper in yet?
>
> **Die Sonne ging auf.**
> The sun rose.
>
> **Wollen Sie bitte in den zweiten Stock hinaufgehen?**
> Would you please go up to the third floor?
>
> **Wir haben Sie im Hotel Zeppelin untergebracht.**
> We've put you up at the Hotel Zeppelin.
>
> **Ihre Koffer habe ich schon hinunterbringen lassen.**
> I've already had your suitcases brought down.

hin and **her** in "Prepositional Brackets"

The sentence

> **Wir fuhren durch den Panamakanal**

expresses the idea

> We went through the Panama Canal.

In order to strengthen the feeling of spatial motion, the preposition **durch** can be reinforced by adding the verbal complement **hindurch.**

> **Wir fuhren *durch* den Panamakanal *hindurch*.**

This **durch . . . hindurch** acts as a prepositional bracket enclosing the noun. Other frequently used brackets are:

Er kam *aus* **dem Haus** *heraus.*
Er ging *in* **das Haus** *hinein.*
Er stieg *auf* **den Turm** [tower] *hinauf.*

Frequently **her,** without a preposition, forms the second bracket; it then expresses continuous motion.

Er lief hinter mir her.
Er lief neben mir her.
Er lief vor mir her.

This tendency to "bracket" is so strong in German that it is found even in such syntactical units as **von Berlin aus,** *from Berlin;* **von da an,** *from then on;* **von mir aus,** *as far as I'm concerned.*

170 Comparison of Adjectives and Adverbs

Forms of the Comparative and the Superlative

Both German adjectives and adverbs form their comparative and superlative forms by adding **-er** and **-(e)st** to the stem, parallel to the English pattern in *fast, fast-er, fast-est:*

schnell, schneller, schnellst-

The English patterns *interesting, more interesting, most interesting,* and *quickly, more quickly, most quickly* are not possible in German:

interessant, interessanter, interessantest-

The **-e-** in the superlative forms is added whenever the **-st-** ending alone would be hard to pronounce—for example, **weitest-, ältest-, kürzest-.** An exception is the superlative form of **groß:**

groß, größer, größt-

Many monosyllabic adjectives add an umlaut in both the comparative and superlative:

alt, älter, ältest-	old
arm, ärmer, ärmst-	poor
hart, härter, härtest-	hard
jung, jünger, jüngst-	young
kalt, kälter, kältest-	cold
kurz, kürzer, kürzest-	short
lang, länger, längst-	long
oft, öfter, öftest-	often
schwarz, schwärzer, schwärzest-	black
stark, stärker, stärkst-	strong

Adjectives ending in **-el** and **-er** lose the **-e-** in the comparative:

dunkel, dunkler, dunkelst-
teuer, teurer, teuerst-

The adjective **hoch** loses the **-c-** in the comparative:

hoch, höher, höchst-,

and the adjective **nah** adds a **-c-** in the superlative:

nah, näher, nächst-;

gut and **viel** have irregular forms:

gut, besser, best-
viel, mehr, meist-,

and the adverb **gern,** which has no comparative and superlative forms of its own, substitutes the forms of the adjective **lieb:**

gern, lieber, liebst-.

Superlatives cannot be used without an ending; therefore the superlative forms above are followed by hyphens.

Use of Comparison

In comparisons implying equality, **so . . . wie** is used:

> **Er ist so alt wie ich.**
> **Er ist nicht so alt wie ich.**
> **Er ist so schnell gekommen, wie er nur kommen konnte.**

If the comparison expresses inequality, the comparative form of the adjective is used, followed by **als**:

> **Er ist älter als ich.**
> **Er kann nicht älter sein als ich.**
> **Er ist älter, als ich dachte.**

As *attributive adjectives,* comparative and superlative forms are treated like any other adjective; that is, they add normal adjective endings to the **-er** and **-st** suffixes:

> **Einen interessanteren Roman habe ich nie gelesen.**
> **Ein interessanteres Buch habe ich nie gelesen.**
> **Heute ist der längste Tag des Jahres.**

As *adverbs,* comparative forms do not take an ending, and superlative forms always use the pattern **am** (adjective) **-sten.**

> **Mit deinem Mercedes kommen wir bestimmt schneller nach München als mit meinem VW-Bus.**
> **Können Sie mir sagen, wie ich am schnellsten zum Flugplatz komme?**
> **Da nehmen Sie am besten ein Taxi.**

As *predicate adjectives,* comparative forms do not take an ending. Superlatives use attributive forms preceded by an article if a noun can be supplied; otherwise they follow the **am** (adjective) **-sten** pattern.

> **Meyers finde ich ja ganz nett, aber Schmidts sind doch netter.**
> **Von seinen drei Töchtern ist Ingrid zwar die intelligenteste, aber nicht die schönste (Tochter).**
> **Ich reise ja sehr gerne, aber zu Hause ist es doch am schönsten.**

Some Special Forms

1. A few comparatives are used with reference to their opposites. For example,

> **Wir haben längere Zeit in Berlin gewohnt**

means: we did not live there a long time, but longer than a short time. Similarly, **eine ältere Dame** (an elderly lady) does not mean that the lady is old, but that she is no longer young.

2. To express a high degree of a certain quality, German can use **höchst** as the equivalent of English *most*. Observe the degrees:

Das war ganz interessant.	(quite *interesting*)
Das war interessant.	(*interesting*)
Das war sehr interessant.	(*very* interesting)
Das war aber höchst interessant.	(*most* interesting)

3. Where English repeats the comparative to indicate an increase in degree, German uses **immer** with the comparative:

It was getting warmer and warmer.

Es wurde immer wärmer.

171   Nouns Derived from Adjectives

German, like English, has a number of suffixes which can be used to derive nouns from adjectives.

The Suffix -e

A number of adjectives may be changed into feminine nouns by adding the suffix **-e** and by umlauting when possible. These nouns correspond in meaning to English nouns in *-th* (*strong, strength; long, length*), *-ness* (*weak, weakness; great, greatness*), or *-ty* (*brief, brevity*).

breit	**die Breite**	breadth
frisch	**die Frische**	freshness
früh	**die Frühe**	morning
groß	**die Größe**	greatness; size
gut	**die Güte**	goodness, good quality
hart	**die Härte**	hardness
heiß	**die Hitze**	heat
hoch	**die Höhe**	height
kalt	**die Kälte**	cold(ness) *
kurz	**die Kürze**	shortness, brevity
lang	**die Länge**	length
nah	**die Nähe**	nearness, proximity
rot	**die Röte**	redness
schwach	**die Schwäche**	weakness
stark	**die Stärke**	strength
still	**die Stille**	peacefulness, calm, quiet
warm	**die Wärme**	warmth

* But *cold* in the medical sense: **die Erkältung.**

The Suffixes **-heit, -keit, -igkeit**

Many feminine abstract nouns corresponding to English derivatives in
-th, -ity, and *-ness* can be formed by adding one of these three suffixes;
they form their plurals in **-en.** Feel free to use the nouns listed, but do
not try to invent your own: they may not exist. Of high frequency are
the formations in **-keit** added to derivatives in **-bar, -ig,** and **-lich,** and
formations in **-igkeit** added to **-los.**

	dunkel	die Dunkelheit	darkness
	frei	die Freiheit	freedom
	gesund	die Gesundheit	health
	krank	die Krankheit	sickness
	möglich	die Möglichkeit	possibility
	müde	die Müdigkeit	tiredness
	neu	die Neuheit	newness, novelty
		die Neuigkeit	news
	richtig	die Richtigkeit	correctness
	schön	die Schönheit	beauty
	sicher	die Sicherheit	security
	vergangen	die Vergangenheit	past
	wahr	die Wahrheit	truth
	wahrscheinlich	die Wahrscheinlichkeit	probability
	wichtig	die Wichtigkeit	importance
	wirklich	die Wirklichkeit	reality
	zufrieden	die Zufriedenheit	contentment
	unfähig	die Unfähigkeit	inability
	unzufrieden	die Unzufriedenheit	discontent
	unsicher	die Unsicherheit	insecurity
der Freund, –e	freundlich	die Freundlichkeit	friendliness
der Hof, ̈-e	höflich	die Höflichkeit	politeness
der Mensch, –en	menschlich	die Menschlichkeit	humaneness
		die Menschheit	mankind, humanity
die Sache, –n (thing, fact, cause)	sachlich (objective)	die Sachlichkeit	objectivity, matter-of-factness
sterben	sterblich	die Sterblichkeit	mortality
	unsterblich	die Unsterblichkeit	immortality
die Hoffnung	hoffnungslos	die Hoffnungslosigkeit	hopelessness
der Schlaf	schlaflos	die Schlaflosigkeit	sleeplessness, insomnia
der Dank	dankbar	die Dankbarkeit	gratitude
halten (to last, to hold up)	haltbar (durable)	die Haltbarkeit	durability

teilen	teilbar	die Teilbarkeit	divisibility
(to divide)	(divisible)		
	unteilbar	die Unteilbarkeit	indivisibility
	(indivisible)		

Note the following special cases:

die Kindheit	childhood
die Gottheit	deity
die Flüssigkeit	liquid
die Seltenheit	rarity

die Einheit	unit, unity
die Einigkeit	accord, being of one mind, unity
einig	in agreement, in accord
vereinigt	united
die Vereinigten Staaten	the United States
die Wiedervereinigung	the reunification
einsam	lonely
die Einsamkeit	loneliness, solitude
einzeln	single (apart from the rest)
die Einzelheit	detail
einzig	single, unique, sole
einfach	simple
die Einfachheit	simplicity

172   The Rhetorical **nicht**

If a speaker asks for a positive confirmation of a statement he makes, he adds *don't you?, aren't you?, haven't you?* etc., in English and **nicht?** or **nicht wahr?** in German.

> **Du warst doch gestern abend mit Inge im Kino, nicht?**
> You and Inge were at the movies last night, weren't you?

This rhetorical **nicht** can be moved into the inner field (between items of news value and items of no news value) if the statement is transformed into a rhetorical question. The normal question

> **Warst du gestern abend mit Inge im Kino?**

thus becomes the rhetorical

> **Warst du nicht gestern abend mit Inge im Kino?**

This rhetorical **nicht** appears only in yes-or-no questions. It is never stressed; it is always followed by the stress point of the sentence; and if followed by **ein,** it cannot be replaced by **kein.** An affirmative answer to such rhetorical questions can be either **Ja** or **Doch.** However, even though the speaker always expects a confirmation, the answer can, of course, also be **Nein.**

Haben Sie nicht einen Bruder?   You have a brother, don't you?
Answer: *Ja, Doch,* or *Nein.*

Haben Sie keinen Bruder?   Don't you *have* a brother?
Answer: *Doch* or *Nein,* but never *Ja.*

Haben Sie einen Bruder?   Do you have a brother?
Answer: *Ja* or *Nein,* but never *Doch.*

Further examples:

Warum hast du denn den *Mey*er nicht besucht?
(Real question; stress point precedes *nicht.*)

Hast du den Meyer letzte Woche *nicht* besucht?
(Real question; *nicht* is stressed.)

Hast du nicht letzte Woche den *Mey*er besucht?
(Rhetorical question; stress point follows unstressed *nicht.*)

173 Numbers over 100—Decimals—Ordinal Numbers—Fractions

100	**hundert** (**einhundert**)
101	**hunderteins**
102	**hundertzwei**
110	**hundertzehn**
121	**hunderteinundzwanzig**
200	**zweihundert**
600	**sechshundert**
1.000	**tausend** (**eintausend**)
7.625	**siebentausendsechshundertfünfundzwanzig**
1.000.000	**eine Million**
2.000.000	**zwei Millionen**
1.000.000.000	**eine Milliarde** (one billion)

Note that German uses periods where English uses commas: 2.325.641. Conversely, in *decimal numbers,* German uses commas where English uses periods.

0,3	**null komma drei**
12,17	**zwölf komma siebzehn**
6,5342	**sechs komma fünf drei vier zwei**

German *ordinal numbers* are attributive adjectives:

der erste
der zweite

der *dritte*
der vierte
der fünfte
der sechste
der siebte
etc.
der neunzehnte
der zwanzig*ste*
der einundzwanzig*ste*
der dreißig*ste*
etc.

To make a figure indicate an ordinal number, German uses a period.

der 4. Juli
the Fourth of July

NOTE:

Heinrich I. (Heinrich der Erste)
Friedrich Wilhelm IV. (Friedrich Wilhelm der Vierte)
Er war ein Sohn Friedrichs II. (Friedrichs des Zweiten)

Series are expressed as follows:

1. erstens
2. zweitens
3. drittens
4. viertens
5. fünftens
6. sechstens
7. siebtens
etc.
„Erstens bin ich zu alt, und zweitens bin ich zu müde.“

Fractions:

die Hälfte, –n
das Drittel, –
das Viertel, –
das Fünftel, –
das Sechstel, –
das Siebtel, –
etc.

halb can be inflected:

Ich hätte gerne ein halbes Pfund Butter.

All other fractions are uninflected:

Ich hätte gerne ein viertel Pfund Butter.

½	**ein halb**
⅓	**ein drittel**
¾	**drei viertel**
⅞	**sieben achtel**

174 Time

In *colloquial* German, the following terms are used to tell time.

8.00 Uhr	acht Uhr
8.05 Uhr	fünf nach acht
8.10 Uhr	zehn nach acht
8.15 Uhr	viertel nach acht
8.20 Uhr	zwanzig nach acht
8.25 Uhr	fünf vor halb neun
8.30 Uhr	halb neun
8.35 Uhr	fünf nach halb neun
8.40 Uhr	zehn nach halb neun
8.45 Uhr	dreiviertel neun, viertel vor neun
8.50 Uhr	zehn vor neun
8.55 Uhr	fünf vor neun

In a railway station or an airport, the following pattern is used:

0.10 Uhr	null Uhr zehn (12:10 A.M.)
8.05 Uhr	acht Uhr fünf (8:05 A.M.)
20.05 Uhr	zwanzig Uhr fünf (8:05 P.M.)
24.00 Uhr	vierundzwanzig Uhr (midnight)

EXERCISES

A. Express in German. All German sentences must contain a form of **lassen.**

1. That leaves me cold.
2. Why didn't you leave your books at home?
3. I don't want to let him take me home. (Use reflexive pronoun plus *von ihm.*)
4. He has his letters written by his wife. (Use reflexive pronoun plus *von seiner Frau.*)
5. You shouldn't let him go to Africa.
6. I must get myself a haircut.
7. Why don't you have your hair cut?
8. He went downtown to get a haircut.
9. She has left her coat here again.

10. You should leave her in peace.
11. We are having a house built in Cologne. (Use reflexive pronoun.)
12. We want to have Overbeck build us a house. (Use reflexive pronoun plus *von Overbeck.*)
13. I wish we had had Overbeck build us a house. (Use reflexive pronoun plus *von Overbeck.*)

B. Restate the following sentences in the perfect.

1. Ich blieb oft vor Alis Haus stehen.
2. Er riet mir, an die Nordsee zu fahren.
3. Wir ließen gestern abend den Arzt kommen.
4. Er braucht *doch* nicht nach Berlin zu fahren.
5. Wir dachten damals daran, nach Köln zu ziehen.
6. Um sechs Uhr gingen wir essen.
7. Der Müller war einfach nicht zu verstehen.
8. Gegen Abend fing es dann an zu regnen.
9. Er lief aus dem Haus, ohne ein Wort zu sagen.

C. Transform the following pairs of sentences into sentences with **ohne . . . zu** or **statt . . . zu.**
Note that the negation disappears in the infinitive phrase.

> **Er fuhr nach Afrika. Er nahm seine Frau nicht mit.—ohne**
> **Er fuhr nach Afrika, ohne seine Frau mitzunehmen.**

1. Er fuhr nach Afrika. Er nahm seine Frau nicht mit.—ohne
2. Er fuhr nach Afrika. Er blieb nicht zu Hause.—statt
3. Er schrieb ihr einen Brief. Er rief sie nicht an.—statt
4. Er war in Berlin. Er hat mich nicht besucht.—ohne
5. Er kaufte sich einen Wagen. Er hatte nicht das Geld dafür.—ohne

D. Express in German:

1. Where is your coat?—Oh, I left it (hanging) at the Meyers.
2. Perhaps you should try once more to call him.
3. This chair you must leave (standing) in the living room.
4. Now the apartment is in order again at last.—No, you have forgotten to put the chairs back into the living room.
5. He finally had to promise his wife not to go to Africa again.
6. He suggested that my wife should go to the North Sea this year.

E. Change to comparatives:

> **Ich bin nicht so alt wie er. Er ist älter als ich.**

1. Unser Haus ist nicht so groß wie eures.
2. Bei uns ist es nicht so kalt wie bei euch.
3. Glas ist nicht so hart wie ein Diamant.
4. Der Weg war nicht so lang wie ich dachte. (Use *kurz.*)
5. Ich gehe nicht so oft ins Theater wie du.
6. Amerikanisches Bier ist nicht so stark wie deutsches Bier.
7. Von Köln bis Bonn ist es nicht so weit wie von Frankfurt bis Bonn.
8. Ich kann nicht so viel essen wie du.
9. Bier trinke ich nicht so gerne wie Wein.
10. Ich finde ihn nicht so interessant wie seine Frau.

F. Change the adjectives to superlatives:

1. Hans hat viel getrunken.
2. München ist eine schöne Stadt.
3. In München gibt es gutes Bier.
4. Im Dezember sind die Tage kurz.
5. Im Juni sind die Tage lang.
6. Der 21. Juni ist ein langer Tag.
7. Giganto ist ein starker Mann.
8. Ich wäre jetzt gern in Deutschland.
9. In Alaska ist das Obst teuer.

G. Read aloud:

21   32   43   54   65   76   87   98   109   120
213   324   435   546   657   768   801
1.003   1.011   1.021   1.248   1.349   1.492
14.395   128.473   847.666   3.492.716
0,3   7,43   421,7   3.746,4519
DM 0,25   DM 7,50   DM 300,00   DM 16.500,00   DM 1.000.000.000
$\frac{2}{3}$ $\frac{3}{4}$ $\frac{7}{8}$ $\frac{15}{16}$ $\frac{19}{20}$

H. Imagine that you have a cousin, Hildegard, who lives in Munich and knows no English. You
want to visit her during your stay in Germany, so you decide to write her a letter while on the
train to Koblenz. For lack of anything profound to say (owing to your lack of that kind of
German), you tell her about your adventures at the Frankfurt railroad station.

The envelope, incidentally, would be addressed as follows.

Fräulein
Hildegard Pfeilguth

    8   <u>München 13</u>
           Tengstraße 40

After duly addressing her as "Liebe Hildegard!" you tell her that you arrived in Frankfurt after a good flight. Because you wanted to go to Koblenz on the same day, you took a taxi to the station. Then you describe what happened to you until the Hellas-Express finally started moving.

You sign off by writing,

Viele herzliche Grüße

Dein John

BASIC VOCABULARY

allerdings however
ändern to change
aufgehen to rise (sun, moon); to open
aussprechen to pronounce, utter
bedeuten to mean, signify
bereit ready
besetzen to occupy
　besetzt busy (telephone)
besonder– special
beweisen to prove
die Bibliothek, –en library
damit' (conjunction) so that
deshalb for that reason, therefore
der Dezember, – December
der Dollar, –s dollar
　zwanzig Dollar twenty dollars
das Drittel, – third (fraction)
erhalten to receive, sustain
erlauben to allow, permit
der Februar, –e February

fernsehen to watch TV
　der Fernseher TV set
　das Fernsehen television
gestatten to permit, allow
es gibt there is (are) available
die Hälfte, –n half
hart hard
hübsch pretty
die Karte, –n map, ticket
　die Fahrkarte, –n (train) ticket
　die Rückfahrkarte, –n round-trip ticket
　der Flugschein, –e plane ticket
　die Landkarte, –n map
die Klasse, –n class
das Komma, –s comma
langweilig dull, boring
die Milliarde, –n billion
die Million, –en million
der Mittwoch, –e Wednesday
nah near, close

die Nähe proximity, nearness, closeness
nachher afterwards
der Norden the north
　nördlich northern
der Osten the east
　östlich eastern
der Süden the south
　südlich southern
der Westen the west
　westlich western
sobald (conjunction) as soon as
der Teil, –e part
unbedingt by all means
untergehen to sink, perish; to set (sun, moon)
verlangen demand
vorhin a while ago
der Vorschlag, ⁓e suggestion, proposal
　vorschlagen to propose, suggest
wagen to dare

ADDITIONAL VOCABULARY

die Alpen the Alps
auskommen to get along
die Bühne, –n stage
einholen to catch up with
die Flut, –en flood

der Handschuh, –e glove
die Handtasche, –n handbag
der Herzog, ⁓e duke
lochen to punch (ticket)
die Lokomoti've, –n loco-

motive
die Möbel (pl.) furniture
die Nordsee (no pl.) North Sea
die Partei, –en party

Prozent percent
  zwei Prozent two percent
reservieren to reserve
der Schalter, – (ticket)
  window
der Schuß, die Schüsse shot
das Semester, – semester

der Spiegel, – mirror
der Tabak, –e tobacco
das Testament, –e last will
todschick elegant, "great"
unterbringen to put up, lodge
unterkommen to find a place
  to stay

das Vermögen, – wealth,
  fortune, estate
der Zaun, ̈e fence
die Zeile, –n line (of print,
  poetry, verse)
der Zwerg, –e dwarf

IRREGULAR VERBS

beschließen to decide, determine
  beschloß, hat beschlossen,
  er beschließt
beweisen to prove

  bewies, hat bewiesen, er
  beweist
erhalten to receive; sustain
  erhielt, hat erhalten, er
  erhält

vorschlagen to propose,
  suggest
  schlug vor, hat vorge-
  schlagen, er schlägt vor

UNIT 12: Reflexive Verbs—Imperatives

[1] Unstressed Reflexive Objects

Ich will mir ein *Haus* bauen.

Du willst dir ein *Haus* bauen?

Er will sich ein *Haus* bauen.

Sie will sich ein *Haus* bauen.

Wir wollen uns ein *Haus* bauen.

So, ihr wollt euch ein *Haus* bauen?

Meyers wollen sich ein *Haus* bauen.

Sie wollen sich ein *Haus* bauen, Herr Meyer?

Ich habe mich schon ge*ba*det.

Hast du dich schon ge*ba*det?

Er hat sich schon ge*ba*det.

Sie hat sich schon ge*ba*det.

Wir haben uns schon ge*ba*det.

Habt ihr euch schon ge*ba*det?

Die Kinder haben sich schon ge*ba*det.

SEE ANALYSIS 139, 175 (pp. 283-284, 396-398)

Er hat mich noch nicht gefragt, ob ich ihn heiraten will, und ich frage mich oft, ob er der richtige Mann für mich ist.

Ich hole mir ein Glas Wasser. Darf ich dir auch eins holen?

VARIATIONS

Using the phrases

> **sich** (accusative) **im Spiegel sehen**
> to look at oneself in the mirror

> **sich** (dative) **einen Bart wachsen lassen**
> to grow a beard

form sentences of your own, beginning with simple sentences like

> **Ich sehe mich im Spiegel.**
> **Ich lasse mir einen Bart wachsen.**

and advancing to more complicated structures like

> **Du solltest dich mal im Spiegel sehen.**
> **Ich wollte, er hätte sich keinen Bart wachsen lassen.**

(*Facing*) **Schuhputzer in Berlin**

[2] Stressed Reflexive Objects

SEE
ANALYSIS
139, 175

(pp. 283-284,
396-398)

Erkenne dich *selbst.* (Know thyself.)

Ich habe Angst vor dem Leben; vielleicht weil ich Angst vor mir *sel*ber habe.

Den Meyer habe ich nicht eingeladen; der hat sich *sel*ber eingeladen.

Du solltest auch einmal an dich (selbst) denken.

Professor Schnarf hat nur ein Thema: sich *selbst.*

VARIATIONS

In the following sentences, change the objects to stressed reflexive objects; use
selbst or **selber** in all cases.

Er hat Angst vor mir.

Wir helfen euch.

Das habe ich für meine Frau gekauft.

Ich kann dich nicht mehr verstehen.

[3] selbst and selber Emphasizing a Noun or Pronoun

SEE
ANALYSIS
175

(pp. 396-398)

Das weiß ich *selbst.*

Ihrer Frau geht es also wieder gut—und wie geht es Ihnen *selbst?*

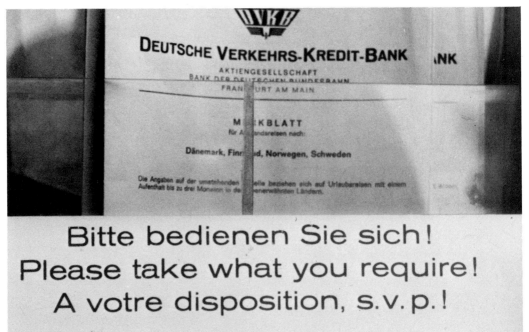

Ich wollte eigentlich meine Sekretärin nach Berlin schicken; aber ich fahre doch besser *selber* hin.

Bei diesem Brief kann ich dir nicht helfen; den mußt du *selber* schreiben.

Ich habe nicht mit Meyers Frau gesprochen; ich habe mit ihm *selbst* gesprochen.

Meine Frau hat nicht mit ihm gesprochen; ich habe *selbst* mit ihm gesprochen.

VARIATIONS

Insert **selbst** or **selber** in the appropriate place in the second clause of each sentence.

Das kann ich erst glauben, wenn ich es gesehen habe.

Nein, das hat mir nicht seine Sekretärin gesagt, das habe ich von ihm gehört.

Seine Frau ist ja ganz nett, aber mit Meyer will ich nichts zu tun haben.

[4] Special Cases of **selbst** and **selber**

Dabei brauchst du mir nicht zu helfen; das kann ich *selber* machen.

Was, du mußt den Kleinen immer noch *füttern*? Kann der sich denn noch nicht *selber* füttern?

Muß *ich* denn jeden Morgen zuerst aufstehen? Kannst du dir das Frühstück nicht mal *selber* machen?

SEE ANALYSIS 175

(pp. 396-398)

VARIATIONS

To each of the following sentences, add another one containing **selber** in the meaning of *without help.*

> **Du brauchst doch die Kinder nicht zu baden.**
> **Die können sich doch selber baden.**

Danke, du brauchst mir den Koffer nicht zu tragen.

Du brauchst doch den Kaffee nicht zu kochen.

Warum soll *ich* denn deiner Frau schreiben?

Er *selbst* ist ja ganz *nett;* aber mit seiner *Mutter* könnte ich nicht *leben.*

Andere hat er ge*rettet,* aber sich *selbst* kann er nicht retten.

Uns schickt Vater jeden Sonntag in die *Kirche,* aber er *selber* bleibt zu *Hause* und liest die Zeitung.

VARIATIONS

To each of the following sentences add a contrasting statement containing **selbst:**

> **Ihre *Mutter* hat *viel* Geld; aber sie *selbst* hat *kein* Geld.**

Mein *Mann* ist schon *oft* in Paris gewesen.

Uns schickt Vater jeden Sommer an die *Nordsee.*

Ihre *Schwes*tern haben alle ge*hei*ratet.

Ich habe *sel*ber kein Geld.

Ich habe *auch* kein Geld.

Ich kann dir nicht helfen; ich habe *sel*ber viel zu tun.

VARIATIONS

To each of the following sentences add a statement containing **selber** meaning **auch.**

Wir können euch kein Geld schicken. Wir haben _____.

Ich bin gar nicht erstaunt, daß Sie meinen Mann nicht verstehen. Ich kann _____

_____.

Er hat immer gelacht, wenn ich Detektivromane gelesen habe; und jetzt _____

_____.

[5] selbst, sogar, auch meaning *even*

SEE
ANALYSIS
176

(p. 398)

Selbst (sogar, auch) *das* ist ihm zu viel.

Selbst (sogar, auch) Herrn Dr. Müller, der sonst immer da ist, konnte ich diesmal nicht sprechen; der war auch in Berlin.

In Berlin sprechen selbst (sogar, auch) kleine Kinder Deutsch.

Selbst (sogar, auch) von seiner Frau läßt er sich nichts sagen.

VARIATIONS

Restate the following sentences, starting with **selbst.**

> **Seiner Frau hat er auch nichts davon gesagt.**
> **Selbst (sogar, auch) seiner Frau hat er nichts davon gesagt.**

In Rom hat es heute *auch* geschneit.

Mein Vater raucht *auch* nicht mehr.

Tante Amalie will *auch* nicht mehr ins Museum.

[6] Reciprocal Pronouns

Note the use of **sich, einander** and **gegenseitig.**

Hat er sie zuerst geküßt oder hat sie ihn zuerst geküßt?—Das weiß ich nicht. Aber es ist sicher, daß sie sich geküßt haben.

„Sie fühlten sich zueinander hingezogen. Sie schauten sich in die Augen; ihre Lippen trafen sich, und ihre Herzen hatten einander gefunden." (Ingelheim)

So, ihr wollt beide ein Wochenendhaus bauen? Wenn ihr euch gegenseitig helft, dann ist das gar nicht so schwer.

Im Sommer hat er ihr das erste Mal geschrieben, und seitdem schreiben sie sich jede Woche zweimal, und mindestens einmal im Monat rufen sie sich an.

Heute abend gehe ich mit ihr ins Theater.—Wo triffst du sie denn?—Wir treffen uns am Bahnhof.

SEE ANALYSIS 177

(pp. 398-399)

[7] Reflexive Verbs

SEE ANALYSIS 178–180

(pp. 399-402)

sich verlieben in: verliebt sein in
to fall in love with: to be in love with

Er ist verliebt.
In wen hat er sich denn diesmal verliebt?
Er soll sich in seine Lehrerin verliebt haben.
Er soll in seine Lehrerin verliebt sein.
Mit einem verliebten jungen Mann ist nichts Vernünftiges anzufangen.

sich verloben mit: verlobt sein mit
to become engaged to: to be engaged to

Ich höre, die Emma soll sich verlobt haben.
Ich dachte, sie wäre schon lange verlobt. Wer ist denn ihr Verlobter?
Darf ich Ihnen meine Verlobte vorstellen, gnädige Frau?
Ich gratuliere dir zu deiner Verlobung. Deine Emma ist wirklich ein nettes Mädchen.

heiraten: sich verheiraten: verheiratet sein mit
to marry: to get married: to be married to
Ich höre, Sie haben sich verlobt. Wann wollen Sie denn heiraten?
Die jüngste Tochter soll sich auch schon verheiratet haben.
Mit wem ist sie denn verheiratet?
Wann heiratest *du* denn, Monika?—Ich muß erst jemanden *finden*, der mich heiraten will.
Sie soll schon dreimal verheiratet gewesen sein.
Ich brauche eine neue Sekretärin; eine verheiratete wäre mir lieber als eine unverheiratete.

sich scheiden lassen von: geschieden sein
to get a divorce from: to be divorced
Kurz nach dem Krieg ließ sich seine erste Frau von ihm scheiden.
Eine geschiedene Frau hat oft ein schweres Leben.
Anton und Emma waren einmal verheiratet; jetzt sind sie geschieden.

sich umziehen: umgezogen sein
to change (clothes): to have changed (clothes)
Ich muß mich noch umziehen, bevor wir ins Theater gehen.
Ich brauche mich nicht umzuziehen, ich bin schon umgezogen.

But note: **umziehen, zog um, ist umgezogen** *to move*
Ich höre, Sie sind umgezogen.—Ja, wir wohnen jetzt in der Ingelheimer Straße.

sich anziehen: angezogen sein
to get dressed: to be dressed
Hast du den Kleinen schon angezogen?
Der kann sich jetzt schon selbst anziehen; den brauche ich nicht mehr anzuziehen.
Er ist schon angezogen; er hat sich selber angezogen.

sich ausziehen: ausgezogen sein
to get undressed: to be undressed
Als er nach Hause kam, zog er sich schnell aus und legte sich ins Bett.
Heute abend bin ich zu müde, um noch ins Kino zu gehen. Ich bin schon ausgezogen und
   möchte mich nicht noch einmal anziehen.

sich ausruhen: ausgeruht sein
to take a rest: to be rested
Du hast in der letzten Zeit viel zu viel gearbeitet; du solltest dich endlich einmal ausruhen.
Ich habe heute morgen bis zehn geschlafen und bin ganz ausgeruht.
Nach vier Wochen an der Riviera sollte er sich eigentlich gut ausgeruht haben.

sich ausschlafen: ausgeschlafen sein
to get enough sleep: to have had enough sleep
Nächsten Sonntag kann ich mich endlich einmal ausschlafen.
Warum stehst du denn heute so früh auf?—Ich konnte nicht mehr schlafen. Ich bin ausgeschlafen.

sich erholen: erholt sein
to get a rest (to recover one's strength): to be recovered
Du bist so überarbeitet. Du solltest einmal irgendwohin fahren und dich ein bißchen er-
   holen.
Ich war vier Wochen an der See und habe mich gut erholt.
Als er aus dem Schwarzwald zurückkam, war er gut erholt.

sich rasieren: rasiert sein
to shave: to have shaved, to be shaved
Natürlich mußt du dich noch einmal rasieren, bevor wir zu Erdmanns gehen.
Aber ich habe mich doch heute schon einmal rasiert.
Wenn du nicht rasiert bist, kannst du in diesem Hotel unmöglich ins Frühstückszimmer
   gehen.

sich aufregen über: aufgeregt sein
to get excited (upset) about: to be excited (upset)
Frau Meyer hat über tausend Mark im Kasino verloren, und Meyer hat sich furchtbar darüber aufgeregt.
Warum ist Meyer denn so aufgeregt?—Weil seine Frau schon wieder tausend Mark verloren hat.
Meyer soll furchtbar aufgeregt gewesen sein.
Meyer soll sich furchtbar aufgeregt haben.

sich beruhigen: beruhigt sein
to calm down: to be calmed down
Natürlich ist Meyer sehr aufgeregt, aber wie ich ihn kenne, wird er sich auch wieder beruhigen.
Seine Frau hat ihm versprochen, nie wieder ins Kasino zu gehen.—Na ja, dann kann er ja beruhigt sein.

sich entschließen zu: entschlossen sein zu
to make up one's mind to: to have made up one's mind, to be determined
Lieber Johannes, ich habe mich dazu entschlossen, mich von dir scheiden zu lassen.
Ich bin fest entschlossen, mich von dir scheiden zu lassen.

sich erkälten: erkältet sein
to catch a cold: to have a cold
Bei Niedermeyers gestern abend war es so kalt, daß ich mich erkältet habe.
Hannelore ist auch erkältet. War die auch bei Niedermeyers?

sich gewöhnen an: gewöhnt sein an
to get accustomed (used) to: to be accustomed (used) to
An das Klima hier in Kairo kann ich mich einfach nicht gewöhnen.
An das Klima bin ich jetzt ganz gewöhnt.

sich überzeugen von: überzeugt sein von
to become convinced of: to be convinced of
Ich habe ihm lange nicht geglaubt, aber jetzt habe ich mich davon überzeugen müssen, daß er recht hat.
Ich bin fest davon überzeugt, daß er recht hat.

sich verändern: verändert sein
to change: to have changed, to be changed
Ich habe ihn fast nicht erkannt, so sehr hat er sich verändert.
Seit dem Tod seiner Frau ist er ganz verändert.

sich vorbereiten auf: vorbereitet sein auf
to prepare for: to be prepared for
Er macht morgen sein Examen.—Hat er sich auch gut darauf vorbereitet?
Ist er auch gut darauf vorbereitet?

sich öffnen: geöffnet sein
to open: to be open

„Die Natur ist ein Buch mit sieben Siegeln [seals], das sich nur dem öffnet, der darin zu
  lesen versteht.“

Es ist nur dem geöffnet, der es versteht, darin zu lesen.

sich schließen: geschlossen sein
to close: to be closed

Und hinter ihm schloß sich das Tor.

Das Tor war noch geschlossen, als wir ankamen.

entschuldigen: sich entschuldigen: entschuldigt sein; verzeihen
to excuse oneself: to be excused; to pardon

Ich glaube, Sie sitzen auf meinem Platz.   Oh, ich bitte um Verzeihung.
    I think you're sitting in my seat.   I'm sorry. *or:* I beg your pardon.
Oh, entschuldigen Sie, Sie haben recht.   (for example, for stepping on your foot).
    Excuse me, you're right.
Oh, Entschuldigung, Sie haben recht.   Oh, Verzeihung.
    Excuse me, you're right.   I beg your pardon.
Oh, ich bitte um Entschuldigung.   Oh, verzeihen Sie.
    Excuse me.   I beg your pardon.

Entschuldigen Sie mich einen Augenblick; ich muß mal eben telephonieren.

Entschuldigen Sie, gnädige Frau, daß ich so spät komme.—Sie brauchen sich gar nicht zu
  entschuldigen, bei dem Regen ist das ja kein Wunder.

Sie kommen allein, Edgar?—Meine Frau läßt sich entschuldigen; sie hat sich erkältet und
  wollte lieber zu Hause bleiben.

Ich kann ja vieles verstehen; aber daß du mich am Frühstückstisch mit Gisela anredest, das
  ist nicht zu entschuldigen.

Meyer kommt nicht; er ist entschuldigt, er mußte nach Berlin.

VARIATIONS

Change the following actions into states:

    Sie hat sich in ihren Lehrer verliebt.   Hast du dich schon angezogen?
    Sie hat sich mit ihm verlobt.   Meyer soll sich furchtbar darüber
    Sie soll ihn geheiratet haben.   aufgeregt haben.
    Sie hat sich scheiden lassen.   Ich hoffe, du hast dich gut ausgeruht.

Change the following states into action; use the perfect:

    An das Klima bin ich schon gewöhnt.   Mein Mann ist wirklich überarbeitet.
    Ist er schon wieder nicht rasiert?   Ich bin davon überzeugt, daß sie
                                   gut küssen kann.

[8] sich setzen, sich stellen, sich legen

SEE
ANALYSIS
181
(pp. 402-403)

sitzen—setzen—sich setzen

Wer sitzt denn da bei euch am Tisch?—Den kenne ich auch nicht. Der hat sich einfach an unseren Tisch gesetzt.

Nein, unter *die*sen Brief setze ich meinen Namen *nicht*.

Ich wollte mich gerade in die erste Reihe setzen, als ich sah, daß Frau Meier da saß; und da habe ich mich in die letzte Reihe gesetzt.

stehen—stellen—sich stellen

Wer steht denn da bei Frau Schmidt? Ist das nicht Dr. Gerhardt?

Diese amerikanischen Cocktailparties machen mich wirklich müde. Ich habe stundenlang stehen müssen und war froh, als ich mich endlich setzen konnte.

Bitte, gnädige Frau, wie wäre es, wenn Sie sich hier auf diesen Stuhl setzten? Und Sie stellen sich links neben Ihre Frau, Herr Doktor. Und der Kleine kann rechts von Ihrer Frau stehen.—So, und jetzt bitte recht freundlich!

In der Zeitung steht, daß Ingelheim spurlos verschwunden ist.—Auf welcher Seite steht das denn?

liegen—legen—sich legen

Ich hatte mich gerade ins Bett gelegt, als Erich anrief. „Liegst du etwa schon im Bett?" sagte er.

Ich lag noch nicht lange im Bett, als Erich anrief. „Hast du dich etwa schon ins Bett gelegt?" sagte er.

Wo hast du denn mein Buch hingelegt?—Ich habe es auf deinen Schreibtisch gelegt. Liegt es denn nicht mehr dort?

Köln liegt am Rhein. Wolframs-Eschenbach liegt in der Nähe von Nürnberg.

VARIATIONS

Ich habe den Wein auf den Tisch _____.
Der Wein _____ auf dem Tisch.

Ich habe die Kleine schon in ihren Stuhl _____.
Die Kleine _____ schon in ihrem Stuhl.

Ich habe den Kleinen schon ins Bett _____.
Der Kleine _____ schon im Bett.

Warum hast du dich noch nicht ins Bett _____?
Warum _____ du noch nicht im Bett?

Warum hast du dich denn in die letzte Reihe _____?
Warum _____ Reihe?

[9] Imperative, **du**-Form

SEE
ANALYSIS
182–185
(pp. 403-409)

Ruf mich bitte *nicht* vor *acht* an!   Bitte bring mir doch etwas zu *lesen* mit!

Bitte ruf mich *nicht* vor *acht* an!   Bring mir doch bitte etwas zu *lesen* mit!

Aber bitte ruf mich *nicht* vor *acht* an!   Bring mir doch etwas zu *lesen* mit, *bitte*!

Aber ruf mich bitte *nicht* vor *acht* an!   Fahr doch mit uns in den *Schwarzwald*!

Ruf mich aber bitte *nicht* vor *acht* an!   Sei mir nicht böse, aber ich muß jetzt nach Hause.

Aber ruf mich *nicht* vor *acht* an, bitte!   Sei doch nicht so nervös!

Ruf sie doch noch einmal *an*. Vielleicht ist sie jetzt zu *Hause*.

Bitte ruf sie doch noch einmal *an*!

Ruf sie doch noch mal *an*, bitte!

Bitte sei doch so gut und fahr mich mal eben in die Stadt.

Rede doch nicht so dumm, Anton; du verstehst ja doch nichts davon.

Tu nicht so, als ob du mich nicht gehört hättest.

Sei so gut, Klaus, und trag mir mal meinen Mantel.

Fritzchen, gib dem Onkel die Hand und sag schön „guten Tag"!

Fritzchen, nimm die Finger aus dem Mund!

Lauf doch nicht so schnell, Hans, ich kann ja gar nicht mitkommen.

Fürchte dich nicht; denn ich bin bei dir.

Steh *du* doch mal zuerst auf.

Rede *du* mal mit Meyer, du kennst ihn doch besser als ich.

Bleib *du* doch wenigstens vernünftig.

Arbeite *du* mal acht Stunden im Büro; dann kannst du verstehen, daß ich abends hunde-
müde bin.

VARIATIONS

Change the following sentences into du-form imperatives; use **doch, doch mal,**
or **mal** where appropriate:

Ich bringe dir ein Glas Wasser.
Ich gehe in den Garten.
Ich besuche euch in München.

Ich gebe dir das Buch morgen.
Ich nehme mir eine Taxe.
Ich sehe mal nach, ob Meyer schon da ist.

[10] Imperative, **ihr**-Form

Kinder, vergeßt nicht, euch die Hände zu waschen.

Bitte vergeßt nicht, euch die Hände zu waschen.

Vergeßt bitte nicht, euch die Hände zu waschen.

Es war schön, daß ihr kommen konntet; besucht uns bald mal wieder.

Seid mir nicht böse. Aber ich muß jetzt wirklich nach Hause.

Also auf Wiedersehen. Und ruft uns an, wenn ihr nach Hause kommt.

Während der Woche haben wir nicht viel Zeit. Aber besucht uns doch mal an einem Sonntag!

Geht ihr ruhig ins Theater. Ich muß noch arbeiten.

Warum ich sonntags immer zu Hause bleibe? Arbeitet *ihr* einmal jeden Tag zehn Stunden,
dann wißt ihr warum.

SEE
ANALYSIS
183
(pp. 404-405)

VARIATIONS

Change to **ihr**-form imperatives:

Wir kommen bald wieder.
Wir geben doch nicht so viel Geld aus.
Wir trinken doch nicht so viel Kaffee.
Wir sind euch nicht böse.

Wir bringen euch ein paar Blumen mit.
Wir lassen uns das Frühstück aufs
   Zimmer bringen.
Wir bleiben noch ein bißchen hier.

[11] Imperative, **wir**-Form

Wo sollen wir denn essen, Rosemarie?—Gehen wir doch mal ins Regina, Klaus, da waren
wir schon so lange nicht mehr.

Müssen wir denn heute schon wieder zu Müllers?—Natürlich müssen wir.—Also schön,
fahren wir wieder zu Müllers.

Was, schon wieder Fisch, Maria?—Aber Karl, Fisch ist doch jetzt so billig.—Also gut,
essen wir wieder Fisch.

SEE
ANALYSIS
183
(pp. 404-405)

VARIATIONS

Change to the **wir**-form, starting with **Schön,** . . .

Ich möchte nach München fahren.
Schön, fahren wir doch nach München.

Ich möchte zu Hause bleiben.

Ich möchte heute im Hotel Berlin essen.

Ich möchte heute schwimmen gehen.

[12] Imperative, Sie-Form

SEE
ANALYSIS
183
(pp. 404-405)

Bitte, Fräulein, geben Sie mir Zimmer 641.

Seien Sie herzlich gegrüßt von Ihrem Hans Meyer.

Seien Sie vorsichtig, Herr Professor, und überarbeiten Sie sich nicht.

Bitte glauben Sie mir, ich habe alles getan, was ich tun konnte.

Entschuldigen Sie bitte, gnädige Frau; Ihr Ferngespräch nach Hamburg ist da.

Es gibt keine bessere Kamera. Fragen Sie Ihren Fotohändler.

Informieren Sie sich in unserem großen Photo-Katalog.

Lassen Sie sich unser neuestes Modell zeigen.

Wenn Ihnen die starken Zigaretten zu stark und die leichten zu leicht sind, so rauchen Sie
    PRIVAT, die Zigarette des Mannes von Format.*

Freude am Leben! Wundervolle Urlaubstage, in farbigen Kodakbildern! Und natürlich
    MARTINI† „on the rocks". Machen Sie Ihren Gästen eine Freude, mit MARTINI,
    Schluck für Schluck.

[13] Impersonal Imperative

SEE
ANALYSIS
183
(pp. 404-405)

Alles aussteigen.

Einsteigen bitte.

Bitte einsteigen.

Nicht öffnen, bevor der Zug hält.

Langsam fahren.

Nicht rauchen.

Bitte anschnallen.

Nicht mit dem Fahrer sprechen.

Eintreten ohne zu klingeln.

Nicht stören.

Bitte an der Kasse zahlen.

Nach rechts einordnen.

„Und natürlich Martini ‚on the rocks'."

* **Ein Mann von Format** a man of distinction

† This does not mean what you think it means. It means vermouth (distilled by Martini)
on the rocks.

Impersonal imperatives

Ein Wort über deutsche Hotels

Wie überall in der Welt gibt es in Deutschland teure und billige Hotels, große und kleine, gute und weniger gute. In den Großstädten gibt es internationale Hotels, in denen man so komfortabel wohnen kann wie in internationalen Hotels der ganzen Welt. Im Berlin Hilton oder im Hotel Berlin, im Frankfurter Hof oder im Hotel 5 Intercontinental in Frankfurt, im Hotel Vier Jahreszeiten in Hamburg und im Hotel Vier Jahreszeiten in München brauchen Sie kein Deutsch zu können, um sich Ihr Frühstück aufs Zimmer bringen zu lassen oder um einen Luftpostbrief nach Chicago aufzugeben. Wenn Sie aber in einem kleineren Hotel wohnen wollen oder in einer 10 Pension, oder wenn Sie in einer Kleinstadt oder auf dem Land in einem Dorfgasthof ein Zimmer haben wollen, dann ist das schon etwas anderes. Sie können dann natürlich mit den Händen reden, aber besser ist es doch, wenn Sie Deutsch sprechen. Doch dazu brauchen Sie ein bißchen Hotel-Jargon. 15

Wir wollen annehmen, daß Sie in Koblenz übernachten wollen, denn dorthin haben wir Sie ja mit dem Hellas-Express geschickt. In Koblenz gibt es etwa 30 Hotels und 25 Gasthöfe und Pensionen. Es ist nicht immer ganz einfach, den Unterschied zwischen einem Hotel und einem Gasthof zu sehen. Hotels sind größer als Gasthöfe, und 20 Gasthöfe sind kleiner als Hotels. (Aber das ist natürlich keine Definition.) Das größte Hotel in Koblenz hat 120 Betten, der kleinste Gasthof hat 5 oder 6 Betten. Eine Pension ist etwas, was es in Amerika nicht gibt. Die meisten Pensionen sind Privathäuser, in denen man, ganz ähnlich wie in Gasthöfen, übernachten kann und 25 in denen man Frühstück bekommt. Zum Gasthof gehört noch eine Gaststätte, ein Restaurant (oft ähnlich wie in England die *neighborhood pubs*), wo man abends hingeht, um ein Glas Wein oder ein Bier zu trinken. Die „Gaststätten" heißen in vielen Gegenden Deutschlands „Wirtschaften" oder „Wirtshäuser". Auf dem Land 30 haben solche Gasthäuser oft Namen wie „Zum Löwen", „Zum Oschsen", „ Zum Goldenen Lamm", „Zum Deutschen Kaiser".

Außer den Hotels, Gasthöfen und Pensionen gibt es in Koblenz auch eine Jugendherberge mit 540 Betten und einen Campingplatz für etwa 1000 Personen, aber da Sie Ihre erste Nacht in Deutschland 35 weder in einer Jugendherberge noch auf einem Campingplatz verbringen wollen, so gehen Sie in eines der besseren Hotels. In Ihrem Hotelführer haben Sie eins gefunden: Zimmerpreis DM 15,00–18,00, Frühstück DM 3,00, Halbpension DM 18,50–21,50, Vollpension DM 24,00–30,00, und dann heißt es unter „Comfort": *Flw B PB Z G P L* 40 *T*. Das alles verstehen Sie natürlich erst, wenn Sie unten auf der

die Jahreszeit, –en season

einen Brief aufgeben to mail a letter

die Pension, –en tourist home
der Gasthof, ̈e inn

der Jargon' pronounced as in French

der Löwe, –n lion
der Ochse, –n ox
das Lamm, ̈er lamb

die Jugendherberge, –n youth hostel

Zwei Gasthöfe und eine Pension

Seite lesen: T—Zimmertelephon, L—Lift (das normale deutsche
Wort für *Lift* ist *Aufzug*), P—Parkplatz, G—Garage (das interessiert
Sie nicht, denn Sie sind ja nicht mit Ihrem eigenen Wagen gekommen), Z—Zentralheizung, PB—Privatbad (von den dreißig
Hotels haben nur siebzehn Zimmer mit Bad, und von den Gast- 5
höfen nur drei), B—Bad (das heißt, es gibt ein oder mehrere Bäder,
aber diese Bäder gehören nicht zum Zimmer, und man bezahlt zwei
oder drei Mark extra dafür), Flw—ganzjährig fließendes warmes
Wasser. Vollpension heißt, daß man alle Mahlzeiten im Hotel ißt,
bei Halbpension ißt man nur eine Mahlzeit im Hause (entweder 10
Mittag- oder Abendessen). Frühstück ist in allen deutschen Hotels
obligatorisch; d.h., man muß dafür bezahlen, ob man frühstückt oder
nicht. Zum Standard-Frühstück in Deutschland gehören Brötchen,
Butter, Marmelade und Kaffee oder Tee.

So, jetzt haben Sie Ihren Reiseführer lange genug studiert; Sie geben 15
dem Gepäckträger, der Ihre Koffer vor den Bahnhof getragen hat,
eine Mark Trinkgeld und nehmen ein Taxi zum Hotel. Der Mann,
der Ihnen am Hotel mit Ihrem Gepäck hilft, ist aber kein Gepäckträger, sondern ein Hausdiener. Er bringt Ihre Koffer zum Empfang,
und der Mann, der Sie dort empfängt, ist der Portier (oder in 20
manchen größeren Hotels der Empfangschef).

Es folgt ein imaginäres Gespräch zwischen Ihnen und dem Portier.

„Ich habe für heute nacht ein Zimmer bestellt."
„Auf welchen Namen, bitte?"

„Ray, aus New York."
„Einen Augenblick, bitte,—und würden Sie inzwischen schon das
Anmeldeformular ausfüllen?"
„Sie wollten ein Zimmer mit Bad, Mr. Ray? Leider habe ich nur ein
Zimmer mit Dusche, wenn Sie nichts dagegen haben?"
„Das ist mir schon recht. Wie teuer ist denn das Zimmer?"
„18 Mark, plus 15% Bedienung."
„Gut. Und gibt es ein Telefon auf dem Zimmer? Ich muß nämlich
noch ein paar Ferngespräche führen."
„Aber sicher. Rufen Sie nur die Zentrale an; die Telefonistin ver-
bindet Sie dann. So, hier ist Ihr Schlüssel,—Zimmer 318. Der Aufzug
ist hier drüben links, bitte. Das Gepäck lasse ich Ihnen nach oben
bringen."

Es gibt keinen Liftboy, sondern es ist ein Aufzug mit Selbst-
bedienung. Im dritten Stock gehen Sie einen langen Korridor hinunter und suchen Zimmer 318. Nach Zimmer 315 kommt eine Tür 40
mit „H", dann eine mit „D" und dann kommt erst 316. (Statt H und
D finden Sie vielleicht auch nur eine Tür mit 00). Zimmer 318 ist

---

der Aufzug, ⁀e ele-
vator

d.h. = das heißt
das Brötchen, –
(hard) roll
Marmelade, any kind
of jam
der Gepäckträger, –
porter
das Trinkgeld, –er
tip
der Hausdiener, –
bellhop
der Portier, –s desk
clerk
der Empfangschef, –s
head clerk

anmelden to register;
das Formular, –e
form
ausfüllen to fill out

die Dusche, –n
shower
bedienen to wait on,
serve; die Bedienung
service charge
ein Ferngespräch
führen to make a
long-distance call
die Zentrale, –n
switchboard

ganz nett, vielleicht ein bißchen altmodisch, aber doch komfortabel. Am interessantesten finden Sie das Federbett, aber wir müssen Sie warnen: Solche Federbetten sind für die meisten Amerikaner erstens zu warm und zweitens zu kurz; wenn man unter einem Federbett schläft, hat man entweder kalte Füße oder kalte Schultern. Sie ⁵ klingeln also dem Zimmermädchen und bitten sie, Ihnen statt des Federbettes eine Wolldecke zu bringen. Dann wollen Sie telefonieren; zuerst Köln, und dann Ihre Freundin Barbara, die in Augustdorf bei Detmold wohnt.

die Feder, –n feather
warnen to warn

die Wolle wool

Ferngespräche

Sie nehmen also den Hörer ab, und dann hören Sie die Stimme der ¹⁰ Telefonistin: „Zentrale."
„Ja, Fräulein, ich hätte gerne Köln, 20 37 88 (zwo-null, drei-sieben, acht-acht)."
Am Telephon sagt man immer „zwo" statt „zwei."
„Köln, 20 37 88—bitte legen Sie wieder auf; ich rufe Sie zurück." ¹⁵ Nach zwei Minuten klingelt das Telefon.
„Die Nummer ist leider besetzt. Soll ich es in ein paar Minuten noch einmal versuchen?"
„Ja, bitte."
Fünf Minuten später klingelt es wieder. ²⁰
„Ihr Gespräch nach Köln. Einen Augenblick, bitte; ich verbinde."

(den Hörer) auflegen to put down the receiver

Dann hören Sie am anderen Ende eine Frauenstimme: „Hier bei Doktor Fischer", und weil die Stimme „*bei* Doktor Fischer" sagt, wissen Sie, daß das das Dienstmädchen sein muß. Sie sagen also:

das Dienstmädchen, – maid

„Kann ich bitte Herrn Doktor Fischer sprechen?" ²⁵
„Darf ich Sie um Ihren Namen bitten?"
„John Ray,—aus New York."
„Einen Augenblick, bitte, Herr Reh."

Ihr Gespräch mit Herrn Fischer ist natürlich Ihre Privatsache, und wir wollen es hier nicht abdrucken. Aber nachdem das Gespräch ³⁰ zu Ende ist, sprechen Sie wieder mit der Telefonistin, denn Sie wollen ja Ihre Freundin Barbara auch noch anrufen.

abdrucken to print

„Sagen Sie, Fräulein, kennen Sie dieses Augustdorf bei Detmold?"
„Nein, nie davon gehört; das muß irgendein Dorf sein."
„Ich hatte den Namen auch noch nie gehört, aber so klein kann es ³⁵ nicht sein, denn die Telefonnummer ist eine Meile lang."
„Was ist denn die Nummer?"
„05237258."
„Nein, nein", lacht die Telefonistin. (Lacht sie über Ihren amerikanischen Akzent oder darüber, daß Sie über deutsche Telefon- ⁴⁰

die Meile, –n mile

nummern nicht Bescheid wissen?) „Da haben Sie die Vorwahlnummer mit dazu genommen. Augustdorf ist bestimmt ein Dorf,
denn die Nummer ist 258. Die Vorwahl ist 05237. Ihre Kölner
Nummer ist mit der Vorwahlnummer noch länger. Köln hat die
Vorwahl 0221;—das heißt, die Nummer, die ich vorhin gewählt habe, 5
war 0221203788."

Bescheid wissen to know, be informed
die Vorwahlnummer, –n area code

"Das wußte ich nicht—unsere amerikanischen Vorwahlnummern
haben nur drei Zahlen. Aber versuchen Sie doch jetzt mal Augustdorf."

„Gut,—und bleiben Sie doch bitte gleich am Apparat."

10 **am Apparat** on the line

Aber Sie haben kein Glück. Die Nummer ist zwar nicht besetzt,
aber es antwortet auch niemand. „Da meldet sich leider niemand",
sagt die Telefonistin.

sich melden to answer (the phone)

„Soll ich es später noch mal versuchen?"
„Nein danke. Ich möchte mir jetzt erst einmal ein bißchen die Stadt 15
ansehen."
„Dann können Sie es ja von der Post aus noch mal versuchen."
„Gute Idee. Ich will sowieso noch einen Brief aufgeben. Vielen
Dank, Fräulein."

Sections VIII–X of *Ein Mann kommt nach San Franzisko* appear after Unit 13
but may be read in conjunction with this unit.

ANALYSIS

175 Reflexive and Emphatic Pronouns

The English pronouns *myself, himself, oneself,* etc., can be used in three
different ways:

1. as unstressed reflexive objects:

    I almost *killed* myself.

2. as stressed reflexive objects:

    I must also think of my*self*.

3. as emphatic pronouns repeating a preceding noun or pronoun (subject
or object):

    I saw Meyer my*self*.
    I saw Meyer him*self*.

Unstressed Reflexive Objects

While English uses the compounds *my-self, him-self, one-self,* etc., German uses the reflexive **sich** for all third-person forms and the normal personal pronouns **mir, mich, dir, dich, uns,** and **euch** for first- and second-person forms. (See **139.**)

Er hat sich ver*gif*tet.	He *poisoned* himself.
Sie hat sich ver*gif*tet.	She *poisoned* herself.
Sie haben sich ver*gif*tet.	They *poisoned* themselves.
Ich hole mir eine Zeitung.	I'm getting myself a *newspaper.*
Du holst dir eine Zeitung.	You're getting yourself a *newspaper.*
Wir holen uns eine Zeitung.	We're getting ourselves a *newspaper.*
Ihr holt euch eine Zeitung.	You're getting yourselves a *newspaper.*

Stressed Reflexive Objects

In such English sentences as

I must also think of my*self,*

the reflexive is the stress point of the sentence. German can either stress the reflexive pronoun

Ich muß auch mal an *mich* denken,

or add an undeclinable **selbst** or **selber** which carries the main syntactical stress:

Ich muß auch mal an mich *selbst* denken.

Emphatic Pronouns

The English reflexive pronouns *myself, yourself, himself,* etc., sometimes merely repeat, for emphasis, a preceding noun or pronoun. When so used, they again carry the main syntactical stress, but nevertheless they are not independent syntactical units.

He said it him*self.*
They did it them*selves.*

German cannot repeat a preceding noun or pronoun. Instead, German uses the strongly stressed particles **selbst** or **selber** to emphasize these nouns or pronouns. **Selbst** and **selber** are interchangeable. They always follow the word to be emphasized, either immediately or at the end of the inner field.

Das weiß ich *selbst.*	I know that my*self.*
So! Ihrer Frau geht's gut.	So your wife is fine.
Und wie geht's Ihnen *selbst?*	And how are you your*self?*

Ich fahre morgen *selbst* nach Berlin.   I am going to Berlin my*self* tomorrow.
Das war der Direktor *selber*.   That was the boss him*self*.

NOTE:

1. When emphasizing the subject at the end of the inner field, **selber** frequently assumes the meaning "without help" or "others don't have to."

Du könntest dir das Frühstück auch   You really could get your *own* breakfast,
  einmal *selber* machen.   for a change.
Das kann ich doch *selber* machen.   I can do that *myself*.

2. If **selbst** (or **selber**) appears in the front field, contrast intonation is used, and a contrast with others, of whom the opposite statement is true, is implied.

Sie *selbst hat* kein Geld; aber ihre *Mut*ter hat *viel* Geld.
Er *selber* bleibt zu *Hause: uns* schickt er in die *Kir*che.
Sich *selbst kann* er nicht retten; *an*dere hat er ge*ret*tet.

3. If **selbst** (or **selber**) appears in the inner field, it may also be a substitute for **auch** and express the notion "just like others."

Ich bin *selber* arm, so arm wie du.
Ich bin *selbst* nicht glücklich, ich bin so unglücklich wie ihr.

176   selbst, sogar, and auch meaning *even*

Selbst, sogar, and **auch,** without stress, may form a syntactical unit with an immediately following stressed word. If so used, they mean *even,*

Selbst (sogar, auch) *das* ist ihm zu viel.
Er *will* einfach nicht, und solange jemand nicht *will,* kann ihm selbst
  (sogar, auch) *Gott* nicht helfen.

Compare:

Der brave Mann denkt an sich *selbst* zu*letzt*. (Schiller)
A brave man thinks of himself last.
Der brave Mann denkt an *sich,* selbst zu*letzt*.
A brave man thinks of himself, even at the very end.

177   Reciprocal Pronouns

Normally, the reflexive plural pronouns can also be used as reciprocal pronouns, and it is not necessary to make a distinction. No one will misunderstand: **Sie küßten sich.** This can only mean *They kissed each other,* not *They kissed themselves.*

If it is desirable to express reciprocity, **einander** and **gegenseitig** can be

used. **Einander** is literary and replaces the reflexive; **gegenseitig** follows
the reflexive.

> Es waren zwei Königskinder, die hatten einander so lieb.*
> Wenn ihr euch nicht gegenseitig helft, dann werdet ihr nie fertig.

178 Reflexive Verbs

Many German verbs can be used with either a reflexive or a non-
reflexive pronoun object:

REFLEXIVE:	**Ich habe mich gebadet.**	I took a bath.
	Ich habe mich ins Bett gelegt.	I went to bed.
	Er hat sich erschossen.	He shot (and killed) himself.
NONREFLEXIVE:	**Ich habe ihn gebadet.**	I gave him a bath.
	Ich habe ihn ins Bett gelegt.	I put him to bed.
	Er hat ihn erschossen.	He shot (and killed) him.

Neither the syntactical structure of the sentence nor the meaning of the
verb **erschießen** is changed, when **er erschoß sich** is changed to **er
erschoß ihn.** In both cases, the verb is **jemanden erschießen,** *to shoot
somebody;* and sometimes, this "somebody" is the subject itself. A genuine reflexive verb is a verb with a reflexive pronoun which is either not
replaceable at all or not replaceable without a change of meaning. Take,
for instance, English *to enjoy oneself.* It is possible to say

> Good-bye, Mrs. Smith. I had a wonderful time. I really enjoyed myself;
> and your steaks were delicious.

But I cannot say

> Good-bye Mrs. Smith. I had a wonderful time. I really enjoyed myself
> and your steaks.

The two sentences *I enjoyed myself* and *I enjoyed it* (*the steak*) are not
parallel. In *I enjoyed it, to enjoy* is a normal transitive verb, meaning
"to derive pleasure from"; and the *it* is a real object. But in *I enjoyed
myself, to enjoy oneself* means "to have a good time" and the *myself* is
not an object, but an irreplaceable part of the verbal pattern *to enjoy
oneself.*

From a linguistic point of view, the *to enjoy onself* used in the sentence
I really enjoyed myself last night is a genuine reflexive verb. English has
only a few such verbs. German has hundreds. Compare:

TRANSITIVE:	**Sie konnte die Hand nicht bewegen.**	She could not move her hand.
REFLEXIVE:	**Die Erde bewegt sich um die Sonne.**	The earth moves around the sun.
TRANSITIVE:	**Hast du die Eier schon umgedreht?**	Have you turned the eggs over?
REFLEXIVE:	**Du darfst dich jetzt nicht umdrehen.**	You must not turn around now.

* First line of a folk song: There were (once upon a time) two king's children (a prince and
a princess); they loved each other very much.

Very often, the reflexive verb is distinguished from the transitive verb by a prefix:

lieben (transitive), *to love*   Ich liebe meine Frau.
sich verlieben in (reflexive), *to fall in*   Ich habe mich in Inge verliebt.
     love with

179 The Forms of the Reflexive Verb

ACTIONAL INFINITIVE:	sich erkälten	to catch a cold
	sich erkältet haben	to have caught a cold
ACTIONAL PRESENT:	ich erkälte mich	I am catching a cold
	du erkältest dich	you are catching a cold
	er erkältet sich	he is catching a cold
	wir erkälten uns	we are catching a cold
	ihr erkältet euch	you are catching a cold
	sie erkälten sich	they are catching a cold
ACTIONAL IMPERATIVE:	erkälte dich nicht	don't catch a cold
	erkältet euch nicht	don't catch a cold
	erkälten Sie sich nicht	don't catch a cold
ACTIONAL PAST:	ich erkältete mich	I caught a cold
ACTIONAL PERFECT:	ich habe mich erkältet	I have caught a cold
STATAL PRESENT: (see below)	ich bin erkältet	I have a cold (I am under the weather with a cold)
STATAL PAST:	ich war erkältet	I had a cold
STATAL PERFECT:	ich bin erkältet gewesen	I've had a cold
STATAL INFINITIVE:	erkältet sein	to have a cold

The terms "actional" and "statal" used in this table need an explanation. You are familiar with the fact that intransitive verbs which denote a change in the condition or location of the subject form their compound tenses with **sein**:

Die Preise sind gestiegen.   The prices went up. (or: are up)
Die Preise sind gefallen.   The prices came down. (or: are down)

Forms like **sind gefallen** denote *both* the past event *and* the new present state created by this past event. The difference between action or event (compare English *has gone*) and state (compare English *is gone*) cannot be expressed in German with such intransitive verbs.

However, in the case of reflexive verbs denoting a transition from one state of affairs to another, the difference between event (or action) and state must be expressed. Thus, **sich verlieben,** meaning *to fall in love,* forces the speaker to distinguish between

THE PAST EVENT (OR ACTION):   **Er verliebte sich in Erika.**
He fell in love with Erika.

Er hat sich in Erika verliebt.
He fell in love with Erika.

Er hatte sich in Erika verliebt.
He had fallen in love with Erika.

AND THE STATE CREATED BY THIS EVENT: **Er ist in Erika verliebt.**
He is in love with Erika.

Er war in Erika verliebt.
He was in love with Erika.

One can only say:

    Er ist seit drei Wochen in Erika verliebt

and

    Er hat sich vor drei Wochen in Erika verliebt,

but not

    [Er hat sich seit drei Wochen in Erika verliebt]

or

    [Er ist vor drei Wochen in Erika verliebt.]

180   Reflexives Which Denote Transition to a New State

As stated above, such reflexives distinguish between a past event and the state reached by this event. Some of these reflexives can also be used as transitive verbs.

sich anziehen	to get dressed
angezogen sein	to be dressed
sich aufregen über	to get excited (upset) about
aufgeregt sein	to be excited (upset)
sich ausruhen	to take a rest
ausgeruht sein	to have taken a rest, to be rested
sich ausschlafen	to get enough sleep
ausgeschlafen sein	to have had enough sleep
sich ausziehen	to get undressed
ausgezogen sein	to be undressed
sich baden	to take a bath
gebadet sein	to have taken a bath, to be bathed
sich beruhigen	to calm down
beruhigt sein	to have calmed down
sich entschließen zu	to make up one's mind
entschlossen sein zu	to be determined

sich entschuldigen	to excuse oneself
entschuldigt sein	to be excused
sich erholen	to get a rest (to recover one's strength)
erholt sein	to be well rested (recovered)
sich erkälten	to catch a cold
erkältet sein	to have a cold
sich gewöhnen an	to get accustomed to
gewöhnt sein an	to be accustomed to
sich öffnen	to open (intransitive)
geöffnet sein	to be open
sich rasieren	to shave
rasiert sein	to have shaved, be shaved
sich scheiden lassen	to get a divorce
geschieden sein	to be divorced
sich schließen	to close (intransitive)
geschlossen sein	to be closed
sich überarbeiten	to overwork
überarbeitet sein	to be overworked
sich überzeugen von	to become convinced of
überzeugt sein von	to be convinced of
sich umziehen	to change (clothes)
umgezogen sein	to have changed
sich verändern	to change
verändert sein	to have changed
heiraten	to marry
sich verheiraten	to get married
verheiratet sein mit	to be married to
sich verlieben in	to fall in love with
verliebt sein in	to be in love with
sich verloben mit	to become engaged to
verlobt sein mit	to be engaged to
sich vorbereiten auf	to prepare for
vorbereitet sein auf	to be prepared for

NOTE: Reflexives like **sich öffnen,** which denote transition into a new state without reference to any agent, frequently correspond to English intransitive verbs.

Die Tür öffnete sich.	The door opened. (process)
Die Tür ist geöffnet.	The door is open. (state)

181   sich legen, sich setzen, sich stellen

The verbs **sitzen, stehen,** and **liegen** describe a state, not an event. They are intransitive—that is, they cannot take an accusative object—and they are strong verbs.

> sitzen, saß, hat gesessen, er sitzt
> stehen, stand, hat gestanden, er steht
> liegt, lag, hat gelegen, er liegt
> Anton und Emma saßen auf der Bank vor dem Haus.
> Das Haus stand am Rhein.
> Auf dem Tisch lag ein Buch.

The weak reflexive verbs **sich setzen, sich stellen,** and **sich legen** describe the action leading to the state of **sitzen, stehen,** and **liegen.**

> Er hat sich auf die Bank gesetzt;   jetzt sitzt er auf der Bank.
> Er hat sich vor die Haustür gestellt;   jetzt steht er vor der Tür.
> Er hat sich ins Bett gelegt;   jetzt liegt er im Bett.

When the weak verbs **setzen, stellen,** and **legen** are used with a non-reflexive accusative object, they also describe an action, again leading to the state of **sitzen, stehen,** and **liegen.**

> Sie hat das Kind auf die Bank gesetzt.   Das Kind sitzt auf der Bank.
> Er hat die Flasche auf den Tisch ge-   Die Flasche steht auf dem Tisch.
>   stellt.
> Er hat das Buch auf den Tisch gelegt.   Das Buch liegt auf dem Tisch.

NOTE: If a prepositional phrase is used with these verbs, (**sich**) **setzen,** (**sich**) **stellen,** (**sich**) **legen** require the accusative (**auf die Bank**) and **sitzen, stehen, liegen** require the dative (**auf der Bank**).

182   The Forms of the Imperative

The imperative is that form of a verb which is used for the expression of a command or a request. The following forms occur:

Weak Verbs

du-form:	sag(e)	rede	antworte	entschuldige
ihr-form:	sagt	redet	antwortet	entschuldigt
wir-form:	sagen wir	reden wir	antworten wir	entschuldigen wir
Sie-form:	sagen Sie	reden Sie	antworten Sie	entschuldigen Sie

Impersonal form: identical with infinitive

The **Sie-**form was introduced in Unit 3. Of the personal forms, only the **du-**form is not identical with the corresponding forms of the present indicative. The impersonal form is the infinitive used with imperative force.

In principle, the ending **-e** of the **du-**form is optional. However, verbs whose stems end in **-d** (**reden**) or **-t** (**antworten**), or in the suffix **-ig** (**entschuldigen**) are not usually used without the **-e** ending.

Strong Verbs

du-form:	geh(e)	frag(e)	finde	gib	lauf
ihr-form:	geht	fragt	findet	gebt	lauft
wir-form:	gehen wir	fragen wir	finden wir	geben wir	laufen wir
Sie-form:	gehen Sie	fragen Sie	finden Sie	geben Sie	laufen Sie

Impersonal form: identical with infinitive

du-form:	nimm	sieh	sei	fahre	werde
ihr-form:	nehmt	seht	seid	fahrt	werdet
wir-form:	nehmen wir	sehen wir	seien wir	fahren wir	werden wir
Sie-form:	nehmen Sie	sehen Sie	seien Sie	fahren Sie	werden Sie

Impersonal form: identical with infinitive

Again, only the **du**-form is not identical with the present indicative. The change of vowel from **a** to **ä** (**ich fahre, du fährst**), from **au** to **äu** (**ich laufe, du läufst**), and from **o** to **ö** (**stoßen, du stößt**) does not occur in the imperative. However, the change from **e** to **ie** or **i** (**ich gebe, du gibst; ich sehe, du siehst**) must be observed. These changed-vowel forms never show the ending **-e** in the **du**-form. The **du**-form **werde** is irregular, as are the forms of **sein**. In principle, the ending **-e** of the **du**-form is again optional.

183   The Use of the Various Forms of the Imperative

The Use of the **du**-Form

The **du**-form is used when the persons involved say **du** to each other. It is also used in advertisements.

> **Bring mir bitte Zigaretten mit,**
> **Bring mir doch bitte Zigaretten mit,** } **wenn du in die Stadt fährst!**
> **Bitte bring mir Zigaretten mit,**
>
> **Mach mal Pause, trink Coca-Cola!**

This form can be used together with a **du** immediately following the imperative. This **du** always establishes a contrast between the person addressed and someone else.

> **Steh** *du* **doch mal zuerst auf!** (wife to husband; she usually gets up first)
>
> **Rede** *du* **mal mit Meyer!** (wife to husband; she has talked with Meyer already)

This pattern is sometimes expressed in English by "Why don't *you* . . ."

The **ihr**-Form

Like the **du**-form, the **ihr**-form is used between persons who say **du** to each other.

Kinder, vergeßt nicht,
Kinder, bitte vergeßt nicht,   } daß ihr um zehn zu Hause sein sollt.
Kinder, vergeßt bitte nicht,

The use of **ihr** is parallel to the use of **du** with the **du**-form.

Geht ihr schon! *Ich* komme *später.*

Versucht *ihr* doch mal, mit Meyer zu reden. *Mir glaubt* er nicht.

The **wir**-Form

The **wir**-form can only be used if the speaker includes himself among the persons addressed:

Wo wollen wir denn essen? Im Regina? Gut, fahren wir ins Regina!

The **Sie**-Form

The **Sie**-form is used (with or without **bitte**) between persons who say **Sie** to each other.

(Bitte) bringen Sie mir noch ein Glas Wein.

In advertising it is used without **bitte**.

Versuchen Sie SUNIL. Sie werden bestimmt zufrieden sein.

The Impersonal Form

The impersonal form is the infinitive used to express a request. It is used to give instructions to the public. It therefore appears on traffic signs, at airports, in planes, in railroad stations, etc. It is also used in advertising and in modern cookbooks, without exclamation marks.

Alles aussteigen.
Bitte aussteigen.
Aussteigen bitte.
Nicht öffnen, bevor der Zug hält.
Langsam fahren.
Nicht rauchen.
Bitte anschnallen.
Nicht benutzen, während der Zug hält.

Bitte nicht stören!
Do not disturb please!
Ne pas déranger s.v.p.!

184   The Intonation of Imperatives

The imperative as a command is distinguished from the imperative as
a polite request by level of intonation.

The imperative expressing a command follows the usual 2-3-1 assertion
pattern; that is, the intonation curve goes up to level 3 and then sinks
to level 1:

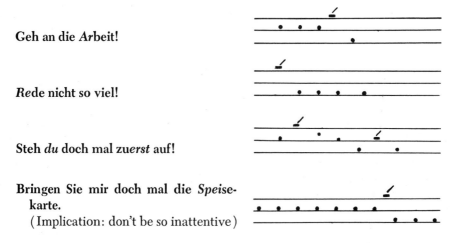

Geh an die *Arbeit!*

Rede nicht so viel!

Steh *du* doch mal zu*erst* auf!

Bringen Sie mir doch mal die *Speise*-
karte.
(Implication: don't be so inattentive)

In a polite request using imperative forms, the unstressed syllables preceding the stress-point are usually arranged in a downward trend toward
level 1, and then the first stressed syllable is raised only to level 2, not
to level 3:

Sei mir nicht *böse!*

Bitte bring mir etwas zu *lesen* mit!

Geben Sie mir doch mal etwas zu
trinken. (Request by patient, not order to nurse.)

Bleib ruhig im *Bett!* (Why don't you
stay in bed! Not: Be quiet in bed!)

Bringen Sie mir doch mal die *Speise*-
karte. (Would you be so kind as to
bring me the menu?)

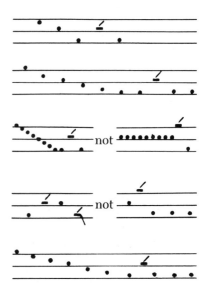

Einfahrt freihalten
Parken im Hof verboten

Be-u. Entladen v. 19-16 h
erlaubt.

GEPÄCKBAHNSTEIG
NICHT AUSSTEIGEN

How to express commands and requests is not so much a question of grammatical correctness as of correct social behavior. Nobody likes to be ordered around, and nobody wants to gain the reputation of being "bossy." You are therefore advised to express requests either by questions or by those forms of the imperative which are marked by intonation as requests.

185 The Syntax of the Imperative

The personal forms of the imperative begin the sentence and can be preceded only by **bitte.**

> **Bring mir etwas zu lesen mit!**
> **Bitte bring mir etwas zu lesen mit!**
> **Bring mir bitte etwas zu lesen mit!**
> **Bring mir etwas zu lesen mit, bitte!**

Since the impersonal imperatives are infinitives, they stand at the end of the imperative phrase:

> **Langsam fahren!**
> **Hinten einsteigen!**
> **Bitte die Türen schließen!**
> **Bitte von der Bahnsteigkante zurücktreten!**

When imperatives are negated, **nicht** stands, as usual, at the end of the inner field. Since the impersonal imperative is an infinitive, it must always follow the **nicht.** Thus the sentence

> **Man darf nicht mit dem Fahrer sprechen**

becomes the impersonal imperative

> **Nicht mit dem Fahrer sprechen!**

> **Bitte fahr morgen nicht nach Berlin!**
> **Sei doch nicht so ungeduldig!**
> **Warte heute nicht auf mich!**
> **Vergiß mich nicht!**
> **Bitte ruf mich morgen nicht an!**
> **Nicht hinauslehnen.**

Any imperative constitutes direct discourse. In order to report, by indirect discourse, that a request was made or a command given, **sollen** is used:

IMPERATIVE:

Fahren Sie doch einmal an die See.

INDIRECT DISCOURSE:

Der Arzt meinte, ich solle (sollte) doch einmal an die Nordsee fahren.
Der Arzt meinte, er solle (sollte) doch einmal an die Nordsee fahren.
Der Arzt meinte, wir sollten doch einmal an die Nordsee fahren.

186 doch einmal, doch mal

When **einmal** or the shorter **mal** is used in assertions and requests, they may mean *once, for once,* or *for a change:*

> **Ich will dieses Jahr nicht an die Nordsee. Ich möchte mal in die Berge fahren.**
> I don't want to go to the North Sea this year. I'd like to go to the mountains for a change.

> **Steh *du* doch mal zuerst auf.**
> Why don't you get up first for a change?

Very often, however, the short **mal** loses its literal meaning and expresses simply a note of casualness.

> **Ich geh' mal in die Stadt.**
> **Ich muß mal telefonieren.**

In requests, this casual **mal** is usually preceded by an unstressed **doch**.

> **Mach uns doch mal eine Tasse Kaffee.**
> How about fixing us a cup of coffee?

Noch (ein)mal and **doch noch (ein)mal** always mean *once more* or *again*.

> **Ruf sie doch noch mal an.**
> Call her up again.

187 eben and gerade

If **eben** is used with a full lexical meaning, it means either *flat, even,* or *just (a while ago):*

ebenes (flaches) Land	flat land
die Ebene, -n	the plain
die Norddeutsche Tiefebene	the North German Plain
er ist eben gekommen	he just came

Eben can also be used as a sentence adverb meaning "it won't take long; I hope you won't mind the interruption." In this function, it minimizes the significance of the action, and for this reason is frequently used in connection with the casual **mal**. As a sentence adverb, **eben** is never stressed.

> **Ich muß mal eben in die Stadt.**
> I've got to run downtown for a minute. (Nothing important; I'll be right back.)
>
> **Entschuldigst du mich einen Augenblick? Ich muß mal eben telefonieren.**
> Will you excuse me for a minute? I just want to make a quick phone call.

If **gerade** is used with full lexical meaning, it means *straight:*

> **eine gerade Linie**   a straight line

In connection with numbers, one speaks of **gerade Zahlen** and **ungerade Zahlen** (even and odd numbers). It can also mean *just then* or *just now* (see **eben** above):

> **er ist gerade gekommen**   he just came
> **Ich war gerade (eben) nach Hause gekommen, als das Telefon klingelte.**

188   ruhig

German **ruhig** can be used either as an adjective or as a sentence adverb. As an adjective, it means *calm, quiet.*

> **Sei ruhig.**   Be quiet.
> **Nun sei mal ganz ruhig, Gerda, und versuche, uns zu erzählen, was passiert ist.**

If used as a sentence adverb, **ruhig** denotes that the speaker will remain "quiet" and has no objections.

> **Bleib du ruhig im Bett; ich frühstücke im Flughafen.**
> Don't bother to get up for me; I'll have breakfast at the airport.
>
> **Ihr könnt ruhig laut sein, Kinder, ich will jetzt *doch* nicht schlafen.**
> I won't mind your being loud; I don't want to sleep now anyway.

EXERCISES

A. In the following sentences, insert **selbst** or **selber** in as many places as possible and translate the resulting sentences into English. The number of possibilities is indicated in parentheses.

1. Erika fährt nicht. (4)
2. Ich wollte, ich könnte einmal mit Meyer reden. (4)
3. Warum denkst du eigentlich nie an dich? (1)
4. Meyer geht jeden Sonntag in die Kirche. (3)
5. Ich habe Angst gehabt. (3)
6. Mit Erika könnte ich, wenn nötig, ins Museum gehen. (5)

B. Restate the following sentences by using the subject indicated in parentheses. Be sure to distinguish between dative and accusative reflexives.

1. Natürlich haben sie sich schon einmal geküßt. (wir)
2. Kann er sich schon selber anziehen? (du)
3. Und dann sah er sich im Spiegel. (ich)
4. Ich muß mir morgen eine Wohnung suchen. (wir) (ihr)
5. Das können sie sich nicht kaufen. (ich) (du) (er) (Erika)
6. Sie trafen sich am Bahnhof. (wir)
7. Du mußt auch einmal an dich selbst denken. (Sie)
8. Kannst du dir das Frühstück nicht einmal selber machen? (er)
9. Sie hat sich in ihn verliebt. (er)
10. Hat er sich schon umgezogen? (du)

C. Restate the following sentences containing a statal present by using the corresponding perfect of the reflexive.

1. Ich bin gut ausgeruht.
2. Er ist schon rasiert.
3. Er ist seit einer Woche mit meiner Schwester verlobt.
4. Er ist in Rosemarie verliebt.
5. Ich bin schwer erkältet.

D. Restate the following sentences by replacing the reflexives by a statal present.

1. Mit wem hat er sich denn verlobt?
2. Warum hat er sich denn so aufgeregt?
3. Hat Hans sich vorbereitet?
4. Hast du dich schon wieder erkältet?
5. Ich habe mich entschlossen, das Haus zu kaufen.

E. In the following sentences, fill in the blanks by using the correct form of **setzen, sitzen; stellen, stehen; legen, liegen.**

1. Als ich nach Hause kam, _____ meine Frau schon im Bett.
2. Als ich nach Hause kam, hatte meine Frau sich schon ins Bett _____.
3. Hast du die Schuhe schon vor die Tür _____?
4. Meine Frau geht nur dann ins Theater, wenn sie in der ersten Reihe _____ kann.
5. Ich hatte einen guten Platz. Aber dann _____ sich der dicke Meyer vor mich, und ich konnte nichts mehr sehen.
6. Gestern im Theater habe ich neben Rosemarie _____.
7. Heute möchte ich eigentlich gern im Garten _____.
8. Ich habe deinen Mantel aufs Bett _____.

9. Der Zug war so voll, daß ich keinen Sitzplatz finden konnte, und ich mußte von Köln bis nach Frankfurt _____.
10. Wir haben den Tisch jetzt an die Wand _____.

F. In the following sentences, replace the transitives **setzen, stellen, legen** or the reflexives **sich setzen, sich stellen, sich legen** with the intransitives **sitzen, stehen, liegen,** or vice versa. Observe the difference in tense and, in some cases, the change of subject; remember also that you have to change case in the prepositional phrase.

> **Sie liegt schon im Bett.**
> **Sie hat sich schon ins Bett gelegt.**

1. Er hat sich neben sie gesetzt.
2. Wir saßen in der ersten Reihe.
3. Sie sitzen alle im Garten.
4. Warum hast du dich denn noch nicht ins Bett gelegt?
5. Er muß sich schon ins Bett gelegt haben.
6. Sie hatte sich direkt neben den Zollausgang gestellt.
7. Er stand am Fenster.
8. Er hat das Buch auf den Nachttisch gelegt.
9. Ich habe meine Schuhe vor die Tür gestellt.
10. Er saß schon am Frühstückstisch.
11. Vor ihm stand eine Tasse Kaffee. (New subject: Ingrid)
12. Er legte die Bibel vor sich auf den Tisch.
13. Wo hast du denn meinen Hut hingelegt?
14. Wo sitzt denn deine Frau? (Start new question with *Wo*)
15. Wo steht denn mein Wagen? (Start question with *Wohin?*; new subject: *du*)

G. Express in German by using a reflexive verb.

1. Why don't you go to bed?
2. Did you shave this morning?
3. They got engaged.
4. They got a divorce.
5. Can't Fritzchen take a bath by himself now?
6. You ought to change before Tante Amalie comes.
7. I broke my arm and I can't undress my*self.*
8. Have you had enough sleep?
9. Did you have a good rest?
10. He always gets so excited.
11. Did she finally calm down?

H. By placing **bitte** in the front field, inner field, and end field, repeat the following sentences three times.

1. Sei doch nicht so aufgeregt!
2. Laß mich in Ruhe!
3. Sprechen Sie etwas lauter!
4. Ruf mich nicht vor acht an!
5. Komm nicht wieder erst um zwei nach Hause!

I. Change the following sentences to imperative sentences, using **doch mal** in the inner field.

1. Könntest du uns eine Tasse Kaffee machen?
2. Würdest du mir etwas zu lesen mitbringen?
3. Könnten Sie uns an einem Sonntag besuchen?
4. Muß *ich* denn immer das Licht ausmachen?
5. Ich rate Ihnen, an die See zu fahren, gnädige Frau.

J. Change the following complaints into imperatives. Use **doch bitte** in the inner field.

1. Du rauchst zuviel.
2. Du gibst zuviel Geld aus.
3. Du bist immer so unfreundlich.
4. Können Sie mir kein Zimmer mit Bad geben?
5. Kannst du nicht mal vernünftig sein?

K. Change the following imperatives to the **du**-form. Use **du** and **ihr** only when **Sie** is italicized.

1. Seien Sie doch nicht so aufgeregt!
2. Stehen Sie doch morgen etwas früher auf!
3. Bringen Sie mir ruhig noch eine Tasse Kaffee!
4. Gehen *Sie* doch mal mit Tante Amalie ins Museum!
5. Sprechen Sie ruhig lauter!
6. Gute Nacht, schlafen Sie gut.
7. Ich weiß, dies ist kein schönes Zimmer. Aber finden Sie hier mal ein besseres!
8. Denken Sie mal, wen ich gestern getroffen habe!
9. Fahren Sie doch mal eben zur Post.
10. Verbieten Sie ihm doch einfach, daß er Sie zu Hause anruft.
11. Schlagen *Sie* mir mal etwas vor.
12. Bringen Sie die Bücher bitte in die Bibliothek zurück.
13. Nehmen Sie uns doch bitte mit.
14. Schreien Sie doch nicht so laut!
15. Schwimmen *Sie* doch mal über den Rhein!

L. Change the following imperatives to indirect discourse, starting with **Er sagte, . . .** Use both forms of the subjunctive where possible.

1. Fahren Sie doch mal an die See.

2. Sei nicht so unfreundlich.
3. Schicken Sie mir den Brief nach.
4. Geht doch mit ins Theater.
5. Seid vorsichtig, und macht dem Wolf nicht die Tür auf.

M. Composition.

After you have spent your first night in a German hotel, you decide to write to your cousin Hildegard again. This time, describe what happened to you after your arrival in Koblenz; how you took a taxi to your hotel, and how surprised you were at the difference between this German hotel and American hotels. Tell her what an American motel is like; are there any motels in Germany at all? Then tell her that you have tried to call your friend Barbara, but haven't been able to reach her yet. You will try again and you hope that you'll be able to visit her. Ask Hildegard to write to you in Augustdorf and to let you know whether it is all right with her if you come to Munich in about two weeks.

Restrict yourself to the vocabulary and to the patterns you know. The reading selections of Units 10–12 should provide you with all you need; review them before you start writing.

BASIC VOCABULARY

ähnlich similar
sich anziehen to get dressed
sich aufregen über to get excited about
der Augenblick, –e moment, instant
sich ausruhen to rest; to get a rest
sich ausschlafen to get enough sleep
aussteigen to get out (of a vehicle)
sich ausziehen to undress
der Bart, ⸚e beard
benutzen to use
(sich) beruhigen to calm down
  beruhigt sein to be calmed down
billig inexpensive; cheap
ein bißchen a bit, a little
die Decke, –n ceiling; blanket
Deutsch können (here used in the sense of "to know," "to have a mastery of," as a language. Thus: **Er kann Deutsch, Er kann Französisch**, etc.)
einander each other

empfangen to receive
  der Empfang, ⸚e reception
sich entschließen zu to make up one's mind to
  entschlossen sein zu to be determined
(sich) entschuldigen to excuse (oneself)
  entschuldigt sein to be excused
sich erholen to get a rest (to recover one's strength)
  erholt sein to be well rested (recovered)
sich erkälten to catch a cold
  erkältet sein to have a cold
falsch false, wrong
farbig in color, colored
fest firm(ly)
fließen to flow
der Führer, – guide; leader
sich fürchten vor to be afraid of
gegenseitig each other, mutual
gnädige Frau formal way of addressing a married woman
sich gewöhnen an to get used to

gewöhnt sein an to be used to
die Großstadt, ⸚e large city; metropolis
  die Kleinstadt, ⸚e small town
inzwischen meanwhile, in the meantime
das Land, ⸚er country
  auf dem Land in the country
legen to lay
  liegen to lie
  sich legen to lie down
die Luft, ⸚e air
  die Luftpost air mail
der Mund mouth
  mündlich oral
(sich) öffnen to open
  geöffnet sein to be open
sich rasieren to shave
retten to save
schauen look, gaze
sich scheiden lassen von to get a divorce from
  geschieden sein to be divorced
(sich) schließen to close
  geschlossen sein to be closed

selbst, selber (*indeclinable*) self (see **175**); even (see **176**)
setzen to set
  sitzen to sit
  sich setzen to sit down
sogar even
sowieso anyhow, anyway
stark strong
stellen to place
  sich stellen to place oneself (to stand)
der Stock, ⁔e stick; floor (of a building)
  im ersten (zweiten, etc.) Stock on the first (second, etc.) floor
stören to disturb
der Tod, –e death

das Tor, –e gate
treffen to hit; to meet
(sich) überzeugen von to convince (oneself) of
  überzeugt sein von to be convinced of
sich umziehen to change (clothes)
sich verändern to change
  verändert sein to be changed, different
verbinden to connect
sich verheiraten to get married
sich verlieben in to fall in love with
  verliebt sein in to be in love with

sich verloben mit to get engaged to
  verlobt sein mit to be engaged to
der Verlobte, –n fiancé
die Verzeihung pardon
verzeihen to pardon, excuse
voll full
vor allem above all
sich vorbereiten auf to prepare for
vorstellen introduce (socially)
wachsen to grow
  erwachsen (*adj.*) grown up, adult
das Wunder, – miracle, wonder
die Zahl, –en number

ADDITIONAL VOCABULARY

altmodisch old-fashioned
anreden mit to address by
sich anschnallen to fasten seat belts
  die Schnalle, –n buckle
anzeigen to announce
der Aufzug, ⁔e elevator
bedienen to serve
  die Bedienung service
das Ei, –er egg
sich einordnen (traffic) to get into the correct lane; to merge
sich erkundigen to inquire
die Geduld (*no pl.*) patience
  geduldig patient

das Gepäck (*no pl.*) baggage
das Geschäft, –e business, store
der Händler, – dealer
heizen to heat
  die Heizung heating system, radiator
  die Zentralheizung central heating
die Kasse, –n cash register, cash box
das Klima, –s climate
das Konzert', –e concert
sich leisten to afford
die Lippe, –n lip
nervös' nervous

reißen to tear
schlucken to swallow
  der Schluck sip
schneien to snow
  der Schnee (*no pl.*) snow
die Schulter, –n shoulder
der Schwarzwald Black Forest
das Tal, ⁔er valley
das Thema, die Themen topic; subject; theme
der Urlaub furlough; vacation
die Vorsicht (*no pl.*) caution
  vorsichtig careful; cautious

IRREGULAR VERBS

empfangen to receive
  empfing, hat empfangen, er empfängt
fließen to flow
  floß, ist geflossen, er fließt
reißen to tear
  riß, hat gerissen, er reißt
schließen to close

schloß, hat geschlossen, er schließt
treffen to hit; to meet
  traf, hat getroffen, er trifft
sich umziehen to change clothes
  zog sich um, hat sich um-

gezogen, er zieht sich um
verzeihen to pardon, excuse
  verzieh, hat verziehen, er verzeiht
wachsen to grow
  wuchs, ist gewachsen, er wächst

UNIT 13: The Passive—**es** in the Front Field—
Pre-Noun Inserts

PATTERNS

[1] Reflexives Denoting a (Mental) State

SEE
ANALYSIS
189
(pp. 431-434)

langweilen—sich langweilen—gelangweilt sein

Meine Damen und Herren, ich hoffe, ich langweile Sie nicht, aber der Oedipuskomplex ist wirklich ein sehr wichtiges Problem.

Meine Damen und Herren, ich sehe, Sie sind gelangweilt. Sie scheinen nicht zu verstehen, daß der Oedipuskomplex ein sehr wichtiges Problem ist.

sich bemühen um—bemüht sein

Gnädige Frau, wir haben uns sehr bemüht, ein Zimmer für Sie zu finden, aber wir haben nichts finden können.

Er behauptet, daß er mich liebt, und er ist sehr bemüht (er bemüht sich sehr), Mama davon zu überzeugen.

sich interessieren für—interessiert sein an (plus dative)

Interessieren Sie sich nicht für moderne Tänze?

An einem Chronometer bin ich nicht interessiert.

ärgern, sich ärgern über

Der Meyer ist wirklich ein Dummkopf. Ich habe mich gestern abend furchtbar über ihn geärgert.

Es ärgert mich, daß Meyer immer zu spät kommt.

Ich ärgere mich auch immer darüber, daß er so spät kommt.

erinnern an—sich erinnern an

Ich bin Renate Pfeiffer, Herr Professor. Sie erinnern sich sicher nicht mehr an mich, aber ich war vor zwanzig Jahren in Ihrem Faust-Seminar.

Oh doch, ich erinnere mich sehr gut an Sie, Fräulein Wilke. Sie kamen immer zehn Minuten zu spät.

*Da*ran kann ich mich aber nicht mehr erinnern, Herr Professor.

Du mußt mich morgen unbedingt daran erinnern, daß ich den Mehrens anrufen muß.

(*Facing*) Zwei alte Frankfurter in Sachsenhausen

417

Ihre Frau hat gerade angerufen; sie wollte Sie daran erinnern, daß Sie heute abend Gäste
haben.—Oh, das erinnert mich, ich muß noch Zigarren kaufen; Dr. Mertens raucht
keine Zigaretten.

sich freuen auf

Du kommst doch auch nächsten Samstag zu unserer Party?—Ja, ich freue mich schon
darauf.

Also, lieber Herr Raschke, wir erwarten Sie am Freitag gegen vier; wir freuen uns sehr
auf Ihren Besuch.

sich freuen über

Und vielen Dank für die Blumen; ich habe mich sehr darüber gefreut.

Vater hat sich sehr darüber gefreut, daß du seinen Geburtstag nicht vergessen hast.

fürchten—sich fürchten vor

Ich fürchte, Herr Meyer ist schon nach Hause gegangen.

Ich habe mich wirklich davor gefürchtet, mit ihm in einem Büro sitzen zu müssen. Aber
jetzt sind wir gute Freunde.

Wirklich? Ich habe mich nie vor ihm gefürchtet.

sich wundern über

Ich habe mich doch gestern abend über den Fritz gewundert. Daß der gar nichts getrunken
hat! Früher hat er immer zu viel getrunken.

sich verlassen auf

Wenn du den Nolte nach Berlin geschickt hast, kannst du beruhigt sein. Auf den kann man
sich verlassen.

Kann ich mich darauf verlassen, daß du um fünf zu Hause bist?

sich beschäftigen mit—beschäftigt sein mit

Meyer kennt nur eine Beschäftigung: Geld verdienen. Augenblicklich ist er damit beschäftigt (beschäftigt er sich damit), das Land, das er letztes Jahr billig gekauft hat,
teuer zu verkaufen.

Herr Dr. Müller ist jetzt leider nicht zu sprechen; er ist beschäftigt.

Womit ist er denn beschäftigt?

VARIATIONS

Complete the following sentences:

1. sich ärgern

Hast du _____ heute wieder _____ müssen im Büro?

Über _____ hast du _____ denn heute _____?

Ja, heute habe ich _____ über Meyer geärgert.

Ich glaube, du bist nicht glücklich, wenn du dich nicht _____ kannst.

2. sich freuen

Ich habe mich sehr _____ gefreut, daß sie gekommen ist.

Ich freue mich sehr _____, daß sie morgen kommt.

[2] Reflexives Denoting Physical Motion

sich bewegen

Der Mond bewegt sich um die Erde, und die Erde bewegt sich um die Sonne.

Ich war so müde, ich konnte mich kaum bewegen.

SEE
ANALYSIS
189
(pp. 431-434)

sich eilen—sich beeilen

Ich brauche mindestens zehn Minuten, um mich umzuziehen.—Kannst du dich nicht mal ein bißchen eilen (beeilen)?

Eilt euch, Kinder, der Vater wartet schon.

sich verfahren—sich verlaufen

Natürlich brauchen wir eine Straßenkarte, sonst verfahren wir uns wieder.

In München kann man sich leicht verlaufen.—Wieso denn? Ich habe mich in München noch nie verlaufen.

sich umdrehen

Sie hat sich nach mir umgedreht.

VARIATIONS

Complete the following sentences:

1. sich verfahren

Wo bleibt er denn? Ob er sich schon wieder _____ hat?

Ich brauche keine Straßenkarte; ich _____ mich nie.

2. sich umdrehen

Als er mich sah, hat er sich sofort _____.

Aber Anton, du brauchst dich doch nicht immer _____, wenn ein hübsches Mädchen vorbeigeht.

[3] Dative Reflexives

Ich stelle mich vor—ich stelle mir vor

Darf ich mich vorstellen? Ich bin Dr. Ingelheim.

Gnädige Frau, darf ich Ihnen Herrn Dr. Ingelheim vorstellen?

Ich kann mir nicht vorstellen, daß Ingelheim ein guter Soldat gewesen ist.

SEE
ANALYSIS
189
(pp. 431-434)

Ich hatte mir das alles viel leichter vorgestellt.

sich etwas einbilden—eingebildet sein

Das stimmt doch gar nicht; das bildest du dir nur ein.

Und er hat sich eingebildet, ich wollte ihn heiraten.

Den Erich heirate ich nicht; der ist mir viel zu eingebildet.

sich etwas denken

Du kannst dir gar nicht denken, wie ich mich darauf freue, Dich endlich wiederzusehen.

Ich habe mir gar nichts dabei gedacht, als ich sie fragte, wie es ihrem Mann ginge. Wie
   konnte ich denn wissen, daß sie geschieden ist?

sich etwas überlegen

Ich überlege mir oft, ob es nicht besser wäre, wenn wir nach Heidelberg zögen.

Wie wäre es, wenn Sie auch in die Stadt zögen?—Das muß ich mir erst noch überlegen.

sich etwas ansehen—sich etwas anschauen

Ich wollte mir den Hitchcock Film eigentlich gar nicht ansehen; aber du kennst ja Tante
   Amalie. Sie interessiert sich nur noch für Hitchcock und Picasso.

Schau dir das an! Da kommt Edith Maschke mit ihrem neuen Freund.—Die hat sich ja ganz
   verändert! Seit wann ist sie denn blond?

VARIATIONS

Complete the following sentences:

Vater freut sich _____ Weihnachten.

Das kann ich _____ nicht vorstellen.

Ich habe _____ noch nicht vorgestellt; ich bin Hans Ingelheim.

Ich kann _____ gar nicht denken, was er _____ dabei
   gedacht hat.

Das solltest du _____ gut überlegen.

Er soll _____ eingebildet haben, ich wollte _____ heiraten.

Was kann er _____ nur dabei gedacht _____?

Habt ihr _____ schon überlegt, welchen Film _____ euch
   anschauen wollt?

Hast du	dir schon	die Zähne	geputzt?
Darf ich	mir mal	die Hände	waschen?
Wo kann ich	mir hier	die Haare	schneiden lassen?
Erika hat	sich	den Arm	gebrochen.
Fritz läßt	sich tatsächlich	einen Bart	wachsen.

[4] Impersonal Reflexives

Es stellte sich heraus, daß Erich das Geld gestohlen hatte.
Es erwies sich, daß das Problem *so* nicht zu lösen war.
Es zeigte sich, daß auch die Elektronen sich um ihre Achse drehen.

Worum handelt es sich denn eigentlich?
Es handelt sich um ein wichtiges Problem.

Mein Vater hat mit Diamanten gehandelt.
Wovon handelt dieser Roman denn?
Ich hatte keine Zeit, darüber nachzudenken; ich mußte sofort handeln.

SEE
ANALYSIS
189

(pp. 431-434)

[5] The Active Voice of Transitive and Intransitive Verbs; Actional and Statal Forms of the Passive

This is a presentation of basic forms. Study these examples *after* you have read
190–192.

SEE
ANALYSIS
190–192

(pp. 434-437)

PRESENT

INTRANSITIVE	Kochen die Kartoffeln schon?
TRANSITIVE	Mutter kocht jeden Tag Kartoffeln.
ACTIONAL PASSIVE	Bei uns werden jeden Tag Kartoffeln gekocht.
STATAL PASSIVE	Sind die Kartoffeln schon gekocht?

PAST

INTRANSITIVE	Als ich nach Hause kam, standen die Kartoffeln schon auf dem Herd und kochten.
TRANSITIVE	Mutter kochte damals jeden Tag fünf Pfund Kartoffeln.
ACTIONAL PASSIVE	Bei uns wurden früher jeden Tag fünf Pfund Kartoffeln gekocht.
STATAL PASSIVE	Als ich nach Hause kam, waren die Kartoffeln schon gekocht. Wenn die Kartoffeln schon gekocht gewesen wären, hätten wir sofort essen können.

PERFECT

INTRANSITIVE	Die Kartoffeln haben noch gar nicht gekocht.
TRANSITIVE	Hast du auch genug Kartoffeln gekocht?
ACTIONAL PASSIVE	Bei uns sind noch nie soviel Kartoffeln gekocht worden wie in den letzten Tagen.

INFINITIVES

Ingelheim will *Die Frau mit dem Flamingo* an den Exotica-Verlag verkaufen.
Ingelheim soll *Die Frau mit dem Flamingo* an den Exotica-Verlag verkauft haben.

Das Wasser kocht, die Hausfrau lacht, weil JUNO vieles leichter macht

Das Kochendwassergerät von JUNO liefert im Handum-
drehen warmes, heißes oder kochendes Wasser, ganz nach
Wunsch und Menge von 0,5 - 5 Liter. Ein Liter kocht in
ca. 3 Minuten. Stromkosten: 1 Pfennig!
Näheres über JUNO-Elektro-Heißwasserbereiter im Fach-
geschäft. Prospekte – auch über JUNO-Öfen, Herde, Wasch-
vollautomaten – durch JUNO 6348 Herborn/Dillkreis

**JUNO bringt
Komfort
ins Haus**

In Kanada darf *Die Frau mit dem Flamingo* nicht verkauft werden.

Im letzten Jahr sollen über 100.000 Exemplare verkauft worden sein.

Die ganze erste Auflage soll schon verkauft sein.

Haben Sie gehört, die ganze erste Auflage soll schon nach vier Wochen verkauft
gewesen sein.

[6] Distinction between Actional and Statal Passive Forms

SEE
ANALYSIS
191–192

(pp. 435-437)

Bei uns werden alle Briefe mit der Maschine geschrieben.

Diese Briefe sind mit der Maschine geschrieben.

Wann ist das Pulver denn erfunden worden?

Das weiß ich nicht. Als ich geboren wurde, war es schon erfunden.

Dieses Zimmer ist aber kalt. Ist das Zimmer nicht geheizt, oder kann es nicht geheizt
werden?

*Die Trans-Pacific-Eisenbahn
wurde nicht an einem Tag gebaut*

**Auch die
Frankfurter Stadtbahn
braucht ihre Bauzeit**

Ich höre, das Haus neben der Kirche soll verkauft werden.
Es ist schon verkauft.

VARIATIONS

Change the following statal passive sentences to the actional passive.

> Das Haus ist schon verkauft.
> Ist die Stadt wiederaufgebaut?
> Das müßte verboten sein.
> Ist meine Schreibmaschine schon repariert?

[7] "Transformations" from Active Voice to Actional Passive

Wer hat denn den Bunsenbrenner erfunden?
Der Bunsenbrenner ist von Bunsen erfunden worden.
Bunsen soll den Bunsenbrenner erfunden haben.
Der Bunsenbrenner soll von Bunsen erfunden worden sein.

SEE
ANALYSIS
193
(pp. 437-438)

Wer hat Amerika entdeckt?
Amerika ist von Kolumbus entdeckt worden.
Schon die Wikinger sollen Amerika entdeckt haben.
Amerika soll schon von den Wikingern entdeckt worden sein.

Die Polizei sucht ihn.
Die Polizei soll ihn suchen.
Er wird von der Polizei gesucht.
Er soll von der Polizei gesucht werden.
Die Polizei suchte ihn überall.
Er wurde von der Polizei gesucht.
Hat ihn die Polizei nie gefunden?
Ist er nie gefunden worden?
Doch! Die Polizei soll ihn gestern gefunden haben.
Doch! Er soll gestern gefunden worden sein.

Eine einzige Bombe hat das Haus zerstört.
Das Haus ist durch eine einzige Bombe zerstört worden.
Das Haus soll durch eine einzige Bombe zerstört worden sein.
Eine einzige Bombe soll das ganze Haus zerstört haben.

VARIATIONS

Transform the following sentences to the statal and the actional passive. Leave out the agent.

Man hat die ganze Stadt zerstört.

Er hat das Haus verkauft.

Er soll das Haus schon verkauft haben.

Wir haben ihn gerettet.

[8] Dative Objects

SEE
ANALYSIS
194
(p. 438)

Wir konnten ihm nicht helfen.

Dem Manne kann geholfen werden. (Schiller, *Die Räuber*)

Ihm ist nicht zu helfen.

Man half ihm sofort.

Ihm wurde sofort geholfen.

Jemand hat mir gesagt, ich sollte um drei Uhr hier sein.

Mir wurde gesagt, ich sollte um drei Uhr hier sein.

Es wurde mir gesagt, ich sollte um drei Uhr hier sein.

[9] Passive Forms to Express Activity as such

SEE
ANALYSIS
195
(pp. 438-439)

Wir waschen nur mit Persil.

Bei uns wird nur mit Persil gewaschen, denn Persil bleibt Persil.

Hier wird gearbeitet.

Jeden Samstag abend wird dort getanzt.

In meinem Elternhaus ist viel musiziert worden.

In Kalifornien wird fast nur mit Gas geheizt.

Bei euch im Büro wird viel zu viel geredet.

Wann wird denn hier morgens gefrühstückt?

In diesem Hotel wird nur vom 15. September bis zum 1. Mai geheizt.

Ingelheim ist mir zu sentimental; in seinen Romanen wird auf jeder dritten Seite
geweint.

Es wird gebeten, nicht zu rauchen.

VARIATIONS

Change to actional passive, expressing "activity as such."

Wir arbeiten hier schwer.

Man hat hier noch nie getanzt.

Und um eins essen wir hier zu Mittag.

In unserer Familie lachen wir viel.

[10] Syntactical Variations

zeigen

SEE
ANALYSIS
190–197

(pp. 434–440)

Der neue schwedische Film wird jetzt auch in Deutschland gezeigt.

Könnte man ihn nicht auch in den Vereinigten Staaten zeigen?

Während der internationalen Filmfestspiele in Berlin wurde auch der neue schwedische Film gezeigt.

Der Film soll sehr gut sein, aber in Amerika ist er noch nicht gezeigt worden.

Es wäre besser, wenn dieser Film auch in Berlin nicht gezeigt worden wäre.

Es tut mir leid, daß der Film gezeigt wird. Ich wollte, er würde nicht gezeigt.

When is it supposed to be shown here? _____

It can never be shown here. _____

einladen

So, ihr seid schon wieder bei Schultes eingeladen?

So, Schultes haben euch schon wieder eingeladen?

Ich werde leider nie eingeladen.

Mich haben sie noch nie eingeladen.

Warum warst du denn gestern abend nicht bei Schultes?

Ich war nicht eingeladen.

Ich wollte, ich würde auch einmal eingeladen.

Ich wollte, ich wäre damals auch eingeladen gewesen.

Den Eugen Wilke treffe ich wahrscheinlich heute bei Schultes. Er soll auch eingeladen sein.

Karola Kirchhoff soll eingeladen worden sein, in Stuttgart die Desdemona zu spielen.

Natürlich freue ich mich darüber, daß ich eingeladen bin, hier in Stuttgart die Desdemona zu spielen. Aber ich bin nicht überrascht. Ich wäre sehr enttäuscht gewesen, wenn ich nicht eingeladen worden wäre.

I wish they would invite us.   Ich wollte, _____.

I wish we were invited.   Ich wollte, _____.

I wish Ingrid had invited us.   Ich wollte, _____.

I wish we had been invited by Ingrid. Ich wollte, _____.

I wish we had been invited.   Ich wollte, _____.

reden

Meine Herren, Sie wissen, ich bin hier neu; aber eines habe ich schon festgestellt. Hier wird zu viel geredet, zu viel geraucht, zu viel Kaffee getrunken und zu wenig gearbeitet.

Auf dem Weg nach Hause redeten wir kaum ein Wort miteinander.

Auf dem Weg nach Hause wurde kaum geredet.

Auf dem Weg nach Hause wurde kaum ein Wort geredet.

Express in the actional passive:

Wir haben genug geredet; jetzt müssen wir etwas tun.

lösen

Es wurde zwar schon im Altertum angenommen, daß sich die Materie aus gewissen „Elementen" zusammensetzt, aber das Problem, aus welchen Elementen die Materie tatsächlich zusammengesetzt ist, konnte viele Jahrhunderte lang nicht gelöst werden.

Man konnte das Problem lange nicht lösen.

Das Problem war einfach nicht zu lösen.

Man glaubte, das Problem wäre nicht zu lösen.

Das Problem ließ sich lange nicht lösen.

Das Problem ist erst vor wenigen Jahren gelöst worden.

Das Problem konnte erst vor wenigen Jahren gelöst werden.

Ohne die Entdeckung des Radiums hätte das Problem nie gelöst werden können.

Im Mittelalter war das Problem noch nicht gelöst.

Erst die moderne Wissenschaft hat das Problem gelöst.

Heute ist das Problem gelöst.

ändern   *to change something, to enforce change*

sich ändern   *to become different, to change in nature or character*

sich verändern   *to change in physical appearance or behavior*

Ich habe meine Meinung geändert.

Der Mantel ist mir viel zu groß; den muß ich ändern lassen.

Haben Sie meinen Mantel schon geändert?

Ja, der Mantel ist schon geändert.

Bei uns gibt es nichts Neues; bei uns ändert sich nie etwas.

Der Marktplatz ist noch immer der alte, und nichts scheint sich hier geändert zu haben. Aber die Menschen, die hier wohnen, die haben sich sehr geändert.

Morgen soll sich das Wetter endlich ändern.

Du hast dich aber verändert, Otto.

Gnädige Frau, Sie haben sich gar nicht verändert.

Die Maria hat sich aber verändert; die muß ja mindestens fünfundzwanzig Pfund abgenommen haben.—Ja, verändert hat sie sich, aber geändert hat sie sich nicht; es ist immer noch dieselbe alte Maria.

Of course I've changed; I'm ten years older.	Natürlich _____.
Karl has really changed; he doesn't drink any more.	Karl hat _____
	_____.

[11] The Impersonal **es**

Be prepared to produce these and similar sentences orally.

Niemand war zu Hause.
Es war niemand zu Hause.

SEE
ANALYSIS
198

(pp. 440-443)

Jemand hat heute nachmittag nach Ihnen gefragt.
Es hat heute nachmittag jemand nach Ihnen gefragt.

Leider meldete sich niemand.
Es meldete sich leider niemand.

Jetzt werden wieder Häuser gebaut.
Es werden jetzt wieder Häuser gebaut.

Viele Leute waren nicht *da*.
Es waren nicht viele *Leu*te da.

Ach Emma, du bist's!
Wer ist denn da?—Ich bin's, Emma.
Meyer kann es nicht gewesen sein.

Es regnet schon seit Tagen.
Hier regnet es schon seit Tagen.

Es hat schon wieder gehagelt.
Hier hat es heute schon wieder gehagelt.

Es hat die ganze Nacht geschneit.
Heute morgen hat es ein bißchen geschneit.

Es hat stundenlang gedonnert und geblitzt, aber geregnet hat es nicht.

Wie geht es denn deinem Vater?—Danke, es geht ihm gut.
Dem Anton geht's immer gut.
Mir geht es heute gar nicht gut; mir geht's schlecht.
Guten Tag, Herr Müller. Ich habe Sie lange nicht gesehen; wie geht's Ihnen denn?

Vor hundert Jahren gab es noch keine Flugzeuge.
Da oben ist ein Flugzeug.

Es gibt jeden Tag Schweinebraten.
Das ist doch kein Schweinebraten, das ist Kalbsbraten.

Wieviele Hotels gibt es denn hier?
Heute gibt es nicht mehr viele Familien mit neun Kindern.
Was gibt's denn zum Mittagessen?

[12] The Impersonal **es** Anticipating a Subject Clause

SEE
ANALYSIS
198

(pp. 440-443)

Es ist nicht gestattet, während der Fahrt mit dem Wagenführer zu sprechen.

Natürlich ist es nicht gestattet, während der Fahrt mit dem Wagenführer zu sprechen.

Es ist leider nicht erlaubt, vor dem Rathaus zu parken.

Leider ist es nicht erlaubt, vor dem Rathaus zu parken.

Es ist verboten, die Türen während der Fahrt zu öffnen.

Ist es verboten, die Türen während der Fahrt zu öffnen?

Es wurde berichtet, daß Ingelheim spurlos verschwunden wäre.

Heute wird aus Kairo berichtet, daß die erste Meldung auf einem Irrtum beruhte.

Es muß leider angenommen werden, daß er nicht mehr am Leben ist.

Leider muß angenommen werden, daß er nicht mehr am Leben ist.

Es wurde vorgeschlagen, eine neue Brücke über den Rhein zu bauen.

Von allen Seiten wurde vorgeschlagen, eine neue Brücke über den Rhein zu bauen.

Es wird oft behauptet, daß Männer besser Auto fahren können als Frauen.

Früher wurde oft behauptet, daß Männer besser Auto fahren könnten als Frauen.

Es wurde beschlossen, endlich eine neue Klinik zu bauen.

Gestern abend wurde beschlossen, endlich eine neue Klinik zu bauen.

Leider konnte nicht festgestellt werden, wer der Dieb ist.

Es konnte nicht festgestellt werden, wer der Dieb ist.

Wer der Dieb ist, konnte bis jetzt nicht festgestellt werden.

Invent anticipating clauses with **es** for the following subject clauses.

_____ das Kind in eine Privatschule zu schicken.

_____ Ingelheim hätte sich scheiden lassen.

_____ daß er nicht gerettet worden ist.

_____ hier ein Bürohaus zu bauen.

[13] Pre-Noun Inserts

SEE
ANALYSIS
200

(pp. 444-446)

Mein Chef, der gottseidank nicht sehr intelligent ist, weiß gar nicht, daß es in Berlin auch billigere Hotels gibt.

Mein (gottseidank nicht sehr intelligenter) Chef weiß gar nicht, daß es in Berlin auch billigere Hotels gibt.

Der Winter, der selbst für Norwegen ungewöhnlich kalt war, wollte gar kein Ende nehmen.

Der (selbst für Norwegen ungewöhnlich kalte) Winter wollte gar kein Ende nehmen.

Die Fluggäste, die soeben mit Lufthansa Flug Nummer 401 aus Frankfurt angekommen
sind, werden gebeten, den Warteraum nicht zu verlassen.

Die (soeben mit Lufthansa Flug Nummer 401 aus Frankfurt angekommenen) Fluggäste
werden gebeten, den Warteraum nicht zu verlassen.

Karthago, das von den Römern zerstört wurde, ist nicht wiederaufgebaut worden.

Das (von den Römern zerstörte) Karthago ist nicht wiederaufgebaut worden.

Aloys Hinterkofer, der seit Wochen von der Polizei gesucht wird, soll gestern in der
Regina-Bar gesehen worden sein.

Der (seit Wochen von der Polizei gesuchte) Aloys Hinterkofer soll gestern in der Regina-
Bar gesehen worden sein.

Die Züge, die im Sommer von München nach Italien fahren, sind meistens überfüllt.

Die (im Sommer von München nach Italien fahrenden) Züge sind meistens überfüllt.

Alle Studenten, die sich für das Projekt interessierten, das Professor Behrens vorgeschlagen
hatte, wurden gebeten, sich am nächsten Tag auf dem Sekretariat zu melden.

Alle (an dem von Professor Behrens vorgeschlagenen Projekt interessierten) Studenten
wurden gebeten, sich am nächsten Tag auf dem Sekretariat zu melden.

If you can figure out the next sentence, you have really mastered the last few
lessons:

Meine Damen und Herren, es handelt sich hier um ein (von der Wissenschaft bis heute
noch kaum beachtetes und, soweit ich das aufgrund meiner Untersuchungen beurteilen
kann, immer wichtiger werdendes) mathematisches Problem.

―――――――――――――――

Sections XI–XIV of *Ein Mann kommt nach San Franzisko* appear after Unit 13
but may be read in conjunction with this unit.

READING

Wie oft läßt sich ein Körper teilen?

Die Frage, wie oft sich ein Körper teilen läßt, ist schon im Altertum
gestellt worden. Was geschieht zum Beispiel, so fragte man, wenn
man ein kleines Körnchen Salz mit immer feineren Messern in immer
kleinere Teile teilt? Auch das kleinste Teilchen wäre ja kein mathe-
matischer Punkt. Auch von dem kleinsten Teilchen müßte immer ⁵
noch ein gewisser, wenn auch sehr kleiner, Raum ausgefüllt werden;

das Körnchen, – little
grain

und rein theoretisch müßte sich dieser Raum, und damit der Körper,   **rein** pure(ly)
von dem dieser Raum ausgefüllt ist, weiter teilen lassen.

Nach Demokrit kann ein Körper nicht unendlich oft geteilt werden.
Bei einem letzten Schnitt entstehen zwei Teile, die sich nicht weiter
teilen lassen. Diese kleinsten Teilchen nannte er Atome; und er   5
scheint gelehrt zu haben (seine Lehre ist uns nur durch die   **die Lehre, –n** teaching
Schriften seiner Gegner überliefert), daß es außer diesen Atomen   **der Gegner, –** opponent
nur blinde Kräfte, wie z.B. die Gravitation, gibt, aber keinen Geist,   **überliefern** transmit
der „über" der Materie steht.   **die Kraft, ⸚e** force

    der Geist, –er spirit

Aristoteles ging von dem Gegensatz zwischen „Form" und „Stoff" 10   **die Materie** matter
aus. Nach dieser Lehre, von der auch das Denken des Mittelalters   **der Stoff, –e** substance, matter
beherrscht war, ist der Unterschied zwischen dem Element Wasser   **beherrschen** to rule
und dem Element Luft auf den Unterschied zwischen der „Form"   **der Tropfen, –** drop
(oder Struktur) des Wassers und der „Form" (oder Struktur) der
Luft zurückzuführen. Wird z.B. ein Tropfen Wasser immer weiter 15
geteilt, so muß schließlich ein Augenblick kommen, wo die für das
Wasser charakteristische Struktur zerstört wird. Das letzte Teilchen
Wasser kann also zwar noch geteilt werden, aber das Resultat wären
nicht zwei noch kleinere Tröpfchen Wasser, sondern vielleicht zwei
Teilchen Luft oder Feuer, von denen jedes die für die Luft oder 20
für das Feuer charakteristische „Form" (oder Struktur) hätte. Nach
dieser Lehre kann die formlose oder strukturlose Materie, die   **enthalten** to contain
materia prima, nicht als solche existieren. Alle Körper enthalten
zwar *materia prima,* aber sie sind das, was sie sind (Luft, Feuer,
Erde, Wasser, Gold), nicht durch die in ihnen steckende Materie, 25   **steckend** existing, contained
sondern durch die für sie charakteristische Form.

    das Blei lead

Bei den Versuchen der Alchimisten, Blei in Gold zu verwandeln,   **verwandeln** transform
war die Lehre von dem Gegensatz zwischen *materia prima* und
forma stets vorausgesetzt. Wir wissen heute, daß die Alchemisten
im letzten Grunde recht hatten. Die von ihnen vorausgesetzte Ein- 30   **die vorausgesetzte Einheit** the presupposed unity
heit alles Stofflichen ist heute sichergestellt, ja, sogar die Verwand-
lung eines Metalls in ein anderes, z.B. von Natrium in Magnesium,   **sicherstellen** to secure
ist bereits Tatsache geworden.   **das Natrium** sodium

    das Magnesium magnesium

Aber den Alchimisten fehlte die wissenschaftliche Methode, d.h.   **die Tatsache, –n** fact
eine Methode, die Natur durch gut ausgedachte Experimente dazu 35
zu zwingen, eine ihr gestellte Frage so zu beantworten, daß diese
Antwort durch weitere Experimente geprüft und bestätigt werden   **prüfen** to test
kann.   **bestätigen** to confirm

Vor allem aber fehlte den Alchimisten die Geduld. Sie wollten das   **das Verdienst, –e** merit
Gebäude der Wissenschaft sozusagen mit dem Dach anfangen. Es 40
ist das große Verdienst Robert Boyles (1627–1691), seine Kollegen   **der Bau, –ten** building, construction
dazu gebracht zu haben, daß sie sich zunächst einmal mit dem Bau
des Fundamentes beschäftigten, d.h. mit der Frage, wieviele Ele-   **das Fundament, –e** foundation

mente es denn eigentlich gibt. Wir können uns heute kaum noch vorstellen, wieviel Boyle von seiner Zeit verlangte, als er das Spekulieren über die *materia prima* beiseite schob und lehrte: In dem roten Mineral Zinnober stecken tatsächlich die beiden Stoffe Schwefel und Quecksilber. Der Zinnober besteht aus ihnen, so wie etwa ein Haus 5 aus Steinen und aus Holz besteht. Diese Behauptung schien paradox zu sein, denn von den Eigenschaften beider „Elemente" ist ja nichts mehr wahrzunehmen, sobald sie sich „verbunden" haben.

Aber erst als man sich entschloß, dieses Paradox zunächst einmal— obwohl noch ungelöst—zu vergessen, wurde es möglich, durch lang- 10 same Arbeit die 92 Elemente zu entdecken, aus denen die materielle Welt besteht. Als mit dieser Entdeckung das wissenschaftliche Fundament gelegt war, konnte die Frage gestellt werden, ob diese 92 Elemente vom Wasserstoff bis zum Uran sich vielleicht doch noch weiter „teilen" lassen. 15

das Spekulieren speculation
beiseite aside
der Zinnober cinnabar
der Schwefel sulphur
das Quecksilber mercury, quicksilver
die Eigenschaft, –en characteristic
wahrnehmen to observe, perceive, notice

der Wasserstoff hydrogen

Die Suche nach dem Glück

Wir wollen hier nun endlich die Frage stellen, ob das Suchen nach dem Glück wirklich ein sinnvolles Suchen ist. Das Glück hängt ja nicht nur von materiellen Dingen ab, es hängt vor allem ab von der Empfänglichkeit des Menschen, davon, ob er fähig ist, glücklich zu sein. Diese Glücksfähigkeit aber leidet unter dem Suchen nach 20 Glück: Sie ist am größten, wenn ein geschenktes Gut nicht gesucht war; sie ist am geringsten, wenn dieses Gut leidenschaftlich gewünscht wurde. Das Wünschen selbst, so scheint es, zerstört den Glückswert des Gewünschten, und das Erreichen wird illusorisch, weil das Erreichte für den Wünschenden nicht mehr dasselbe Glück 25 ist, das er suchte und das er erwartete. Das wirkliche Glück kommt immer von einer anderen Seite als man es meint; es liegt immer da, wo man es nicht sucht. Es kommt immer als Geschenk und läßt sich dem Leben nicht abzwingen. Denn das Glück liegt in den Werten des Lebens, die zwar immer da sind, die aber nur der findet, der 30 diese Werte selbst sucht und nicht das Glück, das sie versprechen. Das Glück begleitet diese Werte, aber wer nur dem Glück nachläuft und nicht die Werte selbst sucht, dem bleibt das Glück für immer ein Phantom.

die Empfänglichkeit, –en receptivity

am geringsten least
leidenschaftlich passionate(ly)
der Wert, –e value

(nach Nicolai Hartmann, *Ethik*)

ANALYSIS

189 Other Reflexive Verbs of High Frequency

The reflexives introduced in Unit 12 all denote transition from one state to another. Not all reflexives can be classified as "transitional." The following four groups are found very frequently.

Verbs Denoting a Mental State with an Accusative Reflexive Pronoun

sich ärgern über	to be mad, annoyed, angry, peeved
sich erinnern an	to remember
sich freuen auf	to look forward to
sich freuen über	to be glad about
sich fürchten vor	to be afraid of
sich verlassen auf	to rely on
sich wundern über	to be amazed at (about)
sich bemühen um	to be trying hard
bemüht sein um	to be trying hard
sich beschäftigen mit	to occupy oneself with
beschäftigt sein mit	to be occupied with
sich langweilen	to be bored
gelangweilt sein	to be bored
sich interessieren *für*	to be interested in
interessiert sein *an*	to be interested in

Note that some of these verbs have a statal as well as a reflexive form. For all practical purposes, these two forms are synonymous, for all the verbs in this group are "durative verbs."

Durative verbs are verbs denoting action without a built-in end. While the action described by verbs like **sterben** or **ankommen** must by definition come to an end, that of verbs like **lieben** or **wohnen** can, at least theoretically, go on indefinitely. Verbs like **sterben** and **ankommen** are called perfective verbs.

The reflexives introduced in Unit 12 are all perfective. Thus the activity of **sich verlieben** (*falling in love*) cannot go on indefinitely, but must end in the state of **verliebt sein** (*being in love*). On the other hand, there is very little difference between **sich beschäftigen** (*to occupy oneself*) and **beschäftigt sein** (*to be occupied, to be busy*). The reflexive itself (**sich beschäftigen**) denotes a continuous action, and the state (**beschäftigt sein**) does not follow upon the completion of the action, but is simultaneous with it.

NOTE: **sich wundern über** cannot be used as the equivalent of English *to wonder:*

Beware!	[Ich wundere, wo er ist.]
Americanism!	
Correct:	**Ich möchte wissen, wo er ist.**
Correct:	**Darüber wundere ich mich gar nicht.**
	(I am not at all surprised at that.)

Verbs Denoting Physical Motion with an Accusative Reflexive Pronoun

sich bewegen	to move
sich eilen or sich beeilen	to hurry
sich verlaufen	to lose one's way (walking)
sich verfahren	to lose one's way (driving)
sich umdrehen	to turn around

Verbs with a Dative Reflexive Pronoun

A small number of German reflexives are used with a dative pronoun.

sich etwas anschauen, sich etwas ansehen   to (take a) look at something

> **Hast du dir den Film schon angesehen?**

sich etwas überlegen   to think (meditate) about something

> **Willst du mit uns nach Italien fahren?**
>
> **Das muß ich mir überlegen.**
> I must think about that.

sich etwas denken (bei)   to think, to imagine, to have thoughts about something

> **Ich kann mir nicht denken, daß sie ihn heiraten will.**
> I can't imagine that she is going to marry him.
>
> **Was hast du dir denn dabei gedacht?**
> What in the world did you think you were doing (or saying)?

sich etwas einbilden   to imagine something falsely

> **Das stimmt doch gar nicht; das bildest du dir nur ein.**
> That's not so at all; you're just imagining it.
>
> **Und er hat sich eingebildet, ich wollte ihn heiraten.**
> And he imagined that I was going to marry him.

NOTE: **eingebildet sein** means *to be conceited.*

sich etwas vorstellen   to imagine, to form a mental picture of something

> **Ich kann mir nicht vorstellen, daß Ingelheim Lehrer geworden ist.**
> I can't imagine that Ingelheim has become a teacher.

NOTE: **vorstellen** can also be used with the accusative; it then means *to introduce:*

> **Darf ich mich vorstellen? Ich bin Dr. Ingelheim.**
> **Gnädige Frau, darf ich Ihnen Herrn Dr. Ingelheim vorstellen?**
> **Darf ich vorstellen? Herr Dr. Ingelheim—Fräulein Wedemeyer.**

To this group belong a number of verbs which call for a dative reflexive where English uses a possessive pronoun. A German would say: "She washed herself the hands" instead of "She washed her hands." Some of these verbs have already been used.

sich die Zähne putzen	to brush one's teeth
sich die Schuhe putzen	to polish one's shoes
sich die Hände waschen	to wash one's hands
sich die Haare schneiden lassen	to have one's hair cut
sich den Arm brechen	to break one's arm
sich einen Bart wachsen lassen	to grow a beard
sich die Haare kämmen	to comb one's hair
sich den Mantel anziehen	to put on one's coat

Impersonal Reflexive Verbs

Es zeigte sich, daß ...   It became apparent that ...
Es stellte sich heraus, daß ...   It turned out that ...
Es erwies sich, daß ...   It was proved that ...

Es handelte sich um   It was a matter of, we were dealing with
    Es handelt sich um Geld.   It is a matter of money.
    Es handelt sich hier um eine wichtige Sache.
    We are dealing here with an important problem.

But note:

    Er handelt *mit* Bananen.
    He sells bananas; he is in the banana business.
    Sein neuer Roman handelt *von* den Kämpfen in der Normandie.
    His new novel deals with the battles in Normandy.
    Wir haben lange genug geredet. Jetzt müssen wir handeln.
    We've talked long enough; now we must act.

190   Active Voice and Passive Voice

Compare these two groups of sentences:

We feed him once a day.	He is fed once a day.
We fed him once a day.	He was fed once a day.
We have always fed him once a day.	He has always been fed once a day.
We ought to feed him once a day.	He ought to be fed once a day.
We ought to have fed him once a day.	He ought to have been fed once a day.

The comparison shows that the forms of the transitive verb *to feed* (*a dog*)—that is, of a verb that can take a direct object—fall into two groups, called the "active voice" and the "passive voice":

	ACTIVE VOICE	PASSIVE VOICE
PRESENT	he feeds	he is fed
PAST	he fed	he was fed
PRESENT PERFECT	he has fed	he has been fed
PRESENT INFINITIVE	to feed	to be fed
PAST INFINITIVE	to have fed	to have been fed

It is easy to see why the terms "active" and "passive" were chosen to identify these forms. In sentences like *We feed our dog,* the grammatical subject acting upon the object is an "active agent," whereas in *Our dog is fed once a day,* the grammatical subject plays the role of a "passive patient" who "suffers" the agent's activity.

191 Action and State

The phrase *was fed* in the two sentences

The dog was fed well

and

The dog was well fed

refers to two fundamentally different situations; for *was fed well* expresses the repeated action of feeding the dog, whereas *was well fed* refers to the state resulting from this action. However, though the difference between state and action is expressed in this particular case by word order, English has not developed a system which forces the speaker to differentiate at all times between an action and the state resulting from this action. Thus the sentence

The house was built on a hill

can refer both to the action of building the house "from scratch" and to the accomplished fact that the house had been built and was sitting on a hill.

In contrast to English, German forces the speaker to select his passive-voice forms in such a way that they refer either to an action or to the state resulting from this action. An ambiguous form comparable to English *was built* simply does not exist. Actions are expressed by the "actional passive"—a form of **werden** plus a participle—and the resulting state is expressed by the "statal passive"—a form of **sein** plus a participle.

ACTION	STATE
Das Haus wird morgen verkauft.	
Das Haus ist gestern verkauft worden.	**Das Haus ist schon verkauft.**

The forms of the actional passive and those of the statal passive are never interchangeable. Occasionally the difference between the statal passive and the actional passive is quite dramatic. Thus the statal forms of **erschießen,** *to shoot and kill,* and of **erschlagen,** *to slay,* have developed a metaphorical meaning:

> **Ich bin erschossen, ich bin erschlagen.**
> I am shot, I am pooped, I am dead tired.

The actional forms

> **Ich bin erschossen worden.**   I have been shot dead.
> **Ich bin erschlagen worden.**   I have been slain.

could only be used at the Pearly Gates.

In the case of some verbs, the actional passive and the statal passive occur with equal frequency. Thus it makes linguistic sense to say *either*

> **Die Stadt war zerstört**   The city was (already) destroyed
>   (as the result of previous bombings)

or

> **Die Stadt wurde zerstört.**   The city was destroyed (during the war by
> **Die Stadt ist zerstört worden.**   bombing).

However, in cases like **Das Haus war nicht versichert,** *The house was not insured,* the speaker is usually more interested in the state; and therefore the actional passive

> **Das Haus wurde versichert**   The house was (going through the act of
>   being) insured

hardly ever occurs.

192   The Forms of the Statal and Actional Passive

	STATAL PASSIVE	ACTIONAL PASSIVE
PRESENT	ist enttäuscht	wird enttäuscht
PAST	war enttäuscht	wurde enttäuscht
PERFECT	ist enttäuscht gewesen	ist enttäuscht worden
FUTURE	wird enttäuscht sein	wird enttäuscht werden
INFINITIVE	enttäuscht sein	enttäuscht werden
	enttäuscht gewesen sein	enttäuscht worden sein

NOTE: The participle of **werden,** when used as an auxiliary, is **worden,** not **geworden.**

193   Choice between Active and Passive Voice

In order to describe the difference between *His father punished him* and *He was punished by his father,* it is sometimes stated that the direct object (*him*) of an active verb becomes the grammatical subject (*he*) of the passive verb. This is true. However, it is necessary to point out two things.

First, the German passive is used only if there is a situation in which an "active agent" somehow focuses his action or attention on an object. German is much more rigid in this respect than English. It is perfectly acceptable English to say

Ingelheim was killed in an accident,

although this statement does not mean that some "active agent" killed him. German, on the other hand, because there is no "active agent" involved, cannot use a passive and will use the intransitive verb **verunglücken,** *to die in an accident,* instead:

Ingelheim ist gestern verunglückt.

Second, if the sentence *My sister has adopted a child,* which does contain both an agent and a patient being acted upon, is transformed into the statement *A child was adopted by my sister,* this indicates a change in the speaker's focus of attention.

When I say *My sister adopted a child, my sister* is not only the grammatical subject, but also the focus of my attention. I am making a statement about my sister, not a statement about a child. Conversely, the attention of a nurse in a home for orphans is focused on the children under her care. She might, therefore, say, *Last week we got six babies; three have already been adopted. One was adopted by my sister.*

Nobody ever mentally forms an active sentence and then transforms it into a passive sentence. Such transformations are only classroom exercises. Nevertheless, the term "transformation" is not useless, as long as one realizes that one does not transform an active sentence into a passive sentence, but rather shifts the focus of attention from the "agent" to the "patient."

194 Dative Objects

The event reported by the English sentence *They gave him a pill* can also be reported by saying *He was given a pill.* The indirect object *him* of the active clause has been "transformed" into the grammatical subject *He* of the passive clause.

In German, no dative object can be transformed into a nominative subject. Not ever! **Nie!**

    Americanism!   [Ich wurde sofort geholfen.]
    CORRECT: **Der Arzt half mir sofort.**

However, to shift the focus from the doctor to myself, the active sentence **Der Arzt half mir sofort** can be changed into **Mir wurde sofort geholfen.** The result is a sentence without a subject; **wurde geholfen** is an impersonal form not depending on **mir.**

If the speaker wants to place this **mir** in the inner field, he cannot leave the front field empty; for that would change the statement into the question

    Wurde mir sofort geholfen?

The declarative force of **mir wurde sofort geholfen** can be maintained in such a case by putting the meaningless "filler" **es** into the front field:

    Es wurde mir sofort geholfen.

This **es** has only one function: it preserves verb-second position. It disappears as soon as the front field is occupied:

    Natürlich wurde mir sofort geholfen.

195 Use of the Actional Passive to Express Activity as Such

German verbs like **arbeiten, tanzen, schießen, warten** do not normally govern an accusative object and can therefore not be used to describe situations in which an agent acts upon a patient. One would not expect them, therefore, to appear in passive sentences. But they do!

The question *What is going on here?* is frequently answered in German by a form of the actional passive.

QUESTION **Was ist denn hier los?**
ANSWER **Hier wird gearbeitet.**
Hier wird getanzt.

Note that such short sentences do not contain a grammatical subject. The form **wird gearbeitet,** structurally not possible in English, denotes the activity of **arbeiten** as such. **Hier wird gearbeitet** means "The activity of working is going on here."

Further examples:

In meinem Elternhaus wurde viel musiziert.
Bei uns wird auch sonntags gearbeitet.
Seit heute morgen wird zurückgeschossen.
(Hitler, on September 1, 1939)

196 The Use of **von, durch,** and **mit** in Passive Sentences

A large percentage of German passive sentences contain only the "passive patient" (the grammatical subject) and no active agent.

If a *personal* agent is mentioned, **von** is used:

Jerusalem wurde von den Römern zerstört.
Jerusalem was destroyed by the Romans.

Mit is used for the instrument "handled" by a personal agent:

Abel wurde von Kain mit einem Stein erschlagen.
Abel was slain by Cain with a rock.

Das ganze Zimmer war mit Blumen geschmückt.
The whole room was decorated with flowers.

Abstract causes, impersonal causes, and impersonal means of destruction are introduced by **durch:**

Sie wurden durch ein neues Gesetz gezwungen, das Land zu verlassen.
They were forced by a new law to leave the country.

Lissabon wurde durch ein Erdbeben zerstört.
Lisbon was destroyed by an earthquake.

Dresden wurde durch Bomben zerstört.
Dresden was destroyed by bombs.

197 Examples Illustrating the Difference between
Action and State

The difference between action and state was introduced in **179** in connection with the reflexives. It was pointed out that **Fritzchen ist schon gebadet** denotes the state resulting from **Fritzchen hat sich gebadet.** We now have to point out that **ist gebadet** may also be the state resulting from the actional passive **Er ist gerade gebadet worden.** Of course, **Fritzchen ist schon gebadet** can also denote the state resulting from an active statement such as **Ich habe Fritzchen schon gebadet.**

	EVENT	STATE
ACTIVE VOICE	Die Polizei hat ihn gerettet. (Perfect)	
ACTIONAL PASSIVE	Er ist gerettet worden. (Perfect)	Er ist gerettet. (Present)
REFLEXIVE	Er hat sich gerettet. (Perfect)	
ACTIVE VOICE	Sein Vater hatte ihn gut vorbereitet. (Pluperfect)	
ACTIONAL PASSIVE	Er war gut vorbereitet worden. (Pluperfect)	Er war gut vorbereitet. (Past)
REFLEXIVE	Er hatte sich gut vorbereitet. (Pluperfect)	

198 The Impersonal **es** in the Front Field

Before discussing the impersonal **es** in the front field, it is necessary to recall that an **es** in the front field cannot be a normal accusative object. For if the **es** in the sentence

>   **Ich weiß es nicht**

is shifted into the front field, it becomes **das:**

>   **Das weiß ich nicht.**

Compare English *I don't know it* and *That I don't know.*

The impersonal **es** in the front field has one of three functions: It can (a) be a meaningless "filler" to preserve verb-second position; it can (b) be the grammatical subject of impersonal verbs; and it can (c) be used to anticipate a following dependent clause.

The Use of **es** as a Filler

In a short sentence like

>   **Niemand war zu Hause**

the inner field is empty. Both **war,** the first prong, and **zu Hause,** the second prong, are position-fixed. If the speaker, in order to put greater news value on **niemand,** decides to put **niemand** in the inner field, he must put something else in the front field; otherwise he would come up with the question

War niemand zu Hause?

Verb-second position, in these cases, can be preserved by filling the front field with a meaningless **es:**

Es war niemand zu Hause.
Es hat niemand angerufen.

This use of **es** as a filler is rather frequent in connection with the passive voice:

Es werden wieder Häuser gebaut.
Es wird wieder gearbeitet.

In all these cases, **es** disappears when the front field is occupied by another unit:

Gestern war niemand zu Hause.
Gestern hat niemand angerufen.
Hier werden wieder Häuser gebaut.
Hier wird wieder gearbeitet.

NOTE:

1. The **es** used in identification sentences was discussed in **73.** This **es** is not a meaningless filler that disappears when the front field is filled; it can appear either in the front field or as the second prong.

Es war nicht mein Bruder.
Mein Bruder war es nicht.

In short sentences like **Ich bin's, du bist's, wir sind's,** etc., the **es** means "the thing to be identified." **Ich bin's** corresponds to *it's me,* which cannot be expressed by [**Es bin ich**] or [**Es ist ich**].

2. **Es** as a filler is also used in the standard introduction of German fairy tales and folksongs. **Es war einmal ein König** corresponds to *Once upon a time there was a king.* Since the entire news value is concentrated in **ein König,** the subject cannot stand in the front field.

Es war einmal eine alte Geiß.
Es war ein König in Thule.
Es waren zwei Königskinder.
Es steht ein Baum im Odenwald.

es as the Grammatical Subject of Impersonal Verbs

The verbs most frequently used with the impersonal subject **es** are:

> **Es regnet, es schneit, es donnert, es hagelt**
> **Es geht mir (ihm, ihr, etc.) gut**
> **Es geht mir (ihm) schlecht**
> **Es ist mir zu warm (zu kalt, zu heiß)**
> **Es ist zehn Uhr (schon spät, noch früh)**
> **Es gelingt mir**

In all these cases, the **es** must appear in the inner field if the front field is occupied by some other unit:

> **Es hat gestern geregnet.**   **Gestern hat es geregnet.**
> **Es schneit schon wieder.**   **Schneit es schon wieder?**
> **Es ist mir hier zu warm.**   **Hier ist es mir zu warm.**

Also, the idiom **es gibt** belongs to this group of "impersonal verbs." **Es gibt,** translatable by either *there is* or *there are,* and roughly meaning "the situation provides," governs the accusative. In connection with a food term, it expresses what will be served. In other cases, it expresses that certain things exist as a permanent part of the environment or of nature.

> **Heute mittag gibt es Kartoffelsuppe.**
> **In Afrika gibt es noch immer wilde Elefanten.**
> **Gibt es hier ein Hotel?**

Unlike the English *there is,* **es gibt** can never be used to point at a specific thing or person:

> *Americanism!*   [Da oben gibt es ein Flugzeug.]
> CORRECT: **Da oben ist ein Flugzeug.**

The Anticipating **es**

The use of **es** to anticipate a following dependent clause is comparable to the use of English *it* in

> I have *it* on good authority that Smith will be our next boss.
> *It* simply is not true that she has gone to college.

where the *it,* which cannot be left out, anticipates the following *that-*clause.

The German anticipatory **es** refers forward to a dependent (subject) clause, and **es** is the grammatical subject of the main clause.

> **Es ist möglich, daß Ingelheim noch lebt.**
> **Es ist nicht wahrscheinlich, daß Ingelheim noch lebt.**
> **Es ist nicht leicht, mit einer Frau wie Ilse verheiratet zu sein.**
> **Es tut ihm leid, daß ich gestern nicht kommen konnte.**

> Es wird berichtet, daß Ingelheim spurlos verschwunden ist.
> Es freut mich, daß Sie kommen konnten.

As long as this anticipatory **es** precedes the clause it anticipates, it does not disappear when the front field is occupied by some other unit:

> Natürlich ist es auch möglich, daß Ingelheim noch lebt.
> Wahrscheinlich ist es allerdings nicht, daß Ingelheim noch lebt.
> Natürlich tut es mir leid, daß ich gestern nicht kommen konnte.

Only the actional passive in such phrases as **Es wird berichtet, daß** . . . becomes **Gestern wurde berichtet, daß** . . .

If the dependent clause precedes the main clause, the anticipatory **es** disappears, because there is nothing left to anticipate.

> Daß Ingelheim noch lebt, ist ganz unwahrscheinlich.

199 jetzt and nun

Though both **jetzt** and **nun** are frequently equivalent to English *now*, they are not always interchangeable. **Jetzt** is an adverb of time without any implications.

> Es ist jetzt zwölf Uhr fünfzehn.
> Meyer wohnt jetzt in München.

Nun, on the other hand, always implies a reference to something which precedes; it therefore contains the idea that one state of affairs is superseded by another:

> Und nun wohnt er in München.
> (He used to live elsewhere.)
> Und nun ist er schon drei Jahre tot.
> (He used to be so full of life.)
> Bist du nun zufrieden?
> (I know you were dissatisfied before.)
> Und nun hören Sie zum Abschluß unserer Sendung „Eine kleine Nacht-
>   musik" von Wolfgang Amadeus Mozart.
> And now we conclude our broadcast with Mozart's "Eine kleine Nacht-
>   musik."

Because of the connotation "this is something new," **nun mal** (**nun einmal**) has the flavor "you might as well get used to it."

> Das *ist* nun einmal so.
> That's the way it is.
> Ich *bin* nun mal nicht so intelligent wie du.
> You might as well accept the fact that I'm not as intelligent as you are.

Na und? Ich bin nun mal kein Genie.
So what? I'm not a genius, and that's that.

200 Pre-Noun Inserts

Syntactical units like *a child* can be separated by adjectives, which are placed between the article and the noun. We shall call such inserted adjectives "pre-noun inserts." For the sake of clarity and illustration, pre-noun inserts are placed within parentheses in this section.

In English, one can speak of *a (healthy) child* or even of *a (healthy but somewhat retarded) child.* However, one cannot speak of

>   a (by a series of unfortunate childhood experiences somewhat retarded, but otherwise quite healthy) child.

English speakers don't have that long a syntactical breath. In German, pre-noun inserts of considerable length are a standard characteristic of expository prose and academic lectures:

> *Man sollte dieses* (**durch eine Reihe von unglücklichen Kindheitserlebnissen leider etwas zurückgebliebene, aber sonst ganz gesunde**) *Mädchen nicht der Gefahr aussetzen, von* (**gleichaltrigen, nicht zurückgebliebenen**) *Kindern unfreundlich behandelt zu werden.*

> *One should not expose this girl,* (who, though quite healthy, is unfortunately retarded by a number of unhappy childhood experiences,) *to the danger of being treated in an unfriendly way by children* (of the same age who are not retarded).

Both in English and in German, pre-noun adjective inserts can be viewed as "shorthand" versions of dependent clauses, usually relative clauses. Thus

>   This . . . . .child, who is   really very beautiful

becomes:

>   This   really very beautiful   child

and

>   Dieses . . . . .Kind, das   wirklich sehr schön   ist,

becomes:

>   Dieses   wirklich sehr schöne   Kind.

The example shows that

1. When a German dependent clause is transformed into a pre-noun insert, it drops its subject and the inflected verb belonging to it.

2. Since this transformation changes a predicate adjective or a participle into an attributive adjective, the adjective acquires an ending.

As far as German is concerned, pre-noun inserts, with the exception of (5) below, consist of an inner field plus a second prong. The usual word order is preserved. Pre-noun inserts can originate in the following ways:

1. The second prong is a predicate adjective:

> Dieses . . . . Mädchen, das   sehr intelligent   ist, . . ,

becomes:

> Dieses   sehr intelligente   Mädchen . . .

2. The second prong is the participle of an intransitive verb like **ankommen, fallen, sterben,** or **zurückbleiben,** which forms its compound tenses with **sein:**

> Dieses . . . . Kind, das   leider etwas zurückgeblieben   ist,

becomes:

> Dieses   leider etwas zurückgebliebene   Kind . . .

3. The second prong is the participle used to form the actional or statal passive:

> Diese Stadt, die   während des letzten Krieges zerstört   wurde (Actional Passive)

becomes:

> Diese   während des letzten Krieges zerstörte   Stadt . . .

> Diese Stadt, die   noch nicht wiederaufgebaut   ist (Statal Passive)

becomes:

Diese   noch nicht wiederaufgebaute   Stadt . . .

Diese (während des letzten Krieges zerstörte) und (noch nicht wiederaufgebaute)
Stadt war einmal ein wichtiges Kulturzentrum.

4. The second prong is the participle belonging to a reflexive verb:

Der Gast, der sich   betrunken   hat (event)

The guest who got drunk

and

Der Gast, der   betrunken   ist (state)

The guest who is drunk

become:

Der   betrunkene   Gast

5. As long as it makes sense, any present and past form of the *active* voice
may be changed into a **-d** adjective. This **-d** adjective, preceded by its
inner field, can then be used as a pre-noun insert.

Das Kind, das   laut schrie

becomes:

Das   laut schreiende   Kind

Die allgemeine Frage, die (hinter diesem speziellen Problem steckt), . . .
The general question which stands behind this special problem . . .
   Die (hinter diesem Problem steckende) allgemeine Frage . . .

Die Bevölkerung Chinas, die (immer schneller wächst), . . .
The population of China, which is growing faster and faster . . .
   Die (immer schneller wachsende) Bevölkerung Chinas . . .

Der Weg, der (vom Dorf aus in den Wald) führt, . . .
The path which leads from the village to the forest . . .
   Der (vom Dorf aus in den Wald führende) Weg . . .

EXERCISES

A. Express the following sentences in German. These sentences all contain reflexives introduced in Units 12 and 13. Do not use statal forms.

1. Are you still interested in her?
2. Think of yourself for a change.
3. I was really mad at him last night.
4. She fell in love with her teacher.
5. We have never been so bored.
6. I've bought myself a new coat.
7. They want to get a divorce.
8. May I introduce myself?
9. Just imagine: after twenty years he still remembered me.
10. I know she has nothing against you; you just imagine that.
11. I am looking forward to seeing her again.
12. We want to have a look at Meyer's new house.
13. I haven't changed yet, and I still have to shave.
14. Hurry up!
15. Don't get so excited.
16. Has she calmed down again?
17. I simply can't get used to his Russian accent.
18. Did you lose your way again? (Hiking) (Driving)
19. It turned out that Erich wasn't the thief at all.
20. We are dealing with people, gentlemen, and not with machines.

B. Change the following short sentences from the active voice to the actional passive. Do not change the tense. Omit the subject of the active sentence.

> **Man brachte ihn zurück.**
> **Er wurde zurückgebracht.**

1. Man führte uns durch den Garten.
2. Man trennte die Kinder von ihren Eltern.
3. Um acht Uhr schloß man das Tor.
4. Mich nimmt man nie mit.
5. Man suchte ihn, aber man fand ihn nicht.
6. Man schickte ihn nach Hause.
7. Man hielt ihn für einen Spion und erschoß ihn.
8. Man brachte uns im „Löwen" unter.
9. Man hat uns wieder im „Löwen" untergebracht.
10. Man hat ihn schon wieder gebeten, eine Rede zu halten.

C. In the following sentences, change the present actional passive forms into
  (a) Present statal passive forms and
  (b) Perfect actional passive forms.

> **Die Stadt wird zerstört.**
> **(a) Die Stadt ist zerstört.**
> **(b) Die Stadt ist zerstört worden.**

  1. Die Brücke wird schon gebaut.
  2. Die Schweine werden gefüttert.
  3. Der Brief wird schon geschrieben.
  4. Es wird beschlossen.
  5. Es wird gefunden.
  6. Die Tür wird geschlossen.

D. Change the following active sentences into actional passive sentences. Omit the subject of the active sentence.

> **Wir zeigen den Film jetzt auch in Deutschland.**
> **Der Film wird jetzt auch in Deutschland gezeigt.**

  1. In den Vereinigten Staaten trinkt man mehr Bier als in Deutschland.
  2. Mich lädt nie jemand ein.
  3. In unserem Elternhaus haben wir viel musiziert.
  4. Kolumbus hat Amerika 1492 entdeckt.
  5. Sie konnten nur wenige retten.
  6. Wann hat Ihr Vater denn dieses Haus gebaut?

E. In the following sentences, supply **von, mit,** or **durch.**
  1. Die Stadt wurde _____ ein Erdbeben völlig zerstört.
  2. Die Stadt wurde _____ einen Bombenangriff völlig zerstört.
  3. Die Stadt wurde _____ den Russen zerstört.
  4. Er ist _____ einem Stein erschlagen worden.
  5. Er ist _____ seinem Bruder erschlagen worden.
  6. Der Brief ist mir _____ meinem Vater nachgeschickt worden.
  7. Er hat den Brief zwar unterschrieben, aber der Brief ist nicht _____ ihm selbst geschrieben worden.
  8. Er hat alle seine Briefe _____ der Schreibmaschine geschrieben.
  9. Ich wurde _____ meinem Chef nach Afrika geschickt.
  10. Amerika ist _____ Kolumbus _____ Zufall entdeckt worden.

F. In the following sentences, supply either a form of **werden** or a form of **sein**.

1. Daß die Erde sich um die Sonne bewegt, _____ schon lange bewiesen.
2. Die Stadt _____ im Jahre 1944 zerstört.
3. Im Jahre 1950 _____ die Stadt noch nicht wieder aufgebaut.
4. Der weiße Mercedes _____ schon verkauft.
5. Das Haus neben der Kirche soll nächste Woche verkauft _____.
6. Der Film hat mir gar nicht gefallen. Ich _____ wirklich enttäuscht.

G. Change the following relative clauses into pre-noun inserts.

1. Der Zug, der soeben aus München angekommen ist, fährt in zehn Minuten weiter.
2. Für einen jungen Menschen, der in einem Dorf in den bayerischen Alpen großgeworden ist, ist es nicht leicht, sich an die Großstadt zu gewöhnen.
3. Hans ist jetzt Arzt, aber sein Bruder, der viel intelligenter ist, hat nie seinen Doktor gemacht.
4. Ingrids Vater war ein Architekt, der auch in Amerika bekannt war.
5. Die Städte, die während des Krieges zerstört wurden, sind heute fast alle wieder aufgebaut.
6. Die Douglas-Maschinen, die in Amerika gebaut werden, sieht man heute auf allen deutschen Flughäfen.
7. Der Juwelendieb, der seit Wochen von der Polizei gesucht wird, soll gestern in München gesehen worden sein.
8. Der Preis, der für diesen Rembrandt bezahlt worden ist, ist nach meiner Meinung viel zu hoch.
9. Seine Mutter, die noch immer in Berlin wohnte, hatte er seit Jahren nicht gesehen.
10. Er sah sie mit einem Blick an, der viel sagte.

BASIC VOCABULARY

abhängen von to depend upon
sich ändern to change
sich etwas anschauen, sich etwas ansehen to look at something
sich ärgern über to be angry, mad at
auf (die Tür) zu toward (the door)
augenblicklich momentarily; instantly
sich bemühen um, bemüht sein um to be concerned about, with
berichten to report

sich beschäftigen mit to occupy oneself with
beschäftigt sein to be occupied, employed
die Beschäftigung, –en occupation
beschließen to decide, determine
bestehen aus to consist of
beurteilen to judge, to make a judgment
sich bewegen to move
die Bewegung, –en movement; motion; exercise
blitzen to lighten, flash
der Blitz, –e lightning

brennen to burn
das Dach, ⸚er roof
sich etwas denken to imagine
Was hast du dir denn dabei gedacht? What in the world did you think you were doing?
Ich habe mir gar nichts dabei gedacht I didn't think a thing of it
das Ding, –e thing
donnern to thunder
der Donner (*no pl.*) thunder
sich eilen, sich beeilen to hurry

sich etwas einbilden to imagine something
   eingebildet sein to be conceited
   es fällt mir ein I remember
entdecken to discover
entstehen to originate, come into being
enttäuschen to disappoint
die Erde, –n earth
erfinden to invent
erfreut sein to be pleased, glad
erinnern an to remind of
   sich erinnern an to remember
fähig capable
feststellen to determine; find out; conclude
das Feuer, – fire
eine Frage stellen to ask a question
   eine Frage beantworten to answer a question
sich freuen auf to look forward to
sich freuen über to be happy (glad) about
das Gebäude, – building
geboren werden to be born
gefallen to please
   das gefällt mir I like it (that pleases me)
der Gegensatz, ⸚e contrast
gelingen to succeed
   es gelingt mir I succeed
gewöhnlich usual
der Grund, ⸚e reason, ground
   aufgrund (*prep. with gen.*) on the basis of

handeln to act
   sich handeln um to be a matter of
   handeln mit to deal with (objects)
   handeln von to deal with (subject matter)
sich herausstellen to turn out, to become apparent
hinten (*adverb*) in the back
das Holz, ⸚er wood
sich interessieren für, interessiert sein an to be interested in
der Irrtum, ⸚er error
das Jahrhundert, –e century
jedenfalls at any rate
der Körper, – body
langweilen to bore
   sich langweilen, gelangweilt sein to be bored
   langweilig boring
leer empty
leid tun to feel sorry
   sie tat ihm leid he felt sorry for her
   es tut mir leid I am sorry
leiden to suffer
das Lied, –er song
los loose
   was ist los? what's the matter? what's going on?
der Markt, ⸚e market(place)
die Meinung, –en opinion
das Messer, – knife
das Mittelalter Middle Ages
putzen to clean
der Raum, ⸚e room; space
mit Recht rightfully
reisen to travel

schießen to shoot
sinken to sink
soeben just, just now
die Sprache, –n language
stimmen to be correct
   das stimmt nicht that's wrong
die Suche, –n search
der Tanz, ⸚e dance
überlegen (**sich**) to think about, meditate
unendlich infinite
sich verbinden to unite, compound
die Vereinigten Staaten the United States
sich verfahren to lose one's way (driving)
sich verlassen auf to depend or rely upon
sich verlaufen to lose one's way (walking)
die Verwandlung, –en change, metamorphosis
vorbeigehen to pass
sich vorstellen (*dat.*) to imagine
   sich vorstellen (*acc.*) to introduce (oneself)
Weihnachten Christmas
wiederaufbauen to reconstruct
die Wissenschaft, –en science
   wissenschaftlich scientific
sich wundern über to be amazed at
der Zahn, ⸚e tooth
sich zeigen (*impersonal*) to turn out, show

ADDITIONAL VOCABULARY

die Achse, –n axle; axis
das Altertum antiquity
die Auflage, –n printing
beachten note, notice
beruhen auf to be based on
die Bombe, –n bomb
braten to roast, fry

der Braten, – roast
der Schweinebraten pork roast
der Kalbsbraten veal roast
der Chef, –s boss
sich drehen um to turn (around something), to

revolve; to concern, to be a matter of
sich umdrehen to turn around
das Element', –e element
sich erweisen to turn out, show

das Exemplar', –e copy (of a book, etc.)
die Fabrik', –en factory
färben to color; dye
das Filmfestspiel, –e film festival
das Gas, –e gas
hageln to hail
der Herd, –e stove
Indien India
    der Inder, – (East) Indian

der Indianer, – (American) Indian
kämmen to comb
die Kartoffel, –n potato
lösen to solve, dissolve
die Mate'rie matter
sich melden to report (to somebody); to answer (the phone)
mitteilen to report (something)

musizieren to make music
das Pulver, – powder; gunpowder
das Salz, –e salt
überfüllt overflowing
der Verlag, –e publishing house, publisher
das Visum, die Visen visa
sich zusammensetzen aus to be composed of

IRREGULAR VERBS

beschließen to decide, determine
    beschloß, hat beschlossen, er beschließt
bestehen aus to consist of
    bestand aus, hat aus . . . bestanden, es besteht aus
braten to roast, fry
    briet, hat gebraten, er brät
brennen to burn
    brannte, hat gebrannt, er brennt
entstehen to originate
    entstand, ist entstanden, er entsteht

erfinden to invent
    erfand, hat erfunden, er erfindet
sich erweisen to turn out, show
    erwies sich, hat sich erwiesen, es erweist sich
gefallen to please
    gefiel, hat gefallen, er gefällt
gelingen to succeed
    es gelang, es ist mir gelungen, es gelingt
leid tun to be sorry
    tat . . . leid, hat . . . leid getan, es tut . . . leid

leiden to suffer
    litt, hat gelitten, er leidet
schießen to shoot
    schoß, hat geschossen, er schießt
sinken to sink
    sank, ist gesunken, er sinkt
sich verbinden to unite, compound
    verband sich, hat sich verbunden, er verbindet sich
sich verlassen auf to depend (rely) upon
    verließ sich auf, hat sich verlassen auf, er verläßt sich auf

FURTHER READING: *Ein Mann kommt nach San Franzisko* von Mathias Koch

I Epilog als Vorspiel

das Vorspiel prologue

Flughafen San Franzisko, November 1962

Die Lufthansa-Maschine aus Frankfurt ist gerade angekommen: Abflug in Frankfurt um zwei Uhr, kurze Zwischenlandung in Montreal, am gleichen Abend in Kalifornien,—was sind schon† zwölftausend Kilometer. Man kauft sich eine Flugkarte, steigt ein, ißt zwei Mahlzeiten, schläft ein bißchen, und dann ist plötzlich nur noch der Zoll da, der einen von der neuen Welt trennt.

ein bißchen a bit, a little
einen accusative of **man**
trennen to separate

Vor dem Zollausgang stehen zehn, zwölf Leute und warten: eine Frau wartet auf ihren Mann, Eltern auf ihre Kinder; ein Mädchen wartet auf ihren Vater, eine Braut auf ihren Bräutigam. Endlich kommen die ersten Fluggäste aus dem Zoll; zuerst eine große blonde Frau, dann ein junger Mann, dann wieder eine Frau, eine Familie mit vier Kindern, dann zwei junge Leute, Touristen, wie es scheint, man sieht es an ihren Koffern. Alle reden und lachen, man hört Englisch und Deutsch, und langsam verlieren sich alle den langen, hellen Korridor hinunter.

die Braut, ̈-e bride
der Bräutigam, –e bride-groom
zuerst first, at first

langsam slow
hell light, bright

Minutenlang bleibt die Tür zum Zoll geschlossen. Dann öffnet sie sich noch einmal, langsam diesmal, so langsam, als hätte der, der sie öffnet, Angst davor, das Flugzeug zu verlassen und in eine Welt zu treten, die er nicht kennt. Für ihn war der Flug sicher keine Reise, wie man sie so macht, wenn man Geld und Zeit dazu hat. Grau ist er, der Mann, der jetzt in der Tür steht, und er sieht aus, als fröre er. Seine Augen sind müde; Angst ist darin, als er jetzt nach links sieht und dann nach rechts. Seine Hände zittern, als ob ihm Koffer und Tasche zu schwer wären. Oder zittert er, weil er Angst hat? Lange steht er so. Dann sieht er noch einmal nach links und nach rechts und geht langsam weiter.

sich öffnen to open

grau gray
frieren to freeze

link- left
links left, on the left side

Da kommt plötzlich ein junger Mann den Korridor herunter, und hinter ihm eine junge Frau. Der junge Mann mag fünfunddreißig Jahre alt sein, höchstens vierzig, und sie muß ungefähr fünfund-

---

* In this text, we have purposely retained certain grammatical constructions, such as reflexives and passives, which are introduced systematically in Units 11–13. These constructions, as well as some other grammatical points and some vocabulary, appear in the margins.

† **schon** here: *a mere* (used as a sentence adverb expressing a shoulder-shrugging so-what attitude of the speaker).

zwanzig sein. Sie laufen auf den alten Mann zu. Der sieht sie nicht   **auf ... zu** toward
kommen. Sie bleiben vor ihm stehen; sie sprechen mit ihm, aber er
scheint sie nicht zu hören. Die Angst ist immer noch in seinem
Gesicht, in seinen Augen und in seinen zitternden Händen. Der   **das Gesicht, –er** face
junge Mann nimmt ihm den Koffer aus der Hand. Der alte Mann ⁵
will es nicht, aber als das Mädchen (oder ist es die Frau des
jungen Mannes?) auch noch seine Tasche nimmt, läßt er es geschehen. Wie ein Kind führen ihn die beiden den Korridor hinunter.
Dort, wo der Korridor in das Empfangsgebäude hineinführt, stehen
zwei Kinder, ein Junge und ein Mädchen, vielleicht drei Jahre alt, ₁₀
und bei ihnen steht ein älteres Ehepaar.   **das Ehepaar, –e**
married couple

Als die letzten Fluggäste den Korridor herunterkommen, sehen sie   **knien** to kneel
den Mann auf dem Boden knien, in jedem Arm eines der beiden
Kinder. Von dem kleinen Mädchen sieht er hinauf zur Mutter (es
muß die Mutter sein), und von der Mutter wieder zur Tochter, und ₁₅
zu beiden sagt er immer wieder: „Barbara!", so, als hätte er den
Namen noch nie gehört. Der junge Mann und das ältere Ehepaar
stehen dabei und lächeln, und der Mann sieht gar nicht mehr so
grau und müde aus, und auch nicht mehr so alt wie vor ein paar
Minuten, als er dort unten durch die Tür kam. Er steht plötzlich ₂₀
auf, zieht ein Stück Papier aus der Tasche und gibt es dem jungen   **das Papier, –e** paper
Mann. „Hier", sagt er, „hier, das ist es. Wenn ich das nicht gehabt
hätte, hätte ich euch nie gefunden". Er zittert wieder, aber die
Angst ist aus seinen Augen verschwunden.

II

Mai 1945

Angefangen hatte es damit, daß Paul Suhl aus St. Louis, nachdem ₂₅
er ein Jahr lang Japanisch gelernt hatte, nach Deutschland geschickt   **geschickt wurde** was
wurde. Zur Landung in der Normandie war er zu spät gekommen; sent
im November 1944 kam er zu einer Infanterie-Kompanie in der   **die Nähe** proximity,
Nähe von Aachen. Danach verpaßte er nichts mehr; die Ardennen- closeness, nearness
schlacht, den Rheinübergang bei Remagen, und dann die Kapitu- ₃₀   **verpassen** to miss
lation. Überall zerstörte Brücken und Dörfer, zerbombte Städte.   **die Ardennen** Forest
Quer durch Deutschland fuhr er seinen Jeep, vom Rhein nach of Ardennes; **die**
Kassel, von Kassel nach Leipzig. Es wurde Frühling, während er **Ardennenschlacht**
mit dem Krieg nach Osten fuhr. Die braune Erde wurde grün; Battle of the Bulge
manchmal sah man Frauen auf den Feldern arbeiten, oder alte ₃₅   **der Übergang, ⁼e**
Männer oder Kinder; auf den Straßen zogen deutsche Soldaten nach crossing
Westen in die Kriegsgefangenenlager.   **quer durch** straight
across
Am 20. April, an Hitlers letztem Geburtstag, besetzten die Ameri- **nach Osten** eastward
kaner Leipzig. Am 21. April, seinem eigenen Geburtstag—einund- **die Erde, –n** earth
zwanzig Jahre wurde er alt—, fuhr Paul Suhl mit seiner Kompanie ₄₀ **grün** green
wieder nach Südwesten, in den Thüringer Wald. Manchmal, wenn **manchmal** sometimes
das Feld, –er field
das Kriegsgefangenen-
lager P.O.W. camp
20. = zwanzigsten
nach Südwesten
southwestward

er die Straßenschilder las, dachte er an seinen Großvater, der aus dieser Gegend gekommen war (er war in Saalfeld an der Saale geboren und in den neunziger Jahren nach Amerika ausgewandert): „Naumburg 12 km, Jena 23 km, Weimar 39 km", las er auf einem Schild; und später: „Gotha 45 km, Eisenach 61 km." ₅

Das Dorf lag im Thüringer Wald, nicht weit von Ilmenau, an der Eisenbahn von Erfurt nach Meiningen. In einem langen Tal, Wald auf beiden Seiten, zog es sich an der Straße hin, alt und grau; im Zentrum das Rathaus, die Schule, eine einfache Kirche; daneben das Pfarrhaus, vor dem selbst in diesem Frühling ein paar Blumen ₁₀ blühten. Von den Bewohnern sah man nicht viel, als Paul das erste Mal mit seinem Jeep durch das Dorf fuhr; sie hielten sich zurück, wußten nicht, was sie von den fremden Soldaten denken sollten.

Die Soldaten wurden in der Schule untergebracht, aber die Schule war nicht groß genug für die ganze Kompanie. Paul und zwei andere ₁₅ wohnten in einem Haus nicht weit vom Pfarrhaus. Der Bauer, ein alter Mann, sagte etwas von einem gefallenen Sohn und von Stalingrad; dann machte er den Mund nicht mehr auf; auch seine Frau sagte kein Wort. Paul, Bill und Joe bewohnten das Wohnzimmer und das Schlafzimmer. Wo der Bauer und seine Frau schliefen, wußten ₂₀ sie nicht; irgendwo mußte wohl noch ein Zimmer sein, vielleicht das Zimmer des gefallenen Sohnes. Am nächsten Morgen merkten sie, daß noch andere Menschen bei dem Bauern wohnten; in der Scheune lebten zwei oder drei Flüchtlingsfamilien, aus dem Osten wahrscheinlich, vielleicht auch aus Berlin oder Leipzig. Paul sah ₂₅ die Frauen manchmal über den Hof gehen, sie kamen ihm vor wie dürres Laub, das der Wind über die Straße fegt. Auf einer Bank vor der Scheune saß ein alter Mann und blickte ins Leere. Er bemerkte nicht einmal die Kinder, die auf dem Hof und auf der Straße spielten. ₃₀

III

Für die Amerikaner: No fraternizing; Fraternisieren verboten. Für die Deutschen: No loitering; Herumstehen verboten.—Wer die Bestimmungen der Militärregierung übertritt, wird bestraft.—Den Anordnungen des amerikanischen Ortskommandanten ist unbedingt Folge zu leisten, Zuwiderhandelnde werden bestraft. ₃₅

Nur die Kinder waren von Anfang an ausgenommen.

Das Mädchen mochte neun Jahre alt sein. Sie blieb immer im Hintergrund, wenn die anderen zu den Soldaten kamen. Paul hatte sie zum ersten Mal gesehen, als er mit Joe und Bill abends auf der Bank vor dem Haus saß. Die Flüchtlingskinder aus der Scheune, die auf ₄₀ dem Hof gespielt hatten, zögerten zuerst, als Joe mit ihnen sprach; aber als er ihnen Schokolade hinhielt, kamen sie doch. Die Soldaten

---

Straßenschild road sign
in den neunziger Jahren in the (18)90's **auswandern** to emigrate

das Tal, ⸚er valley

zog . . . hin it stretched along the road

das Pfarrhaus, ⸚er parsonage
selbst even
der Bewohner, – inhabitant; **bewohnen** to inhabit
wurden . . . untergebracht were billeted

der Bauer, –n peasant, farmer

die Scheune, –n the barn
die Flüchtlingsfamilie, –n refugee family
sie kamen ihm vor they looked to him
dürres Laub dry leaves
fegen to sweep
leer empty; **ins Leere** into space
Wer . . . bestraft Whoever transgresses the orders of the military government will be punished.
von (jetzt) an from (now) on
der Hintergrund, ⸚e background
Den Anordnungen . . . bestraft Orders issued by the American local commander are to be obeyed under all circumstances; offenders will be punished.
ausgenommen exempted
zögern to hesitate

lachten, und Bill meinte, man hätte den ganzen Krieg mit Schokolade führen sollen, alle Deutschen wären mit Schokolade zu kaufen.
Nur das schlanke dunkelblonde Mädchen wollte nicht näherkom-
men. „Was ist denn mit Eurer Freundin los?" fragte Paul. „Will die
denn keine Schokolade?" „Ach die", sagte eines der Mädchen, „die 5
weint immer nur, weil ihre Mutti tot ist.—Mein Vater ist auch tot,
aber ich kriege bald einen neuen." „Mein Pappi ist auch in Rußland
gefallen", rief ein sechs- oder siebenjähriger Junge dazwischen, „und
mit der Barbara spielen wir gar nicht mehr." Joe und Bill wollten
wissen, wovon die Kinder sprachen, aber Paul konnte sich nicht 10
dazu bringen zu übersetzen. Aber von da an beobachtete er die
kleine Barbara. Sie war fast immer allein; und auch, als die Soldaten
anfingen, jeden Morgen zwei oder drei der Kinder im Jeep mitzunehmen, wenn sie zur Schule fuhren, wollte sie nie mitfahren.

Bis Paul und Bill sie eines Nachmittags allein vor dem Haus fanden. 15
„Na, Barbara, möchtest du nicht auch mal ein Stück mitfahren? Du
brauchst doch keine Angst vor uns zu haben", sagte Paul und hielt
ihr ein Stück Schokolade hin. „Hör auf, Mensch", meinte Bill, „die
kannst du auch mit Schokolade nicht kaufen; das ist so'n richtiger
kalter Fisch." Das Kind mußte gefühlt haben, daß Bill ihm da kein 20
Kompliment machte. Sie drehte sich um und rannte die Straße hinunter. Man konnte sehen, daß sie weinte. Bill lachte und ging ins
Haus. Paul stieg in den Jeep und fuhr hinter ihr her. Sie mußte ihn
kommen hören, aber sie drehte sich nicht um. Er hielt neben ihr, sie
sah zu ihm herüber, ohne etwas zu sagen; dann mußte sie lächeln. 25
Langsam kam sie zu ihm und setzte sich wortlos neben ihn in den
Wagen. Paul fuhr aus dem Dorf hinaus; die Straße führte neben der
Eisenbahn ins Tal. Er wußte nicht recht, was er sagen sollte. Er
konnte ihr ja nicht erklären, daß sie ihm leid tat, weil ihre Mutter
tot war, und daß sie ihn an seine kleine Schwester erinnerte. Dieser 30
verdammte Krieg—aber sie war ja nur ein Kind und hatte mit all
dem nichts zu tun. Und irgend jemand mußte sich doch um sie kümmern. Man sollte einen Brief nach Hause schreiben: Liebe Eltern,
ich habe ein Kind gefunden, erinnert mich an Kathy, Mutter tot, wo
der Vater ist, weiß ich nicht. Man kann das Kind doch nicht einfach 35
allein lassen. Aber mitnehmen kann ich sie auch nicht, sie ist doch
eine Deutsche. „Du, ich weiß, wo es hier Walderdbeeren gibt", sagte
Barbara plötzlich, dann fuhren sie eine Seitenstraße hinauf in den
Wald. Eine halbe Stunde suchten sie unter den Bäumen herum,
Erdbeeren fanden sie nicht, aber er war froh, daß sie „du" zu ihm 40
sagte. Er hatte ihr eigentlich die Schokolade wieder anbieten wollen,
aber dann dachte er daran, wie Bill gesagt hatte, man könne alle
Deutschen mit Schokolade kaufen; und er ließ die Schokolade in
der Tasche.

die Schokola'de, —n chocolate

schlank slender, slim

Was ist los? What's the matter?

Rußland Russia

überset'zen to translate
beobachten to observe, watch

hör auf stop (leave her alone)
das ist . . . Fisch she's a real cold fish
sich umdrehen to turn around

nicht recht not quite
leid tun to feel sorry
sie tat ihm leid he felt sorry for her
es tut mir leid I am sorry
erinnern an to remind of
verdammt damn

sich kümmern um to take care of

die Erdbeere, —n strawberry
es gibt there are

anbieten to offer

IV

Juli 1945

„Woher können Sie eigentlich so gut Deutsch? Das haben Sie doch nicht während der paar Wochen hier im Dorf gelernt."

Deutsch können (here used in the sense of "to know," "to have a mastery of," as a language.

„Ja, wissen Sie, Herr Pfarrer, meine Großeltern kommen aus Deutschland, hier aus dieser Gegend. Mein Großvater ist nach Missouri ausgewandert, und mein Vater ist lutherischer Pfarrer in 5 St. Louis. Bei uns zu Hause haben wir immer viel Deutsch gesprochen; bis zum Krieg hat mein Vater sogar noch Deutsch gepredigt. In den letzten zwei Jahren habe ich allerdings Japanisch lernen müssen."

predigen to preach

„Und deshalb hat man Sie wohl nach Deutschland geschickt. Aber 10 Spaß beiseite. Sie haben da einen Vorschlag gemacht, und Sie wollen meinen Rat wissen. Glauben Sie denn, daß Sie das überhaupt machen können?"

Spaß fun, kidding
beiseite aside

„Doch, bestimmt. Ich habe Ihnen ja gesagt, wir haben Verwandte in Frankfurt,—einen Vetter mit seiner Frau,—denen habe ich ge- 15 schrieben, und sie haben zurückgeschrieben und haben ja gesagt. Meine Kompanie fährt in ein paar Tagen nach Frankfurt; Sie wissen ja, die Amerikaner ziehen sich ganz aus Thüringen zurück, Thüringen gehört ja zur russischen Zone."*

der Vetter, –n cousin (male)

sich zurückziehen to withdraw

„Ja, leider! Thüringen gehört zur russischen Zone. Dann ist es wohl 20 auf jeden Fall besser, wenn Sie Barbara mitnehmen. Und dem Kind wird es in Frankfurt besser gehen als hier, wo die Kleine ganz allein ist. Wenn nur die Mutter nicht gestorben wäre! Ich kannte sie ja kaum, die beiden waren erst ein paar Wochen hier, aus Breslau kamen sie. Dieses Flüchtlingselend ist furchtbar; wir haben zweimal 25 soviel Flüchtlinge im Dorf wie Einwohner. Wohin das noch führen soll!"

der Flüchtling, –e refugee
das Elend (no pl.) misery
furchtbar frightful, terrible
der Einwohner, – inhabitant

„Ich habe lange darüber nachgedacht, Herr Pfarrer. Ich habe meinem Vater davon geschrieben, und er meinte, ich solle tun, was ich für richtig halte; wir hätten ja jetzt lange genug gehaßt. Und wenn 30 ich sehe, wieviel Haß es hier noch gibt; die Bauern hassen die Flüchtlinge, weil die ihnen das Brot wegessen; die Flüchtlinge hassen die Bauern, weil es denen besser geht als ihnen, und sie alle hassen die Amerikaner, weil die ihnen das Land zerstört haben.

---

* At the end of the war, British and American troops had occupied large parts of what later became East Germany. In August 1945, these troops were withdrawn to a demarcation line which had been agreed upon at Yalta. This line became the "Iron Curtain."

Die Barbara hat mir neulich davon erzählt. ‚Ich soll dich auch hassen‘, hat sie gesagt, ‚aber das will ich nicht!‘ "

„Sie dürfen nicht vergessen, daß der Krieg erst seit acht Wochen zu Ende ist. Geben Sie uns Zeit, Herr Suhl. Sie sind ja noch sehr jung; aber ich bin ein alter Mann, ich weiß, daß es kein Gefühl gibt, das 5 die Zeit nicht ändern kann. Nehmen Sie die Kleine mit nach Frankfurt,—und wir wollen hoffen, daß sie noch jung genug ist, um zu vergessen, was hinter ihr liegt."

Am 15. Juli zog Barbara in ein Haus in der Bettinastraße in Frankfurt, von dem nur noch das Erdgeschoß und der erste Stock standen. 10 Wenn es regnete, lief' an allen Wänden das Wasser herunter. Aber Ernst und Irene Suhl, Pauls Verwandte, waren froh, überhaupt ein Dach über dem Kopf zu haben, auch wenn es nur die Decke ihrer Wohnung war. „Das wird sich schon finden", meinte Ernst, als Paul ihn fragte, wie er sich denn eigentlich den nächsten Winter vor- 15 stelle; und als sie über die Zukunft der kleinen Barbara sprachen, hatte Ernst die gleiche optimistische Antwort.

Bei seinem letzten Gespräch mit dem alten Pfarrer in Thüringen hatte Paul Namen und Adresse seiner Verwandten auf ein Stück Papier geschrieben, und darunter seine eigene I.D.-Nummer. „Die 20 Armee weiß immer, wo ich bin", hatte er gesagt, „und auf jeden Fall können Sie mich über meine Frankfurter Verwandten erreichen."

V

Frankfurt, September 1948

In der Bettinastraße läuft zwar das Wasser nicht mehr an den Wänden herunter, aber das Haus besteht noch immer nur aus Erdgeschoß und erstem Stock. Ernst und Irene Suhl sind ganz gut durch 25 die wilden Jahre nach dem Krieg durchgekommen; Paul hat nach seiner Entlassung aus der Armee von Amerika aus geholfen.

Die Zeit der Care-Pakete und der Lebensmittelkarten: Wer Freunde in Amerika hatte, brauchte nicht zu hungern; die anderen bekamen, wenn sie Glück hatten, alle vier Wochen ein Ei; und die Milch war 30 so blau wie der Himmel im November,—was wurde eigentlich aus der Butter? Die öffentlichen Bibliotheken waren überfüllt, weil es da warm war. Auf der Universität saßen die Studenten in alten Soldatenmänteln und froren. Aber es ist nie so viel gearbeitet worden wie in den ersten Semestern nach dem Kriege. Die Studenten froren, 35 und die Professoren froren mit ihnen. Im Theater fror das Publikum, und die Schauspieler froren auf der Bühne. Und wenn† dann endlich der Sommer kam, fror man zwar nicht mehr, aber man hungerte immer weiter.

---

neulich recently

das Erdgeschoß, –e ground floor
der Stock, ⸚e stick; floor(of a building)im ersten (zweiten, etc.) Stock on the first (second, etc.) floor
die Decke, –n ceiling
das Dach, ⸚er roof
das wird sich schon finden it'll work out all right
sich vorstellen to imagine, picture
die Zukunft (no pl.) future
das Gespräch, –e conversation
die Armee', –n army

bestehen aus to consist of
wild wild
die Entlassung discharge
das Paket,–e package
die Lebensmittelkarte, –n ration card
das Ei, –er egg
die Milch (no pl.)milk
blau blue
öffentlich public
der Schauspieler, – actor
es ist . . . worden never has so much work been done
das Publikum audience, public

der Markt, ⸚e market(place)

---

† wenn rather than als is used here, because more than one summer is involved.

Frankfurt/Main, An der Hauptwache

Care-Pakete, Lebensmittelkarten, Schwarzer Markt. Frankfurt war eine Zentrale des Schwarzen Marktes in Deutschland, und der Schwarze Markt war das Fieberthermometer von Westdeutschland. Am Anfang kostete eine Zigarette fünfzig Pfennig,—dann stiegen die Preise, aber die Währung war nicht etwa die Mark, sondern die amerikanische Zigarette. Ein Pfund Butter für 200 Zigaretten, ein Paar Nylonstrümpfe für 300 Zigaretten. Als Paul Suhl im März 1948 nach Deutschland zurückkam, stand die Zigarette bei etwa 4 bis 5 Mark, im Juni war sie auf 10 Mark gestiegen. Und bewacht wurde das alles von der Militärregierung,—HICOG, was die Deutschen wie „Hickock" aussprachen. HICOG war eine Maschine mit vielen Rädchen, und eines dieser Rädchen hieß seit März 1948 Paul Suhl. Nachdem er sein Studium beendet und sein Japanisch völlig vergessen hatte, bekam er eine Stellung bei der Militärregierung in Deutschland und hatte nun ein Büro im I. G. Hochhaus‡ in Frank- 15 furt.

‡ **I. G. Hochhaus** Administration Building of I. G. Farben, the largest German chemical trust until 1945. After the war, the building was used as headquarters by the Americans.

die Zentra'le, –n center
das Fieber fever
die Währung, –en medium of exchange, currency
der Strumpf, ⸚e stocking
bewacht wurde was watched over
HICOG High Commissioner of Germany
das Rad, ⸚er wheel
das Studium, die Studien studies; course of study
beenden to conclude, finish
völlig completely
die Stellung, –en position; job

Auf der Kaiserstraße und im Hauptbahnhof beobachtete er oft die Schwarzmarkthändler; er wanderte zu Fuß durch die zerstörte Stadt und kletterte auf den Ruinenbergen zwischen dem Römer und dem Dom herum, in dem viele deutsche Kaiser gekrönt worden waren. Während der Hauptverkehrszeit stand er oft an der Hauptwache, [5] gegen fünf Uhr nachmittags, wenn die Straßenbahnen überfüllt waren, um zu hören, worüber die Menschen sprachen. Und abends besuchte er seinen Vetter Ernst, um mit ihm endlos zu diskutieren.

So wurde es April, und Mai, und Juni.—Das Fieberthermometer kletterte immer mehr in die Höhe, und der Patient wäre gestorben,[10] wenn die Militärregierung nicht die Währungsreform§ befohlen hätte. Am Montag, dem 20. Juni, gab es statt der alten „Reichsmark" die neue „Deutsche Mark", und wer an dem Tage auf zehntausend Reichsmark saß statt auf tausend Zigaretten, der hatte nur einen Haufen nutzloses Papier, mit dem man noch nicht einmal gut Feuer[15] anmachen konnte.

§ The currency reform was a drastic devaluation of the currency. Each German, on that day, could receive no more than 40 new "Deutsche Mark."

der Händler, – dealer
klettern to climb
der Römer (name of the Frankfurt city hall)
gekrönt worden waren had been crowned
der Verkehr traffic
die Hauptwache (square in the center of Frankfurt)
diskutieren (here) to have a bull session

die Höhe, –n height
in die Höhe upward

der Haufen, – heap, pile
nutzlos useless
Feuer anmachen to light a fire

,,und hatte nun ein Büro im I. G. Hochhaus in Frankfurt''.

Und so wurde es Juli, und August, und September, und an diesen Sommernachmittagen geschah es oft, daß, wenn Paul in die Bettinastraße fuhr, Barbara vor dem Haus auf ihn wartete. Sie kam dann zu seinem Wagen gerannt, steckte den Kopf durch das offene Fenster und sagte: „Fahren wir heute ein bißchen?" Und dann [5] fuhr er mit ihr vor die Stadt, irgendwohin, wo es Felder gab und Wiesen und Blumen und Bänke, auf denen man sitzen konnte und wo Barbara lachen mußte, wenn Paul manchmal einschlief. „Erdbeeren essen gehen" nannten sie diese Expeditionen, und Barbara fand das viel schöner als die „olle Schule", womit sie die Bettina- [10] Schule meinte, ein Gymnasium für Mädchen. Sie war in der Quarta und erzählte Paul immer wieder, wie ihr Englischlehrer den amerikanischen Akzent nachahmte. (Er hatte in Oxford studiert.) Aber auch Paul erzählte in diesem Sommer viel, von Schiffen auf dem Atlantik, von New York, von tagelangen Fahrten mit der Eisenbahn, [15] von St. Louis und von seinen Eltern, von seiner Schwester Kathy, die auch zwölf Jahre alt war und auch immer Geschichten über ihre Lehrer erzählte. An einem Freitagnachmittag, als er gerade versucht hatte, ihr zu erklären, wie breit der Mississippi ist, sagte sie auf einmal: „Du, weißt du, da möchte ich auch mal hin." „Ja, dann [20] müssen wir ja wohl mal darüber reden", meinte er.

die Wiese, –n meadow

olle = alte

die Quarta third year of the Gymnasium (seventh grade)
nachahmen to imitate

die Eisenbahn, –en railroad

VI

Ernst Suhl war fünfzehn Jahre älter als sein Vetter Paul. Er war Diplomingenieur und hatte während des Krieges bei einer Frankfurter Firma gearbeitet, die irgendwelche kriegswichtigen Maschinen herstellte. Ernst hatte daher nie Soldat zu werden [25] brauchen. Neunzehnhundertdreiundvierzig war er Chefingenieur geworden und hatte einige Erfindungen gemacht, die seine Firma noch kriegswichtiger machten als vorher. Aber nach dem 8. Mai 1945 brauchte in Deutschland kein Mensch mehr einen Chefingenieur, und ganz bestimmt keinen, der kriegswichtige Erfindungen gemacht [30] hatte. Eine Zeitlang tat Ernst gar nichts; dann, kurz nachdem Barbara nach Frankfurt gekommen war, arbeitete er ein paar Monate lang bei den Amerikanern in einer Soldatenküche, wo er Englisch lernte. Später bekam er eine Stellung als technischer Zeichner bei der Eisenbahn; eine Möglichkeit, in seinen alten Beruf zurück- [35] zukommen, gab es nicht. Schon lange bevor Paul wieder nach Deutschland gekommen war, hatten Ernst und Irene daran gedacht auszuwandern, sobald das wieder möglich sein würde. Und während der Sommermonate 1948 hatte Paul sie davon überzeugt, daß Ernst in Amerika eine neue Zukunft finden könnte. Hatte man nicht [40] schon gleich nach dem Krieg viele deutsche Wissenschaftler in die Staaten gebracht, die da weiterarbeiten durften, wo sie am Ende des Krieges aufgehört hatten? Warum sollte Ernst das nicht können?

der Diplomingenieur engineer with a graduate degree from a technical university
die Firma, die Firmen firm
herstellen to produce
der Chef, –s boss
die Erfindung, –en invention

der Zeichner, – draftsman
der Beruf, –e profession

überzeugen to convince

der Wissenschaftler, – scientist

aufhören to stop

Die Frage war nur, was aus Barbara werden sollte. Das Leben in Frankfurt war in der ersten Zeit nach dem Kriege nicht leicht gewesen für Barbara. Es hatte lange gedauert, bis sie sich in der Bettinastraße zu Hause fühlte. Zuerst hatte sie kaum gesprochen, wenn sie mit Irene allein war, gelacht hatte sie nur manchmal, wenn ⁵ Ernst da war. Aber dann hatte sie sich doch an die beiden gewöhnt, und nach ein paar Monaten war sie ein völlig normales Kind geworden. Ihr Vater blieb verschwunden; alle Versuche, ihn zu finden, waren erfolglos. Ernst hatte drei- oder viermal an den Pfarrer in Thüringen geschrieben, aber der wußte nichts von Barbaras Vater. ₁₀ Nach Breslau, an die alte Adresse, konnte man ja nicht schreiben: Breslau hieß jetzt Wroclaw und war polnisch. Auch beim Roten Kreuz konnten sie nichts erfahren, und so mußte man annehmen, daß er, wie tausend andere, irgendwo in Osteuropa umgekommen war. Im Juni, ein paar Tage vor der Währungsreform, machte Paul ₁₅ einen letzten Versuch und schrieb noch einmal nach Thüringen. Aber der Brief kam zurück: „Adressat verstorben." Der alte Pfarrer, der einzige, der von der Sache wußte, war tot, und als die Blockade Berlins begann, gab es überhaupt keine Verbindung mehr nach drüben, zum Osten Deutschlands, zur russischen Zone. ₂₀

Wenn Irene und Ernst nach Amerika auswanderten, dann wollten sie Barbara mitnehmen, und das ging nur, wenn sie sie adoptierten. Es war ein schwerer Entschluß, denn sie wußten ja nicht bestimmt, ob Barbaras Vater nicht doch noch lebte. Aber sie konnten sich ihr Leben ohne Barbara nicht mehr vorstellen, und an dem Tage, an ₂₅ dem Barbara auf dem Rückweg in die Stadt zu Paul gesagt hatte: „Du, weißt du, da möchte ich auch mal hin", beschlossen sie, mit ihr darüber zu sprechen. Nach dem Abendessen fing Paul ganz harmlos an: „Sag mal, Barbara, wie wäre es, wenn wir nächstes Jahr mal in St. Louis Erdbeeren essen gingen?" ₃₀

VII

Januar 1952

Viele von den deutschen Soldaten, die mit Oswald Kerner aus Rußland zurückgekommen waren, waren so schnell wie möglich nach Westdeutschland weitergefahren. Andere fuhren zu ihren Familien in der Sowjetzone. Die meisten hatten seit Monaten oder Jahren nichts von zu Hause gehört und hatten keine Ahnung, wo ₃₅ sie ihre Eltern, ihre Frauen, ihre Kinder finden würden.

Kerner war im Februar 1945 in Pommern gefangengenommen worden. Ein paar Tage vorher hatte er den letzten Brief von seiner Frau bekommen. Sie war mit ihrer kleinen Tochter aus Breslau geflüchtet und wohnte in einem Dorf im Thüringer Wald. Seitdem ₄₀

---

sich gewöhnen an to get used to
der Versuch, –e try, attempt; experiment
der Erfolg, –e success

polnisch Polish
das Rote Kreuz the Red Cross

₁₅ umkommen to perish

Adressat verstorben addressee deceased
einzig (adjective) only, sole
₂₀ die Verbindung, –en connection, link

der Entschluß, ¨–e decision

beschließen to decide, determine

₃₅ die Ahnung, –en idea; premonition, hunch
Pommern Pomerania, a province of Eastern Germany
war . . . gefangengenommen worden had been taken prisoner

hatte er nichts mehr gehört, aber er war trotzdem nach Thüringen gefahren. Zwei Tage lang war er von einem Haus zum anderen gegangen, aber niemand wußte etwas von seiner Frau und seinem Kind. Schließlich hatte er den Bauern gefunden, in dessen Haus Paul Suhl gewohnt hatte, und der konnte sich an die junge Frau aus 5 Breslau erinnern, die damals mit den anderen Flüchtlingen in seiner Scheune gewohnt hatte. Schon bei ihrer Ankunft sei die Frau krank gewesen und dann wäre sie auch bald gestorben; dann seien die Amerikaner gekommen, und die hätten die Tochter mitgenommen. Der Bauer wußte auch noch, daß einer der amerikanischen Soldaten 10 oft im Pfarrhaus gewesen war. Und so saß Oswald Kerner dann dem Pfarrer gegenüber, im gleichen Stuhl, auf dem Paul gesessen hatte. Nur war es nicht mehr derselbe Pfarrer.

„Ich kann Ihnen nur sagen, Herr Kerner, daß Ihre Frau am 28. März 1945 gestorben ist. Von Ihrer Tochter steht in unseren 15 Büchern nichts. Möglich, daß mein Vorgänger wußte, was aus ihr geworden ist, aber der alte Herr ist vor vier Jahren gestorben und hat keine Papiere hinterlassen. Ich bin erst nach seinem Tod hier ins Dorf gekommen. Es tut mir leid, Herr Kerner. So gerne ich es möchte, ich kann Ihnen leider nicht helfen." 20

Kerner sagte kein Wort. Er saß und starrte ins Leere. Der Krieg war seit sieben Jahren vorbei, aber für ihn kam das Ende erst jetzt. Als er ins Dorf gekommen war, war er schwach und hungrig gewesen, aber was ihn sieben Jahre lang am Leben gehalten hatte, hatte ihn immer noch getrieben: die Hoffnung auf ein Ende und auf 25 einen neuen Anfang. Das Ende war jetzt gekommen, aber statt eines neuen Anfangs—nichts. Sieben Jahre Leben hatte er verloren, und er hatte fast vergessen, was es heißt, sein eigenes Leben zu leben. Aber das wäre alles nicht so schlimm gewesen, er hätte es vergessen können. Aber jetzt? 30

„Verstehen Sie, was das bedeutet, Herr Pfarrer? Sieben Jahre warten; sieben Jahre lang jeden Tag daran denken, wie es sein wird, wenn— Und dann gibt es auf einmal kein ‚wenn' mehr. Wissen Sie, Herr Pfarrer, daß ich eine fünfzehnjährige Tochter habe, und ich kenne sie gar nicht, und wenn ich zu ihr sage: Bar- 35 bara, ich bin dein Vater, dann denkt sie, wer ist der Mensch und was will er von mir? Aber ich habe ja gar keine Tochter mehr; die ist bei den Amerikanern, wenn sie überhaupt noch lebt. Nach Hause kommen, wieder zu Hause sein, das alles war nur ein Traum, Herr Pfarrer, wissen Sie: Lagerpsychose, Fata Morgana. Was ist richtig, 40 ‚Das Leben ein Traum' oder ‚Der Traum ein Leben'?"

„Was sind Sie eigentlich von Beruf, Herr Kerner?"

---

schließlich finally, after all

sich erinnern an to remember

dem Pfarrer gegenüber opposite the pastor. (The noun governed by **gegenüber** usually precedes the preposition.)

der Vorgänger, – predecessor

der Tod, –e death

ins Leere starren to stare into space

treiben to drive

der Traum, ⸚e dream
die Lagerpsychose prison psychosis
die Fata Morgana mirage
„Das Leben ein Traum" title of a play by Calderón
„Der Traum ein Leben" title of a play by Grillparzer

„Sie meinen, was *war* ich von Beruf? Ich war Lehrer, Studienrat in Breslau, Deutsch und Geschichte. Neunzehnhundertvierzig bin ich Soldat geworden, und meine Schüler schrieben im Abitur über das Thema: „Der ideale Mensch im idealen Staat.“

„Sie sollten das alles vergessen, Herr Kerner, und von vorne an- 5 fangen. Gehen Sie wieder in Ihren Beruf, man braucht doch überall Lehrer. Sie können noch so viel Gutes tun in ihrem Leben, Herr Kerner, unsere Jugend braucht Männer wie Sie, Männer, die nicht nur das Leben kennen, sondern auch den Tod.“

„Danke, nein, Herr Pfarrer, das mache ich nicht mehr mit. Soll ich 10 etwa meine Schüler wieder über den idealen Menschen und den idealen Staat schreiben lassen? Ich könnte doch nur sagen, Kinder, glaubt den Unsinn nicht; am Ende kommt nie eine bessere Welt, sondern einfach nichts.—Nein, nein,—ich bleibe hier im Dorf, ir- gendeine Arbeit werde ich schon finden.“   15

Im Dorf fand er zwar keine Arbeit, aber vierzehn Tage später holte ihn Fritz Müller, Schreinerei, Möbel- und Sarglager VEB in die kleine Nachbarstadt. Als junger Mann hatte Oswald Kerner in seiner Freizeit für Barbara Kindermöbel gemacht. Jetzt machte er vierzehn Monate lang Särge. „Sechs Bretter und zwei Brettchen“, das war 20 schließlich auch klassische deutsche Literatur.

Was sind Sie von Beruf? What is your profession? **der Studienrat, ⸚e** fully certified Gymnasium teacher **von vorne** from the beginning

die Jugend (*no pl.*) youth (the early years of life; young people collectively) **etwas mitmachen** to take part in something

Schreinerei, Möbel- und Sarglager carpenter's shop, furniture and coffin depot **VEB = Volkseigener Betrieb** business owned by the people. (Many firms in East Germany had been nationalized by that time.) **das Brett, ‒er** board; this is a line from Bürger's ballad *Lenore*. (Six boards and two little boards are needed to make a coffin.)

VIII

März 1953

Der Pfarrer hatte einen Brief geschrieben, und Kerner wußte plötz- lich, warum er nicht in den Westen gegangen war. Irgendwo in seinem Unterbewußtsein mußte er gewußt haben, daß er in Thü- ringen doch etwas über Barbara erfahren würde. Nicht, daß er von 25 Barbara selbst gehört hätte, so viel Glück hatte er nicht; aber der Pfarrer hatte das Stück Papier gefunden, auf das Paul Suhl Namen und Addresse seines Vetters in Frankfurt geschrieben hatte. Darüber stand in der zitternden Handschrift des alten Pfarrers: „Barbara Kerner, zu erreichen bei“. Lange betrachtete Kerner das Stückchen 30 Papier, das jemand wahrscheinlich aus einem Taschenkalender ge- rissen hatte. Er sah nur den Namen und die Adresse; Pauls I.D. Nummer beachtete er nicht. Und er überlegte sich, daß Barbara im August siebzehn Jahre alt werden würde.

Der Pfarrer schlug vor, daß Kerner zunächst einmal an die Adresse 35 in Frankfurt schreiben sollte. Wenn Barbara dort noch zu erreichen

das Unterbewußtsein the subconscious

die Handschrift handwriting **betrachten** to look at, observe

beachten note, notice **sich überlegen** to think about, meditate, consider

wäre, dann könnte er sie ja zu sich kommen lassen. Aber daran dachte Kerner nicht. Da er politisch unverdächtig war,—er war weder für noch gegen das Regime und dachte nur manchmal, daß es in Deutschland jetzt zwei „ideale Staaten" gäbe—, fiel es ihm nicht schwer, eine Reisegenehmigung nach Ost-Berlin zu bekommen. 5 Er hatte gesagt, daß er dort seinen Schwager besuchen wolle. Und so fuhr er an einem Freitagmorgen im April 1953 mit dem Fahrrad zum letzten Mal zu Fritz Müller VEB. Es war Frühling in der Luft, während er seinen letzten Sarg machte. Auf der Fahrt nach Hause regnete es, und am nächsten Vormittag stieg er in einen Personenzug 10 der Deutschen Reichsbahn,* die im Westen jetzt Deutsche Bundesbahn* hieß. Zwischen Leipzig und Berlin kontrollierte ein humorloser Polizist seine Papiere, aber die waren in Ordnung. Er hatte keinen Koffer mitgenommen, denn wer damals mit einem Koffer nach Berlin fuhr, war sofort verdächtig. Am Abend kam er an, es regnete immer 15 noch, aber statt zu seinem Schwager zu gehen (er hatte tatsächlich einen Schwager in Ost-Berlin), setzte er sich in die S-Bahn und fuhr kurz hinter dem Bahnhof Friedrichstraße über die Grenze zwischen Ost- und West-Berlin.

Auch im Westen regnete es, aber die Neonlichter ließen den Regen 20 in allen Farben schillern. Im Flüchtlingslager allerdings war der Regen wieder grau, doch das störte Kerner nicht. Er wußte jetzt, was er wollte; und als man ihn ein paar Wochen später von Berlin nach Frankfurt flog, träumte er davon, daß er mit Barbara in eine kleine Wohnung ziehen wollte und daß er wieder Lehrer werden 25 und an einem Gymnasium in Frankfurt unterrichten würde. Eines Tages würde Barbara dann heiraten,—und er dachte über seine Rolle als zukünftiger Großvater nach. Als sie über Thüringen flogen, dachte er an den Pfarrer da unten in einem der kleinen Täler und überlegte sich, ob der wohl für den „idealen Staat (Ost)" oder für 30 den „idealen Staat (West)" wäre. Dann dachte er daran, daß er Barbara seit fast zehn Jahren nicht gesehen hatte, und er hatte plötzlich Angst vor seiner erwachsenen Tochter.

IX

Frankfurt, April 1953

Care-Pakete, Lebensmittelkarten und Schwarzer Markt sind vergessen; man kann mit gutem Geld kaufen, was man will. Während 35 man vor der Währungsreform mit amerikanischen Zigaretten alles und ohne amerikanische Zigaretten nichts kaufen konnte, bekommt man jetzt in jedem Geschäft jede Menge Zigaretten,—zehn oder

---

* The East-German railroad has retained the old name "Imperial Railways," whereas the West-German term is "Federal Railways."

Margin glosses:

unverdächtig not under suspicion, not suspect; **verdächtig** suspect

es fällt mir schwer it is hard for me

die Genehmigung, –en permission, permit

der Schwager, ⸚ brother-in-law

das Fahrrad, ⸚er bicycle

der Personenzug local train

kontrollieren to check

S-Bahn = Stadtbahn city railroad

die Grenze, –n border

schillern to shimmer, sparkle

das Flüchtlingslager, – refugee camp

träumen to dream

unterrich'ten to teach, instruct

die Währungsreform currency reform

die Menge, –n quantity, mass, crowd

jede Menge any amount

zwölf Stück für eine Deutsche Mark. Man fährt jetzt mit dem Motorrad zur Arbeit; und wer es sich leisten kann, fährt einen Volkswagen. Der Mercedes wird zum Standessymbol. In der Universität sitzen keine Soldaten mehr, sondern neunzehn- oder zwanzigjährige Studenten, für die der Krieg anfängt, Geschichte zu werden. Ins 5 Theater oder ins Konzert geht man im dunklen Anzug, und in der Pause trinkt man Coca-Cola oder Sekt. Das Leben ist wieder „normal" geworden; was HICOG war, wissen nur noch wenige, man lebt jetzt in der Bundesrepublik Deutschland. Der Hunger ist vergessen, und gäbe es nicht noch so viele Ruinen zwischen den neuge- 10 bauten modernen Häusern, so hätte man wahrscheinlich auch die Bomben längst vergessen. Daß die amerikanischen Soldaten, die man überall in der Stadt sieht, vor acht Jahren als Feinde ins Land kamen, daran denkt man auch nicht mehr oft.

Das Haus in der Bettinastraße ist auch wieder aufgebaut. Vier 15 Stockwerke hoch, moderne Komfortwohnungen, drei Zimmer mit Bad und Küche. Daß hier einmal das Wasser an den Wänden heruntergelaufen ist, kann man sich nicht mehr vorstellen. Im Erdgeschoß wohnt ein Arzt, im ersten Stock ein Pfarrer, im zweiten ein Geschäftsmann und darüber ein Schauspieler. Im ganzen Haus 20 wohnt nicht ein Frankfurter; alle sind erst nach dem Krieg in die Stadt gezogen.

Als Oswald Kerner gegen drei Uhr nachmittags an der Tür des Arztes klingelte, machte ihm die Sprechstundenhilfe auf. Als er versuchte, ihr zu erklären, daß er nicht krank sei, sondern den Arzt in 25 einer persönlichen Sache sprechen möchte, meinte sie nur, der Herr Doktor hätte jetzt für private Dinge keine Zeit, und ließ ihn einfach vor der Tür stehen. Im ersten Stock war niemand zu Hause, und die Frau des Geschäftsmannes im zweiten Stock öffnete die Tür nur ein bißchen, sagte: „Ich kaufe nichts", und machte die Tür wieder 30 zu. Aber die Frau des Schauspielers, klein, rundlich, mit einem freundlichen Mondgesicht, vielleicht Mitte dreißig, ließ ihn nicht vor der Tür stehen. Er hatte kaum angefangen, ihr zu erklären, was er wollte, als sie ihn bat, er möchte doch hereinkommen. Sie sei nämlich auch Breslauerin, und da müßte man sich doch einmal über 35 alte Zeiten unterhalten. Außerdem könne ihr Mann ihm bestimmt helfen; der kenne nämlich so viele Leute hier in der Nachbarschaft, und irgend jemand müsse sich doch an diesen Herrn Suhl erinnern können.

Kerner nickte nur müde und resigniert. Als er unten vor der 40 Haustür die Namen an den Briefkästen studiert hatte und den Namen, der allein ihm wichtig war, nicht finden konnte, da war die Welt, von der er geträumt hatte, ganz plötzlich zusammenge-

---

das Motorrad, ⸚er
motorcycle
das Standessymbol, –e
status symbol

der Anzug, ⸚e suit
der Sekt champagne

der Feind, –e enemy

das Stockwerk, –e
story

sich vorstellen
imagine

die Sprechstundenhilfe, –n receptionist
in a doctor's office
persönlich personal
das Ding, –e thing

rundlich plump
Mitte dreißig in her
mid-thirties

sich unterhalten
to converse,
have a conversation
die Nachbarschaft
neighborhood

nicken to nod
der Kasten, ⸚ box

zusammenbrechen
to collapse

brochen, und er wußte auf einmal, daß er Barbara nicht finden
würde. Dr. med. H. Jagow. Pfr. Gerhard Maschke. Die Namen
interessierten ihn nicht. Joseph Schmidhuber, das war der Geschäftsmann im zweiten Stock, und der Schauspieler hieß Jürgen
Cramer. Kerner hatte keinen der Namen behalten; er wußte nur, daß 5
kein Ernst Suhl hier einen Briefkasten hatte. Zuerst hatte er gleich
weitergehen wollen, und als er dann doch beschloß, sich im Haus zu
erkundigen, ob vielleicht jemand wüßte, was aus einem gewissen
Herrn Suhl geworden war, da tat er es ohne Hoffnung auf Erfolg.
„Ich hätte es mir doch denken können", dachte er, als er jetzt bei 10
Cramers im Wohnzimmer saß und einen Cognac trank.

„Aber Herr Kerner, geben Sie doch nicht so schnell auf", meinte Herr
Cramer. „Dieser Suhl kann doch nicht einfach aus der Welt verschwunden sein, der muß doch zu finden sein.—Warten Sie, ich rufe
einmal nebenan bei Schreiners an, die haben schon im Krieg hier 15
gewohnt. Vielleicht wissen die etwas." Cramer griff zum Telefon,
wählte, Frau Schreiner meldete sich. „Stimmt", hörte Kerner ihn
sagen, „der muß es gewesen sein, ja, ja, das Mädchen war damals
zehn oder elf.—Ausgewandert? Nach Amerika? Da muß doch wohl
über das Konsulat etwas zu erfahren sein.—Vielen Dank für die 20
Auskunft, Frau Schreiner, Wiederhören."

„Sehen Sie", sagte Kerner, „ich wußte es ja", aber er ließ sich von
Cramer doch dazu überreden, zunächst auf die Polizei und dann
zum Konsulat zu gehen. Suhl hatte sich, seine Frau und seine
adoptierte Tochter Barbara am 3. Mai 1949 polizeilich abgemeldet, 25
ohne eine Adresse in Amerika zu hinterlassen. Auf dem Konsulat
versprach man ihm, sich um die Sache zu kümmern, aber erst
Monate später erhielt er einen Brief, in dem ihm mitgeteilt wurde,
die gegenwärtige Adresse des Herrn Ernst Suhl sei leider nicht
festzustellen. Von Paul Suhls Rolle in der ganzen Sache hatte er 30
keine Ahnung.

In der Innenstadt, ganz in der Nähe des Doms, hatte er ein Zimmer
gefunden. Ab und zu besuchte er den Schauspieler Cramer, der
immer wieder versuchte, ihn dazu zu überreden, wieder Lehrer zu
werden. Aber Oswald Kerner wollte nicht mehr; „Erstens", meinte 35
er, „bin ich seit vierzehn Jahren in keiner Schule mehr gewesen, und
zweitens weigere ich mich, den Kindern Dinge zu sagen, an die ich
selbst nicht mehr glaube."

Fünf kurze Jahre hatte er unterrichtet, von 1935 bis 1940; dann war
er fünf Jahre lang Soldat gewesen und hatte ganz Europa gesehen. 40
Die sieben Jahre, die er als Kriegsgefangener in Rußland verbracht
hatte, waren in seiner Erinnerung zu einer Unendlichkeit geworden:

Glossary (right margin):

Pfr. = Pfarrer

behalten to retain, remember, keep

gewiß certain
die Hoffnung hope

nebenan next door

sich melden to answer (the telephone)

die Auskunft, ⁔e information

überreden to persuade

sich polizeilich ab-melden to cancel one's registration with the police
hinterlassen to leave behind
sich kümmern um to take care of; to be concerned with
ihm mitgeteilt wurde he was informed
gegenwärtig present
feststellen to determine; find out; conclude
ab und zu off and on

sich weigern to refuse

die Erinnerung, –n memory
unendlich infinite

endlose Arbeit, endloser Hunger, endloses Heimweh. Nur der jähr-
liche Wechsel zwischen Sommerhitze und Winterkälte hatte dem
Leben einen Rhythmus gegeben. Als er dann nach der hoffnungs-
vollen Rückfahrt nach Deutschland der Wirklichkeit gegenüber-
stand, war das, was während der sieben langen Jahre für ihn das 5
einzig Wirkliche gewesen war, zu etwas Unwirklichem geworden:
seine Frau war tot, seine Tochter verschwunden. Und so hatte er
vierzehn Monate lang Särge gemacht, als Hilfsarbeiter bei der
Firma Fritz Müller VEB, bis er noch einmal eine hoffnungsvolle
Reise machte, nur um auch dieses Mal zu erfahren, daß Träume 10
und Wirklichkeit nicht dasselbe sind.

So wurde Oswald Kerner wieder Hilfsarbeiter. Durch den Schauspieler bekam er eine Stellung als Schreiner beim Theater in Frankfurt. Statt Särge zu machen, baute er jetzt Träume, den Kerker für
*Fidelio,** die Hölle für *Don Giovanni,*† den Serail für die *Ent-* 15
führung‡ und einen fahrbaren Schwan für *Lohengrin.*§ Und abends
stand er hinter den Kulissen, um dafür zu sorgen, daß der Schwan
auch richtig fuhr.

X

Frankfurt, Juni 1958

Ein warmer Frühsommerabend; während der Pause konnte man auf
der Opernterrasse eine Zigarette rauchen. Es gab Glucks *Orpheus,* 20
mit deutschem Text und dem von Gluck angehängten Happy End.‖
„Ich finde das ganz richtig", meinte Barbara. „Jede Liebesgeschichte
sollte ein Happy End haben." Paul lachte. „Du bist ja erst drei
Wochen verheiratet. Warte nur ein paar Jahre, dann tut es dir
bestimmt leid, daß du mich alten Mann geheiratet hast." „Du armer 25
alter Mann! Komm, ich helfe dir auf deinen Platz zurück." Immer
noch lachend ließ er sich von ihr sanft über die Terrasse schieben.

Während des letzten Aktes stand Oswald Kerner wie immer in den
Kulissen. „Hoffentlich fällt die Sonne nicht herunter", sagte er zu
einem Kollegen. Die Sonne war das Glanzstück der Aufführung; in 30
ihr wurde Amor aus dem Theaterhimmel herabgelassen, um Orpheus
nach dem zweiten Tod der Eurydike vor dem Selbstmord zu bewahren. Kerner hatte immer Angst, daß Amor eines Tages mit der
Sonne auf die Bühne fallen könnte; aber er vergaß seine Angst
jedesmal, wenn kurz vorher Orpheus seine letzte Arie sang. „Ach, 35

---

* opera by Beethoven
† opera by Mozart
‡ *The Abduction from the Seraglio,* opera by Mozart
§ opera by Wagner
‖ In Gluck's opera, after the second death of Eurydice, with which the Greek
myth ends, Amor (Cupid) prevents Orpheus from committing suicide, and
Orpheus and Eurydice are happily reunited.

Glossary (margin):

das Heimweh home-sickness
der Wechsel,– change
die Hitze (*no pl.*) heat
die Kälte (*no pl.*) cold

der Hilfsarbeiter, – unskilled laborer

der Schreiner carpenter
der Kerker, – dungeon
die Hölle hell
der Serail seraglio, harem
einen fahrbaren Schwan a mobile (i.e., on wheels) swan
die Kulisse, –n wings, drop
sorgen für to see to it

sanft soft

der Kolle′ge colleague
das Glanzstück, –e showpiece
die Aufführung, –en performance
wurde . . . herab-gelassen was lowered
der Selbstmord, –e suicide
bewahren to save, protect

ich habe sie verloren", heißt es da im deutschen Text, „all mein
Glück ist nun dahin." Es war Kerners Lieblingsstelle in der ganzen
Oper, und manchmal dachte er dabei an die Frau und die Tochter,
die er vor Jahren einmal gehabt hatte. Hier müßte die Geschichte
des Orpheus eigentlich aufhören, dachte Kerner und fand, daß das 5
glückliche Ende falsch wäre, selbst in einer Oper.

dahin (here) gone
die Stelle, –n place

„Würdest du wegen mir auch in die Unterwelt steigen?" flüsterte
Barbara. „Aber sicher", flüsterte Paul zurück, „nur könnte ich nicht
so gut singen." Barbara schob ihre Hand in Pauls Hand. „Vorher
gehen wir aber noch oft Erdbeeren essen", sagte sie.   10

flüstern whisper

Noch während des Beifalls verließ Kerner das Theater. Er wollte
noch in Sachsenhausen ein Glas Apfelwein trinken. Über dem Main
hing ein romantischer Vollmond; darunter stand, wie eine Kulisse,
das Sachsenhäuser Ufer mit der Dreikönigskirche. Auf dem Eisernen
Steg blieb Kerner lange stehen und starrte aufs Wasser. „Komisch", 15
dachte er, „wenn der Pfarrer damals nicht den Zettel gefunden
hätte, wäre ich wahrscheinlich heute noch in Thüringen und machte
Särge."

der Beifall (no pl.)
applause
der Apfelwein hard
apple cider
das Ufer, – bank,
shore
starren to stare
komisch funny, odd;
comical
der Eiserne Steg
(name of a bridge)

Frankfurt. Blick von Sachsenhausen zum Eisernen Steg und Dom

„Wenn du damals nicht von mir weggelaufen wärst, hätte ich dich
sicher nie nach Frankfurt gebracht", sagte Paul. Sie hatten beschlossen, zu Fuß in ihr kleines Hotel bei der Universität zurück-
zugehen, und auf dem Weg dorthin waren sie in die Nähe der
Bettinastraße gekommen. Obwohl die ganze Straße sich so sehr 5
verändert hatte, erkannte sie das Haus wieder. Sie fing an zu er-
zählen, unterbrach sich immer wieder mit „Weißt du noch?—Erin- **(sich) unterbrechen** to interrupt (oneself)
nerst du dich?" Dann sprachen sie über Barbaras Auswanderung
mit Ernst und seiner Frau. Sie hatten zuerst bei Pauls Eltern in St.
Louis gewohnt, dann hatte Ernst eine Stellung in New York ge- 10
funden, während Paul nach seiner Rückkehr aus Deutschland in **die Rückkehr** return
Chicago arbeitete. Sieben Jahre hatten sie einander nicht gesehen.
Paul und Ernst schrieben sich manchmal Briefe, und Paul wußte,
daß Barbara 1954 aufs College gegangen war. Trotzdem war er über- **überraschen** to surprise
rascht, als Ernst ihm ein Bild von Barbara schickte,—dieses Bild 15
trug dazu bei, daß er beschloß, im Sommer 1956 seine Ferien mit **beitragen zu** to contribute to
Ernst zu verbringen und daß er sich ein halbes Jahr später von **die Ferien** (*pl.*) vacation
seiner Firma nach New York schicken ließ. **verbringen** to spend (time)

Während Barbara und Paul im Hotel noch ein Glas Wein tranken,
saß Oswald Kerner in Sachsenhausen an seinem Stammtisch, trank 20 **der Stammtisch, –e** table reserved for reg-
Apfelwein und unterhielt sich mit ein paar Bekannten. Er war jetzt ular guests at a tavern
einundfünfzig Jahre alt, sah aber älter aus; er war nicht mehr so **die Katastro′phe** catastrophe
zynisch wie vor fünf Jahren, aber die Katastrophen in seinem Leben
hatte er nie überwinden können. Daß er einmal Lehrer gewesen **überwinden** to over-
war, das hatte er fast vergessen. Es ging ihm nicht schlecht, und er 25 come, get over
war ganz zufrieden damit, daß er für den Rest seines Lebens Opern-
kulissen machen würde.

XI

Frankfurt, Dezember 1960

„Was ich nicht verstehen kann, Herr Kerner, ist, daß Sie damals nicht
weitergesucht haben. Als Sie vom Konsulat diesen negativen Brief
bekamen, hätten Sie einfach wieder hingehen sollen. Irgendwo 30
hätten die Ihre Tochter schon gefunden."

„Das sagen Sie so, Herr Müller, aber Sie dürfen nicht vergessen, daß
ich gerade aus dem Osten gekommen war. Und außerdem hatte ich
zum zweiten Mal alles verloren. Nein, ich habe damals einfach auf-
gegeben; es hatte ja doch alles keinen Sinn mehr. Ich habe auch nie 35 **der Sinn, –e** sense
wieder davon gesprochen. Heute war eigentlich das erste Mal, daß
ich die ganze Geschichte wieder erzählt habe. Komisch, wie man sich
plötzlich wieder an Dinge erinnern kann, an die man seit Jahren
nicht mehr gedacht hat."

Es war wieder ein Samstagabend, und Kerner saß mit seinen Bekannten an seinem Sachsenhäuser Stammtisch beim Apfelwein.
Irgend jemand hatte angefangen, vom Krieg zu sprechen; Müller
hatte davon erzählt, daß seine Frau bei dem Luftangriff auf Dresden
umgekommen war,—und das hatte ganz unerwartet bei Kerner viele 5
Erinnerungen wachgerufen. Er hatte von den paar Jahren vor dem
Krieg erzählt, als er in Breslau Lehrer gewesen war, von seinen
Erlebnissen in ganz Europa während des Krieges, von seiner Ver-
wundung vor Stalingrad und von seiner Gefangennahme in Pommern. Über die Jahre der Gefangenschaft wußte er nicht viel zu 10
sagen, aber an die beiden Fahrten, die mit Hoffnung begonnen und
mit Enttäuschung geendet hatten, nach Thüringen und nach Frankfurt, wußte er sich genau zu erinnern.

„Ich kenne den Kerner ja schon seit Jahren", meinte Müller, „aber
so viel wie heute habe ich ihn noch nie reden hören." 15

Kerner hatte seine Brieftasche aus der Jacke gezogen. „Ja, sehen Sie,
ich hatte ja nur die Adresse hier",—er zeigte den anderen Paul Suhls
Zettel, „da ist heute bestimmt nichts mehr mit zu machen. Und
selbst wenn ich die Barbara finden könnte,—das Kind hat doch
schon längst vergessen, daß ich einmal ihr Vater war. ,Das Kind' sage 20
ich, dabei ist sie vierundzwanzig Jahre alt und ist wahrscheinlich
verheiratet. Vielleicht bin ich sogar schon Großvater, ohne es zu
wissen." Der Gedanke schien seine gute Laune gestört zu haben.
„Reden wir nicht mehr davon; das macht einen ja direkt melan-
cholisch." 25

„Darf ich Sie doch noch etwas fragen, Herr Kerner?" Der jüngere
Mann, der Kerner gegenüber an dem großen runden Tisch saß, hatte
sich gerade Pauls Zettel sehr intensiv angesehen. „Wissen Sie, was
das für eine komische Zahl ist hier unten?"

„Ach, diese Zahl", sagte Kerner. „Ich habe mir damals oft überlegt, 30
was das sein könnte; aber die steht wahrscheinlich nur aus Zufall da."

„Das glaube ich nicht. Ich habe doch jahrelang bei den Amerikanern
gearbeitet, und ich weiß, daß die Soldaten alle so eine lange Nummer
haben."

„Na ja, und?" 35

„Das könnte doch sehr gut die Nummer von dem Soldaten sein,
der die Adresse geschrieben hat,—ist doch die gleiche Handschrift.
Wissen Sie was, Herr Kerner, lassen Sie mich die Nummer abschreiben. Ich habe einen Bekannten auf dem amerikanischen Konsulat, den werde ich fragen, ob man damit etwas machen kann." 40

„Von mir aus". Kerner zuckte die Achseln. „Da wird doch nichts
draus."

der Angriff, –e attack,
raid
umkommen to perish
wachrufen to awaken

das Erlebnis, –se
experience, adventure

die Brieftasche, –n
billfold
die Jacke, –n jacket
der Zettel, – slip of
paper

dabei at that, actually

die Laune mood,
humor

gegenüber (*with
dative*) opposite
rund round

abschreiben to copy
die Achseln zucken
to shrug one's
shoulders
da wird nichts draus
nothing will come of it

Kerner sagte nichts mehr. Dann stand er abrupt auf: es sei spät und
er müsse nach Hause, die anderen möchten ihn entschuldigen, aber
es ginge ihm schon den ganzen Tag nicht gut. Er bezahlte und ging.
Es ärgerte ihn, daß seine Bekannten ihm wieder Hoffnung gemacht   **es ärgerte ihn** it made
hatten,—Hoffnung auf etwas, woran er seit Jahren kaum mehr ge- ₅   him mad
dacht hatte. Aber noch mehr ärgerte er sich darüber, daß er überhaupt geredet hatte. Warum hatte er diesen Leuten seine Ge-
schichte erzählt, verdammt noch mal. Er hätte ja auch den Mund   **verdammt noch mal**
halten können.   dammit

Er beschloß, nicht mehr samstagabends nach Sachsenhausen zu ₁₀
gehen.

Aber wenn der Herr Kerner nicht mehr an seinem Stammtisch erschien, so mußte eben der Stammtisch zu Herrn Kerner kommen.
Wochen später standen eines Abends Herr Müller und der Mann,
der die I.D. Nummer abgeschrieben hatte, aufgeregt vor Kerners ₁₅   **aufgeregt** excited
Tür. Neuigkeiten hatten die beiden, und Oswald Kerner war so   **die Neuigkeit, –en**
überrascht, daß er zunächst kein Wort herausbringen konnte. Da-   news
nach kämpfte Kerner drei Tage lang mit sich selbst,—„Soll ich oder
soll ich nicht?"—und schließlich setzte er sich an einem Sonntag-
vormittag hin und schrieb einen Brief.   ₂₀

XII

Frankfurt, 21. April 1961

Sehr geehrter Herr Suhl!

Durch Zufall bin ich in den Besitz Ihrer Adresse gelangt und   **der Besitz** possession;
schreibe Ihnen in der Hoffnung, daß Sie mir vielleicht etwas über   **in den Besitz ge-**
meine Tochter Barbara Kerner mitteilen können.   **langen** to acquire

Meine Frau und meine Tochter waren kurz vor Ende des Krieges
aus Breslau in den Thüringer Wald geflüchtet. Nach dem Tod ₂₅   **flüchten** to flee
meiner Frau sollen amerikanische Soldaten, als die Russen nach
Thüringen kamen, meine Tochter mit nach Frankfurt genommen
haben.

Als ich nach sieben Jahren russischer Gefangenschaft selbst nach
Thüringen kam, war der einzige Hinweis auf das weitere Schicksal ₃₀ **der Hinweis, –e** indi-
meiner Tochter ein Zettel mit der Adresse eines Herrn Ernst Suhl   cation, clue, hint
in Frankfurt. Da der Pfarrer, in dessen Papieren der Zettel gefunden **das Schicksal** fate
worden war, nicht mehr lebte, konnte ich nichts weiteres erfahren.
Vor allem wurde mir nicht klar, daß die Zahl, die außer der Adresse
noch auf dem Zettel stand, die I.D. Nummer eines amerikanischen ₃₅
Soldaten war.

Als es mir 1953 gelang, nach dem Westen zu kommen, mußte ich
leider erfahren, daß meine Tochter von Herrn und Frau Suhl
adoptiert worden war und mit ihren Adoptiveltern nach Amerika
ausgewandert war. Aber es gelang mir nicht, die Adresse meiner
Tochter in den Staaten festzustellen. Seitdem lebe ich in Frankfurt, 5 **feststellen** to ascertain
wo ich bei den Städtischen Bühnen als Bühnenarbeiter beschäftigt
bin.

Die Hoffnung, meine Tochter wiederzufinden, hatte ich längst auf-
gegeben, als ein Bekannter, dem ich den Zettel mit Herrn Ernst
Suhls Adresse zeigte, in der langen Zahl eine amerikanische Sol- 10
datennummer erkannte. Durch einen Herrn auf dem amerikanischen
Generalkonsulat hat mein Bekannter dann Ihre Adresse in St. Louis
finden können.

Ich habe lange gezögert, bevor ich mich endlich doch entschloß,
Ihnen zu schreiben. Für meine Tochter sind Herr und Frau Suhl 15
seit vielen Jahren die „richtigen" Eltern, und ich dachte zuerst, daß
ich Barbara bei dem Glauben lassen sollte, daß ihr Vater, den sie
kaum gekannt hat, irgendwo im Osten umgekommen ist. Ich weiß
nicht, was mich zwingt, Ihnen doch zu schreiben. Zweimal bin ich   **handgreiflich** within
enttäuscht worden, als ich Barbara schon handgreiflich vor mir sah; 20 reach
und so treibt es mich, einen dritten Versuch zu machen. Als ich   **treiben, trieb, ge-**
Barbara das letzte Mal sah, war sie acht Jahre alt; im kommenden   **trieben** to drive
August wird sie fünfundzwanzig.

Verzeihen Sie einem alten Mann, daß er Sie belästigt. Vielleicht   **belästigen** to bother
wissen Sie gar nicht, was aus meiner Tochter geworden ist. Sollten 25
Sie aber doch etwas von ihr wissen, dann wäre ich Ihnen dankbar,
wenn Sie mich wissen lassen wollten, wo und wie sie lebt.

Ihr

Oswald Kerner

XIII

San Francisco, den 8. Mai 1961

Mein lieber Vater,

Wie seltsam das klingt,—„Mein lieber Vater". Aber du bist ja mein   **klingen** to sound
Vater, und ich bin Deine Tochter, auch wenn ich seit vielen Jahren
geglaubt habe, Du wärst tot.   30

Verzeih mir, daß ich so anfange. Wie beginnt man einen solchen
Brief? Sollte ich schreiben, „Lieber Vater, ich habe mich sehr ge-
freut, endlich von Dir zu hören"? Nein, gefreut habe ich mich nicht.
—Aber das ist auch falsch. Natürlich habe ich mich gefreut. Aber als

Pauls Eltern uns Deinen Brief von St. Louis aus nachgeschickt
haben, konnte ich zuerst gar nicht begreifen, was geschehen war. **begreifen** to
Dann habe ich geweint, bis Ernst (das ist mein Vater,—mein comprehend
Adoptivvater) sagte, „Aber Kindchen, jetzt hast du eben zwei Väter,
—und es gibt nicht viele Menschen, die das von sich behaupten ₅
können."

Verstehst Du, wie schwer das alles für mich ist? Ich muß mich erst
daran gewöhnen, daß ich wirklich zwei Väter habe. Ich kann mich
ja kaum an Dich erinnern. Ich weiß noch, wie Du im Krieg einmal
auf Urlaub gekommen bist; ich saß in der Küche, als plötzlich die ₁₀
Tür aufging und ein großer fremder Mann in Uniform hereinkam,
und ich hatte Angst vor Dir, und Mutti sagte immer wieder, Bär-
belchen, kennst du denn deinen Vater nicht mehr? Seltsam, daß mir
diese Szene in Erinnerung geblieben ist. Ich muß noch sehr klein
gewesen sein, vielleicht vier oder fünf.—Doch ich glaube, daß ich ₁₅
mich an vieles werde erinnern können, nur brauche ich Zeit. Es ist
ja so viel passiert in den letzten fünfzehn Jahren.

Kurz nachdem Mutti gestorben ist, habe ich Paul kennengelernt. Er **das Mitleid** pity,
hatte wohl Mitleid mit mir; er hat mir erzählt, daß ich ein ver- sympathy
ängstigtes, scheues kleines Mädchen gewesen wäre, und daß die ₂₀ **verängstigt** timid,
anderen Kinder nicht mit mir spielen wollten. Paul war damals scared
einundzwanzig und hat mich dann mit nach Frankfurt genommen, **scheu** shy
zu seinem Vetter, obwohl er das eigentlich gar nicht hätte tun
dürfen. Paul und Ernst haben damals alles versucht, Dich zu finden,
aber Du warst und bliebst verschwunden, und als Irene und Ernst ₂₅
nach Amerika auswandern wollten, haben sie mich adoptiert. Wir
haben dann lange in New York gewohnt. Paul habe ich erst sieben
Jahre später wiedergesehen, als ich schon auf dem College war, und
dann habe ich mich in ihn verliebt, und 1958 haben wir geheiratet.
Im September 1959 sind unsere Kinder geboren, Paul Jr. und Bar- ₃₀
bara. Du bist also der Großvater von Zwillingen. Seit 1959 wohnen **der Zwilling, –e** twin
wir hier in San Francisco, und seit einem halben Jahr wohnen Irene
und Ernst ganz hier in der Nähe.

Jetzt habe ich plötzlich das Gefühl, daß ich Dir noch Seiten und
Seiten schreiben könnte, aber das tue ich lieber das nächste Mal. ₃₅
Dieser Brief soll jetzt schnell auf die Post.

Plötzlich habe ich auch tausend Fragen. Wo warst Du am Ende des
Krieges? Wie hast Du gewußt, daß ich in Thüringen war? Warum
hat man Dir auf dem Konsulat nicht gesagt, was die Nummer auf
dem Zettel bedeutete? Was hast Du in den zwei Jahren in Thüringen ₄₀
gemacht? Hast Du wieder unterrichtet? Und warum bist Du in
Frankfurt nicht wieder Lehrer geworden? Weißt Du, daß wir auf

unserer Hochzeitsreise auch in Frankfurt waren, und wir waren auch   **die Hochzeit, –en**
zwei oder drei Mal im Theater. Wer weiß, vielleicht haben wir ein-   wedding
ander sogar gesehen.

Lieber Vater, sei mir nicht böse, daß ich so unzusammenhängend
schreibe. Ich bin immer noch verwirrt und kann nicht recht glauben, ₅ **verwirrt** confused
daß das alles wahr ist. Für Dich wird mein Brief sicher auch ein
Schock sein. Wir müssen uns eben langsam an den Gedanken gewöhnen, daß wir für einander nun wieder existieren. Ernst sagt
immer, Kinder, das wird sich schon finden; und ich weiß, daß er
recht hat.   ₁₀

Herzlich,

Deine Barbara

P.S. Ich lege ein Bild von den Kindern bei. Von Paul und mir habe
ich im Moment kein gutes.

XIV

San Franzisko, November 1962

Die Lufthansa-Maschine aus Frankfurt ist gerade angekommen. Die
Fluggäste drängen zum Ausgang; alle wollen so schnell wie möglich   **drängen** to push
durch den Zoll kommen. Die meisten werden draußen erwartet, von ₁₅
ihren Eltern, oder ihren Kindern. Ein paar Geschäftsleute sind unter   **die Geschäftsleute**
den Fluggästen, die von ihren Frauen abgeholt werden; andere   (*pl.*) businessmen;
haben in Deutschland Verwandte besucht; auch ein paar typische   **der Geschäftsmann**
Touristen sind dabei.   (*sing.*)

Oswald Kerner wartet, bis alle anderen das Flugzeug verlassen ₂₀
haben. Er hat Angst,—Angst vor dem neuen Land, Angst vor der
fremden Sprache. Er fürchtet sich vor den Menschen, die da draußen
auf ihn warten, er fürchtet sich vor allem vor der jungen Frau, die
seine Tochter ist, und als er jetzt zum Zoll geht, merkt er auf einmal,
daß ihm die Hände zittern. Ganz grau ist er geworden, und er denkt ₂₅
wieder, wie so oft in diesen letzten Monaten, daß er hätte in
Deutschland bleiben sollen, daß es ein Fehler gewesen war, den
ersten Brief an Paul zu schreiben. War er denn nicht zufrieden gewesen mit seinem Leben? Warum hatte er sich in das Leben dieser
Menschen drängen müssen, auch wenn einer dieser Menschen seine ₃₀
eigene Tochter war?

     einsprechen auf to
Bei der Paßkontrolle sprach ein Beamter auf ihn ein, und er verstand   talk (intensely) to
kein Wort. Als sein Koffer kontrolliert wurde, dachte er, jetzt   **einfallen** to occur
schicken sie dich bestimmt wieder zurück,—und plötzlich fiel ihm   (to one's mind)
der Polizist ein, der damals im Zug seine Papiere kontrolliert hatte, ₃₅   **es fällt mir ein**
     I remember

als er von Thüringen nach Berlin fuhr. Aber der amerikanische
Beamte war sehr freundlich und mußte mehrere Male "OK, Sir"
sagen, bevor Kerner begriff, daß er gehen konnte. Er war der letzte,
und als er jetzt auf die Tür zuging, durch die die anderen Fluggäste
verschwunden waren, überfiel ihn wieder die Angst. Langsam öff- 5
nete er die Tür. Der Korridor war leer, er sah ängstlich nach links
und nach rechts und wußte nicht, in welche Richtung er gehen sollte.

Dann kamen plötzlich zwei junge Leute den Korridor herunter-
gerannt, ein junger Mann und eine junge Frau. Kerner wußte sofort,
das waren Barbara und Paul; aber als sie ihn begrüßten und auf ihn 10
einsprachen, konnte er kein Wort sagen. Er hielt sich an seiner
Tasche und an seinem Koffer fest und wollte sich nicht helfen lassen.
Dann ließ er es aber doch geschehen, daß sie ihm Tasche und Koffer
abnahmen, daß sie ihn zwischen sich nahmen und langsam den
Korridor hinunterführten. Dort unten, am Eingang zum Empfangs- 15
gebäude, standen Irene und Ernst mit den beiden Kindern.

Ein paar Minuten später,—die anderen Fluggäste waren längst in
die Empfangshalle verschwunden,—kniete Oswald Kerner auf dem
Boden, hatte in jedem Arm eines der beiden Kinder, blickte immer
wieder von dem kleinen Mädchen zur Mutter und von der Mutter 20
zur Tochter und sagte „Barbara, Barbara." Er lächelte und schien
gar nicht mehr so alt und grau wie vor zehn Minuten. Dann stand
er auf, zog den Zettel aus seiner Brieftasche, gab ihn Paul und sagte:
„Hier, das ist es. Ohne dieses Stück Papier hätte ich euch nie
gefunden." 25

überfallen to over-
come

die Richtung, –en
direction

abnehmen to take
away; to lose
weight

PRINCIPAL PARTS OF STRONG AND IRREGULAR VERBS

NOTE: Many compound verbs, such as **aufmachen** and **ausgehen,** are not included in this table. The principal parts of such verbs will be identical in basic form with those of the corresponding simple verbs (**machen, gehen**).

abhängen von to depend upon
  hing ab von, hat abgehangen von, es hängt ab von
anfangen to begin, start
  fing an, hat angefangen, er fängt an
ankommen to arrive
  kam an, ist angekommen, er kommt an
annehmen to accept; to assume
  nahm an, hat angenommen, er nimmt an
anrufen to call up (on the telephone)
  rief an, hat angerufen, er ruft an
aufstehen to get up, to rise
  stand auf, ist aufgestanden, er steht auf

backen to bake
  backte (also **buk**), **hat gebacken, er bäckt**
befehlen to order, command
  befahl, hat befohlen, er befiehlt
beginnen to begin, start
  begann, hat begonnen, er beginnt
begreifen to comprehend
  begriff, hat begriffen, er begreift
behalten to keep, retain; to remember

behielt, hat behalten, er behält
bekommen to get, receive
  bekam, hat bekommen, er bekommt
beschließen to decide, determine
  beschloß, hat beschlossen, er beschließt
beweisen to prove
  bewies, hat bewiesen, er beweist
bitten to ask for, request
  bat, hat gebeten, er bittet
bleiben to stay, remain
  blieb, ist geblieben, er bleibt
braten to roast; to fry
  briet, hat gebraten, er brät
brechen to break
  brach, hat gebrochen, er bricht
brennen to burn
  brannte, hat gebrannt, er brennt
bringen to bring
  brachte, hat gebracht, er bringt

denken to think
  dachte, hat gedacht, er denkt
dürfen to be permitted to
  durfte, hat gedurft, er darf
einladen to invite
  lud ein, hat eingeladen, er lädt ein

empfangen to receive
  empfing, hat empfangen, er empfängt
empfehlen to recommend
  empfahl, hat empfohlen, er empfiehlt
sich entschließen to decide, make up one's mind
  entschloß sich, hat sich entschlossen, entschließt sich
entsprechen to correspond to
  entsprach, hat entsprochen, es entspricht
entstehen to originate, come into being
  entstand, ist entstanden, er entsteht
erfahren to find out, learn
  erfuhr, hat erfahren, er erfährt
erfinden to invent
  erfand, hat erfunden, er erfindet
erhalten to receive; to sustain
  erhielt, hat erhalten, er erhält
erkennen to recognize
  erkannte, hat erkannt, er erkennt
erscheinen to appear
  erschien, ist erschienen, er erscheint
erschrecken to be frightened
  erschrak, ist erschrocken, er erschrickt
ertrinken to drown

ertrank, ist ertrunken, er ertrinkt
sich erweisen to turn out, show
erwies sich, hat sich erwiesen, es erweist sich
essen to eat
aß, hat gegessen, er ißt

fahren to drive, go (by train, boat, plane, car)
fuhr, ist gefahren, er fährt
fallen to fall
fiel, ist gefallen, er fällt
finden to find
fand, hat gefunden, er findet
fliegen to fly
flog, ist geflogen, er fliegt
fliehen to flee, escape
floh, ist geflohen, er flieht
fließen to flow
floß, ist geflossen, er fließt
fressen to eat (said of animals)
fraß, hat gefressen, er frißt
frieren to freeze; to be cold
fror, hat gefroren, er friert

geben to give
gab, hat gegeben, er gibt
gefallen to please
gefiel, hat gefallen, er gefällt
gefangennehmen to capture, take prisoner
nahm gefangen, hat gefangengenommen, er nimmt gefangen
gehen to go, walk
ging, ist gegangen, er geht
gelingen to succeed
gelang, ist gelungen, es gelingt
geschehen to happen, occur
geschah, ist geschehen, es geschieht
gewinnen to win
gewann, hat gewonnen, er gewinnt
greifen to grasp
griff, hat gegriffen, er greift

haben to have
hatte, hat gehabt, er hat
halten to hold; to stop
hielt, hat gehalten, er hält
heissen to be called, to mean
hieß, hat geheißen, er heißt
helfen to help
half, hat geholfen, er hilft

kennen to know, be acquainted with
kannte, hat gekannt, er kennt
klingen to sound
klang, hat geklungen, es klingt
kommen to come
kam, ist gekommen, er kommt
können to be able to
konnte, hat gekonnt, er kann

lassen to let; to leave
ließ, hat gelassen, er läßt
laufen to run
lief, ist gelaufen, er läuft
leiden to suffer
litt, hat gelitten, er leidet
lesen to read
las, hat gelesen, er liest
liegen to lie (flat); to be situated
lag, hat gelegen, er liegt
lügen to tell a lie
log, hat gelogen, er lügt

mögen to like
mochte, hat gemocht, er mag
müssen to have to
mußte, hat gemußt, er muß

nachdenken to reflect, meditate
dachte nach, hat nachgedacht, er denkt nach
nehmen to take
nahm, hat genommen, er nimmt
raten to advise, to guess
riet, hat geraten, er rät
reißen to tear
riß, hat gerissen, er reißt
rennen to run

rannte, ist gerannt, er rennt
rufen to call
rief, hat gerufen, er ruft

scheinen to seem; to shine
schien, hat geschienen, er scheint
schieben to push, shove
schob, hat geschoben, er schiebt
schießen to shoot
schoß, hat geschossen, er schießt
schilaufen to ski
lief Schi, ist schigelaufen, er läuft Schi
schlafen to sleep
schlief, hat geschlafen, er schläft
schlagen to beat; hit
schlug, hat geschlagen, er schlägt
schließen to close
schloß, hat geschlossen, er schließt
schneiden to cut
schnitt, hat geschnitten, er schneidet
schreiben to write
schrieb, hat geschrieben, er schreibt
schreien to scream, cry
schrie, hat geschrie(e)n, er schreit
schweigen to be silent, say nothing
schwieg, hat geschwiegen, er schweigt
schwimmen to swim
schwamm, ist geschwommen, er schwimmt
sehen to see
sah, hat gesehen, er sieht
sein to be
war, ist gewesen, er ist
senden to send;
sandte, hat gesandt, er sendet
singen to sing
sang, hat gesungen, er singt
sinken to sink
sank, ist gesunken, er sinkt
sitzen to sit
saß, hat gesessen, er sitzt
sollen to be supposed to

sollte, hat gesollt, er soll
spazierengehen to go for a
walk
ging spazieren, ist spa-
zierengegangen, er geht
spazieren
sprechen to speak, talk
sprach, hat gesprochen, er
spricht
springen to jump
sprang, ist gesprungen, er
springt
stehen to stand
stand, hat gestanden, er
steht
stehenbleiben to stop (walking or moving)
blieb stehen, ist stehengeblieben, er bleibt stehen
stehlen to steal
stahl, hat gestohlen, er
stiehlt
steigen to climb
stieg, ist gestiegen, er
steigt
sterben to die
starb, ist gestorben, er
stirbt
streichen to spread; to stroke;
to paint
strich, hat gestrichen, er
streicht

tragen to carry
trug, hat getragen, er trägt
treffen to meet; to hit
traf, hat getroffen, er trifft
treten to step
trat, ist getreten, er tritt

trinken to drink
trank, hat getrunken, er
trinkt
tun to do
tat, hat getan, er tut

sich unterhalten to converse,
have a conversation
unterhielt sich, hat sich
unterhalten, er unterhält
sich

verbieten to forbid
verbot, hat verboten, er
verbietet
verbinden to unite; to compound
verband, hat verbunden,
er verbindet
verbringen to spend (time)
verbrachte, hat verbracht,
er verbringt
vergessen to forget
vergaß, hat vergessen, er
vergißt
verlassen to leave
verließ, hat verlassen, er
verläßt
verlieren to lose
verlor, hat verloren, er
verliert
verschwinden to disappear
verschwand, ist ver-
schwunden, er ver-
schwindet
versprechen to promise
versprach, hat versprochen,
er verspricht
verstehen to understand

verstand, hat verstanden,
er versteht
verzeihen to pardon, excuse
verzieh, hat verziehen, er
verzeiht
vorschlagen to suggest; to
propose
schlug vor, hat vorge-
schlagen, er schlägt vor

wachsen to grow
wuchs, ist gewachsen, er
wächst
waschen to wash
wusch, hat gewaschen, er
wäscht
werden to become
wurde, ist geworden, er
wird
werfen to throw
warf, hat geworfen, er
wirft
wissen to know
wußte, hat gewußt, er weiß
wollen to want to
wollte, hat gewollt, er will
wiegen to weigh
wog, hat gewogen, er wiegt

ziehen to move (from one
place to another)
zog, ist gezogen, er zieht
ziehen to pull
zog, hat gezogen, er zieht
zwingen to force
zwang, hat gezwungen, er
zwingt

VOCABULARY: German – English

This vocabulary is intended primarily for quick reference; it is not meant to be a substitute for a dictionary of the German language. The English equivalents given here do not include all the meanings of the corresponding German words that are found in a German dictionary. Most of the translations are limited to the meanings in which the German words are used in this book.

NOUNS

All nouns are preceded by the definite article to show their gender and are followed by an indication of the plural form. Thus the entries

der Mann, ̈er	man
die Blume, –n	flower
das Fenster, –	window

mean that **Mann** is masculine and its plural is **Männer, Blume** is feminine and its plural is **Blumen**, and **Fenster** is neuter and is unchanged in the plural. Nouns for which no plural form is shown are not used in the plural. If two case endings are listed, the first indicates the genetive singular and the second the nominative plural.

ACCENTUATION

An accent mark shows the pronunciation of words with an unusual accentuation in German (e.g. **Schokola′de**). If the stress shifts to another syllable in the plural, the complete plural form is shown with an accent mark indicating the stress (**der Doktor, die Dokto′ren**). Stress is not indicated for words in which the first syllable is an unaccented prefix such as **be-** or **er-** or for compound verbs.

VERBS

The vowel changes of "regular" strong verbs are indicated (e.g. **schreiben, ie, ie**), the vowels given being respectively the stem vowels of the past indicative and the past participle. With verbs that have a change of stem vowel in the present, the third person singular present is also given (e.g. **schlafen, ie, a, er schläft**). "Irregular" strong verbs have their principal parts given in full (e.g. **stehen, stand, gestanden**). For further reference a summary list of strong and irregular verbs used in this text precedes this vocabulary.

Verbs that require the auxiliary **sein** to form the perfect tenses are indicated by (**ist**) [e.g. **bleiben, ie, ie,** (**ist**) stay].

480

In compound verbs written as one word a dot between the complement and the verb (aus·gehen, nach·denken) indicates that the two parts are separated in the present and past tenses (er geht aus, er denkt nach).

With irregular or strong verbs that have separable prefixes the prefix is not repeated, but the principal parts are given thus: auf·stehen, stand –, –gestanden.

ABBREVIATONS

The following abbreviations are used in the entries:

acc.	= accusative		*gen.*	= genitive
adv.	= adverb		*pers.*	= person, personal
colloq.	= colloquial		*prep.*	= preposition
conj.	= conjunction		*sent. adv.*	= sentence adverb
dat.	= dative		*trans.*	= transitive
demonstr.	= demonstrative			

ab off
ab und zu now and then; off and on
der **Abend, –e** evening
  abends evenings
  gestern abend yesterday evening, last night
  heute abend this evening, tonight
  morgen abend tomorrow evening
das **Abendessen, –** supper
aber but; however
ab·fahren, u, a, (ist), er fährt ab to depart, leave
ab·hängen, i, a, von to depend upon
ab·holen to pick up
das **Abitur'** final examination in secondary school
ab·nehmen, nahm –, –genommen, er nimmt ab to lose weight
ach oh
  ach so oh, I see
die **Achse, –n** axle, axis
acht eight
achtzehn eighteen
achtzig eighty
adressie'ren to address
  die **Adres'se, –n** address
Ägyp'ten Egypt
ähnlich similar
die **Ahnung, –en** idea; pre-

monition; hunch
alle all, all of us
  alle all gone
allein alone
allerdings' however; admittedly
alles everything
die **Alpen** the Alps
als than; when; as
also therefore; well; in other words
alt old
das **Altertum** antiquity
alt'modisch old-fashioned
der **Amerika'ner, –** American
an on; at
ander- other
  anders different
(sich) **ändern** to change
an·fangen, i, a, er fängt an to begin, start
  der **Anfang, ˝e** beginning, start
an·gehen, ging –, –gegangen, (ist) to begin, go on
der **Anglist', –en, –en** Anglicist
die **Angst, ˝e** fear, anxiety
  Angst haben vor to be afraid of
an·kommen, kam –, –gekommen, (ist) to arrive
  die **Ankunft** arrival

an·nehmen, nahm –, –genommen, er nimmt an to accept; to assume, take on
an·reden mit to address by
an·rufen, ie, u to call up (on the telephone)
sich etwas an·schauen to look at something
an·schnallen to fasten seat belts
  die **Schnalle, –n** buckle
an·sehen, a, e, er sieht an to look at
  sich etwas an·sehen to look at something
die **Ansicht, –en** view, opinion
antworten (*plus dat. of pers.*) to answer
  die **Antwort, –en** answer, reply
an·zeigen to announce
sich an·ziehen, zog –, –gezogen to get dressed
  angezogen sein to be dressed
  der **Anzug, ˝e** suit
der **Apfel, ˝** apple
der **April'** April
arbeiten to work
  die **Arbeit, –en** work
sich ärgern über to be angry about, mad at
arm poor

der **Arm**, −e arm
die **Armee'**, die **Arme'en**
army
der **Arzt**, ⁔e physician, doctor
der **Ast**, ⁔e branch
auch also, too
auf on, on top of; up; open
auf sein to be up, open
auf (die Tür) zu toward
(the door)
die **Aufführung**, −en performance
auf·geben, a, e, er **gibt auf**
to give up; mail, post (a
letter)
auf·gehen, ging −, −gegangen, (ist) to rise (sun,
moon); to open
aufgrund' (*prep. with gen.*)
on the basis of
auf·hören to stop
die **Auflage**, −n printing
auf·machen to open
die **Aufnahme**, −n picture,
photo
sich **auf·regen über** to get excited about
aufgeregt sein über to be
excited about
auf·schreiben, ie, ie to write
down, note
auf·springen, a, u, (ist) to
jump up
auf·stehen, stand −, −gestanden, (ist) to get up,
stand up
der **Aufzug**, ⁔e elevator
das **Auge**, −n eye
der **Augenblick**, −e moment,
instant
augenblicklich momentarily; instantly
der **August'** August
aus out, out of
aus·geben, a, e, er **gibt aus** to
spend
aus·gehen, ging −, −gegangen, (ist) to go out
aus·kommen, kam −, −gekommen, (ist) to get along
die **Auskunft**, ⁔e information
aus·lachen to laugh at, make
fun of
das **Ausland** foreign countries
er lebt im Ausland he lives
abroad

sich **aus·ruhen** to rest; to get
a rest
ausgeruht sein to be rested
(sich) **aus·schlafen**, ie, a, er
schläft (sich) aus to get
enough sleep
aus·sehen, a, e, er **sieht aus**
to look, appear
außer besides, except for
außerdem moreover
aus·sprechen, a, o, er **spricht
aus** to pronounce, utter
aus·steigen, ie, ie, (ist) to get
out (of a vehicle)
aus·wandern to emigrate
sich **aus·ziehen**, zog −, −gezogen to undress
ausgezogen sein to be undressed
das **Auto**, −s car

backen, backte or buk, gebacken to bake
der **Bäcker**, − baker
baden to bathe
das **Bad**, ⁔er bath
die **Badewanne**, −n bathtub
der **Bahnhof**, ⁔e railway station
zum Bahnhof to the station
im Bahnhof within the station
auf dem Bahnhof on the
platform
bald soon
die **Bank**, ⁔e bench
die **Bank**, −en bank
der **Bart**, ⁔e beard
der **Bauch**, ⁔e stomach, belly
bauen to build
der **Bauer**, −n peasant, farmer
der **Baum**, ⁔e tree
beachten to note, notice
der **Beamte**, −n, −n civil servant, (government) official
die **Beamtin**, −nen official
(female)
beantworten (*trans.*) to answer (a letter)
bedeuten to mean, signify
bedienen to serve
die **Bedienung** service
beenden to conclude, finish
befehlen, a, o, er **befiehlt**
(*plus dat. of pers.*) to

command, order
beginnen, a, o to begin, start
begleiten to accompany
begreifen, begriff, begriffen
to comprehend
behalten, ie, a, er **behält** to
keep, retain
behaupten to maintain, claim
bei at, at the home of; near;
with
bei Schmidts at the
Schmidts'
beim Essen while eating
beide both
das **Bein**, −e leg
das **Beispiel**, −e example
zum Beispiel (z.B.) for example
bekannt well-known
der **Bekannte**, −n, −n acquaintance
bekommen, bekam, bekommen to get, receive
bellen to bark
bemerken to notice, mention,
note, say
sich **bemühen um**, bemüht
sein um to be concerned
about, with
benutzen to use
beobachten to observe, watch
bereit ready
der **Berg**, −e mountain
berichten to report
der **Beruf**, −e profession
Was sind Sie von Beruf?
What is your profession?
beruhen auf to be based on
(sich) **beruhigen** to calm
down
beruhigt sein to be calmed
down
sich **beschäftigen mit** to occupy oneself with
beschäftigt sein to be occupied, employed
die **Beschäftigung**, −en occupation
beschließen, beschloß, beschlossen to decide, determine
besetzen to occupy
besetzt busy (telephone)
besonder- special

besonders especially
besser better
bestehen aus, bestand, bestanden to consist of
bestellen to order
bestimmt definitely
besuchen to visit
der **Besuch, –e** visit
betrachten to look at, observe
das **Bett, –en** bed
beurteilen to judge, make a judgment
bevor (*conj.*) before
sich **bewegen** to move
die **Bewegung, –en** movement
beweisen, ie, ie to prove
bezahlen to pay
die **Bibliothek', –en** library
das **Bier, –e** beer
das **Bild, –er** picture
billig inexpensive; cheap
bis until, up until; up to, as far as
bis gestern until yesterday
bis Köln as far as Cologne
bis zum Winter (up) until winter
bis zum Bahnhof as far as the station
zwei bis drei two to three
ein **bißchen** a bit, a little
die **Bitte, –n** request
bitte please
bitten um, bat, gebeten to request, ask for
blau blue
bleiben, ie, ie, (ist) to stay, remain
blicken to look, glance
der **Blick, –e** look, glance; view
blitzen to lighten
der **Blitz, –e** lightning
blühen to bloom, blossom, flower
die **Blume, –n** flower
der **Boden, –** ground; floor
die **Bombe, –n** bomb
böse mad, angry at; evil
(jemandem) **böse sein** to be angry (mad) at somebody
braten, ie, a to roast, fry

der **Braten, –** roast
der **Kalbsbraten, –** veal roast
der **Schweinebraten, –** pork roast
brauchen to need
braun brown
die **Braut, ÷e** bride
der **Bräutigam, –e** bridegroom
brechen, a, o, er bricht to break
breit broad, wide
brennen, brannte, gebrannt to burn
der **Brief, –e** letter
die **Brieftaube, –n** carrier pigeon
der **Briefträger, –** mailman
bringen, brachte, gebracht to bring
ich bringe dich nach Hause I'll take you home
das **Brot, –e** bread
die **Brücke, –n** bridge
der **Bruder, ÷** brother
der **Brunnen, –** well, fountain
das **Buch, ÷er** book
der **Buchstabe, –n, –n** letter (of the alphabet)
die **Bühne, –n** stage
die **Bundesregierung** Federal Government (of Germany)
das **Büro', –s** office
der **Bus, –se** bus
die **Butter** butter

das **Café, –s** café
der **Chef, –s** boss

da there; then; under these circumstances; (*conj.*) since
da drüben over there
das **Dach, ÷er** roof
daher therefore; from there, from that place
dahin there, toward that place
damals at that time
die **Dame, –n** lady, woman
damit (*conj.*) so that
dankbar grateful, thankful
danken (*plus pers. dat.*) to thank

danke thank you, thanks
danke schön thank you very much
vielen Dank thank you very much
dann then
darum for that reason
das that (*demonstr.*)
daß that (*conj.*)
dauern to last, take (time)
die **Decke, –n** ceiling; blanket
denken, dachte, gedacht to think
sich etwas denken to imagine
denn for (*conj.*)
dersel'be the same (see **158**)
deshalb therefore
Deutsch German (language)
Deutschland Germany
Deutsch können to know German
der **Dezember** December
der **Dieb, –e** thief
dieser, diese, dieses this
das **Ding, –e** thing
doch (see **36**)
der **Dok'tor, die Dokto'ren** doctor
der **Dollar, –s** dollar
der **Dom, –e** cathedral
donnern to thunder
der **Donner** (*no pl.*) thunder
der **Donnerstag, –e** Thursday
das **Dorf, ÷er** village
dort there
draußen (*adv.*) outside
sich drehen um to turn (around something), to revolve; to concern, to be a matter of
dumm stupid, dumb
der **Dummkopf, ÷e** dumbbell, fool
dunkel dark
durch through
sich um·drehen to turn around
drei three
dreißig thirty
dreizehn thirteen
das **Drittel, –** third
drüben over there
drucken to print

durch·machen to go through, suffer

durstig thirsty

der Durst (*no pl.*) thirst

dürfen, durfte, gedurft (see 49 ff.)

eben just

die Ecke, –n corner

egoi'stisch egotistic, selfish

das Ei, –er egg

eigen (*adj.*) own

eigentlich actually, really

sich eilen, sich beeilen to hurry

einander each other

sich etwas ein·bilden to imagine something

eingebildet sein to be conceited

eineinhalb one and a half

einfach easy, simple

ein·fallen, fiel –, –gefallen, (ist), es fällt ein to remember, occur (to one's mind)

es fällt mir ein I've just remembered

ein·holen to catch up with

einige some, several, a few

ein·laden, u, a, er lädt ein to invite

einmal (*colloq.* mal) once, at some time

zweimal twice

dreimal three times

viermal four times

etc.

(noch) nicht' einmal not even

nicht ein'mal not once

noch einmal once more

sich ein·ordnen (traffic) to get into the correct lane; to merge

eins one (cardinal number)

ein·schlafen, ie, a, (ist), er schläft ein to fall asleep

ein·steigen, ie, ie, (ist) to enter, board (a plane or train)

ein·wandern to immigrate

der Einwohner, – inhabitant

die Einzelheit, –en detail

einzig only, sole

die Eisenbahn, –en railroad

das Element', –e element

elf eleven

die Eltern (*no singular*) parents

empfangen, i, a, er empfängt to receive

der Empfang, ⁀e reception

empfehlen, a, o, er empfiehlt to recommend

das Ende, –n end

zu Ende to an end, to a conclusion

endlich at last, finally

eng narrow

entdecken to discover

entfernt distant

sich entschließen zu, entschloß, entschlossen to decide, make up one's mind

entschlossen sein zu to be determined

(sich) entschuldigen to excuse oneself

entschuldigt sein to be excused

entsprechen (*plus dat.*), a, o to correspond

entstehen, entstand, entstanden (ist) to originate, come into being

enttäuschen to disappoint

entweder . . . oder either . . . or

die Erde, –n earth

erfahren, u, a, er erfährt to find out, learn; experience

erfinden, a, u to invent

die Erfindung, –en invention

der Erfolg, –e success; result

erfreut sein to be pleased, glad

erhalten, ie, a, er erhält to receive

sich erholen to get a rest

erholt sein to be well rested

erinnern an to remind of

sich erinnern an to remember

die Erinnerung, –en memory

sich erkälten to catch a cold

erkältet sein to have a cold

erkennen (an), erkannte, erkannt to recognize (by)

erklären to explain

sich erkundigen to inquire

erlauben to allow, permit

erleben to experience

erreichen to reach, attain, achieve

erscheinen, ie, ie, (ist) to appear

erschrecken, erschrak, erschrocken, (ist), er erschrickt to be frightened

erst first; not until, only

erst dann not until then, only then

erst gestern not until yesterday, only yesterday

zuerst at first, first

erstaunt astonished, amazed

erstens first(ly)

zweitens second(ly)

drittens third(ly)

viertens fourth(ly)

etc.

ertrinken, a, u, (ist) to drown

erwachsen (*adj.*) grown-up, adult

erwarten to expect

sich erweisen, ie, ie to turn out, show

erzählen to tell, relate

essen, aß, gegessen, er ißt to eat

das Essen, – food, meal

etwa about; by any chance

etwas something; somewhat

Euro'pa Europe

europä'isch European

das Exemplar', –e copy (of a book, etc.)

die Fabrik', –en factory

fähig capable

fahren, u, a, (ist) er fährt to drive, go (by train, boat, plane, car)

fahren lernen to learn to drive

die Fahrkarte, –n (train) ticket

das **Fahrrad**, ⁻er bicycle
fallen, fiel, gefallen, (ist) er fällt to fall, drop
  der **Fall**, ⁻e case, fall
  auf jeden Fall in any case, at any rate
  auf keinen Fall in no case, under no circumstances
falsch false, wrong
die **Fami′lie**, –n family
die **Farbe**, –n color
  die **Lieblingsfarbe**, –n favorite color
  färben to color; dye
  farbig in color, colored
fast almost
der **Februar** February
der **Fehler**, – mistake
fein fine
der **Feind**, –e enemy
das **Feld**, –er field
das **Fenster**, – window
die **Ferien** (*no singular*) vacation
fern far away, distant
  die **Ferne** distance
fern′·sehen, a, e, er sieht fern to watch TV
  das **Fernsehen** television
  der **Fernseher**, – TV set
fertig ready, complete, finished
fest firm(ly)
fest·stellen to determine; find out; conclude
das **Feuer**, – fire
  das **Feuerwerk**, –e fireworks
der **Film**, –e movie, film
das **Filmfestspiel**, –e film festival
finden, a, u to find
der **Finger**, – finger
fischen to fish
  der **Fisch**, –e fish
das **Fleisch** (*no pl.*) meat
fliegen, o, o, (ist) to fly
  der **Flieger**, – flyer
  der **Tiefflieger**, – strafing plane
fliehen, o, o, (ist) to escape, flee
fließen, o, geflossen, (ist) to flow

der **Flug**, ⁻e flight
  der **Abflug**, ⁻e departure
  der **Fluggast**, ⁻e passenger
  der **Flughafen**, ⁻ airport
  der **Flugschein**, –e plane ticket
  das **Flugzeug**, –e airplane
flüstern to whisper
die **Flut**, –en flood
folgen (*with dat.*) to follow
fort away
fragen to ask
  die **Frage**, –n question
  eine Frage stellen to ask a question
  eine Frage beantworten to answer a question
Frankreich France
die **Frau**, –en woman, wife; Mrs.
  das **Fräulein**, – young lady, Miss
frei free, unoccupied
der **Freitag**, –e Friday
freiwillig voluntary
fremd strange, alien
fressen, a, e, er frißt to eat (said of animals)
die **Freude** joy, pleasure
  sich freuen auf to look forward to
  sich freuen über to be happy (glad) about
der **Freund**, –e friend (male)
  die **Freundin**, –nen friend (female)
frieren, o, o to freeze
frisch fresh
froh glad, gay
früh early
  früher earlier; formerly
  frühestens at the earliest
der **Frühling**, –e spring
frühstücken to breakfast, have breakfast
  das **Frühstück**, –e breakfast
fühlen to feel
  das **Gefühl**, –e feeling
führen to lead, guide
  der **Führer**, – leader; guide
füllen to fill
fünf five
fünfzehn fifteen
fünfzig fifty

für for
furchtbar terrible, frightful
fürchten to fear
  sich fürchten vor to be afraid of
der **Fuß**, ⁻e foot
  der **Fußabdruck**, ⁻e footprint
füttern to feed

ganz whole, entire
  ganz gut pretty good, not bad
gar nicht (kein, nichts) not (no . . . , nothing) at all
der **Garten**, ⁻ garden
das **Gas**, –e gas
der **Gast**, ⁻e guest
das **Gebäude**, – building
  das **Hauptgebäude**, – main building
geben, a, e, er gibt to give
  es gibt there is (are) available
  aus·geben, a, e, er gibt aus to spend (money)
geboren born
  ich bin geboren I was born
  geboren werden to be born
die **Geburt**, –en birth
  der **Geburtstag**, –e birthday
der **Gedanke**, –ns, –n thought, idea
  auf den Gedanken kommen to hit upon the idea
die **Geduld** (*no pl.*) patience
geduldig patient
die **Gefahr**, –en danger
gefährlich dangerous
gefallen, gefiel, gefallen, er gefällt to please
  das gefällt mir I like it (that pleases me)
der **Gefallen**, – favor
gefangen·nehmen, nahm –, –genommen, er nimmt gefangen to capture, take prisoner
gegen against
  gegen sechs Uhr around six o'clock
die **Gegend**, –en area
der **Gegensatz**, ⁻e contrast
gegenseitig each other, mutual

gegenü'ber (*with dat.*) opposite

die **Gegenwart** (*no pl.*) present; presence

gegenwärtig present

geheim secret

das **Geheimnis, –se** secret

gehen, ging, gegangen, (ist) to go, walk

gehorchen to obey

gehören (*plus pers. dat.*) to belong to (property)

gehören zu to belong to (membership)

die **Geiß, –en** goat

der **Geist** intellect, mind, spirit; ghost

das **Geld** money

gelingen, a, u, (ist) to succeed

es gelingt mir I succeed

das **Gemüse, –** vegetable

genau exact

der **General', ⁼e** general

genug enough

das **Gepäck** (*no pl.*) baggage

gerade just, straight

gern(e) gladly

ich esse gern(e) I like to eat

ich möchte gern(e) etwas essen I'd like to eat something

der **Gesandte, –n** ambassador, envoy

das **Geschäft, –e** business; store

geschehen, a, e, (ist), es geschieht to happen, occur

das **Geschenk, –e** present, gift

die **Geschichte, –n** story, history

das **Gesetz, –e** law

das **Gesicht, –er** face

das **Gespräch, –e** conversation

gestatten to permit, allow

gestern yesterday

gestern abend last night, yesterday evening

gesund well, healthy

gewinnen, a, o to win

gewiß certain

sich gewöhnen an to get used to

gewöhnt sein an to be used to

gewöhnlich usual

das **Glas, ⁼er** glass

der **Glaube, –ns** (*no pl.*) belief, faith

glauben to think, believe

glauben an (*with acc.*) to believe in

gleich equal, same, like; (*time adv.*) immediately, presently

das **Glück** (*no pl.*) happiness; luck, good luck; fortune

Glück haben to be lucky

glücklich happy

glücklicherwei'se fortunately, happily

gnädige Frau formal way of addressing a married woman

der **Gott, ⁼er** god

Gott God

gottseidank' thank heavens, thank goodness

gratulie'ren to congratulate

grau gray

greifen, griff, gegriffen to grasp, reach out (for something)

die **Grenze, –n** border

groß big, great, tall

die **Großstadt, ⁼e** large city, metropolis

der **Großvater, ⁼** grandfather

grün green

der **Grund, ⁼e** reason, ground

aufgrund' (*with gen.*) on the basis of

grüßen to greet

der **Gruß, ⁼e** greeting

gut good

das **Gymna'sium, die Gymna'sien** German secondary school, grades 5–13)

das **Haar, –e** hair

haben to have

hageln to hail

halb half

die **Hälfte, –n** half

die **Halle, –en** hall, lobby

halten, ie, a, er hält to hold, stop

halten für to consider

halten von to think of

die **Hand, ⁼e** hand

handeln to act

sich handeln um to be a matter of

handeln mit to deal with (objects)

handeln von to deal with (subject matter)

der **Händler, –** dealer

die **Handschrift** handwriting

der **Handschuh, –e** glove

die **Handtasche, –n** handbag

hart hard

hassen to hate

das **Haus, ⁼er** house

ich gehe nach Hause I go home

ich bin zu Hause I am at home

heilen to heal

geheilt healed, well

heiraten to get married, marry

verheiratet married

ich bin verheiratet I am married

heiß hot

heißen, ie, ei to be called; to mean

heizen to heat

die **Heizung** heating system, radiator

die **Zentral'heizung** central heating

helfen (*plus pers. dat.*)**, a, o, er hilft** to help

hell light, bright

das **Hemd, –en** shirt

her toward the speaker (in the sense of *hither*)

heraus' out

herbei' here

herein' in

her·kommen to come here

sich heraus·stellen to turn out, become apparent

der **Herd, –e** stove

der **Herr, –en** (*gen., dat. and acc. sing.* **Herrn**) gentleman

herum' around

das **Herz**, –ens, –en (*dat.:* dem **Herzen**) heart
der **Herzog**, ⸚e duke
heute today
  heute abend this evening, tonight
  heute morgen this morning
hier here
die **Hilfe** help
der **Himmel** heaven, sky
  himmlisch heavenly
hin away from the speaker
  hinein' in
  hin·fahren, u, a, (ist), er **fährt hin** to go there
hinten (*adv.*) in the back
hinter (*prep.*) behind, beyond, on the other side of
der **Hintergrund**, ⸚e background
hinun'ter down
  den (**Rhein**) **hinunter** down the (Rhine)
die **Hitze** (*no pl.*) heat
hoch high
  höchstens at the most
der **Hof**, ⸚e court, yard
  der **Hofgarten** the Royal Gardens
hoffen to hope
  hoffentlich I hope (*sent. adv.*)
die **Höhe**, –n height
  in die Höhe upward
holen to get, fetch
das **Holz**, ⸚er wood
hören to hear
  der **Hörer**, – telephone receiver; listener
das **Hotel'**, –s hotel
hübsch pretty
der **Hund**, –e dog
hundert hundred
der **Hunger** hunger
  ich habe Hunger I am hungry
  hungrig hungry
der **Hut**, ⸚e hat

die **Idee'**, die **Ide'en** idea
immer always
  immer noch, noch immer still
  immer wieder again and again
in in
In'dien India
  der **In'der**, – (East) Indian
  der **India'ner**, – (American) Indian
der **Ingenieur'**, –e engineer
intelligent' intelligent
  die **Intelligenz'** intelligence, intellect
interessant' interesting
sich interessie'ren für, interessiert sein an to be interested in
inzwi'schen meanwhile, in the meantime
irgendetwas something, anything
irgendwo somewhere
  irgendwohin somewhere
der **Irrtum**, ⸚er error
Ita'lien Italy
  italie'nisch Italian

ja yes; indeed
das **Jahr**, –e year
  das **Jahrhun'dert**, –e century
der **Januar** January
je, jemals ever
jedenfalls at any rate
jeder, jede, jedes each, every
jemand somebody, someone
jetzt now
die **Jugend** (*no pl.*) youth (*collective noun*); time of youth
der **Ju'li** July
jung young
der **Junge**, –n boy
der **Ju'ni** June

der **Kaffee** coffee
kalt cold
  die **Kälte** (*no pl.*) cold
kämmen to comb
kämpfen to fight
  der **Kampf**, ⸚e fight, battle
das **Kapi'tel**, – chapter
die **Karte**, –n map; ticket
  die **Landkarte**, –n map
  die **Fahrkarte**, –n (train) ticket
  die **Rückfahrkarte**, –n round-trip ticket
die **Kartof'fel**, –n potato
die **Kasse**, –n cash register, cash box
der **Kasten**, ⸚ chest, box
kaufen to buy
kaum hardly
kein no (not any)
der **Kellner**, – waiter
  der **Oberkellner**, – headwaiter
  "Herr Ober" normal way of addressing a waiter
kennen, kannte, gekannt to know, be acquainted with
kennen·lernen to meet, become acquainted with
das **Kind**, –er child
das **Kino**, –s movie house
die **Kirche**, –n church
  ich gehe in die Kirche I go to church
klar clear
die **Klasse**, –n class
das **Kleid**, –er dress
klein little
klettern to climb
das **Klima** climate
klingeln to ring (bell)
klingen, a, u to sound
klopfen to knock
  an·klopfen to knock (at the door)
kochen to cook, boil
der **Koffer**, – suitcase
komisch funny; odd; comical
das **Komma**, –s comma
kommen, kam, gekommen, (ist) to come
der **König**, –e king
können, konnte, gekonnt, er kann (see 49 ff.)
das **Konzert'**, –e concert
der **Kopf**, ⸚e head
  die **Kopfschmerzen** (*pl.*) headache
der **Körper**, – body
kosten to cost
krank sick
die **Kreide** chalk
der **Krieg**, –e war
kriegen (*colloq.*) = **bekom-**

men to get
die Küche, –n kitchen
die Kugel, –n ball, globe; bullet
  der Kugelschreiber, – ball-point pen
sich kümmern um to take care of; to be concerned with
kurz short
die Kusi′ne, –n (female) cousin
küssen to kiss

lächeln to smile
  das Lächeln smile
lachen to laugh
  das Lachen laughter
das Land, ⸚er country; land
  auf dem Land in the country
landen to land
die Landkarte, –n map
lang long
  lange for a long time
  jahrelang for years
  fünf Jahre lang for five years
langsam slow
längst, schon längst for a long time, a long time ago
lang′·weilen to bore
  sich langweilen, gelangweilt sein to be bored
  langweilig boring
der Lärm (*no pl.*) noise; din
lassen, ie, a, er läßt to let, leave
  die Kinder zu Hause lassen to leave the children at home
die Later′ne, –n street light
laufen, ie, au, er läuft to run
laut loud
leben to live, be alive
  das Leben, – life
  am Leben sein to be alive
  ums Leben kommen to lose one's life
das Leder leather
leer empty
legen to lay, place
  sich legen to lie down
lehren to teach
  der Lehrer, – teacher

leicht easy; light (in weight)
leiden, litt, gelitten to suffer
leider unfortunately (*sent. adv.*)
leid tun to be sorry
  es tut mir leid I am sorry
  er tut mir leid I am sorry for him
leise soft, without noise
sich leisten to afford
lernen to learn
lesen, a, e, er liest to read
letzt– last
  letzten Mai last May
  letzte Woche last week
  letztes Jahr last year
leuchten to shine
die Leute (*pl. only*) people
der Leutnant, –e lieutenant
das Licht, –er light
lieb dear
  lieber rather (*adv.*)
  am liebsten (to like) most of all
  lieb·haben to love
lieben to love
  die Liebe love
lieblich lovely
der Liebling, –e darling, favorite
das Lied, –er song
liegen, a, e to lie (flat); to be situated
link– left
  links to the left
die Lippe, –n lip
lochen to punch (a ticket)
  das Loch, ⸚er hole
die Lokomoti′ve, –n locomotive
los loose
  was ist los what's the matter
lösen to solve, dissolve
die Luft, ⸚e air
  die Luftpost airmail
lügen, o, o to tell a lie

machen to make; to do
  es macht nichts it doesn't matter
  an·machen to turn on
  aus·machen to turn off
das Mädchen, – girl
die Mahlzeit, –en meal
der Mai May

das Mal time
  dieses Mal this time
  diesmal this time
  einmal once
  zweimal twice
  noch einmal once more
  manchmal sometimes
  jedesmal every time
  zwei mal zwei two times two
man (*dat.:* **einem** *acc.:* **einen**) one (*pronoun*)
mancher many a (see **152**)
  manchmal sometimes
der Mann, ⸚er man, husband
der Mantel, ⸚ coat, overcoat
die Mark mark
  zwei Mark two marks
der Markt, ⸚e market; market place
die Maschi′ne, –n machine; typewriter
die Mate′rie (*no pl.*) matter
die Mathematik′ mathematics
die Medizin′ medicine; science of medicine
das Mehl flour
mehr more
  mehr als more than
  nicht mehr no longer
mehrere several
die Meile, –n mile
meinen to mean, be of the opinion, say, have an opinion
  die Meinung, –en opinion
meist– most
meistens usually, mostly
sich melden to report (to somebody); to answer (the phone)
die Menge, –n quantity, mass, crowd
  jede Menge any amount
der Mensch, –en, –en man, human being
merken to notice
das Messer, – knife
das Meter, – meter
die Milch (*no pl.*) milk
mild mild
die Milliar′de, –n billion
die Million′, –en million
mindestens at least

die **Minu'te**, –n minute
mit with, along
mit·machen to go along, cooperate
der **Mittag**, –e noon
der **Nachmittag**, –e afternoon
das **Mittagessen**, – dinner
(noon meal, the main
meal in Germany)
mit·teilen to inform, let
know, report (some-
thing)
das **Mittelalter** Middle Ages
Mitternacht midnight
der **Mittwoch**, –e Wednesday
die **Möbel** (*pl.*) furniture
modern' modern
**mögen, mochte, gemocht, er
mag** (see **137** ff.)
möglich possible
unmöglich impossible;
(*sent. adv.*) not possibly
möglicherweise possibly
die **Möglichkeit**, –en possibility
der **Mo'nat**, –e month
der **Mond**, –e moon
der **Montag**, –e Monday
der **Morgen**, – morning
heute morgen this morning
morgen tomorrow
morgen abend tomorrow
evening
das **Motorrad**, ¨-er motorcycle
müde tired
der **Müller**, – miller
der **Mund** mouth
mündlich oral
das **Muse'um, die Muse'en**
museum
musizie'ren to make music
**müssen, mußte, gemußt, er
muß** (see **49** ff.)
die **Mutter**, ¨ mother
Mutti Mom, Mommy

na well
na sowas! (expression of
astonishment) you don't
mean it, what do you
think of that

na und? so what?
nach to, toward; after
der **Nachbar**, –ns, –n neighbor
nachdem' (*conj.*) after
**nach·denken über, dachte –,
–gedacht** to reflect,
meditate about
nachher afterwards
der **Nachmittag**, –e afternoon
der **Nachname**, –ns, –n last
name
nach·schicken to forward
(mail)
nächst- next
nächstes Jahr next year
nächstens in the near future
die **Nacht**, ¨e night
heute nacht this coming
night; last night
but: **gestern abend** last
night (before going to
bed), yesterday evening
nah near, close by
die **Nähe** proximity, closeness, nearness
nähen to sew
der **Name**, –ns, –n (*dat.:* **dem
Namen**; *acc.:* **den
Namen**) name
der **Vorname**, –ns, –n first
name
der **Nachname**, –ns, –n
last name
nämlich namely; that is to
say; you know
die **Nase**, –n nose
die **Natur'** nature
natür'lich naturally, of
course
neben next to, beside
der **Nebel** fog
neblig foggy
nebenan' next door
nee (*colloq.*) = **nein** no
**nehmen, nahm, genommen,
er nimmt** to take
nein no
nervös' nervous
nett nice
neu new
das ist mir neu that's news
to me
die **Neuigkeit**, –en news

neulich recently
neun nine
neunzehn nineteen
nicht not
nicht mehr no longer
noch nicht not yet
nichts nothing
nicken to nod
nie never
niemand nobody, no one
nirgends nowhere
noch still
noch nicht not yet
noch einmal once more
der **Norden** the north
nördlich northern
die **Nordsee** the North Sea
normalerweise normally
Norwegen Norway
der **November** November
null zero
die **Nummer**, –n number
nun now
nur only
nutzlos useless

ob whether, if
oben up (above); upstairs,
on top
das **Obst** (*no pl.*) fruit
obwohl although
oder or
öffentlich public
der **Offizier'**, –e officer
(**sich**) **öffnen** to open
geöffnet sein to be open
offen (*adj.*) open
oft often
ohne (*with acc.*) without
der **Onkel**, – uncle
die **Oper**, –n opera; opera
house
die **Ordnung** order
in Ordnung in order, all
right, O.K.
der **Osten** the east
östlich eastern

das **Paar**, –e pair, couple
ein paar a few
das **Paket'**, –e package,
parcel
das **Papier'**, –e paper
die **Partei'**, –en party
der **Paß, die Pässe** passport;
pass

passieren to happen
die **Pause, –n** pause, intermission, break
(das) **Persil'** a German detergent
die **Person', –en** person
 persön'lich personal
 der **Perso'nenzug, ¨-e** local train
der **Pfarrer, –** pastor
der **Pfennig, –e** pfennig, penny
das **Pfund, –e** pound
die **Physik'** (no pl.) physics
der **Plan, ¨-e** plan
die **Platte, –n** (phonograph) record, plate, flagstone
der **Platz, ¨-e** place, plaza, square; seat
 der **Sitzplatz, ¨-e** seat
 Platz nehmen to sit down, have a seat
plötzlich suddenly
plus plus, and
Polen Poland
 polnisch Polish
die **Polizei'** (no pl.) police
 der **Polizist', –en** policeman
die **Post** mail; post office
der **Preis, –e** price; prize
prima (colloq.) wonderful
das **Problem', –e** problem
der **Profes'sor,** die **Professo'ren** professor
Prozent' percent
die **Psychologie'** psychology
das **Pulver, –** powder; gunpowder
der **Punkt, –e** point, period
putzen to clean

das **Rad, ¨-er** wheel
sich **rasie'ren** to shave
 rasiert sein to be shaved
raten, ie, a, er rät to advise; give counsel; guess
 der **Rat** advice, counsel; council; councilor
 das **Rathaus, ¨-er** town (city) hall
rauchen to smoke
der **Raum, ¨-e** room; space
reagie'ren auf to react to
recht right; correct

rechts to the right
 das ist mir recht that's all right with me
 recht haben to be right
 mit Recht rightfully
rechtzeitig on time
reden to talk, speak
die **Regie'rung, –en** government
 die **Bun'desregierung** Federal Government (of Germany)
regnen to rain
 der **Regen** rain
reich rich
die **Reihe, –n** row; series
 ich bin an der Reihe it's my turn
reisen to travel
 die **Reise, –n** trip
 eine Reise machen to take a trip
reißen, riß, gerissen to tear
rennen, rannte, gerannt (ist) to run
reservie'ren to reserve
retten to save
der **Rhein** the Rhine
richtig correct, accurate
die **Richtung, –en** direction
der **Ring, –e** ring
rollen to roll
der **Roman, –e** novel
die **Rose, –n** rose
rot red
die **Rückfahrkarte, –en** round-trip ticket
rufen, ie, u to call
ruhig quiet, restful; (sent. adv.) it won't bother me, I'll stay calm about it
 unruhig restless
 die **Ruhe** rest; quietness
 in aller Ruhe at leisure
rund round
russisch Russian
Rußland Russia

die **Sache, –n** thing, matter
sagen to say
das **Salz, –e** salt
der **Samstag, –e** Saturday
 samstags on Saturdays
sanft soft
der **Sänger, –** singer

schade too bad
der **Schalter, –** (ticket) window
der **Schauspieler, –** actor
schauen to look, gaze
sich **scheiden lassen von** to get a divorce from
 geschieden sein to be divorced
scheinen, ie, ie to seem; to shine
 er scheint zu schlafen he seems to be asleep
schenken to give (as a present), present
 das **Geschenk, –e** present, gift
schicken to send
schieben, o, o to push, shove
das **Schiff, –e** ship, boat
schi·laufen to ski
der **Schinken, –** ham
schlafen, ie, a, er schläft to sleep
schlagen, u, a, er schlägt to beat, hit
schlank slender, slim
schlecht bad
(sich) **schließen, schloß, geschlossen** to close
 geschlossen sein to be closed
schließlich finally, after all
schlucken to swallow
 der **Schluck** sip
der **Schluß,** die **Schlüsse** end; conclusion
der **Schlüssel, –** key
die **Schnalle, –n** buckle
schnarchen to snore
der **Schnee** (no pl.) snow
schneiden, schnitt, geschnitten to cut
 der **Schnitt, –e** cut
schneien to snow
schnell fast, rapid
die **Schokola'de** chocolate
schon already
schön beautiful, pretty; good, O.K.
der **Schrank, ¨-e** cupboard, wardrobe
schreiben, ie, ie to write
schreien, ie, ie to scream, cry

der **Schrei,** –e scream
der **Schriftsteller,** – writer
der **Schuh,** –e shoe
die **Schule,** –n school
  auf der Schule in school
der **Schüler,** – pupil, (Gymnasium) student
die **Schulter,** –n shoulder
der **Schuß,** die **Schüsse** shot
schwach weak
der **Schwager,** ⸚ brother-in-law
schwarz black
der **Schwarzwald** Black Forest
schweigen, ie, ie to be silent, say nothing
das **Schwein,** –e pig; swine
  das **Schweinefleisch** (*no pl.*) pork
die **Schweiz** Switzerland
schwer hard, heavy, difficult
die **Schwester,** –n sister
schwimmen, a, o, (ist) to swim
  das **Schwimmbecken,** – swimming pool
sechs six
sechzehn sixteen
sechzig sixty
die **See** (*no pl.*) sea, ocean
sehen, a, e, er **sieht** to see
sehr very
sein, war, gewesen, (ist), er **ist** to be
seit since
  seitdem (*conj.*) since; (*adv.*) since then, since that time
  seit langem for a long time
  seit Anfang Mai since the beginning of May
die **Seite,** –n page, side
der **Sekretär',** –e secretary
selbst, selber –self (see **175**); even (see **176**)
selten rare, seldom
seltsam strange, peculiar
das **Seme'ster,** – semester
senden, sandte, gesandt to send; broadcast
  der **Sender,** – sender; broadcasting station
der **September** September

setzen to set
  sich setzen to sit down
sicher certain, sure; probably
sieben seven
siebzehn seventeen
singen, a, u to sing
sinken, a, u, (ist) to sink
der **Sinn,** –e sense
die **Situation',** –en situation
sitzen, saß, gesessen to sit
  der **Sitzplatz,** ⸚e seat
so so
  so etwas something like this
sobald' (*conj.*) as soon as
soe'ben just, just now
sofort' at once, immediately
sogar' even
der **Sohn,** ⸚e son
solan'ge (*conj.*) as long as
solcher such (see **153**)
der **Soldat',** –en, –en soldier
sollen (see **49** ff.)
der **Sommer,** – summer
sondern but
die **Sonne,** –n sun
der **Sonntag,** –e Sunday
  jeden Sonntag every Sunday
  sonntags on Sundays, every Sunday
sonst otherwise
soviel so much, as much; (*conj.*) as far as
sowieso anyhow, anyway
spät late
spätestens at the latest
spazie'ren·fahren, u, a, (ist), er **fährt spazieren** to go for a ride
spazie'ren·gehen, ging –, –gegangen, (ist) to go for a walk
der **Spiegel,** – mirror
spielen to play
der **Sport** (*no pl.*) sport, sports, athletics
sprechen, a, o, er **spricht** to speak, talk
  die **Sprache,** –n language
springen, a, u, (ist) to jump
  auf'springen to jump up
die **Spur,** –en trace
  spurlos without a trace
der **Staat,** –en state

die **Stadt,** ⸚e town, city
stark strong, heavy
starren to stare
statt (*with gen.*) instead of
  statt . . . zu (kaufen) instead of (buying)
stecken to stick, put
stehen, stand, gestanden to stand
  auf·stehen, (ist) to arise, stand up, get up, rise
stehen·bleiben, ie, ie, (ist) to stop
stehlen, a, o, er **stiehlt** to steal
steigen, ie, ie, (ist) to climb
  ein·steigen to enter, board (a train or plane)
der **Stein,** –e stone
stellen to place, put (upright)
  die **Stelle,** –n place
  die **Stellung,** –en position; job
sterben, a, o, (ist), er **stirbt** to die
still quiet, still
die **Stimme,** –n voice
stimmen to be correct
  das stimmt nicht that's wrong
der **Stock,** ⸚e stick; floor (of a building)
  im ersten (zweiten, etc.) Stock on the first (second, etc.) floor
der **Stolz** (*no pl.*) pride
stolz proud
stören to disturb
die **Straße,** –n street
die **Straßenbahn,** –en streetcar
streichen, i, i to spread; to stroke; to paint
das **Stück,** –e piece; play
  das **Goldstück,** –e gold coin
der **Student,** –en, –en student (masculine)
  die **Studentin,** –nen student (feminine)
studie'ren to study
  das **Stu'dium,** die **Stu'dien** studies, course of study
der **Stuhl,** ⸚e chair
die **Stunde,** –n hour
suchen to look for, seek, search
  die **Suche** search

der **Süden** the south
südlich southern
die **Suppe**, **–n** soup

der **Tabak**, **–e** tobacco
der **Tag**, **–e** day
das **Tal**, **–̈er** valley
die **Tante**, **–n** aunt
tanzen to dance
der **Tanz**, **–̈e** dance
die **Tasche**, **–n** pocket; bag,
handbag; briefcase
die **Tasse**, **–n** cup
tatsächlich actual(ly), indeed,
as a matter of fact
tausend thousand
das **Taxi**, **–s**; die **Taxe**, **–n**
taxi
der **Tee** tea
teilen to divide
geteilt durch divided by
der **Teil**, **–e** part
das **Telefon**, **–e** telephone
telefonie′ren (mit) to talk
on the phone (with), to
make a phone call (to)
die **Terras′se**, **–n** terrace
das **Testament′**, **–e** last will
teuer expensive
das **Thea′ter**, **–** theater
das **Thema**, die **Themen**
topic; subject; theme
das **Tier**, **–e** animal
der **Tisch**, **–e** table
die **Tochter**, **–̈** daughter
der **Tod**, **–e** death
todschick elegant, "great"
das **Tor**, **–e** gate
tot dead
tragen, **u**, **a**, **er trägt** to carry;
to wear
träumen to dream
der **Traum**, **–̈e** dream
treffen, **traf**, **getroffen**, **er trifft**
to meet; to hit
trennen to separate
treten, **a**, **e**, (ist) **er tritt** to
step
trinken, **a**, **u** to drink
trotz (*prep.*) in spite of
trotzdem (*adv.*) in spite of,
despite, nevertheless
tun, **tat**, **getan** to do
die **Tür**, **–en** door

über over
überall everywhere
überfüllt′ overflowing
sich **überle′gen** to think
about, meditate, consider
überra′schen to surprise
überre′den to persuade
überset′zen to translate
die **Überset′zung**, **–en**
translation
(sich) **überzeu′gen** to convince (oneself)
überzeugt sein von to be
convinced
übrigens by the way, incidentally
die **Uhr**, **–en** clock, watch
sechs Uhr six o'clock
wieviel Uhr what time
um around; about; at
um ... zu in order to
um·kommen, **kam –**, **–gekommen**, (ist) to perish
um·werfen to knock over
um·ziehen, **zog –**, **–gezogen**,
(ist) to move
sich **um·ziehen** to change
(clothes)
umgezogen sein to be
changed
unbedingt absolute(ly), by all
means
und and
unendlich infinite
ungefähr approximate(ly),
about
die **Universität**, **–en** university
unmöglich impossible
unruhig restless
der **Unsinn** nonsense
unten (*adv.*) down, down
below, downstairs
(sich) **unterbre′chen**, **a**, **o**, **er
unterbricht** to interrupt
unter·bringen, **brachte –**,
–gebracht to put up,
lodge
unter·gehen, **ging –**, **–gegangen**, (ist) to sink,
perish; to set (sun, moon)
sich **unterhal′ten**, **ie**, **a**, **er
unterhält sich** to con-
verse, have a conversa-
tion

unter·kommen, **kam –**, **–gekommen**, (ist) to find a
place to stay
unterrich′ten to teach, instruct
der **Unterschied**, **–e** difference
untersu′chen to investigate
der **Urlaub** (*no pl.*) furlough;
vacation

die **Vase**, **–n** vase
der **Vater**, **–̈** father
sich **verändern** to change
verändert sein to be
changed, different
verbieten, **o**, **o** to forbid, prohibit
(sich) **verbinden**, **a**, **u** to
unite; to compound; to
connect
verbringen, **verbrachte**, **verbracht** to spend (time)
verdienen to earn, deserve
die **Vereinigten Staaten** the
United States
sich **verfahren**, **u**, **a**, **er ver-
fährt sich** to lose one's
way (driving)
vergessen, **vergaß**, **vergessen**
er vergißt to forget
vergiften to poison
sich **verheiraten** to get married
verkaufen to sell
der **Verkehr** traffic
der **Verlag**, **–e** publishing
house, publisher
verlangen to demand
verlassen, **verließ**, **verlassen**
er verläßt to leave
(somebody or something)
sich **verlassen auf** to depend,
rely upon
sich **verlaufen**, **ie**, **au**, **er ver-
läuft sich** to lose one's
way (walking)
der **Verleger**, **–** publisher
sich **verlieben in** to fall in
love with
verliebt sein in to be in
love with
verlieren, **o**, **o** to lose

sich verloben mit to get engaged to
    verlobt sein mit to be engaged to
    verlobt engaged
    der Verlobte, –n fiancé
das Vermögen, – wealth, fortune, estate
die Vernunft reason (intellect)
    vernünftig reasonable
verrückt crazy
verschwinden, a, u, (ist) to disappear
    verschwunden (*adj.*) lost
die Verspätung, –en delay
    Verspätung haben to be late, not on schedule
versprechen, a, o, er verspricht to promise
der Verstand (*no pl.*) mind, reason
verstehen, verstand, verstanden to understand
versuchen to try, attempt
    der Versuch, –e try, attempt; experiment
die Verwandlung, –en change, metamorphosis
verwandt related
    der Verwandte, –n, –n relative
verwunden to injure, wound
verzeihen, ie, ie to pardon, excuse
    die Verzeihung pardon
der Vetter, –n cousin (male)
viel much
    viele many
    soviel so much, as much
    zuviel too much
vielleicht' perhaps
vier four
vierzehn fourteen
vierzig forty
das Visum, die Visen visa
das Volk, ̈er people
voll full
völlig completely
von from
    von (Paris) aus from (Paris)
vor before; in front of; ago
    vor einem Jahr a year ago

vor allem above all
vorbei' (*adv.*) gone, past
vorbei'·gehen, ging –, –gegangen, (ist) to pass
sich vor·bereiten auf to prepare for
    vorbereitet sein auf to be prepared for
vorgestern day before yesterday
vorher (*adv.*) before, earlier
vorhin' a little while ago
der Vorname, –ns, –n first name
vorne in front
vor·schlagen, u, a, er schlägt vor to propose, suggest
    der Vorschlag, ̈e suggestion, proposal
die Vorsicht (*no pl.*) caution
    vorsichtig careful
sich vor·stellen (*dat. reflexive*) to imagine
(sich) vor·stellen (*acc. reflexive*) to introduce (oneself)

wachsen, u, a, (ist), er wächst to grow
    erwachsen (*adj.*) grown-up, adult
wagen to dare
der Wagen, – car; wagon
wählen to choose; to dial
wahr true
während during (*prep.*), while (*conj.*)
wahrschein'lich probably
der Wald, ̈er woods, forest
die Wand, ̈e wall
wandern to wander, migrate, hike
    aus·wandern to emigrate
    ein·wandern to immigrate
wann when
warm warm
warten auf (*with acc.*) to wait for
warum why
was what
    was für what kind of (see **159**)
waschen, u, a, er wäscht to wash
das Wasser water

der Wechsel, – change
weder . . . noch neither . . . nor
weg away
    weg·fahren, u, a, (ist), er fährt weg to drive away, leave
der Weg, –e way, path
wegen because of
sich weigern to refuse
Weihnachten Christmas
weil (*conj.*) because
der Wein, –e wine
weinen to cry, weep
weiß white
weit far
welcher which
die Welt, –en world
wenig little
    weniger minus, less
    wenigstens at least
wenn when, whenever, if
wer who
werden, wurde, geworden (ist), er wird to become
werfen, a, o, er wirft to throw
    um·werfen to knock over
der Westen the west
    die Westfront Western Front
    westlich western
das Wetter weather
wichtig important
wie as; like; how
    wie gesagt as I said
wieder again (i.e., second or third time); back (to the place of origin)
wiederauf'bauen, ich baue wieder auf to reconstruct
wiederho'len to repeat
wieder·sehen, a, e, er sieht wieder to see again
    auf Wiedersehen good-by
    auf Wiederhören good-by (telephone)
wiegen, o, o to weigh
Wien Vienna
die Wiese, –n meadow
wieviel how much
    wieviel Uhr what time
wild wild
der Winter, – winter
    im Winter in the winter

wirklich really
  die **Wirklichkeit, –en** reality
der **Wirt, –e** innkeeper, landlord
wissen, wußte, gewußt, er weiß to know (as a fact)
  wissen Sie you know (*sent. adv.*)
  das **Wissen** knowledge
die **Wissenschaft, –en** science
  wissenschaftlich scientific
wo where
die **Woche, –n** week
woher from where
wohin where, where to (direction)
wohl well; probably
wohnen to reside, live
  die **Wohnung, –en** apartment
der **Wolf, ⁼e** wolf
wollen, er will (see 49 ff.)
das **Wort, ⁼er** (*also* **–e**) word
die **Wunde, –n** wound
das **Wunder, –** miracle, wonder
wunderbar wonderful, marvelous
sich wundern über to be amazed at
der **Wunsch, ⁼e** wish
wünschen to wish
die **Wurst, ⁼e** sausage, cold cuts
das **Würstchen, –** sausage
wütend mad, angry

zahlen to pay (in a restaurant)
zählen to count
  die **Zahl, –en** number
der **Zahn, ⁼e** tooth
der **Zaun, ⁼e** fence
zehn ten
zeigen to show
  sich zeigen (*impersonal*) to turn out, show
die **Zeile, –n** line (of print, poetry, verse)
die **Zeit, –en** time
  eine Zeitlang for a while (*not:* for a long time)
die **Zeitung, –en** newspaper
zerstören to destroy
ziehen, zog, gezogen to pull; (**ist**) to move (from one place to another)
  er hat gezogen he has pulled
  er ist nach (**Köln**) **gezogen** he has moved to (Cologne)
die **Zigaret′te, –n** cigarette
die **Zigar′re, –n** cigar
das **Zimmer, –** room
zittern to tremble, shake

zögern to hesitate
der **Zoll, ⁼e** customs; duty
zu to; too; at
  zuviel too much
zuerst first, at first
der **Zufall, ⁼e** accident, coincidence
  durch Zufall by accident
  zufällig by coincidence, by chance, accidentally
zufrie′den (*adj.*) satisfied, content
der **Zug, ⁼e** train
die **Zugspitze** highest mountain in Germany
zu·hören to listen to
die **Zukunft** (*no pl.*) future
zunächst′ first, first of all
zurück′ back
  wieder zurück back, back again
zusam′men together
sich zusam′men·setzen aus to be composed of
zwanzig twenty
zwar to be sure
zwei two
der **Zwerg, –e** dwarf
zwingen, a, u to force
zwischen between
zwölf twelve

VOCABULARY: English–German

able: to be able to können
to accept annehmen
accidentally zufällig
to act (as if) tun (als ob)
afraid: to be afraid (of) Angst
   haben (vor)
after all doch
again wieder
airport der Flughafen
alone allein
along mit
already schon
also auch
although obwohl
always immer
to answer antworten
apartment die Wohnung
approximately ungefähr
arm der Arm
to arrive ankommen
to ask fragen
aunt die Tante
away weg

back zurück
bank die Bank, -en
to bathe, take a bath (sich)
   baden
beautiful schön
because weil
to become werden
bed das Bett
to begin anfangen
  beginning der Anfang
to believe glauben, denken
  to believe in glauben an
to belong to gehören
bench die Bank, ⁀e
birthday der Geburtstag
book das Buch
bored: to be bored sich
   langweilen
to break brechen
breakfast das Frühstück
brother der Bruder

to build bauen
but aber; sondern
to buy kaufen

to call (up) anrufen
called: to be called heißen
to calm down sich beruhigen
car der Wagen
to catch a cold sich erkälten
chair der Stuhl
to change (sich) ändern,
   (sich) verändern
to change (clothes) sich
   umziehen
child das Kind
church die Kirche
city die Stadt
coat der Mantel
coffee der Kaffee
cold kalt
to come kommen
correct: to be correct
   stimmen
to count zählen
of course natürlich
cup die Tasse

darling Liebling
daughter die Tochter
day der Tag
dead tot
to deal with sich handeln um
   (impersonal)
dear lieb
to decide sich entschließen
to die sterben
different(ly) ander-, anders
dinner das Essen, das
   Mittagessen, das
   Abendessen
to disappear verschwinden
divorce: to get a divorce sich
   scheiden lassen
to do tun
doctor der Arzt, der Doktor

dog der Hund
door die Tür
downtown in die Stadt
to drink trinken
to drive fahren
dumbell der Dummkopf

each jeder, jede, jedes
early früh
to eat essen
end das Ende
engaged: to get engaged sich
   verloben
every jeder, jede, jedes
everything alles
excited: to get excited (about)
   sich aufregen (über)
to expect erwarten
expensive teuer
to experience erfahren
eye das Auge

far weit
father der Vater
to feel fühlen
few wenige
  a few ein paar, einige
to fight kämpfen
finally endlich, schließlich
flower die Blume
to fly fliegen
footprint der Fußabdruck
for (conj.) denn
to forget vergessen
free frei
friend der Freund, die
   Freundin

garden der Garten
girl das Mädchen
to give geben
to go gehen
goldpiece das Goldstück
good gut

haircut: **to get a haircut** sich die Haare schneiden lassen
to **happen** geschehen, passieren
happy glücklich
hat der Hut
to **have** haben
    to **have to** müssen
healthy gesund
to **hear** hören
to **help** helfen
here hier
hole das Loch
home (*adv.*) nach Hause
    at home zu Hause
to **hope** hoffen
hot heiß
hour die Stunde
house das Haus
how wie
human being der Mensch
hungry hungrig
to **hurry up** sich eilen, sich beeilen
husband der Mann

if wenn
to **imagine** sich vorstellen, sich (etwas) einbilden
immediately sofort
important wichtig
instead of statt . . . zu
intelligent intelligent
to **intend to** wollen
interested: to be interested in sich interessieren für
interesting interessant
to **introduce (oneself)** (sich) vorstellen
to **invite** einladen

just gerade

key der Schlüssel
to **knock** klopfen
to **know** (a person) kennen
    to **know** (facts) wissen

large groß
last letzt-; zuletzt
    at last endlich
late spät

law das Gesetz
to **learn** lernen
least: at least mindestens, wenigstens
to **leave** lassen; abfahren
to **let** lassen
letter der Brief
to **lie** liegen
life das Leben
light das Licht
little klein; wenig
to **live** wohnen; leben
living room das Wohnzimmer
long lang; (*adv.*) lange
to **look** aussehen
to **look forward to** sich freuen auf
to **lose one's way** sich verlaufen, sich verfahren
to **love** lieben
to **fall in love with** sich verlieben in

mad: to be mad at sich ärgern über
to **make** machen
many viele
married: to be married verheiratet sein
to **marry, to get married** heiraten
to **meet** kennenlernen
mistake der Fehler
moment der Augenblick
money das Geld
more mehr
mother die Mutter
movie (house) das Kino
much viel

to **need** brauchen
never nie
new neu
newspaper die Zeitung
nice nett
nobody niemand
not nicht
    not until erst
    not yet noch nicht
nothing nichts
novel der Roman
now jetzt
o'clock: at (three) o'clock um

(drei) Uhr
often oft
old alt
once einmal; früher
only nur; erst
order: in order in Ordnung
in order to um . . . zu
other ander-
overcoat der Mantel

to **pay** bezahlen
people die Leute
perhaps vielleicht
permitted: to be permitted to dürfen
to **pick up, meet** abholen
picture das Bild
please bitte
to **prepare (oneself) for** (sich) vorbereiten auf
to **promise** versprechen
to **put** setzen; stellen; legen

quite ganz

to **rain** regnen
rather lieber
to **reach** erreichen
to **read** lesen
really wirklich
to **remember** sich erinnern an
to **rest** sich ausruhen
restless unruhig
to **ring** (a telephone) klingeln
reason die Vernunft
    reasonable vernünftig
to **recognize** erkennen
relative der Verwandte
room das Zimmer

shoe der Schuh
school die Schule
to **scream** schreien
to **see** sehen
to **seem** scheinen
to **send** schicken
several mehrere
to **shave** sich rasieren
to **show** zeigen
sick krank
silent: to be silent schweigen
simple einfach
sister die Schwester
to **sit** sitzen
to **sleep** schlafen

to **get enough sleep** (sich) ausschlafen
small klein
to **smoke** rauchen
soldier der Soldat
some einige, ein paar, manche; etwas
somebody jemand
something etwas
somewhere irgendwo, irgendwohin
son der Sohn
to **speak** sprechen
to **stand** stehen
station der Bahnhof
to **stay** bleiben
still noch
stone der Stein
stop halten, stehenbleiben
story die Geschichte
student der Student, die Studentin
to **study** studieren
such solch
suddenly plötzlich
to **suggest** vorschlagen
Sunday der Sonntag
supposed: to be supposed to sollen
swimming pool das Schwimmbecken

to **switch off** ausmachen

table der Tisch
to **take** nehmen
to **talk** reden, sprechen
teacher der Lehrer
to **tell** sagen; erzählen
thank danken
thief der Dieb
to **think** (**of**) denken (an)
tile die Platte
time die Zeit
    at the time damals
tired müde
today heute
tomorrow morgen
tonight heute abend
too auch
trace die Spur
    without a trace spurlos
train der Zug
to **try** versuchen
to **turn off** (light) ausmachen
to **turn out** sich herausstellen (*impersonal*)

to **understand** verstehen
to **undress** sich ausziehen
unfortunately leider
until bis

to **get used to** sich gewöhnen an

very sehr
to **visit** besuchen

to **wait for** warten auf
wall die Wand
to **want to** wollen
war der Krieg
watch die Uhr
week die Woche
weekend das Wochenende
well gesund; gut
when wann
where wo; wohin
whether ob
why warum
wife die Frau
wine der Wein
winter der Winter
without ohne
woman die Frau
to **work** arbeiten
writer der Schriftsteller

year das Jahr
yesterday gestern
young jung

INDEX